W9-BGK-720

LABOR GUIDE TO LABOR LAW

THIRD EDITION

Bruce S. Feldacker
Attorney-at-Law, J.D., LL.M.

PRENTICE HALL, *Englewood Cliffs, New Jersey 07632*

Library of Congress Cataloging-in-Publication Data

FELDACKER, BRUCE S.
    Labor guide to labor law / Bruce S. Feldacker.—3rd ed.
        p. cm.
    Includes bibliographical references.
    ISBN 0-13-517731-6
    1. Labor laws and legislation—United States.   2. Trade-unions—
Law and legislation—United States.   I. Title.
KF3369.F44 1990
344.73′01—dc20
[347.3041]
                                                89-27565
                                                CIP

**Editorial/production supervision and
    interior design:** Alison D. Gnerre
Cover design: Wanda Lubelska
Manufacturing buyer: Peter Havens

To my wife Barbara
and my children Robert, Deborah, and Caryl Beth
for their patience, understanding, and support

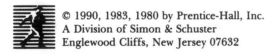

© 1990, 1983, 1980 by Prentice-Hall, Inc.
A Division of Simon & Schuster
Englewood Cliffs, New Jersey 07632

All rights reserved. No part of this book may be reproduced, in any form or by any means, without
permission in writing from the publisher.

Printed in the United States of America
10 9 8 7 6 5 4 3

ISBN 0-13-517731-6

Prentice-Hall International (UK) Limited, *London*
Prentice-Hall of Australia Pty. Limited, *Sydney*
Prentice-Hall Canada Inc., *Toronto*
Prentice-Hall Hispanoamericana, S.A., *Mexico*
Prentice-Hall of India Private Limited, *New Delhi*
Prentice-Hall of Japan, Inc., *Tokyo*
Simon & Schuster Asia Pte. Ltd., *Singapore*
Editora Prentice-Hall do Brasil, Ltda., *Rio de Janeiro*

CONTENTS

4 PROTECTION OF THE EMPLOYEE'S RIGHT TO UNION REPRESENTATION, 102

5 THE DUTY TO BARGAIN, 139

6 STRIKES, STRIKER RIGHTS, AND LOCKOUTS, 184

9 ENFORCEMENT OF COLLECTIVE BARGAINING AGREEMENTS AND THE DUTY TO ARBITRATE, 271

10 UNION MEMBERSHIP AND UNION SECURITY, 299

11 RIGHTS AND RESPONSIBILITIES OF UNION MEMBERS, 327

12 THE DUTY OF FAIR REPRESENTATION, 348

13 UNIONS AND EQUAL EMPLOYMENT OPPORTUNITY, 362

14 FEDERAL-STATE RELATIONSHIPS IN LABOR RELATIONS, 409

PREFACE

Labor studies programs, in which union members study labor relations from the perspective of labor, are now established in many colleges and universities across the nation as well as part of the internal training programs of many international and local unions. When I first began teaching labor law in such a program at St. Louis Community College, there was no suitable text. Law school labor law texts are too technical and emphasize many procedural points that are of no interest to a lay person. Most graduate labor law texts are intended for business school use. They are written from management's perspective, and they tend to emphasize issues of interest to management rather than labor.

This book is intended to fill the gap. It is a comprehensive survey of labor law in the private sector, written from the labor perspective for labor relations students and for unions and their members. Thus, issues of greatest importance to unions are emphasized, just as texts intended for management emphasize issues of importance to management. Where the law permits a union to make certain tactical choices, those choices are pointed out. Included is material on internal union matters, which tends to be either ignored or noted only briefly in management texts; examples are drawn from the workplace.

Labor Guide to Labor Law is intended for use in either a one- or two-semester course in labor law. The chapters are arranged in progression covering applicable labor law principles from a union's initial organizing campaign to the mature bargaining relationship, the use of labor's economic weapons, and internal union regulation. Each chapter contains a summary and review questions, with answers at the back of the book. Each chapter also includes a review section of "Basic Legal Principles" where each key case discussed in the text is fully cited for the reader who wishes to read the full opinions or do additional research. The cases cited expand on the basic legal points. Each chapter also contains a list of recommended reading on the subjects covered.

I generally cover the basic material included in the first seven chapters thoroughly in a single thirty-hour course, and include an introductory survey on selected subjects covered in Chapters Eight, Nine, and Ten. The material included in Chapters Eight through Fourteen is covered in detail in a second thirty-hour course. Other instructors may prefer a different order or pace, or they may choose to select portions for seminars or training programs.

In my teaching, I frequently supplement a chapter with one or two key court or NLRB cases on recent developments pertaining to the material covered. I considered including the full text of selected cases in the book. However, based on my experience in teaching both law and labor studies students, I believe that the text method is the better approach to use in a course that labor leaders and students take to learn the labor law principles they need to know for use in their work rather than to acquire the technical skills of an attorney in reading and analyzing cases. In addition, cost considerations are also important. More material can be presented more consisely through text rather than by cases and keeping *Labor Guide to Labor Law* affordable for union officers and members is an overriding consideration. Space and cost considerations also prevent including a separate glossary of terms. However, I have hopefully compensated for this by including a detailed index referring readers to the pages where key concepts and basic terms are defined.

Labor Guide to Labor Law is also a useful reference and review for full-time union officers and representatives who have a working knowledge of labor law but wish to brush up on certain points. A union faced with a particular legal problem will find that reading the material included here on that issue will help the union to understand the issue and take appropriate action. However, this book is not intended to take the place of an attorney. Labor law is a changing field. Although this book is as accurate as possible, a few principles will undoubtedly change. Thus, the book cannot take the place of up-to-the-minute advice based on the latest developments and the specific facts of a case.

ABOUT THE THIRD EDITION

The first edition of *Labor Guide to Labor Law*, published in 1980, summarized the law regulating the labor-management relations process as of the end of the 1970s. It is therefore appropriate that this third edition summarizes the law as it has developed during the 1980s. This ten-year period has been a tumultuous one in labor law, brought on by changing economic conditions as well as by a National Labor Relations Board dominated by Reagan appointees and an increasingly conservative federal judiciary. The Board decisions during this period, with a few rare exceptions, have generally strengthened the position of employers in labor management relations.

Although it would be easy to focus on the bias of the Board in recent years, I have tried to avoid the temptation. The purpose of *Labor Guide to Labor Law* is to provide union officers and members and labor relations students with a straightforward unbiased explanation of labor law principles. Therefore, although I have pointed out the inconsistencies and illogical reasoning in some of the more flagrant Board decisions in recent years, I have remained focused on my primary goal of providing up-to-date and practical information on the law as it is for labor leaders to use in their work. However, where appropriate, I have summarized the law as it existed before certain principles were changed by more recent Reagan Board or court decisions in the hope that a more moderate Board may return to the prior law on some of the points.

References in the text to the "Reagan Board" are to decisions issued during the 1981 to 1988 period when Board members appointed by President Reagan comprised a Board majority. Of course, the Board composed of members appointed by President Bush will almost certainly lean toward management views on controversial issues just as Board majorities appointed by Democratic presidents have tended to favor the labor view. Still, the early decisions of the "Bush Board" indicate that it will be more balanced and fairer than its predecessor.

Labor law has grown increasingly complex and sophisticated in the last ten years. But, in my experience, labor leaders and students in labor relations courses have also grown more sophisticated to meet the challenge. Therefore, although this third edition continues to follow the pattern of the prior editions in discussing legal principles in understandable lay terms, I have included more technical discussions of legal principles and of specific Board and court cases where understanding the underlying technical points will enable users to apply the law more effectively in their work.

There are many persons whose assistance I appreciate in preparing the third edition. My good friend and client, William Stodghill, an international vice-president of the Service Employees International Union and president of Local 50 of the Service Employees, encouraged me to complete work on this edition despite the time pressures of practice. As Bill well knows, many of the examples in this book are based on cases involving his local. My law firm partner, attorney Bruce Cohen, and associates, attorneys Marie Durbin and Jerald Hochsztein, and law school student Melinda Baum provided invaluable assistance in updating the chapters; and, of course, the third edition could not have been completed without the hard work of my secretaries Kathryn Dukes, Patti Hadfield, and Terri Harrison. I also appreciate the suggestions of St. Louis civil rights attorney Mary Anne Sedey, who reviewed Chapter Thirteen.

Finally, since 1984 I have been privileged to serve as an instructor in the college degree program sponsored by the AFL-CIO George Meany Labor Studies Center in conjunction with Antioch College. The hardworking students in this program are full-time labor officials studying in what should be time off from their busy work schedules for a college degree in labor studies to serve their union and the community more effectively. *Labor Guide to Labor Law* is intended for just such persons, and I am very pleased that they have found the text useful in their union duties and in their studies. It is to these students who represent the best traditions of the labor movement and its future that this third edition is dedicated.

Bruce Feldacker
St. Louis, Missouri

EXPLANATION OF LEGAL CASE
AND STATUTORY CITATIONS

Each chapter in this book concludes with a section of Basic Legal Principles citing leading cases of the National Labor Relations Board, the United States Supreme Court, the United States Courts of Appeals, and the United States Federal District Courts discussed in the chapter.

There are twelve United States Courts of Appeals. Eleven of these courts serve separate geographic areas (each called a circuit) composed of a number of states. These Courts are referred to as the First through Eleventh Circuits. There is a twelfth Court of Appeals for the District of Columbia only, which is known as the District of Columbia Circuit. Each state is served by one or more United States Federal District Courts. The number of districts per state is generally based on the state's population. There is also a separate District Court for the District of Columbia.

Decisions of the United States Supreme Court are published in bound volumes called the United States Reports (abbreviated U.S.) or the Supreme Court Reporter (abbreviated S.Ct.). Decisions of the United States Courts of Appeals are reported in the Federal Reporter, Second Series (abbreviated F.2d). Decisions of the United States District Courts are reported in the Federal Supplement (abbreviated F.Supp.). Decisions of the National Labor Relations Board are reported in the National Labor Relations Board Decisions and Orders, abbreviated NLRB.

Citations to the United States Reports (U.S.), the Federal Reporter Second Series (F.2d), and the Federal Supplement (F.Supp.) follow a uniform numbering system. The first number, before the name of the reporter, indicates the volume of the reporter in which a decision is published. The second number, following the reporter's name, indicates the page in the volume where the decision begins. This number is followed by a citation in parentheses to the court and year of the decision. Thus, the citation "*Smith v. Jones*, 178 F.2d 220 (4th Cir., 1949)" means that the case decision is found in Volume 178 of the Federal Reporter, Second Series, beginning at page 220. The decision was rendered by the United States Court of Appeals for the Fourth Circuit in 1949. The opposing parties were Smith versus Jones. A decision such as "410 F.Supp. 948 (E.D. Mo., 1976)" means that the decision is found in Volume 410 of the Federal Supplement beginning at page 948, and that the decision was rendered by the United States District Court for the Eastern District of Missouri in 1976.

Citations to National Labor Relations Board decisions use the same basic numbering sequence: the volume followed by either a case number or a volume page number. Thus, a reference to 234 NLRB No. 162 means that the decision is found in volume 234 of the National Labor Relations Board Decisions and Orders, and is Case No. 162.

Several reporting services report federal and state court decisions on labor law issues and the decisions of the National Labor Relations Board in the same volumes. The Bureau of National Affairs (BNA), Washington, D.C., publishes two widely used reporting services: the Labor Relations Reference Manual (abbreviated LRRM), which reports federal and state court labor decisions and NLRB decisions; and the Fair Employment Practice Cases Reporter (FEP Cases), which reports civil rights cases. As a convenience to readers, citations in *Labor Guide to Labor law* are to both the official reporters and to the appropriate BNA reporter. These reporters are also cited first by volume and then by page number. Thus, a case reference such as "429 U.S. 1037, 94 LRRM 2202" means that the decision is found in Volume 429 of the United States Reporter at page 1037, and that the same case is reprinted in Volume 94 of the Labor Relations Reference Manual beginning at page 2202.

Some cases discussed in this book were decided so close to the book's publication date that the complete case citations were not yet available. These cases are cited only to the appropriate BNA Reporter. A reference such as ____ F.2d ____ or ____ U.S. ____ indicates the citation to these volumes was not available at the time of printing.

Federal statutes are published in the United States code (U.S.C.). The code is divided into sections corresponding to the sections of the law as passed by Congress. Most labor laws are found in Title 29 of the Code. Civil rights legislation is found in Title 42 of the Code. Thus, as an example, Section 301 of the Labor-Management Relations Act (discussed in Chapter Nine) is frequently cited as 29 U.S.C. Section 185. This means that the provision is found in Title 29 of the United States Code, Section 185.

Throughout this book, the Labor Management Relations Act of 1947 as amended, the primary statute governing labor relations in the private sector, is abbreviated as "LMRA."

Citation to legal periodicals and law journals are also given by volume number, periodical names, and page number. Thus, the citation "25 *Lab. L.J.* 418" means that the particular article can be found in Volume 25 of the *Labor Law Journal* beginning at page 418. The abbreviation "L. Rev." refers to a law review published by a law school. Law review articles are written either by law professors, practicing lawyers, or by students under a professor's direction.

The case reporters and legal journals cited in this book can be found in virtually any law school library, most of which are open to the public. Most bar associations in larger cities and counties also maintain complete libraries, and the regional offices of the National Labor Relations Board maintain libraries containing most of the cited material as well.

chapter 1

FEDERAL REGULATION OF LABOR-MANAGEMENT RELATIONS: A STATUTORY AND STRUCTURAL OVERVIEW

This book is a practical guide to labor law in the private sector. The first ten chapters present a discussion of legal principles primarily based on the Labor Management Relations Act (LMRA) 1947, as amended, commonly referred to as the "Act." The remaining chapters discuss principles based on the Labor Management Reporting and Disclosure Act and the Civil Rights Act of 1964, as amended, as well as on the LMRA. The appendix contains pertinent sections of these statutes, and it should be referred to as these sections are discussed in the text.

This chapter begins with a brief historical survey of federal labor legislation leading to the passage of the LMRA in the current form studied in this book. This survey is followed by an introductory overview of the major provisions of the LMRA, which are considered in detail in subsequent chapters, and by an explanation of the structure and procedures of the National Labor Relations Board, the agency administering the Act.

PART I: THE HISTORICAL DEVELOPMENT OF THE LABOR MANAGEMENT RELATIONS ACT

A. COLLECTIVE BARGAINING BEFORE THE STATUTORY ERA

Before the passage of the federal labor legislation discussed in this book, regulation of labor relations was left largely to the states. The law governing labor relations was primarily developed by state courts on a case by case basis. This process of judicial development is known as the "common law," in contrast to statutory law (laws made by the legislature) or administrative law (laws made by administrative agencies).

Workers began to organize into workers' associations, the historical forerunner of today's unions, in America in the late 1700s. The concept of workers uniting together to improve their working conditions was initially greeted by hostility in the courts. Thus, in the historically important Philadelphia Cordwainers' case, decided in 1806, the court ruled that it was an unlawful conspiracy for workers to form an organization in which the membership agreed that none of them would work as shoemakers except at certain specified prices higher than the price which had previously been paid. The doctrine that an organization of workers formed to better their working conditions constituted an unlawful conspiracy was frequently followed in the United States until the mid-1850s. However, in 1842, the Massachusetts Supreme Court issued an important decision upholding the right of workers to form associations, and this viewpoint gradually was adopted in other states.

Although the state courts began to recognize the rights of workers to form labor organizations, the courts continued to restrict the methods that unions could use to accomplish their goals as the labor movement grew in the second half of the nineteenth century. Some courts distinguished between the right to strike and the right to picket. These courts upheld the right of workers to withhold their own services in order to force a change in their working conditions. But such courts, reasoning that an employer had the right to continue operations during a strike and that employees who chose to had the right to continue working, frequently issued injunctions prohibiting unions from picketing in support of their strike on the theory that even peaceful picketing coerced and interfered with the rights of the employer to continue operation and of employees to continue working. Obviously, this approach seriously undermined the effectiveness of strike activity. Even those state courts that upheld the right of workers to strike and to picket under some circumstances frequently issued injunctions limiting the scope of union conduct if the judge did not approve of the conduct or the purpose of the strike. This was known as the *ends/means test*. Thus, in some states, picketing in support of a union's claim to certain work in a jurisdictional dispute was held to be for an unlawful purpose (end), and the state court would enjoin the picketing. Product boycotts in support of a strike were sometimes enjoined as being an unlawful method.

The American economy in the second half of the nineteenth century and early in this century was philosophically based on the concept of open competition, unfettered by governmental restrictions, commonly referred to as *laissez-faire* (French words meaning "to do as one pleases") government. The conservative pro-business courts of the period applied this philosophy in determining the lawfulness of union conduct. For example, strikes protesting an employer's unilateral change in production methods, resulting in a loss of jobs for the affected employees, were enjoined by the courts on the grounds that such strikes were for the unlawful purpose of interfering with the employer's right to determine the manner of production. In many states, collective bargaining agreements, once entered into, were valid and binding. However, an employer was under no obligation to engage in collective bargaining, nor to sign a collective bargaining agreement. Thus, in such states, a court would enjoin a strike to compel an employer to sign a collective bargaining agreement, on the grounds that such a strike was for the unlawful purpose of interfering with the employer's right to enter or not enter into such an agreement on a voluntary basis.

Of course, the rights of employees and labor unions during this pre-statutory era varied according to the social and political climate of the state. Labor unions engaged in a broader range of permissible conduct in those states where the judges were more progressive, or where the labor movement had greater political strength. In every state, however, the pro-business legal doctrines applied in determining the legality of union conduct and the broad discretion that individual judges had under the common law in applying these doctrines placed unions under restraints varying from court to court and from case to case, with many resultant inconsistencies between decisions and principles that they applied.

The federal courts also interfered in the organization and conduct of labor unions. With the passage of the federal Sherman Antitrust Act in 1890 (see Chapter Eight, Part IV), the federal courts frequently issued injunctions against union strike activity or boycotts of employers involved in a labor dispute on the grounds that such union conduct interfered with the free flow of goods in commerce and was thus a combination or conspiracy in restraint of trade violating the antitrust laws. As discussed below and in Chapter Eight, the passage of the Norris-LaGuardia Act in 1932 restricted the federal courts' right to enjoin union conduct on the grounds that it violated the antitrust laws.

This, then, was the generally unfavorable legal climate in which labor functioned through the 1920s until the beginning of the modern statutory era.

B. THE RAILWAY LABOR ACT

The Railway Labor Act, passed by Congress in 1926, was the first comprehensive federal statutory regulation of labor-management relations. It originally covered only railroad employees, but was amended in 1936 to cover airlines as well. The Railway Labor Act is important to all employees because it was the first comprehensive federal legislation specifically recognizing the right of employees to form unions and engage in collective bargaining.

C. THE NORRIS-LaGUARDIA ACT

In 1932, Congress passed the Norris-La-Guardia Act, a fundamental turning point in federal statutory regulation. The Act prohibited federal courts from issuing injunctions in any labor dispute regardless of the strike's purpose. The law prevented judges from engaging in the previously common practice of enjoining a strike because the judge did not approve of the strike's goals or methods. However, the law did not guarantee the employees any collective bargaining rights. Bargaining rights, except in the railroads, were still won in a test of economic strength between an employer and a union. But with the Norris-LaGuardia Act, the federal courts' injunctive power was removed as a weapon against labor.

D. THE NATIONAL LABOR RELATIONS ACT

In 1935, Congress passed the National Labor Relations Act (NLRA), frequently referred to as the Wagner Act after the New York Senator who sponsored the legislation. The Supreme Court upheld the NLRA's constitutionality in 1937. The NLRA was enacted as part of President Franklin Roosevelt's New Deal legislation during the depression, and was, in effect, a peaceful revolution in labor relations.

The NLRA established employee rights to organize, join unions, and engage in collective bargaining. The NLRA established employer unfair labor practices, making it unlawful for an employer to interfere with an employee's right to join a union and engage in concerted (union) activities. Employers were required to bargain in good faith with the union and were prohibited from discharging or otherwise discriminating against employees because they engaged in union activities.

The NLRA also established procedures by which employees may elect their bargaining agent. Before passage of the NLRA, employees could secure bargaining rights only if their employer voluntarily agreed to recognize the union or if the employees struck and forced recognition. The NLRA thus dramatically paved the way for peaceful unionization, especially of industrial workers whose employers had consistently opposed organizing efforts until then. The provisions first enacted in the NLRA remain the basic franchise of American workers.

Beyond establishing employee rights and employer unfair labor practices, the NLRA established the National Labor Relations Board to enforce its provisions. Today it is common for federal laws to be enforced by administrative agencies, as the NLRB was established to enforce the NLRA. But until the 1930s, it was far more common for the courts to enforce all laws. Congress established the NLRB because it mistrusted the manner in which the courts, which were historically associated with employer interests, might enforce the law. Congress also felt the need for a specialized agency to develop and apply expertise in the unique field of labor relations.

E. THE TAFT-HARTLEY ACT (THE LABOR MANAGEMENT RELATIONS ACT)

In 1947, Congress passed the Taft-Hartley Act, named after Senator Taft and Congressman Hartley, who cosponsored the legislation. The Taft-Hartley Act extensively revised the NLRA and renamed it the Labor Management Relations Act (LMRA), 1947. The LMRA, incorporating the original NLRA as amended by the Taft-Hartley Act in 1947, is the basic statute studied in this book. The term NLRA is still used sometimes to refer to the provisions of the original NLRA that were continued as part of the LMRA (basically the employer unfair labor practices now found in LMRA Section 8(a)).

The original NLRA was pro-labor, establishing employee rights and restricting employer acts. Congress intended for the Taft-Hartley Act to embody what it regarded as a better balance between labor and management. For example, the NLRA established the right of employees to engage in collective bargaining and other mutual aid and protection; the Taft-Hartley Act added a provision that employees also have the right to refrain from any or all such activities. The NLRA established employer unfair labor practices now contained in LMRA Section 8(a); the Taft-Hartley Act added Section 8(b), union unfair labor practices, which prohibits unions from interfering with employee rights, prohibits unions from coercing or discriminating against employees because of their union activities, and requires unions to bargain in good faith— provisions that place the same restrictions on unions as the NLRA placed on employers. The restrictions on secondary boycotts

and on picketing (see Chapter Seven) are all an outgrowth of the Taft-Hartley Act.

F. THE LANDRUM-GRIFFIN ACT

In 1959, Congress passed the Landrum-Griffin Act, named after the congressional cosponsors, formally entitled the Labor Management Reporting and Disclosure Act (LMRDA). The LMRDA primarily regulates internal union matters. It established the so-called Bill of Rights for union members; internal union election procedures; and reporting and disclosure requirements for unions, union officers, and employers (see Chapter Eleven).

The LMRDA also amended the LMRA by adding additional restrictions on picketing, closing certain "loopholes" in Taft-Hartley, and by adding Section 8(e) of the LMRA, prohibiting "hot cargo" clauses prohibiting one employer from dealing with other employers who are nonunion or who are on strike (see Chapter Eight). After 1959, the formal name of the LMRA was changed to the "Labor Management Relations Act, 1947, as amended," the present formal title.

G. THE POSTAL REORGANIZATION ACT

Chapter 12 of the Postal Reorganization Act of 1970 established the collective bargaining rights of postal workers. The Reorganization Act placed the United States Postal Service under the jurisdiction of the National Labor Relations Board for determining employee representation issues and also provided that labor relations in the Postal Service would be governed by the Labor Management Relations Act to the extent not inconsistent with the Reorganization Act itself. Two major differences between the rights of postal workers and private sector employees covered by the LMRA are that the postal workers, as federal employees, do not have the right to strike; and the Reorganization Act forbids required union membership (a "union shop") as a condition of employment (see Chapter Ten). The Reorganization Act also provides for final and binding arbitration if the parties are unable to agree upon the terms of their collective bargaining agreement (called *interest arbitration*), which is not required under the LMRA (see Chapter Nine).

H. THE HEALTH CARE AMENDMENTS

In 1974, the LMRA was amended to delete the provision previously included in Section 2(2) of the Act excluding nonprofit hospitals from the Act's coverage. This means that both profit and nonprofit hospitals are now covered. In addition to extending coverage to nonprofit hospitals, the 1974 amendments also enacted special provisions for the health care industry, both profit and nonprofit, as to bargaining notice requirements (Section 8(d)) and the right to picket or strike (Section 8(g)).

I. THE RELIGIOUS BELIEF EXEMPTION

The 1974 Health Care Amendments added Section 19 to the Act that as initially enacted provided that a health care industry employee who has religious objections to joining a labor union cannot be required to join or financially support a union as a condition of employment. Effective December 24, 1980, Section 19 was extensively revised, and the religious objection exemption was extended to all employees, not just to those in the health care industry. To qualify for the exemption, an employee must be a member of a bonafide religious organization that historically holds conscientious objection to joining or financially supporting a labor union (see Chapter Ten).

PART II: AN OVERVIEW OF THE LABOR MANAGEMENT RELATIONS ACT IN CURRENT FORM

A word of caution and encouragement is in order before reviewing the LMRA in its present form. This is an introductory overview providing a general understanding of the structure and coverage of the Act. Do not expect to understand all of the statute at first reading. The statute is complex. Some of it is of interest only to lawyers, and other parts are understandable only in the light of subsequent court decisions interpreting the language discussed in later chapters. Sections briefly highlighted here are discussed in detail in subsequent chapters.

A. BASIC STRUCTURE AND DEFINITIONS: SECTIONS 1 THROUGH 6

Section 1 of the Act contains basic findings and policies stating the background reasons for which Congress originally passed the NLRA. Section 2 of the Act includes the definitions used throughout the Act. Note the definition of employer in Section 2(2). Federal and state governmental agencies are excluded from coverage under the Act. Labor organizations are covered by the Act when acting as an employer for their own employees. For example, the secretaries of a labor union have the rights of employees. Note the definition of employee in Section 2(3). An employee who is on strike is still entitled to the protection of the Act. Agricultural and domestic employees are excluded from the Act, as are people employed by their own parent or spouse, independent contractors, and supervisors (see Chapter Two).

Section 2(11) defines the term "supervisor" and Section 2(12) defines the term "professional employees." Supervisors are excluded from coverage under the Act, and professional employees have the right to a bargaining unit of their own (see Chapter Two).

Sections 3, 4, 5, and 6 of the Act all pertain to the establishment and structure of the National Labor Relations Board (see Part III of this chapter).

B. SECTIONS 7 AND 8: THE UNFAIR LABOR PRACTICE SECTIONS

Section 7 of the Act establishes the basic right of employees to bargain collectively. Section 8 is the heart of the Act. Section 8(a) establishes employer unfair labor practices, and Section 8(b) establishes union unfair labor practices. Sections 8(a)(1) through 8(a)(5) and Sections 8(b)(1) through 8(b)(3) generally prohibit either employers or unions from taking certain actions against each other or against employees. Thus, Section 8(a)(1) and Section 8(b)(1)(A) respectively prohibit an employer and a union from interfering with employee rights under Section 7. Section 8(a)(3) prohibits an employer from discriminating against an employee because of union membership, but permits mandatory union membership ("union security agreements") under certain circumstances (see Chapter Ten). Section 8(b)(2) prohibits a union from causing the employer to violate Section 8(a)(3). Sections 8(a)(5) and 8(b)(3) require both an employer and a union to engage in good-faith bargaining (see Chapters Three through Six).

Section 8(b)(4) contains the secondary boycott provisions of the Act. Section 8(b)(5) prohibits excessive or discriminatory union initiation fees. Section 8(b)(6) attempts to prohibit "feather-bedding." Section 8(b)(7) regulates union picketing for recognition or organizational purposes (see Chapters Seven and Eight).

Section 8(c) is the so-called "free speech" provision under which employers are permitted to express their opinion about union representation for their employees (see Chapter Three). Section 8(d) defines good-faith bargaining and establishes notice requirements before a contract can be terminated or modified (see Chapter Five).

Section 8(e) prohibits hot cargo provisions (see Chapter Eight). Section 8(f) permits certain pre-hire contracts in the construction industry and shortens the period after which an employee may be required to join a union to seven days after hiring in the construction industry, in contrast to the 30-day requirement in other industries. Section 8(g) contains the special notice requirements for a strike or for picketing in the health care industry.

C. SECTION 9: ELECTION PROCEDURES

Section 9 governs union election procedures leading to the certification of a union as the employees' bargaining representative (see Chapter Two). Under Section 9(a), the certified representative is the exclusive representative of the employees (see Chapter Four). Under Section 9(b), the Board has very broad discretion in determining the appropriate bargaining unit. However, Section 9(b)(1) gives professional employees the right to a separate vote before they can be included in a unit that includes nonprofessionals; Section 9(b)(2) places certain restrictions on the Board's right to include craft employees in a broader unit; and Section 9(b)(3) requires that guards be certified separately in a unit composed only of guard employees.

Sections 9(c)(1) through 9(c)(5) regulate the election process. Section 9(c)(3) prohibits a valid election from being held more than once a year, establishes the right of economic strikers to vote in an election, and establishes the procedure for runoff elections if no choice initially receives a majority of the valid votes counted. Section 9(e)(1) permits employees whose contract contains a union security clause to hold a deauthorization election rescinding the clause.

D. SECTION 10: ENFORCEMENT OF THE UNFAIR LABOR PRACTICE PROVISIONS

Under Section 10(a) the NLRB is established as the authority for enforcing the unfair labor practice provisions found in Section 8.

Under Section 10(b) an unfair labor practice charge must be filed within six months after an unfair labor practice has occurred. Sections 10(b), (c), and (d) establish trial procedures in unfair labor practice cases. Sections 10(e) and (f) of the Act set the procedures that the Board follows in enforcing its decisions or that a party may follow to appeal a Board decision to the courts.

Contrast Sections 10(j) and Section 10(l) of the Act. Under Section 10(j), the Board has discretionary authority to request a federal district court to issue an injunction prohibiting certain unfair labor practices after the Board has issued a complaint alleging that the conduct violates the Act. In contrast, under Section 10(l), the Board is required to seek an injunction even before a complaint is issued if the regional director has reasonable cause to believe that a charge alleging violations of Section 8(b)(4), 8(b)(7), or 8(e) of the Act is true. Note that the mandatory provisions of Section 10(l) apply to only union unfair labor practices. Unions have frequently complained that there are no employer unfair labor practices for which the Board must seek an injunction.

Section 10(k) is a unique provision giving the Board authority to determine the merits of a work assignment dispute if any party to the dispute threatens to strike, picket, or engage in other concerted activities in order to force a work assignment (see Chapter Eight). Section 11 sets out the investigatory powers of the Board, the manner in which Board documents are served, and other procedural matters. Section 12 makes it a criminal act to interfere with the Board's processes.

E. PROTECTION OF THE RIGHT TO STRIKE: SECTION 13

Section 13 preserves the right to strike. Two other important sections deal with the right to strike. Section 8(b)(4) provides that "nothing contained in this subsection (b) shall be construed to make unlawful a refusal by any person to enter upon the premises of any employer (other than his own employer), if the employees of such employer are engaged in a strike ratified or approved by a representative of such employees whom such employer is required to recognize under this Act. ..." Under the provisions of Section 502 an individual employee cannot be required to work without his consent, and employees who quit in good faith because of abnormally dangerous conditions are not considered to be on strike (see Chapter Six).

Section 14(a) permits supervisors to be members of a labor organization. However, employers are not required to bargain about the working conditions of supervisors or to recognize a supervisor's union.

Section 14(b) permits individual states to pass so-called "Right-to-Work" laws. Section 19, as discussed above, exempts employees with a religious objection to joining or financially supporting a union from required union membership under a contractual union security clause (see Chapter Ten).

F. TITLES II AND III OF THE ACT

Title II of the Act establishes the Federal Mediation and Conciliation Service and defines its authority.[1]

Section 301 authorizes the enforcement of collective bargaining agreements. Section 301 has encouraged the growth of arbitra-

---

[1] This book does not discuss the Federal Mediation and Conciliation Service in detail except as the agency's activities relate to statutory matters such as bargaining notice requirements. Most of the agency's activities relate to the bargaining process beyond the scope of this text.

tion rather than the courts or strikes as the primary method of resolving contractual disputes (see Chapter Nine).

Section 302 restricts employer payments to union representatives. This section prohibits union representatives from receiving gifts from employers and prohibits an employer from giving financial support to a union (see Chapter Four). Important subsections include Section 302(c)(4), which permits an employer to deduct union dues from an employee's wages; and Section 302(c)(5), which establishes the basic structure and purpose of jointly-administered fringe benefit trust funds. The establishment and operation of employee fringe benefit funds are extensively regulated by the Employee Retirement Income Security Act (ERISA), effective Labor Day 1974.

Section 303 permits a court to award damages against a union engaging in unfair labor practices in violation of Section 8(b)(4) (the secondary boycott provisions). Sections 301, 302, and Section 303 are all enforced by the courts rather than the NLRB.[2]

PART III: STRUCTURE AND PROCEDURE OF THE NATIONAL LABOR RELATIONS BOARD

The NLRB administers the LMRA following set procedures in unfair labor practice and representation cases established by the statute and by regulations issued by the Board. Most of the principles discussed in this book were developed by the NLRB in decisions made through the procedures outlined here. This outline gives the basic information needed to understand the process should you or your union be involved in Board proceedings. Do not expect to remember the details of these procedures at first reading. Read this part now to get a general understanding of the Board's structure and procedures. Then review this material as you study the following chapters.

A. THE NATIONAL LABOR RELATIONS BOARD AND THE GENERAL COUNSEL

The National Labor Relations Board, located in Washington, D.C., has five members. The members, who serve for five-year terms, are appointed by the president and approved by a vote of the Senate. One of the five is appointed as Board chairman by the President with Senate confirmation. Usually the Board decides cases using three-member panels, but important cases can be decided by all five members (en banc).

In addition to the Board, the Labor Management Relations Act established a separate, independent general counsel, also appointed by the president and approved by the Senate for a four-year term. Figure 1 is an organizational chart of the National Labor Relations Board and of the Office of the General Counsel.[3]

To understand the functions of the five-member Board and the general counsel, think of the relationship between a prosecutor and a judge. In unfair labor practice cases (Section 8), the Board acts as the judge and it decides whether the charged party (the defendant) has violated the Act. Judges do not decide cases unless a prosecutor brings a charge alleging a violation of the law. The Board functions in a similar way, hearing only cases in which a complaint has been filed alleging an unfair labor practice. The general counsel fills the prosecutor function. Anyone may file a charge with the general counsel alleging that the Act has been violated.[4] The general counsel inves-

---

[2] The relationship between the NLRB and federal courts in administering the Act is discussed in Chapter Fourteen.

[3] The charts and other documents reproduced in Figures 1 through 8 are publications of the National Labor Relations Board reprinted with the agency's permission.

[4] People frequently refer to filing a charge with the Board but a charge is actually filed with the general counsel.

NATIONAL LABOR RELATIONS BOARD

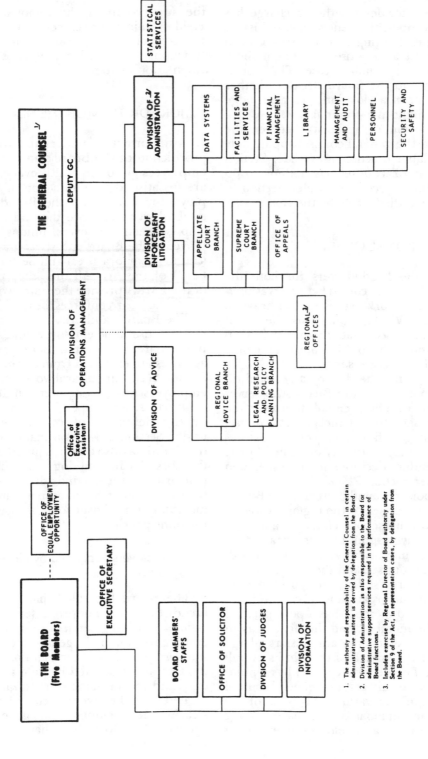

1. The authority and responsibility of the General Counsel in certain administrative matters is derived by delegation from the Board.

2. Division of Administration is also responsible to the Board for administrative support services required in the performance of Board functions.

3. Includes exercise by Regional Director of Board authority under Section 9 of the Act, in representation cases, by delegation from the Board.

FIGURE 1.

9

tigates and decides whether a charge has merit. If it does, the general counsel issues a complaint charging that the Act has been violated, just as a prosecutor might file a complaint in a criminal case. The case is then tried and the Board decides whether there has been a violation, just as a judge (or jury) might in a criminal case.

The division of authority between the Board and the general counsel applies only to unfair labor practice cases under Section 8. The general counsel has nothing to do with election procedures under Section 9; those are handled solely by the Board.

B. THE REGIONAL OFFICES

Although the headquarters for both the Board and general counsel are in Washington, D.C., the work load is far too heavy to handle from Washington. Thus, the Board has regional offices that administer the Act. Figure 2 shows the location of each regional office and the area it serves.

Each region is headed by a regional director appointed by the Board who serves two functions. The regional director is the local representative of the general counsel in processing unfair labor practice charges and, pursuant to authority delegated by the Board, renders decisions in representation cases under Section 9.

This book frequently refers to the Board, the general counsel, or the regional director as taking certain action. That is because they are ultimately responsible for certain decisions. Remember, however, that the Board, the general counsel, and the regional director all have large staffs to support them. As indicated in the organizational chart (Figure 1), each Board member has a personal staff to assist the member, and the Board has an executive secretary who administers a large office staff to assist the Board in its overall functions. The general counsel has a number of associate and assistant general counsel in charge of the various functions of the office. The regional offices have a large staff of attorneys and field examiners under

the supervision of the regional director. Field examiners are career civil servant employees performing primarily investigatory functions in unfair labor practice and representation matters.

C. JURISDICTION OF THE NLRB

It is important to understand the limited jurisdiction of the Board's authority. Some employees go to the NLRB every time they are dissatisfied with an action of their employer or union. But the Board was not established to regulate the entire relationship between employers, unions, and employees. The Board enforces only Section 8 (unfair labor practices) and Section 9 (elections) of the Act. All the other provisions of the LMRA provide the framework within which the Board enforces these two sections.

The Board's authority is even more limited because some employers and some employees are not covered. State and federal agencies are excluded from coverage under Section 2(2). Agricultural workers, domestic employees in a private home, independent contractors, and supervisors are excluded by the definition of covered employees under Section 2(3). As a matter of policy, the Board has also declined jurisdiction over the horse racing and dog racing industries, primarily on the grounds that those industries are subject to extensive state control including control over some aspects of labor relations policies.

1. Employers Supported by Government Funds

The Board has ruled that it will assert jurisdiction over nonprofit service organizations providing services to or for an exempt governmental agency, such as head start programs, child care, and medical clinics, that are supported by state and/or federal funds. Some of these organizations have argued that they were excluded from the Act by the exemption for governmental agencies. The Board held that such agencies

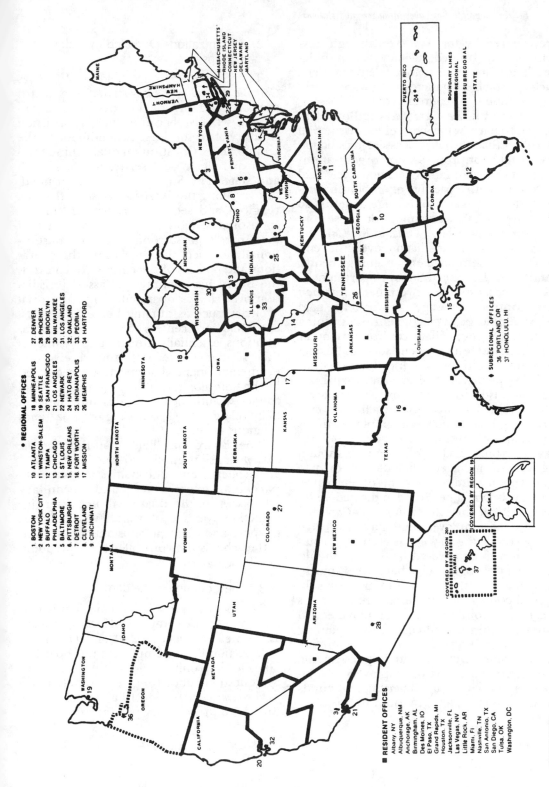

FIGURE 2.

are covered by the Act, even though governmentally funded, if they retain independence in labor-management matters, such as establishing wages, hours, and working conditions of their employees.

However, in *Res-Care, Inc.* the Board appeared to narrow the scope of its jurisdiction by ruling that it would not assert jurisdiction over such nonprofit service organizations unless the organization retained the "final say on the entire package of employee compensation, i.e. wages and fringe benefits" so that "meaningful bargaining" on those core subjects was possible.[5] Thus, in *Res-Care* the Board declined jurisdiction over the employer (an employment training center funded by the United States Department of Labor) because the government retained final control over wages and benefits paid to the employees even though the training center had independent control over other conditions of employment such as hiring, working conditions, and disciplinary action.

Subsequently, however, the Board asserted jurisdiction over a private employer who retained control over such economic terms and conditions of employment as health and life insurance, vacations, holiday pay, overtime, and sick leave even though a governmental agency had the authority to limit the maximum amount of employee compensation. The Board indicated in so deciding that the statement in *Res-Care* that the private employer must have the final say on the *entire package* of employee compensation to be covered by the Act should not be applied literally, but rather meant only that an employer had to exercise substantial control over the economic as well as the noneconomic terms of employment in order for meaningful collective bargaining to take place. Thus, *Res-Care,* as now applied by the Board, should not unduly restrict the representation rights of employees of employers supported by governmental funds as the case originally appeared to do.

2. Organizations Operated by Religious Groups

The Supreme Court held in *NLRB v. Catholic Bishop of Chicago*[6] that the Board cannot assert jurisdiction over church-operated schools, because such jurisdiction would violate the First Amendment to the United States Constitution establishing freedom of religion and separation of church and state. The Supreme Court concluded, in overruling the Board's decision, that the religious and secular purposes of church-sponsored schools are so interwoven that the Board's jurisdiction would unconstitutionally interject the Board into the operations and policies of the church. In contrast, the Board has continued to assert jurisdiction over church-operated, nonprofit social agencies, such as nursing homes, hospitals, and child-care centers, because such organizations essentially function the same as their secular counterparts; they receive governmental financial support, are regulated by the state along with other nonprofit social agencies, and their activities only tangentially relate to the sponsoring organization's religious mission.

The Board has held that the *Catholic Bishop* decision applies to religiously affiliated colleges and universities as well as to parochial, elementary, and secondary schools. Also, the Board will not assert jurisdiction over schools that have a religious purpose and object in substantial part even if the schools are controlled by a predominently lay-board.

3. The Commerce Standard

The Board's jurisdiction covers only employers whose operations affect commerce as defined in Sections 2(6) and (7) of the Act. Section 9(c)(1) empowers the Board to hold elections only if it determines that there is a question concerning representation *affecting commerce.* Section 10(a) empowers the Board "to prevent any person from engag-

---

[5] See legal principle 10.

[6] See legal principle 10.

ing in any unfair labor practice [listed in Section 8] *affecting commerce"* (emphasis added). Why does the statute have these restrictions and what do they mean?

The federal government has limited constitutional authority. Some conduct is not subject to federal regulation. The broadest scope of Congress's constitutional authority is that Congress, under the commerce clause of the Constitution (Article 1, Section 8), can regulate any activity that affects commerce among the states. This is the clause under which most federal legislation in the fields of labor, education, and social welfare is upheld. The Labor Management Relations Act was originally upheld on the legal theory that labor unrest disrupts commerce. Goods will not flow in commerce between states if there is a strike. Thus, Congress can regulate labor relations to maintain industrial peace and prevent disruption of commerce.

Since the LMRA applies to any employer or unfair labor practice affecting commerce, the statute has the broadest possible constitutional reach, covering most small employers. For example, the operation of a small business whose customers are all located within the same state as the business would still "affect commerce" if the business purchases supplies produced in another state. A business that purchases all of its supplies within the state would still affect commerce if it has customers in or if its products are sold in another state. A business that operates solely within a state may still affect commerce if a labor dispute at the business would affect the operations of another employer that does engage in interstate commerce. For example, a small manufacturer may supply a part to another manufacturer in the same state for a product shipped to other states. If the manufacturer of the part is shut down by a labor dispute, the interstate manufacturer will not be able to produce the product, and the flow of goods in interstate commerce will be disrupted. The operations of the parts manufacturer, therefore, affect commerce under the Act. How-ever, some employers' operations may be so small that they might not affect commerce. Thus, although the operations of almost all employers would affect commerce as the courts have interpreted this term, employees must be aware that some employers may not meet the standard.

4. The Board's Jurisdictional Standards

In addition to the constitutional and statutory requirement that an unfair labor practice or representation matter affect commerce under Section 8 or 9, the Board has set certain monetary jurisdictional standards that an employer must meet before the Board will assert jurisdiction. Because so many small employers meet the constitutional and statutory requirement of affecting commerce, the Board established these jurisdictional standards to avoid being engulfed with more cases than it can possibly handle. These standards apply to both unfair labor practice and representation cases.

The monetary standards that an employer must meet before the Board will assert jurisdiction vary by industry, and may be based either on the amount of sales or on gross revenue. Nonretail businesses must either have $50,000 in direct or indirect sales outside their state, or make direct or indirect purchases of supplies from businesses in other states in that amount. Direct sale or purchase means that the transaction is directly with the out-of-state consumer or supplier. Indirect sale or purchase means that the employer sells to or buys from another company within the same state that meets one of the Board's direct jurisdictional standards. A nonretail business must meet either the sales or supply standard. Costs of sales and supplies cannot be combined to meet the $50,000 standard.

The general retail enterprise standard is at least $500,000 annual volume of business. Hotels and taxicab companies must also meet the $500,000 standard. Other industries have different annual volume of business jurisdictional requirements: $250,000 for public utilities and transportation companies; $200,000 for newspapers; $100,000 for communication companies; $100,000 for nursing homes; $250,000 for all other health care institutions; and $1,000,000 for private colleges and symphony orchestras.

Interstate transportation companies must meet a $50,000 annual income requirement. The Board will assert jurisdiction over defense contractors that affect commerce and have a substantial defense impact, regardless of the monetary amount. The Board has established a jurisdictional standard of $250,000 annual revenue for all social service organizations other than those for which there is another specific standard applicable for the type of activity in which the organization is engaged. For example, the specific $100,000 standard would still apply for a nursing home.

Thus, if an employer commits an act that you believe may violate the LMRA or if you are about to organize a new employer, first consider whether the employer meets the definition of an employer covered by the Act and whether the employees meet the definition of an employee under the Act. Be sure alleged employer misconduct is the type covered by the Act, not for example, just a contract violation. Then consider whether the employer meets both the statutory standard of affecting commerce and the appropriate Board monetary jurisdictional standard. Proceed to the Board only after reasonably satisfying yourself on all these matters.

D. PROCESSING AN UNFAIR LABOR PRACTICE CHARGE

1. Filing the Charge

The procedures followed in unfair labor practice cases are outlined in Figure 3. The first step is filing a document called a "charge." The Board has a standard form for filing a charge (Figure 4) that is used in all regional offices. The person filing a charge, called the charging party, states the facts constituting a violation of the Act. Anyone—an employer, an employee, or a union—can file a charge. Usually the facts alleged in a charge are set forth in general terms rather than in great detail. The regional office will assist the charging party in filing the charge. A charge must be filed within six months of the date of the alleged unfair labor practice or else it will be barred as untimely under Section 10(b).

A charge is filed in the regional office in the region in which the unfair labor practice occurred. A copy of the charge must be served, usually by mail, on the charged party. The regional director cannot refuse to accept a charge even though the facts alleged are clearly outside the Board's jurisdiction. A charge is simply an allegation; the fact that a charge is filed is not an indication that the facts alleged are true or that they constitute a violation of the Act.

All regional offices use a standard case numbering system. The first two numbers indicate the region in which the charge is filed; the next two letters indicate whether the charge is against an employer or a union and the provision of Section 8 allegedly violated. The final numbers are the numerical sequence of the charge within the region. For example, in the number 14–CA–1085, 14 indicates that the charge was filed in the fourteenth region, C indicates that the case is an unfair labor practice charge, and A indicates that the charge alleged a violation of Section 8(a), a charge against an employer. The 1085 is the sequence number within the region. Figure 5 is an NLRB chart of the types of cases and the lettering system that the Board uses in both unfair labor practice and representation cases. Unfair labor practice cases begin with a C. For this reason, unfair labor practice charges are frequently referred to by labor practitioners as "C cases."

2. Regional Determination and Appeal

After a charge is filed in the regional office, it is referred to either an attorney or

NATIONAL LABOR RELATIONS BOARD
BASIC PROCEDURES IN CASES INVOLVING
CHARGES OF UNFAIR LABOR PRACTICES

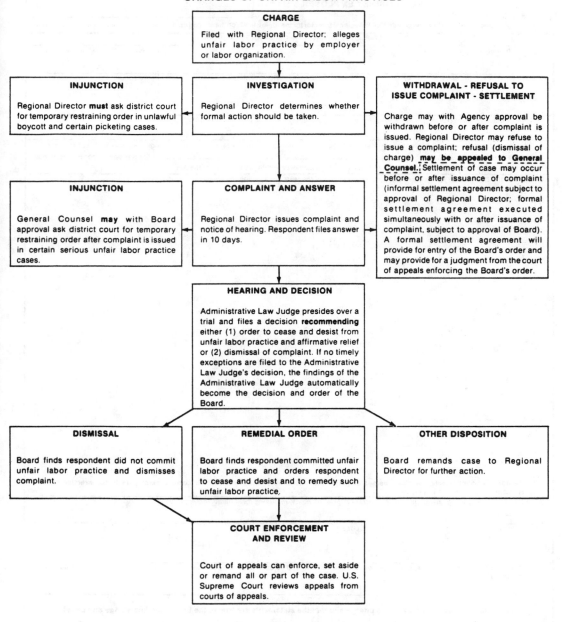

CHARGE

Filed with Regional Director; alleges unfair labor practice by employer or labor organization.

INJUNCTION

Regional Director **must** ask district court for temporary restraining order in unlawful boycott and certain picketing cases.

INVESTIGATION

Regional Director determines whether formal action should be taken.

WITHDRAWAL - REFUSAL TO ISSUE COMPLAINT - SETTLEMENT

Charge may with Agency approval be withdrawn before or after complaint is issued. Regional Director may refuse to issue a complaint; refusal (dismissal of charge) may be appealed to General Counsel. Settlement of case may occur before or after issuance of complaint (informal settlement agreement subject to approval of Regional Director; formal settlement agreement executed simultaneously with or after issuance of complaint, subject to approval of Board). A formal settlement agreement will provide for entry of the Board's order and may provide for a judgment from the court of appeals enforcing the Board's order.

INJUNCTION

General Counsel **may** with Board approval ask district court for temporary restraining order after complaint is issued in certain serious unfair labor practice cases.

COMPLAINT AND ANSWER

Regional Director issues complaint and notice of hearing. Respondent files answer in 10 days.

HEARING AND DECISION

Administrative Law Judge presides over a trial and files a decision **recommending** either (1) order to cease and desist from unfair labor practice and affirmative relief or (2) dismissal of complaint. If no timely exceptions are filed to the Administrative Law Judge's decision, the findings of the Administrative Law Judge automatically become the decision and order of the Board.

DISMISSAL

Board finds respondent did not commit unfair labor practice and dismisses complaint.

REMEDIAL ORDER

Board finds respondent committed unfair labor practice and orders respondent to cease and desist and to remedy such unfair labor practice.

OTHER DISPOSITION

Board remands case to Regional Director for further action.

COURT ENFORCEMENT AND REVIEW

Court of appeals can enforce, set aside or remand all or part of the case. U.S. Supreme Court reviews appeals from courts of appeals.

December 13, 1984

FIGURE 3.

FORM NLRB-501
(11-88)

FORM EXEMPT UNDER 44 U.S.C. 3512

UNITED STATES OF AMERICA
NATIONAL LABOR RELATIONS BOARD
CHARGE AGAINST EMPLOYER

DO NOT WRITE IN THIS SPACE	
Case	Date Filed

INSTRUCTIONS:
File an original and 4 copies of this charge with NLRB Regional Director for the region in which the alleged unfair labor practice occurred or is occurring.

1. EMPLOYER AGAINST WHOM CHARGE IS BROUGHT

a. Name of Employer		b. Number of workers employed
c. Address *(street, city, state, ZIP code)*	d. Employer Representative	e. Telephone No.
f. Type of Establishment *(factory, mine, wholesaler, etc.)*	g. Identify principal product or service	

h. The above-named employer has engaged in and is engaging in unfair labor practices within the meaning of section 8(a), subsections (1)
and *(list subsections)* _____ of the National Labor Relations Act,
and these unfair labor practices are unfair practices affecting commerce within the meaning of the Act.

2. Basis of the Charge *(set forth a clear and concise statement of the facts constituting the alleged unfair labor practices)*

By the above and other acts, the above-named employer has interfered with, restrained, and coerced employees in the exercise of the rights guaranteed in Section 7 of the Act

3. Full name of party filing charge *(if labor organization, give full name, including local name and number)*

4a. Address *(street and number, city, state, and ZIP code)*	4b. Telephone No.

5. Full name of national or international labor organization of which it is an affiliate or constituent unit *(to be filled in when charge is filed by a labor organization)*

6. DECLARATION
I declare that I have read the above charge and that the statements are true to the best of my knowledge and belief.

By _____   _____
         (signature of representative or person making charge)   *(title if any)*

Address _____   _____   _____
                                                                                          (Telephone No.)   *(date)*

WILLFUL FALSE STATEMENTS ON THIS CHARGE CAN BE PUNISHED BY FINE AND IMPRISONMENT (U. S. CODE, TITLE 18, SECTION 1001)

FIGURE 4.

a field examiner within the office for investigation. The investigator reviews the facts, researches the law, and takes formal statements (affidavits) from witnesses. The investigator asks the charged party for a statement of its position and any evidence it wishes to offer in its defense. The charged party must decide whether and to what extent it will cooperate with the investigation.

Sometimes a charge filed with a regional office involves a unique question or a legal area in which the Board's position is unclear. In that case, the regional director may refer the charge to the Advice Section of the Office of the General Counsel. This office advises the regional directors on difficult or unique cases. Occasionally the Advice Section issues memorandums or directives to the regional directors on how to handle cases raising certain issues. Sometimes the general counsel requires that all cases raising a certain issue be forwarded to the Advice Section for consideration. This insures that similar problems arising throughout the country are handled uniformly.

If a case is referred to the general counsel for a decision, the local Board agent assigned to the case informs the charging party that the case is "on advice."

The regional director is required by Section 10(1) to seek a federal court injunction against certain union unfair labor practices if, after investigation, the regional director has reasonable cause to believe the charge is true. These are primarily cases in which the union is alleged to be engaged in unlawful picketing, secondary boycotts, or unlawful hot cargo agreements. Cases in which the Board is required to seek an injunction have priority for investigation. Sometimes a union voluntarily ceases the alleged unlawful conduct after such a charge is filed. In that case, the regional director does not have to seek an injunction.

If the regional director, after investigation, or consultation with advice, determines that the charge lacks merit, the Board agent conducting the investigation will contact the charging party and suggest that the charge

be withdrawn. This is basically a face-saving gesture to avoid a formal dismissal. If the charging party will not withdraw the charge, and the regional director has determined that it lacks merit, the regional director dismisses the charge. If the charge is dismissed, the charging party can appeal the dismissal to the General Counsel Office of Appeals.

If the charging party is not planning to appeal, it is best in most cases to withdraw the charge rather than having it formally dismissed. The only exception might be if the charging party wants detailed reasons for the regional director's decision. A union, for example, might want to present its members with the regional director's detailed reasons if the regional director dismisses a union charge on issues the members consider to be very significant.

The regional director uses one of two dismissal formats: a short or long form. The short-form dismissal briefly states that the charge has been dismissed and can be appealed, without giving any detailed reasons for the dismissal. The long form gives a detailed explanation of the reasons. The charging party's choice is again a tactical one. The charging party is allowed to choose the format the regional director uses. The long form gives the charging party a more detailed statement of the regional director's reasons, and may make the appeal slightly more effective. On the other hand, the long form frequently contains strong statements supporting the charged party. A union might not want a strong statement upholding the employer's position on the record, and should therefore request the short form. Fewer than 10 percent of the regional directors' decisions that are appealed to the general counsel are reversed. The general counsel's decision is final. There is no further appeal to the Board.

A general counsel's decision upholding the regional director's dismissal is not binding on either an arbitrator or a court should there be proceedings before either on the same issue giving rise to the unfair labor practice charge. Still, there may be an ad-

TYPES OF CASES

1. CHARGES OF UNFAIR LABOR PRACTICES (C CASES)

Charge Against Employer		Charge Against Labor Organization	
Section of the Act CA	Section of the Act CB	Section of the Act CC	Section of the Act CD
8(a)(1) To interfere with, restrain or coerce employees in exercise of their rights under Section 7 (to join or assist a labor organization or to refrain).	8(b)(1)(A) To restrain or coerce employees in exercise of their rights under Section 7 (to join or assist a labor organization or to refrain).	8(b)(4)(i) To engage in, or induce or encourage any individual employed by any person engaged in commerce or in an industry affecting commerce, to engage in a strike, work stoppage, or boycott, or (ii) to threaten, coerce, or restrain any person engaged in commerce or in an industry affecting commerce, where in either case an object is:	(C) To force or require any employer to recognize or bargain with a particular labor organization as the representative of its employees if another labor organization has been certified as the representative.
8(a)(2) To dominate or interfere with the formation or administration of a labor organization or contribute financial or other support to it.	8(b)(1)(B) To restrain or coerce an employer in the selection of its representatives for collective bargaining or adjustment of grievances.	(A) To force or require any employer or self-employed person to join any labor or employer organization or to enter into any agreement prohibited by Sec. 8(e).	(D) To force or require any employer to assign particular work to employees in a particular labor organization or in a particular trade, craft, or class rather than to employees in another trade, craft, or class, unless such employer is failing to conform to an appropriate Board order or certification.
8(a)(3) By discrimination in regard to hire or tenure of employment or any term or condition of employment to encourage or discourage membership in any labor organization.	8(b)(2) To cause or attempt to cause an employer to discriminate against an employee.	(B) To force or require any person to cease using, selling, handling, transporting, or otherwise dealing in the products of any other producer, processor, or manufacturer, or to cease doing business with any other person, or force or require any other employer to recognize or bargain with a labor organization as the representative of its employees unless such labor organization has been so certified.	
8(a)(4) To discharge or otherwise discriminate against employees because they have given testimony under the Act.	8(b)(3) To refuse to bargain collectively with employer.		
8(a)(5) To refuse to bargain collectively with representatives of its employees.	8(b)(5) To require of employees the payment of excessive or discriminatory fees for membership.		
	8(b)(6) To cause or attempt to cause an employer to pay or agree to pay money or other thing of value for services which are not performed or not to be performed.		

2. PETITIONS FOR CERTIFICATION OR DECERTIFICATION OF REPRESENTATIVES (R CASES)

By or in Behalf of Employees		By an Employer
Section of the Act RC	Section of the Act RD	Section of the Act RM
9(c)(1)(A)(i) Alleging that a substantial number of employees wish to be represented for collective bargaining and their employer declines to recognize their representative.*	9(c)(1)(A)(ii) Alleging that a substantial number of employees assert that the certified or currently recognized bargaining representative is no longer their representative.*	9(c)(1)(B) Alleging that one or more claims for recognition as exclusive bargaining representative have been received by the employer.*

* If an 8(b)(7) charge has been filed involving the same employer, these statements in RC, RD, and RM petitions are not required.

Charges filed with the National Labor Relations Board are letter-coded and numbered. Unfair labor practice charges are classified as "C" cases and petitions for certification or decertification of representatives as "R" cases. This chart indicates the letter codes used for "C" cases and "R" cases, and also presents a summary of each section involved.

FIGURE 5.

Section of the Act CG	Section of the Act CP	**Charge Against Labor Organization and Employer** Section of the Act CE
8(g) To strike, picket, or otherwise concertedly refuse to work at any health care institution without notifying the institution and the Federal Mediation and Conciliation Service in writing 10 days prior to such action.	8(b)(7) To picket, cause, or threaten the picketing of any employer where an object is to force or require an employer to recognize or bargain with a labor organization as the representative of its employees, or to force or require the employees of an employer to select such labor organization as their collective-bargaining representative, unless such labor organization is currently certified as the representative of such employees: (A) where the employer has lawfully recognized any other labor organization and a question concerning representation may not appropriately be raised under Section 9(c). (B) where within the preceding 12 months a valid election under Section 9(c) has been conducted, or (C) where picketing has been conducted without a petition under 9(c) being filed within a reasonable period of time not to exceed 30 days from the commencement of the picketing; except where the picketing is for the purpose of truthfully advising the public (including consumers) that an employer does not employ members of, or have a contract with, a labor organization, and it does not have an effect of interference with deliveries or services.	8(e) To enter into any contract or agreement (any labor organization and any employer) whereby such employer ceases or refrains or agrees to cease or refrain from handling or dealing in any product of any other employer, or to cease doing business with any other person.

3. OTHER PETITIONS

By or in Behalf of Employees	By a Labor Organization or an Employer	
Section of the Act UD	Board Rules UC	Board Rules AC
9(e)(1) Alleging that employees (30 percent or more of an appropriate unit) wish to rescind an existing union-security agreement.	Subpart C Seeking clarification of an existing bargaining unit.	Subpart C Seeking amendment of an outstanding certification of bargaining representative.

Revised 12/78

verse psychological effect if the general counsel refuses to proceed. Thus, the decision to appeal the regional director's determination must be carefully considered. An appeal should be taken only if the case is sufficiently important and there is a reasonable likelihood of success.

3. Settlement or Issuance of a Complaint

If the regional director determines, based upon the investigation, that a charge has merit, the director will usually advise the charged party of this determination and propose a settlement. A settlement is an agreement in which the violator, whether an employer or a union, agrees to cease the particular unfair labor practice and take whatever action may be necessary to correct the wrong, including back pay if appropriate. A written settlement may be either informal or formal. An informal settlement is approved by the regional director. A formal settlement is approved by the Board, usually in conjunction with the issuance of a complaint. Formal settlements are usually used only in aggravated or extensive unfair labor practice cases. If the charged party is unwilling to enter into such a settlement, the regional director issues a complaint. A complaint is a detailed legal document, drafted with the same care and precision as a suit to be filed in court. It contains detailed allegations to show that the Board's jurisdictional standards are met, summarizes the facts giving rise to the violation, and lists the provisions of the Act that have been violated. Even after a complaint has been issued, the Board will still try to settle the case if possible.

A charge can be filed by anyone and does not indicate that the facts are true or that the charge has merit. In contrast, a complaint is issued only if the regional director determines that the charge has merit. Basically, a complaint describes in greater detail the facts generally alleged in the charge. However, a complaint may allege acts that were not even mentioned in the charge, and that the charged party might not have even known about. The Board is permitted to base its complaint on the charges alleged, and on any additional violations that the Board investigator discovers during the course of the investigation that are reasonably related to the charge. Sometimes, to avoid any question of the relationship, the regional director will ask a charging party to file an amended charge alleging additional violations discovered during the course of the investigation.

A charge must be filed within six months of the date of the alleged unfair labor practice. However, there is no maximum time limit between when a charge is filed and a complaint is issued. Sometimes many months may elapse between the filing of a charge and the issuance of a complaint, especially in complex cases that have been referred to Advice for a decision or in which a complaint is issued pursuant to successful appeal to the Office of Appeals.

4. Trial Procedures and Board Decision

After a complaint is issued, there is a hearing before an administrative law judge, commonly referred to as an ALJ (previously known as Trial Examiner). The administrative law judge, a civil service appointee, is independent of the Board and hears the case independently. Unfair labor practice cases are tried in the region where the case arose. Administrative law judges are permanently stationed in Atlanta, New York, Washington, D.C., and San Francisco but travel to the regions for hearings.

The trial of an unfair labor practice case is similar to a typical civil trial, except there is no jury. The ALJ functions very much like a federal judge. An unfair labor practice trial is a formal proceeding, very different from typically informal arbitration hearings. Section 10(b) of the Act provides that the federal rules of evidence apply in an unfair labor practice case hearing.

At the trial, the general counsel has the burden of proving that the Act has been violated as alleged in the complaint. An attorney from the regional office representing the general counsel tries the case. The charging party is not required to have its own attorney, although it is permitted to have one at its own expense. Even if the charging party has an attorney, the general counsel's attorney has the primary responsibility for trying the case. The charging party's attorney can, however, give valuable assistance to the Board's attorney because of familiarity with the case. At trial, the charged party, termed the respondent, is entitled to an attorney at its own cost.

There is one important difference between the role of an ALJ and a federal judge. District court judges enter binding decisions that can be appealed. However, an administrative law judge simply makes a *recommended* decision and order for the Board. This decision is not binding unless approved by the Board.

The ALJ's decision contains recommended findings of fact and conclusions of law as to whether the facts constitute a violation of the Act. If the ALJ finds a violation, the ALJ issues a recommended order listing the actions the respondent must undertake to cure the effects of its unlawful actions, such as requiring back pay for a discharged employee. Either the charging party, the general counsel, or the respondent has an absolute right to appeal the ALJ's decision to the Board. The Board then makes a binding decision.

A party files an appeal of the ALJ's decision by filing "exceptions" to the ALJ's decision. This is a formal document listing the alleged errors the ALJ made in factual conclusions, legal conclusions, or in the proposed remedy. Briefs and counter-briefs are filed. The Board makes the final decision and order based on the transcript of the hearing, the exhibits, and the briefs. There is not another full trial before the Board. The Board's decision is a binding, enforceable order.

5. Appeal Procedures

After the Board's decision, the case can be appealed to a United States Court of Appeals. Figure 6 illustrates the enforcement process. There are eleven courts of appeals, each serving an appellate circuit composed of a number of states, and one appellate court for the District of Columbia. The party losing before the Board can appeal the decision to the court of appeals covering the state where the alleged unfair labor practice occurred, where the appealing party resides or transacts business, or in the United States Court of Appeals for the District of Columbia.

On the other hand, the respondent can simply refuse to obey the Board's decision. In that case, the general counsel can file a petition in the appropriate court of appeals to enforce the Board's decision.

There is no new trial before the court of appeals. The court bases its decision upon the transcript and exhibits of the hearing before the ALJ and the Board's decision. The Supreme Court has held that a court of appeals must uphold the Board's decision if it is based on substantial evidence on the record as a whole. This means that if there is substantial evidence to support the Board's decision, the court of appeals cannot reverse the Board even though the court might have reached a different conclusion on the same evidence. This standard is applied because in establishing the NLRB, Congress intended the Board, not the courts, to be the primary agency to interpret and apply the Act.

The court of appeals can enforce the Board's decision and order in full, modify the Board's decision in some aspect and enforce the decision as modified, or vacate the Board's entire decision. Sometimes the court may remand a case to the Board for reconsideration in light of some point raised by the court of appeals that the court feels the Board should consider before further action is taken. Overall, most of the Board's decisions are upheld on appeal. Practically,

NLRB ORDER ENFORCEMENT CHART

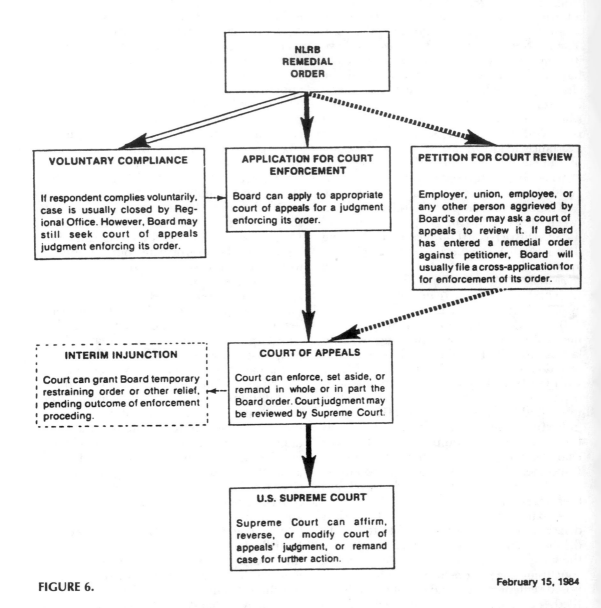

FIGURE 6.

February 15, 1984

there is little chance of reversing the Board on appeal if the only issue is one of fact, such as whether an employee was discharged for cause or for union activity. There is a greater likelihood of success on appeal if the issue pertains to the law's meaning. The substantial evidence rule discourages the courts from substituting their judgment for the Board's on fact issues.

There is a unique relationship between the NLRB and the courts of appeals that is sometimes difficult for lay persons to understand. The Board is bound by only Supreme Court interpretations. The Board is bound by a court of appeals decision in a particular case affirming, denying, modifying, or remanding the Board's decision. However, the Board is not bound by any general interpretations of the Labor Management Relations Act that a court of appeals may make. Sometimes a particular court of appeals' interpretation will differ from the Board's on a specific point. The Board may continue to issue decisions applying one view of the law that the court of appeals consistently reverses because the court has a different interpretation. Sometimes some courts of appeals may agree with the Board's interpretation while other courts of appeals may not. This means that some courts of appeals will affirm the Board's decision on a given point while other courts of appeals will refuse to enforce the Board's decision on the same issue. That conflict may continue until such time as the Board changes its view, the courts of appeals finally reach agreement with the Board, or the Supreme Court issues a binding decision.

A party appealing a Board's decision usually has a choice as to where to appeal; and because courts of appeals may disagree with the Board or among themselves, a party may maneuver to file its appeal in a court of appeals that would interpret the law favorably. This is called *forum shopping*. Generally, the court of appeals in which an appeal is first filed has jurisdiction over the case. Sometimes parties engage in a "race to the courthouse" attempting to file their respective appeals as quickly as possible in a court of appeals favorable to their position. Although forum shopping or courthouse races do occur in important or unique cases, appeals in most cases are routinely filed in the court of appeals where the unfair labor practice occurred.

a. Appeal to the Supreme Court. Following a court of appeals decision, it is possible to appeal to the Supreme Court. In contrast to the court of appeals, which must consider every case appealed to it, the Supreme Court has discretion as to whether it will consider a case. The technical term for requesting the Supreme Court to hear a case is a Petition for Writ of Certiorari (abbreviated "Cert"). A petition for Cert describes the basic facts of the case and the reasons why the Supreme Court should consider it. The petition is reviewed by the Court, and if at least four of the justices agree to hear the case, the petition is granted. The case is then placed on the Court's appeal calendar. There is no trial before the Supreme Court; the appeal is based on the trial transcript, the Board's decision, and the parties' briefs.

The Supreme Court usually does not hear a case just because the facts are complicated. Normally, the Supreme Court considers only a case involving a unique issue of law or if the courts of appeals have reached conflicting decisions on the same issue and the Court wants to resolve the uncertainty that the conflict creates. Sometimes, however, an issue may be so controversial that the Court will simply prefer not to consider the matter at that time until the ramifications are clear. Denial of a Writ of Certiorari does not indicate that the Court agrees or disagrees with the lower court decision; it simply means that the Court, for whatever reason, chose not to hear that particular case.

Supreme Court action, either in denying a Writ of Certiorari, or in affirming or reversing the decision of the court of appeals on the merits, is the final step in the judicial process. Of course, sometimes the same case may be before a court of appeals or the Supreme Court more than once. A court of appeals, for example, may modify or remand a Board decision, and the case may come back to a court of appeals for a second time. Similarly, the Supreme Court may remand a case to the court of appeals for reconsideration in light of a principle stated by the Supreme Court. The decision on remand may be reappealed to the Supreme Court after the court of appeals issues its second opinion.

6. Compliance Proceedings

After an unfair labor practice charge is finally resolved, either by settlement, by a Board decision, or by a final appellate court decision, the case goes to the compliance stage. Each regional office has a compliance officer who ensures that the Board's order or the terms of a settlement agreement are complied with. That includes making sure that required notices have been posted, that any backpay has been paid, or that any other actions required have been taken.

An unlawfully discharged employee is entitled to backpay based on the difference between what would have been earned and what was earned, on a quarterly basis, after discharge. If there is a disagreement on the amount of backpay under a Board decision that the parties cannot settle, the matter is resolved in a backpay specification hearing. The regional director issues a backpay specification alleging the amount of backpay the regional director has determined the employee should receive. The employer has the burden of proving that the amount claimed is erroneous and that a lesser amount is due. These cases usually involve issues such as whether the employee was actively looking for work while unemployed, as the law requires; or whether the employee would have been legitimately terminated before the date the Board ordered the reinstatement (such as by a legitimate economic layoff), so that the backpay period should end prior to the date the Board ordered reinstatement. Backpay specification hearings follow the same procedures followed in an unfair labor practice case and are heard by an ALJ. There is again an absolute right to appeal the ALJ's decision to the Board and ultimately to a court of appeals.

Usually, the compliance officer simply checks with the charging party about sixty days after the Board's decision has been rendered or a case has been settled to make sure that the Board's decision or settlement is being complied with. If so, the case is routinely closed. If a settlement is not being complied with, the settlement can be set aside and the case will be resumed as a formal proceeding. If an employer fails to follow a Board decision, the matter can be appealed to a court of appeals by the Board. If there has been a court decision enforcing the Board's award, and the respondent is not complying with the court decision, the Board can request the court of appeals to find the respondent in contempt of court.

The Board decides whether or not a respondent is complying with a Board order and what action to take if it is not. Suppose that an employer has been ordered to bargain in good faith with a union. The compliance officer will contact the union about the employer's compliance. If the union believes that the employer is not bargaining in good faith, the compliance officer will investigate the facts. The regional director, acting for the general counsel, determines whether the employer is complying.

If the regional director decides that the employer is complying, notwithstanding the union's assertion that it is not, what can the union do? Can the union seek court enforcement or contempt of court if the employer is failing to comply? No, it is the general counsel's decision; he or she controls the case. If the general counsel does not act, the union cannot go to court on its own. There have been several cases involving flagrant employer violations, in which the general counsel has settled pending court actions over the union's objection that the general counsel accepted a settlement that was too lenient. The unions involved could protest, but they could not prevent the general counsel from taking such action.

7. Unfair Labor Practice Processing Time

A charge has to be filed within six months of the unfair labor practice, although there is an exception for what is called a "continuing violation." For example, an employer's pattern of bad-faith bargaining may continue for a long time. The time limit for filing a charge over a continuing violation is six months from the last unlawful act, which might be the last bargaining session. A discharge is not a continuing violation, so a charge must be filed within six months from the date of the discharge. It is best, however, to file a charge within six months of the first violation. Do not rely upon the Board's concluding that the violation is a continuing one.

The regional director's processing in the typical unfair labor practice charge case usually takes approximately forty-five days from the filing of a charge to issuance of a complaint. In that time, the regional director either dismisses a charge that lacks merit or attempts to settle a meritorious case. More time is taken in a complicated case or cases sent to the general counsel for advice. If the regional director is unable to settle a meritorious case, and a formal complaint and trial are necessary, a case is usually set for trial between three to six weeks from the date the complaint was issued.

Allowing time for all parties to file briefs with the administrative law judge, and for the ALJ to consider the case, the ALJ decision is usually issued approximately four months after the hearing. If the ALJ's decision is appealed to the Board, it takes about one year from the ALJ's decision for the Board to issue its decision.

These time limits are the average for a typical case. If a case is complicated, or if the Board members are divided over it, the Board may hold the case for a longer time, perhaps for several years. If a case raises an issue that the Board is reconsidering, other cases raising that issue may be held up for long periods while the Board decides the point.

If a case is appealed to a circuit court of appeals, it takes close to a year (longer in some circuits) after the appeal is filed before the court's decision is rendered. That time includes time for filing the Board's case record with the appellate court, filing briefs, oral argument, and court consideration. The courts of appeals also, of course, have a backlog of cases to consider. If a case is appealed to the Supreme Court and the Court agrees to hear the case, it may take at least another year before the Court reaches a decision.

Thus, some labor cases may take three years to resolve: one year to process the case through the Board, a second year to go through the court of appeals, and a third year if the case reaches the Supreme Court.

In some cases, employers will take advantage of the time lag and attempt to destroy employee rights by illegally delaying the process even longer. Some employers will risk a court of appeals contempt citation because it is cheaper for them to pay fines than to pay the higher wages a union may have won for its employees. Most cases, however, do not go through this entire process. In fiscal year 1987, 92.7 percent of all meritorious unfair labor practice charges were settled. Contested Board decisions were issued in only 4.5 percent of the cases. Only 0.7 percent of all charges filed went all the way to a court of appeals decision.[7]

E. PROCEDURE IN REPRESENTATION CASES

The form filed to start a representation proceeding is a petition (see Figure 7). Figure 8 is a chart of the representation proceedings process. Just as unfair labor practice cases have a "C" letter designation, representation cases also have letter designations. A petition filed by a union to represent employees has the designation "RC." Figure 5 shows the types of representation petitions and the designations used. Representation petitions use the same numbering system as used in unfair labor practice cases: the regional number, the letter code, and the case number. Representation cases are commonly referred to as "R" cases.

1. Administrative Investigation— The "Showing of Interest"

Representation matters are governed by Section 9 of the Act. A representation pe-

---

[7] Source: Office of the General Counsel, National Labor Relations Board, Office Systems Management Branch.

FORM NLRB-502
(5-85)

UNITED STATES GOVERNMENT
NATIONAL LABOR RELATIONS BOARD
PETITION

FORM EXEMPT UNDER 44 U.S.C. 3512

DO NOT WRITE IN THIS SPACE

Case No.	Date Filed

INSTRUCTIONS: Submit an original and 4 copies of this Petition to the NLRB Regional Office in the Region in which the employer concerned is located. If more space is required for any one item, attach additional sheets, numbering item accordingly.

The Petitioner alleges that the following circumstances exist and requests that the National Labor Relations Board proceed under its proper authority pursuant to Section 9 of the National Labor Relations Act.

1. PURPOSE OF THIS PETITION (*If box RC, RM, or RD is checked and a charge under Section 8(b)(7) of the Act has been filed involving the Employer named herein, the statement following the description of the type of petition shall not be deemed made.*)   **(Check One)**

☐ **RC-CERTIFICATION OF REPRESENTATIVE** - A substantial number of employees wish to be represented for purposes of collective bargaining by Petitioner and Petitioner desires to be certified as representative of the employees.

☐ **RM-REPRESENTATION (EMPLOYER PETITION)** - One or more individuals or labor organizations have presented a claim to Petitioner to be recognized as the representative of employees of Petitioner.

☐ **RD-DECERTIFICATION** - A substantial number of employees assert that the certified or currently recognized bargaining representative is no longer their representative.

☐ **UD-WITHDRAWAL OF UNION SHOP AUTHORITY** - Thirty percent (30%) or more of employees in a bargaining unit covered by an agreement between their employer and a labor organization desire that such authority be rescinded.

☐ **UC-UNIT CLARIFICATION** - A labor organization is currently recognized by Employer, but Petitioner seeks clarification of placement of certain employees: (*Check one*) ☐ In unit not previously certified. ☐ In unit previously certified in Case No. _____

☐ **AC-AMENDMENT OF CERTIFICATION** - Petitioner seeks amendment of certification issued in Case No. _____ *Attach statement describing the specific amendment sought.*

2. Name of Employer	Employer Representative to contact	Telephone Number

3. Address(es) of Establishment(s) involved (*Street and number, city, State, ZIP code*)

4a. Type of Establishment (*Factory, mine, wholesaler, etc.*)	4b. Identify principal product or service

5. Unit Involved (*In UC petition, describe **present** bargaining unit and attach description of proposed clarification.*)	6a. Number of Employees in Unit:
Included	Present
	Proposed (By UC/AC)
Excluded	6b. Is this petition supported by 30% or more of the employees in the unit? * ____ Yes ____No *Not applicable in RM, UC, and AC

(*If you have checked box RC in 1 above, check and complete EITHER item 7a or 7b, whichever is applicable*)

7a.☐ Request for recognition as Bargaining Representative was made on (*Date*) _____ and Employer declined recognition on or about (*Date*)_____ (*If no reply received, so state*).

7b.☐ Petitioner is currently recognized as Bargaining Representative and desires certification under the Act.

8. Name of Recognized or Certified Bargaining Agent (*If none, so state*)	Affiliation
Address and Telephone Number	Date of Recognition or Certification

9. Expiration Date of Current Contract, If any (*Month, Day, Year*)	10. If you have checked box UD in 1 above, show here the date of execution of agreement granting union shop (*Month, Day, and Year*)

11a. Is there now a strike or picketing at the Employer's establishment(s) Involved? Yes ____ No ____	11b. If so, approximately how many employees are participating?

11c. The Employer has been picketed by or on behalf of (*Insert Name*) _____, a labor organization, of (*Insert Address*)_____ Since (*Month, Day, Year*) _____

12. Organizations or individuals other than Petitioner (*and other than those named in items 8 and 11c*), which have claimed recognition as representatives and other organizations and individuals known to have a representative interest in any employees in unit described in item 5 above. (*If none, so state*)

Name	Affilation	Address	Date of Claim (*Required only if Petition is filed by Employer*)

I declare that I have read the above petition and that the statements are true to the best of my knowledge and belief.

_____
(*Name of Petitioner and Affilation, if any*)

By _____   _____
   (*Signature of Representative or person filing petition*)   (*Title, if any*)

Address _____   _____
   (*Street and number, city, State, and ZIP Code*)   (*Telephone Number*)

WILLFUL FALSE STATEMENTS ON THIS PETITION CAN BE PUNISHED BY FINE AND IMPRISONMENT (U. S. CODE, TITLE 18, SECTION 1001)

FIGURE 7.

tition filed by a union must be supported by a "showing of interest" that at least 30 percent of the employees in the proposed unit want an election. This rule prevents the Board from getting bogged down in elections that the union has no chance of winning. Usually a union showing of interest is made by authorization cards signed by 30 percent of the employees in the bargaining unit stating that they wish union representation. However, cards are not the only method that can be used. Employees can simply sign a petition circulated by the union. However, cards are undoubtedly the preferred method. Cards must be dated to be accepted by the Board and as a matter of good practice, they should also be initialed by the person getting the signatures. In that way, if there is ever any question about the authenticity of the card, a witness can verify it.

The Board makes an "administrative investigation" to determine whether the petition is supported by the 30 percent showing. Someone from the regional director's office conducts the investigation usually by verifying the number of cards against a payroll list submitted by the employer to the regional office. The Board has consistently held that the question of a "showing of interest" is an internal matter for the Board to resolve. That means that there is no hearing on the question of showing of interest. Rather, if showing of interest is disputed, either side may informally submit evidence on the question to the regional director for consideration.

Another union may intervene in a representation case proceeding if it has at least one valid representation card signed by a bargaining unit employee, or on the basis of a collective bargaining contract purportedly covering the proposed unit.

2. Consent Elections

If, after preliminary investigation, the regional director determines that the petition raises a question concerning representation (that the petition is properly supported by a "showing of interest" and that the Board appears to have jurisdiction as discussed above), a regional office staff member normally contacts the union and the employer to determine whether the parties can agree to the terms of an election. If so, the parties may enter into a consent election agreement that includes a description of the appropriate unit, the employee classifications to be included and excluded, the time and place of the election, and the payroll eligibility date (the date by which a person must be employed in order to vote). These issues are discussed in detail in Chapter Two.

There are two types of consent election agreements. Under one type, the Agreement for Consent Election, the regional director's decision on postelection matters is final with no appeal to the Board. Under the second type, a Stipulation for Certification Upon Consent Election, the regional director issues a report on postelection challenges and objections, which summarizes the facts and recommends a decision. This report can be appealed to the Board. Most parties who agree to a consent election execute the Stipulation Agreement to retain the right to appeal.

The terms for a consent agreement are frequently worked out by phone. If an agreement is reached, the Board agent may arrange a mutually convenient time for the parties to sign the consent agreement form or may simply mail copies to the parties for signature. Sometimes, if the preliminary discussions indicate that an agreement may be possible, the regional director will schedule an informal conference between the parties at the regional office or elsewhere to work out the details. If there is not a prompt agreement for an election, the regional director will send out a notice of hearing. Even then, however, the regional office will usually continue its efforts to work out a consent agreement including a pre-hearing conference for that purpose on the day of the hearing.

OUTLINE OF REPRESENTATION PROCEDURES UNDER SECTION 9(c)

Revised 12/78

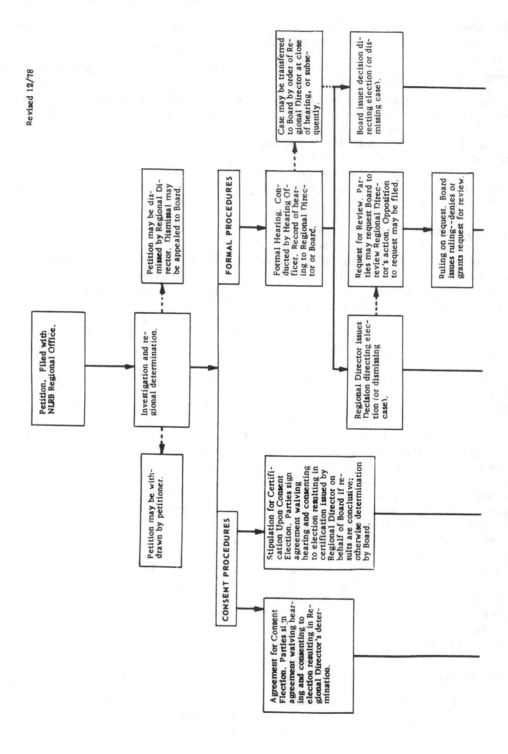

Petition. Filed with NLRB Regional Office.

Investigation and regional determination.

Petition may be withdrawn by petitioner.

Petition may be dismissed by Regional Director. Dismissal may be appealed to Board.

CONSENT PROCEDURES

Agreement for Consent Election. Parties sign agreement waiving hearing and consenting to election resulting in Regional Director's determination.

Stipulation for Certification Upon Consent Election. Parties sign agreement waiving hearing and consenting to election resulting in certification issued by Regional Director on behalf of Board if results are conclusive; otherwise determination by Board.

FORMAL PROCEDURES

Formal Hearing. Conducted by Hearing Officer. Record of hearing to Regional Director or Board.

Regional Director issues Decision directing election (or dismissing case).

Case may be transferred to Board by order of Regional Director at close of hearing, or subsequently.

Board issues decision directing election (or dismissing case).

Request for Review. Parties may request Board to review Regional Director's action. Opposition to request may be filed.

Ruling on request. Board issues ruling--denies or grants request for review.

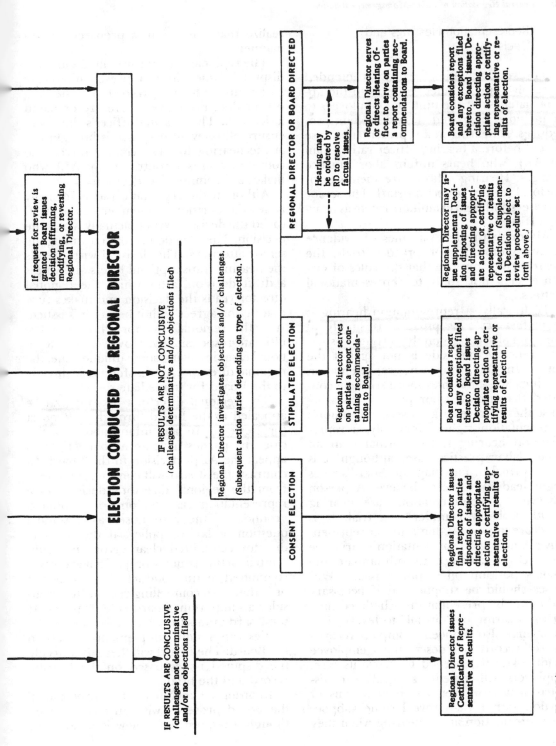

ELECTION CONDUCTED BY REGIONAL DIRECTOR

If request for review is granted Board issues decision affirming, modifying, or reversing Regional Director.

IF RESULTS ARE NOT CONCLUSIVE
(challenges determinative and/or objections filed)

Regional Director investigates objections and/or challenges.
(Subsequent action varies depending on type of election.)

IF RESULTS ARE CONCLUSIVE
(challenges not determinative and/or no objections filed)

CONSENT ELECTION

Regional Director issues final report to parties disposing of issues and directing appropriate action or certifying representative or results of election.

STIPULATED ELECTION

Regional Director serves on parties a report containing recommendations to Board.

Board considers report and any exceptions filed thereto. Board issues Decision directing appropriate action or certifying representative or results of election.

REGIONAL DIRECTOR OR BOARD DIRECTED

Hearing may be ordered by RD to resolve factual issues.

Regional Director may issue supplemental Decision disposing of issues and directing appropriate action or certifying representative or results of election. (Supplemental Decision subject to review procedure set forth above.)

Regional Director serves or directs Hearing Officer to serve on parties a report containing recommendations to Board.

Board considers report and any exceptions filed thereto. Board issues Decision directing appropriate action or certifying representative or results of election.

Regional Director issues Certification of Representative or Results.

FIGURE 8.

29

3. Representation Hearings and Decisions

The representation hearing is intended to resolve any disputed issue as to the appropriateness of the unit, the employees to be included or excluded, and election procedures. A hearing in a representation case is held before a hearing officer rather than an ALJ, who hears unfair labor practice charges. Hearing officers are members of the local regional director's staff. The senior attorneys and field examiners rotate as hearing officers.

Although the federal rules of evidence apply to unfair labor practice trials, the Board's rules provide that the rules of evidence shall not apply to representational matters.

Technically, a representation hearing is "nonadversary"; its purpose is simply to bring out all the facts on the disputed issues. Theoretically, one side is not against the other. In fact, however, representation hearings are sometimes more strongly contested than unfair labor practice cases because they involve basic issues of the union's representation rights. Generally, a representation hearing is less formal than an unfair labor practice case, although it is more formal in fact than the Board's rules might lead someone to believe. A person observing a representation case hearing would probably consider it a trial. It is therefore important that a union representative handling a representation hearing be prepared in advance to substantiate the union's position on disputed issues. Witnesses should be subpoenaed if necessary and either be present at the scheduled time for the hearing or "on-call" to testify. The union may also subpoena company records (payroll records, job descriptions, employee handbooks, etc.) needed to prove its case. Employers will sometimes stipulate to disputed issues or even agree to a consent election rather than reveal some subpoenaed information at the hearing when they realize that the union is prepared in this manner.

The regional director usually decides the disputed issues in a representation case based on the hearing record. The hearing officer does not make or even recommend a decision. The hearing officer's duty is to ensure all relevant evidence is brought out at the hearing for the regional director to consider. This is in contrast to the ALJ, who makes a recommended decision.

Although the regional director formally issues the decision, a member of the staff, called the decision writer, actually writes the decision. This function is rotated among the senior attorneys. The decision writer reads the hearing transcript and briefs and writes a draft decision, after which the regional director reads the decision and makes sure that he/she agrees with it before it is issued. It is the regional director who bears the ultimate responsibility. However, in exceptional cases involving some unique issue, the regional director can transfer a case directly to the Board for immediate decision.

The regional director's decision can be appealed to the Board through a "Request for Review." In an unfair labor practice case, the parties have an absolute right to appeal the ALJ's decision to the Board. In contrast, the Board will consider an appeal from the regional director's decision in a representation case on only four limited grounds: if the case raises a substantial question of law or policy; if the regional director committed clear error on a substantial factual issue; if prejudicial error was committed in the conduct of the hearing; or if there are compelling reasons to reconsider an important Board rule or policy. If the Board grants the request for review, the parties can submit supplemental briefs to the Board. The Board will thereafter decide the disputed issues based on the hearing record and the briefs.

In order to expedite election procedures, the Board proceeds with an election even though a request for review is pending or has been granted. Under this procedure, the ballots are impounded pending the outcome of the request. If the request for review is denied or the regional director's decision upheld on review, the ballots are counted and the result is certified as in any other election. If the Board overrules the regional director's decision upon review, the ballots are not counted.

The general counsel does not have a role in representation proceedings. In an unfair labor practice case, the charging party files the charge. If the regional director, acting for the general counsel, finds merit in the charge, the general counsel issues a complaint and prosecutes the case. In a representation case, however, the petitioner is on its own. The regional director will investigate a petition to ensure it raises a question of representation, may suggest changes in the unit description, and will try to work out a consent election between the parties if they are agreeable. But if there is a hearing on disputed issues, the petitioner presents its own case. The hearing officer is required to make a complete record, but the Board does not act on behalf of either party. The decision of the regional director or the Board resolves the disputed issues and either dismisses the petition or directs an election in the appropriate unit.

4. Postelection Proceedings

At the time of the election, whether pursuant to a consent agreement or an order after hearing, either party can challenge the ballot of an employee who the party believes is ineligible to vote. If there is any unlawful conduct during the election campaign, either party can file objections to the election within seven days after the election.[8] If there are no challenges or objections, the regional director certifies the results, and the matter

[8] See Chapter Two for a discussion of the grounds for challenging a voter and for setting aside an election because of campaign misconduct.

is closed.

If there are objections or challenges, the regional director can investigate them administratively without a hearing. In that case, the parties simply submit their evidence to the regional director, and the director issues a decision based on the evidence as submitted. If the evidence is conflicting or there are issues of witness credibility, the regional director will order a hearing on the challenges or objections to the election. The regional director has discretion to choose between an administrative investigation or hearing (see Figure 8).

If there is a hearing on postelection challenges or objections, it is held before a hearing officer following the same procedures used in a preelection hearing. The action the regional director takes following the hearing depends upon whether the election was by consent or was directed by a regional director or Board order after a hearing. If the parties entered into a stipulation consent agreement as discussed above, the regional director issues a report on challenges and objections that summarizes the facts and recommends a decision. This report can then be appealed to the Board. If the parties entered into an Agreement for Consent Election, the regional director issues a final decision which is not appealable.

In a directed election the regional director can either issue a recommended report on the challenges or objections, as in a consent election, or can direct the hearing officer to issue such a report. In that case, the report can be appealed to the Board. The regional director can also issue a formal decision from which there is no automatic right to appeal. Rather, the parties can request review, as in the case of a regional director's decision in a preelection hearing. In most cases regional directors issue a final decision rather than just a recommended report.

The final step in the representation process is certification of the election results. Certification is made by the regional director of the Board following resolution of any postelection objections or challenges. When employees refer to a union as being certified, they are referring to a union that has won an election. Actually, though, the results are certified whether the union wins or loses.

5. Appellate Review of Representation Decisions

Although the Board's decision in an unfair labor practice case may be appealed to the court of appeals, there is no direct right of judicial review in representation cases. What can an employer do if a union wins an election, but the employer believes that the Board's decision on the unit, election challenges, or election procedures was in error? An elaborate ritual ensues.

The only way the employer can challenge the representation proceedings is by refusing to bargain with the union on the grounds it was improperly certified due to the Board's erroneous decision in the representation case. The union must then file an unfair labor practice charge alleging a violation of Section 8(a)(5) of the Act (refusal to bargain). The case is processed through the unfair labor practice procedures discussed above. The case is handled more quickly, though, because the Board does not permit an employer to relitigate the issues that were raised previously in the representation case. The Board normally reaffirms its prior rulings in the disputed representation case and orders the employer to bargain.

The employer can then appeal the Board's decision in the unfair labor practice case to the court of appeals. The court of appeals can review the Board's ruling on the representation issues as part of its review of the unfair labor practice case. The court can either rule that the employer properly refused to bargain because the union was improperly certified or it can affirm the Board's decision and order the employer to bargain.

This appeal procedure may seem to be a cumbersome process, as it allows an employer to drag things out for a long time. On the other hand, because the process is cumbersome and expensive, most employers, even if dissatisfied with the result, simply accept the NLRB's decision in representation cases and forego an appeal. Thus, in many cases, the employer and union bargain sooner than if there were a direct appeal of a representation case decision.

6. Representation Case Processing Time

If the parties do not enter into a consent agreement, a hearing is usually held within thirty days from the date a petition was filed. In that time the regional director must make an administrative investigation into the union's showing of interest, explore the possibility of a consent agreement, and then arrange a hearing date if consent is not possible. The regional director's decision after a hearing, allowing time for briefs, is usually issued quickly in representation cases, frequently within two or three weeks after the hearing. Thus, even in a contested election, the regional director's determination is usually made within forty-five days from the date the petition was filed. Elections are normally held twenty-five to thirty days after an election directed by a regional director or thirty days from the date of a Board-directed election.

The processing is quicker in a consent election. The realistic minimum for an election would be about four weeks after a petition is filed. A consent agreement might be entered into within a week or two after a petition is filed. An employer has to submit a list of the employees who are in the proposed unit to the union (see Chapter Two) and has seven days after a consent agreement is executed, or after an election is directed following a hearing, to file the list of names with the Board. The election cannot be scheduled for less than ten days after the list is due. Thus, seventeen days from the date of a consent agreement is the absolute minimum amount of time. As a practical matter, a certain week or day of the week may be the best time to hold the election for all parties so the election may be scheduled three or four weeks after consent date. If there is a hearing, and the employer requests review of the regional director's decision, the process takes longer. It might take the Board thirty days to rule on the request for review. If the Board grants review, a Board decision may take four to six months or more if the case is unusually complex or novel. Neither the filing of a Request for Review nor the granting of such a request by the Board stays holding the election unless the Board specifically so orders. Rather, in such cases, the election proceeds as scheduled, but the ballots are impounded without being counted until the Board rules. If, after an election is held, challenges and/or objections are filed, the process takes more time, depending upon whether the postelection disputes are resolved by the Board or regional director. Postelection processing takes about as long as the preelection procedures discussed above—four to six weeks in simple cases, but a minimum four to six months in complicated ones. In a strongly contested representation case the entire process may take close to a year, after which the employer can seek judicial review by refusing to bargain after the union is certified. That will easily add another year to the process.

But most representation cases, even those with disputed issues, are handled expeditiously. According to the General Counsel's "Summary of Operations for Fiscal Year 1987," the regions conducted 4,173 initial elections in fiscal year 1987 of which 83 percent were held pursuant to agreement of the parties. There were 6,874 representation and related petitions filed in 1987. Formal decisions by a regional director were issued in only 905 of these cases and only 54 cases reached the Board for a full decision. In fiscal year 1987, the median time to process an election petition from the date of filing to the election day was 48.4 days.

This figure varies by only a few days from year to year. Although most election cases are handled informally and quickly, the procedures can be abused by employers who use every delaying tactic to gain time to undermine the union.

7. Other Types of Representation Petitions

The procedures outlined above are used when a union files a representation petition for an election. Employees may also file a petition either for a union to represent them or to decertify (revoke the representation rights) their existing union. Employees may file a petition to revoke the union security clause of their collective bargaining agreement (see Chapter Ten). An employer can also file a petition for an election (an RM petition), but only if the employer has a good-faith doubt, based on objective considerations, that the union no longer represents a majority of the unit's employees (see Chapter Five). The procedures discussed above are used in processing all types of representation petitions. However, a showing of interest is not required for an employer petition.

A union may also file a petition to amend its certification (an AC petition). This petition may be filed if there has been a change in the name of the employer or the union, but no change in the bargaining unit. For example, if the local number of a union has been changed, the union can file a petition to amend its certification to the new number.

A unit clarification (UC) petition may be filed if the employer and the union disagree about whether certain employee classifications should be included within an existing unit. This situation occurs most frequently when an employer adds new jobs after a unit has been certified and the parties are unable to agree whether the new classifications are within the existing unit or are entitled to separate representation.

If there is a question of representation,

rather than just a simple change of name, a unit amendment petition cannot be used. If a union wants to represent additional employees, it must file either a unit clarification petition or a representation petition, as appropriate (see Chapter Two). The procedures followed in unit amendment or clarification cases are basically the same as in election cases except that no showing of interest is required.

F. CONSOLIDATED UNFAIR LABOR PRACTICE AND REPRESENTATION PROCEEDINGS

Frequently, improper conduct during an election campaign may be grounds both for setting aside the election in a representation case and an unfair labor practice charge. For example, an employer might discharge an employee during an election campaign because the employee favored the union. In such a case the union would file an objection to the election and an unfair labor practice charge against the employer. The cases would be consolidated for hearing. Consolidated cases are heard before an ALJ and are processed the same as unfair labor practice cases, using the procedures discussed above.

G. OTHER AGENCIES ADMINISTERING LABOR LAW

Although this chapter has emphasized the role of the National Labor Relations Board, a number of other agencies are also important in labor law. The Department of Labor administers portions of the Labor Management Reporting and Disclosure Act (see Chapter Eleven), as well as the Fair Labor Standards Act, the Occupational Safety and Health Act, and portions of the Employee Retirement Income Security Act. The Equal Employment Opportunity Commission (EEOC) (see Chapter Thirteen) administers Title VII of the Civil Rights Act. The EEOC also administers the Equal Pay and the Age Discrimination in Employment Acts, acts formerly administered by the Department of Labor.

Finally, despite the emphasis on federal law in this text, the states still play an important role in labor relations. State courts have retained their traditional jurisdiction to prevent violent conduct during a labor dispute and have concurrent jurisdiction with the federal courts, applying federal law to enforce the terms of collective bargaining agreements. The states also have authority to enforce state labor laws over employers not covered by federal law (see Chapter Fourteen).

Summary   The Railway Labor Act, passed in 1926, was the first comprehensive federal statutory regulation of labor-management relations. It specifically recognized the right of employees to engage in collective bargaining. This act was followed by the Norris-LaGuardia Act, passed in 1932, prohibiting federal courts from issuing injunctions in labor disputes.

The National Labor Relations Act (NLRA), passed in 1935, established the basic legislative framework protecting employee collective bargaining rights. The Act protects the right of employees to join unions and engage in collective bargaining, prohibits employer unfair labor practices, provides election procedures for determining the employees' bargaining agent, and created the National Labor Relations Board to enforce the Act.

In 1947, Congress passed the Taft-Hartley Act to counterbalance the strength of unions under the NLRA. The entire Act was renamed the Labor Management Relations Act (LMRA).

The Taft-Hartley Act established union unfair labor practices to match the employer unfair labor practices prohibited by the NLRA. Other provisions of Taft-Hartley extensively regulate union picketing and secondary activity. The Taft-Hartley Act also amends Section 7, giving employees the right to refrain from, as well as engage in, union activities.

Section 8 is the heart of the LMRA as it established employer and union unfair labor practices. Section 9 established election procedures. Section 10 established NLRB jurisdiction and procedures in unfair labor practice cases. In addition to the Board, the Labor Management Relations Act established a separate independent general counsel who functions like a prosecutor in unfair labor practice cases.

The first step in an unfair labor practice case is the filing of a charge. If the general counsel finds merit in a charge, a complaint is issued. There may be a trial before an administrative law judge (ALJ) with an appeal to the Board and, ultimately, to the courts, but most cases are settled without going through the entire process.

A representation proceeding is started by filing a petition. Most representation proceedings are handled by consent. However, there may be formal proceedings before the regional director with the right to appeal to the Board. There is no right to appeal a Board's decision on a representation matter directly to court. An employer may refuse to bargain following a Board's decision in a representation case and ultimately obtain judicial review of the decision in the representation proceeding by appealing the unfair labor practice case.

The Board, general counsel, and regional director all have sizable staffs. Thus, when they take a certain action, it is usually taken by a staff member acting in their behalf, even though the Board, general counsel, or regional director can review the action and does bear ultimate responsibility.

Finally, the National Labor Relations Board has limited jurisdiction. It has authority only to prevent unfair labor practices under Section 8 and administer elections under Section 9. These are very important functions, but they are not all of labor law. Furthermore, the Board has jurisdiction over only employers and employees covered by the Act. It has further limited its own jurisdiction by establishing monetary standards that an employer must meet before the Board will assert jurisdiction over a dispute within its statutory authority.

Review Questions

1. What was the importance of the Norris-LaGuardia Act?
2. What was the purpose of the Taft-Hartley Act?
3. How does the function of the five-member Board differ from the function of the general counsel?
4. Does the Board assert jurisdiction in every case in which the employer's operations affect commerce as defined in the Act?
5. What is the first step in an unfair labor practice case?
6. Who can file a charge with the NLRB?

6 mo - P. 7

7. What is the time limit for filing a charge? <u>6 mo - P. 7</u>

8. What is the purpose of a representation hearing?

9. What is a "showing of interest"?

10. How is a regional director's decision in a representation case appealed to the Board?

(Answers to review questions are at the end of the book.)

Basic Legal Principles

1. The first step in an unfair labor practice proceeding is to file a charge with a regional office of the Board alleging a violation of the LMRA by an employer or a labor organization. *NLRB Rules and Regulations* §102.9.

2. A charging party can appeal a regional director's dismissal of an unfair practice charge to the Office of the General Counsel in Washington, D.C. If the appeal to the general counsel is denied, there is no further appeal to the Board. The general counsel's decision to dismiss a charge is final and not reviewable by the courts. *United Electrical Contractors Assn. v. Ordman*, 366 F.2d 776, 63 LRRM 2223 (2nd Cir. 1966), cert. denied 385 U.S. 1026, 64 LRRM 2158 (1967); *RWDSU Local 310 v. NLRB*, 745 F.2d 358, 117 LRRM 2576 (6th Cir. 1984).

3. Either the charging party, the general counsel, or the respondent has an absolute right to file exceptions with the Board to an administrative law judge's decision in an unfair labor practice case. Only the Board makes a binding decision. *NLRB Rules and Regulations* §102.46.

4. Only final orders of the NLRB in unfair labor practice cases are subject to review by the courts of appeals. Decisions in representation cases are not final orders and can be reviewed only in an appeal in an unfair labor practice proceeding. *AFL v. NLRB*, 308 U.S. 401, 5 LRRM 670 (1940). However, federal district courts can set aside NLRB certification orders if the Board has plainly exceeded its statutory authority. *Leedom v. Kyne*, 358 U.S. 184, 43 LRRM 2222 (1958); *Physicians National House Staff Ass'n. v. Murphy*, 100 LRRM 3055 (D.C. Cir. 1979); *NLRB v. Action Automotive, Inc.*, 469 U.S. 490, 118 LRRM 2577 (1985).

5. A court of appeals must uphold the Board's decision on appeal if the decision is based on substantial evidence on the record as a whole, including the evidence opposed to the Board's conclusions. A court of appeals cannot reverse the Board even though the court might have reached a different conclusion on the same evidence. *Universal Camera Corp. v. NLRB*, 340 U.S. 474, 27 LRRM 2373 (1951); *NLRB v. Jack August Enterprises, Inc.*, 583 F.2d 575, 99 LRRM 2582 (1st Cir. 1978); *NLRB v. Transportation Management Corp.*, 462 U.S. 393, 113 LRRM 2857 (1983); *Metropolitan Edison Co. v. NLRB*, 460 U.S. 693, 112 LRRM 3265 (1983).

6. If the regional director has ordered a representation election, a party may request that the Board review the decision. There are only four limited grounds on which the Board will accept review: if the case raises a substantial question of law or policy; if the regional director committed

clear error on a substantial factual issue; if prejudicial error was committed in the conduct of the hearing; or if there are compelling reasons to reconsider an important Board rule or policy. *NLRB Rules and Regulations* §102.67(c).

7. Either the Board agent or an employer or union observer may, for good cause, challenge the eligibility of any voter. Persons challenged are allowed to vote, but their ballots are impounded by the Board agent. The challenged ballots are not resolved unless there are enough to affect the results of an election. *NLRB Rules and Regulations* §102.69.

8. If a representation election is conducted pursuant to a Stipulation for Certification for Consent Election and there are postelection objections or challenges, the regional director merely issues a recommended report on objections and challenged ballots. The Board makes the final ruling. If the parties hold an election pursuant to an Agreement for Consent Election, the regional director's decision on postelection matters is absolutely final with no appeal to the Board. *NLRB Rules and Regulations* §102.62(a) and (b).

9. A trial in an unfair labor practice case is an adversary proceeding governed by the federal rules of evidence. A representation case proceeding is technically nonadversary, and the rules of evidence do not apply. *NLRB Rules and Regulations* §§102.38–39 and §102.66.

10. The Board's statutory jurisdiction applies to covered employers whose activities affect commerce, the broadest possible constitutional jurisdiction; but, to limit its case load to manageable proportions, the Board has set certain monetary jurisdictional standards that an employer must meet before the Board will assert jurisdiction in either an unfair labor practice or a representation proceeding. *American Gypsum Co.*, 231 NLRB No. 152, 97 LRRM 1069 (1977); *Ogden Food Service Corp.*, 234 NLRB No. 69, 97 LRRM 1190 (1978); *United Services for the Handicapped*, 239 NLRB No. 140, 100 LRRM 1057 (1978); *Hispanic Federation for Social and Economic Development*, 284 NLRB No. 50, 125 LRRM 1201 (1987) (most recent Board decision establishing a new $250,000 annual revenue standard for jurisdiction over social service organizations other than those for which there is another specific applicable standard). However:

(a) the Board cannot assert jurisdiction over church-operated schools, as it would violate the First Amendment to the United States Constitution establishing freedom of religion and separation of church and state. *NLRB v. Catholic Bishop of Chicago*, 440 U.S. 490, 100 LRRM 2913 (1979). See also *Trustee of St. Joseph's College*, 282 NLRB No. 9, 123 LRRM 1281 (1986) (*Catholic Bishop* decision applies to religious-affiliated colleges and universities as well as to parochial elementary and secondary schools); *Jewish Day School of Greater Washington*, 283 NLRB No. 106, 125 LRRM 1033 (1987) (jurisdiction will not be asserted over schools having a religious purpose and function in substantial part even if school is controlled by predominantly lay-board);

(b) The Board will assert jurisdiction over private agencies that are funded by exempt governmental agencies only if the private employer retains substantial control over the economic as well as the noneconomic terms of employment so that meaningful bargaining is possible on these core subjects. Compare *Res-Care, Inc.,* 280 NLRB No. 78, 122 LRRM 1265 (1986) with *Community Transit Services, Inc.,* 290 NLRB No. 154, 129 LRRM 1185 (1988).

Recommended
Reading

Aldrich, "Practice Before the NLRB," 5 *Litigation* 20 (1979).

Casebeer, "Drafting Wagner's Act: Leon Keyserling and the Precommittee Drafts of the Labor Disputes Act and the National Labor Relations Act," II *Industrial Relations Law Journal* 73 (1989).

Gould, "Fifty Years under the National Labor Relations Act: A Retrospective View," 37 *Lab. L.J.* 235 (1986).

Gregory and Katz, *Labor and the Law* (3d ed., 1979).

Hogler, "Law History and Critical Labor Law: An Interdisciplinary Approach to Worker's Control," 30 *Labor History* 165 (1989).

Kammholz and Strauss, *Practice and Procedure before the National Labor Relations Board* (4th ed., 1987).

McGuiness and Norris, *How to Take a Case before the National Labor Relations Board* (5th ed., 1986).

Zimmerman, "Restoring Stability in the Implementation of the National Labor Relations Act," 1 *Lab. Lawyer* 1 (1985).

chapter 2

THE COLLECTIVE BARGAINING UNIT

Unions represent and bargain for employees in appropriate bargaining units. To understand the bargaining process, it is necessary to understand the appropriate bargaining unit concept. This chapter discusses how the appropriate bargaining unit is determined, which employees may be part of a unit, and election rules and procedures.

The rules applying to appropriate bargaining units in certain industries or occupations can be very detailed. Entire books have been written on collective bargaining units and representation issues. This chapter is necessarily limited to general principles and the issues most frequently faced by unions. If you understand these general principles, you should be able to handle most specific situations as well. Remember, the principles discussed in this chapter assume that the employer is subject to the Board's jurisdiction as discussed in Chapter One and that the union has the required showing of interest in the appropriate unit it seeks to represent (see Chapter One.)

A. DETERMINING THE APPROPRIATE BARGAINING UNIT

An employer may voluntarily agree to recognize and bargain with a union, in which case the parties mutually determine the bargaining unit. Generally, the Board permits a union to represent the employees in any unit the employer and union voluntarily agree or consent to, provided the unit does not violate basic Board policies and statutory requirements covering an appropriate unit as discussed below.

1. The Community-of-Interest Principle

The most important factor used in determining an appropriate unit is the existence of a community of interest among the employees. A community of interest refers to what the employees have in common. The more the employees have in common, the more likely it is that the Board will find that they have a community of interest and are thus an appropriate unit for bargaining. Several factors are considered in determining the existence of a community of interest. Do the employees (1) perform similar types of work and have similar training and skills, such as craft work, clerical work, or production and maintenance work; (2) work in the same location and/or interchange and have regular work contact with each other; (3) perform integrated production or service functions; (4) enjoy similar working conditions, such as working the same hours or shift schedules, using the same locker room and cafeteria facilities, or being subject to the same personnel policies or work rules; (5) have similar wage and benefits schedules; and (6) have common supervision or centralized control over personnel policies or day-to-day operations?

The Board also considers the scope of any existing bargaining unit that represents the employees, the organizational structure of the employer, and the bargaining history in the industry. No one factor is controlling; any evidence showing common interest will be considered by the Board in determining community of interest. While the factors listed above are frequently considered, they are by no means all-inclusive.

Suppose, for example, a plant has had no union. Both salaried and hourly employees work on an assembly line. Obviously, the salaried employees and the hourly workers have different wage conditions. If, however, they are all performing similar work, are at the same location, and work the same shift schedule, they may still have a sufficient community of interest so that both the salaried and hourly employees would be in the same appropriate unit.

2. Multiple Appropriate Units

It is possible for one union to represent all the employees in a plant in one unit. Production employees in one department may share a community of interest with those in other departments, and with the maintenance and craft employees, based on the factors discussed above, to make a plant-wide unit appropriate. All employees, for example, might work the same hours, have similar working conditions, and have common supervision. Frequently, however, there is more than one union representing employees in a plant because there is more than one appropriate unit. Craft employees, production and maintenance employees, technical employees, or employees in a particular department may each have a separate distinct community of interest among themselves. Under these conditions each employee group would be an appropriate unit.

Generally, the Board allows employees to bargain in any appropriate unit even though other units may also be appropriate. A unit does not have to be the "best" or most appropriate in terms of employer efficiency or bargaining convenience. A bargaining unit can be compared to a pie that can be cut up in many different ways. The employees can be divided up any way as long as the individual piece is an appropriate unit.

a. Extent of Organization. Section 9(c)(5) of the LMRA provides that in determining the appropriateness of a unit for collective bargaining, the extent to which the employees have organized shall not be controlling. This means that the Board cannot decide that a unit is appropriate just because a group of employees have joined a union and wish to be represented by it. Rather, the Board must consider whether these employees have a separate community of interest among themselves. The Board has held that as long as it does not treat extent of organization as the controlling factor, it can consider extent of organization in determining community of interest along with the other factors discussed above.

3. Unit Segments

There may be a number of possible bargaining units, but the union cannot represent a segment of an appropriate unit; it must represent all the employees in the unit. Assume that a union sought a unit consisting only of craft employees in one of two plant departments. However, the craft employees regularly work interchangeably in both departments, have common supervision, and share a common wage structure. The Board would probably conclude that the craft employees in the two departments were so interrelated that the appropriate unit would have to include both departments. The Board would not permit an election in only one of the departments, even if all the craft employees in the department wanted the union to represent them because a union cannot represent only a segment of an appropriate unit. If the Board permitted the union to do so, it would be giving controlling weight to the extent of organization contrary to Section 9(c)(5).

As an exception to the general community-of-interest standards, if most of the employees of an employer have been organized in appropriate bargaining units, but there are small scattered groups that are not included in any of the existing units, a petitioning union may be permitted to represent the remaining employees in a single bargaining unit, even though they do not have a common community of interest applying the usual criteria. This is known as a residual bargaining unit. The Board reasons that a residual unit is appropriate because the included employees, who would otherwise not be included in any existing collective bargaining unit, should not be deprived of the right to collective bargaining.

Because one person cannot engage in collective bargaining alone, the Board has held that a bargaining unit must have a minimum of two employees and it will not certify a one-employee unit. However, this rule does not prevent an employer from voluntarily recognizing a union as a representative for a single employee. Single employee contracts are most frequently found in the construction industry, where a craft union may have contracts with a number of small employers.

4. Commonly Accepted Bargaining Units

Over the years, the Board has recognized that certain groups of employees, because of their distinct community of interest, almost always comprise a separate appropriate unit. These are called *presumptively appropriate units.*

If an employer or union opposes bargaining in one of the presumptive units, it must establish that there are special circumstances for which the usual rule does not apply. Thus, for example, a unit composed of an employer's production and mainte-

nance employees is presumptively appropriate as is a unit of an employer's office clerical employees. Clerical employees who work in the employer's production area (such as shipping clerks) are classified as plant clerical employees and are included in a production and maintenance unit, not in the office clerical unit. Because office clerical employees have a separate and distinct community of interest from production and maintenance employees, the Board ordinarily will include these two groups in a single unit only by the consent of the parties.

If an employer operates multiple plants or facilities, the Board presumes that separate bargaining units are appropriate at each facility. If either the employer or the union wants a multi-facility unit, the burden is on that party to prove that the employees in the two facilities share a community of interest.

If the Board finds that both a single-plant or a multi-plant unit are appropriate, the union can choose which unit to represent, provided, of course, the union has a 30 percent showing of interest in the combined unit if it seeks the broader representation. (In that case, there is no need to have a 30 percent showing of interest in each facility to be included in the unit.) Remember, as long as the union is seeking to represent an appropriate unit, it cannot be compelled to represent a different one. Thus, the union could not be required to represent employees on a multi-plant basis except when only a multi-plant unit is appropriate.

The structure of some industries makes certain units presumptively appropriate. The appropriate unit for public utilities is usually systemwide. Thus if a union seeks a smaller unit, such as a single geographic division, it must show that the structure of the particular company is unique, or that there is some special factor in the employees' community of interest setting them apart from the usual industry pattern. In the printing trades, the printing and bindery departments are traditionally in separate units. In contrast, warehouse department employees in a retail industry are entitled to separate representation only if the warehouse operation is geographically separate from the retail store operations, there is no substantial integration of warehouse employees with other employees in performing their ordinary duties, and the warehouse employees are separately supervised.

Technological change reducing the differences in skills between employees is resulting in changes in some traditional bargaining patterns. Thus, meat department employees were traditionally in a separate unit from the clerical employees in a grocery store. However, due to the increased use of precut meats so that meat department employees no longer perform traditional butchering skills, meat department employees are now frequently included in overall units. In the past, hotel maintenance employees were usually entitled to separate representation from the service employees, but in most recent cases, the Board has ruled that the only appropriate unit, based on community-of-interest factors, must include both the service and maintenance employees.

Historically the Board also has presumed that a single store in a retail chain (e.g., a grocery or drug store) or a single branch of a bank is appropriate for bargaining. Unions frequently had a choice of either representing the employees at a single facility or an overall unit including all the facilities in the area because both units were appropriate. However, in a number of recent cases the Board has held that the evidence of the employees' overall areawide community of interest overcame the single facility presumption, so that the *only* appropriate unit had to include all the stores in a district or regional area. In part, these decisions have reflected the Reagan Board's general preference for larger bargaining units, but they also result from the "computer revolution," so that stores that once functioned fairly independently are now subject to centralized control over personnel policies and practices in a way that was not previously feasible. Thus, although the Board has not

expressly overruled prior cases establishing a presumption favoring single-store units, unions as a practical matter should seek as broad a unit as possible. Certainly, however, in some cases a single store will still constitute an appropriate unit or the union will have a choice as in the past of either a single- or areawide unit based on community-of-interest principles.

Obviously, there are important tactical decisions for both the employer and the union in fashioning a bargaining unit. Both parties will seek a unit in which they can win a representation election, and there are many representation election hearings in which the parties seek to add or delete certain employees from the bargaining unit on community-of-interest grounds when the underlying reason is to gain an advantage in the election.

5. Health Care Bargaining Units

In 1974 the Labor Management Relations Act was amended to cover employees of nonprofit health care institutions. Until then, Section 2(2) of the LMRA had excluded nonprofit hospitals from coverage under the Act. When Congress passed the health care amendments, both the Senate and House committee reports on the legislation contained statements that the Board should guard against a proliferation of bargaining units in the health care field. However, the actual language of the amendments as passed does not include any special restrictions on health care bargaining units.

In the initial representation cases before the Board on health care industry bargaining units, employers argued, based on the legislative history, that facility-wide bargaining units had to be preferred for bargaining. The Board disagreed. It concluded that the congressional statements against proliferation meant only that there should not be separate representation for each craft as in the construction industry. Thus, the Board held that it would follow the same community-of-interest standards for health care employers as it applied to industrial plants.

However, in subsequent years, health care industry employers continued to press for larger bargaining units. The Board did not articulate clear standards for appropriate bargaining units in the industry, and representation hearings were frequently long, complex, and bitterly contested. Courts of appeals frequently reversed Board unit determinations on the grounds that the Board had not given sufficient weight to the congressional concerns against undue unit proliferation. Finally, in the landmark case of *St. Francis Hospital* (Memphis, Tennessee), the Board attempted to clarify its position.[1] In that case, the International Brotherhood of Electrical Workers filed a representation petition in 1979 seeking a bargaining unit of the hospital's maintenance employees. In a decision not issued until December 1982 the Board held that the maintenance unit was appropriate. In its decision, the Board reviewed the legislative history and its decisions to that date as to appropriate units, and identified seven potentially appropriate units: physicians; registered nurses; other professional employees; technical employees; business office clerical employees; service and maintenance employees; and maintenance employees. The Board stated that these units would be considered as commonly found employee groups that might warrant separate representation if they actually possessed a distinct community of interest separate and apart from other hospital employees under the usual community-of-interest criteria.

St. Francis Hospital refused to bargain with the IBEW after the union was certified so that it could seek judicial review of the Board's decision. (The procedure that must be followed to challenge a Board certification is discussed in Chapter One.) When the case reached the Board a second time in the unfair labor practice proceedings, the Board issued a new decision (known as *St. Francis II*)[2] in which it dramatically changed

its approach to health care bargaining units. In this 1984 decision, the Board, relying on the legislative history, stated that it would apply a "disparity-of-interest" test in determining appropriate units under which only overall units of all professional or all nonprofessional employees are presumptively appropriate. If a union seeks a lesser unit, (such as solely service and maintenance employees or nurses) it must establish a *disparity of interest* between those employees and the employees the union seeks to exclude. The Board defined disparity as "sharper than usual differences" between the wages, hours, and working conditions of the requested employees and those in an overall professional or nonprofessional unit.

The Union appealed the Board's decision in *St. Francis II* to the United States Court of Appeals for the District of Columbia. In March 1987, eight years after the union's original petition had been filed, the court of appeals issued a decision refusing to enforce the Board's decision. The court of appeals reasoned that the Board had given undue weight to the legislative history and had improperly interpreted the 1974 health care amendments as mandating a disparity-of-interest standard and compelling a presumption that only two bargaining units were appropriate in the health care industry.

Historically the Board has decided bargaining unit issues on a case-by-case basis. However, in July 1987 the Board announced that it intended to issue general rules establishing appropriate bargaining units in the health care industry rather than continuing to resolve such issues on a case-by-case basis in the hope that it would be able to adopt standards acceptable to both labor and management. The Board also announced that in the meantime it would continue to follow the disparity-of-interest standard adopted in *St. Francis II* notwithstanding the District of Columbia Court of Appeals decision. Subsequently, the Board also issued a decision in *St. Francis III*[3] on

[1] See legal principle 1.C.
[2] See legal principle 1.C.
[3] See legal principle 1.C.

remand from the courts of appeals reaffirming its analysis as to the appropriate bargaining units in the health care industry and the disparity-of-interest test.

Following extensive hearings in which representatives of both labor and management participated, the Board issued a Final Rule on April 21, 1989, regulating bargaining units for "acute care" hospitals, which the Board defined in general as a short-term hospital with an average length of patient stay of less than thirty days. The Board excluded nursing homes and hospitals primarily devoted to psychiatric care or rehabilitation from the rule, and will continue to determine bargaining units for such employers on a case-by-case basis. The Board's rule establishes eight bargaining units for acute care hospital employees. Three bargaining units are permitted for the professional employees: (1) registered nurses; (2) physicians; and (3) all other professional employees (e.g., pharmacists, medical technologists). Five units are established for all other nonprofessional acute care hospital employees: (1) technical employees (e.g., LPNs, laboratory technicians); (2) skilled maintenance workers; (3) business office clericals; (4) all other nonprofessional and service employees; and (5) guards. The Board indicated that it would also approve units comprised of all professional or nonprofessional employees (excluding guards), but that it would decide whether any of the authorized units could be combined together in any other way (i.e., a single unit of technical and all other nonprofessional and service employees) on a case-by-case basis. Also, the Board will permit the parties to stipulate to a bargaining unit even if it varies from the units established by the rule as long as the stipulated unit does not violate any express statutory provision or established Board policy, the same policy the Board applies to a stipulated bargaining unit in all other industries. Absent a stipulation, units different from those established by the rule will be permitted only under "extraordinary" circumstances. The rule provides that a unit of five or fewer employees constitutes an extraordinary circumstance so that the appropriateness of such a unit will be determined on a case-by-case basis. The Board emphasized, however, that other exceptions will be very rare.

Labor organizations representing health care employees have generally approved of the rule's approach, but some employers have protested that the rule permits too many bargaining units. The American Hospital Association filed a suit challenging the rule, and a federal District Court issued an injunction against the rule on the grounds that it permitted undue proliferation of bargaining units. This decision has been appealed, and the Board is continuing to follow the disparity-of-interest test on a case-by-case basis until the suit is resolved. Thus the law pertaining to health care bargaining units will undoubtedly remain uncertain for some time pending the outcome of the litigation, congressional action to amend the law, or a definitive Supreme Court decision as to the appropriate standard for determining bargaining units in the health care industry.

6. Multi-Union and Globe Elections

If more than one union wants to represent a particular unit, each union is on the ballot along with the choice of no union. One of the choices (the competing unions or no union) must receive a majority of all valid votes cast in the election. If there is no majority, a runoff election is held between the top two choices.

Suppose that there are 100 employees in the unit and that 70 employees cast valid ballots in the election. The election results are 35 votes for union A, 33 votes for union B, and two votes for no union. There is no winner because none of the choices on the ballot received the necessary majority of 36 votes or more. A runoff election would have to be held between the two top choices, union A and union B. There would not be a no union choice. If the top two choices in the first election had been union A and no union, the second election would have been between only those two choices, and union B would not have been on the ballot at all.

a. Globe Elections. Suppose there are two departments, A and B, which could either be separately represented or comprise a single bargaining unit such as the warehouse and production departments of a plant that are geographically separate. Suppose union X wants to represent only the employees in department A while union Y wants to represent the employees in both departments. In such a case, there would be a "globe election," named after the case (*Globe Machine & Stamping Co.*)[4] setting down this procedure.

In a globe election, the employees in department A would receive a ballot listing union X, union Y, and no union because both unions want to represent those employees. The employees in department B would have a choice between union Y or no union. Union X would not appear on the department B ballot because it does not seek to represent those employees. The votes of each department are tallied separately. If a majority of the employees in department A vote to be represented separately by union X, which sought to represent them separately, then union X will be certified as the representative of those employees, regardless of the vote of the employees in department B.

If union X does not receive a majority of the votes in department A, the votes in departments A and B will be counted together to determine whether union Y will represent both departments as a single unit. Thus, what if the vote in department A had been four for union X, four for union Y, and two for no union; and the vote in department B was 14 for union Y and 16 for no union? Since union X failed to receive the majority in department A that it sought to represent separately, department A would not have separate representation. Therefore, the votes in department A would be counted in the overall unit of depart-

ments A and B. The final tally in the combined voting group would be four votes for union X, 18 for union Y (the combined tally of 4 Y votes in department A and 14 Y votes in department B), and 18 for no union. Since there is a tie between Y and no union there would be a runoff election between these two top choices.

Employees in department A would be able to vote in the runoff election, but they would no longer be able to vote for union X. If union Y received the majority of votes cast in the overall unit during the runoff election, it would be certified as the representative of a unit consisting of departments A and B.

Sometimes two unions will seek joint certification. That may happen if two unions decide to combine their efforts in a particular organizing campaign or if each union has strength in only a segment of the employees in an appropriate bargaining unit and must unite to achieve majority support for representation.

The Board permits unions to be jointly certified. However, two unions that are jointly certified are not permitted to divide the employee group between themselves after the election. Instead, both unions have an obligation to represent the entire work force. If one of the jointly certified unions refuses to represent a segment of the jointly certified bargaining unit, the Board may revoke the joint certification.

7. Accretions to Bargaining Units

Once a union is certified as the representative of the bargaining unit, other employees may be added to the unit without being entitled to vote for union representation. Employees added in this manner are called an accretion to the bargaining unit. This occurs when an employer expands operations and the new employees have the same community of interest as those already in the unit. Among the key factors that the Board considers are the frequency of interchange among employees in the new and existing groups; the amount of common supervision or centralized control over labor relations; the degree of physical, functional, and administrative integration of the two employee groups; geographic proximity; and the degree of similarity in working conditions, skills, and functions.

For example, if a union is the certified representative for an employer's production employees and the employer adds an additional assembly line with new employees, the new employees would have the same community of interest as the employees already working on the other lines. The new employees would be added to the bargaining unit as an accretion without a vote on union representation. Sometimes employees working at a new facility can be added as an accretion to an existing facility's bargaining unit if the employees at the old and new facility have a common community of interest and the two facilities have closely integrated operations. Thus, for example, if a union represents a multi-store bargaining unit, and the employer opens a new store, that store may be an accretion to the existing unit. If, in contrast, two separate facilities are consolidated, the smaller workforce may constitute an accretion to the larger one so that the union that had represented the larger force will represent the combined unit. However, if separate workforces historically represented by different unions are combined, and neither workforce is substantially larger than the other, the Board will direct an election to determine the bargaining representative for the employees at the combined facility.

If an employer disputes the inclusion of new employees in the unit, the union may file a clarification petition (a UC petition) with the Board for a determination. If the Board finds that the employees are an accretion, they will be added to the unit without a vote. If the Board concludes that the employees are not an accretion, the union must obtain authorization cards (a showing of interest) from the employees in dispute and file an election petition if it wishes to represent the employees. Elections are the preferred way of determining representa-

tion. The Board has ruled, therefore, that a unit will not be clarified to include additional employees if there is doubt about the employees' community of interest. Also, as a general principle, employees will not be added to a unit through the clarification method if the disputed employee classifications existed at the time of the union's original certification and could have been included in the original unit. Such employees are entitled to an election before being added to the unit.

Unit clarification petitions are a valuable aid to unions, but such petitions may be used by employers as well. Thus, employers have successfully filed petitions to remove certain job classifications from a bargaining unit on the grounds that the employees are in fact supervisors or managerial or confidential employees (discussed below). The Board will exclude such persons from a bargaining unit even though they have historically been included.

8. Craft and Departmental Severance Elections

On occasion, craft or departmental employees initially included in an overall production and maintenance unit seek separate representation. At one time, the Board permitted craft units to be severed from a larger unit if the proposed unit was a true craft unit (meaning the employees in the unit exercised craft level skills rather than routine work) and the union seeking to represent the craft unit traditionally represented craft employees. Similarly, the Board permitted severance of a department under the same factors if the department traditionally had separate representation such as maintenance shop departments. In *Mallinckrodt Chemical*, decided in 1966, the Board changed this approach and ruled that it would no longer grant automatic craft severance.[5] The Board listed six illustrative factors it would apply in determining whether a craft unit or a department unit

[5] See legal principle 3.

would be severed from a broader unit. Those six factors are:

1. Whether or not the proposed unit consists of a distinct and homogeneous group of skilled journeymen craftsmen performing the functions of their craft on a nonrepetitive basis or of employees constituting a functionally distinct department working in trades or occupations for which a tradition of separate representation exists.
2. The history of collective bargaining among the employees and at the plant involved, and at other plants of the employer, with emphasis on whether the existing patterns of bargaining produce stability in labor relations, and whether such stability will be unduly disrupted by the destruction of the existing pattern of representation.
3. The extent to which the employees in the proposed unit have established and maintained their separate identity during the period of inclusion in a broader unit, and the extent of their participation or lack of participation in the establishment and maintenance of the existing pattern of representation and prior opportunities, if any, afforded them in obtaining separate representation.
4. The history and pattern of collective bargaining in the industry involved.
5. The degree of integration of the employer's production processes, including the extent to which the continued normal operation of the production processes depends upon the performance of the assigned functions of the employees in the proposed unit.
6. The qualifications of a union seeking to carve out a separate unit, including that union's experience in representing employees like those involved in the severance action.

Since the adoption of the *Mallinckrodt* principles, the Board has usually denied petitions seeking to sever craft and departmental employees from an existing unit. Unions have been successful only if there is clear evidence that the employees have maintained a separate identity. Such evidence might be shown by the retention of special rights, such as the right to select special representatives on a bargaining committee or the right to vote separately on a contract.

Unions have been far more successful in obtaining separate craft or departmental units if the employees to be represented are not already included in a broader bargaining unit. Under those circumstances, there is, of course, no history of bargaining in a broader unit, and the petitioning union is frequently able to prove that the craft or departmental employees have a separate and distinct community of interest. Also, the Board is more likely to find a separate unit appropriate if no other union is seeking to represent the employees as part of a broader unit so that the only alternative to separate representation is no representation at all.

9. Multi-plant and Multi-employer Units

A multi-employer unit is an association of separate employers who have come together to bargain with a union. Multi-employer units are established voluntarily between the employers and the union. Multi-employer bargaining is discussed further in Chapter Five.

Once a multi-plant or multi-employer bargaining unit is established, another union cannot seek a bargaining unit composed of employees at only a single plant or a single employer, as long as the multi-plant or multi-employer bargaining unit remains in effect. The multi-plant or employer unit is regarded as the only appropriate unit for the covered employees. This is an important advantage to an incumbent union because any other union challenging the incumbent's status must organize on the multi-plant or multi-employer basis and not rely upon its strength at a single location.

Multi-plant and multi-employer bargaining units are usually voluntarily established by contractual agreement between the union and the employer(s). If the union and the employer(s) do not agree to continue their multi-plant or multi-employer bargaining relationship when their contract expires, or if the union or an employer properly withdraws from a multi-employer bargaining unit at the end of the contract, the plants no longer covered by the multi-plant or multi-employer agreement would once again be presumably appropriate for bargaining as separate facilities and other unions could then seek to represent the employees at each facility.

B. EXCLUSION OF EMPLOYEES FROM THE BARGAINING UNIT

In addition to determining the appropriate bargaining unit, the parties, or the Board in a contested case, must determine whether certain persons are to be included or excluded from the unit. There are four general categories of persons who are excluded from a bargaining unit: (1) employees whom the LMRA requires or permits to have separate representation; (2) individuals excluded from the LMRA definition of employee (Section 2(3)) and thus not entitled to representation at all; (3) employees excluded from the unit because they do not regularly perform bargaining unit work; and (4) employees the Board excludes as a matter of policy because their interests are more closely aligned with management than with the bargaining unit.

A word of caution for bargaining purposes. There is a distinction between whether certain employees are in the bargaining unit and whether they may do bargaining unit work. The fact that the Board finds that a particular individual should be excluded from the unit does not prevent that person from performing bargaining unit work. As many unions have learned the hard way, Board certification establishes only that the union represents a particular group of employees in an appropriate unit for bargaining. The Board has held in many cases that certification is not a guarantee that employees will perform any particular work or that the work may not be subcontracted. The bargaining unit's work is a matter of negotiations. If the union wants to prevent nonbargaining unit employees from performing its work, or prevent subcontracting, it must negotiate contract clauses providing this protection—certification alone is insufficient.

1. Employees Entitled to or Required to Have Separate Representation

a. Professional Employees and Technical Employees Professional employees are not excluded from collective bargaining rights, but special rules do apply to them. Section 9(b)(1) provides that the Board shall not find a unit containing both professional and nonprofessional employees appropriate unless a majority of the professional employees vote for inclusion in the broader unit.

The term professional employee under LMRA Section 2(12) generally refers to someone who performs work of a predominantly intellectual, nonstandardized nature. The work must require the use of discretion and independent judgment and knowledge of an advanced type in a field of science or learning customarily acquired in an institution of higher learning. Lawyers, doctors, teachers, and certified public accountants (CPAs) are examples of professional employees.

A person who has a professional degree is classified as a professional under the Act only if he is functioning in a position requiring the use of professional training. A CPA doing routine bookkeeping rather than skilled accounting work would not be a professional.

PROFESSIONAL ELECTION PROCEDURES. The voting procedures in an election involving professional employees are similar to those in a globe election. Professionals vote by ballot, first on whether they wish to be included in an overall unit, and second on whether they wish to be represented by the petitioning union. If a majority vote for inclusion in the larger unit, their votes are counted with the votes of the other employees in determining whether the union has won the election. If a majority of the professional employees vote for separate representation and also for the union, the union can represent the professional employees separately if it desires. The union can also represent the other employees separately if a majority of them vote for representation. Thus, the union can end up separately representing two units of employees.

TECHNICAL EMPLOYEES. A distinction must be made between professional and technical employees. Technical employees do not meet the qualifications for a professional, but perform work of a technical nature requiring the use of independent discretion and special training. Such training is usually acquired in college or technical schools, but may be acquired on the job. Technical employees are not entitled to vote separately on representation. At one time the Board permitted technical employees to be represented separately, just as craft employees were. The Board also routinely excluded technical employees from a production and maintenance unit if either party requested it. The Board no longer follows this rule, but applies traditional community-of-interest factors to technical employees to determine whether their community of interest is with the production and maintenance employees, the office clerical employees, or is separate.

b. Guards. Section 9(b)(3) provides that the Board shall not find a unit appropriate if it includes, together with other employees, anyone employed as a guard. A guard is someone who enforces rules to protect the property of the employer or protects the safety of persons on the employer's premises against employees and others. The section also requires that a guard's union not be affiliated with a union that admits employees other than guards. Congress included these provisions because it believed that guards, whose job is to protect employers' property in part from other employees and to enforce rules or take action against their fellow employees, might be reluctant to do so if both groups were in the same union. Security guards employed by an outside firm to protect the property of another employer are classified as guards under the Act even though they do not protect their own employer's property.

Unarmed courier service drivers, armored car drivers, fire fighters who enforce company fire safety rules, and even maintenance employees whose duties include patrolling the employer's premises at night or checking employees in and out at a shift change have also been so classified based on their duties.

Although a union cannot be certified as the bargaining agent for guards if it is affiliated directly or indirectly with any organization that represents employees other than guards, a unit consisting of guards and nonguards is not illegal. The Board cannot certify such a unit, but an employer and a union may voluntarily agree to a unit including both groups. At one time, if an employer voluntarily recognized a unit comprised of both guards and nonguard employees, and another union filed a representation petition seeking to represent *only* the guards, the Board permitted the mixed guard/nonguard union to intervene in the election. The Board would not certify the mixed union as the employee's bargaining agent if it won the election, but it would certify the arithmetic result. However, the current rule is that the mixed guard/nonguard union cannot even be on the ballot.

2. Individuals Excluded from the Definition of Employee

Only employees are entitled to be members of a bargaining unit. Section 2(3) excludes certain persons from coverage as employees under the Act: (1) agricultural laborers or people in the domestic service of a family or person in a home; (2) persons employed by a parent or spouse; (3) independent contractors; and (4) supervisors.

A person who is excluded from the definition of employee is not subject to the various protections the Act gives employees. Such individuals, for example, may be fired for attempting to form a union.

a. Agricultural Laborers and Domestics. An agricultural laborer is one who works with an agricultural or horticultural product in its natural state. A person who changes a raw product in some way, such as processing wheat into flour or canning vegetables, is classified as a manufacturing employee and is covered by the Act. Domestic employees (such as housekeepers) are excluded from the Act if they are employed by a family or person at his home. Individuals doing domestic type work but employed by an outside contractor, such as a cleaning service, are classified as employees under the Act.

b. Individuals Employed by a Parent or Spouse The spouse or child of an employer is not classified as an employee under Section 2(3) and is therefore excluded from the bargaining unit. Other relatives, such as mothers, brothers, or daughters-in-law of the employer, are not specifically excluded from the definition of employee under Section 2(3). However, the Board has held that other relatives may be excluded if it finds that their interests are more closely aligned with the employer than with the other employees. They are then classified as managerial employees (discussed below). Exclusion is not automatic. The Board determines whether such relatives have a special relationship with the employer other than being related. For example, the brother or sister of an employer who performed the same work on the same schedule as other employees and received no special consideration from the employer would be included in the bargaining unit. A brother or sister who could come and go freely, attended management meetings, or enjoyed special privileges would be excluded as a managerial employee because of this special status. In contrast, an employer's child, even working under the same conditions as the other employees, would automatically be excluded under Section 2(3).

THE CLOSELY HELD CORPORATION· Corporations raise different issues. Because a corporation is not a natural person and cannot have children or a spouse, the statutory exclusion for individuals employed by a parent or spouse does not apply. What if all the corporate stock is owned by one person whose children work in the business? Is it right that the son of a person who owns a business outright is excluded from the bargaining unit, but the daughter of a stockholder who owns 100 percent of a corporation is included? To deal with this situation, the Board has held that the spouse or children of the principal stockholders of a closely held corporation must be excluded from a bargaining unit as managerial employees, just as if the employer were an individual. Other relatives, such as the mother, brother, or daughter-in-law of the stockholder, are not automatically excluded. The same test is applied to these relatives as to those of an individual owner. They will be in the unit unless they have a special relationship with management, as shown by special privileges, etc., making their interests more closely aligned with management than with their coworkers.

Similarly, relatives of a corporate officer who is not a principal stockholder or of a supervisor are included in a bargaining unit unless they have special privileges. It does not matter that they would almost certainly vote against the union as long as they work within the unit without special privileges.

c. Independent Contractors. Independent contractors are excluded from the definition of employee under Section 2(3). Independent contractors are generally distinguished from employees based on the amount of control the employer exercises over how a person does his work. The more an employer controls how the work is done, the more likely it is that the individual will be classified as an employee. On the other hand, if the employer specifies only the result, but not the method of work, the person is an independent contractor. For example, a taxicab driver who pays the company a flat fee to use a cab but is otherwise free to determine his or her own schedule and to work anywhere in the company's service area would undoubtedly be classified as an independent contractor.

A distinction must be made between an

independent contractor and an employee who—because of experience, skill, and ability—is given greater working freedom. Such an employee is not an independent contractor, as the employee remains subject to the same wages, hours, and working conditions as the other employees in the bargaining unit. The employer still controls the method of operation as well as the result, even though the senior employee knows the procedures well and thus requires little or no supervision.

d. Supervisors. Many employees believe that a supervisor is someone who has authority to hire or fire; however, the statutory definition is much broader. Section 2(11) of the LMRA defines a supervisor as "any individual having authority, in the interest of the employer, to hire, transfer, suspend, lay off, recall, promote, discharge, assign, reward, or discipline other employees, or responsibly to direct them, or to adjust their grievances, or effectively to recommend such action, if in connection with the foregoing the exercise of such authority is not of a merely routine or clerical nature, but requires the use of independent judgment." A person with the authority to perform even one of these twelve functions, even if it is not exercised, is classified as a supervisor.

EFFECTIVE AUTHORITY TO RECOMMEND ACTION. Section 2(11) does not require that a person have the independent authority to take any of the actions listed above in order to be a supervisor. An employee who cannot take action alone, but has effective authority to recommend supervisory action, is also classified as a supervisor. Effective authority means that an employer acts on the employee's recommendations without making an independent investigation and determination. Employees whose duties include evaluating the performance of other employees may be classified as supervisors if the employer relies upon these evaluations in determining such matters as promotions, pay increases or bonuses, discipline, etc.

For example, suppose a leadperson tells the employer that a probationary employee is not performing satisfactorily and should be let go. If the employer fires the probationary employee based on the leadperson's recommendation without making a further investigation of the facts, the leadperson making the recommendation is a supervisor because he or she has effective authority to recommend a supervisory act—the power to fire.

If the employer asks other employees or the foreman about the new employee's performance and then decides to fire the employee based on all the facts, however, then the employee making the recommendation is not a supervisor because the employer made a separate investigation and did not as a matter of course follow the employee's recommendation.

EXERCISE OF INDEPENDENT JUDGMENT. An employee is not a supervisor if the authority exercised does not require independent judgment, but is routine or clerical. A supervisor must use independent judgment in at least one of the factors listed in Section 2(11). An employee who fires another employee on instructions from higher management is not a supervisor because no discretion is exercised. But, if the same employee is instructed to discipline another employee and given discretion as to the penalty, the employee would be a supervisor because of that discretion.

An employee who is told by higher management that the employee may allow other employees to go home early if their work is finished or they are ill is not a supervisor because the employee is simply carrying out rules established by higher authority and lacks the discretionary judgment to be a supervisor. In contrast, if the employee can allow others to leave early for any reason the employee approves, the employee would probably be classified as a supervisor.

An experienced employee who assists or directs less-skilled junior employees in their work is not a supervisor. The Board holds that an employee whose authority is based on a knowledge of how certain work is to be performed and that does not involve the exercise of independent judgment is not a supervisor. Similarly, professional or technical employees who direct less-skilled employees in order to carry out their duties are not classified as supervisors if the authority is of a routine professional nature. Thus, a licensed practical nurse (LPN) in a nursing home who directs nurse's aides and orderlies in the course of the LPN's patient care duties based on the LPN's higher technical training and experience would not be a supervisor. If, however, the LPN in fact exercised independent judgment in exercising any of the statutory criteria for a supervisor (such as the authority to discipline the aides or orderlies), the LPN would be a supervisor.

An employee's duties, not the title, control whether the employee is classified as a supervisor. An employee may be called a supervisor or foreman by the employer, but may not be classified as a supervisor by the Board if the employee does not exercise statutory supervisory control. Most leadpersons, for example, lack the discretionary judgment to be classified as supervisors. But if the leadperson does have the required discretionary authority, the leadperson will be classified as a supervisor regardless of the title.

Sometimes the Board looks at the ratio of alleged supervisors to employees in a unit to determine which employees are supervisors. If classifying an employee as a supervisor results in an unusually low supervisor–employee ratio and the employee's supervisory status is questionable, the Board might conclude that the employee is not a supervisor. However, there have been cases in which the Board has excluded an individual from the bargaining unit as a supervisor although the individual supervised only one employee.

Remember that a person must have discretionary control over employees to be classified as a supervisor. Thus, a person working in a department alone with no employees under his or her control (such as "storeroom supervisor" in a one-person storeroom) would not be classified as a supervisor regardless of the title. As discussed below, however, the employee might be classified as a managerial employee.

Questions frequently arise as to the supervisory status of employees who usually perform bargaining unit work, but who take the place of a supervisor when the supervisor is absent. Are such part-time "supervisors" classified as supervisors under the Act, and thus excluded from the bargaining unit? The Board's approach to this issue is to analyze the actual authority of the temporary supervisor. If an employee is left "in charge" but is given detailed instructions and must contact higher management if anything out of the ordinary occurs, then the employee is not a supervisor because the employee exercises only routine authority. If, however, the temporary supervisor can in fact exercise the discretionary authority of the full-time supervisor in the supervisor's absence, the employee would be excluded from the bargaining unit, even though the employee does bargaining unit work most of the time.

Also, an employee who *regularly* performs a supervisory function will be excluded from the bargaining unit even though that function takes only a small percentage of the employee's work time. However, an employee who only performs supervisory duties sporadically (such as if the supervisor is out sick) or temporarily at infrequent intervals (such as the supervisor's annual vacation) is usually included in the bargaining unit. Even in those cases, the Board may exclude the employee from the bargaining unit if the evidence establishes that the employee, in fact, exercises full supervisory authority during such periods.

3. Employees not Regularly Employed in the Bargaining Unit

Regular part-time employees are included in a bargaining unit and entitled to vote in an election. At one time the Board held that an employee had to work a certain percentage of the work week to be classified as a regular part-time employee, but that rule is no longer followed. Now an employee is included in a unit if the employee works a sufficient number of hours on a regular basis to have a substantial interest in the wages, hours, and working conditions in the unit. Thus, an employee who works only one day a week every week, as a weekend relief, is included in the bargaining unit. On the other hand, an employee who works only as needed and who has no regular schedule is not included in the unit, but classified as an irregular or casual employee. An on-call employee could be included in a bargaining unit if the employee worked regularly, such as for a large employer where there were absences every week to be filled.

There are Board cases in which an employee has worked for 10 percent or less of the work week, but was included in the unit because the work was on a regular schedule. In addition to regularity, the Board considers whether the employee performs the same duties and receives the same benefits as full-time employees.

a. Dual-Status Employees. Employees who work part time in the bargaining unit and part time for the employer out of the unit are classified as dual-status employees. An example would be an employee who works three days a week in the office doing clerical work and two days a week as a production worker. The determining factors for a dual-status employee are the same as those applied to part-time employees. A dual-status employee who works regularly in a bargaining unit is included in it. This means, for example, that an employee may actually be included in two or more bargaining units because the employee regularly works in them.

b. Seasonal Employees. Seasonal workers (e.g., people hired for the summer at a resort) may be included in a bargaining unit of regular full-time employees if the seasonal employees have a reasonable expectation of returning each season. On the other hand, if the employees are hired for

only one season, with no expectation of returning the next year, they are not included in the unit. Since these employees have no expectation of future employment and have no great interest in the wages, hours, or working conditions, they lack a community of interest with the full-time and returning seasonal employees.

c. Students, Retirees, Trainees, and Probationary Employees. Students may be included in a bargaining unit depending upon their community of interest. A student working after school on a regular schedule can be included in the unit as a regular part-time employee. But a student who works one season at a summer resort or in a factory with no reasonable expectation of returning the next summer is excluded from the bargaining unit.

At one time the Board held that retirees who work part time in a unit would be excluded if they limited the number of hours they worked in order to make maximum social security benefits. This rule has now been changed. A retiree who works regularly will be in the bargaining unit even if working a limited number of hours. A retiree's unit eligibility is determined by the same criteria as any other part-time employee.

The eligibility of employees hired as management trainees is determined by their reasonable expectations of becoming managers. If trainees have a reasonable expectation of becoming part of management within a reasonably short period, they will be excluded from the unit. On the other hand, if promotion to management is uncertain or far in the future, the Board looks to the current status of the trainee and may include the trainee in the bargaining unit. Probationary employees with a reasonable expectation of completing their probationary period and being permanently hired are included in a bargaining unit.

Questions have arisen as to whether employees working for an employer under governmental manpower training programs or employees working under special programs for the handicapped should be included in a bargaining unit. The Board, applying the usual standards used for other unit employees, includes such employees in the bargaining unit provided they have substantially the same community of interest.

d. Illegal Aliens. Questions have also arisen as to the bargaining unit status of illegal aliens. Although an employee may be in the United States illegally, the employee is entitled to the statutory protection of the Act. Thus, illegal aliens employed in the bargaining unit would be included in the unit and are eligible to vote in representation elections.

4. Individuals Excluded Because of Their Relationship to Management

a. Managerial Employees. The Board has long recognized that there are employees who do not meet the definition of supervisor, but whose interests are far different from rank-and-file employees. A company treasurer, for example, might not supervise, but would have interests obviously aligned with management and not with the bargaining unit. To cover these types of employees, the Board developed the concept of the managerial employee.

There are two types of managerial employees: (1) Those whose interests, based on community-of-interest factors, are closely aligned with management and (2) those who are involved in the formulation, determination, and effectuation of management policy. The Board has held that these individuals, although not specifically excluded from the definition of employees in the Act, should be excluded from a unit. Managerial employees are not entitled to separate representation. Thus, the status of managerial employees differs from that of guards or professional employees who may be excluded from an overall unit, but are still entitled to representation in their own right.

ENJOYMENT OF SPECIAL PRIVILEGES. The first type of managerial employee, those with special privileges who align them with management rather than co-employees, was discussed above in regard to the exclusion of an employer's relatives from a unit. The key to this determination is whether an individual has a special relationship with management as evidenced by the receipt of special privileges not usually afforded other employees, or different terms or conditions of employment.

PARTICIPATION IN COMPANY POLICIES. The second type of managerial employee is involved in making company policy or exercises discretion and independent judgment in carrying out such policy. For example, a head buyer who determines the products a retailer will sell is a managerial employee because the buyer helps formulate company policy. A buyer who is told which goods to buy, but has discretion in carrying out the policy such as selecting the supplier and negotiating the contract price would also be classified as managerial. In general, an employee who has discretionary control over more than a minimal amount of purchases is considered managerial.

There is often a narrow line between a professional employee exercising professional skills and the performance of duties which would classify an employee as managerial under the Act. For example, in the *Yeshiva University* decision,[6] the Supreme Court, reversing an NLRB decision, held that the full-time faculty members at the university were managerial employees, and thus had no statutory right to engage in collective bargaining. The Court noted that the faculty had absolute authority in academic matters, such as deciding which courses would be offered, when they would be scheduled, and to whom they would be taught. The faculty determined admission, retention, and graduation requirements. The Supreme Court rejected the Board's argument that the faculty's authority simply constituted the routine exercise of professional skill.

Of course, *Yeshiva* does not mean that the professional faculty at all schools will be

---

[6] See legal principle 8.A.

barred automatically from collective bargaining. That would depend upon whether the faculty exercises the collective decision-making power that the faculty in *Yeshiva* exercised. Furthermore, the Supreme Court specifically noted that its decision was not intended as a wedge to sweep all professional employees outside the Act. Thus, the Court favorably noted other Board decisions holding that professional architects and engineers, functioning as project captains, were employees under the Act, despite substantial responsibility, because the responsibility (although important) was limited to the routine discharge of professional duties.

Some employers have organized their employees into employee-led teams or "quality circles" that purportedly give employees a greater voice in determining management policy. Are employees who take part in such programs managerial employees because they share in the decision-making process, or is the team leader a supervisor? So far, the Board has basically held that the employees who lead or participate in such programs have only routine authority and lack the discretion and independent judgment necessary to be either a supervisor or a managerial employee.

b. Confidential Employees. Confidential employees are also excluded from the bargaining unit because of their relationship with management. A confidential employee acts in a confidential capacity to a person who formulates, determines, and effectuates *labor policy*. The person who formulates the policy might be a supervisor or a managerial employee. Under this definition, many personal secretaries, who commonly have confidential company information, are not classified as confidential for bargaining purposes if their information does not pertain to labor policy. In the prior example of the head buyer, the buyer would undoubtedly have confidential information about the company's future purchases and be classified as managerial. If the buyer, however, did not formulate, determine, and

effectuate labor policy, the buyer's secretary would not be a confidential employee, even though the secretary might have access to important trade secrets. The confidential employee exclusion only applies to a person having confidential information about labor matters.

Working in the personnel department does not mean that an employee is automatically excluded from a unit. Payroll clerks, for example, may not have any confidential information. A secretary who simply types routine notices to employees would probably not be classified as confidential, but a secretary who types letters from the company's personnel director to the company's labor attorney or types minutes of personnel policy meetings would be confidential because the secretary has access to labor relations policy information before it becomes known to the union or the employees concerned.

Finally, to be classified as confidential, an employee must be regularly engaged in confidential work. Thus, if an employer had a secretarial pool of ten employees, each of whom might occasionally type a confidential letter on labor relations, none of the ten would be classified as confidential. All would be eligible for union representation. On the other hand, if the employer regularly used only one of the ten employees for all labor relations matters, that one employee would probably be excluded as confidential.

Many employers had urged the Board to broaden the scope of the confidential employee category to include employees having access to confidential business information (such as the company's financial situation or trade secrets) unrelated to labor relations matters. The Board, however, refused to broaden the definition, pointing out that any broader scope would deny many white-collar workers doing routine work the benefits of collective bargaining. Ultimately, the Supreme Court in the *Hendricks County Rural Electric Membership Corporation* decision upheld the Board's approach.[7]

---

[7] See legal principle 8.A.

C. ELECTION TIMING AND PROCEDURES

In addition to determining the appropriate unit and the placement of employees within the unit, the time when an election may be held is another important issue in representation proceedings.

1. New or Expanding Units

Unions frequently seek to organize newly opened plants. How long must a union wait after a new plant is opened before an election can be held? What if a union files a petition when only 100 employees out of a potential workforce of 1,000 are present? Is it fair that 100 employees determine whether the plant will be unionized? But, what if it will take five years for the new plant to reach the full workforce? Is it right that the current employees should be denied representation when they may need it most only because more employees may be hired in the future?

The Board has had to develop a principle balancing the respective rights of present and future employees. The Board has ruled that an election may be held if the existing workforce is a substantial and representative employee complement. The Board considers the relationship between the duties and functions of the current employees and of the workforce after the contemplated expansion to determine whether the current employees will adequately represent future employees as well. The employer's prediction about the total number of employees and job classifications that the plant will eventually have must be based on a reasonable period of time. The employer cannot consider a potential expansion five years in the future to set figures. Also, the expansion plans cannot be speculative. Usually the Board will consider evidence of expansion only within the year.

There is no hard and fast rule as to the percentage of the potential employee workforce that must be employed before an election can be held in a new or expanding workforce. However, as discussed later in this chapter in regard to the "contract bar" doctrine, at least 30 percent of the employees in 50 percent of the total job classifications must have been employed in the bargaining unit at the time a contract was executed for it to bar a representation election petition. The Board has said that these percentage requirements may be used as a guideline (but not mechanically applied in all cases) to determine whether there is a representative workforce for the purpose of holding an election at a new or expanding facility.

2. The Twelve-Month Election Rule

Section 9(c)(3) provides that "no election shall be directed in any bargaining unit or in any subdivision within which, in the preceding twelve-month period, a valid election shall have been held." This provision, commonly known as the twelve-month rule, has some exceptions.

First, the provision applies only if there has been a *valid* election. If an election has been set aside because of some irregularity, the union involved or another union can seek another election within the year.

Second, the twelve-month rule applies only to elections held in a particular bargaining unit or subdivision of the unit. If a union seeks to represent a different unit that is not merely a subdivision of the first, then an election could be held within twelve months. Thus, if one union lost an election in a proposed craft unit, a second union seeking to represent an overall production and maintenance unit including the craft employees could have an election within twelve months of the first, because the unit is neither the same nor a subdivision of the bargaining unit involved in the previous election.

Because the twelve-month rule applies only to an election, it has no effect on union organizing. A union may begin soliciting cards again the day after it loses an election. A petition for an election may be filed as early as sixty days before the end of the twelve-month period, and the Board will begin processing the petition as long as the election is not held before the year is up.

The twelve-month rule also does not prohibit an employer from voluntarily recognizing a union in the same unit within twelve months of an election. Nor does it prohibit a union from striking for recognition. (For some general restrictions on recognition picketing that would apply, see Chapter Seven.)

3. Certification Bar and Recognition Bar

The twelve-month election rule is a statutory requirement. As a matter of policy, the Board has established a similar rule if a union wins an election. The Board will not permit another election in the bargaining unit, or its subdivision, within twelve months of a union's certification. This is called certification bar. The purpose of this rule is to promote stability in the bargaining relationship by giving the parties a reasonable bargaining period without the interference of an election campaign. As a related rule, an employer is required to bargain with a union in good faith for a full year after a union is certified. The union's majority status is irrebuttable for that period (see Chapter Five).

The Board also prohibits an election in a unit for a reasonable period of time (anywhere up to twelve months) after an employer voluntarily recognizes a union as the bargaining agent. This prohibition is called recognition bar. Again, the employer is also required to bargain with the union in good faith for this period.

4. The Contract Bar Doctrine

The certification and recognition bar periods of up to a year apply to the time before a company and union enter into a contract. Once a contract is executed, the Board usually does not permit an election in a unit covered by the contract until that contract expires, up to a maximum period of three years. This rule, called the contract bar doctrine, applies to a petition filed by another union to represent the employees (an RC petition), a petition filed by the employees to decertify the union (an RD petition), or a petition filed by the employer (an RM petition). The contract bar rules do not apply to a petition to clarify or amend the unit's certification (UC and UA petitions), as those petitions do not require elections. The purpose of the contract bar doctrine, as for the recognition and certification bar, is to promote stability in the bargaining relationship by prohibiting an election during the contract's duration. The Board strikes a balance between the employee's right to free choice and bargaining stability.

a. Basic Requirements for Contract Bar. There are four basic requirements for a contract to be a bar. First, the contract must be in writing and signed by both parties in order to be a bar. However, the Board has held that a tentative agreement, which the parties have initialed pending the execution of their formal contract, is sufficient. Also, an exchange of telegrams in which the parties confirm their agreement may meet this requirement. The contract would be a bar as of the date of the telegram confirming the parties' agreement, although the contract is not signed until a later date. What if both a local union and its parent international are parties to the collective bargaining agreement? In that case, both the local union and the international union, as well as the employer, must sign the agreement before it will be a bar. In contrast, if the contract is only between an employer and the local, but is subject to approval by the international office, the contract is a bar as soon as it is duly signed by the employer and the local union even though it has not been approved by the international.

Second, the contract must contain substantial terms and conditions of employment to be a bar. A contract, for example, which simply recognizes the union as the bargaining agent, but does not contain provisions on wages, hours, or working conditions, might constitute a recognition bar for its first year, but would be insufficient as a contract bar beyond that period. However, the document that the parties sign need not set out the entire terms of their agreement to be a bar if the terms are set forth in sufficient detail in another written document. For example, if an employer and union have an existing collective bargaining agreement and sign a simple one-paragraph document renewing their prior agreement except for the listed changes, the contract would be a bar even though the renewal agreement does not set out all terms of the agreement. If an employer submits a written contract proposal to the union and the union sends a letter or telegram accepting the offer, the contract would be a bar even though the union's letter or telegram does not list the terms of the agreement, because the terms can be definitely determined from the company's written offer that has been accepted. In some cases, a contract may be a bar if the parties execute an agreement setting forth those items on which they agree and agree to binding arbitration of the remaining open issues. This is known as "interest arbitration" (see Chapter Nine). Thus, for example, if the parties agree on all terms of their agreement except a pay increase, and submit that issue to arbitration, the contract would constitute a bar. However, the Board has held that an agreement of the parties to submit all issues pertaining to their new contract to binding arbitration is not a bar. In that case, the Board concluded that there was, in fact, no contract, and the submission of all unresolved issues to binding arbitration did not promote industrial stability, the basic purpose of the contract bar doctrine.

Third, a contract must be for a definite duration. If the contract does not contain a termination date, an election may be held at any time as long as twelve months have elapsed since the last valid election, because a bargaining agreement without a set period does not promote bargaining stability. Similarly, if the parties agree to extend their current contract beyond its expiration date

pending the execution of a new agreement, the contract would not be a bar during the extension period, because the extension agreement would be for an indefinite duration. In contrast, if the parties agree to renew their agreement for a one-year period (because, for example, the company is going through an economic period that would make meaningful bargaining difficult), the one-year extension, being for a definite period, would constitute a bar for the year. However, a contract or extension agreement must be in effect for a definite period of at least ninety days to be a bar. The Board regards a contract of lesser duration as too short to provide industrial stability.

Fourth, as mentioned above, a contract is only a bar for up to a three-year period. A longer period would unduly deprive employees of a free choice in their bargaining unit. This means, for example, that if the union and the employer negotiate a five-year contract, another union could seek an election after three years even though two years remain on the first contract. A contract for longer than three years is lawful, and it would still be a bar for the first three years. If no election is held or if the contracting (incumbent) union wins an election, the parties are still bound by the contract until it expires.

If a collective bargaining contract is not a bar to an election and another union wins an election that is held, the newly certified union has the choice of keeping the old contract or negotiating a new one. The Board permits renegotiation in this situation because it reasons that a new union was not a party to the old agreement and it would not promote stable labor relations to bind employees to a contract negotiated by a union they have repudiated.

By combining a certification or recognition bar with a contract bar, no election might be held for up to four years. That could happen if a union and employer did not negotiate their first contract until the recognition bar period was nearly up and then entered into a three-year agreement.

b. The Insulated and Open Periods. The Board has established time limits within which a representation petition may be filed at the end of a contract that has been a bar.

Under Section 8(d), the parties to a contract must serve a notice of their desire to terminate or amend the agreement sixty days before the end of their contract. The Board has ruled that no representation petition can be filed in the sixty days before a contract expires so that this period may be devoted exclusively to bargaining rather than election campaigning. This sixty-day period is called the insulated or closed period because it is insulated from a petition being filed. The Board has further ruled that a petition may not be filed more than ninety days before a contract expires. The sixty- to ninety-day period before the contract expires is referred to as the open period.

Section 8(d) requires that in the health care industry, a notice to terminate or amend a collective bargaining agreement be served ninety days before the end of a contract, thirty days earlier than in other industries. For this reason, the Board has moved the contract bar periods back by thirty days in the health care industry. Thus, to be timely, a representation petition must be filed in the 120- to 90-day period before the contract expires. Other than this time change, the other principles of the contract bar doctrine apply to the health care industry.

These time rules for filing a petition apply only if a contract is a bar. Thus if a contract is of an indefinite duration, or after a contract has been in effect for more than three years, a petition can be filed at any time. Also a rival union may seek recognition cards during the period of the incumbent's contract. It does not have to wait until the open period to begin solicitation. However, the cards must be less than a year old to be valid as a showing of interest.

At one time, the Board held that if a rival union filed a valid representation petition during the open period, the employer and incumbent union had to cease negotiations for a new contract until the representation case proceedings were terminated or an election was held and the results certified. Now, however (as discussed in Chapter Four), the Board permits the employer and incumbent union to continue negotiations and to execute a new collective bargaining agreement. If the rival union is certified as the employees' bargaining representative, any contract negotiated between the employer and the prior union is null and void.

If no representation petition is filed during the ninety-day to sixty-day open period and the parties execute a new contract during the sixty-day closed period, no petition can be filed. The new contract is once again a bar. If, however, the parties fail to execute a new agreement during the closed period and the contract expires, a petition may be filed at any time until a new agreement is executed. The filing period is open again after the contract expires. This is often a strong incentive for an incumbent union to agree to a contract if it sees another union collecting cards and getting ready to file a petition as soon as the contract expires. If a contract is executed before a petition is filed, the contract is once again a bar for its duration up to three years.

c. Ratification and Contract Bar. If the effectiveness of a contract is not expressly contingent on membership ratification, the contract is a bar as soon as it is signed. This rule applies even though the parties understand that the contract is subject to a ratification vote. If a contract is rejected by the membership, there is another open period for the filing of a petition until another contract is signed.

d. Premature Contract Extensions. What if an incumbent union anticipates that another union may challenge it either at the time its contract expires or at the end of the three-year contract bar period? Can it prevent the filing of a rival petition by prematurely negotiating a new contract before the old contract expires in order to extend the bar? No. If a contract is prematurely extended for any reason, a petition is still timely if it is filed during the open period based on the original contract's expiration date.

e. Exceptions to Contract Bar

1. UNLAWFUL CONTRACT CLAUSES. In some instances the Board may permit an election before three years are up even though the contract is in effect. First, a contract will not be a bar if the contract contains a union security clause or a checkoff provision that is unlawful on its face. An example would be a union security clause requiring employees to join the union on their first day of work (see Chapter Ten). What if the language of a contract union security clause appears to be lawful but, in fact, a union unlawfully requires employees to join on the first day of employment? The Board will not consider evidence that a union security clause is being unlawfully applied in a representation case hearing. It will only consider the express language, and the contract will therefore still be a bar. If the clause is being unlawfully enforced, an unfair labor practice charge must be filed because the Board does not permit unfair labor practice issues to be resolved in representation cases, due to the different procedures and rules of evidence that apply.

What if a contract contains no unlawful clauses, but was entered into unlawfully, such as at a time when the union did not represent a majority of the employees? The contract will not be set aside as a bar in a representation proceeding. The challenging party must file an unfair labor practice charge that the contract was unlawfully executed. If the challenger prevails on the unfair practice case, the contract will be set aside. Until then, it would remain a bar.

2. SCHISMS AND DEFUNCT UNIONS. A contract is also not a bar if there is a schism in the union. A schism is a basic split over fundamental policy within the union that results in the presentation of conflicting representation claims to the employer. There must be a basic split—the formation of a dissident group within a union is not sufficient.

Another exception to the contract bar rule is if a union is defunct, if it has ceased to function as a bargaining agent. The union must be unable or unwilling to function. The Board will not set aside a contract, however, if the union is attempting to function even though it is weak and ineffective.

3. EXPANDING UNITS. A contract does not bar an election if there has been a substantial expansion in the plant since the contract was executed or if it was executed prematurely. To be a bar, at least 30 percent of the employees who will eventually work in the bargaining unit in 50 percent of the total job classifications must have been employed in the unit at the time a contract was executed. If a plant was to eventually have 100 employees in 20 job classifications, a contract would not be a bar unless there were at least 30 employees in 10 of the job classifications working at the time of execution. The 30 percent requirement applies only to the total number of employees in the unit. There is no requirement that each classification be at least 30 percent filled, only that the overall percentage be met.

f. Contract Bar Following a Merger, Consolidation, or Sale.

Contract bar problems frequently arise following a merger or consolidation of two or more plants. The Board has ruled that a contract is not a bar to an election following a merger or consolidation of one contracting employer with another employer, or of two or more plants owned by the same employer, if the nature of the enterprise changes because of the merger. The Board reasons that a merger that changes the nature of the operation creates an unstable bargaining situation. The contract is not a stabilizing factor and the purpose of the contract bar doctrine, to preserve a stable relationship, is not served. In that case, if a rival union tries to represent the employees, an election to determine the bargaining representative may lead to greater stability than preserving the existing contract.

Whether a merger has the effect of changing the nature of a business is a question of fact. Sometimes two companies merge, but each plant continues to operate independently. In that case, each contract remains a bar. Sometimes one plant closes and employees are transferred to the remaining facility and covered by its contract. A newly purchased plant may simply be added as an accretion to an older plant's bargaining unit covered by an existing contract because of the close community of interest between the new and old facilities.

In some cases, however, substantial numbers of employees previously represented by different unions at different locations may be relocated to the same facility. Which union's contract should control? The Board has an easy solution: The Board reasons that since neither union clearly represents the employees, neither contract promotes stability and neither contract should be a bar. Thus, the two competing unions (or any other unions wishing to intervene) are free to file a representation petition to determine majority status.

As discussed in Chapter Five, an employer purchasing a company, called a successor employer, normally is not obligated to assume the existing collective bargaining agreement between the old employer and existing union. The successor employer's only obligation is to bargain in good faith with the prior union if it still represents a majority of the employees.

Since a successor employer is normally not obligated to assume the existing collective bargaining agreement, the Board has held that an existing agreement is not a contract bar if there is a successor employer. The only exception is that the contract will be a bar if the successor expressly assumes it. This distinction arises because of the underlying contract bar policy of promoting stability in the bargaining relationship. If a successor employer is not obligated to assume an existing collective bargaining agreement, and does not do so, the contract is not a stabilizing factor. On the other hand, if the successor employer expressly assumes the agreement, applying the contract bar doctrine promotes stability.

D. VOTER ELIGIBILITY

Voter eligibility is another important issue. After a representation election is directed, the Board establishes a payroll eligibility date, the date by which an employee must be on the employer's payroll in order to be eligible to vote. Normally, the payroll eligibility date is the payroll period immediately preceding the direction of election or the execution of a consent election agreement. To be eligible, an employee must be employed on the payroll eligibility date and also on the date of the election; both dates must be met.

The employer is required to give the union a list of the names and addresses of all employees who are eligible to vote as of the payroll eligibility date. This list must be furnished within seven days after the Board directs an election. The list is called the Excelsior list, after the case (*Excelsior Underwear, Inc.*) in which the Board first adopted this requirement.[8] Normally, the union must possess the list ten days before an election. The Excelsior list gives a union the opportunity to contact the employees before the election. Failure of the employer to provide the list or the presence of so many inaccuracies that the list cannot reasonably be used may be grounds for setting aside an election.

1. Voting Rights of Striking and Replacement Employees

Elections may be held during a strike. This occurs most frequently when employees who did not join the strike and/or strike replacements file a petition to decertify the union while other employees continue to strike. Who votes in the election: the striking employees, their replacements, or both the strikers and replacements? The answer depends on the type of strike and the length of the strike.

a. Unfair Labor Practice versus Economic Strikers. There are two types of strikers: unfair labor practice strikers and economic

[8] See legal principle 12.

strikers (see Chapter Six). An unfair labor practice striker is on strike protesting an employer's unfair labor practices. An economic striker is on strike over an economic issue such as grievances or a new collective bargaining agreement.

The Board has held that unfair labor practice strikers are entitled to reinstatement to work any time if they unconditionally offer to return. Although an employer can continue to operate during an unfair labor practice strike, unfair labor practice strikers cannot be permanently replaced. The Board has reasoned that since unfair labor practice strikers may return to work at any time and cannot be permanently replaced, they are entitled to vote in any election held during the strike. Furthermore, their replacements are ineligible to vote.

REPLACED ECONOMIC STRIKERS AND THEIR REPLACEMENTS. In contrast to unfair labor practice strikers, economic strikers may be replaced permanently. An employee hired by an employer to replace an economic striker whom the employer intends to retain after the strike is over is called a permanent replacement. Temporary replacements are employees who do the strikers' work only while the strike lasts, such as supervisor or a nonbargaining unit employee or a student. A permanently replaced economic striker is not entitled to reinstatement at the end of a strike, but is placed on a recall list, to be reinstated as jobs become available (see Chapter Six).

An economic striker's right to vote is determined by whether the striker has been permanently replaced by another employee. An economic striker who has *not* been permanently replaced has the right to vote in any election, as does an unfair labor practice striker. However, under Section 9(c)(3), economic strikers who have been permanently replaced, and are thus not entitled to immediate reinstatement, are eligible to vote only in elections held within twelve months after a strike begins. This rule applies even though the striker still has recall rights after twelve months.

Permanent replacements for economic strikers are eligible to vote from their date of hire. Temporary replacements are not eligible to vote regardless of the election date. Thus, during the first twelve months of an economic strike, both economic strikers and permanent replacements may vote. After twelve months, only permanent replacements and economic strikers who have not been permanently replaced are eligible. (Of course bargaining unit employees who never joined the strike or returned to work during the strike are also eligible.)

If a representation petition is filed before twelve months are up, the Board generally expedites an election so that permanently replaced economic strikers will be eligible to vote. If an election is held within the twelve-month period but set aside because of meritorious objections to its conduct (see Chapter One), replaced economic strikers who were eligible to vote in the initial election are still eligible to vote in the rerun even if it is held more than twelve months after the strike began.

b. Loss of Voting Eligibility. Either an economic or unfair labor practice striker who is eligible to vote in an election may lose eligibility if the striker abandons the prior job and obtains permanent employment elsewhere; if the striker's job is permanently discontinued during the strike; or if the striker has been discharged for strike misconduct such as picket line violence. These are basically the same grounds for which strikers may lose their recall or reinstatement rights at the end of a strike (discussed in detail in Chapter Six).

There is a presumption that a striker's employment during a strike is temporary and that replacements hired during the strike are permanent. Thus, the employer has the burden of proving that a striking employee is not eligible to vote, but the union has the burden of proving that replacements are only temporary and thus ineligible. There must be a mutual understanding between the employer and the replacement that the replacement is permanent in order for the replacement to be so classified. Thus, noncommittal statements by an employer to replacements that they *might* be retained after a strike is over may be insufficient to establish that the replacement is permanent. At one time, the Board applied a fairly lenient standard that an employee could be discharged only for serious strike misconduct. However, as discussed in Chapter Six, the Reagan Board substantially broadened the employer's right to discharge employees for misconduct that prior Boards would have considered minor.

Employees discharged during a strike may vote subject to challenge. Whether their discharge was lawful is decided in an unfair labor practice proceeding, which is usually consolidated with the pending representation case. If the discharge is unlawful, then the employee's ballot will be counted. If the Board decides that the employee was lawfully discharged, the ballot will not be counted.

2. Employees on Layoff or Sick Leave

The voting eligibility of an employee on layoff is determined by the reasonable likelihood of the employee's returning to work with the employer in the near and foreseeable future. The Board considers such factors as the employer's past history in recalling employees to work; the employer's future plans; the circumstances of the layoff (e.g., was it due to the permanent shutdown of a department or only a seasonal work fluctuation); and what the employer told the employee at the time of the layoff about the possibility of recall.

An employee placed on indefinite layoff under a contract that preserves the employee's seniority recall rights for one year would probably be able to vote in any election held within the year. In some cases, however, even an employee with contractual recall rights may be ineligible to vote if, based on the specific facts, it is clear that the employee has no reasonable likelihood of being recalled to work within the contractual recall period. An employee placed on layoff with the understanding that the employee would

be recalled if a large order scheduled the following month came in would most likely be permitted to vote since the recall is fairly definite. An employee whose department was permanently closed and who was told only that someday, if the company expanded, the employee would be recalled, would probably not be eligible because the expansion might never occur and the employee would have no reasonable likelihood of returning to work.

The voting status of an employee on an indefinite leave of absence would also basically be determined by whether that employee has a reasonable likelihood of returning to work.

The Board applies a special eligibility formula for elections in the construction industry. An employee is eligible to vote if the employee has been employed by the employer for a total of thirty days or more within the twelve-month period immediately preceding the election eligibility date or has had some employment with the employer in that period and had been employed forty-five or more days within the twenty-four-month period immediately preceding the eligibility date. Employees terminated for cause or who quit work voluntarily prior to the completion of the last job for which they were employed are not eligible to vote. The Board applies this special rule because of the sporadic nature of employment in the construction industry to assure that those employees who have a reasonable expectation of future employment will be eligible to vote.

There is some confusion in the standard for determining the voting eligibility of employees on sick or maternity leave. Some Board decisions appear to base eligibility on the same criteria used for employees on layoff, that is, whether the employee has a reasonable likelihood of returning to work in the foreseeable future. However, in more recent cases the Board has stated that an employee on sick or maternity leave is presumed to continue in that status and is eligible to vote unless the employee has been discharged or has resigned. Under this approach, employees whose medical condition makes it highly unlikely that they will ever return to work might be eligible to vote.

Employees on military leave can vote if they appear in person at the poll. No absentee ballots are permitted.

3. Voter Challenge Procedure

The Board prefers that voter eligibility issues be resolved at a representation hearing prior to the election if the parties know such issues exist. Then the Board can rule on both eligibility issues and the appropriate unit at the same time. However, an employee's right to vote may be challenged by either party or the Board agent on the grounds that the employee is not properly in the unit or ineligible for one of the reasons discussed above at the time the employee votes. It is the parties' responsibility to make their challenges at the time an employee votes. An employee cannot be challenged after voting.

A challenged employee is allowed to vote subject to challenge. The ballot is set aside in a sealed envelope rather than placed in the ballot box. After all employees have voted, the unchallenged ballots are counted first. If the results of the election would not be affected by the number of challenged ballots, the Board will not even rule on the challenges. What, then, is the status of these employees? Are they in the unit or not? The unit status would be left to collective bargaining between the parties. If no agreement is reached, then the union might file a union clarification petition with the Board to determine their status.

Summary

The appropriate bargaining unit concept is fundamental to understanding the bargaining process as unions represent and bargain for employees through appropriate bargaining units. The most important factor in determining the appropriate unit is the community of interest among the employees. A bargaining unit is appropriate if it has a separate community of interest. Generally, the Board allows employees to bargain in any unit that is appropriate even though other units may also be appropriate. The unit does not have to be the best or most appropriate. Special rules restricting the number of bargaining units apply in the health care industry.

Because of their distinct community of interest, certain groups of employees, called presumptively appropriate units, almost always comprise a separate appropriate unit. An office clerical employees unit and a production and maintenance employees unit are typical examples. Craft employees and departmental employees were at one time entitled to separate representation, but they are now so entitled under only specific circumstances. Generally, if an employer has more than one plant or facility, each plant or facility is a separate appropriate unit. However, if either the employer or the union wants a multi-facility unit, the burden is on the party requesting it to prove that the employees in the two facilities share a community of interest. In some cases both a single- or multi-facility unit might be appropriate. In recent years, although the Board has not changed these principles, it has tended to favor larger bargaining units over smaller ones, and in some cases, has held that only a multi-plant or multi-facility bargaining unit was appropriate because of the employer's centralized control over labor relations at the facilities, etc.

Multi-employer units are established voluntarily between the employers and the union. However, once an employer has voluntarily joined a multi-employer group, it cannot withdraw from the group after negotiations have begun.

An employer and a union have some discretion in determining the employees included in a unit. However, certain categories are excluded because the LMRA specifically prohibits them from being included in a unit with other employees. They may be excluded from the definition of employees and therefore not entitled to union representation; they may not regularly work in the bargaining unit; or they may have a special relationship with management and thus lack a community of interest with their fellow employees. Persons falling within these categories are not included in a bargaining unit and are not permitted to vote in a Board election. These categories include supervisors; managerial employees; casual, part-time, and temporary employees; confidential employees; the children or spouse of the owner; independent contractors; and agricultural laborers.

The twelve-month election rule (Section 9(c)(3)) prohibits an election in any bargaining unit or subdivision if a valid election has been held within the preceding twelve months. The rule applies only to an election. It does not prohibit union organizing or voluntary employer recognition during the period. In addition to an election bar, the Board, as a matter of policy, has established similar rules if a union is voluntarily recognized. The Board will not permit another election in a bargaining unit within twelve months of the union's certification or for a reasonable period of time after an employer voluntarily recognizes a union.

Once a contract is executed, the Board, applying the contract bar doctrine, usually does not permit an election in the unit covered by the contract until it expires up to a maximum of three years. This rule applies to a petition filed by another union to represent the employees, a petition filed by the employees to decertify the union, or a petition filed by the employer.

To be eligible to vote in an election, an employee must be on the payroll on the payroll eligibility date and also on the date of the election. The employer is required to provide the union with a list of the names and addresses of all employees who are eligible to vote as of the payroll eligibility date.

Elections may be held while employees are on strike. The basic rules are that an unfair labor practice striker can vote in a Board election regardless of how long the employee has been on strike. An economic striker who has been replaced can vote only in an election held within the first year of the strike. Unreplaced economic strikers can vote indefinitely. Permanent replacements for economic strikers can vote, but temporary replacements or replacements for unfair labor practice strikers cannot vote.

An employee on layoff is eligible to vote if there is a reasonable likelihood the employee will return to work with the employer and thus shares a community of interest with the other active employees.

An employee's right to vote may be challenged at the time of voting by either party or the Board agent. The Board will rule only on the challenged ballots if the number of challenged ballots affects the outcome of the election.

Review Questions

1. What is a community of interest?
2. Will the Board allow an election in a unit that is appropriate for bargaining although other units are more appropriate?
3. Will the Board certify a one-employee unit?
4. Who is a professional employee under the LMRA?
5. Is an employee who is called a guard by the employer automatically excluded from a unit that includes nonguard employees?
6. What persons are excluded from the definition of employee under Section 2(3) of the Act?
7. How is an independent contractor distinguished from an employee under the Act?
8. Can a person who does not have the authority to hire or fire employees be classified as a supervisor under the Act?
9. Can seasonal workers (for example, persons hired for the summer season at a resort) be included in a bargaining unit of regular full-time employees?
10. What is the contract bar doctrine?
11. How long is an unfair labor practice striker eligible to vote in a representation election?
12. What are the insulated and open periods for filing a representation petition?

(Answers to review questions are at the end of the book.)

Basic Legal Principles

1.A. A labor organization may represent employees in any bargaining unit that is appropriate for bargaining. A unit is appropriate if the employees within it have a separate and distinct community of interest. A unit need be only an appropriate unit for bargaining, not the best or most appropriate. *Dinah's Hotel Corp.*, 295 NLRB No. 127, 131 LRRM 1797 (1989); *Dezcon Inc.*, 295 NLRB No. 19, 131 LRRM 1675 (1989) (construction industry); *Livingstone College,* 290 NLRB No. 41, 129 LRRM 1079 (1988); *Gibbs & Cox, Inc.,* 280 NLRB No. 110, 123 LRRM 1034 (1986); *Atlantic Hilton,* 273 No. 9, 118 NLRB 1032 (1984); *KJAZ Broadcasting, Inc.,* 272 NLRB No. 21, 117 LRRM 1177 (1984).

1.B. In general, a single plant or facility is presumed to be an appropriate bargaining unit, but recently the Board has tended to favor larger bargaining units including several plants or facilities as the only unit appropriate for bargaining. *Coplay Cement Co.,* 288 NLRB No. 21, 128 LRRM 1038 (1988); *Hilton Hotel Corp.,* 287 NLRB No. 36, 127 LRRM 1141 (1987); *New England Telephone & Telegraph,* 280 NLRB No. 16, 122 LRRM 1202 (1986) (system-wide unit); *Ramada Beverly Hills,* 278 NLRB No. 95, 121 LRRM 1237 (1986) (hotel); *Hall's Super Markets, Inc.,* 281 NLRB No. 150, 123 LRRM 1158 (1986); *Kobacker Stores,* 274 NLRB No.

132, 118 LRRM 1427 (1985) (multi-store unit); *Emporium-Capwell,* 273 NLRB No. 89, 118 LRRM 1348 (1984); *Queen City Distributing Co.,* 272 NLRB No. 98, 117 LRRM 1320 (1984) (multi-store unit); *Airco, Inc.,* 273 NLRB No. 53, 118 LRRM 1052 (1984) (single-plant unit).

1.C. Special rules apply in the health care industry limiting the number of appropriate bargaining units. *St. Francis Hosp. I,* 265 NLRB No. 120, 112 LRRM 1153 (1982); *St. Francis Hosp. II,* 271 NLRB No. 160, 116 LRRM 1465 (1984), (disparity-of-interest test), enforcement denied *Electrical Workers Local 474 v. NLRB and St. Francis Hospital,* 814 F.2d 697, 124 LRRM 2993 (D.C. Cir. 1987); *St. Francis Hosp. III,* 286 NLRB No. 123, 126 LRRM 1361 (1987); *St. Vincent Hospital,* 285 NLRB No. 64, 125 LRRM 1329 (1987); *St. Anthony's Hospital v. NLRB,* 884 F. 2d 518, 132 LRRM 2055 (10th Cir. 1989). See NLRB Final Rule, Collective-Bargaining Units in the Health Care Industry, Vol. 29 Code of Federal Regulations (C.F.R.) Part 103. But see *American Hospital Assn. v. NLRB,* 718 F. Supp. 704, 132 LRRM 2033 (N.D. Ill., 1989) (decision enjoining implementation of rule currently on appeal to United States Court of Appeals for Seventh Circuit).

2. The primary factors in determining community of interest are (1) the distinctiveness or integration of the employees into the overall work-force; (2) bargaining history in the industry and of the parties before the Board; (3) common supervision and similarity of duties, skills, interests, wages, and working conditions; (4) organizational structure of the company including the degree to which there is centralized control over personnel policies; and (5) desires of the employees. See cases cited in legal principles 1.A., B., and C.

3. In determining whether craft or departmental employees are entitled to separate representation, the Board considers (1) the distinctness and homogeneity of a group; (2) the collective bargaining history; (3) the craft's or department's separate identity from the larger employee groups; (4) the industry's bargaining practice; (5) the integration of production and craft functions; and (6) the qualifications of the union seeking representation. *Mallinckrodt Chemical Works,* 162 NLRB No. 48, 64 LRRM 1011 (1966); *International Foundation of Employee Benefit Plans, Inc.,* 234 NLRB No. 51, 97 LRRM 1144 (1978); *NLRB v. Metal Container Corp.,* 660 F.2d 1309, 108 LRRM 2625 (8th Cir. 1981); *Dodge City of Wauwatosa,* 282 NLRB No. 71, 124 LRRM 1038 (1986); *Westin Hotel,* 277 NLRB No. 172, 121 LRRM 1105 (1986); *Longcrier Co.,* 277 NLRB No. 62, 120 LRRM 1343 (1985); *Charrette Drafting Supplies,* 275 NLRB No. 177, 119 LRRM 1301 (1985).

4. If one union seeks to represent an overall production and maintenance unit and another union seeks to represent a separate craft group, both of which are appropriate, the Board will hold a self-determination election for the employees to decide their preference. *Globe Machine and Stamping Co.,* 3 NLRB No. 25, 1 LRRM 122 (1937); *Columbia Transit Corp.,* 237 NLRB No. 201, 99 LRRM 1114 (1978).

5. Once a union is certified as the representative of a bargaining unit, other employees may be added to the unit as an "accretion" without a vote if the employees of a new, expanded, or merged facility have the same community of interest as those already in the bargaining unit. However, the doctrine does not apply if previously separate workforces have historically been represented by different unions and neither workforce is substantially larger than the other so that neither union clearly predominates over the other. In general, employees may not be added to a unit by accretion if the employee classifications existed at the time of the union's original certification and could have been included in the original bargaining unit. *Save Mart of Modesto Inc.*, 293 NLRB No. 135, 131 LRRM 1791 (1989); *George V. Hamilton, Inc.*, 289 NLRB No. 165, 129 LRRM 1067 (1988); *Super Valu Stores, Inc.*, 283 NLRB No. 24, 124 LRRM 1294 (1987); *Special Machine & Engineering, Inc.*, 282 NLRB No. 172, 124 LRRM 1219 (1987); *NLRB v. Stevens Ford, Inc.*, 773 F.2d 468, 120 LRRM 2589 (2d Cir. 1985); *Martin Marietta Chemicals*, 270 NLRB No. 114, 116 LRRM 1150 (1984).

6. A person is classified as a supervisor if the person can exercise any of the twelve powers listed in LMRA Section 2(11) or can effectively recommend such action provided that the person is exercising independent judgment. *Washington Post Co.*, 254 NLRB 168, 106 LRRM 1404 (1981). Compare *Northwood Manor, Inc.*, 260 NLRB No. 110, 109 LRRM 1226 (1982) (charge nurses are supervisors) with *Mt. Airy Psychiatric Center*, 253 NLRB 1003, 106 LRRM 1071 (1981) (charge nurses not supervisors and properly included in bargaining unit); *Anamag*, 284 NLRB No. 72, 125 LRRM 1287 (1987) (quality team leaders not supervisors); *Bowne of Houston*, 280 NLRB No. 132, 122 NLRB 1347 (1986) (sporadic duties); *St. Louis Credit Union*, 273 NLRB No. 90, 118 LRRM 1079 (1984); *Albany Medical Center*, 273 NLRB No. 75, 118 LRRM 1318 (1984); *Aladdin Hotel*, 270 NLRB No. 122, 116 LRRM 1155 (1984); *Detroit College of Business*, 296 NLRB No. 40, 132 LRRM 1081 (1989) (supervision of non-unit employees); *Baltimore Sun Co.*, 296 NLRB No. 131, 132 LRRM 1210 (1989) (timing of unit clarification petition to exclude supervisors).

7. Part-time or dual-status employees who are regularly employed in the unit have a substantial community of interest with the unit's full-time employees and are included in the unit. Regularity of employment rather than the number of hours is controlling. *Sears, Roebuck & Co.*, 172 NLRB No. 132, 68 LRRM 1469 (1968); *Leaders-Nameoki, Inc.*, 237 NLRB No. 202, 99 LRRM 1132 (1978); *L & B Cooling*, 267 NLRB No. 2, 113 LRRM 1119 (1983) (seasonal employees); *Alpha School Bus Co.*, 287 NLRB No. 71, 127 LRRM 1150 (1987); *Tri-State Transportation Co.*, 289 NLRB No. 38, 128 LRRM 1246 (1988).

8.A. Confidential and managerial employees and independent contractors are excluded from coverage under the LMRA. The confidential employee exclusion is narrowly applied to only those employees acting in a confidential capacity to a person who formulates, determines, and effectuates labor policy. *NLRB v. Hendricks County Rural Electric Membership Corp.*, 454 U.S. 170, 108 LRRM 3105 (1981); *Crest Mark Packing Co.*, 283

NLRB No. 151, 125 LRRM 1139 (1987); *Intermountain Rural Electric Assn.,* 277 NLRB No. 3, 120 LRRM 1245 (1985); *Associated Day Care Services,* 269 NLRB No. 32, 115 LRRM 1217 (1984). Managerial employees formulate, determine, and effectuate management policy, or are otherwise closely aligned with management. Professional employees carrying out the routine duties of their profession are not managerial. *NLRB v. Yeshiva University,* 444 U.S. 672, 103 LRRM 2526 (1980); *NLRB v. Action Automotive,* 469 U.S. 490, 118 LRRM 2577 (1985); *NLRB v. Lewis University,* 765 F.2d 616, 119 LRRM 2993 (7th Cir. 1985); *Sampson Steel & Supply, Inc.,* 289 NLRB No. 59, 128 LRRM 1230 (1988); *FHP, Inc.,* 274 NLRB No. 168, 118 LRRM 1525 (1985). See also *Roadway Package System,* 288 NLRB No. 22, 128 LRRM 1016 (1988) (independent contractors).

8.B. Guards are entitled to representation under the LMRA, but the Board cannot certify a union to represent guards if it represents employees other than guards or is directly or indirectly affiliated with a union admitting nonguards to membership. *Teamsters Local 851 v. NLRB,* 732 F.2d 43, 116 LRRM 2386 (2d Cir. 1984); *University of Chicago,* 272 NLRB No. 126, 117 LRRM 1377 (1984); *Teamsters Local 807 v. NLRB,* 755 F.2d 5, 118 LRRM 2613 (2d Cir. 1985); *Wells Fargo Alarm Services,* 289 NLRB No. 74, 128 LRRM 1217 (1988).

9.A. Whether employees who are not actively at work, but who retain employee status (e.g., laid-off employees) are included in a bargaining unit depends upon whether they have a reasonable expectation of returning to work in the near and forseeable future. *Sullivan Surplus Sales, Inc.,* 152 NLRB No. 12, 59 LRRM 1041 (1965); *East Bay Newspapers, Inc.,* 225 NLRB No. 128, 93 LRRM 1102 (1976); *Tenneco Automotive,* 273 NLRB No. 14, 118 LRRM 1054 (1984); *S & G Concrete Co.,* 274 NLRB No. 116, 118 LRRM 1420 (1985); *Data Technology Corp.,* 281 NLRB No. 136, 123 LRRM 1192 (1986); *Amoco Oil Co.,* 290 NLRB No. 37, 131 LRRM 1088 (1989). But see *Red Arrow Freight Lines,* 278 NLRB No. 137, 121 LRRM 1257 (1986) (employee on sick or maternity leave is presumed to continue in that status and is eligible to vote unless the employee has been discharged or has resigned).

9.B. In the construction industry only, an employee is eligible to vote if the employee has been employed by the employer for a total of thirty days or more within the twelve-month period immediately preceding the election eligibility date or has had some employment with the employer in that period and has been employed forty-five or more days within the twenty-four-month period immediately preceding the eligibility date unless the employee was terminated for cause or quit work voluntarily prior to the completion of the last job for which employed. *Daniel Construction Co.,* 167 NLRB No. 159, 66 LRRM 1220 (1967); *Wilson & Dean Construction Co.,* 295 NLRB No. 54, 131 LRRM 1583 (1989).

10. Both replaced economic strikers and their permanent replacements may vote in an NLRB election held during the first year of a strike. Thereafter employees who are permanently replaced are ineligible to vote. Unfair labor practice strikers remain eligible to vote regardless of the strike's length. *Pacific Tile & Porcelain Co.,* 137 NLRB No. 169, 50

LRRM 1394 (1962); *W. Wilton Wood, Inc.*, 127 NLRB No. 185, 46 LRRM 1240 (1960); *Larand Leisurelies, Inc.*, 222 NLRB No. 131, 91 LRRM 1305 (1976); *K & W Trucking Co.*, 267 NLRB No. 21, 113 LRRM 1134 (1983); *JELD-WEN*, 285 NLRB No. 19, 125 LRRM 1307 (1987); *Lamb-Grays Harbor Co.*, 295 NLRB No. 40, 131 LRRM 1550 (1989); *St. Joe Mining Co.*, 295 NLRB No. 59, 132 LRRM 1108 (1989). See also, *Harter Equipment Inc.*, 293 NLRB No. 79, 131 LRRM 1059 (1989) (since locked out employees cannot be permanently replaced, they are eligible to vote in a representation election even after the first year of a lockout; their temporary replacements are ineligible).

11. To serve as a contract bar, a contract must be signed and contain substantial terms and conditions of employment sufficient to stabilize the bargaining relationship. A collective bargaining agreement can bar an election for up to three years. A contract for a longer period, although not a bar after three years, remains in effect and is binding on the parties to it for its full period unless a representation election is held and another union is duly certified as the bargaining agent. A contract must be for a fixed duration of at least ninety days to be a bar for any period. *Appalachian Shale Products Co.*, 121 NLRB 1160, 42 LRRM 1506 (1958); *Stur-Dee Health Products*, 248 NLRB No. 138, 104 LRRM 1012 (1980); *USM Corp.*, 256 NLRB 996, 107 LRRM 1358 (1981); *Crompton Co.*, 260 NLRB No. 69, 109 LRRM 1161 (1982); *Crothall Hosp. Services, Inc.*, 270 NLRB No. 195, 117 LRRM 1072 (1984); *Kent Corp.*, 272 NLRB No. 115, 117 LRRM 1333 (1984); *Georgia Kaolin Co.*, 287 NLRB No. 50, 127 LRRM 1051 (1987); *Corporation de Servicios Legales*, 289 NLRB No. 79, 128 LRRM 1270 (1988); *NLRB v. Mississippi Power & Light*, 769 F.2d 276, 120 LRRM 2302 (5th Cir. 1985); *Brown Transport Corp.*, 296 NLRB No. 157, 132 LRRM 1219 (1989).

12. Within seven days after the Board directs a representation election the employer is required to give the union a list of the names and addresses of all employees who are eligible to vote in the election. *Excelsior Underwear Inc.*, 156 NLRB No. 111, 61 LRRM 1217 (1966).

Recommended Reading

"A Comparison of the Selection of Bargaining Representatives in the United States and Canada." 10 Comp. Lab. L. J. 65 (1988).

Ashlock, "The Bargaining Status of College and University Professors under the National Labor Relations Laws," 35 *Lab. L. J.* 103 (1984).

CCH Editorial Staff, "When Has Substantial Agreement Been Reached for Application of the Contract Bar Doctrine?" 33 *Lab. L. J.* 121 (1982).

Delaney and Sockell, "Hospital Unit Determination and the Preservation of Employee Free Choice," 39 *Lab. L. J.* 259 (1988).

"Development of the Craft Severance Doctrine," 11 *St. Louis U. L. J.* 615 (1967).

Dyleski-Najjar, "Professional Unions in the Health Care Industry," 17 *Loyola U. Chi. L. J.* 383 (1986).

Krent, "Collective Authority and Technical Expertise: Re-examining the Managerial Employee Exclusion," 56 *NYU L. Rev.* 694 (1981).

Scott and Odewahn, "Multi-Union Elections Involving Incumbents: The Legal Environment," 40 *Lab. L. J.* 403 (1989).

chapter 3

UNION ORGANIZING RIGHTS AND EMPLOYER RESPONSE

This chapter describes permissible union and employer tactics in organizing employees and conducting an election campaign. It also discusses the unique blend of Section 8 unfair labor practices and Section 9 acts that may interfere with an election, which together govern union organizing rights and employer responses.

The rights and obligations of unions, employees, and employers in organizing and in election campaigns are regulated by Sections 8 and 9 of the LMRA. Some of the actions discussed below are either protected or prohibited as unfair labor practices under Section 8. However, in addition to the unfair labor practice restrictions, the Board, under its authority to administer elections pursuant to Section 9, has determined that an election must be conducted under "laboratory conditions." The Board prohibits an employer or union from engaging in misconduct that destroys the laboratory conditions and interferes with the employees' right to a free-choice election. An election may be set aside for acts that the Board concludes interfere with an election under Section 9, even though those acts may not constitute an unfair labor practice under Section 8.

A. OBTAINING RECOGNITION CARDS

Union organizational drives usually begin by having employees sign recognition cards authorizing the union to represent them; these cards are submitted to the NLRB for an election. Cards are not the only method of obtaining an NLRB election. The union can circulate a petition asking for an election. The Board will hold an election if 30 percent of the employees in the appropriate unit sign cards or a petition. Cards are far more common and convenient and cause fewer legal problems that could disrupt the election process.

In representation campaigns, the union frequently obtains recognition cards from a majority of the employees in the proposed unit and then seeks voluntary recognition from the employer. The union may propose that the employer verify the cards against the payroll records or have them verified by an independent person such as a local minister. However, a union need not request recognition before filing a representation petition at the Board, but may go directly to the Board.

The Supreme Court has held that an employer has an absolute right to an election. An employer does not have to recognize a union voluntarily even if the union has obtained cards from a majority of the employees, but can simply decline recognition. In that case the union has no choice but to file a representation petition using the cards as a showing of interest except in the rare case of a recognition strike.

1. Single-Purpose versus Dual-Purpose Cards: Bargaining Orders

There are two types of recognition cards: single-purpose and dual-purpose cards. The single-purpose card expressly authorizes the union to represent the employee signing the card. Its sole purpose is recognition. The single-purpose card customarily states: "I hereby authorize Local——to represent me for the purpose of collective bargaining with my employer."

The dual-purpose card is for recognition and an election. These cards typically state: "I want an NLRB election, and I authorize Local——to represent me for purposes of collective bargaining."

The Board accepts both single- and dual-purpose cards for a showing of interest. Most cards now are single-purpose recognition cards only because of the Supreme Court's decision in *Gissel Packing Company*.[1] In *Gissel,* the union had single-purpose recognition cards signed by a majority of the employees in the unit. The union alleged that it lost an election because the employer engaged in unfair labor practices that undermined the union's support. The Supreme Court, upholding the Board's position, held that if a union has the support of a majority of the employees in the unit before an election, as shown by single-purpose authorization cards signed by a majority of the unit employees, but loses the election because of employer unfair labor

practices that undermined the union's strength, the employer can be ordered to bargain with the union even though the union lost the election.

The Board will not base a bargaining order on dual-purpose cards. This is because a bargaining order requires proof that a majority of the employees wanted the union to represent them at one point. With a single-purpose card, which expressly authorizes the union to represent the employee, there is no question of the employee's intent. But the Board reasons that an employee who has signed a dual-purpose card may have signed the card just to get an election, although the card refers to both recognition and an election. The clear intent of a single-purpose card is lacking. So that the union will have an opportunity for a bargaining order if it should lose an election, most unions have abandoned the dual-purpose card and use only single-purpose cards.

2. Employee Intent in Signing a Recognition Card

What if a union organizer hands an employee a single-purpose card, but tells the employee that the card will be filed with the NLRB to get an election? Can that card be used to prove the union represented a majority of the employees at one time? The employee might not have paid attention to the wording of the card as it related to recognition or might have signed the card only because the employee thought that the other employees deserved an election if they wanted it. Is the employee's intent in favor of representation clear?

The Board rejects the approach of reading an employee's mind. The express wording of the card controls. The employee's subjective understanding, or even misunderstanding, of what the card means, or what the card could be used for, does not matter.

One of the primary reasons for this rule is that it prevents an employer from intimidating employees into testifying that they either did not understand what the card

---

[1] See legal principle 12.A.

meant or that they were misled by the union. Also, the employees may simply have forgotten what they were told at the time. Thus, the card's wording, if it clearly states the purpose is recognition, not the employee's subjective interpretation, is a better indication of the employee's intent at the time of signing.

The only exception to this rule is that a single-purpose card will not be counted in determining the union's majority status if the employee is told that the *only* purpose is an election. Then the card would not indicate the employee wanted union representation. Thus, a union organizer can tell an employee who signs a single-purpose card that the union will first seek voluntary recognition from the employer, but will seek an NLRB election if the employer declines. The card will count in determining the union's majority status because the employee was not told the card's only purpose is an election. But what if an employee tells an organizer that the employee does not want a union, but is willing to sign a card so that other employees can have an election? The organizer replies: "Don't worry about it; the only purpose of this card is to get an election." In that case, the Board would not count the card for bargaining order purposes because the employee was misled into believing the card would be used only for an election, even though the card referred to recognition.

3. Recognition Card Procedures

Employees frequently ask the union if their employer will see the signed recognition cards. This question should be answered forthrightly. Yes, the employer may see the card under some circumstances. The employer does not see the cards when they are filed with the Board or during the course of representation election proceedings. However, if the union loses the election and files an unfair labor practice charge seeking a bargaining order, the union must prove that it represented a majority of the employees at one time. That is done by intro-

ducing the cards at the trial where the employer can examine them. If the union wins the election or does not file unfair labor practice charges after a defeat, the cards will not be revealed to the employer. Of course it is an unfair labor practice for an employer to retaliate against an employee for signing a recognition card.

The Board requires that recognition cards be dated. A card over a year old is not counted in determining a union's showing of interest. Although not required, it is a good idea to have each card witnessed and initialed by the witness so that the union knows who solicited a card in case its validity is in dispute. Also, each solicitor should be given detailed instructions on what to tell employees about the card's purpose when it is signed. In that way the union may prevent employees from being improperly told that the only purpose of a card is an election, which, as discussed above, would invalidate the card for purposes of a bargaining order.

4. Solicitation by Supervisors

Occasionally, supervisors, especially those at lower supervisory levels who used to work in the bargaining unit, support a union's organizational efforts. A supervisor's support of the union does not necessarily invalidate recognition cards obtained with the supervisor's help unless there is evidence that the supervisor used the position to coerce employees, or that the employees regarded the supervisor as speaking for the employer rather than expressing a personal viewpoint. In some cases, working foremen or leadpersons, who regard themselves as bargaining unit employees, and are so regarded by the other employees, are active in a union's campaign. What if the employer challenges the status of these persons, and the Board determines that they are, in fact, supervisors as defined in the Act? (See Chapter Two.) Is the union's entire organizational effort tainted by the supervisory involvement? In such cases, the Board looks at the actual relationship between the employees and the involved supervisors. If the employees looked upon these supervisors as co-employees until the Board determined that they were, in fact, statutory supervisors, and if there is no evidence of any coercive conduct by the supervisors, the Board will uphold the validity of any recognition cards the supervisors obtained, and uphold the results of an election that the union won even though the supervisors supported the union's efforts.

B. UNION SOLICITATION AND DISTRIBUTION OF CAMPAIGN LITERATURE

Where can a union solicit employee support? The workplace is the logical choice, but there are restrictions on where and when this may be done. The Board has developed two basic sets of principles governing union organizing rights: one set for oral solicitation and the other for the distribution of literature. These rules are based on LMRA Section 8(a)(1), which protects an employee's right to engage in concerted activities under Section 7. Concerted activity includes the right to organize. Handing an employee a recognition card and talking to the employee about the union is considered oral solicitation and is governed by the rules for solicitation, although the card is obviously literature.

It is an unfair labor practice under Section 8(a)(1) for an employer to impose an unlawfully broad rule against solicitation or distribution interfering with the employee's statutory rights to engage in concerted activity, as discussed below. It is also a violation for the employer to discipline, or threaten to discipline, employees who engage in lawfully protected solicitation or distribution in violation of the employer's unlawful restrictions. Also, the imposition of an unlawful restriction, or the discipline or threat of discipline against employees for violating such a restriction, interferes with the laboratory conditions that the Board insists must be maintained during an election. Such a

rule, or its enforcement, is grounds for setting aside an election.

1. Oral Solicitation of Union Support

As a general rule an employee can orally solicit for the union in working and nonworking areas, but only on the employee's own nonwork time. An employee can talk to co-employees on the production line about union matters, and can solicit recognition cards, if the employees have a break with no work to do. The employee is not limited to formal breaks such as a coffee break or lunch time. If employees have idle time where they stand around and talk about sports, etc., they can stand around and talk about union activities instead. An employee's own time means time when the employee is not actively working, so-called "free time," even though it is paid company time. The Board terms a company rule prohibiting solicitation on the employee's own time as "presumptively invalid." This means that such a rule is unlawful unless the employer can establish some unique circumstances, as discussed below, to justify the rule.

If an employer allows the employees to engage in casual conversation while they are actually working, the employees could discuss union matters as long as production is not interrupted. An employer who allows the employees to talk about anything but union activities is interfering in the employees' rights to engage in concerted (union) activities.

The right of a union supporter to wear a union button is considered a form of oral solicitation. Except under unusual circumstances, an employer cannot prohibit employees from wearing union buttons on their work clothes in their work area. For example, an employer may be able to ban union buttons if it can prove that any insignia pinned on a worker's clothes would be a unique safety hazard (e.g., they could catch in equipment). That an employer's customers may possibly disapprove of an employee wearing a union button does not usually override the employee's statutorily protected right to express his or her support of the union. However, in some cases, an employee dealing with the public, and wearing a standard uniform, may be prohibited from wearing a union button if the button is clearly out of place on the uniform.

Although the union has the right to distribute campaign buttons urging its support, the employer has no right to pass out buttons with anti-union slogans for the employees to wear. The Board regards the distribution of anti-union buttons by the employer as coercion and as improper surveillance of union activity because the employees are, in effect, forced to reveal their views on the union to their employer by either accepting or rejecting the buttons.

2. Distribution of Literature

As with oral solicitations, union literature can be distributed only on an employee's own time. Although oral solicitation can take place in work areas, employers can limit the distribution of literature to nonwork areas. A company rule that prohibits the distribution of union literature on an employee's own time in nonwork areas is presumptively unlawful. This distinction between oral solicitation and the distribution of literature is permitted because the distribution of literature is more likely to create litter, disrupt operations, and cause accidents. The employer has a right to keep the work area free of these hazards. A nonwork area is any area not related to production, such as a break area, locker room, coffee machine area, or company parking lot.

Sometimes employers have general rules governing all types of solicitation or distribution of literature in the plant including solicitation for charities or sports pools. These general rules, however, cannot override an employee's statutory rights. A rule prohibiting the distribution of literature in the plant, even in nonwork areas, is valid for other literature. But employees still have the statutory right to distribute

union literature on the employee's own time in nonwork areas.

Although an employer cannot restrict an employee's right to distribute union literature, an employer's rules may expand that right. If an employer has always permitted distribution of literature in production areas the employer cannot suddenly prohibit the distribution of literature after a union organizing campaign begins. That would be unlawful discrimination. If an employer's rules on solicitation or distribution of literature are more permissive than the statute requires, they must be evenly applied. However, an employer may be permitted a few reasonable limited exceptions to its general rules, for example, allowing solicitation for the United Fund to take place during work time, without having to extend that same right to solicitation on union matters.

3. Exceptions to the General Distribution and Solicitation Rules

In a few cases an employer might be able to prove the existence of unique conditions justifying a broader "no distribution" or "no solicitation" rule than otherwise permitted. Department stores may establish rules prohibiting employees from soliciting on the sales floor, even on an employee's own time, provided that employees are generally prohibited from casual conversation in that area because customers waiting for service may take offense at seeing employees talking to each other.

Exceptions approved by the Board are very rare and the general rules apply in almost every case. For example, some employers have sought to limit the distribution of literature pertaining to controversial issues within the bargaining unit on the grounds that the literature will undermine discipline and disrupt production. The Board has insisted upon actual evidence of a disruptive impact rather than mere employer speculation to justify any such limitation. Thus, the Board held in one case that an employer unlawfully removed a notice referring to union members who had crossed a picket line during a strike as scabs, even though the notice was offensive to those employees, because there was no evidence that the notice provoked a serious threat to discipline. In contrast, in another case, the Board upheld an employer's right to prohibit employees from wearing buttons referring to strike breakers as scabs because the strike had been violent and the buttons were likely to provoke a confrontation.

Many hospitals have argued that they should be permitted to establish broader rules prohibiting solicitation in any areas where patients may be, including cafeteria areas that both employees and patients share. Hospitals wanted employee union activities limited to exclusive nonpatient areas such as locker rooms. The Supreme Court, however, has upheld the Board's position that health care employees should be permitted to engage in union solicitation in areas other than the immediate patient-care areas, such as lobbies, lounges, and cafeterias, even though patients may use those areas as well. A rule banning solicitation in these areas is presumptively unlawful. The hospital would have the burden of establishing special circumstances justifying the ban. Solicitation may be prohibited in patient-care areas such as patient rooms, operating rooms, treatment areas, and adjoining corridors and sitting rooms where solicitation could disturb patient care or disrupt health services.

Any rule that an employer establishes limiting employees' rights to solicit and distribute literature must be clear. The Board has consistently held that ambiguous rules that an employee might interpret to prohibit statutorily protected rights are unlawful. At one time the Board held that a rule prohibiting employees from engaging in union activity during "work time" or "work hours" was presumptively invalid because an employee might erroneously interpret the rule to mean that union solicitation was prohibited during lunch or break periods during the course of the work day. However, the Reagan Board modified this principle. At

present, rules prohibiting solicitation during "working time" are presumptively *lawful*. In the Board's view, such a rule correctly implies that solicitation is permitted during nonworking time during the work day. However, a rule prohibiting solicitation during "working hours" is still presumptively invalid because that rule erroneously implies that an employee cannot engage in solicitation during the employee's own time, such as lunch and break periods during the work day.

4. Organizing Rights of Outside Organizers and Off-Duty Employees

The rights to solicit and distribute union literature on company property are employee rights only. Normally, an employer can prohibit outside union organizers from entering its premises for these purposes. The union must rely on employees for its organizing efforts. As an exception, if an employer permits other solicitors to enter the plant, it cannot exclude union organizers. Also, outside union organizers have the right to meet with off-duty employees in the public areas of a facility such as a hotel, department store, or hospital as long as the organizer's use conforms with the normal use of the area and is not disruptive to customers or normal operations. Thus, for example, organizers can meet with off-duty employees in the restaurants or lounges of a hotel or department store or even in the public cafeteria of a hospital. As another exception, organizers may be able to distribute leaflets and handbills to employees on company parking lots generally open to the public under the same principles which apply to picketing or handbilling on private property during a labor dispute, as discussed in detail in Chapter Seven.

Some unions have one of their professional organizers hire on as an employee. The organizer would then have the same right as any other employee to solicit and distribute union literature.

Does an off-duty employee have the right to enter the plant while on off-duty time to engage in union organizing? If employees are prohibited from entering the interior or other work areas while off duty, they may be prohibited from reentering for union activity. However, if an employer permitted off-duty employees to reenter the plant before a union began its organizing effort, the employer cannot prevent reentry after the union campaign begins. The employees must be aware of any rule prohibiting reentry in advance. Furthermore, if employees are permitted back into the plant for any reason, they cannot be prohibited from returning for union activity.

Although the employer can validly prohibit off-duty employees from reentering the plant or other work areas, off-duty employees cannot be prohibited from union activity on company property outside the plant in nonwork areas unless there are special circumstances justifying a total prohibition. Thus, off-duty employees can engage in union activities in company parking lots or at the plant gates. Finally, employees cannot be prohibited from remaining after the end of their shift to engage in union activity if they are allowed to remain after their shift for other reasons.

a. Inaccessible Employees. The principal, but narrow, exception to the employer's right to prohibit outside union organizers from entering the plant is that a union has the right to enter the company's property to talk to employees if there is no other way to reach the employees. This exception is restricted primarily to company towns where employees live on company premises or to the maritime industry where a union may not be able to reach employees except on the ship where they work. If the gate to an enclosed plant is far from the employees' parking lot, employees can speed through the gate at 50 m.p.h. Union organizers, standing on the edge of the property trying to hand out cards to the employees, have little chance of success. Still, these organizers generally would not have the right to enter the company's property and go to the parking lot area because the organizers probably

have other ways to reach the employees. They can take down license plates and find out the owners, follow employees home, go to nearby taverns, or even put ads in local newspapers. These other methods are certainly not easy or convenient, but they are sufficient alternatives so that organizers would not have the right to enter the property.

5. Organizing in Shopping Centers

Questions frequently arise about a union's right to enter a shopping center to organize employees. Unions have argued that shopping centers should be treated as public places and that union organizers should be able to enter them to organize employees as a matter of constitutional free speech. The Supreme Court rejected this argument in the *Central Hardware* case, holding that a shopping center is private property and is not to be treated as a public block.[2]

The Court said that the rules applied to organizing employees working in a shopping center should be the same as those applied to outside organizers entering any other plant. This means that if a union has other reasonable methods of reaching employees who work in a shopping center besides entering the center, it must use those methods. However, the Board has recognized that there are frequently no reasonably effective means to identify and communicate with employees working within a shopping center unless the organizers are permitted on the property. Thus, the Board has upheld the right of union organizers to distribute handbills or leaflets to employees within shopping centers in areas generally open to the public (such as at a store entrance) or on adjoining walkways or parking lots under the same principles which in many cases permit picketing or handbilling within a center during a labor dispute (see Chapter Seven).

---

[2] See legal principle 6.

6. Post-Recognition Solicitation and Distribution Rights

The employees' rights to solicit for the union and distribute literature apply not only to initial organizing, but after union recognition as well. Employees have a continuing right to discuss union matters in their work areas on company time, and to wear union buttons and distribute literature in nonwork areas. These are employee as well as union rights.

In the *Magnavox* case, an employer and union negotiated a provision that restricted the right to distribute literature to certain bulletin boards.[3] The employer prohibited employees from distributing literature in nonwork areas, relying on the contract provision that restricted notices to the bulletin board. The Supreme Court upheld the Board's decision that the contract provision was unlawful and that the union could not contractually waive the employees' right to distribute literature. Similarly, the Supreme Court has held that employers cannot allow an encumbent union to post notices but prohibit other unions or employee groups from doing so. Some bulletin boards may be reserved exclusively for the encumbent union's use, but other space must be made available for notice by other employee groups as well.

The right to discuss union matters and distribute union literature pertains to all collective bargaining activities and subjects, including related political activity and internal union matters that may have impact on working conditions, such as union officer elections or changes in the union's constitution and bylaws, etc. Thus, the Supreme Court has held that a union may circulate literature in the plant against right-to-work laws because the abolishment of such laws is a political act designed to further the union's collective bargaining goals. Can an employer prohibit employee political activity unrelated to the union's collective bargaining activities? Yes, because the em-

ployer has a statutory obligation to permit employee solicitation and distribution pertaining to collective bargaining activities on the company's premises, but the employer has no statutory or constitutional obligation to permit any other political activity. The constitutional provisions protecting free speech apply only to governmental bodies, not to a private employer.

C. EMPLOYER ANTI-UNION SPEECHES ON COMPANY TIME

1. The Captive Audience Doctrine

Although unions are limited in campaigning on company time and property, employers are not. Under the *Peerless Plywood* rule, an employer has the right to speak to employees against the union on company time and require employees to attend the meeting.[4] This is the so-called "captive audience" doctrine. A union does not have the right to reply on company time. The union must limit its activities to the employees' own time off premises or to the employees' own solicitation and distribution of literature. The only exception under which a union might be able to give a speech on company premises is in the rare situation (such as a retail store) in which an employer can enforce a broad no solicitation–no distribution rule. In that limited situation, if an employer gives a speech on company time the union can be permitted to reply on premises because otherwise the union has no effective way to reply. Usually, however, the employer may give a speech and the union has no right to reply on company time.

2. The Twenty-Four-Hour Rule

The one general exception to the captive audience doctrine is the "twenty-four-hour rule." The Board sets aside an election if an employer gives a speech on company

---

[3] See legal principle 4.

[4] See legal principle 7.

time to a mass employee audience in the last twenty-four hours before an election.

The twenty-four-hour rule does not prohibit all campaigning against the union, only an employer speech to a mass audience. It is lawful for a foreman to go around during the last twenty-four hours before an election and talk to the employees individually or in small groups against the union. The employer can have a picnic after work within the twenty-four hours before the election, even on paid time, as long as no mass speech is given. If attendance at the picnic is voluntary and not on company time, the employer can give a speech to the employees present without violating the twenty-four-hour rule.

The Board strictly enforces the twenty-four-hour rule. Even if an employer's speech before a mass audience on company time starts before the beginning of the twenty-four-hour period and runs for only a few minutes into the twenty-four-hour period, the Board will set aside the election. The Board reasons that if it makes exceptions for short violations, the rule will be gradually undermined with exceptions. On the other hand, the twenty-four-hour rule is not violated if an employer ends his speech before the twenty-four-hour period begins, but answers questions from employees who voluntarily remain afterwards causing the meeting to end less than twenty-four hours before the election.

3. Speeches in Management Authority Areas

One other exception to the employer's right to speak to employees is that an employer cannot at any time speak to small groups of employees about the union in an area of management authority, that is, an area where employees normally do not go except on management matters, such as a supervisor's office or a board room. The Board feels that an employee may be intimidated in an area of management authority. The employee might couple the employer's anti-union remarks with the surroundings, which would remind the employee of the employer's authority to hire or fire. The small group rule applies even if the employer's remarks are perfectly legal and noncoercive. The setting itself is regarded as coercive regardless of what is said.

The Reagan Board did not formally abolish the restrictions on meetings in areas of management authority, but it narrowly restricted the rule's application. Thus, for example, the Board upheld the right of a company president to meet individually with each employee in the plant manager's office to encourage the employees to vote against the union. The Board reasoned that the employees knew that the president was meeting with virtually every employee, thus lessening the impact, and the employees had met with the president in the plant manager's office before for other reasons and were therefore familiar with the setting. It is probable, based on past decisions, that prior Boards would have ruled that this conduct was grounds for setting aside the election.

D. FREE UNION MEMBERSHIP AS A CAMPAIGN TECHNIQUE

Unions used to offer free union membership during election campaigns to employees who signed recognition cards before the election. This helped a union get a showing of interest and majority support for a bargaining order. An employee who waited until after the election to join the union had to pay, so there was a strong incentive to join early.

In the *Savair* case, the Supreme Court held that a union cannot limit free membership offers to those signing before the election date.[5] That would be an employer ground for an objection setting aside an election. However, the Court did not invalidate free membership as an organizing technique altogether. A union can still offer

---

[5] See legal principle 1.

free membership if it is allowed both before and for a reasonable time after an election. The most common practice now, which the Board has upheld, is to offer free membership to anyone who joins the union up to the time the first contract is executed.

What the Supreme Court feared in *Savair* was that an employee who had to sign a recognition card before the election in order to get free membership might feel compelled to vote for the union. By offering free membership up to the time of the contract, the union avoids that misunderstanding. An employee then realizes that the employee's vote has no effect on the right to free membership.

Can the union offer free membership only if the union wins the election? In a sense, that gives the employees an incentive to vote for the union. That offer is legal, provided it remains open until the first contract, because the employees know they can be out of the union if they vote against it. That is different from telling employees they can only join the union up until the election. Thus, signing the card does not put pressure on the employee to vote for the union, as the Supreme Court hoped to eliminate in *Savair*.

E. INCENTIVES TO ATTEND CAMPAIGN MEETINGS AND PAYMENTS TO UNION SUPPORTERS

Unions want to get large employee turnouts at meetings during organizing drives. Can a union offer incentives, such as a television set as a door prize, for employees to attend a campaign rally? Employers would argue that this technique is an attempt to buy votes for the union. However, the Board has held that attendance prizes are lawful techniques as long as the prizes are not excessive, amounting to a bribe. Of course, this rule works both ways. An employer can also have a meeting with door prizes, as long as they are not excessive. Obviously, outright payments of money or something of value to

influence a vote is not permitted. Paying $25 to everybody who attended a meeting would be grounds for setting aside the election.

In one case, the union gave out jackets with the union's emblem on them to union supporters between voting sessions on the day of the election. The Board set aside the election for this reason even though the jackets were given out only to employees who openly favored the union. The Board reasoned that other employees who had not yet voted might regard the jackets as a reward for voting for the union and thus be improperly influenced in their vote. It is quite probable, however, that the Board would still uphold a union's right to distribute jackets and other relatively inexpensive items as a bona fide campaign technique during the course of a campaign rather than under the unusual circumstances of this case.

If employees miss work time and lose pay to assist in a union organizing drive or to attend a Board hearing, it is lawful for the union to reimburse the employees for lost time. However, if a union pays an employee not only for lost time, but also for his inconvenience, that can be construed as an unlawful bribe and therefore grounds for setting aside the election. Payments should be limited to an employee's lost time and out-of-pocket expenses only.

F. BOARD REGULATION OF CAMPAIGN STATEMENTS

1. Substantial Misrepresentations as Grounds for Setting Aside an Election

The Board's goal in elections is to maintain laboratory conditions in order to maintain the employees' free choice. Nonetheless, the Board recognizes that, as in a political election campaign, both the employer and the union must be permitted a broad range of permissible campaign tactics, promises, and propaganda.

The Board has had to draw a line between

the parties' right to free expression and the need to maintain free choice for employees. However, the Board's approach to the question has changed several times as its membership has changed. Thus, in the *Hollywood Ceramics* decision in 1962, the Board, emphasizing the goal of a free election based on truthful campaign information, held that an election would be set aside because of false campaign statements by either an employer or a union if (1) there is a substantial misrepresentation (2) on a material fact (3) made at a time when the other party has inadequate time to respond and correct the misrepresentation.[6] All three of these factors had to be present for an election to be set aside. This principle remained in effect until the Board's 1977 decision in *Shopping Kart Food Market, Inc.*,[7] overruling *Hollywood Ceramics*. Under *Shopping Kart* an election is set aside for false campaign statements only if a party uses fraudulent documents, thus preventing an employee from recognizing a misrepresentation as false campaign propaganda, or for abuse of Board processes (explained more fully below).

In late 1978 following a change in Board membership, the Board reversed itself in *General Knit of California*[8] and returned to the *Hollywood Ceramics* doctrine. But, in 1982, following yet another change in Board membership, the Board reversed itself again and held in *Midland National Life Insurance* that it would return to the *Shopping Kart* rule under which an election is set aside only for the abuse of Board processes or the use of fraudulent documents.[9]

The opinion of the three-member Board majority in the *Midland National* decision emphasized the importance of free speech in election campaigns and stressed the majority's belief that employees are sufficiently sophisticated to recognize and evaluate misrepresentations. In contrast, the two dissenters stressed the need to preserve the integrity of the electoral process and the need to protect workers, despite their relatively high level of education, from unscrupulous campaigners and professional opinion molders who devise campaigns to defeat union organizing efforts. The return to the *Shopping Kart* rule has been heavily criticized by unions, but the Board has continued to adhere to it. Remember, however, even under the *Shopping Kart* approach, elections will still be set aside for such other campaign misconduct as employer threats or promises of benefits.

2. Abuse of Board Processes

The remaining principal ground for setting aside an election is either party's abuse of Board processes by making it appear that the Board favors one side. This issue most frequently arises in the use of sample ballots. At one time the Board applied a strict rule prohibiting either side from sending out a sample ballot that looked like the official Board ballot with an "X" mark in the voting box favoring one party. The Board reasoned that reproducing the official ballot with the "X" mark made it appear that the Board backed one side over the other. However, in accord with its overall approach of loosening campaign restrictions, the Board now permits an altered reproduction of an official ballot unless the ballot in fact is likely to mislead employees into believing that the Board favors one party to the election. An altered ballot that clearly identifies the party who prepared it is not objectionable. However, if a sample ballot is not clearly identified, the Board will examine the materials to determine whether it has the tendency to mislead employees. Thus, if a sample ballot is reproduced as part of a leaflet that is clearly partisan in tone so the employees could reasonably be expected to understand that the leaflet was produced by a party rather than by the Board, the election will not be set aside even though the source of the ballot is not clearly identified.

The parties may not make statements in an election campaign that make it appear

[6] See legal principle 9.
[7] See legal principle 9.
[8] See legal principle 9.
[9] See legal principle 9.

the Board backs one side over the other. The union cannot make statements, for example, that make it appear the Board prefers that employees be organized. Technically, the Board takes no position on whether employees should or should not be represented by a union. The Board's only function is to insure a free and fair election so the employees can make their own choice. But, the union can truthfully state the Board's role to protect employee rights. The union can tell employees that the law protects their right to join a union and that it is unlawful for an employer to discriminate against an employee for union activity.

At one time, the Board held that an election would be set aside if one party misrepresented the results of NLRB proceedings to make it appear that the other party had been found guilty of unlawful conduct when, in fact, the Board had made no such finding. Thus, for example, an election could be set aside if the union distributed leaflets stating that the employer had been found guilty of an unfair labor practice when, in fact, the regional director had issued only a complaint charging a violation or the employer had settled a charge without admitting a violation. However, following the *Midland National* decision, discussed above, the Board reversed its position and held that such misrepresentations are to be treated the same as any other misrepresentation of fact and thus are not objectionable, provided there is no fraud or other abuse of Board processes.

What if only a small percentage of the eligible employees actually vote in an election? The Board will certify the election, notwithstanding the low turnout, as long as all eligible voters had an adequate opportunity to vote. The election will be set aside only if employees were prevented from voting by the conduct of a party or by unfairness in the scheduling or mechanics of the election. Thus, for example, an election might be set aside if an employer prevented employees from leaving their workstations to vote or if a substantial number of employees were unable to vote be-

cause of unusual circumstances beyond the parties' control, such as a snowstorm's preventing employees from getting to work.

3. Employer Free Speech

A recurring issue in election campaigns is the right of employers to express their views on the union's campaign. In theory, it can be argued that an employer should not be able to express any views at all during an election campaign, as the election is the employees' concern only. However, that is not the law. Congress has recognized that employers have a legitimate right to express their opinion as to whether their employees should be unionized.

a. Employer Threats. Section 8(c) of the Labor Management Relations Act states that the "expressing of any views, arguments or opinions or the dissemination thereof, whether in written, printed, graphic or visual form, shall not constitute or be evidence of an unfair labor practice under any provision of this Act, if such expression contains no *threat of reprisal or force or promises of benefits*" (emphasis added).

This provision, known as the free speech amendment, was added in 1948 as part of the Taft-Hartley Act. The amendment nullified prior Board cases that set aside elections based on statements employers had made. Section 8(c) was intended to make it clear that an employer has the right to speak against the union.

The most important part of Section 8(c) is the last phrase (emphasized above), that the employer's remarks can contain neither threats of reprisal or force nor promises of benefit. Some threats are obvious, such as if an employer blatantly says it will discharge certain employees or close the plant if the union wins an election. However, most employers campaigning against a union are more sophisticated in their techniques. Thus, what if the employer tells its employees that it expects costs to go up if the work force is unionized, that it might lose customers as a result, and that it might therefore be forced to lay off employees or even move to another location where costs will be lower? Are such statements of adverse consequences an unlawful threat of reprisal or simply a statement of fact that the employer has a right to make under Section 8(c)? For many years, the Board, with court approval, based its determination of lawfulness of such employer predictions on whether the prediction was of some consequence within the employer's control. An employer's prediction of an adverse effect outside its control was regarded as a permissible expression of opinion under Section 8(c), but a prediction within its control, requiring an act the employer could carry out or not, was considered an unlawful threat not protected by Section 8(c). For example, an employer's prediction that customers would be lost if the union won an election is not a matter within the employer's control and was therefore a lawful matter of opinion. In contrast, however, an employer can control whether employees are laid off. Therefore, prior Boards have held that employer statements that employees might be laid off or that the plant might be closed if the union won the election were unlawful threats of retaliation violating Section 8(a)(1), not just a permissible expression of opinion protected by Section 8(c).

The Reagan Board applied a broader interpretation to Section 8(c) giving employers greater leeway in the statements they may make. It held that an employer may present its views on the "economic realities" of unionization as long as the employer's predictions are supported by what the Board termed as "objective fact." For example, what if an employer points to other cases in which an employer laid off employees or even closed a facility after it was unionized? Or what if the employer tells the employees about its prior experiences with the same union at other facilities in which "excess labor costs" eventually led to layoffs? The employer then predicts that the same adverse consequences may occur at the present facility if the employees vote for the union. Prior Boards almost certainly

would have found such employer predictions to be unlawful because, regardless of what had happened elsewhere, the employer still had control at the present facility over the decision to lay off employees or cease operations. In contrast, however, the Reagan Board upheld an employer's right to make such statements on the grounds that the employer was simply presenting its views as to the economic realities of unionization supported by "objective fact," that is, the experience that the employer or other employers have had with unions.

Under this approach an employer with any degree of sophistication at all in its tactics will be able to convey a very negative image as to the adverse consequences of unionization on the employees without fear that the statements will either violate Section 8(a)(1) of the Act or be grounds for setting aside an election.

Some employers as a campaign tactic state that if the union wins the election, bargaining for a collective bargaining agreement will start "from scratch" or from "ground zero," thus implying that employees may lose existing benefits if the union wins. Prior Boards have held that such comments are unlawful threats by the employer to reduce benefits unilaterally if the union wins. The Reagan Board, however, held that such statements are lawful because they convey the economic reality of the bargaining process to the employees, that is, a union cannot guarantee the retention of present benefits because they are subject to negotiation. Currently such statements are unlawful only if the employer makes an outright statement that benefits will be (rather than may be) reduced or if the statements are made in the context of an overall coercive campaign.

An employer's statement that an employee's signed recognition card may be disclosed to the employer under some circumstances may be unlawful under Section 8(a)(1), especially if the employer has indicated that it opposes the union's organizing efforts. Such statements may be an implied threat of retaliation against employees who sign cards and thus have an unlawful chilling effect on the employee's right to representation.

Threatening or coercive remarks, which are not protected by Section 8(c), are both an unfair labor practice under Section 8 and grounds for setting aside the election under Section 9. Remember that an election is set aside only if the Board determines, based on the totality of conduct, that laboratory conditions to insure employee free choice have been interfered with. Thus, whether a specific coercive statement justifies setting aside an election might depend upon the employer's overall conduct of the election campaign. If an employer who conducted a fair campaign gave a speech that was generally noncoercive but contained an isolated threatening remark, the election would probably not be set aside. On the other hand, if an employer who had engaged in other unlawful conduct, such as discharging union supporters, gave the same speech containing the isolated threat, the Board would probably find the speech coercive in its overall context. The Board reasons that employees will tend to discount an isolated threat made by an employer who has otherwise conducted a fair campaign, but could be intimidated by a threat in a speech made by an employer engaging in other unlawful conduct.

b. The Futility Doctrine.

Another limitation on employer speech is the futility doctrine. An employer cannot indicate that voting for a union is a futile act, that it will lead inevitably to strikes, that collective bargaining will not bring any benefits, or that even with a union nothing is going to improve. Such statements may not contain any threat of retaliation or promise of benefit under Section 8(c). However, Section 8(c) provides that only certain statements cannot be unfair labor practices under the Act. The section does not deal with election procedures governed by Section 9. Thus, although a statement conveying the futility of bargaining may not be an unfair labor practice under Section 8(a), because of the exceptions contained in Section 8(c), it may

still be grounds for setting aside an election under the Board's responsibility under Section 9 to ensure a fair election.

The current Board has not formally abandoned the futility doctrine, but it has narrowly circumscribed its application. In line with its general policy giving employers much greater campaign leeway, the Board has upheld employer statements that go very far in conveying the possible adverse consequences (futility) of unionization as long as the employer provides "objective facts" to support its contentions and does not state that the adverse consequences are *inevitable* rather than just a *possibility*.

c. Racial appeals.

Appeals to racial prejudice can be grounds for setting aside an election. An employer might try to play black and white workers off against each other by saying that a union would benefit one race at the expense of the other. Such statements are probably not unfair labor practices because there is no promise of benefits or threat of reprisal. But the statements could be grounds for setting aside an election because by playing upon racial hostility, the employer has destroyed employee free choice.

In contrast, the Board has held that unions may appeal to racial pride. If a workforce has a high percentage of blacks, women, or Hispanics, a union can appeal to their pride as a group and their goals of group improvement as a reason for favoring the union. These are considered bona fide campaign arguments. Thus, appeals to racial pride are permissible, but appeals to racial prejudice are not.

d. Employer Promises of Benefits.

Although threats are a common union-busting technique, Section 8(c) also prohibits employers from promising benefits if the union loses the election. The Supreme Court has referred to such promises as "a velvet glove over an iron fist." That is because the employees understand that although the employer has promised benefits if the union loses (the velvet glove) the employer can take those benefits away if the union wins (the iron fist). Promises of benefits and threats of reprisal are frequently coupled together. An employer may state that it has been thinking about increasing vacation weeks, but is not sure that it can afford the increase if there is a union. Such a statement promises a benefit (to increase vacations) if the union loses and a threat if the union wins. Also, since vacation benefits are within the employer's control, the statement is not merely a prediction protected by Section 8(c), but also constitutes an unfair labor practice.

Sometimes employers faced with an organizing drive call a meeting of their employees to ask them what conditions led them to form a union. It is objectionable conduct for an employer to solicit grievances from employees during an election campaign with either an express or implied promise to correct the unsatisfactory conditions without a union. The solicitation is like promising a benefit to the employees if the union is defeated. Similarly, the employer cannot initially establish an employee's grievance committee during the campaign to deal with complaints as this implies improved conditions for the employees if the union is defeated.

If an employer regularly held meetings with its employees before a union began organizing, the employer would not be prohibited from holding meetings during the campaign. The burden would be on the employer, however, to show that the meetings held during the union's election campaign and the promises the employer made were no different from those made before the organizing drive began.

The whipsaw effect, coupling promises of benefits if the union loses with coercive acts during the campaign, is a technique frequently used by employers who wish to defeat a union. It is effective because it brings home sharply the overall force of management to the employees. Such conduct, if proven, is both an unfair labor practice and grounds for setting aside an election. Unfortunately, however, because of the weakness in the Board's remedies,

some employers willingly run the risk of purposely engaging in unlawful conduct in order to defeat a union.

G. BENEFIT CHANGES DURING AN ELECTION CAMPAIGN

The Board permits an employer to give benefit increases during an election campaign only if the employer can prove that the benefit increase was planned or regularly scheduled before the election. Also if an employer decides to place a certain benefit into effect companywide, it may do so even at facilities where an election campaign is underway as long as the benefit is implemented companywide in a normal business fashion and there is no evidence that the benefit was granted with the intent to interfere with the election. The burden is on the employer to establish that benefits granted during an election campaign were properly granted as an exception to the general rules prohibiting such conduct.

It is unlawful retaliation under Section 8(a)(1) for an employer to fail or refuse to give employees a scheduled increase in benefits, or to rescind existing benefits, simply because a union is seeking to represent the employees. Such conduct would also be grounds for setting aside the election. It is also unlawful for an employer to condition participation in a pension plan on the employees remaining unorganized.

H. EMPLOYER DISCRIMINATION DURING AN ELECTION CAMPAIGN

It is unfair labor practice under Sections 8(a)(1) and 8(a)(3) of the LMRA for an employer to discriminate against its employees as to their hiring, tenure, or conditions of employment, in order to encourage or discourage their membership in or activity for or against a union. Examples of such conduct include discharging or disciplining employees who support the union, denying such employees promotions, or otherwise discriminating in benefits between those employees who support or do not support a union's organizing drive. Closing down a department where the employer believes a union is strong, or transferring work to another plant in retaliation for the employees' organizational activities, are other examples. Such employer misconduct, occurring during an election campaign, obviously undermines employee free choice and the laboratory conditions the Board seeks to maintain during an election campaign. Thus, such misconduct, provided it occurs in the period between the date the union files its election petition and the date of the election, is grounds for setting aside the election. Remember, however, that an isolated discriminatory act may not be grounds for setting aside the election, even if it is an unfair labor practice, if the Board finds that the conduct did not destroy laboratory conditions based upon the totality of the employer's conduct. Employer discrimination as an unfair labor practice, apart from an election campaign, is discussed further in Chapter Four.

I. INTERROGATION, SURVEILLANCE, AND THE IMPRESSION OF SURVEILLANCE

The Board's position on an employer's right to question (interrogate) employees about their union activities has varied through the years depending upon the Board's membership. At one time, in the 1950s and 1960s, the Board held that an employer could lawfully question employees who openly supported the union about union activities, because such questioning would not have a coercive effect on employees who were open in their pro-union sympathies. However, in a series of cases in the middle and late 1970s, the Board changed its position, and held that even the questioning of open union supporters was unlawful. The Board reasoned that the questioning might discourage union activity in the future, especially by other employees who were not as open in their support who witnessed or heard about the questioning.

The Reagan Board, in the *Rossmore House* decision, returned to the older view that an employer may lawfully question employees who openly support the union about union activities.[10] The Board stated that the proper test to determine whether questioning violates the Act is whether under all the circumstances the interrogation reasonably tended to restrain, coerce, or interfere with rights guaranteed by the Act. The Board listed four key factors it would consider:

1. The background of the questioning—had the employer engaged in unlawful activity creating an overall hostile environment?
2. The nature of the information sought—did the employer ask a casual question about the employee's support or detailed questions about the union activities of the employee or other employees?
3. The identity of the questioner—was the questioning by a supervisor with whom the employee had an informal relationship or by someone whom the employee would regard as an authority figure?
4. The place and method of interrogation—was the employee questioned in the work area or in a management area? Did the employee answer voluntarily or did the employer press for information that the employee was reluctant to provide?

Rossmore House involved interrogation of an open union supporter. However, the Board subsequently ruled that the *Rossmore* principles would also apply to the questioning of employees who were not active union supporters. Even the current Board has continued to find employer interrogations unlawful in some cases under the *Rossmore* criteria. However, it has also upheld interrogation techniques that earlier Boards in all probability would have found to be coercive.

Surveillance—keeping track of the em-

---

[10] See legal principle 10.

ployee's union activities—may also be unlawful. For example, an employer cannot photograph employees talking to union organizers at the plant gate, eavesdrop on employees discussing union matters, or ask an employee to attend union meetings and report back who attended and what was said. Such conduct is an implied threat that there will be retaliation against employees for joining or supporting the union.

Giving employees the impression of surveillance may violate the Act, even though the employer actually may not be checking up on union activity at all. An employer might intentionally give the impression of surveillance in order to intimidate employees into refraining from union activity. Thus, an employer may tell an employee: "I heard that you were at the union meeting last night," while only guessing that the employee was at the meeting. But by making the statement, the employer is giving the employee the impression that the employer is keeping track of those who favor the union and may retaliate against them. However, under the Board's current *Rossmore* approach, statements conveying the impression of surveillance may not be an unfair labor practice or grounds for setting aside an election unless there is evidence that a statement reasonably tended to restrain or coerce employees in the exercise of their right to engage in union activities.

1. Polling Employees

As an exception to the restrictions on questioning employees, if a union requests voluntary recognition, an employer may lawfully poll its employees to determine if they support the union. There are strict rules on such polls. The poll must be conducted for the purpose of determining the truth of a union's claim of majority status; the employer must tell the employees that the purpose is to determine the union's majority status; the employer must give assurances against reprisals; and the employees must be polled by secret ballot. Also, the poll must be conducted in an atmosphere free from employer coercion. If an employer polls its employees and determines that a majority favor the union, the employer is bound by the result of the poll and must recognize and bargain with the union without an election.

J. UNION OR EMPLOYEE MISCONDUCT

This chapter has focused on employer misconduct constituting an unfair labor practice or grounds for setting aside a representation election. However, misconduct by the union or even by rank-and-file employees may also be grounds for setting aside an election. Thus, although such cases are rare, assaults or threats against employees who do not support the union would be an unfair labor practice under Section 8(b)(1) of the Act and also grounds for setting aside an election if the conduct occurred in the critical period between the date a representation petition was filed and the election. As with employer misconduct, the Board evaluates the overall impact of union or employee misconduct to determine whether it tended to interfere with the employees' free and uncoerced choice in an election. Thus a single act, although an unfair labor practice, might not be sufficient to set aside the election. In evaluating union or employee misconduct, the Board considers such factors as the number and severity of the incidents; the likelihood that the incidents would create a general atmosphere of fear and coercion; the number of employees directly subjected to the misconduct and the extent to which those not directly affected had knowledge of it; the closeness of the misconduct to the election date; the likelihood that the coercive impact would persist in the minds of the employees; and the closeness of the vote.

The Board applies slightly different standards in determining whether an election should be set aside depending upon whether the union was responsible for the misconduct or whether it was the unauthorized acts of individual employees. If the conduct is unauthorized, the election will be set aside only if the acts created such an atmosphere of fear and coercion as to render employee free choice *impossible*. In contrast, if the union was directly responsible, the election will be set aside if the misconduct *reasonably tends* to interfere with the employee's free and uncoerced choice.

The Board has also held that a union is responsible for the statements employees soliciting authorization cards make about union fee waivers or other union policies. As discussed earlier in this chapter, a union may offer free union membership as an incentive to join the union only if the offer remains open for a reasonable time after the election (the *Savair* doctrine). The Board has held that it may set aside an election because of statements made by employees gathering authorization cards that are improper under the *Savair* standard (e.g., that membership will be free only for employees who join the union before a representation election petition is filed) although the union did not authorize or instruct the employees to make the erroneous promises. However, a union may avoid responsibility for the improper statements if it clearly publicizes a lawful fee-waiver policy in a manner reasonably calculated to reach unit employees before they sign authorization cards, such as a statement of the fee-waiver policy on the authorization card itself.

K. CONDUCT OF OUTSIDE PARTIES

Although it does not occur often, an election can be set aside because of the conduct of an outside person (commonly called a third party) not connected with either an employer or union. For example, in a small rural area, the town newspaper may carry an editorial against the union's election campaign threatening that the plant will probably close if the union wins. Such a threat might be an unfair labor practice if the employer had made it. But unless there is

proof that the employer instigated the newspaper article, the employer probably will not be held responsible for the paper's remarks in an unfair labor practice case. However, if the third party's statement contains a serious threat, the Board might still rule that the comments interfered with the employees' free choice. The election can be set aside even though the employer is not in any way responsible for the statement.

L. ELECTION PROCEDURE AND CONDUCT DURING THE ELECTION

Irregularities in election procedures (see Chapter One) or the parties' conduct during the election itself may be grounds for an objection to an election. Thus, as discussed in Chapter One, the employer must provide the union with a list (the *Excelsior* list) of the names and addresses of the employees eligible to vote in the election within seven days after an election consent agreement is entered into or an election is directed following a hearing. The election cannot be scheduled for less than ten days after the list is due. The failure of the employer to provide the list on time or errors in the names and addresses on the list may be grounds for setting aside the election if the employer's failure to comply was in bad faith, was the result of gross negligence, or if the errors were so substantial as to prejudice the union in its efforts to contact the employees.

Questions used to arise as to whether an employer had properly posted the official Board Notice of Election in sufficient time before the election to assure the employee's proper notice. To resolve this issue, the Board issued a rule requiring that copies of the official Notice of Election be posted in conspicuous places at least three full working days prior to 12:01 A.M. of the day of the election and that the notices remain posted until the end of the election. The term "working day" is defined as an entire twenty-four-hour period excluding Saturdays, Sundays, and holidays. If a substantial number of workers do not understand English, the Board will provide election notices and ballots in the appropriate languages. Failure to do so may be grounds for setting aside an election.

Both the employer and the union can designate an employee or employees as observer(s) at the election to verify the vote, make challenges, and ensure fair procedures. The number permitted depends upon the size of the bargaining unit, the number of shifts, etc. The employer's observer cannot be a supervisor or a person closely identified with management. No campaigning is permitted in the polling area or the area where employees wait in line to vote while the polls are open. Union representatives can stand outside the plant the morning of an election and the employer can go around and talk to employees in small groups (provided it is not in an area of management authority), but neither party can pass out literature or solicit in the voting area. The parties are prohibited from engaging in prolonged conversations with employees waiting in line to vote.

The Board also prohibits the parties from making an unofficial list of those voting while the balloting is in process on the grounds that the existence of such a list, if known to the employees, might have an intimidating effect on their individual decision to vote or not in the election.

M. PROCEDURES FOR CHALLENGING AN ELECTION

An election is challenged by filing objections to the conduct of the election. The NLRB requires that the objections be filed within seven days after the tally of the ballots is furnished to the parties. The tally is usually furnished immediately after the ballots are counted on the election day. The objections list the acts that occurred during the campaign that interfered with the employees' right to a free election. The Board has held that only acts occurring between the date

the union filed its petition and the election are grounds for setting aside the election.

The objections are processed by the regional director (see Chapter One). As previously discussed in this chapter, many of the grounds for setting aside an election under Section 9 are also unfair labor practices under Section 8. However, the Board sets aside an election only if timely objections are filed. Unions frequently file both objections and unfair labor practice charges based on the same conduct, although filing an unfair labor practice charge alone is insufficient to have the election set aside.

N. REMEDIES FOR EMPLOYER UNFAIR LABOR PRACTICES: THE BARGAINING ORDER

What happens if an election is set aside for employer misconduct? Will there simply be another election or should a union be entitled to bargaining rights without going through another election?

The Board has a number of specific remedies for unlawful employer acts. It can issue a cease and desist order requiring the employer to cease an unlawful tactic or to assure employees that their rights are protected. The Board can remedy specific unfair labor practices by ordering the reinstatement of employees or ordering the reinstitution and back payment of benefits unlawfully denied. In cases in which an employer has committed outrageous and pervasive unfair labor practices to undermine the union's organizing efforts (by engaging in multiple unlawful acts as discussed in this chapter and Chapter Four), the Board can order so-called extraordinary remedies requiring an employer to: allow the union to post notices on employee bulletin boards and to meet with employees in nonwork areas of the plant on their nonwork time; give the union notice of and the right to respond to any employer speeches to its employees about union representation; allow the union to give a speech on working time prior to any scheduled NLRB election;

and supply the union upon request with an up-to-date list of employee names and addresses.

The Board has long taken the view that even though a union loses an election, the Board can order an employer to bargain with the union if the employer's unfair labor practices undermined the union's majority status as proven by single-purpose authorization cards signed by a majority of the employees. The Board is not limited to remedying the specific violations and ordering a new election.

1. Misconduct Justifying a Bargaining Order: The *Gissel* Decision

In the landmark 1969 *Gissel* case, the Supreme Court upheld the Board's approach in favor of bargaining orders under some circumstances.[11] The Court held that, although signed recognition cards are not preferable to an uncoerced election, single-purpose cards can adequately reflect a union's majority status.

Once the Supreme Court decided that an employer could be ordered to bargain with a union based on a card majority, it determined what type of misconduct warranted a bargaining order. First, the Court emphasized that in the absence of unfair labor practices undermining the union, an employer has an absolute right to an election. No bargaining order should be issued, even if the union has cards from all the employees, if the employer simply refuses recognition. As previously discussed, the only exception would be if the employer verifies the union's majority status, thus waiving its right to an election.

The Court divided employer misconduct into three categories. The first category consists of pervasive unfair labor practices of such a nature that the coercive effect cannot be eliminated by lesser remedies and a fair election cannot be held. In such cases a bargaining order is an appropriate remedy.

[11] See legal principle 12.A.

The second category of employer misconduct consists of less pervasive unfair labor practices that still have a tendency to undermine the union's majority strength and impede the election process. The Board in such cases must weigh the seriousness of the misconduct against the effectiveness of its remedies to ensure a fair rerun. The Board considers the extensiveness of the employer's unfair labor practices in terms of their past effect on election conditions and the likelihood of the recurrence in the future. The Court stated:

If the Board finds that the possibility of erasing the effects of past practices and of ensuring a fair election (or a fair rerun) by the use of traditional remedies, though present, is slight and that employee sentiment once expressed through cards would, on balance, be better protected by a bargaining order, then such an order should be issued.

The Supreme Court emphasized, however, that "there is a third category of minor or less extensive unfair labor practices which, because of their minimal impact on the election machinery, will not sustain a bargaining order." An employer's isolated threat to discharge an employee for union activity, which is not carried out, is an example of this third category.

The Board's decisions applying *Gissel* follow the Supreme Court's pattern. First, the Board decides whether an employer's conduct falls into the first (pervasive), second (serious), or third (minor) category. If a case falls within the first category and the union has a valid card majority, the Board issues a bargaining order. If a case falls into the second category, the Board analyzes the impact of the unfair labor practices versus the possibility of a free election through lesser remedies. If a case falls into the third minor misconduct category, the Board issues an order remedying the specific violations.

Hard and fast rules are not possible in determining the situations in which the Board will issue a bargaining order. Each case is based on the specific facts of the employer's violations. Generally, cases involving the discharge, reassignment, or demotion of active union supporters or other reprisals against bargaining unit employees, plant closings, or changes in the benefits that employees receive (either improving benefits to eliminate the conditions that started the employees' union activities, or decreasing benefits in reprisal) fall into the first or second category under *Gissel,* justifying a bargaining order, depending upon their extent. The Board and the courts refer to such conduct as "hallmark" violations. Even the unlawful threat of a plant closing or of serious adverse consequences if the union wins the election have justified bargaining orders in some cases. However, cases involving only general threats of adverse consequences if the union wins, or promises of benefits if the union loses, or cases involving only interrogation or surveillance of employees in which no actual adverse action is taken against employees, generally fall into the third minor misconduct category. In those cases, the Board enters an order remedying the specific violations, requires the employer to post a notice in which it agrees to cease the unlawful conduct, and orders a new election, usually held after a sixty-day compliance period.

In deciding whether to enter a bargaining order, the Board considers not only the nature of the unlawful acts, but also the timing, extent, and repetitiveness of the unlawful conduct; the level of management involved in the unlawful conduct; and the size of the bargaining unit. Thus, the Board is more likely to enter a bargaining order if the employer's unlawful campaign begins soon after the union requested recognition (or filed its election petition) and continues throughout the campaign, than if there are only a few isolated unlawful acts. The Board is more likely to enter a bargaining order if the employer's action is directed at a large percentage of the workforce than if the conduct is directed at only a few individuals. However, the Board presumes that reprisals directed against a few key union supporters have a widespread coercive effect even though only a relatively few employees are directly involved. The Board is also more likely to enter a bargaining order if higher management is directly involved in an anti-union campaign than if only low-level supervisors are involved, because of the greater coercive impact on the employees. The Board is more restrictive now in issuing bargaining orders than in the past. However, it still applies the same basic criteria and has issued bargaining orders in a number of cases.

Some courts of appeals have set aside Board bargaining orders in part on the grounds that the number of years since the election and the employee turnover make it inappropriate to grant bargaining rights to the union for employees who were not even working when the union's organizing drive began. Such decisions are particularly disturbing to unions because they encourage employers to use delay as a tactic to undermine employee rights. In a few cases that courts of appeals have remanded (returned) to the Board for consideration of this issue, the Board has set aside a bargaining order that it had previously issued in part because of the long time (more than four years) between the date of the union's organizing campaign and the Board's ultimate order. However, in general, even the current Board has refused to consider the amount of time or employee turnover as grounds for denying a bargaining order where the employer's misconduct otherwise justified the order.

As a general principle of administrative law, the courts of appeals are supposed to give deference to the Board's interpretation and application of the LMRA because Congress established the Board to administer the Act, and the courts should defer to the Board's expertise in labor-management relations. However, there is a tendency for the courts of appeals to reverse a higher percentage of Board decisions in bargaining order cases than on other issues, especially in cases involving high employee turnover or a prolonged time lapse. Thus, these issues may have to be resolved by the Supreme Court.

A bargaining order is based on the commission of unfair labor practices. If acts occurring during the election campaign interfere with employee free choice but are not unfair labor practices, the election is set aside. There is not a bargaining order; the only remedy is a rerun.

2. Procedures for Obtaining a Bargaining Order

Generally, a bargaining order dates from the date the employer began to engage in unfair labor practices, provided the union can demonstrate a card majority by that date. If an employer engaged in unfair labor practices before the union obtained majority status, the bargaining order starts from the date the union obtained majority status.

Although unions frequently request voluntary recognition from an employer before filing a representation petition with the Board, a request for recognition is not necessary to get a bargaining order. If an employer engages in unfair labor practices warranting a bargaining order under the *Gissel* criteria, the Board issues a bargaining order even if the union never requested voluntary recognition, provided the union had a card majority. Thus a union that does not bother with requesting voluntary recognition because it realizes the futility of such a request does not forfeit its right to a bargaining order. The advantage to requesting recognition is that a union has greater certainty as to the date it achieved majority status. This is important in determining the date of an employer's bargaining obligation under a bargaining order.

Procedurally, to obtain a bargaining order, a union that has lost an election must file timely objections to the election and also file unfair labor practice charges against the employer's misconduct. The representation and unfair labor practice cases are consolidated for hearing (see Chapter One). If the Board finds that the objections have merit,

the Board sets aside the election. If the Board also finds that the unfair labor practices are serious enough under the *Gissel* criteria, the Board issues a bargaining order. If the unfair labor practices are not sufficient, the Board simply orders a rerun election and issues an order remedying the specific violations. No bargaining order is issued unless the Board sets aside the election based on the objections.

a. Choice of Proceeding with an Election. A union does not have to go ahead with an election in the face of serious unfair labor practices that the union feels make an election futile. Instead, the union can file unfair labor practice charges against the employer before the election is held. The representation election does not proceed while the unfair labor practice charges are pending. A charge filed while a representation case is pending is called a "blocking charge." The Board can issue a bargaining order, even though an election was never held, if the employer's unfair labor practices warrant a bargaining order under the *Gissel* criteria.

In most cases, a union goes ahead with a pending election in the hope of winning anyhow, despite the employer's serious unfair labor practices during the election campaign. A union can file charges and then sign a "request to proceed," permitting the representation case to proceed even though there are unfair labor practice charges pending. If the union wins despite the employer's unlawful acts, there is no need for a bargaining order. If, however, the union loses the election, it can still file objections to the election, proceed with the unfair labor practice charges, and seek a bargaining order.

b. Weakness of the Bargaining Order Remedy. There are weaknesses in bargaining orders as a remedy. The bargaining order is just that, an order that the employer bargain with the union. Even if the employer is ordered to bargain, the union may have been permanently weakened by the employer's misconduct. Many union supporters might have left the company before the bargaining order was issued. Thus, the time needed to process a case through the Board might result in a practical victory for the employer although the union wins the legal battle. An employer who is determined to defeat the union can drag out bargaining after the bargaining order is issued, further frustrating the employees' rights. As also discussed in Chapter Five, legislative changes are needed to expedite the representation election process and strengthen the remedies against employers who flaunt the law.

3. Bargaining Orders without Union Majority Status

As the Board's membership has changed through the years, the Board has remained divided over whether it has the authority to issue a bargaining order under *Gissel* if a union never obtained a card majority of the employees in the proposed unit. The Board members opposing a bargaining order if the union lacks majority card support argue that it is contrary to the principle of majority rule to impose a union upon bargaining unit employees if the union never obtained majority status. The Board members favoring a bargaining order have argued that such an order is necessary, even in the absence of the union's majority status, in those cases in which the employer's pervasive unfair labor practices have destroyed the possibility of a free election, in order to prevent the employer from reaping the benefits of its own unlawful conduct.

The first time this issue was presented to the Board in the 1979 *United Dairy Farmers Coop. Assn.* case, the Board split three ways on this issue.[12] Two of the Board members stated the opinion that the Board could issue a bargaining order even if a union never obtains a card majority. One Board member was of the opinion that the Board lacked the authority to issue a bargaining

order in the absence of the union's majority status regardless of the pervasiveness of the employer's unfair labor practices. The other two Board members stated that the Board might have the authority, but refused to render a definite opinion until faced with what they regarded as an appropriate case. The *Dairy Farmers* decision was appealed to the United States Court of Appeals for the Third Circuit. The court held that the Board does have authority to issue a bargaining order, although the union never obtained majority status, in exceptional cases where the employer's outrageous and pervasive unfair labor practices eliminated any reasonable possibility of holding a free and uncoerced election.

In the 1982 *Conair Corp.* decision,[13] the Board (following a change in three members since the *Dairy Farmers* decision) held in a three to two decision that it does have authority to issue a bargaining order in a nonmajority status situation if the employer's misconduct fell into the category of pervasive unfair labor practices of such a nature that the coercive effects cannot be eliminated by lesser remedies. The two dissenting members held to the position that the bargaining order was contrary to the principle of majority rule. The Board's decision in *Conair* was appealed to the United States Courts of Appeals for the District of Columbia. The court refused to enforce the bargaining order on the grounds that the Board lacked statutory authority to enter a bargaining order if the union never attained majority status. Subsequently, the Board, following another change in its membership, ruled three to one in *Gourmet Foods* (1984) that it lacked authority to issue a bargaining order in any case in which the union had never attained majority status.[14] The Board majority thus followed the reasoning of the District of Columbia Court of Appeals in the *Conair* case and rejected the reasoning of the Court of Appeals for the

---

[12] See legal principle 12.B.

[13] See legal principle 12.B.
[14] See legal principle 12.B.

Third Circuit in the *Dairy Farmers* decision that held that the Board did have such authority in extraordinary cases.

It is possible that with future membership changes the Board will once again rule that it does have authority to issue a bargaining order even if the union never attained majority status. Since the courts of appeals have disagreed on the question, the issue may remain open until such time as the Supreme Court rules or (as has been proposed) the Labor Management Relations Act is amended to give the Board specific authority to issue a bargaining order in such a case. It would appear, however, that even if the Board's authority is ultimately upheld, bargaining orders in cases in which a union never attained majority status will be rare and limited to instances of extremely pervasive unlawful employer conduct.

Summary   The rights and obligations of unions, employees, and employers in organizing and conducting elections are regulated by both Sections 8 and 9 of the Act. Some tactics by an employer or a union may be protected or prohibited as unfair labor practices under Section 8. In addition to the unfair labor practice restrictions, an employer and a union are prohibited from engaging in certain misconduct that destroys the "laboratory conditions" necessary to protect the employees' right to a free-choice election under Section 9. An election may be set aside for election misconduct even if there was no unfair labor practice.

Section 8(c) allows employers to express their views on whether their employees should be unionized, as long as the employer's remarks do not contain a threat of reprisal, force, or promise of benefit. Threatening or coercive remarks are both an unfair labor practice and grounds for setting aside the election. However, the Board's decision on setting aside an election is based upon the totality of an employer's or union's conduct. Thus, a single remark may not be grounds for setting aside an election even though it was an unfair labor practice. In general, the current Board has given employers far greater leeway than in the past to engage in aggressive campaigns against union representation without committing acts that would be grounds for setting aside an election.

To be grounds for setting aside an election, objectionable conduct must occur after the union has filed its representation petition. Objectional conduct may include:

1. Certain company restrictions on employees distributing union literature and soliciting for the union;
2. Interrogation or surveillance of employees' union activities if, under all the circumstances, the interrogation or surveillance reasonably tends to restrain, coerce, or interfere with employee rights guaranteed by the Act;
3. A company speech within the twenty-four-hour period preceding the election to a mass assembly of employees on company time or to small groups of employees in an area of management authority at any time during the campaign;
4. Use of fraudulent documents preventing an employee from recognizing

a misrepresentation as false campaign propaganda or abuse of Board processes;

5. Threats of adverse consequences if the union wins (but an employer has the right to present its views on the "economic realities" of unionization as long as the employer's predictions are supported by "objective fact");

6. Granting new or additional benefits during the election campaign;

7. Coercion or denial of benefits during the campaign;

8. Interference with the Board's conduct of the election.

Although most election cases pertain to employer misconduct, union misconduct may also be grounds for setting aside an election the union has won, such as free union membership to employees who join the union before the election is held, improper gifts to union supporters, or coercive conduct by the union or, in some cases, by employees supporting the union against employees who oppose the union.

   The employer may sometimes, however, commit unfair labor practices during a campaign that are so serious that a rerun election is an insufficient remedy. In such cases, the Board can order the employer to bargain with the union even though it lost the election. The Supreme Court held in the *Gissel* decision that a bargaining order is an appropriate remedy for two types of employer misconduct: pervasive unfair labor practices of such a nature that the coercive effect cannot be eliminated by lesser remedies, so that a fair election cannot be held; and less pervasive unfair labor practices that still have a tendency to undermine the union's majority strength and impede the election process. The Board's current position is that it does not have authority to issue a bargaining order, regardless of the pervasive nature of the employer's unlawful practices, if the union never attained majority status in the bargaining unit. A signed single-purpose authorization card is a valid indication of an employee's support unless the employee was told that the card's only purpose was for an election.

Review Questions

1. Is an employer obligated to recognize a union that can prove its majority support without an election?

2. What are the two types of recognition cards?

3. Will the Board base a *Gissel* bargaining order on a majority proven through dual-purpose cards?

4. Should recognition cards be dated?

5. When will the Board reject a single-purpose recognition card as a basis for proving majority support?

6. Can an employee hand out recognition cards and talk to other employees during his free time in working areas?

7. Can a union offer free membership in the union as a campaign technique?

8. Is there a First Amendment right of free speech to engage in political campaigning at work?

9. Is an employer's statement that there might be layoffs if the union wins an election grounds for setting aside the election?

10. Can an employer give employees benefit increases during the election campaign?

11. Can an unfair labor practice be committed during an election campaign, but not be grounds for setting aside an election?

12. If a union loses an election, how many days after the election does it have to file objections to the employer's alleged misconduct?

(Answers to review questions are at the end of the book.)

Basic Legal Principles

1. An employer and a union are prohibited from engaging in election misconduct that destroys laboratory conditions and undermines the employee's right to a free-choice election. An election may be set aside for such acts even though they may not constitute an unfair labor practice. *General Shoe Corp.,* 77 NLRB 124, 21 LRRM 1337 (1948); *Newport News Shipbuilding,* 239 NLRB No. 14, 99 LRRM 1518 (1978); *General Dynamics Corporation,* 250 NLRB 719, 104 LRRM 1438 (1980); *Adams Super Markets Corp.,* 274 NLRB No. 194, 118 LRRM 1552 (1985); *Lovilia Coal Co.,* 275 NLRB No. 186, 120 LRRM 1005 (1985); *YMCA of San Francisco,* 286 NLRB No. 98, 126 LRRM 1329 (1987); *S.E. Nichols, Inc.,* 284 NLRB No. 55, 127 LRRM 1298 (1987); *Madison Industries,* 290 NLRB No. 160, 129 LRRM 1323 (1988).

As to union misconduct, see *NLRB v. Savair Mfg. Co.,* 414 U.S. 270, 84 LRRM 2929 (1973); *Newport News Shipbuilding,* 239 NLRB No. 14, 99 LRRM 1518 (1978); *Davlan Engineering, Inc.,* 283 NLRB No. 124, 125 LRRM 1049 (1987) (union liable for erroneous statements made by employees soliciting cards); *Mike Yurosek & Son,* 292 NLRB No. 124, 130 LRRM 1308 (1989); *McCarty Processors, Inc.,* 286 NLRB No. 69, 126 LRRM 1211 (1987); *Y.K.K. (U.S.A.), Inc.,* 269 NLRB No. 8, 115 LRRM 1186 (1984); *Westwood Horizons Hotel,* 270 NLRB No. 116, 116 LRRM 1152 (1984); *Owens-Illinois,* 271 NLRB No. 194, 117 LRRM 1104 (1984) (gift of union jackets to employees on election day between voting sessions grounds for setting aside election); *Mailing Services, Inc.,* 293 NLRB No. 58, 130 LRRM 1465 (1989) (election set aside because union made free medical screenings available to all employees during election campaign). See also *Electra Food Machinery, Inc.,* 279 NLRB No. 40, 122 LRRM 1046 (1986) (interference by outside party in election).

2. Generally an employee can solicit for the union in working areas on the employee's own time. Literature can be distributed on an employee's own time, but only in nonworking areas. *Republic Aviation Corp. v. NLRB,*

324 U.S. 793, 16 LRRM 620 (1945); *Stoddard-Quirk Mfg. Co.,* 138 NLRB 615, 51 LRRM 1110 (1962); *Norris K. W. Printing Co.,* 231 NLRB No. 156, 97 LRRM 1080 (1977); *United Parcel Service, Inc.,* 234 NLRB No. 11, 97 LRRM 1212 (1978); *NLRB v. Baptist Hospital, Inc.,* 442 U.S. 773, 101 LRRM 2556 (1979) (discussing hospital rules on solicitation and distribution of literature); *Burger King Corp. v. NLRB,* 725 F.2d 1053, 115 LRRM 2387 (6th. Cir. 1984) (right to wear union insignia); *NLRB v. Harper Grace Hospitals,* 737 F.2d 576, 116 LRRM 3001 (6th Cir. 1984); *Harold's Club v. NLRB,* 758 F.2d 1320, 119 LRRM 2141 (9th Cir. 1985) (right of off-duty employees to engage in organizing activities on company premises); *NLRB v. Pizza Crust Co.,* 862 F.2d 49, 129 LRRM 3002 (3d Cir. 1988) (off-duty employees).

3. Rules that an employer establishes limiting employees' rights to solicit and distribute literature must be clear. Ambiguous rules, which an employee might interpret to prohibit statutorily protected rights, are unlawful. *G. C. Murphy,* 171 NLRB No. 45, 68 LRRM 1108 (1968); *NLRB v. Charles Miller & Co.,* 341 F.2d 870, 58 LRRM 2507 (2d Cir. 1965); *Tri-County Medical Center,* 222 NLRB No. 174, 91 LRRM 1323 (1976); *T.R.W., Inc.,* 257 NLRB No. 47, 107 LRRM 1481 (1981). The Board permits an employer rule to prohibit solicitation during "working time" because the rule correctly implies that solicitation is permitted during nonworking time during the workday, but a rule prohibiting solicitation during "working hours" is presumptively invalid because it erroneously implies that an employee cannot engage in solicitation during the employee's own time during the workday. *Our Way, Inc.,* 268 NLRB No. 61, 115 LRRM 1009 (1983).

4. The right to discuss union matters and distribute union literature pertains to all legitimate collective bargaining activities and subjects, including internal union matters and related political activity (e.g., distribution of literature against right-to-work laws). *Eastex Inc. v. NLRB,* 437 U.S. 556, 98 LRRM 2717 (1978); *U.S. Postal Service,* 269 NLRB No. 170, 116 LRRM 1179 (1984); *Southwestern Bell Telephone Co.,* 276 NLRB No. 110, 120 LRRM 1145 (1985); *Machinists District Lodge 91 v. NLRB,* 814 F.2d 876, 125 LRRM 2011 (1987). A union cannot contractually waive the employees' statutory right to distribute union literature. *NLRB v. Magnavox,* 415 U.S. 322, 85 LRRM 2475 (1974).

5.A. Normally outside union organizers are not allowed into an employer's premises to solicit and distribute literature even though other means of reaching employees may not be as easy or convenient. *NLRB v. Babcock & Wilcox Co.,* 351 U.S. 105, 38 LRRM 2001 (1956); *New Process Co.,* 290 NLRB No. 83, 131 LRRM 1508 (1989); *North Star Drilling Col.,* 290 NLRB No. 91, 131 LRRM 1294 (1988). But see *Sahara Tahoe Hotel,* 292 NLRB No. 86, 131 LRRM 1021 (1989) (outside union organizers may distribute literature on company's unfenced employee parking lot since there was no other reasonably effective way to communicate with employees). Compare *A. R. Zachry Co. v. NLRB,* ___F.2d ___, 132 LRRM 2377 (4th Cir. 1989) (employer may refuse to hire applicant it knows is a paid union organizer who will remain on union payroll and engage in organizing efforts on employer's premises if hired). See also legal principle 6.

5.B. Union organizers have the right to meet with off-duty employees in the public areas of a facility such as a hotel, department store, or hospital as long as the organizers' use conforms with the normal use of the area and is not disruptive to customers or normal operations. *Montgomery Ward & Co. v. NLRB,* 728 F.2d 389, 115 LRRM 3134 (6th Cir. 1984) (use of snack bar); *NLRB v. Methodist Hospital of Gary, Inc.,* 732 F.2d 43, 116 LRRM 2327 (7th Cir. 1984) (use of hospital cafeteria for organizing purposes); *NLRB v. National Broadcasting Co.,* 797 F.2d 75, 123 LRRM 2182 (2d Cir. 1986); *Gilliam Candy Co.,* 282 NLRB No. 89, 124 LRRM 1065 (1987). But see, *Baptist Medical Center v. NLRB,* 876 F.2d 661, 131 LRRM 2565 (8th. Cir. 1989) (hospital may exclude organizers from cafeteria open to general public).

6. A shopping center is private property and union organizers therefore do not have a constitutional free speech right to enter a center to organize employees. In general, the rules as to access are the same as those applied to the private property of any other employer. *Central Hardware Co. v. NLRB,* 407 U.S. 539, 80 LRRM 2769 (1972); *Hutzler Bros. Co. v. NLRB,* 630 F.2d 1012, 105 LRRM 2473 (4th Cir. 1980). However, an organizer may have the right of access to the corridors, walkways, and parking lots of a shopping center which are generally open to the public to distribute leaflets and handbills if there are no other reasonably feasible means of identifying and communicating with employees the union seeks to organize, under the same principles as to access which apply to picketing or handbilling on private property during the course of a labor dispute. *Lechmere Inc.,* 295 NLRB No. 15, 131 LRRM 1480 (1989); *Jean Country,* 291 NLRB No. 4, 129 LRRM 1201 (1988); *Karatjas Family Lockport Corp.,* 292 NLRB No. 92, 130 LRRM 1289 (1989); *Ameron Automotive Center,* 265 NLRB No. 58, 111 LRRM 1641 (1982). (See further discussion, Chapter Seven.)

7. An employer cannot give a speech to a mass employee audience on company time in the last twenty-four hours before an election. Talking to employees individually, in small groups, or at a voluntary meeting is not prohibited. *Peerless Plywood Co.,* 107 NLRB No. 106, 33 LRRM 1151 (1953); *Associated Milk Producers,* 237 NLRB No. 120, 99 LRRM 1212 (1978); *Land o' Frost,* 252 NLRB No. 1, 102 LRRM 1250 (1980); *Flex Products, Inc.,* 280 NLRB No. 61, 122 LRRM 1326 (1986).

8. An employer cannot speak against the union to small groups of employees in an area of management authority at any time during an election campaign. The atmosphere is considered coercive even if the statements made are not. *The Hurley Co.,* 130 NLRB No. 43, 47 LRRM

.293 (1961); *Han-Dee-Pak, Inc.,* 232 NLRB No. 71, 97 LRRM 1054 (1977); *Flex Products, Inc.,* in legal principle 7.

9. An election will be set aside if a party uses fraudulent documents preventing an employee from recognizing a misrepresentation as false campaign propaganda. *Midland National Life Insurance Co.,* 263 NLRB No. 24, 110 LRRM 1489 (1982), overruling *General Knit of California, Inc.,* 239 NLRB No. 101, 99 LRRM 1687 (1978) and *Hollywood Ceramics,* 140 NLRB 221, 51 LRRM 1600 (1962); readopting, *Shopping Kart Food Market, Inc.,* 228 NLRB 1311, 94 LRRM 1705 (1977); *Trailways, Inc.,* 271 NLRB No. 95, 117 LRRM 1023 (1984); *U.S. Ecology, Inc. v. NLRB,* 772 F.2d 1478, 120 LRRM 2779 (9th Cir. 1985).

10. An employer may lawfully question employees about union activities or convey the impression that it is engaging in surveillance of union activities, as long as, under all the facts and circumstances, the interrogation, or impression of surveillance would not reasonably tend to restrain, coerce, or interfere with rights guaranteed by the Act. *Rossmore House,* 269 NLRB 1176, 116 LRRM 1025 (1984); *Sunnyvale Medical Clinic,* 277 NLRB No. 131, 121 LRRM 1025 (1985); *Spencer Industries,* 279 NLRB No. 81, 122 LRRM 1073 (1986); *Golden Fan Inn,* 281 NLRB No. 35, 123 LRRM 1116 (1986); *Southwire Co.,* 282 NLRB No. 117, 124 LRRM 1257 (1987) (polygraph examination regarding drug use unlawfully interrogated employees about union activities).

11. Either party's abuse of the Board's processes by making it appear that the Board favors one side over the other is grounds for setting aside an election. However, an altered reproduction of an official NLRB election ballot may appear in a party's campaign literature unless the ballot in fact is likely to give voters the misleading impression that the Board favors one party to the election. *Gulton Industries,* 240 NLRB No. 73, 100 LRRM 1321 (1979); *Riveredge Hospital,* 264 NLRB No. 146, 111 LRRM 1425 (1982) (party's preelection misrepresentation of NLRB actions against other party to be treated same as any other misrepresentation, not regarded as abuse of Board processes); *SDC Investment, Inc.,* 274 NLRB No. 78, 118 LRRM 1410 (1985); *Krehbiel Co.,* 279 NLRB No. 114, 122 LRRM 1105 (1986); *Worths Stores,* 281 NLRB No. 160, 123 LRRM 1215 (1986); *BIW Employees Credit Union,* 287 NLRB No. 45, 127 LRRM 1098 (1987); *NLRB v. Hyatt Hotels* ____ F.2d ____, 132 LRRM 2630 (6th Cir. 1989).

12.A. An employer can be ordered to bargain with a union that had majority support in the unit before an election as shown by sole-purpose authorization cards, but lost the election, if the employer engaged in pervasive unfair labor practices or extensive unfair labor practices that tended to undermine majority strength and impede the election. *NLRB v. Gissel Packing Co.,* 395 U.S. 575, 71 LRRM 2481 (1969); *Drug Package, Inc.,* 228 NLRB 108, 94 LRRM 1570 (1977); *Montgomery Ward,* 267 NLRB No. 143, 114 LRRM 1114 (1983); *Koon's Ford,* 282 NLRB No. 88, 124

LRRM 1167 (1986); *Fiber Glass Systems, Inc.,* 278 NLRB No. 154, 121 LRRM 1343 (1986); *Madison Industries,* 290 NLRB No. 160, 129 LRRM 1323 (1988).

12.B. The Board's current view is that it does not have authority to issue a bargaining order, regardless of the pervasive nature of an employer's unfair labor practices, unless the union achieved a card majority in the bargaining unit. *Gourmet Foods,* 270 NLRB No. 113, 116 LRRM 1105 (1984); *Conair Corp.,* 261 NLRB No. 178, 110 LRRM 1161 (1982), reversed in part, *Conair Corp. v. NLRB,* 721 F.2d 1355, 114 LRRM 3169 (D.C. Cir. 1983). Compare *United Dairy Farmers Coop. Assn.,* 242 NLRB 1026, 101 LRRM 1278 (1979), reversed in part *NLRB v. United Dairy Farmers Coop. Assn.,* 633 F.2d 1054, 105 LRRM 3034 (3d Cir. 1980), reconsidered by the Board 257 NLRB No. 129, 107 LRRM 1577 (1981).

12.C. In general, neither an unusually long time lapse between the occurrence of an employer's unfair labor practices and the date of the Board's decision nor employee turnover during the period is grounds for denying a bargaining order. Compare, *Salvation Army,* 293 NLRB No. 118, 131 LRRM 1289 (1989), *Coty Messenger, Inc.,* 272 NLRB No. 42, 117 LRRM 1280 (1984), and *U.S. Aviex Co.,* 279 NLRB No. 110, 122 LRRM 1293 (1986) (granting bargaining orders) with *St. Regis Paper Co.,* 285 NLRB No. 39, 126 LRRM 1017 (1987) (denying bargaining order). But see *NLRB v. Atlas Microfilming,* 753 F.2d 313, 118 LRRM 2628 (3d Cir. 1985); *NLRB v. Gordon,* 792 F.2d 29, 122 LRRM 2489 (2d Cir. 1986) (refusing to enforce Board bargaining order decisions due to time lapse).

13. Under LMRA Section 8(c) as currently interpreted by the Board, an employer may present its views on the adverse "economic realities" of unionization as long as the employer's predictions are supported by "objective fact." Thus an employer may now lawfully state that collective bargaining will start "from scratch" or "from ground zero," because such statements lawfully indicate that collective bargaining may result in the decrease as well as the increase of employee benefits. *NLRB v. Gissel Packing Co.* in legal principle 12.A; *Tendico, Inc.,* 232 NLRB No. 118, 97 LRRM 1107 (1977); *Warehouse Groceries Management,* 254 NLRB No. 21, 106 LRRM 1171 (1981); *Auto Workers v. NLRB,* 834 F.2d 816, 127 LRRM 2060 (9th Cir. 1987); *Golden Poultry Co.* 271 NLRB No. 139, 117 LRRM 1127 (1984) (limiting futility of bargaining doctrine); *Michael's Markets, Inc.,* 274 NLRB No. 105, 118 LRRM 1476 (1985); *Pilliod of Mississippi, Inc.,* 275 NLRB No. 117, 119 LRRM 1279 (1985) (bargaining begins "from zero"); *Atlantic Forest Products,* 282 NLRB No. 105, 124 LRRM 1127 (1987) (bargaining "from scratch"); *Black & Decker Corp.,* 282 NLRB No. 156, 124 LRRM 1210 (1987); *Harrison Steel Casing Co.,* 293 NLRB No. 143, 131 LRRM 1815 (1989); *Shaw's Supermarkets v. NLRB,* 884 F.2d 34, 132 LRRM 2634 (1st Cir., 1989).

14. An election may be set aside for procedural irregularity, such as the employer's failure to provide the union with a substantially correct list

of the eligible voters (the *Excelsior* list); failure to post notice of the election at least three work days before the election; electioneering in the voting area while the election is in progress or talking to employees in line to vote; or using a supervisor as an observer. However, a low employee turnout is not grounds for setting aside an election if the employees had adequate notice and an opportunity to vote if the employees were not prevented from voting by the conduct of the parties or unfairness in the scheduling or mechanics of the election. *Thrifty Auto Parts Inc.*, 295 NLRB No. 134, 131 LRRM 1801 (1989); *Pepsi-Cola Bottling Co.*, 291 NLRB No. 93, 129 LRRM 1236 (1988); *Lemco Construction, Inc.*, 283 NLRB No. 68, 124 LRRM 1329 (1987); *Southland Frozen Foods, Inc.*, 282 NLRB No. 106, 124 LRRM 1172 (1987); *Kraft, Inc.*, 273 NLRB No. 184, 118 LRRM 1242 (1985); *Wasatch Medical Management Services, Inc.*, 272 NLRB No. 182, 118 LRRM 1009 (1984); *Del Rey Tortilleria*, 272 NLRB No. 175, 117 LRRM 1449 (1984); *Bio-Medical Applications, Inc.*, 269 NLRB No. 141, 116 LRRM 1036 (1984).

Recommended Reading

Axelrod, "Common Obstacles to Organizing under NLRA," 59 *N.C.L. Review* 147 (1980).

Block, Wolkinson, and Kuhn, "Some are More Equal Than Others: The Relative Status of Employers, Unions and Employees in the Law of Union Organizing," 10 *Industrial Relations Law Journal* 220 (1988).

Bok, "The Deregulation of Campaign Tactics in Representation Elections," 78 *Harv. L. Rev.* 38 (1969).

Changing Labor Union Scene: Shea, "New Approaches in Union Organizing," St. Antoine, "The Legal and Economic Implications of Union-Management Cooperation," 41 NYU Conf. Lab. 7.1–8.23 (1988).

"Disclosure of Union Authorization Cards under the Freedom of Information Act—Interpreting the Personal Privacy Exemptions," 62 *Minn L. Rev.* 949 (1978).

"Discriminatory Discharge in a Sports Context," 53 *Fordham L. Rev.* 615 (1984).

Getman, "Ruminations on Union Organizing in the Private Sector," 53 *U. Chi. L. Rev.* 45 (1986).

Golub, "Propriety of Issuing *Gissel* Bargaining Orders Where the Union Has Never Attained a Majority," 29 *Lab. L. J.* 631 (1978).

Grunewald, "Empiricism in NLRB Election Regulation: *Shopping Kart* and *General Knit* in Retrospect," 4 *Indus. Rel. L. J.* 161 (1981).

Haas and Cox, "Section 7 Update: Balancing Employer Rights vs. Statutory Rights: Where is the Balance Today?" 4 *Lab. Lawyer* 151 (1988).

Maranto, "Corporate Characteristics and Union Organizing," 27 *Industrial Relations* 352 (1988).

"Property Rights and Job Security: Workplace Solicitation by Non-Employee Union Organizers," 94 *Yale L.J.* 374 (1984).

Wolkinson, Hanslowe, and Sperka, "The Remedial Efficacy of *Gissel* Bargaining Orders," 10 *Ind. Rel. L. J.* 509 (1989).

chapter 4

PROTECTION OF THE EMPLOYEE'S RIGHT TO UNION REPRESENTATION

What are the union's rights as the bargaining representative? What are the employee's rights to engage in collective bargaining activities through the union, and how are those rights protected? This chapter examines what happens after a union has obtained bargaining rights, either through a Board-conducted election, voluntary recognition, or perhaps a bargaining order.

The principles discussed in this chapter are primarily based on Sections 7, 8(a)(1), 8(a)(2), and 8(a)(3) of the Act, which should be referred to while reading this material. Section 7 grants employees the right to engage in concerted activity (collective bargaining) or to refrain from such activity. Section 8(a)(1) makes it an employer unfair labor practice to interfere with the employees' rights under Section 7. Section 8(a)(2) prohibits an employer from dominating or interfering in the activities of the employees' labor organization. Section 8(a)(3) prevents the employer from discriminating against employees either because of their union activities or because they choose not to engage in union activities.

Although this chapter emphasizes restrictions on employer conduct, remember that there are similar restrictions on unions. Section 8(b)(1) prohibits a union from interfering with the employees' Section 7 rights. A union cannot force an employee to engage in union activities or to refrain from them. Also, Section 8(b)(2) prevents a union from causing an employer to discriminate against an employee in violation of Section 8(a)(3). The limitations these sections place on union activities are discussed in Chapters Ten, Eleven, and Twelve.

Although employees have a right to engage in concerted activities through a union, the Act protects concerted activity whether through a union or through a less formal employee group. Thus, employees without a union who informally protest unsafe working conditions may also be engaged in concerted activities and enjoy the same statutory protection as union members discussed in this chapter. Remember, therefore, that although this chapter covers employees' rights to engage in union activities, the broader right of concerted activity belongs to all employees whether or not they belong to a labor organization.

A. THE DOCTRINE OF EXCLUSIVE REPRESENTATION

Once a union is either properly recognized voluntarily or certified as the bargaining agent by the NLRB, the union has the right of exclusive representation. This means that the employer cannot deal with any other employee representative about wages, hours, or other terms and conditions of employment. This concept of exclusive representation is fundamental to our system of democratic collective bargaining under which the union, as a representative of the majority, speaks for all employees in the unit.

Exclusive representation prevents an employer from playing the employees off against each other. By preventing an employer from dealing directly with employees, the doctrine prevents an employer from taking advantage of some bargaining unit employees who might otherwise be subject to employer domination. An individual employee cannot be forced to waive contract rights. Thus an employer cannot hire an employee on the condition that the employee accept working conditions less than those provided in the contract or pressure an individual employee to accept lower pay to keep a job. An employer cannot enter into individual contracts with employees containing different provisions than the collective bargaining agreement. However, a contract may expressly permit individual bargaining on some subjects. Theatrical or sports collective bargaining agreements, for example, frequently provide only base pay rates, and the employees may bargain individually for higher rates. In the absence of such exceptions, however, the contract determines the wages, hours, and working conditions for all employees.

The doctrine of exclusive representation is based on Section 9(a)(1), which provides that:

Representatives designated or selected for the purposes of collective bargaining by a majority of the employees in a unit appropriate for such purposes, shall be the exclusive representatives of all the employees in such unit for the purposes of collective bargaining in respect to rates of pay, wages, hours of employment, or other conditions of employment. . . .

Note that Section 9(a) says "designated or selected," not just elected. Thus, a union that is voluntarily recognized is also entitled to exclusive representation.

1. Individual Adjustment of Grievances

There is an exception to Section 9(a) under which any employee or group of employees has the right at any time "to present grievances to their employer and to have such grievances adjusted, without the intervention of the bargaining representative. . . ." However, this exception also provides that the adjustment cannot be inconsistent with the terms of a collective bargaining agreement in effect and that the bargaining representative must be given the opportunity to be present at such an adjustment.

The Supreme Court has interpreted the Section 9(a) exception narrowly. The Court has held that it permits employees to deal directly with the employer outside the grievance procedure if the employer is willing to meet. However, the employer can refuse to meet and can require the employee to use the grievance procedure. Also, talking to the employer directly, even if the employer is willing, may not satisfy the time requirements of the grievance procedure. Thus, if a contract allows only three days to file a grievance and an employee spends five days attempting to resolve the problem directly with the employer, the employee may have lost the right to file a grievance.

2. Direct Employer/Employee Dealings on Civil Rights Issues

The Supreme Court's decision in *Emporium Capwell Co.* is an important demonstration of the scope of the union's authority as the exclusive bargaining representative.[1] In that case, black employees demanded that the employer deal directly with them rather than the union on issues of black minority rights. The employer refused to deal with the black employees, taking the position that the employees should work through the union. The black employees picketed the employer in violation of the contract's no-strike clause, and they were discharged. The employees argued in part that the employer improperly refused to meet directly with them and that they could not lawfully be discharged for protesting the employer's alleged civil rights violations.

The Supreme Court upheld the discharges, holding that under the doctrine of exclusive representation, the black employees had to go through the union. Otherwise, the Court reasoned, every employee group could go directly to the employer with their own special problems. That would undermine the entire concept of majority rule, under which one of the union's functions is to consider the conflicting demands of its members, make a decision, and then present a united approach to the employer.

B. EMPLOYER DOMINATION OR INTERFERENCE WITH A UNION

In order for the doctrine of exclusive representation to function as it should, a union must independently represent the interests of the employees. Primarily for this reason, Section 8(a)(2) makes it an unfair labor practice for an employer to dominate or interfere with the formation or administration of a union or to contribute financial or other support. It is also a violation of Section 8(b)(1)(A) for a union to accept unlawful support.

1. Employer Domination

The Board has held that an employer has unlawful dominant control if the union has no independence. Domination is a

[1] See legal principle 2.

throwback to the company unions that existed back in the 1920s and early 1930s before passage of the Wagner Act. The tactic is still currently used, however, by employers who establish company "unions," in-house employee grievance committees, or quality of work-life programs to thwart legitimate organizing. The Board considers a number of factors in determining if an organization is dominated by the employer. These factors include the employer's role in determining eligibility for membership and in drafting the organization's constitution and bylaws; the employer's participation in meetings; the degree of supervisory participation and influence in the organization either as members or officers; whether the organization meets on company time and receives company financial support; and whether collective bargaining in fact takes place.

Supervisory participation in a union does not constitute employer domination or assistance per se. It is common in some industries for lower-level supervisors to be union members, vote in internal union elections, or even hold office. The Board considers the totality of the circumstances in determining whether such participation violates the Act including the extent of a supervisor's powers as defined under Section 2(11) of the Act; the supervisor's level in the employer's management structure; whether the employees regard the supervisor more as part of management or as a co-union member; whether the supervisory position is included in the bargaining unit under the collective bargaining agreement; and whether the supervisory position is temporary or permanent. Furthermore, a union may be disqualified as the bargaining agent if there is a "clear and present danger" of a conflict of interest between the supervisor's duties for and loyalty to the employer and the supervisor's union activities, especially if supervisors are active in collective bargaining, contract administration, or the grievance procedure for the employer.

If the Board does find that an employer dominates a union, the union is disestablished (dissolved) and its rights to engage in collective bargaining are taken away.

2. Employer Assistance

It is more common for an employer to assist a union than to dominate it. This may occur if an employer realizes that it is unable to dominate a union, but still prefers one union over another. An employer has the free speech right under Section 8(c) to state a preference for one union over another. However, if an employer couples a statement of preference with a threat as to the consequences if the other union wins, the statement constitutes unlawful assistance under Section 8(a)(2) and an unlawful threat under Section 8(a)(1). Other examples of unlawful assistance include using supervisors to obtain recognition cards for a union or requiring that an employee join a union before membership may be required as a condition of employment under Section 8(a)(3) (see Chapter Ten). It is unlawful for an employer to voluntarily recognize a union that it has unlawfully assisted to achieve majority status.

The Board has held that accepting normal social courtesy or amenities is not prohibited by Section 8(a)(2). If the employer and union are meeting at lunch and the employer pays the bill, the company technically might have assisted the union. But this is normal social courtesy between persons, of which the Board approves. If the employer, however, had provided the union leaders with a lavish meal out of all proportion to the meeting occasion, there might be a violation.

If an employer unlawfully assists a union but does not dominate it, the Board may simply order that the unlawful assistance cease. If the assistance is more extensive, the union may be decertified. However, in that case, if the employer ceases the unlawful assistance, the union can obtain new recognition cards and seek certification once again through a Board election.

a. Illegal Assistance versus Benefits Resulting from "Arm's-Length" Bargaining. It is not uncommon for union officials to remain on paid company time during grievance meetings, contract negotiations, or even while conducting internal union business during the work day. Unions may also receive free office space on the company's premises and free use of company equipment such as copiers. Such benefits may be specifically negotiated in the collective bargaining agreement or may exist only as a matter of practice. If Section 8(a)(2) were literally applied, such assistance could be unlawful. However, rather than adopting a per se approach, the Board examines each case to determine whether in fact, the union has been lawfully recognized and if the employer and union maintain an arm's-length relationship without any deeper involvement or intrusion by the employer into union activities. If there is a proper "arm's-length" relationship, the Board regards the use of company time and property to be "friendly cooperation" growing out of an amicable labor-management relationship. Thus the Board has upheld the legality of contract provisions and/or unwritten practices permitting employees paid time off to conduct union business; granting paid time to stewards to process grievances; paying union officers while they are taking part in contract negotiations; holding steward classes on company premises during the work day; and paying printing costs for collective bargaining agreements that the union distributes to its membership. This list of benefits that a union might negotiate or receive is not exhaustive, but it must be emphasized that in each case the Board found that the benefits had a legitimate collective bargaining function, there was an arms-length relationship between the employer and the union, and there was no evidence that the benefits were intended to undermine the union's independence.

3. Section 302 Restrictions on Employer Assistance

In addition to the restrictions of Section 8(a)(2), employer assistance to a union or to the union's officers or employees are also restricted by Section 302 of the Labor Management Relations Act. Section 302(a) prohibits an employer from paying a labor organization or any officer or employee thereof any money or other thing of value, and Section 302(b) prohibits the labor organization or its officers or employees from accepting the payment. Section 302(c) lists important exceptions to these broad restrictions. Thus an employer may pay a union officer, who is also an employee or former employee of the employer, compensation for or by reason of the officer's service as an employee. A union may purchase an article or commodity from the employer at the prevailing market value in the regular course of business. There are also exceptions for money paid and received as a result of a court or arbitrator's decision or in the settlement of a claim or grievance, money properly deducted from the wages of employees in payment of union membership dues (i.e., checkoff arrangements discussed in Chapter Ten), and for money paid to a trust fund jointly administered by employer and union representatives for the purpose of providing pension, medical, and other benefits to employees (the statutory basis for pension and welfare trusts).

The NLRB does not enforce the provisions of Section 302. Rather, the federal district courts have jurisdiction to restrain violations of the section. Also, willful violations of Section 302 are misdemeanors subject to prosecution by the United States Department of Justice. Although Sections 8(a)(2) and 302 are separately enforced, the Board, the Department of Justice, and the courts have attempted to apply the provisions consistently with each other, so that a payment that would be lawful under Section 8(a)(2) is not unlawful under Section 302 or vice versa, in light of the common statutory purposes of maintaining the independence of unions and preventing the corruption of the labor management relations process through the payment or receipt of improper assistance.

Recent decisions involving the *BASF Wyandotte Corporation* have clarified the scope of and the relationship between Section 8(a)(2) and Section 302.[2] The contract between BASF and the union provided that union representatives would be on paid time for attending meetings with the company and also that the union president and/or secretary could have a total of four hours off each day to conduct union business on company property. BASF unilaterally terminated these provisions in mid-contract on the grounds that they constituted unlawful assistance to the union under Section 8(a)(2) of the Act and an unlawful payment of money or other thing of value prohibited by Section 302. The company also unilaterally discontinued practices permitting the union free use of an office in the plant, a telephone to conduct union business concerning BASF's employees, and the free use of BASF's copying machine. The union filed an unfair labor practice charge against the company alleging that the unilateral changes constituted bad-faith bargaining in violation of Section 8(a)(5) (see Chapter Five for a discussion of these Section 8(a)(5) issues). The company's defense was that the payments violated Sections 8(a)(2) and 302 of the Act. In addition, the company filed a federal court suit requesting the court to find that the payments to union officials conducting union business violated Section 302.

Ultimately, both the National Labor Relations Board and the United States Court of Appeals for the Second Circuit upheld the legality of the payments and the benefits the union received under both Sections 8(a)(2) and 302. They concluded that the payments did not violate Section 302 because the union officers were bona fide employees of BASF, and the payments therefore fell within the exception of Section 302(c)(1) for payments to a union officer who is also an employee of the employer as compensation for or by reason for service as an employee. The Board also held that the payments and benefits did not violate Section 8(a)(2) because the union was clearly independent and had a well-estab-

[2] See legal principle 3.B.

lished arm's-length relationship with the company, and the payments and benefits permitted the union to perform its collective bargaining functions more effectively for the benefit of all concerned. The appellate court also noted that no docking provisions were common at the time Section 302 was enacted in 1947 and concluded that Congress would have specifically prohibited the practice if that had been its intent.

Both the Board and Second Circuit Court of Appeals stressed in the BASF cases that the union officers in question were bona fide employees who actually performed services for the employer part of the work day. It is very likely that employer payments to full-time union officers for time spent on union activities would be unlawful under Section 302 even though the officers are technically employees on leave from the employer. Thus, one court of appeals has held that a contract provision requiring the company to make insurance and pension trust fund contributions on behalf of employees on leave of absence to serve in full-time union positions violated Section 302. The Court reasoned that such payments to full-time union officers who may never return to work were not made by reason of their service as an employee of the employer under Section 302(c)(1). Another court of appeals, however, reached a basically contrary conclusion. It held that Section 302 does not prohibit an employer from granting pension credit for the period a former employee is on leave of absence to serve as a union officer *provided* that the credit is openly bargained for and the agreement to grant credit is included as part of the parties' collective bargaining agreement. The court reasoned that Section 302 is intended to prohibit employer payments of benefits which are akin to bribery or which would permit an employer to exercise undue influence over union officials. The court thus required that any policy granting credit be included in the collective bargaining agreement so that it could not be changed unilaterally by an employer and rank-and-file employees would know of the agreement, thus substantially reducing the possibility

that the credit would be granted or manipulated by an employer as a bribe or to exercise undue influence. Because of the conflicting decisions, this issue may ultimately reach the Supreme Court for consideration. Providing benefits to union officers on leave also raises issues under Section 8(a)(3) of the Act that are discussed later in this chapter.

4. Improper Employer Recognition

a. Premature Recognition. Aside from financial or other unlawful assistance, improper employer recognition of a union before the union establishes its uncoerced majority status is a violation of Section 8(a)(2). Also, an employer who has opened a new facility is prohibited from prematurely recognizing a union. To be lawful, an employer must (1) employ a substantial and representative complement of its projected work force (the jobs or job classifications designated for the operation must be substantially filled), and (2) be engaged in normal business operations at the location. In general these criteria are the same ones the Board uses to determine whether a collective bargaining agreement covering employees at a new location would be a contract bar to a representation petition filed by a rival union, discussed in Chapter Two. If a contract is executed prematurely or otherwise results from improper employer assistance, it can be set aside in unfair labor proceedings, and it would thereafter not bar an election.

b. Competing Union Recognition Claims. The right of an employer to recognize and bargain voluntarily with one union at the same time that another union is also seeking to represent the employees has raised recurring issues under Section 8(a)(2). At one time, the Board required that an employer maintain *neutrality* when faced with competing claims for recognition. Thus an employer and incumbent union could not engage in negotiations for, or execute, a new collective bargaining agreement when a timely valid representation petition had been filed by another union. The ban on bargaining remained in effect until the representation petition proceedings were completed. The employer and the incumbent union could continue to meet to administer the existing contract and to adjust grievances even though they could not negotiate a new contract.

In 1982, in two companion cases, *RCA Del Caribe, Inc.* and *Bruckner Nursing Home,* the Board substantially changed the previously established principles.[3] In *Del Caribe,* a case involving the bargaining rights of an incumbent union, the Board ruled that it would no longer require or permit an employer to stop bargaining or refuse to execute a contract with an incumbent union while a valid representation petition was pending. The Board reasoned that prohibiting negotiations until the Board ruled on the pending petition might work an undue hardship on employers, unions, and employees (because there might be important issues that needed resolution), and that the status quo would be better preserved if an employer continued bargaining with the incumbent rather than if bargaining were prohibited. The Board further stated that if the incumbent prevails in the election, any contract executed with it would be valid and binding, but that if the challenging union prevails, any contract executed with the incumbent would be null and void.

In *Bruckner,* involving an employer's right to grant voluntary initial recognition when two or more unions were competing for bargaining rights, the Board held that an employer can grant voluntary recognition to one of the competing unions, provided the union proves its majority status, unless a properly supported representation petition has been filed by one or more of the rivals. The Board abandoned the prior "neutrality" rule prohibiting voluntary recognition of one union where another claim for voluntary recognition is also pending unless the other claim does not raise a substantial question of representation. The Board did emphasize, however, that the employer can give voluntary recognition only if the union requesting it has uncoerced majority support and the employer did not render assistance to the union in its organizing efforts that would otherwise violate Section 8(a)(2).

Under the prior neutrality doctrine, the filing of a valid representation petition did not prohibit an employer from granting voluntary recognition to another union until the employer received notice of the filing. Although the issue is not entirely clear in the decisions to date, it appears that the Board still requires actual notice before the filing of a petition bars voluntary recognition of another union. Therefore, a union that files a representation petition, knowing that another union is also seeking to represent the same employees, should immediately notify the employer that a petition has been filed and not wait for the formal Board notice to be received.

Remember, also, that an employer is normally not obligated to recognize a union voluntarily but can insist on a Board-conducted election (see Chapter Three). Thus, although an employer might be legally permitted to recognize one of the unions requesting it voluntarily, it may choose to deny recognition and require a Board-conducted election.

c. Recognition of the Incumbent Union at a New Location. The relocation of companies is an accepted fact of industrial life. Some employers move to escape the wages and benefits that unions have negotiated. However, a relocation is lawful unless the union can prove that it was made with the *intent* to undermine the union rather than for lawful economic motives (see discussion below) or unless the parties' collective bargaining agreement expressly prohibits the move (see discussion in Chapter Five). Sometimes, however the parties' current collective bargaining agreement may require the employer to recognize the union at any new facility, or the employer and union may negotiate a new contract covering a new facility even before it opens. Do such

---

[3] See legal principle 1.A.

agreements constitute premature recognition in violation of Sections 8(a)(2) (as to the employer) and 8(b)(1)(A) of the Act (as to the union)? Such agreements may be lawful under three circumstances. First, it may be clear from the outset that sufficient employees will transfer from the existing facility to the new one so that the old employees will constitute a majority of the new work force. Second, if the older facility remains in operation, the two facilities may be so functionally integrated that the new facility constitutes an accretion to the existing one (see discussion in Chapter Two). That is unlikely, however, unless the two facilities are in the same geographical area. Third, the Board construes agreements to recognize a union at a new location as only an agreement to recognize the union voluntarily, without a Board conducted election, at such time as the union establishes its majority status at the new location. The union can establish its majority through transferred employees who were union members at the old location and by newly hired employees who voluntarily join. Any contract agreed to would not be effective until the union establishes its majority status and the contract would not bar a representation election among the employees at the new location until it went into legal effect (see discussion in Chapter Two).

One of the most prominent examples of the application of Section 8(a)(2) and Section 8(b)(1)(A) principles is the agreement between the General Motors Corporation and the United Automobile Workers pertaining to General Motors's contemplated Saturn automobile plant. General Motors and the Auto Workers entered into an agreement before the plant was built covering the terms and conditions of employment at the future Saturn facility. This agreement provided that a majority of the initial complement of employees would come from GM-UAW bargaining units and that the company would recognize the UAW as the bargaining agent for these employees at the Saturn complex. Several employer organizations filed unfair labor practice charges alleging that the

agreement constituted unlawful premature recognition of the UAW. However, the General Counsel of the National Labor Relations Board refused to issue a complaint.[4] (As discussed in Chapter One, the General Counsel has full and complete discretion in deciding whether to issue a complaint.) The General Counsel reasoned that General Motors had an obligation to bargain with the union over the *effect* of its decision to open the Saturn plant on the employees represented by the UAW and that the agreement to hire current and laid-off bargaining unit employees at the new location was a legitimate product of the bargaining. As to the issue of premature recognition, the General Counsel concluded that the recognition agreement was, in legal effect, an agreement to recognize the UAW at Saturn only if and when the UAW achieved majority support. Therefore, the agreement was lawful.

d. The Construction Industry Exception for Pre-Hire Agreements. There is one statutory exception to the rule against entering into premature or pre-hire agreements with a union. Section 8(f) expressly allows pre-hire agreements in the construction industry. This means that a construction union does not have to prove its majority status to obtain voluntary employer recognition. However, Section 8(f) also provides that a pre-hire agreement is not a bar to an election petition filed by another union. This means that an election can be held during the term of a pre-hire contract. Until recently, the Board held that an employer may lawfully withdraw from a Section 8(f) agreement at any time until the construction union represents a majority of the employees covered by the agreement.

In the 1987 *Deklewa* decision,[5] in which the Board substantially changed the law pertaining to pre-hire agreements, the Board ruled in part that an employer may no longer unilaterally repudiate a pre-hire agreement during its term. The *Deklewa* decision is discussed fully in Chapter Five.

---

[4] See legal principle 1.B.

[5] See legal principle 4.

C. PROTECTION OF THE RIGHT OF CONCERTED ACTIVITY

Exclusive representation under which the employer is obligated to deal with the union rather than with the employees as individuals is the most fundamental protection that employees have to engage in concerted activities. However, the Labor Management Relations Act does more than protect the union as an entity. Section 7 of the Act also protects the right of each individual employee to engage in concerted activity or to refrain from that activity. Even illegal aliens are considered as employees protected by the Act. Section 8(a)(1) makes it an unfair labor practice for an employer to interfere with, restrain, or coerce employees in these rights. Section 8(b)(1)(A) makes it an unfair labor practice for a union to restrain or coerce an employee in the exercise of these rights.

It is not possible to list all the actions that might constitute employer interference with employee rights in violation of Section 8(a)(1). Union rights to solicit and distribute literature (as discussed in Chapter Three) are rights guaranteed by Section 7 and protected by Section 8(a)(1). Section 8(a)(1) prohibits employer threats of adverse consequences if the employees support a union or promises of benefits if they do not; granting or withholding benefits to discourage union activities; and coercion, such as discipline or harder working conditions, in retaliation for supporting a union because these acts all interfere with the employees' rights. Interrogating employees involuntarily about their union activities, surveillance of an employee's union activities, or transferring an employee to an isolated area of the plant to prevent union activities are other common examples of employer conduct that interfere with an employee's right to engage in concerted activity.

1. Acts of Individuals as Concerted Activity

Usually concerted activity involves conduct by two or more employees acting together. Thus, employees who march into their supervisor's office together to protest working conditions or who engage in a strike are engaged in concerted activity. However, an employee acting alone may also be engaged in concerted activity if the employee is seeking to induce (encourage or initiate) group activity or is acting as a representative of at least one other employee. Thus, for example, suppose an employee complains to co-workers about conditions at their workplace and suggests they need a union. The other workers, however, reject the idea. A supervisor overhears the conversation and discharges the employee. The employee's discharge would be unlawful under Section 8(a)(1) of the Act even though that employee was the *only* one supporting a union because the employee was seeking to induce group support. Similarly, an employee who advocates a strike to other employees or who posts a union meeting notice is engaged in concerted activity because the employee is seeking to induce group activity whether or not anyone else joins the strike or attends the meeting. A union exists only because employees individually decide to form, join, and assist the organization. These individual acts are protected by Section 7 of the Act.

Although it is well established that an employee acting as part of a group or to induce group activity as discussed above is engaged in concerted activity, there has been a question as to whether an employee who protests a working condition that affects other employees as well is engaged in concerted activity if the employee's protest is only by or for that individual employee. For many years the Board has followed the "*Interboro* doctrine"[6] under which an employee acting alone who asserts a contract right is engaged in a Section 7 concerted activity even though the protest is only for that employee. Some courts of appeals refused to enforce Board decisions applying the doctrine, but in *NLRB v. City Disposal*

---

[6] See legal principle 6.A.

Systems, Inc. the United States Supreme Court upheld this *Interboro* doctrine in full.[7]

In *City Disposal,* the collective bargaining agreement provided that an employee could refuse to operate a vehicle that was not in safe operating condition "unless such refusal is unjustified." A driver refused to drive a vehicle on the grounds that something was wrong with the brakes, but he did not specifically refer to the contractual safety clause as the basis for his refusal. The company discharged the driver. The NLRB, applying the *Interboro* doctrine, ruled that the discharge violated Section 8(a)(1). The employer appealed the Board decision to the court of appeals that reversed the Board. The court of appeals took a narrow view that an employee is engaged in concerted activities *only* if the employee is protesting on behalf of other employees as well or is protesting to induce group conduct. The Supreme Court, however, reversed the appellate court and upheld the Board's position in full. The Court held that an employee acting alone asserting a contractual right is engaged in concerted activity even though the complaint concerns only the individual employee if the employee's statement or action is based on a reasonable and honest belief that the employee is being, or has been, asked to perform a task that the employee is not required to perform under the contract.

The Court also decided two other important issues in *City Disposal* as to concerted activity. First, the Court upheld the Board's position that an employee need not specifically refer to the contract to be engaged in concerted activity as long as the nature of the employee's complaint is reasonably clear to the person to whom it is made and the complaint does in fact refer to a reasonably perceived contract violation. Second, the Court also upheld the Board's view that an employee's refusal or protest is concerted whether or not the employee is ultimately proven right or wrong on the issue as long

as the employee acted on an honest and reasonable belief that the employee's contract right had been violated.

As discussed more fully below, sometimes certain conduct may be *concerted* under Section 7 but still not be *protected.* Thus, an employee who strikes in breach of a contractual no-strike clause is engaged in *concerted* activity, but the strike is *unprotected* (and the employee is therefore subject to discipline) because the no-strike clause is a waiver of the right to strike during the term of the contract. In *City Disposal* the Supreme Court stated that although the driver's refusal to drive the truck was concerted because he reasonably and honestly invoked his contractual right, the refusal might not be protected if the contract only permitted a driver to refuse to drive a truck that was in fact unsafe. The Supreme Court remanded (returned) the case to the court of appeals to determine whether the driver's conduct was protected. On remand the court of appeals subsequently ruled that the refusal was protected because the contract permitted a driver to refuse a truck that the driver in good faith believed was unsafe. The discharge was therefore unlawful under Section 8(a)(1).

2. Protests Affecting Other Employees as Concerted Activity

If an employee protests a matter that concerns only that employee, and is not enforcing a contract right as discussed above, the protest is not concerted activity. However, for many years, the Board took the position that if an individual employee protested a working condition that affected other employees as well, the employee was engaged in concerted activity under Section 7 even though no other employee joined in the complaint. The Board *presumed* that the other affected employees supported the individual's actions unless there was evidence that they in fact disavowed the individual's actions. Thus, for example, if a single employee complained to a governmental agency about plant conditions violating fed-

[7] See legal principle 6.A.

eral or state employment standards, and the employer discharged the employee as a result, the discharge would violate Section 8(a)(1) of the Act. In *Meyers Industries* the Board reversed this prior long-standing position.[8] Instead the Board ruled that an employee who individually protests a working condition (except one violating a collective bargaining agreement) is not engaged in concerted activity unless the employee's action is *in fact* engaged in with or on the authority of other employees, not solely by and on behalf of the individual employee.

Furthermore, the employee is not protected unless the employer knows that the employee is not acting solely in the employee's own behalf. Thus in *Meyers* the Board upheld the discharge of a driver who complained to state officials about an unsafe truck. Other employees drove the same truck, but the employee complained only for himself, not with or on the authority of the others.

The Board's narrow interpretation of the protected status of an individual employee's protest has been upheld by the courts of appeals as within the Board's broad discretion to interpret and apply the Act. The Board has, however, softened the impact of *Meyers* to an extent by ruling that an employee may be protected if the employee is acting with the knowledge and implied approval of other employees. Thus if a group of employees discuss their working conditions, and one of the group states that he or she is going to file a complaint over the matter with the appropriate governmental agency, the employee's action would be concerted even though the other employees did not expressly authorize the employee to speak for them as well. Of course, under *Meyers,* the employer must also know that the employee is protesting for the other employees as well for the conduct to be protected.

What if employees discuss a problem among themselves and agree that it should be brought to their employer's attention?

[8] See legal principle 6.B.

One of the employees volunteers to be the spokesperson, but the other employees—while agreeing with the employee's action—ask that the employee not mention their names. Under the Board's prior approach, the employee brave enough to confront the employer without revealing that other employees support the action would be engaged in protected concerted activities if the employee were asserting a right of interest to the group as a whole. Under *Meyers* this employee would not be protected by the Act unless the employer had knowledge in some other way (e.g., a supervisor heard the employees' discussion) that the employee was in fact representing one or more other employees.

Remember that the *Meyers Industries* doctrine does not apply to an employee asserting a contract right. The *City Disposal* decision clearly establishes that even a bargaining unit employee acting alone asserting a contract right is engaged in concerted activities if the employee is reasonably and honestly asserting the right. Furthermore, an individual employee also has the right under Section 502 of the Act to refuse to perform work that is abnormally dangerous (see discussion in Chapter Six).

Finally, even if the discharge of an employee does not violate the Labor Management Relations Act, the employee may have other remedies. The discharge of an employee for filing a charge with the Occupational Safety and Health Administration (OSHA) would violate Section 11(c) of that Act prohibiting employer retaliation for filing a charge. If the discharged employee is covered by a collective bargaining agreement, an arbitrator may find that the employee's discharge was not for just cause even though it did not violate Section 8(a)(1) of the LMRA. In most states, an employee who is not covered by a collective bargaining agreement may be discharged "at will" (for any reason or no reason at all). However, some states have modified this rule so that an employee discharged for protesting unsafe conditions to a governmental agency may be able to sue in state court for wrongful discharge. (As discussed in Chapter Fourteen, however, in regard to the preemption doctrine, employees subject to a collective bargaining agreement may, depending upon the circumstances, be limited to arbitration as the exclusive remedy.)

3. Protection of Supervisors' Rights

Supervisors are excluded from the definition of employee under Section 2(3) of the Labor Management Relations Act, and have no statutory right to engage in collective bargaining. Thus, for example, an employer can discharge a supervisor (meeting the definition under Section 2(11) of the Act) for joining or participating in union activities. At one time the Board took the position that the discharge of a supervisor could violate the Act if the employer discharged the supervisor in order to "chill" the employees' union activity. The Board's current view, however, is that the discharge of a supervisor violates the Act only if it directly interferes with the right of employees to engage in concerted activities. The Board listed three such instances of interference: the discharge of a supervisor for giving testimony adverse to an employer's interest either at an NLRB proceeding or during the processing of an employee's grievance under the collective bargaining agreement; the discharge of a supervisor for refusing to commit unfair labor practices against employees; or discharge because the supervisor fails to prevent unionization of the employees under the supervisor's responsibility. The Board reasoned that the protection of supervisors from employer pressure to engage in such conduct is necessary to vindicate and protect the employees' exercise of their protected rights under Section 7.

4. Right to a Shop Steward in Disciplinary Proceedings

One of the fundamental rights of collective bargaining is that an employee upon request may have a shop steward present if the employee is questioned by the employer about a matter that could lead to disciplinary action against the employee. The right to a steward is a Section 7 right of concerted activity protected by Section 8(a)(1). This is commonly called the *"Weingarten* right," after the Supreme Court decision upholding the Board ruling establishing the basic principle.[9] However, the employee must ask for the steward. The employer has no obligation to tell an employee of the right before questioning begins.

The Board distinguishes between an employer meeting with an employee during a general investigation versus a meeting for possible discipline. An employee does not have a right to a steward if the employer is simply investigating the circumstances of an event that may lead to discipline. If the employee is definitely to be disciplined or if the employer is contemplating such discipline, the employee is entitled to the steward upon request.

How does the employee know the purpose of the meeting? Basically, the employee is entitled to the steward if the investigation is focused on the employee and the employee reasonably believes that the employee may be facing discipline. For example, if an employee has been frequently absent, and the employer calls the employee into a meeting to discuss attendance, the employee can reasonably conclude that the meeting might lead to discipline for poor attendance. The employee would then be entitled to his steward upon request. But if some tools have been stolen and the employer is questioning every employee in the bargaining unit to see what they know, the investigation is not focused on one person and no employee has the right to a shop steward. Of course, at a given point, the investigation may be focused on a few employees who might be disciplined. They would be entitled to a steward upon request.

Because an innocent employee might be the focus of an investigation, the request of a shop steward is certainly not an admission of guilt. Even an innocent employee would

[9] See legal principle 7.A.

be well advised to request his steward. The employee may not be able to explain a situation clearly or may make innocent mistakes of fact that lead the employer to believe erroneously that the employee has committed a disciplinary offense. Having the steward present might avoid this.

a. Employer Choice if an Employee Requests His Steward.
If an employee requests a steward based on a reasonable belief of possible discipline, the employer has three choices: The employer can stop the meeting; call in the shop steward and continue the investigation in the steward's presence; or tell the employee that the meeting will be terminated unless the employee voluntarily agrees to proceed without a steward. Some employees incorrectly believe that if the employer stops the meeting, the employee cannot be disciplined at all. That is not true. The employer cannot discipline the employee for requesting a steward and cannot question the employee in the steward's absence without the employee's consent. However, the employer can discipline the employee for the alleged misconduct based on the information the employer already has. There is no statutory requirement that the employer question an employee before imposing discipline. Of course, if the employee's discipline is arbitrated, the employer has the burden of proving just cause for the discipline taken. If the employer chooses not to interview the disciplined employee with the steward present, the employer might not have sufficient evidence to prove just cause.

b. Steward Opportunity to Meet with the Employee.
If an employee requests a steward, the employee is entitled to meet in private with the steward before the disciplinary meeting is held. The Board reasons that, to be an effective advocate, the steward needs time to find out the facts ahead of time from the employee in order to advise the employee and prepare a defense. The steward has the right to meet with the employee privately for a reasonable period but not to call in other employees or make

a full investigation of the facts. Also, before meeting with the employee, the steward, upon request, may require the employer to state the general subject matter of the employee interview and to identify the misconduct for which the discipline may be imposed. However, the employer does not have to reveal the information it has obtained or the specifics of the misconduct to be discussed.

The employer is not obligated to offer time for the steward to meet with the employee in private. The steward must request it. If the employee requests a steward, and the steward is called into a room with the employer present, the steward should immediately request that the employer state the subject matter of the interview and the misconduct for which discipline may be imposed, and then request a recess to meet with the employee in private. Again, if the employer does not wish to give the steward time, the employer may refuse, stop the interview, and base the decision on the available information if it is sufficient.

Some employers have permitted an employee to have a steward present upon request, but then have demanded that the steward remain silent and only serve as a witness to the interview. It is unlawful to restrict the steward's role in this manner. Rather, the steward has the right to assist and counsel the questioned employee and must therefore be permitted to take an active role. However, the Board has also emphasized that the employee interview is in the nature of an investigation, not an adversary contest or a collective bargaining session. Thus, the employer does have a limited right to restrict the role of the steward to that of defending the employee, and to prevent the steward from turning the interview into a grievance session on the merits of the disciplinary action.

The Board's decisions also emphasize that an employee does not necessarily have a right to the steward of the employee's choice. Thus, for example, if the union has assigned a particular steward to a department, an employee facing a disciplinary interview cannot request another steward whom the employee personally prefers. If the employee refuses the assistance of the assigned steward, the employer can lawfully question the employee without any steward being present. Also, the employee cannot insist on a specific steward, even the one usually assigned to the employee's area by the union, if the steward is unavailable for personal reasons or reasons for which the employer is not responsible and another steward is available. If, in contrast, the requested steward cannot be present because of work duties, a matter within the employer's control, then the employer may be required to wait until the steward is available, unless another authorized steward is available. If, through no fault of the employer, no steward is available within a reasonable time after an employer calls in an employee for a disciplinary interview (such as if the union has not assigned a steward to a particular shift) the employer does not have to postpone the investigation until someone is available. It is the union's responsibility to have a steward present during work hours and to make sure the employee knows the person to contact. However, if no steward is available under these circumstances, the employee may request the presence of another rank-and-file employee unless the collective bargaining agreement prohibits the employee from being represented by anyone but the authorized steward.

The right to have a steward present applies only if the employee is to be questioned. There is no right to a steward if the employer has already made the decision to discipline and simply hands the employee the disciplinary notice or orally tells the employee of the decision without asking any questions. The right to a steward begins at the time of the interview. Thus, an employee asked to leave the work area and report to an office, who suspects disciplinary action, has no right to a steward before leaving, and can be lawfully disciplined for insubordination for refusing to leave. The refusal is unprotected activity. However, if the employee is questioned in the work area, or taken to an office or some other location outside the work area for questioning, the employee is entitled to representation before answering.

Although the Board requires that an employee ask for a steward, nothing prevents the union from negotiating stronger contractual protection. Thus, the contract may require the employer, rather than the employee, to call in the steward whenever an employee is to be questioned or disciplined.

Although the Board cases are not totally clear on the point, the language in some decisions indicates that an employee has the right to request the presence of a co-employee, rather than a shop steward, even if the steward is available, unless the collective bargaining requires the presence of a union representative. Even if the employee has this right, the better practice would certainly be to request the steward, who would be more knowledgeable about the employee's rights, the contract, and the grievance procedure.

For many years, the Board's view was that if an employee was disciplined for conduct that was the subject of an improperly conducted ("tainted") disciplinary interview, it would presume that the disciplinary action was based on the unlawfully obtained information. The Board ordered the employer to rescind the disciplinary action and pay the employee backpay unless the employer could prove that the disciplinary action was not based on the improper information. The Board imposed this remedy even though it required an employer to reinstate an employee who committed an offense that would have otherwise justified disciplinary action. In *Taracorp Industries* the Board reversed this position[10] and held that it would no longer order the reinstatement of an employee discharged for cause even if the evidence was obtained in an improperly conducted interview. It will only order the employer to cease and desist from im-

---

[10] See legal principle 7.B.

proper questioning. The Board based its decision on Section 10(c) of the Act providing that "no order of the Board shall require the reinstatement of any . . . employee who has been suspended or discharged . . . for cause." Note that the term "for cause" in Section 10(c) does not have the same meaning as contractual "just cause." A discharge is "for cause" under Section 10(c) as long as it is not for a reason prohibited by the Act (e.g., discharge for engaging in union activities) even though the grounds might not constitute "just cause" as arbitrators have interpreted the term. The Board did state in *Taracorp*, however, that it will continue to require reinstatement of an employee if an employer discharges the employee for requesting a steward when the employee is legally entitled to representation. The discharge for asserting *Weingarten* rights would not constitute a discharge for cause under Section 10(c).

So far the courts of appeals that have considered the issue have upheld the Board's narrow remedy under *Taracorp* as within the Board's discretion. Obviously, however, the decision encourages employers to interview an employee without a steward over the employee's objection to obtain evidence against the employee. Thus, unions should consider negotiating specific contract provisions requiring that a shop steward be present whenever an employee is questioned. Even without such provisions, some arbitrators, despite the *Taracorp* decision, may not allow employers to use improperly obtained evidence at an arbitration hearing on the grounds that the evidence violates an employee's right to disciplinary due process embodied within the concept of contractual just cause.

c. Rights of Unorganized Employees to Assistance by Another Worker. As discussed above, even unorganized employees have the statutory right to engage in concerted activities. Therefore, the Board initially ruled that even an unrepresented employee has the right to be assisted by a co-worker upon the employee's request if the employee is being questioned about a matter that could lead to disciplinary action to the same extent that an employee represented by a union may request assistance by a shop steward. However, the Reagan Board reversed this position and held that an unrepresented employee has no right to assistance. In reaching this decision, the Board acknowledged that Section 7 could be interpreted to protect unrepresented employees, but decided as a matter of policy that the right to representation should apply only to employees in unionized workplaces. The Board reasoned that the nonunion employer's interest in conducting investigations in accordance with its own practices and procedures and in maintaining efficient operations outweighed the benefit to an unrepresented employee in having another employee present.

The questions of the appropriate remedy if an employee is improperly questioned and the application of the *Weingarten* principles to unrepresented employees are of such importance that they may ultimately reach the Supreme Court.

5. Steward's Right to Free Expression

Protection against employer retaliation for statements made during the course of grievance meetings is an important right for stewards under Section 8(a)(1). Ordinarily, an employee can be disciplined for disrespect to a supervisor. Disrespect may be insubordination. However, the Board has generally held that a steward cannot be disciplined for abusive remarks made to a supervisor or management officials during a grievance meeting or in a bargaining session. The steward may use profanity or even accuse the employer of lying without fear of discipline. The Board applies this rule so that a steward may speak freely without having to weigh every word said or hold back arguments for fear of overstepping the line.

There are, however, a few exceptions to the steward's very broad rights. The steward cannot threaten an employer representative with physical violence. Also, a steward may be disciplined in extremely aggravated situations if the steward is disrespectful to the employer in the presence of rank-and-file employees to the point that an employer is no longer able to exercise proper control over the work force. Such conduct is unprotected.

6. Communications to Third Parties as Protected Activity

Sometimes employees in a dispute with their employer will discuss the matter with customers, write customers to gain their support, or even distribute fliers or take out newspaper advertisements publicizing the dispute to the general public. Employers may try to prohibit such appeals to outsiders (commonly called "third parties") and discipline employees for doing so, on the grounds that going public with a dispute damages the employer's image and harms the business. However, the Board has upheld the employees' right to seek the help of third parties as protected concerted activity if the appeal is related to a legitimate ongoing labor dispute between the employees and their employer, and the communication does not disparage the employer's product or service. The fact that the employer may, however, be embarrassed by the public disclosure of a particular condition does not prohibit the employees from exposing it, if it relates to the ongoing dispute. For example, a union and employer may be disputing the speed at which a given job function should be performed. It would be lawful protected activity for the employees to write customers informing them of the dispute, and expressing the concern that the higher speed the employer is seeking would reduce a product's quality or service to the customer.

7. Refusal to Cooperate in an Employer Investigation as Protected Activity

Employers sometimes try to question employees about the factual basis of a pending unfair labor charge or union grievance against the employer. If an employee, upon questioning, provides the employer with needed information, the union's position in the dispute, as the representative of the employees, may be weakened. Thus, an employer's questioning of individual employees may, in a sense, interfere with the employees' right to engage in concerted activity through their union under Section 8(a)(1). Can the employer require an employee to provide it with information and discipline the employee for refusing?

a. Unfair Labor Practice Matters. The Board has attempted to draw a balance between the right of an employer to question its employees versus the danger that such questioning may interfere with or coerce employees in their right to engage in protected concerted activity. Thus, the Board has held that if an employer wishes to question an individual employee about a pending unfair labor practice charge, in preparation of its defense, the employer must tell the employee the purpose of the questioning, assure the employee that there will be no reprisal, and obtain the employee's participation on a voluntary basis. If the employee agrees to the questioning, the questioning itself must be noncoercive and cannot go beyond the information needed to defend the charge. The employer cannot question the employee generally about the activities of other employees or the employee's own views about the union. These principles are known as the "*Johnnie's Poultry* doctrine"[11] after the lead case on the issues.

If an employee has given a statement to the Board during the course of a Board investigation of an unfair practice charge, the employee cannot be required to provide the employer with a copy. An employer may obtain a copy from the employee voluntarily only if it assures the employee that there will be no retaliation if the employee refuses and the employer needs the statement for its trial preparation. Requiring an employee to answer questions about a pending unfair labor practice charge or to provide the

[11] See legal principle 9.

employer with a copy of the employee's Board statement, except under these limited circumstances, is regarded as unlawful coercion of the employee's right to engage in concerted activity. The Supreme Court has also held that an employer has no right to a copy of an employee's statement in the Board's investigatory file of a charge. The statement is exempt from disclosure under the Freedom of Information Act.

b. Grievance Matters. An employer has broader rights to question an employee about grievance matters. An employer has the general right to question employees about conditions in the plant. Thus, although an employee who is personally subject to disciplinary action may refuse to answer questions without a shop steward being present, an employee who is not the personal subject of the investigation has no statutory right to refuse to answer questions and no right to have a steward present. This is true even though the employee's answers may be harmful to another employee, or contrary to the position of the union on a particular issue. However the employer cannot pry into matters beyond the matter in dispute or seek to uncover internal union positions or strategy.

Stewards have a right to protect the information they obtain in the course of their duties in contract administration, the investigation and processing of grievances, and bargaining. Thus an employer cannot question a steward about the steward's conversation with an employee facing disciplinary action. The Board has stated that a steward's right to talk in private with an employee is one of the basic Section 7 rights and that compelling the steward to disclose the information would have a chilling effect upon the entire bargaining unit. However, even a steward who has firsthand knowledge of a matter as an employee rather than information gathered as a steward might be subject to discipline for refusing to answer employer questions the same as any other employee. The Board has also upheld an employer's right to discipline a steward for advising employees who witnessed an incident that could result in disciplinary action against co-workers not to answer the employer's questions about what happened.

8. Concerted Versus Protected Concerted Activity

Some employees incorrectly believe that all concerted activity is protected from employer retaliation. That is not true. Employee conduct basically falls into three categories under the LMRA. First, there is conduct protected under Sections 7 and 8(a)(1), such as the right to form a union and to solicit and distribute literature in appropriate places. An employer cannot discipline an employee for engaging in such protected activities. Second, there is conduct prohibited by Section 8(b), such as unlawful secondary boycotts (see Chapter Seven). Third, there is conduct that is neither prohibited nor protected by the Act.

An employee engages in conduct in the third category at his or her own risk. It is not an unfair labor practice to engage in such conduct, but, since the activity is not protected, the employer can take disciplinary action in retaliation without committing an unfair labor practice. A union, as a lever in bargaining, might engage in petty harrassment against the employer. Employees might engage in quickie strikes, slowdowns, or sit-ins. That is lawful, concerted activity as long as there is no contractual no-strike clause in effect. However, although this conduct is lawful, it is not protected. This means that an employee who takes part in such conduct is subject to discipline.

The LMRA does not prohibit strikes in breach of a contractual no-strike clause, but such conduct is unprotected and is subject to employer discipline.

Sometimes concerted activity may be unprotected if it is tantamount to insubordination. For example, in one case a nonunion employer adopted a new rule prohibiting employees from leaving the premises during their lunch break. The employees went out for lunch in direct defiance of the rule. The

Board held that this conduct amounted to insubordination and was therefore unprotected. Note, however, that if the employees had demanded a meeting with management to protest the rule or even if they had walked out in protest, their conduct (in the absence of a contractual no-strike clause) would have been upheld as protected concerted activity. The Board said that the employees could not have it both ways—defying the rule while continuing to work.

D. DISCRIMINATION AS TO HIRE, TENURE, OR TERMS AND CONDITIONS OF EMPLOYMENT

Section 8(a)(3) prohibits discrimination regarding hiring, tenure of employment, or conditions of employment with the intent to encourage or discourage membership in a labor organization. This section applies to such conduct as discharging an employee, denying a promotion, denying or reducing an employee's benefits, giving an employee more difficult work, or requiring an employee to work under less favorable conditions than other employees. Section 8(b)(2) prohibits a union from causing or attempting to cause an employer to discriminate against an employee in violation of Section 8(a)(3). It is also a violation of Section 8(b)(1)(A) for a union to accept unlawful support.

One of the most common mistaken beliefs is that the Board has jurisdiction over any unjust discharge regardless of the reason. That is not so. The Board has jurisdiction only over a discharge, or other discrimination, that violates Section 8(a)(3). The discrimination must be with the intent to encourage or discourage membership in a labor organization. Thus disciplinary action may possibly violate a contractual just clause provision but not violate the Act.

1. Section 8(a)(1) versus 8(a)(3) Violations: The Intent Requirement

The acts prohibited by Section 8(a)(3) are narrower than those prohibited by Section 8(a)(1), discussed above. Section 8(a)(1) prohibits any type of employer conduct interfering with, restraining, or coercing employees in the exercise of their rights protected by Section 7. In contrast, Section 8(a)(3) applies only to discrimination in employment or terms of employment. Also, Section 8(a)(3) requires that discrimination be with the *intent* of encouraging or discouraging union membership. The intent to encourage or discourage membership has been interpreted broadly to include intent to encourage or discourage union activity in general. In contrast, Section 8(a)(1) does not expressly require that conduct have an anti-union intent as Section 8(a)(3) does.

The courts and the Board, in comparing the language of Sections 8(a)(1) and (3), have held that there does not have to be an anti-union intent (animus) in order for an employer to violate Section 8(a)(1) if the employer's actions are destructive of employee rights under Section 7. For example, an employer may have a rule barring all solicitation of any kind in the plant. That rule is valid except as applied to union solicitation (see chapter Three). The rule may have been in effect long before there was any union activity and might not have any anti-union intent. Once a union begins an organizing drive, however, the employer violates Section 8(a)(1) by enforcing the rule because the rule infringes on the employees' right to engage in concerted activity.

Note that every violation of Section 8(a)(3) also necessarily violates Section 8(a)(1). Any discrimination with intent to encourage or discourage union activity infringes on the employee's Section 7 rights. On the other hand, every violation of Section 8(a)(1) does not violate Section 8(a)(3). An act might violate Section 8(a)(1) because it interferes with protected concerted activity, but it might not violate Section 8(a)(3) unless discriminatory intent can be proven.

2. Proving Anti-union Intent

How do you prove the anti-union animus (intent) required to prove a Section 8(a)(3) violation? Few if any employers are going to admit their motive. The Board and the courts have established two basic ways to prove the motive. First, there may be direct evidence to establish the employer's unlawful intent. Second, the "natural consequences" of an employer's actions may be so destructive of an employee's right to engage in union activity (or to refrain from such activity) that the employer's intent can be inferred from the conduct itself even though there is no direct evidence of an anti-union animus.

a. Direct Evidence of an Unlawful Intent.
Suppose the union's chief supporter in a plant is discharged for alleged poor work performance. Section 10(c) of the Act provides that the Board cannot order the reinstatement or backpay for an employee discharged or suspended for "cause" (i.e., for any reason not prohibited by the Act). Usually an employer charged with violating Section 8(a)(3) tries to show a lawful cause for its actions, such as the employee's alleged poor work performance, poor attendance, violation of company work rules, or insubordination, etc. The Board considers a number of factors in determining whether the employee was in fact discharged for union activities or for the lawful reason alleged by the employer. The Board considers whether the evidence establishes that the employee in fact engaged in the conduct that the employer has asserted as the lawful reason for discharge or discipline. If, for example, an employer alleges that an employee was discharged for being intoxicated on the job, but the employer lacks proof to substantiate the charge, the Board may very well conclude that the employee was discharged for union activities rather than for the employer's unsubstantiated reason. The Board will also consider whether the employer changes the alleged lawful reasons for the discipline. If, for example, the employer cannot prove that an employee's work performance was unsatisfactory as initially alleged but then asserts that the employee was in fact discharged for insubordination, the Board may conclude that the employer's shift in the alleged reason indicates that the employee's union activity was the true motive.

The Board will also consider whether the employee was first warned before being discharged for the alleged lawful reason and whether the employer departed from its usual disciplinary procedures in the case. Thus, if the employer normally follows progressive discipline, advancing from a warning to a suspension and ultimately to discharge, but discharges a union supporter for the first offense, the Board may regard this unusual action as evidence of unlawful discrimination. That a discharged employee received disparate treatment, that is, harsher discipline than other employees committing the same offense, is strong evidence of a discriminatory intent. The timing of disciplinary action is also important. If the time between the employee's union activity and the disciplinary action is relatively close, the Board is likely to conclude that the union activity, not some intervening event, was the motive for the employer's action. None of the factors listed above is conclusive in every case, but one or more of them taken together may be sufficient to establish the employer's unlawful motive.

The Board will also consider whether the lawful reasons given by the employer for its disciplinary action are a pretext. For example, what if the employer has put up with an employee's poor work performance for a long time without imposing any discipline, but then discharges the employee for poor performance shortly after the employee becomes active in a union's organizing drive? The Board may conclude that the employee was, in fact, discharged because of union activities even if the employer can substantiate that the employee was a poor worker. A reason for discharge that might otherwise be valid may be unlawful under Section 8(a)(3) if it was, in fact, in retaliation for an employee's union activities.

b. Natural Consequences Establishing the Employer's Intent. The Board has also held that an employer's intent can be inferred from the natural consequences of an employer's actions. The leading case in applying the natural consequences test is the *Radio Officers* decision.[12] In this case, the employer, at the union's request, discharged certain employees who had not joined the union or who were disfavored by the union. The employer was charged with violating Section 8(a)(3) by discharging the employees. The union also violated Section 8(b)(2) by causing the employer to engage in the discrimination. The employer argued that it was simply following the union's orders and did not have any anti-union intent to encourage or discourage union membership. The Board, in a decision upheld by the Supreme Court, rejected this argument. It reasoned that Section 8(a)(3) not only prohibits discrimination to encourage union membership, but also discrimination to encourage an employee to be a "good member" who, for example, does not oppose the union's policies. The Board stated the natural consequences of firing an employee improperly at the union's request is to encourage union membership or good membership in violation of Section 8(a)(3), because employees may fear that they will be discharged at the union's request if they incur the union's disfavor.

INHERENTLY DESTRUCTIVE CONDUCT. Board and Court decisions applying the natural consequences test sometimes distinguish between acts that are inherently destructive of an employee's right to engage in union activity regardless of the employer's motive and acts that have a lesser ("comparatively slight") impact. If an action is inherently destructive, the conduct may be unlawful under Section 8(a)(3) of the Act regardless of the employer's business justification if the Board determines that the adverse impact outweighs the justification. There is no need to prove that the employer

acted with an anti-union motive in such a case. Thus, economic strikers cannot be *discharged* regardless of the employer's good faith business reasons for doing so (see Chapter Six) because discharge is so destructive of the employees' right to strike. However, if an employer's conduct falls into the second category of lesser impact, and the employer produces evidence of a legitimate and substantial business reason for its action, the conduct is unlawful only if there is proof that the employer in fact acted with an anti-union motivation rather than for the purported lawful reason. (If the employer does not produce evidence of a legitimate business reason, then "lesser" conduct may also be unlawful in itself, as in the case of inherently destructive conduct.) Thus, employers have the right to *replace* economic strikers permanently because the Board, as upheld by the Supreme Court, has concluded that such replacement falls into this second category of lesser adverse impact and employers have a legitimate and substantial business justification for hiring permanent replacements to remain open during a strike. Such conduct would be unlawful only if there is proof that the employer hired permanent replacements for the purpose of discouraging union activity rather than to maintain operations.

c. Greater Discipline of Union Officers as a Section 8(a)(3) Violation. The Supreme Court's decision in *Metropolitan Edison Co.* is an important example of the application of Section 8(a)(3).[13] In that case, bargaining unit employees at the utility, in violation of a contractual no-strike clause, refused to cross a picket line established at the plant by an outside construction union. Union officers participated in the walkout, but were not strike leaders. In fact the officers tried to convince the picketing construction union to remove its pickets so that the employees could return to work. The company demanded that the union officials cross the line and return to work immedi-

---

[12] See legal principle 5.

[13] See legal principle 5.

ately, but the officers refused because they believed that the other employees would not return while the picket line was up and that it would be more effective for the officers to stay out and persuade the other union to take down the picket line. The company imposed five- to ten-day suspensions on the rank-and-file employees who participated in the work stoppage but it suspended the union officers for twenty-five days. The union officers filed an unfair labor practice charge alleging that imposing greater discipline on them than on the other employees violated Section 8(a)(3) of the Act.

Under the *Precision Castings Co.* doctrine,[14] an employer violates Section 8(a)(3) of the Act if it imposes greater discipline on union officers than on rank-and-file members who have committed the same offense because such disparate discipline discourages employees from becoming officers. The Board applied this doctrine in the *Metropolitan Edison* case and found that the company had violated Section 8(a)(3) by imposing greater discipline on the union officers who had participated in but had not led the strike. The case ultimately reached the United States Supreme Court, which upheld the Board in full. The Court noted that there was no direct evidence that the company had an anti-union intent in imposing greater discipline on the union officers, but the Court said that the intent could be inferred from the conduct itself. The Court upheld the Board's view that imposing greater discipline on union officers has an adverse affect by deterring qualified employees from holding office. The company, however, alleged what it regarded as a legitimate reason for imposing greater discipline on the officers: They had an implied duty to uphold the terms of the collective bargaining agreement. The Court, applying the Section 8(a)(3) balancing test discussed above, balanced the adverse impact on the union officers against the company's business justification, and concluded that the adverse impact outweighed the

justification. The Court noted that the company disciplined the officers because they refused to take the steps (return to work) that the company wanted them to take to end the strike. The Court reasoned that such disciplinary power would give the company too much control over the union's officials in the performance of their duties and place the officers in a conflict between employer pressures and their duty to the union. That would be contrary to the basic statutory principle (discussed above) that labor unions must be free from employer domination to perform their functions properly. Therefore, the court concluded on balance that this adverse impact outweighed the justification so that the discipline violated Section 8(a)(3).

Note that the company could have lawfully imposed greater discipline on the union's officers if they had led the strike. In that case, the discipline would have been based on their conduct, not discriminatorily based on their status as union officers. What if a collective bargaining agreement requires the union's officers to take affirmative steps to end a work stoppage in violation of the contractual no-strike clause? In that case, even under the *Precision Casting* doctrine, an employer can lawfully discipline union officers who fail to live up to their contractual commitment. The Supreme Court specifically held in *Metropolitan Edison* that an agreement requiring union officers to take affirmative steps to end an unlawful work stoppage is lawful and enforceable.

3. Mixed-Motive Employer Conduct

An employer's disciplinary action against an employee may be based on both the employee's union activity (a protected right) and misconduct related solely to the employee's work. For example, an employer might be unhappy about but tolerate an employee's union activities. The employer may be looking for an opportunity to discharge the employee for a lawful reason. The employee commits a work-related offense (such as failing to call in while absent

---

[14] See legal principle 5.

or substandard work performance) and the employer quickly discharges the employee based upon the misconduct. If the employer was looking for a chance to discharge the employee, is the discharge unlawful for that reason, or lawful because it was based upon misconduct unrelated to the employee's union activities?

For many years, the Board took the position that if an employee's discharge is based even in part on the employee's exercise of protected concerted activity, then the discharge is unlawful under Sections 8(a)(1) and (3) even though there were other lawful grounds on which the discharge could have been based. However, many of the courts of appeals regarded this standard as too restrictive on the employer's statutory right under Section 10(c) to suspend or discharge employees for cause.

In response to the appellate court criticism, the Board in the *Wright Line* decision[15] adopted a new approach to mixed-motive cases that was subsequently upheld by the Supreme Court in full. Under *Wright Line,* the Board required the general counsel to make a prima facie (legally sufficient) showing to support the inference that the employee's exercise of protected conduct was a "motivating factor" in the employer's decision to discipline the employee. If protected conduct was a motivating factor, the burden of proof then shifts to the employer to demonstrate that it would have taken the same action even without the employee's protected conduct being considered. If the employee's protected activities were a motivating factor of the employer's action, in that the employer would not otherwise have taken the action, then the relative weight that the activities had in the employer's decision, compared to the other lawful grounds that the employer also considered, does not matter. It is sufficient that the employee's concerted activities be a cause, not that they be a major or dominant cause. As the Board stated in *Wright Line:*

It is enough that the employees' protected activities are causally related to the employer action which is the basis of the complaint. Whether that 'cause' was the straw that broke the camel's back or a bullet between the eyes, if it was enough to determine events, it is enough to come within the proscription of the Act.

Even if the employer does meet the *Wright Line* standard of demonstrating that it would have taken the same action even in the absence of the protected conduct, the employer's action may still be unlawful if the general counsel proves that the employer's purported reason was a pretext, as discussed above, and that the employee was in fact discharged for engaging in protected concerted activities.

4. Proving Employer's Knowledge of Union Activity

In order to prove a Section 8(a)(3) violation, it is necessary to prove that the employer had knowledge of union activity. An employer cannot possibly take an act to discourage or encourage union activity if it does not even know that the activity is taking place. Thus, employers frequently allege as a defense that they were unaware of the union's activity. Usually, however, it is not difficult to prove the employer's knowledge. The employer's knowledge can, for example, be shown through supervisors' statements about the union indicating their knowledge of union activity. Some unions purposely notify an employer when they undertake an organizing drive so there can be no question about the employer's knowledge in case union supporters are later discharged or discriminated against.

The Board also applies the so-called "small shop rule," in which the Board presumes that employers in a small shop (usually employing ten or fewer employees) know if a union organizing campaign is underway. The basis of this rule is the presumption that an employer in a small shop knows what is going on. A union organizing drive is usually open enough

---

[15] See legal principle 11.

that a small shop owner is bound to know about it just as the owner knows about other employee matters. What if employees, fearing reprisal, attempt to hide their organizing activities from their employer? In such a case, the Board may refuse to apply the small shop rule because the presumption of employer knowledge is negated by the circumstances.

5. Constructive Discharges

Most Section 8(a)(3) discharge cases involve situations in which an employee is fired. However, in some cases, an employer may not discharge a union supporter, but may make the employee's working conditions so miserable that the employee resigns. Such conduct, called a constructive discharge, violates Section 8(a)(3) just as if the employer had discharged the employee outright.

6. Backpay Remedies for Section 8(a)(3) Violations

An employee who has been discharged or otherwise discriminated against in violation of Section 8(a)(3) (such as the discriminatory denial of overtime or transfer to a lower-paying job) is entitled to backpay for the monetary loss. In the case of a discharged employee, the Board uses a quarterly system to determine the amount owed the employee. An employee's earnings each quarter after the discharge are subtracted from the amount the employee would have earned in that quarter but for being discharged. The backpay owed per quarter is the difference between what the employee actually earned and would have earned.

The Board uses the quarterly system, rather than basing backpay on the total difference between what an employee earned the entire time after being discharged and would have earned but for the discharge, so that an employee fortunate enough to obtain a higher-paying job toward the end of a long unemployment period does not end up with little or no backpay. The large amount received toward the end might balance the total amount the employee would have earned. Yet, the amount earned after months of unemployment realistically cannot make up for the employee's struggle to get by with no income. The Board has determined that the quarter system is a better measure of the employee's true loss than simply subtracting total interim earnings from what the employee would have earned during the same period but for the discharge. The Board also awards interest on backpay owed at the same rate as the Internal Revenue Services uses for tax refunds.

A discharged employee cannot sit back without looking for work, counting on quarterly backpay. The Board requires that employees actively look for and be available for work. An employee who goes back to school full time and is not looking for work, or an employee who goes on an extended vacation, does not receive backpay for those periods. An employee's right to backpay terminates if the employee rejects a valid offer of reinstatement to the same or a substantially equivalent position with full seniority rights. The offer must be clear and unconditional and the employee must be given a reasonable period to return. The amount of backpay due under a Board decision, if disputed, is determined in compliance procedures (see Chapter One).

7. Superseniority and other Contractual Preferences for Shop Stewards and Union Officers

The rules governing the legality of superseniority clauses in a collective bargaining agreement are an excellent example of the practical application of Sections 8(a)(3) and 8(b)(1)(A) to collective bargaining. A superseniority clause grants contractual benefits to union officers based on their status as officers rather than their actual seniority (length of employment), so that, for example, a shop steward with low seniority is retained during a layoff over a more senior rank-and-file bargaining unit employee. Superseniority clauses have a legitimate purpose in maintaining union officials on the job to administer and enforce the contract for the benefit of all employees. However, the application of such clauses falls within the literal language of Section 8(a)(3) (as to the employer) and Section 8(b)(2) (as to the union) because granting certain benefits only to union officers based on their union status is "discrimination." As discussed above, Section 8(a)(3) prohibits discrimination that either encourages or discourages an employee to participate in union activities or be a "good union member," and it is arguable that a superseniority clause encourages employees to be "good union members" so that they will be selected or elected to union office and enjoy superseniority privileges.

a. Seniority Preference. The Board has determined whether superseniority clauses are lawful under Section 8(a)(3) by balancing the adverse impact of a clause on rank-and-file employees against the union's justification. In several early cases striking this balance, the Board held that a contract clause giving union officers superseniority to protect against a layoff or for recall is lawful because the benefit to all employees in the effective administration of the contract at the plant level outweighed the adverse impact. The Board held, however, that superseniority for any other purpose, such as overtime assignments, vacations, shift preference, or days off, was presumptively unlawful. This means that a union has to establish a special legitimate reason to have superseniority for such purposes.

Initially the Board upheld superseniority for layoff and recall purposes not only for shop stewards or officers performing stewardlike functions, but also for any union officer involved in bargaining, grievance administration, or contract administration, including executive board members involved in the overall administration and determination of union policies. However, in *Gulton Electro-Voice* the Board adopted a narrower rule.[16] It held that superseniority is lawful only for union officers who perform steward or stewardlike functions, that is, on-the-job grievance processing or other on-the-job contract administration responsibilities. Superseniority cannot protect other union officers, regardless of their importance to the union, who do not directly participate in such on-the-job functions. For example, suppose a union president participates in the grievance procedure only at the final step meeting prior to arbitration. Even if the president were on layoff, the president could fulfill this duty by coming back for the grievance meeting. Therefore, the president would not be entitled to superseniority unless the president performs some other on-the-job function that required regular presence at work.

Note that superseniority clauses going beyond layoff and recall protection are only presumptively unlawful and may be upheld by the Board if the union establishes a valid purpose for the protection. Thus, for example, the Board has upheld clauses granting superseniority to protect stewards representing a specific department or job classification from being "bumped" (removed) out of the department or classification by a more senior employee during a layoff. Such clauses are lawful because the steward is needed for on-the-job representation of the employees in the department or work group. Superseniority for stewards assigned to a particular shift may be lawful to assure that a steward is on duty on each shift. Superseniority for a shop steward for overtime, weekend, or holiday work may also be lawful if the union can substantiate that the protection is needed to ensure that a steward is present to enforce the contract during such periods.

b. Other Contract Benefits. In *Mead Packaging Company,* the Board applied Sections 8(a)(3) and 8(b)(2) of the Act to limit the right of union officials on leave of absence from their employer to receive employer benefits while on leave.[17] In that case, the

---

[16] See legal principle 12.A.

[17] See legal principle 12.B.

contract required the company to maintain group insurance coverage and grant pension plan credit for employees on leave to hold union office. Employees on leave for other reasons did not receive these benefits. The Board held that granting special benefits to employees on leave of absence to hold union office unlawfully discriminated in favor of the union officers over other employees in violation of Sections 8(a)(3) and 8(b)(2).

The *Mead* decision was criticized by commentators who argued that continued contract benefits for union officers were needed as an incentive for employees to hold union office, and many contracts continued to provide such benefits even though they were technically illegal. Subsequently, in *IBEW Local 1212*,[18] the Board took the rare action of in effect reversing its decision in *Mead Packaging*. In *Local 1212* the Board upheld a contract clause permitting union officers to take a leave of absence for up to two years, subject to renewal, even though a leave for any other reason was limited to only six months and employees on leave for any other reason could not solicit or accept other employment. The Board stated that under the reasoning of the *Mead* decision, granting a longer leave period to employees holding union office appeared to discriminate in favor of employees engaged in union activities. But the Board went on to conclude that the leave provision did not unlawfully tend to encourage employees to become better union members to hold union office in violation of Section 8(a)(3), but rather merely removed a condition (i.e., the loss of seniority) that would otherwise discourage employees from serving as officers. The Board reasoned that a clause preserving seniority rights for officers on union leave did not have the same adverse effect on other employees under Section 8(a)(3) of the Act as a superseniority clause protecting all officers from a layoff. Thus a superseniority clause may encourage employees to

become union officers to gain additional seniority rights they would not otherwise have; in contrast, a union leave provision preserves only the benefits an officer would have as an employee if the officer remained at work. The Board specifically overruled *Mead Packaging* to the extent that it was inconsistent with the Board's reasoning in *Local 1212*. Thus it appears that under the *Local 1212* decision the Board would now uphold the legality of contract clauses granting union officials on leave the right to receive group insurance coverage and pension plan credit, benefits that the Board held were unlawful in *Mead Packaging*, because such provisions only preserve rather than increase the benefits the union officers would receive anyway as employees.

8. Plant Closing or Transfer as a Section 8(a)(1) or 8(a)(3) Violation

In *Darlington Mfg. Co.*,[19] the Textile Workers Union won a representation election at the only plant of a company that was a subsidiary of another company that operated many other mills. Six days after the election, the board of directors voted to close the plant permanently and it ceased operations soon thereafter. The Supreme Court upheld the NLRB's decision that the shutdown violated Section 8(a)(3) of the Act. The Court stated that a single employer had an absolute right to go out of business permanently for any reason including a desire not to be unionized, but the Court ruled that Darlington's conduct was unlawful because it was part of a larger corporation and the employees at the other plants might be discouraged from union activity because of the discriminatory closure. The Court also stated that an employer cannot threaten in advance to shut down if a union wins an election or state that it will reopen the plant if the employees abandon the

---

[18] See legal principle 12.B.

[19] See legal principle 5.

union. Leaving open the possibility that the plant will remain open would put pressure on the employees in violation of Section 8(a)(1).

Is closing a plant a violation of Section 8(a)(1), Section 8(a)(3), or both? The Supreme Court held that a plant closing is such a basic employer right that it could violate the Act only if the closing were intended to discourage union activities at another one of the employer's plants that remained open. Closing a plant cannot be unlawful just because the natural consequence is to undermine a union. As discussed above, an act may violate Section 8(a)(1) regardless of intent, but Section 8(a)(3) requires proof of discriminatory intent. Since the Court requires a showing of intent for a plant closure to be unlawful, a closing is unlawful only if it violates Section 8(a)(3). Thus although Darlington was part of a larger company, the plant could still have been closed down permanently except for the discriminatory intent. Otherwise, even the right to shut down a single plant in a multi-plant chain is absolute. The Court said in this regard:

The closing of an entire business, even though discriminatory, ends the employer–employee relationship; the force of such a closing is entirely spent as to that business when termination of the enterprise takes place. On the other hand, a discriminatory partial closing may have repercussions on what remains of the business, affording the employer leverage for discouraging the free exercise of Section 7 rights among remaining employees of much the same kind as that found to exist in the "run-away shop" and "temporary closing" cases.

The Court also set down the test for determining when a partial closing violates Section 8(a)(3), stating:

While we have spoken in terms of a "partial closing" in the context of the Board's finding that Darlington was part of a larger single enterprise controlled by the Milliken family, we do not mean to suggest that an organizational integration of plants or corporations is a necessary prerequisite to the establishment of such a violation of Section 8(a)(3). If the persons exercising control over a plant that is being closed for anti-union reasons (1) have an interest in another business, whether or not affiliated with or engaged in the same line of commercial activity as the closed plant, of sufficient substantiality to give a promise of their reaping a benefit from the discouragement of unionization in that business; (2) act to close their plant with the purpose of producing such a result; and (3) occupy a relationship to the other business which makes it realistically foreseeable that its employees will fear that such business will also be closed down if they persist in organization activities, we think that an unfair labor practice has been made out.

Note that the Supreme Court does not require a formal tie between two businesses. If the same person were the majority stockholder in two independent corporations, closing one of the two corporations for anti-union reasons might violate Section 8(a)(3), if it could be proven that the majority stockholder could reap a benefit at the remaining plant by closing the other.

An employer violates both Sections 8(a)(1) and 8(a)(3) by transferring a plant to a new location in retaliation for the employees' exercise of their right to collective bargaining. Such conduct is similar to the partial plant closing prohibited by the *Darlington* decision. However a plant transfer may be lawful even if it is made to escape the terms of a collective bargaining agreement. For example, suppose an employer advises the union that the company is in a poor financial situation, and that unless the union agrees to wage concessions, the employer will be forced to move to a new location where labor costs are lower. The union refuses and the employer carries out its "threat" to move. The move would be lawful under Sections 8(a)(1) and (3) because it was for legitimate financial reasons rather than in retaliation against the employees for union activity, as indicated by the fact that the company was willing to remain at the union facility if the union agreed to the concessions. In contrast, however, if an employer closed a facility after its employees voted for a union and reopened at a new location that was nonunion, the Board would undoubtedly find that the conduct violated Sections 8(a)(1) and (3) in the absence of a very clear lawful economic justification for the action. (See Chapter Five for discussion of the employer's duty to bargain before closing a plant or transferring operations to a new facility.)

a. Remedies for Plant Closings or Transfers. The Board has broad power to remedy either the unlawful closing or transfer of a plant. It can require backpay for the employees and can order a plant reopened at its first location. However, if the costs of reopening are unduly burdensome, the Board does not require reopening. The Board may order the employer to offer the terminated employees employment at the remaining plant or, in the case of a runaway shop, at the new location.

The employer may be required to pay employees their travel and relocation expenses and grant the employees seniority rights at their new location based on their original date of employment at the prior location. If relocation is not practical, the Board may require the employer to pay employees until the date they obtain substantially equivalent employment. If an employer can prove that it would have legitimately closed down by a certain date, the Board may limit the employees' backpay to the date the plant would have lawfully closed. The Board may also order the employer to recognize and bargain with the old union at the new location.

Recall the discussion of Board bargaining orders based upon employer unfair labor practices under the *Gissel* case (see Chapter Three). Violations of Sections 8(a)(1) and 8(a)(3), if occurring during an election campaign after a representation petition has been filed, are the types of unlawful conduct upon which the Board may base a bargaining order, provided the total impact is sufficient under the *Gissel* criteria.

E. PROTECTION FOR TESTIFYING IN BOARD PROCEEDINGS

One other important employee protection is afforded by Section 8(a)(4) that prohibits an employer from discharging or otherwise discriminating against an employee because the employee has filed charges or given testimony under the Act. The Board has broadly applied this section to include protection for giving an affidavit in the course of a Board investigation even if the employee does not actually testify. No specific section of the Act prohibits a union from disciplining employees who testify, but the Board has held that a union violates Section 8(b)(1)(A) if it disciplines an employee for filing charges or testifying at a Board proceeding (see Chapter Eleven). The Board reasons that this conduct interferes with an employee's right to engage in or refrain from concerted activity, protected under Section 7.

The Union should make sure that employees subpoenaed to testify in Board proceedings are properly served to be protected under Section 8(a)(4). In one case, the union advised employees that they would be needed as witnesses and that they would formally receive their subpoenas when they arrived for the hearing. The employees asked their employer for the time off, but the plant manager refused because the employees did not have the subpoenas with them. The employees erroneously believed that the subpoenas were already in effect. They attended the Board hearing over their employer's objection and were discharged. The Board held the discharges violated Section 8(a)(4), but a court of appeals reversed the Board's decision and upheld the discharges in full because the subpoenas had not been duly served on the employees. The court found that the company acted solely to avoid a disruption of its business operations not to retaliate against the employees because they were participating in a Board proceeding.

Summary

This chapter considered a union's authority as the bargaining representative after it obtains bargaining rights, either through a Board-conducted election, voluntary recognition, or a bargaining order. It also considered the employees' rights to engage in collective bargaining activities through their union and how those rights are protected under LMRA Sections 8(a)(1) through (8)(a)(4).

Once a union is either recognized voluntarily or certified as the bargaining agent by the NLRB, it has the right of exclusive representation. This means that the employer cannot deal with any other employee representative on wages, hours, or other terms and conditions of employment. There is an exception in LMRA Section 9(a) under which any employee or group of employees has the right at any time "to present grievances to their employer and to have such grievances adjusted without intervention of the bargaining representative." However, the Supreme Court has interpreted this exception very narrowly, ruling that employees may contact their employer outside the grievance procedure, but the employer is not obligated to deal directly with them.

A union must independently represent the views of the employees. It is unfair labor practice for an employer to dominate or interfere with the formation or administration of a union or to contribute financial or other support to it. However, some employer support, such as contractual provisions permitting union officers to conduct union business on company time or free office space in the employer's facility for the union's use, etc., may be lawful if the union was lawfully recognized by the employer, the union is clearly independent with a well-established history of an arm's-length relationship with the company, and the payments and benefits permit the union to perform its collective bargaining functions more effectively. If an employer dominates a union, the union will be disestablished. If an employer unlawfully assists a union, but does not dominate it, the union will be decertified and the employer will be ordered to cease the conduct constituting unlawful assistance.

Except in the construction industry in which Section 8(f) authorizes pre-hire agreements, it is unlawful for an employer to recognize a union that has not established its majority status. It is not unlawful assistance for an employer to continue contract negotiations with an incumbent union and to execute a collective bargaining agreement with the incumbent while a representation petition filed by a rival union is pending. However, if the rival wins the representation election, the contract negotiated while the representation petition is pending is null and void. It is unlawful assistance for an employer to grant initial voluntary recognition to one union while a valid representation petition filed by another union is pending. An employer may also lawfully recognize the incumbent union at a new location if it is clear from the outset that sufficient employees will transfer from the existing facility to the new one so that the old employees constitute a majority of the new workforce or if the new and old facilities are so functionally integrated that the new facility constitutes an accretion to the existing facility. An employer and union may also agree that the incumbent union is to be recognized at a new location voluntarily without the need for an NLRB election at such time as the union establishes it majority status at the location.

The Labor Management Relations Act not only protects the union as an entity, through the doctrine of exclusive representation, but also protects the right of each employee under Section 7 to engage in concerted activity or to refrain from such activity. It is an unfair labor practice for either an employer or a union to interfere with, restrain, or coerce employees in their rights. Even an employee acting alone may be engaged in protected concerted activities under certain circumstances if the employee is seeking to induce group activity or is acting as a representative of at least one other employee, or if an employee is attempting to enforce a contractual provision if the employee's statement or action is based on a reasonable and honest belief that the employee is being, or has been, asked to perform a task that the employee is not required to perform under the collective bargaining agreement. Remember, however, that some conduct, such as a strike in breach of a contractual no-strike clause, may be unprotected even though it is concerted.

One of the basic employee rights under Section 7, protected by Section 8(a)(1), is that an employee, upon request, may have the shop steward present to protect the employee's interests if the employee reasonably believes that questioning may lead to disciplinary action against the employee. However, the current Board has weakened this right by holding that it will not order the reinstatement of an employee who has been improperly questioned even though the evidence against the employee was gained in the unlawful interview and by limiting the right to representation only to employees represented by a union.

Shop stewards, or other employees engaged in the negotiation and/or the administration of a contract, enjoy special protection under the Act because of their important role in asserting the concerted activity rights of all employees. Thus, the shop steward is treated as the equal of management in grievance and negotiating sessions. The steward cannot be disciplined for acting in an aggressive or disrespectful manner in carrying out steward duties, except for instances of aggravated misconduct, because the discipline might have a "chilling effect" on the rights of all bargaining unit employees. Similarly, a steward may not be questioned by the employer about evidence the steward uncovers during the course of investigating a grievance, because of the "chilling effect" the interrogation might have on the steward and on the employee's willingness to confide in the steward. However, the employer may have the right to question rank-and-file employees about their individual knowledge of matters under investigation, although a grievance is pending, as long as the employer does not question the employee about the union's internal position or strategy. Because of the importance of unhampered employee access to the NLRB to protect concerted rights, an employer cannot question employees about their knowledge of pending unfair labor practice charges against the employer, or obtain a copy of the employee's Board statement, unless the employer obtains the information voluntarily and assures the employee against reprisals if the employee does not wish to be questioned.

Section 8(a)(3) prohibits discrimination because of union activity in hiring, tenure, or conditions of employment. This prohibits such conduct as discharging an employee because of union activity, denying a promotion, denying or reducing an employee's benefits, giving an employee more difficult work to do, or working an employee under less favorable conditions than other employees. Also, Sections 8(a)(3) and 8(b)(2) prohibit employer discrimination that unlawfully encourages union membership or activity. For this reason, superseniority clauses must be limited to union officers, such as stewards, whose presence is needed at work, or in a particular department or shift, in order for them to carry out duties pertaining to the administration of the collective bargaining agreement.

Conduct that interferes with the basic rights of an employee to engage in concerted activity or to refrain from such activity violates the Act (Section 8(a)(1) or 8(b)(1) as appropriate) regardless of the employer's or the union's intent. In contrast, discrimination is unlawful under Sections 8(a)(3) or 8(b)(2) of the Act only if the discriminatory act is taken with the intent to encourage or discourage union membership or activity. This intent may be established by direct evidence of an employer's anti-union animus, such as negative statements against a union's organizing drive, or inferred from the "natural consequences" of an employer's action, such as the imposition of greater discipline on a union officer who participated in but did not lead an unlawful work stoppage.

An employee's discharge, based even in part on union activities, may be unlawful if the employee's exercise of protected rights was a substantial motivating factor in the employer's decision. Also, a reason for discharge that would otherwise be valid may be unlawful under Section 8(a)(3) if it is used as a pretext to discharge an employee for union activities.

The Supreme Court decision in *Darlington Mfg. Co.* is one of the most important cases on the application of Sections 8(a)(1) and 8(a)(3). The Court held that a plant closing violates the Act only if it is closed with the intent of discouraging union activities at another one of the employer's plants that remains open. The Court reasoned that closing a plant is such a basic employer right that intent has to be proven. Thus, in order for a plant closure to be unlawful, it must violate Section 8(a)(3).

Another important employee protection is afforded by Section 8(a)(4), which prohibits an employer from discharging or otherwise discriminating against an employee because the employee has filed charges or given testimony under the Act. The Board has broadly applied this section to include protection covering affidavits given during a Board investigation even if the employee does not actually testify.

1. What rights do employees who are not in a union have to engage in concerted activity?
2. What is the right of exclusive representation?
3. What evidence is needed to prove an employer's intent to discriminate in violation of Section 8(a)(3)?
4. Can an employer express an opinion favoring one union over another?
5. What is the purpose of the Section 8(a)(2) restrictions against employer financial assistance?
6. Can a shop steward be disciplined for insubordinate remarks to the employer during a grievance meeting?
7. Can a contract provide superseniority for shop stewards for purposes of layoff and overtime preference?
8. What is the statutory exception to the rule against an employer entering into a premature or pre-hire agreement with a union?
9. Is an individual employee protesting an employer's contract violation engaged in concerted activity?
10. When can an employee request to have his shop steward present at a meeting with the employer?
11. What options does an employer have if an employee requests a steward based on a reasonable belief that he faces discipline?
12. Under what circumstances may a discharge be unlawful under Section 8(a)(3) although the employer presents an apparently bona fide reason for his action?

(Answers to review questions are at the end of the book.)

1.A. An employer may lawfully continue to bargain with an incumbent union and execute a collective bargaining agreement with the incumbent even though a valid representation petition filed by another union is pending. However, any such contract would be null and void if the rival union wins the representation election and is certified as the employees' bargaining agent. *RCA Del Caribe Inc.*, 262 NLRB No. 116, 110 LRRM 1369 (1982). An employer cannot grant voluntary initial recognition to one union if another union has filed a valid, properly supported, representation petition. If no petition has been filed, an employer may grant voluntary recognition to a union, even though another union is also seeking to represent the employees, provided that the union recognized has uncoerced majority support and the employer has not otherwise rendered unlawful assistance to the union in its organizing efforts. *Bruckner Nursing Home*, 262 NLRB No. 115, 110 LRRM 1374 (1982). See also *Midwest Piping and Supply Co.*, 63 NLRB 1060, 17 LRRM 40 (1945); *Haddon House Food Products v. NLRB*, 764 F.2d 1985, 119 LRRM 3021 (3d Cir. 1985); *Caro Bags*, 285 NLRB No. 97, 128 LRRM 1031 (1987). But see *Rollins Transport. System, Inc.*, 297 NLRB No. 108, 132 LRRM 1185 (1989) (recognition may be lawful under Bruckner, but still not bar filing of rival representation petition [see Chapter Two] if rival union has conducted simultaneous campaign and files a valid representation petition on or within a reasonable time after the date the employer granted voluntary recognition to the other union so long as the petition is based on support gained prior to the grant of recognition).

1.B. An employer may lawfully recognize the incumbent union at an existing facility as the exclusive bargaining representative at a new facility if it is clear at the time that the old employees will constitute a majority of the new workforce or if the old and new facilities are so functionally integrated that the new facility constitutes an accretion to the existing facility. The parties may also enter into a tentative collective bargaining agreement covering the new location and agree that the new agreement will go into effect at such time as the incumbent union lawfully attains majority status at the new location. *NLRB General Counsel Advice Memorandum, General Motors Corp., Saturn Corp.,* 122 LRRM 1187 (1986); *Safeway Stores,* 276 NLRB No. 99, 120 LRRM 1186 (1985); *Harte & Co.,* 278 NLRB No. 128, 122 LRRM 1003 (1986).

2. Once duly certified or lawfully recognized voluntarily by the employer as the employees' majority status representative under Section 9 of the LMRA, a union is entitled to exclusive representation. As an exception, Section 9(a) permits, but does not require, an employer to meet directly with employees to adjust their grievances provided the adjustment is not inconsistent with the agreement and the union has an opportunity to be present. Concerted efforts by employees to bargain directly with their employer are not protected activity if the employees are represented by an exclusive bargaining representative. *Emporium Capwell Co. v. WACO,* 420 U.S. 50, 88 LRRM 2660 (1975); *Certified Grocers,* 273 NLRB No. 196, 118 LRRM 1206 (1985); *U.S. Postal Service,* 281 NLRB No. 138, 123 LRRM 1209 (1986). The union must be free from unlawful employer domination or assistance. *North Shore University Hospital,* 274 NLRB No. 188, 118 LRRM 1585 (1985) (supervisory domination or conflict of interest between union officer's duties for employer and union responsibilities); *Power Piping Co.,* 291 NLRB No. 80, 129 LRRM 1225 (1988) (supervisory participation).

3.A. If an employer unlawfully assists a union, the Board will order the employer to cease recognizing the assisted union and to cease giving effect to any contract between the employer and the union until the union is certified through an election. *Spiegel Trucking Co.,* 225 NLRB No. 26, 92 LRRM 1604 (1976); *Wintex Knitting Mill, Inc., Newport Division,* 223 NLRB No. 195, 92 LRRM 1113 (1976); *Classic Industries, Inc.,* 254 NLRB 1149, 107 LRRM 1046 (1981); *Hilton Inn Albany,* 270 NLRB No. 207, 116 LRRM 1366 (1984).

3.B. Sections 8(a)(2) and 302 of the LMRA do not absolutely ban all forms of assistance from an employer to a union. Thus, permitting union officials to conduct union business on company time or the free use of company office space, etc., may be lawful if the union is clearly independent from the employer with an arm's-length bargaining relationship, and the payments or benefits permit the union to perform its collective bargaining functions more efficiently. *BASF Wyandotte Corp.,* 274 NLRB No. 147, 119 LRRM 1035 (1985), enforced 798 F.2d 849, 123 LRRM 2320 (5th Cir. 1986); *BASF Wyandotte v. ICWU Local 327,* 791 F.2d 1046, 122 LRRM 2750 (2d Cir. 1987); *Coppinger Machinery Services, Inc.,* 279 NLRB No. 85, 122 LRRM 1153 (1986).

3.C. Provisions permitting former employees of an employer on leave of absence to hold union office to receive employer benefits (e.g., pension credit) while on leave may also be lawful under Section 302 of the Act as payments made "by reason of . . . service as an employee" within the Section 302 exemption for such payments. Contrast *Trailways, Inc. v. Trailways Joint Council,* 785 F.2d 101, 121 LRRM 3167 (3d Cir. 1986) (continued employer pension contributions for employees on indefinite leave of absence to hold union office based on employee's salary as union officer unlawful under LMRA Section 302) with *Toth v. U.S.X. Corp.,* 883 F.2d 1297, 132 LRRM 2275 (7th Cir. 1989) (Section 302 permits employer to give pension credit for period former employee is on leave to serve as union officer provided that benefit is openly bargained for and agreement for credit is included as part of the parties' collective bargaining agreement). See also *Communications Workers v. Bell Atlantic,* 670 F.Supp. 416, 126 LRRM 3015 (D.C. Dist. Ct. 1987) (continued employer contributions lawful, based on prior salary as employees and employees may be denied leave if needed for work). See also legal principle 12.

4. Section 8(f) of the LMRA permits a union and employer only in the construction industry to enter into a binding collective bargaining agreement without first establishing the union's majority status. Under current Board law, such a pre-hire agreement is binding for its term whether or not the union attains majority status, but either the employer or the covered employees may file a representation election petition with the Board any time during the term of the agreement challenging the union's representative status. *John Deklewa & Sons,* 282 NLRB No. 184, 124 LRRM 1185 (1987), affirmed 843 F.2d 770, 128 LRRM 2020 (3d Cir. 1988). See further discussion in Chapter Five.

5. Employer or union conduct that interferes with the basic rights of employees under Section 7 of the LMRA to engage in concerted activity, or to refrain from such activity, violates Section 8(a)(1) (employer conduct) or Section 8(b)(1) (union conduct) as appropriate regardless of the party's intent. In contrast, discrimination is unlawful under Section 8(a)(3) (employer conduct) or Section 8(b)(2) of the Act (union misconduct) only if the discrimination is with the intent to encourage or discourage membership in or activity on behalf of a labor organization. There may be direct evidence to establish the unlawful intent, or the intent may be inferred from the "natural consequences" of actions that are destructive of the right to engage in union activity (or to refrain from such activity) even without direct evidence. The impact of a particular action may be so

inherently destructive of employee rights that the employer's business justification for the action does not matter, but if the impact is less, and the employer produces evidence of a legitimate and substantial business justification for the act, actual anti-union motivation must be proven to establish a Section 8(a)(3) violation. *Metropolitan Edison Co. v. NLRB*, 460 U.S. 698, 112 LRRM 3265 (1983), upholding "*Precision Castings* doctrine," 233 NLRB 183, 96 LRRM 1540 (1977); *NLRB v. Erie Resister Corp.*, 373 U.S. 221, 53 LRRM 2121 (1963); *NLRB v. Great Dane Trailers, Inc.*, 388 U.S. 26, 65 LRRM 2465 (1967) (discrimination against strikers); *Electrical Workers Local 1392 v. NLRB*, 786 F.2d 733, 121 LRRM 3259 (6th Cir. 1986); *Radio Officers Union v. NLRB*, 347 U.S. 17, 33 LRRM 2417 (1954); *Alliance Rubber Co.*, 286 NLRB No. 57, 126 LRRM 1217 (1987); *Waco, Inc.*, 273 NLRB No. 101, 118 LRRM 1163 (1984); *National Fabricators Inc.*, 295 NLRB No. 126, 131 LRRM 1761 (1989). Contrast *Sure Tan Inc. v. NLRB*, 467 U.S. 883, 116 LRRM 2857 (1984) (illegal aliens are employees protected by the LMRA) with *Parker-Robb Chevrolet*, 262 NLRB No. 58, 110 LRRM 1289 (1982), affirmed 711 F.2d 383, 113 LRRM 3175 (D.C. Cir. 1983) (supervisors not protected under Act unless action against them interferes with protected employee rights). Compare *Textile Workers v. Darlington Mfg. Co.*, 380 U.S. 263, 58 LRRM 2657 (1965) (specific intent violating Section 8(a)(3) required in case of plant closing); *Purolator Armored Inc. v. NLRB*, 764 F.2d 1423, 119 LRRM 3228 (11th Cir. 1985) (partial plant closing). See also *Lear Siegler Inc.*, 295 NLRB No. 83, 131 LRRM 1763 (1989) (restoration of plant at prior location as remedy for unlawful relocation).

6.A. Usually, concerted activity involves conduct by two or more employees. However, an employee acting alone to induce group activity or acting on behalf of other employees is also engaged in concerted activity. An employee acting alone asserting a contractual right is engaged in concerted activity even though the complaint concerns only the individual employee if the employee's statement or action is based on a reasonable and honest belief that the employee is being, or has been, asked to perform a task that the employee is not required to perform under the collective bargaining agreement. *Interboro Contractors Inc.*, 157 NLRB 1295, 61 LRRM 1537 (1966); *NLRB v. City Disposal Systems, Inc.*, 465 U.S. 822, 115 LRRM 3193 (1984); *City Disposal v. NLRB*, 766 F.2d 969, 119 LRRM 3200 (6th Cir. 1985) (decision on remand from Supreme Court); *Stor-Rite Metal Products, Inc.*, 283 NLRB No. 123, 125 LRRM 1087 (1987); *Salisbury Hotel, Inc.*, 283 NLRB No. 101, 125 LRRM 1020 (1987).

6.B. Under current Board law, an employee who individually protests a working condition that does not violate a collective bargaining agreement is regarded as engaged in concerted activity only if the employee is in fact engaged in, with, or on the authority of other employees, not solely by and on behalf of the individual employee. *Meyers Industries*, 268 NLRB 493, 115 LRRM 1025 (1984), remanded for reconsideration, *Prill v. NLRB*, 755 F.2d 941, 118 LRRM 2649 (D.C. Cir. 1985). Board decision on remand, 281 NLRB No. 118, 123 LRRM 1137 (1986) (adhering to its prior decision). *Millcraft Furniture Co., Inc.*, 282 NLRB No. 83, 124 LRRM

1049 (1987); *Consumers Power Co.*, 282 NLRB No. 24, 123 LRRM 1305 (1986); *Ewing v. NLRB*, 861 F.2d 353, 129 LRRM 2853 (2d Cir. 1988) (approving *Meyers Industries* doctrine).

6.C. Even though employee conduct is concerted, it may still be unprotected and thus subject to employer discipline (e.g., insubordination, "quickie strikes," slowdowns, or the refusal to perform a work assignment in violation of a contractual no-strike clause). *NLRB v. City Disposal Systems, Inc.* in legal principle 6.A.; *Emporium Capwell Co. v. WACO* in legal principle 2; *Bird Engineers*, 270 NLRB No. 214, 116 LRRM 1302 (1984); *Central Motors Corp.*, 269 NLRB No. 27, 115 LRRM 1172 (1984); *National Semiconductor Corp.*, 272 NLRB No. 148, 117 LRRM 1408 (1984). *Carolina Freight Carriers Corp.*, 295 NLRB No. 124, 131 LRRM 1762 (1989); *Roseville Dodge v. NLRB*, 882 F.2d 1355, 132 LRRM 2161 (8th Cir. 1989).

7.A. An employee, upon request, is entitled to have a shop steward present at a meeting with the employer if the investigation is focused on the employee and the employee reasonably believes that he or she may be facing discipline. *NLRB v. J. Weingarten, Inc.*, 420 U.S. 251, 88 LRRM 2689 (1975); *Roadway Express*, 246 NLRB 1127, 103 LRRM 1050 (1979) (no right to specific steward); *Southwestern Bell Tel. Co.*, 251 NLRB 612, 105 LRRM 1246 (1980) (steward cannot be made to remain silent during investigatory interview).

7.B. Currently, the Board will not order an employer to reinstate an employee whose discharge was based on information obtained during an improperly conducted disciplinary interview, but only issue an order requiring the employer to cease and desist from the unlawful conduct. *Taracorp Industries*, 273 NLRB No. 54, 117 LRRM 1497 (1984); *Communications Workers Local 5008 v. NLRB*, 784 F.2d 847, 121 LRRM 3078 (7th Cir. 1986).

7.C. Only employees who are represented by a union have the right to representation in a disciplinary interview. *Sears, Roebuck & Co.*, 274 NLRB No. 55, 118 LRRM 1329 (1985); *E. I. Dupont*, 289 NLRB No. 81, 128 LRRM 1233 (1988); *Slaughter v. NLRB*, 876 F.2d 11, 131 LRRM 2546 (3d Cir. 1989) (ultimately upholding Board position as a reasonable interpretation of the Act).

8. The employee and the steward are entitled to meet in private for a reasonable period before the disciplinary meeting with the employer. *Amax, Inc.*, 227 NLRB No. 154, 94 LRRM 1177 (1977); *Coca Cola Bottling Co.*, 227 NLRB No. 173, 94 LRRM 1200 (1977). Before meeting, the steward may require the employer to state the general subject matter of the employee interview and identify the misconduct for which the discipline may be imposed. *Pacific Tel. & Tel. Co.*, 262 NLRB No. 127, 110 LRRM 1411 (1982), enforced 711 F.2d 134, 113 LRRM 3529 (9th Cir. 1983). See *Chromalloy American Co.*, 263 NLRB No. 22, 110 LRRM 1506 (1982).

9. An employer may question an employee to prepare the employer's defense to an unfair labor practice charge or obtain a copy of the employee's Board statement only if the employer informs the employee

of the purpose of the request, assures him that there will be no reprisal if the employee refuses, and obtains the employee's cooperation voluntarily. *Johnnies Poultry Co.*, 146 NLRB 770, 55 LRRM 1403 (1964); *Bill Scott Oldsmobile*, 282 NLRB No. 140, 124 LRRM 1161 (1987); *W. W. Grainger*, 255 NLRB 1106, 107 LRRM 1147 (1981); *NLRB v. Maxwell*, 637 F.2d 698, 106 LRRM 2387 (9th Cir. 1981). See also *NLRB v. Robbins Tire and Rubber Co.*, 437 U.S. 214, 98 LRRM 2617 (1978) (employee Board statement exempt from disclosure by Board under the Freedom of Information Act). Employees may be required to furnish an employer with information pertaining to a current dispute or grievance between the employer and the union, but a steward may not be required to provide information obtained in the course of his investigation of a grievance or to reveal the union's internal position or strategy. See *Cook Paint & Varnish Co.*, 246 NLRB 646, 102 LRRM 1680 (1979), reversed *Cook Paint & Varnish Co. v. NLRB*, 648 F.2d 712, 106 LRRM 3016 (D.C. Cir. 1981), reconsidered by the Board 258 NLRB No. 166, 108 LRRM 1150 (1981).

10. A steward participating in a grievance meeting or in negotiations is equal in standing to the employer's representative. Thus, the steward cannot be disciplined for his conduct, remarks, or attitude toward the employer during such sessions or for public comments on labor-management issues, except in case of extremely aggravated misconduct. *Sweeney and Co.*, 258 NLRB No. 96, 108 LRRM 1172 (1981); *Alfa Leisure, Inc.*, 251 NLRB 691, 105 LRRM 1121 (1980); *U.S. Postal Service*, 250 NLRB 4, 104 LRRM 1300 (1980); *Mitchell Manuals, Inc.*, 280 NLRB No. 23, 122 LRRM 1195 (1986); *Manville Forest Products Corp.*, 269 NLRB No. 72, 115 LRRM 1266 (1984) (employer may discipline steward for advising employees not to cooperate in an employer's investigation). Compare *Roure Bertrand Dupont, Inc.*, 271 NLRB No. 78, 116 LRRM 1394 (1984) (steward's comments to newspaper reporter protected) with *Stanley Furniture Co.*, 271 NLRB No. 112, 117 LRRM 1030 (1984) (false public statements made to damage employer's reputation not protected). See also *Cincinnati Suburban Press, Inc.*, 289 NLRB No. 127, 129 LRRM 1033 (1988).

11. If an employer's discriminatory action against an employee is for a "mixed motive," the general counsel, in order to establish a violation of Section 8(a)(3), must make a prima facie showing sufficient cause to support the inference that the employee's protected conduct was a "motivating factor" in the employer's decision. If this is established, the burden shifts to the employer to demonstrate that it would have taken the same action even in the absence of the protected conduct. *Wright Line*, 251 NLRB 1083, 105 LRRM 1169 (1980), affirmed in part *NLRB v. Wright Line*, 662 F.2d 899, 108 LRRM 2513 (1st Cir. 1981); *NLRB v. Transportation Management Corp.*, 462 U.S. 393, 113 LRRM 2857 (1983); *Hyatt Hotels Corp.*, 296 NLRB No. 36, 132 LRRM 1130 (1989). See also *Esterline Electronics* Corp., 290 NLRB No. 92, 131 LRRM 1067 (1988) (reinstatement offer to employee discharged in violation of Section 8(a)(3) invalid if letter makes clear on its face that reinstatement is dependent on employee returning to work by unreasonably short date).

12.A. Contract clauses granting union officials superseniority are lawful under Section 8(a)(3) of the Act only if they are limited to shop stewards or other union officials performing steward-like functions whose presence is needed on the job, or in a particular job classification, department, or shift, etc., in order to perform their duties. Granting superseniority for all contractual benefits, including those unrelated to job security, would be unlawful discrimination to encourage union activity. *Gulton Electro-Voice*, 266 NLRB No. 84, 112 LRRM 1361 (1983), enforced *Electrical Workers IUE Local 900 v. NLRB*, 727 F.2d 1184, 115 LRRM 2760 (D.C. Cir. 1984); *Gulton Electro-Voice*, 276 NLRB No. 109, 120 LRRM 1150 (1985); *Wayne Corp.*, 270 NLRB No. 28, 116 LRRM 1049 (1984) (intermittent occasional performance of stewardlike functions insufficient); *Painters Local 1555*, 241 NLRB No. 112, 100 LRRM 1578 (1979); *Dairylea Cooperative, Inc.*, 219 NLRB No. 107, 89 LRRM 1737 (1975).

12.B. Contract clauses granting employees on leave of absence for union business or holding union office continued seniority, health care coverage, or continued pension credit, etc., may be lawful under Section 8(a)(3), even if employees on leave of absence for other reasons do not receive such benefits, since they serve the lawful collective bargaining function of permitting employees to take leave for union business without suffering a loss and do not impermissibly encourage other employees to be "good union members" in order to obtain similar benefits. Compare *Mead Packaging Co.*, 273 NLRB No. 181, 118 LRRM 1184 (1985) (employer may not lawfully continue to maintain group insurance and grant pension plan benefits to employees on leave of absence for union business) with *IBEW Local 1212*, 288 NLRB No. 49, 128 LRRM 1219 (1988), affirmed *WPIX Inc. v. NLRB*, 870 F.2d 858, 131 LRRM 2075 (2nd. Cir. 1989), (upholding continuing seniority credit for employees on leave of absence for union business and overruling *Mead Packaging Co.* to the extent inconsistent therewith). See also legal principle 3.C.

Recommended Reading

Cabot, Jarin, "Third Circuit's New Standard for Strike Misconduct Discharges: NLRB v. W.C. McQuaide, Inc.," 23 *Vill. L. Rev.* 645 (1978).

Dobranski B., "Right of Union Representation in Employer Interviews: A Post-*Weingarten* Analysis," 26 *St. L. U. L. J.* 295 (1982).

Gorman and Finkin, "Individual and the Requirement of 'Concert' under the National Labor Relations Act," 130 *U. Pa. L. Rev.* 286 (1981).

Heshizer and Downing, "The Contracting Weingarten Doctrine: NLRB Policy-making in a Politicized Environment," 36 *Lab L.J.* 707 (1985).

"Intent, Effect, Purpose, and Motive as Applicable Elements to Section 8(a)(1) and Section 8(a)(3) Violations of the National Labor Relations Act," 7 *Wake Forest L. Rev.* 616 (1971).

Mak, "The Evolution of the Requirement of 'Concerted Activity' under the National Labor Relations Act," 2 *Hofstra Lab. L.J.* 265 (1985).

Schatzki, "Majority Rule, Exclusive Representation, and the Interest of Individual Workers: Should Exclusivity Be Abolished?" 123 *U. Pa. L. Rev.* 897 (1975).

chapter 5

THE DUTY TO BARGAIN

The ultimate goal of a union is the successful negotiation and administration of a collective bargaining agreement. This chapter discusses the legal principles governing the collective bargaining process.

The duty to bargain is governed by Sections 8(a)(5), 8(b)(3), and 8(d). It is an unfair labor practice under Section 8(a)(5) for an employer to refuse to bargain collectively with the representative of it employees. Section 8(b)(3) makes it an unfair labor practice for a union to refuse to bargain collectively with an employer whose employees it represents.

Section 8(d) defines the duty to bargain, described as the mutual obligation of the employer and the union to meet at reasonable times and confer in good faith over wages, hours, and other terms and conditions of employment. The duty includes the negotiation of an agreement or any question arising under the agreement. The parties are required to execute a written contract incorporating any agreement reached if requested by either party. Section 8(d) further provides, however, that the duty to bargain does not compel either party to agree to a proposal or make a concession. The duty to bargain exists before and during the negotiation of a collective bargaining agreement, during the administration of the agreement, and upon expiration.

A. INCEPTION AND DURATION OF THE BARGAINING OBLIGATION

1. Bargaining before a Contract is Negotiated

An employer's obligation to recognize and bargain with a union under Section 8(a)(5) may result from certification of a union by the Board following a represen-tation election (see Chapter Two), a bargaining order issued under *Gissel* principles (see Chapter Three), or voluntary recognition.

The duration of an employer's bargaining duty depends upon whether the union has been certified by the Board or voluntarily recognized.

a. The Effect of Board Certification. If the union has been certified by the National

Labor Relations Board, the employer is obligated under Section 8(a)(5) to bargain with it for a full year following certification. There is an irrebuttable presumption that a union has majority status for the year. The one-year rule also applies to bargaining pursuant to a *Gissel* bargaining order (see Chapter Three). A union is entitled to a full year of good-faith bargaining. If an employer fails to bargain in good faith during the certification year, and the Board issues an order requiring the employer to bargain, the employer must bargain in good faith with the union for a full year after the order is entered, even though more than one year has passed since certification.

After one year, there is a rebuttable presumption that the certified union still represents a majority of the employees. However, if the parties have not negotiated a contract after one year of good-faith bargaining, the employer may withdraw recognition if it has a good-faith and reasonable doubt based on objective considerations that the union no longer has majority status.

b. Effect of Voluntary Recognition. If the employer has voluntarily recognized a union, it is obligated to bargain with the union for "a reasonable period of time." If no contract is agreed to after a reasonable period, the employer may withdraw recognition if it has a good-faith and reasonable doubt based on objective considerations that the union no longer represents a majority.

There is no definite period during which an employer must bargain with a union that has been voluntarily recognized. In some cases, the Board has held that a reasonable period is the twelve months required for bargaining with a certified union. However, the Board has upheld the right of an employer to terminate recognition after bargaining with a union for only three months.

2. The Basis for Withdrawing Recognition

a. Effect of a Decertification Petition. As discussed in Chapter Four, the filing of a

rival valid representation petition neither requires nor permits an employer to cease bargaining or refuse to execute a contract with an incumbent union while the rival representation petition is pending. Similarly the mere filing of a decertification petition does not require or permit an employer to withdraw from bargaining or refuse to execute a contract with an incumbent union. Of course, if the incumbent union loses the decertification election, any contract entered into would be null and void.

b. Employer's Good-Faith Doubt of Majority Status. An employer may withdraw recognition at the end of the certification year or after a reasonable period of voluntary recognition if no contract is in effect if it has a good-faith and reasonable doubt based on objective considerations that the union represents a majority of the employees. An uncoerced petition signed by a majority of the employees submitted to the employer stating that the employees no longer wish to be represented by the union is one example of evidence that the union has lost majority status. However, the employer cannot withdraw recognition if the employer's own unlawful acts lead to the union's loss of majority support. Thus, if the employer engages in bad-faith bargaining and the employees, frustrated by the tactics, sign a petition repudiating the union, the employer may not rely on the petition provoked by its misconduct as a basis for withdrawing recognition. Also, the employer may not encourage or assist its employees to sign such a petition. However, if the employees raise the issue, the employer may provide what the Board terms "ministerial" assistance, such as telling the employees the number of signatures necessary to file a decertification petition and where to file.

Evidence that employees are dissatisfied with the union is not sufficient proof that the union no longer represents a majority of the work force. That employees cease paying union dues and cancel their checkoff authorizations is not sufficient proof of lost majority status because the union represents all employees whether they are members or not. A large turnover in the employee work force does not constitute loss of majority status because the new employees are presumed to support the union in the same ratio as the former employees. A deauthorization election in which the employees revoke the union security clause of their contract is not evidence of lost majority status, only an indication that the employees do not wish union membership to be compulsory.

Although none of the factors listed above conclusively establishes that the union has lost its majority status, combined they can be the basis of an employer's good-faith doubt to withdraw recognition. The Board considers each case on its specific facts.

That a majority of the employees abandon a strike and return to work also is not necessarily evidence that the employees do not want the union to represent them. The Board has reasoned that employees may return to work for many reasons, ranging from economic necessity to disagreement with the decision to strike, but still desire union representation. The Board used to apply a presumption that even permanent strike replacements (see Chapter Six) desired representation so that an employer could not withdraw recognition from a striking union because the replacements outnumbered the strikers. Recently, however, the Board ruled that it would no longer apply the presumption, but that an employer would still have to have actual evidence that the replacements did not support the union before withdrawing recognition from the striking union. Some courts of appeals, however, contrary to the Board, have held that an employer may lawfully presume that striker replacements who cross the union's picket line do not support the union, especially if a large number of replacements are hired within a short time period. Thus, this issue may ultimately reach the Supreme Court for final resolution.

3. Withdrawal of Recognition during the Contract's Term

There is a presumption that a union continues to represent a majority of the employees for the duration of a contract. That is true even if a majority of the employees sign a petition that they no longer want the union to represent them. Basically, an employer can withdraw recognition during a contract's term only under the same limited circumstances that the contract would not bar an election (see Chapter Two).

What if an employer moves to a new location during the contractual term? The Board has held that a collective bargaining agreement remains in effect following a relocation, provided operations and equipment remain substantially the same at the new location, and a substantial percentage of the employees at the old plant transfer to the new location. If two facilities are merged at a new location, the employer's obligation to bargain depends upon whether the employees at either facility would constitute an accretion to the other (see discussion in Chapter Two).

4. Withdrawal at the Termination of the Agreement

A union, whether originally certified or voluntarily recognized, has a rebuttable presumption of continued majority status at the termination of a contract. This means that ordinarily an employer has the duty to bargain with the union for a new or modified agreement. (A different rule applies to construction industry pre-hire agreements discussed below.)

However, the employer can withdraw recognition if it has a good-faith and reasonable doubt based on objective considerations as discussed above that the union has continued majority status. An employer can announce its decision to withdraw recognition a reasonable period before the contract expires. The employer must continue to recognize the incumbent union until the contract expires, but it can then cease recognition and unilaterally change the employees' conditions of employment.

If an employer withdraws recognition from the union under any of the circumstances discussed above, it can file a petition for an election (an RM petition) or put the burden on the union to challenge its decision. If the union believes that the withdrawal violated the Act either because of its timing or the lack of a good faith doubt, it can file a Section 8(a)(5) refusal to bargain charge.

5. Multi-employer Bargaining

Multi-employer bargaining is consensual. Employers voluntarily join a multi-employer association and the multi-employer association and union voluntarily enter into negotiations culminating in a contract. Withdrawal, however, is not consensual; each member of a multi-employer association is bound by the contract for its term. Furthermore, upon the contract's expiration, an employer is bound by any renewal of the multi-employer agreement unless the employer serves timely notice to the union of its intent to withdraw from the association. This notice must be received before negotiations begin for a new contract. If the employer does not serve notice, the employer is bound by the new agreement, and violates Section 8(a)(5) by refusing to abide by it. Similarly, a union is obligated to continue the multi-employer relationship unless it serves a timely notice to terminate before negotiations begin for a new agreement. Even if an employer withdraws properly, there is a presumption (except in the construction industry discussed below) that the union continues to represent the employer's employees as a separate bargaining unit. Thus the employer must continue to recognize and bargain with the union for a new contract.

Ordinarily an employer can withdraw from a multi-employer unit after bargaining has begun only with the consent of both the association and the union. An employer can withdraw without mutual consent only in very unusual circumstances, such as if an employer is about to cease existence as a viable business entity, or if so many employers timely withdraw from a multi-employer unit that it is unfair to require the other employers to remain. An employer cannot withdraw from a multi-employer bargaining unit just because there is a bargaining impasse or strike between the association and the union. Such occurrences are not regarded as unusual circumstances. However, after a bargaining impasse has been reached, the union may sign interim agreements with individual employers pending negotiation of a new multi-employer agreement as long as the employer is bound by the eventual unit contract.

There is a distinction between a multi-employer association and a group of employers who bargain together as a convenience. In the multi-employer situation, the employers intend to be bound as a group by the agreement reached between the employers' bargaining committee and the union. In contrast, if employers bargain together as a convenience, the union and the employers understand that each employer will sign an individual contract and that each employer reserves the right to negotiate changes in the pattern agreement. A member of a multi-employer association has no right to make individual changes.

6. Construction Industry Pre-hire Agreements

Section 8(f) of the Act permits a construction union to enter into a collective bargaining agreement with an employer engaged primarily in the building and construction industry covering employees in the industry even though the union does not represent a majority of the employees in the unit at the time. Such agreements are called "pre-hire" contracts. Pre-hire contracts are a statutory exception to the general rule applicable in all other industries that an employer may not sign a contract unless the union represents a majority of the employees under Section 9(a) of the Act as established by a Board-conducted election or authorization cards signed by a majority of the employees in the bargaining unit. The exception was made because of the unique nature of the construction industry in which employment is often short term and the employer looks to the union to furnish skilled labor. In the landmark decision of *John Deklewa & Sons, Inc.*[1] (1987), the Board made major changes in its rules governing the enforcement of pre-hire agreements.

a. The pre-Deklewa rules. Prior to the *Deklewa* decision, the Board's basic rule on Section 8(f) agreements, which the United States Supreme Court had upheld, was that an employer could lawfully withdraw recognition from a union with which it had a Section 8(f) pre-hire agreement and could repudiate the agreement unilaterally until such time as the union represented a majority of the employees in the bargaining unit on the job site to which the agreement applied. The agreement was binding until revoked. However, once the union represented a majority of the employees, the agreement "converted" from a pre-hire contract to a regular fully enforceable majority status agreement. (This principle is known as the "conversion doctrine.") If the employer hired the employees for work on that job site only, the agreement was binding for only that job site. If, however, the employer had a permanent and stable work force that moved from job to job and the union attained majority status in the work force, then the employer was bound by the contract for all work on all job sites for the contract's full term. A union's majority status was usually established when a majority of the employees working under the contract on the job site were union members. A union could also establish its majority status by obtaining signed authorization cards from the employees or through operation of a contractual union security

clause (see Chapter Ten) requiring union membership after seven days of employment as permitted by Section 8(f).

Another important pre-*Deklewa* rule was the so-called "merger" doctrine. Under this doctrine, if an employer signed a pre-hire agreement requiring the employer to become part of a multi-employer bargaining unit in which the union had majority status, the newly covered employees "merged" into the overall unit even though the employees had not authorized the union to represent them and/or were not union members. The employer was bound by the agreement for its full term under the same withdrawal rules that apply to any other multi-employer contract.

b. Deklewa rules. In a major policy change, the Board held in *Deklewa* that an employer may no longer unilaterally repudiate a pre-hire agreement during its term whether or not the union attains majority status. However, even if the union attains a majority, either the employer or covered employees may file a representation election petition with the Board at any time during the contract term challenging the union's representative status. The Board rescinded the conversion doctrine under which a pre-hire agreement became binding for its full term when the union attained majority status. Rather, if the union loses the representation election, the pre-hire agreement is null and void from that point and another pre-hire agreement covering the employees cannot be entered into for at least one year thereafter. If the union wins the election, however, it will be certified as the bargaining agent, and the contract will be binding for its full term the same as any other collective bargaining agreement. An employer cannot withdraw recognition just because a petition has been filed. The agreement remains in full force and effect until and unless the union loses the election. An employer's poll of its own employees, even if conducted in secret and without coercion, cannot be the basis for withdrawing recognition. Only an election will suffice.

[1] See legal principle 1.C.

Under *Deklewa* a pre-hire agreement remains in effect from project to project, whether the contractor has a permanent and stable work force or hires new employees for each job, until the contract expires or the agreement is rescinded by an employee vote. It is no longer necessary to resign a contractor who hires on a "per-job" basis to another contract for each new job site.

However, when the contract expires, an employer may withdraw recognition from the union and unilaterally change conditions of employment without filing an election petition with the Board. But if a pre-hire agreement requires the employer to serve a timely termination notice a specified period before the expiration date, the employer must repudiate during that period or else the agreement will be renewed in accordance with its terms.

The Board also ruled in *Deklewa* that it will no longer follow the "merger doctrine." Now, even if a pre-hire agreement requires the contractor to join a multi-employer unit, the employer or its employees may still file an election petition at any time. The election will be held only among the employees of that employer. If the union loses, the agreement will be null and void for the employees of that employer only.

Note that the Board's new policies announced in *Deklewa* apply only to pre-hire agreements in the construction industry in which the union enters into a contract without first establishing its majority status in an appropriate bargaining unit under Section 9(a) of the Act by either a Board-conducted election or recognition cards. If the union establishes its majority status in an appropriate unit and *then* enters into a collective bargaining agreement, that agreement (a Section 9(a) agreement) will be binding for its full term as in any other industry. Thus some construction unions are now obtaining recognition cards from their members (including those they have in fact represented for many years) to establish the union's majority status in the bargaining unit and then entering into new

contracts expressly recognizing the union as the majority status (Section 9(a)) bargaining representative. The Board has held that for a union to establish Section 9(a) majority status it must unequivocally demand majority status recognition and the employer must unequivocally grant such recognition.

It will undoubtedly take several more years before the full ramifications of the *Deklewa* decision on construction unions are apparent. Thus, the decision may be helpful to unions in "right-to-work" states (see Chapter Ten) where union membership cannot be required as a condition of employment. In those states unions frequently did not attain majority status under a pre-hire agreement so that the contract remained terminable at will under the prior law. *Deklewa* is not helpful to unions in states where construction union collective bargaining agreements legally contain a union security clause or to any union, whether or not in a "right-to-work" state, that is strong enough that a majority of the employees are usually union members on a voluntary basis. The continued usefulness of pre-hire agreements may also depend upon whether contractors begin to file representation (RM) petitions in midterm or simply refuse to negotiate a new agreement when the current agreement expires as *Deklewa* permits. In either case, pre-hire agreements may lose their effectiveness, and construction unions may have to resort to majority status agreements as the only feasible alternative. Ultimately, a case involving the *Deklewa* principles will probably reach the Supreme Court for resolution or legislative action amending Section 8(f) to clarify its scope may be necessary.

B. THE NEGOTIATION PROCESS

1. Statutory Notice Requirements

Besides defining the duty to bargain, Section 8(d) also establishes statutory notice requirements before a contract can be terminated or modified. If there is a collective bargaining agreement in effect, a party seeking to terminate or modify the agreement must serve a written notice of the proposed termination or modification on the other party at least sixty days before the expiration or modification. The party serving the written notice must offer to meet and confer with the other party to negotiate for a new contract or modify the existing agreement. The notice letter can be given by either the union or the employer. Within thirty days after notice to the other side, the party must also provide notice of the dispute to the Federal Mediation and Conciliation Service (FMCS) and to any state agency established to mediate and conciliate labor disputes.

The notice requirements for health care institutions are longer—ninety-days notice to the other party and sixty-days notice to the FMCS. Section 8(d)(A) requires a union representing health facility employees to give thirty-days notice to the FMCS of a dispute pertaining to an initial contract. In other industries, the notice requirements apply to only the termination or modification of an existing agreement, not to the negotiation of an initial agreement. Also, under Section 8(g), a union representing employees at a health care institution must give ten-days notice of its intent to strike beyond the expiration of the applicable notice period.

The notice requirements apply to midterm modification of a contract, such as a wage reopener, as well as to the contract's expiration. However, the Supreme Court has held that the notice requirements do not apply to unfair labor practice strikes. Thus, a union can strike immediately, even during the term of a collective bargaining agreement, if an employer has committed serious unfair labor practices (see Chapter Six).

Section 8(d) establishes the minimum notice periods. If either party wishes, the notices can be sent out sooner than required, such as ninety days before the modification or termination date. Although the law refers to notifying the other party first, and then

the FMCS, it is permissible and common to send out all required notices at the same time. The FMCS has a standard multicopy form that can be used to notify both the employer, the FMCS, and the state mediation agency, if any.

a. Timeliness of the Notices. The Board has held that the required notices must be *received* a *full* sixty days before the date of termination or modification, not counting the date received. To calculate the sixty-day period, start with the expiration date and count back sixty days. The day before the sixtieth day is the last day for timely notice. For example, if a contract expired on June 30, the notice would have to have been received by May 1.

Mailing a notice is sufficient if the notice is mailed in time to be received on the required date in the normal course of the mails.

b. The Ban on Unilateral Changes, Strikes or Lockouts during the Notice Period. Section 8(d) prohibits either party from unilaterally changing the terms of the agreement or engaging in a strike or lockout until the expiration of the sixty-day notice period (ninety days for health care institutions) or the expiration of the contract, whichever occurs later. Although Section 8(d)(4) only refers to the sixty-day-notice provision, the Board has held that the sixty-day period is "tolled" unless the thirty-day notice required by Section 8(d)(3) is also given to the Federal Mediation and Conciliation Service and to the appropriate state mediation agency, if any. Thus both the sixty- and thirty-day-notice requirements (ninety/sixty days for health care institutions) must be complied with. If either party gives the proper notices, both parties are free to engage in a strike or lockout at the termination of the notice period. Thus, if a union gives a sixty- and thirty-days notice, the employer can engage in a lockout. If the employer gives proper notices, the union can strike at the end of the notice period even though it has not given notice. Furthermore, the Board has recently held that the burden of notifying the Federal Mediation and Conciliation Service and any state mediation agency rests with the party that gave the sixty-day notice, so that the other party is free to terminate or modify the agreement or to engage in a strike or lock out at the end of the sixty-day notice period even if the thirty-day notice is not given.

c. Consequences of Failure to Comply with Notice Requirements.

Section 8(d) carries severe penalties for failure to comply with the notice requirements. An employee who takes part in an economic strike before the expiration of the notice periods loses employee status under the Act unless rehired. The employee can be discharged and lose reinstatement rights (see Chapter Six). The employer can lawfully discharge union supporters, while keeping other employees, because the strikers are not considered employees protected by the Act.

A union does not, however, forfeit the right to strike forever by failing to meet the notice requirements. It can give the notice late and strike after waiting the appropriate period. Thus if a union gives proper notice to the employer by the sixtieth day, but forgets to give thirty-days notice to the FMCS, it can give late notice to the FMCS and strike thirty days thereafter.

d. Statutory versus Contractual Notice Requirements.

The Section 8(d) notice requirements must be distinguished from contractual notice requirements. Contracts frequently provide for automatic renewal for another year unless either party serves notice on the other to modify or terminate the agreement. If a union fails to give the contractual notice on time, the contract renews itself and remains in effect in accordance with its terms. The employer has no duty to bargain for a new agreement during the renewal period. If the contract contains a no-strike clause, the union cannot strike even though the statutory notices have been given.

Failure to give the statutory notices has no effect on the contract's expiration—only upon the right to strike. Thus, if a contract has a fixed termination date and no provision for automatic renewal, the contract expires by its terms even if the statutory notices are not given.

Some contracts provide that a contract may be either modified or terminated at the end of the agreement. If the union serves a notice to modify rather than to terminate, and the contract contains a no-strike clause, is the union free to strike if the parties do not agree to the terms of a modified agreement, or does the no-strike clause remain in effect? This problem is best resolved by careful contractual draftsmanship. The agreement should spell out the consequences if the parties are unable to reach agreement, such as providing that either party may terminate the agreement with notice if the parties reach a bargaining impasse, or, perhaps, providing for the arbitration of their unresolved issues. In the absence of express contract language, or bargaining history as to the parties' intent, most courts have held that a party's notice to modify a contract is equivalent to a notice to terminate. Thus, if a union serves a timely notice to modify and the parties are unable to agree upon the terms of the modified agreement, the union would be free to strike after the contract's original expiration date.

2. Selection of the Bargaining Committee

Both the union and the employer have almost an absolute right to choose their respective bargaining committees. Neither party can refuse to bargain because they disapprove of someone on the other side's bargaining committee. There is a narrow exception under which the Board will permit one party to refuse to bargain with someone on the other side's bargaining committee if there is persuasive evidence that the presence of the particular individual will create such ill will as to make good-faith bargaining impossible. For example, if a member of the union's bargaining committee engaged in an unprovoked assault on a member of the employer's committee, the employer might be justified in refusing to bargain with the union while that individual remained a member of the bargaining committee.

a. Coordinated and Coalition Bargaining.
The union's right to choose its own bargaining committee is used by unions to engage in coordinated or coalition bargaining among several unions representing separate bargaining units of the same employer. Since unions can select their own bargaining committees, one union can have representatives from other unions sitting in on the bargaining as part of the contracting union's bargaining committee. Under Section 8(a)(5), it is unlawful for an employer to refuse to meet with a bargaining committee that includes members from another bargaining unit.

Similarly, it is an unfair labor practice for an employer to obstruct the ability of employees from other bargaining units to attend bargaining sessions, such as by insisting that bargaining take place at times or locations that make it difficult for the other employees to attend, or by denying persons from other bargaining units time off from work so that they can attend the bargaining sessions.

There is, however, one limitation. An employer can insist that bargaining be limited to the bargaining issues between the employer and the contracting union. The employer can refuse to discuss any issues pertaining to the other bargaining units even though the employer cannot prevent other unions from being present. The employer has the right to negotiate each contract separately.

3. The Good-Faith Concept

a. Intent to Reach an Agreement. The
LMRA does not require an employer and union to agree to the terms of a collective bargaining agreement. A party's only obligation is to bargain in good faith with an intent to reach an agreement. If an agreement is reached, either party may require that it be written and executed.

The law does not regulate the contents of an agreement, only the bargaining process. Each side in the bargaining process naturally wants to get the best contract it can for itself. The law does not require either party to be "fair" or to compromise its position to reach an agreement. Section 8(d) specifically states that neither party can be required to agree to a proposal or make a concession. A party may lawfully bargain for the most favorable agreement possible. The party with the stronger bargaining power can use that power to get a better agreement as long as it intends to reach an agreement on the terms it has proposed.

b. The Bargaining Impasse. Although
both the employer and the union may bargain in good faith and intend to reach an agreement, they may eventually reach a good-faith deadlock on an issue. A good-faith deadlock is a bargaining impasse, that point in time when the parties are warranted in assuming that further bargaining would be futile. The parties may move on to other issues or break off bargaining altogether at that point. The duty to bargain includes the duty to meet at reasonable times and places. But either an employer or a union can refuse to meet if a bargaining impasse has been reached and neither side is willing to change its position.

However, if an impasse is broken by a change in the position of either party or by a change in circumstances, the parties are once again obligated to meet at the request of either side. The Board frequently regards a strike following an impasse as a changed circumstance. Thus, if an employer breaks off negotiations before a strike begins, the employer may be required to begin bargaining again if the employees strike.

The Board and the courts consider a number of factors in determining whether a *good-faith* impasse has been reached. These include: the parties' bargaining history (e.g., is the bargaining relationship new or long standing?; the attitude of the employer toward the union (does the employer have an anti-union animus?); the length of negotiations; the importance of the issues on which the parties have failed to reach agreement; and the parties' understanding of the state of negotiations (i.e., is any further compromise or agreement possible with further bargaining?). There is no set amount of time the parties must bargain before reaching an impasse. In theory, the parties could be at impasse after only a few minutes of bargaining on a particular subject. That would, of course, be unusual. However, if the parties bargain with the intent to reach an agreement and they are deadlocked in good faith, there is an impasse regardless of the time taken to reach that point. The Reagan Board in particular ruled in a number of cases that a bargaining impasse was reached after only a few bargaining sessions.

As a bargaining tactic to guard against a premature bargaining impasse, union negotiators should avoid statements in bargaining indicating that they will never agree to a particular company proposal regardless of how unacceptable it may appear to be. Such a statement may indicate that an impasse has been reached on that issue, thus permitting the company immediately to implement its proposal unilaterally. Rather, the union, despite misgivings, should indicate that it will consider the proposal so that no immediate impasse is reached. Such tactics will not prevent an impasse from being reached ultimately, but they may deter an employer from acting unilaterally or at least delay action until the union is better prepared to respond.

c. Surface Bargaining: The Totality of Conduct Doctrine.

If an employer simply refuses to meet with a union to negotiate an agreement, the employer is obviously not bargaining in good faith as required by Section 8(a)(5). Most employers, however, are more sophisticated than that. An employer who meets with the union, but goes through only the motions of bargaining with no intent to reach an agreement is using the tactic called "surface bargaining."

No single factor determines whether an employer or a union are bargaining in good faith with an intent to reach an agreement. Good faith is judged on the facts of the particular case based on the totality of a party's conduct.

There are certain bargaining tactics that the Board has traditionally regarded as evidence of surface bargaining. These include:

1. Refusing to meet at reasonable times and places
2. Refusing to give basic information to the union needed for meaningful bargaining
3. Refusing to discuss certain issues at all with the union
4. Agreeing on minor bargaining issues but refusing to give in on any major point (such as agreeing to general contract language but maintaining a fixed position on all major economic issues)
5. Refusing to agree to provisions found in most collective bargaining agreements (such as a just cause clause or seniority provision)
6. Proposing wages and benefits that are no better than before the union was certified
7. Rejecting union proposals without making any counterproposals or indicating why the union's proposals are unacceptable
8. Reintroducing proposals that have previously been withdrawn in order to avoid reaching an agreement

However, no single factor is controlling. Good faith is judged on the facts of the particular case based on the totality of a party's conduct. Thus, for example, an employer may have a perfectly legitimate reason for rejecting union proposals for a union security clause, or proposing a wage freeze or even substantial cutbacks in existing benefits, etc. The Board also gives considerable weight to whether the employer has displayed hostility toward the union or engaged in coercive activities violating the Act.

The Reagan Board applied the surface bargaining concept very narrowly. With very few exceptions, it refused to find surface bargaining violations as long as an employer was going through the motions of bargaining unless the employer engaged in flagrant conduct. The Board as presently constituted has found surface bargaining violations in a few cases that come closer to applying the traditional criteria and it is thus possible that the doctrine will once again have broader application.

d. Circumventing the Union. An employer violates the duty to bargain under Section 8(a)(5) if it attempts to go around the union during bargaining and deals directly with the employees on their terms and conditions of employment. An employer can lawfully keep its employees informed concerning the employer's bargaining position, the reason for its positions, and bargaining progress. The employer cannot, however, solicit grievances with the promise to change conditions if the union goes away. Furthermore, the employer cannot make an offer to the employees that it has not made to the union, urge the employees to abandon the union and deal directly with the employer, or otherwise attempt to undermine the union's bargaining position. However, the Reagan Board upheld the employer's right to survey employees prior to bargaining as to the employee's views on various employee benefits as long as the employer does not question employees about specific issues likely to come up in bargaining.

e. Take it or Leave it Bargaining: Boulwareism. Can an employer adopt a "take it or leave it" attitude on its bargaining proposals, a technique frequently referred to as "Boulwareism"? Boulware was the personnel director for General Electric and developed the technique bearing his name. Under this approach, the company did extensive preliminary research on its bargaining position. Based upon all its research and the union's proposals, the Company devised what it regarded as a "fair but firm offer" that it then presented to the union. The company listened to whatever counterproposals the union made, explained its reasons

for rejecting them, but would not change its position.

The Board held that this technique was unlawful,[2] but for a very narrow reason. The company not only held to a rigid position at the bargaining table, but also circumvented the union through a widespread publicity campaign to convince the employees that the company's offer was best. The company disparaged the union in its literature. The Board held that it was unlawful for the company to make it appear that union representation was futile by acting as if there were no union at all. Thus, the company's conduct was in bad faith because the totality of its conduct, not just the one technique, indicated that it had no true intent to bargain.

f. The Order of Bargaining and Tentative Agreements. In general, collective bargaining breaks down into bargaining on economic and noneconomic subjects. The order in which subjects are discussed is a matter for the parties to decide. They may agree to discuss either economic or noneconomic issues first or proceed clause by clause, etc. Neither party may insist to impasse that particular subjects be discussed first.

During bargaining, either side has the right to keep all agreements tentative until a complete agreement is reached. A party may tentatively agree to a particular contract language or certain benefits during bargaining on the assumption that the overall agreement will be acceptable or that it will win some concession from the other side. If the entire agreement falls short of expectations, a party has the right to revise its total proposal. However, it may be evidence of bad faith if a party puts issues already agreed upon back on the bargaining table at the last moment without any reason.

The Board has held that an offer remains on the bargaining table even after the other party has initially rejected it, until it is expressly withdrawn, and that a party can

---

[2] See legal principle 8.

change its mind and accept an offer until it is withdrawn.

g. Ratification Procedures. Both the employer and the union may condition agreements reached at the bargaining table on higher approval. Thus, the union negotiators can reach an agreement contingent on membership ratification. The employer negotiators can make their agreement contingent upon approval by higher management or the board of directors. However the employer's representative must have sufficient authority to conduct meaningful negotiations for a tentative agreement. It is bad-faith bargaining if the negotiator has to continually check every major point with someone who is not present.

It is assumed that both the employer and the union negotiators have full authority to reach a binding agreement on their own. If a negotiator's agreements are subject to approval, the negotiator must advise the other party of its restriction at the beginning of negotiations. Otherwise a party may be bound by an agreement the negotiator reaches even though it exceeded the negotiator's authority. Neither the employer nor the union is bound by the internal ratification procedures of the other unless it has notice of them or there is a past practice of ratification.

h. Economic Force During Bargaining. The Supreme Court held in the *Insurance Agents*[3] case that economic pressure is not inconsistent with good-faith bargaining. In *Insurance Agents*, the union engaged in a work slowdown. The members refused to fill out paper work, reported to work late and left early, and engaged in other harassing tactics to pressure the employer into accepting the union's bargaining position. The Court held that it was not bad-faith bargaining for the union to use economic pressure to force the other party to concede. It stated:

It must be realized that collective bargaining, under a system where the Government does not

[3] See legal principle 3.B.

attempt to control the results of negotiations cannot be equated with an academic collective search for truth—or even with what might be thought to be the ideal of one. The parties—even granting the modification of views that may come from a realization of economic interdependence—still proceed from contrary and to an extent antagonistic viewpoints and concepts of self-interest. The system has not reached the ideal of the philosophic notion that perfect understanding among people would lead to perfect agreement among them on values. The presence of economic weapons in reserve, and their actual exercise on occasion by the parties, is part and parcel of the system that the Wagner and Taft-Hartley Acts have recognized.... [A]t the present statutory stage of our national labor relations policy, the two factors—necessity for good-faith bargaining between parties, and the availability of economic pressure devices to each to make the other party inclined to agree on one's terms—exist side by side.

Thus, a union has the right to strike or engage in other concerted activity to support its bargaining position. Similarly, the employer has the right to lock out employees in support of its position.

There is a common misunderstanding that a union can strike only if negotiations have reached an impasse following good-faith bargaining. That is not so. As long as a no-strike clause is not in effect and Section 8(d) notice requirements have been met, a union has the right to strike at any time to force an agreement, even though bargaining is still going on and the parties are not deadlocked.

i. Union Bad-Faith Bargaining. Although the emphasis has been on employer conduct constituting bad-faith bargaining, a union can also be guilty of bad-faith bargaining. Suppose a union has a master contract with a multi-employer association that the union wants other smaller independent employers in the same industry to sign. An independent employer suggests a change in the master agreement, but the union insists that all employers sign the same agreement without the change. That may be bad-faith bargaining because the union has no intention of engaging in the give and take of bargaining with the employer, just as an employer using Boulware-ism tactics has no intention of engaging in true bargaining with a union.

C. SUBJECTS FOR BARGAINING

1. Classification of Bargaining Subjects

The Board has divided the subjects for bargaining into three categories: mandatory, permissive, and unlawful subjects for bargaining. Each category has a different bargaining obligation.

The mandatory subjects for bargaining are those listed in Section 8(d) of the Act: wages, hours, and other terms and conditions of employment. The parties have a duty to bargain over mandatory subjects at the request of either party. The parties may bargain to impasse and engage in a strike or lockout over mandatory subjects.

Permissive subjects do not relate directly to wages, hours, and working conditions, but are discussed voluntarily. One party may request bargaining on a permissive subject, but the other party may lawfully refuse to bargain over it. The party may bargain about a permissive subject at first, then unilaterally decide to stop. That is lawful because there is no duty to bargain over permissive subjects. The parties may not bargain to impasse, strike, or lockout over a permissive subject. Thus, if the parties have reached an agreement on all mandatory subjects on which they are bargaining, they must sign a contract incorporating their agreement. A party cannot refuse to sign because agreement was not reached on a permissive subject. If agreement is reached on a permissive subject and incorporated into the contract, the agreement is binding and enforceable. However, a party may retract an agreement on a permissive subject of bargaining at any time until the contract is signed.

Bargaining is prohibited on illegal subjects. An agreement reached on an illegal subject is void and unenforceable. Illegal subjects include such matters as a clause requiring union membership as soon as an employee is hired rather than after thirty days of employment as required by Section 8(a)(3); a clause discriminating between employees on the basis of race or sex; or a clause containing an unlawful hot cargo agreement (see Chapter Eight).

2. Typical Mandatory Subjects

Since a bonus or an incentive plan is a form of wages, bonuses are therefore mandatory subjects of bargaining. Issues such as seniority, job assignments, and promotions are all conditions of employment, and therefore are mandatory subjects.

a. Fringe Benefits. Vacations, holiday pay, and fringe benefits, such as pension and health and welfare plans, are all mandatory subjects of bargaining because they pertain to wages. However, the Supreme Court has held that the subject of increased pension benefits for employees who are already retired is a permissive subject of bargaining. The Court reasoned that retired persons are no longer employees under the Act.

What if a collective bargaining agreement specifies certain hospitalization benefits but does not specify the insurance carrier? Must the employer bargain with the union before changing the carrier? If changing carriers does not result in changing the benefits the employees receive, the employer may make the change unilaterally, because the change does not affect conditions of employment. If, however, the new insurance carrier proposes to implement "cost containment" procedures that might affect contractually negotiated benefits, then the employer must bargain with the union over the change. If the contract specifies the carrier, then, as with any other contractual provision, the employer may not change the carrier during the contract's term without the union's agreement.

b. Conditions of Employment. The Supreme Court has held that vending machine food prices in a company cafeteria used by employees are a mandatory subject of bargaining. Contractual provisions as to discipline (e.g., proposals for discharge only for just cause, warnings before discipline, or progressive discipline) are mandatory subjects of bargaining. A union security clause (see Chapter Ten) is a condition of employment and thus a mandatory subject of bargaining, except in "right-to-work" states in which the clause is illegal. Proposals for the checkoff of union dues and for hiring halls are mandatory subjects. The Board has recently held that the implementation of drug/alcohol testing programs for current employees is a mandatory subject of bargaining but that preemployment testing of job applicants is not a mandatory subject.

Is a proposal that an employer post a bond guaranteeing the employees' wages or payment of fringe benefits a mandatory subject of bargaining? Although a bond relates to the mandatory subject of wages, the Board has held that bonds are a permissive subject because the relationship to wages is too remote.

Issues have arisen recently regarding an employer's right to discontinue bonus programs unilaterally. Thus, in one case, the Board upheld an employer's unilateral right to discontinue giving employees a holiday meal and hams because they were gifts rather than compensation or conditions of employment. The Board ruled in several other cases however that employers violated the Act by unilaterally discontinuing Christmas bonuses that had been regularly paid for many years so that the employees properly regarded the bonus as part of their compensation. In general, a payment or "gift" item is more likely to be considered a mandatory condition of employment that cannot be discontinued unilaterally rather than a gratuity if it has been in effect a long time, has been given consistently regardless of the employer's economic situation, and if it is based upon an individual employee's pay rate, years of service, or productivity rather than the same for all employees.

c. Arbitration Provisions. Grievance and arbitration provisions are mandatory subjects of bargaining because they are considered conditions of employment. Thus, the parties may bargain to impasse over such matters as the method of selecting arbitrators, the issues subject to arbitration, time limits for processing grievances, and the union's access to the plant to investigate and process grievances. The Board has held that recording or transcribing a grievance session is a permissive subject of bargaining, so that neither party may insist to impasse on the issue. The Board reasoned that using a recording device might have a tendency to inhibit free and open discussion of grievances and undermine the informal nature of grievance meetings. In contrast, proposals pertaining to transcribing arbitration sessions are a mandatory subject of bargaining. The Board distinguishes arbitration from grievance procedures because arbitration is an adjudicatory type proceeding that is formal and adversarial so that there is a strong reason for there to be a formal record.

A provision for interest arbitration (arbitration of new contract terms) is classified as a permissive subject of bargaining because interest arbitration has only an indirect impact upon contractual wages, hours, and working conditions.

3. Permissive Subjects of Bargaining

a. Ratification Procedures. The procedures either party uses to approve a contract are a permissive subject of bargaining. The employer can lawfully propose that the union submit the employer's final offer to a full union membership vote. However, the union has the right to decide on its own ratification process and can lawfully refuse to bargain over the employer's proposal. In contrast, the employer cannot condition a wage offer on the union's agreement to submit the offer for ratification or to have a secret ballot. That is improperly conditioning a mandatory subject (wages) on the union's agreement on a permissive subject (the ratification process).

b. Changes in the Bargaining Unit. Attempts to expand, narrow, or modify the bargaining unit are permissive subjects. Suppose a union certified to represent the production and maintenance employees proposes that the contract cover clerical employees as well. The employer could refuse to bargain over expanding the unit and the union could not insist to impasse on expansion.

If a bargaining unit is certified in the name of an international union, but the international assigns the employees to a local, can the international insist that only the local's name appear on a contract? No, because any attempt to modify the international's certification by assigning it to the local is a permissive subject of bargaining. Similarly, if the certification is in only the local's name, an employer's proposal to include the international as a contractual party is a permissive subject.

c. Transcripts of Bargaining Sessions. The Board has held that neither party can insist that there be a stenographic transcript or recording of bargaining sessions, the same rule applied to grievance meetings discussed above, because the recording of bargaining sessions, except by mutual agreement, may undermine the informality and flexibility needed for successful bargaining.

d. Strike Settlement Agreements. A strike settlement agreement on the rights of returning strikers is a permissive subject of bargaining. A union can lawfully propose that the employer take back all strikers including those who have been permanently replaced and not discipline any employees for strike misconduct. But the employer can refuse to bargain on these subjects. Proposals to withdraw NLRB charges or suits are permissive subjects. Thus, if an employer and union have agreed on all mandatory bargaining subjects, a union cannot refuse to sign a contract unless the employer agrees to drop pending charges or a suit.

4. Bargaining Tactics in Light of the Mandatory/Permissive Subject Distinction

Sometimes a subject is very important to a union although it is classified as a permissive subject. If a strike has been marked by violence, the union may need a clause forgiving strike misconduct and dropping pending litigation. What if a union resolves all mandatory subjects of bargaining, but these permissive subjects remain open? Or what if a union does not bring up these matters until all mandatory subjects are resolved? Then the union is in a helpless position, as the employer can refuse to discuss the permissive subjects. Since all mandatory items are already agreed to, the union could be forced to sign the agreement and return to work. Thus, as a tactic, a union must keep both mandatory and permissive subjects of bargaining open on the bargaining table and resolve the permissive subjects at the same time that agreement is reached on the mandatory items.

What if a party submits a package proposal that includes both mandatory and permissive bargaining subjects, such as coupling a wage offer with a proposal for interest arbitration on a midterm wage reopener, and the other side accepts the mandatory subject proposal, but rejects the permissive subject proposal? The Board has held that a party can properly change its position on a mandatory subject proposal because the mandatory subject proposal is conditional on acceptance of the total package.

D. THE EMPLOYER'S DUTY TO BARGAIN BEFORE CHANGING CONDITIONS OF EMPLOYMENT

An employer has the duty to negotiate a collective bargaining agreement covering the employees the union represents. Beyond that, however, an employer has a continuing duty to notify and bargain with the union before making any changes in the employee's wages, hours, or working conditions on a mandatory subject of bargaining. A change an employer makes without the union's consent is called a unilateral change. It is the employer's duty to bargain before making unilateral changes in mandatory conditions of employment. This duty may arise before the parties have negotiated a contract, during a contract's term, or after a contract's expiration.

1. Unilateral Action before a Contract

The duty to bargain arises as soon as a union is certified by the Board or recognized voluntarily by the employer—even before formal contract negotiations begin. The employer must bargain to impasse before making a change in any mandatory subject of bargaining. (Remember, an impasse is a deadlock reached after good-faith bargaining.) The employer cannot put any changes into effect except those discussed in bargaining. It cannot offer employees better or worse conditions than those proposed to the union. In general, an employer must bargain over both the decision to change a mandatory condition of employment and the effect of the decision on the employees. However, as discussed below, an employer may only be required to bargain over the effect of a decision regarding the basic nature or direction of the company.

2. Unilateral Changes during Bargaining

If the parties bargaining in good faith reach a bargaining impasse on the employer's proposals, and there is no contract in effect, the employer can unilaterally implement all or part of its last offer on which there is an impasse. The employer cannot unilaterally impose worse conditions than proposed. If the employer's proposal included an increase in benefits, it can implement any increase up to the amount of its offer. The union's choice at that time might be to accept the changes or strike.

An employer has a right to hire replacements and continue operations during a strike (see Chapter Six). If an employer hires replacements, they can be hired at the terms and conditions contained in the last offer to the union.

3. Bargaining during the Contract's Term

a. Items not Covered by the Contract. After the parties execute a contract, the employer's right to make unilateral changes in working conditions during the contract's term depends upon whether the contract covers the matter that is the subject of the change. Section 8(d) of the Act, defining the duty to bargain under Section 8(a)(5), requires that the parties continue the terms and conditions of their existing contract in effect until the contract's expiration date, and provides that neither party is required to discuss or agree to any modification of the contract's terms and conditions if such modification is to become effective before the contract is subject to reopening under its terms. These provisions forbid an employer from unilaterally changing the terms and conditions of employment embodied in a collective bargaining agreement without the union's consent, even if the employer has given notice to the union and is willing to bargain over the proposed change, and regardless of the employer's good faith and economic need for the change.

An employer can unilaterally take any action the contract permits it to take without notice to and bargaining with the union. If a contract gives an employer the right to lay off employees for lack of work, the employer can unilaterally lay off in accordance with the contract without any further bargaining. If the contract is silent on a particular mandatory condition of employment, the employer has a duty to give the union timely notice of any intended change in the condition and to bargain with the union before making any unilateral change as if there were no contract in effect. The notice must be given sufficiently in advance to allow a union reasonable opportunity to bargain before the change is implemented. Thus, if the contract does not cover the employer's right to lay off, the employer must notify the union and bargain with it before laying off any employees. If the contract is silent, the employer's only obligation is to bargain. After bargaining in good faith to an impasse, the employer can take unilateral action. In contrast, if the issue is covered by the contract, the employer cannot unilaterally change the terms, even after bargaining.

Also, the employer must bargain with the union before instituting new plant rules during the term of a contract or new production standards if the rules are enforced through disciplinary action.

Frequently part of an employer's workforce may be represented by a union, and part may be unorganized. For example, a factory's production and maintenance employees may be represented, but the office clerical employees are not. The Board has held that if an employer grants a new benefit to a group of unrepresented employees (e.g., an improved pension plan), which is a mandatory subject of bargaining and which is not specifically covered by the represented employees' collective bargaining agreement, the employer must bargain with the union over providing the benefit to the represented employees, unless there has been a clear and unmistakable waiver by the union of its bargaining rights. Of course, the employer's only obligation is to bargain in good faith with the union over the matter. It has no obligation to reach an agreement extending the benefit.

b. Reassignment of Work or Plant Transfers as an Unlawful Unilateral Change. During the 1970s, the Board gradually developed the doctrine that the reassignment or transfer of work to outside the bargaining unit during the term of a contract to reduce labor costs, or the transfer of operations to a new location where labor costs were lower, constituted a unilateral modification of the contract in violation of Sections 8(a)(5) and 8(d) of the Act unless the contract permitted such action. The Board reasoned that the contractual recognition, seniority, and wage provisions were an implied limitation on the employer's right to reassign or transfer work, etc. because any such action would deprive the employees of the benefits of the contract that the union had negotiated. Several courts of appeals, however, reversed key Board decisions applying this doctrine. In the *Illinois Coil Spring* decision,[4] the Reagan Board overruled the doctrine altogether. In this case, the company lost a major customer during the term of the contract. The company proposed midterm reductions in wage and benefit levels to the union, and stated that it would transfer work to another, nonunion, location if the union did not agree. The union refused and the company transferred the work to the other location, as it had threatened to do.

The Board rejected the union's argument that the contractual provisions were an implied restriction on the employer's right to transfer or relocate work. The Board held that neither the midterm transfer nor relocation of work constituted a midterm contract modification violative of Section 8(d) unless the action violated a specific express provision of the contract prohibiting such action. This decision was subsequently upheld by the court of appeals. Thus, under current law, an employer may lawfully "threaten" a union that it will move work out of the bargaining unit or even to another nonunion location unless the union agrees to certain midterm concessions. The employer may not unilaterally implement any proposed changes in the contract over the union's objection, but if the union does not agree, the employer is free to reassign or relocate the work as it proposed unless the contract specifically prohibits the action. There are two limitations on the *Illinois Coil Spring* doctrine. First, as discussed below, depending on the reason for the action, an employer may be obligated to bargain over

---

[4] See legal principle 7.

both the decision and the effect of the decision on the bargaining unit employees before implementing it. Second, as discussed in Chapter Four, the reassignment or relocation of bargaining unit work may violate Section 8(a)(3) of the Act if the union can prove that the employer's action was motivated by unlawful anti-union animus rather than for legitimate economic reasons.

c. The Board's Authority to Interpret the Contract. Frequently it is difficult to determine whether or not a contract permits unilateral action without bargaining on a particular matter. The contract language may be ambiguous. Interpreted one way, the employer may have authority to act unilaterally, but interpreted another, the contract may prohibit the employer's actions altogether. A contract may be silent, but past practice between the parties or the bargaining history may establish that the employer is prohibited from taking action or that the union had waived its bargaining rights. Thus, the Board must interpret the contract to determine whether unilateral employer action is permitted or not. In *C & C Plywood* the Supreme Court upheld the Board's authority to interpret a contract as necessary to determine whether an unfair labor practice has occurred.[5]

d. Waiver of Bargaining Rights. Although an employer is usually obligated to bargain over mandatory subjects of bargaining not covered by the contract, the union can waive that right.

(1) WAIVER THROUGH BARGAINING. The most common form of waiver occurs during bargaining if the union proposes a clause limiting the employer's authority, but fails to obtain the desired provision. What if a contract has no clause prohibiting subcontracting and the union proposes a contractual restriction? The matter is negotiated thoroughly but the employer refuses to agree to any contractual restriction. The contract is signed without any subcontract-

ing restrictions and the employer subsequently subcontracts work without bargaining with the union. Since the contract is silent, the employer ordinarily has a duty to bargain with the union before subcontracting. However, the Board would probably conclude that the union waived its right to bargain by proposing, but failing to obtain a contractual restriction.

The Board has stated that a waiver of the right to bargain over matters not covered by the contract must be "clear and unmistakable." This rule follows the general Board principle that a waiver of a statutory right (e.g., the right to bargain over a change in working conditions) must be clear and unmistakable. The Board will not find a waiver unless a subject is fully discussed during bargaining and consciously waived by the union. For example, if a union simply proposes a limit on subcontracting in its written proposals, but does not discuss the matter in bargaining or drops it after only a brief discussion, the union probably has not waived its right to bargain over subcontracting during the contract's term. If a union withdraws a proposal, the better procedure in most cases to avoid waiver is for it to state expressly that it is not waiving its right to bargain on the subject if the employer should take unilateral action.

(2) WAIVER BY UNION INACTION. A union may waive its rights if an employer takes unilateral action and the union fails to protest and request bargaining. However, failure to protest immediately is not a waiver if the employer does not give the union reasonable notice of its intention to act or presents the union with an accomplished fact so that it is clear that a request for bargaining would be futile.

(3) CONTRACTUAL ZIPPER CLAUSES. A union may also waive its right to bargain over a unilateral change by agreeing to a so-called contractual "zipper clause." This is a clause that "zips up" the agreement by stating that the parties have had the right and opportunity to bargain over all mandatory subjects of bargaining and that they

[5] See legal principle 10.A.

waive their right to bargain over any matters during the term of the agreement. If such a clause is applied literally, the employer can take unilateral action on any matter not expressly covered in the contract.

Until recently, the Board refused to apply zipper clauses literally, and took the position that a union could not waive the right to bargain on new matters following the execution of a contract despite broad zipper clause language. Instead, the Board examined all the facts and circumstances of the negotiations to determine whether the union, in fact, had waived the right to bargain on a particular subject. Now, however, the Board has indicated it will apply such clauses more literally. For example, an employer adopted a new savings plan for nonbargaining unit employees. The union requested bargaining over the adoption of the savings plan for the unit employees. The employer refused to bargain on the grounds that the zipper clause did not require bargaining during the contract term. The Board upheld the employer's contention. The Board noted, however, that the employer had not unilaterally changed any contractual terms, but had only refused to bargain over new terms. The Board indicated that a contractual zipper clause can be used as a "shield" by the employer to maintain the contractual status quo, but cannot be used as a "sword" by the employer to prevent bargaining over unilateral changes in contractual terms.[6]

The Board has also recently upheld an employer's unilateral right under a zipper clause to discontinue a bonus that it had given for nearly forty years. However, in that case, the employer had stated in bargaining that the purpose of its proposed zipper-clause language was to permit it to eliminate past practices. Thus, although the Board permitted the clause to be used as a "sword" for a unilateral change, it was clear from the bargaining history that the clause was intended to authorize just such action.

4. The Duty to Bargain over Changes in Business Operations

One of the most controversial issues pertaining to the duty to bargain is the employer's obligation to bargain over changes in business operations, such as subcontracting, reassignment of work, plant transfers, or closing the business.

If the contract either permits or prohibits unilateral action, both the employer and the union are bound by their agreement, as they are to any other term in the contract. If, for example, the contract permits unilateral subcontracting or work reassignments, the employer could subcontract or reassign work without bargaining with the union. But what if the contract is silent? In virtually every case, an employer must bargain with the union about the effect on employees of a decision to change the nature of the operations. The controversial area is the employer's duty to notify the union and bargain over the *decision itself* before it is made rather than just bargain over the effect. The evolving principles governing the scope of an employer's bargaining obligation may be best analyzed by considering the leading Board and Supreme Court cases on the question.

a. The Fibreboard Decision. *Fibreboard Paper Products Corp.*, decided in 1964, was the first leading case to consider the scope of the employer's duty to bargain over certain basic managerial decisions as well as the effect of a decision on the bargaining unit.[7] In *Fibreboard* an employer hired an outside contractor to do plant maintenance work formerly done by bargaining unit employees. The employer notified the union of the decision after it had been made and offered to bargain on the effect on the employees. The Supreme Court upheld the NLRB's decision that the employer had to bargain over the decision itself, not just the effect. The Court, however, limited its decision to the specific facts of the case. It said

---

[6] See legal principle 11.B.

[7] See legal principle 13.

that the employer must bargain over the decision to subcontract, rather than just the effect, if the subcontracting replaces bargaining unit employees with employees of an independent contractor to do the same work under similar conditions of employment.

The Board subsequently further limited *Fibreboard* by holding that subcontracting must have a demonstrable adverse impact on employees in the unit before the employer is obligated to bargain over it. There is no need to bargain over subcontracting of small amounts of bargaining unit work repeatedly subcontracted on a regular basis because of the minimal impact. However, the employer must bargain if the subcontracting varies from past practice or has a significant impact on job tenure, employment security, or anticipated work opportunity.

b. The General Motors Decision. The *General Motors* case, decided in 1971, further restricted the employer's duty to bargain over certain basic decisions.[8] General Motors decided to sell a retail service center. The Board held that the company had no duty to bargain over its decision to sell because it was a basic capital decision on the scope and ultimate direction of the enterprise.

c. The First National Maintenance Corp. Decision. For many years following the *Fibreboard* and *General Motors* decisions, the Board held that an employer's decision to shut down one facility if others remained open (a partial shutdown) is not a basic capital decision, and that there is a duty to bargain over both the decision and the effect of a partial closing. However, the Supreme Court in the *First National Maintenance Corp.* decision in 1981 reversed the Board[9] and held that there is only a duty to bargain over the effect of an economically motivated decision to close part of a business. The Court reasoned that the decision involved a change in the scope and direction of the enterprise, similar to the decision to close a business entirely. The Court stated that the harm likely to an employer's need to operate freely, in deciding whether to shut down part of its business purely for economic reasons, outweighed the benefits that might be gained through the union's participation in the decision-making process.

d. The United Technologies Decision. In *Otis Elevator Co., a subsidiary of United Technologies* (1984) the Board, on which Reagan appointees then held a majority, reconsidered the scope of an employer's bargaining obligation in light of the *First National Maintenance Corp.* decision.[10] In *United Technologies,* the company unilaterally decided to discontinue its research and development functions at two locations, to consolidate all such functions in a facility at another location, and to transfer certain employees from the old facilities to the new location. The facilities to be closed were outdated and performed overlapping functions, and the company hoped to reduce production costs through the consolidation. The Board ruled that the company had no duty to bargain over the *decision* to consolidate operations. However, the four members on the Board at the time split on the reasons for their decision. Two Board members issued a plurality decision singling out *labor costs* as the controlling factor in determining an employer's duty to bargain. They stated that if a decision turns on labor costs and is not a change in the basic scope, direction, or nature of the enterprise, then the employer must bargain over the decision itself as well as over the effect. If, however, labor costs are not the controlling factor, then the employer is not obligated to bargain over the decision but only over the effect. The two-member plurality opinion further stated that this rule would apply in every case involving changes in basic operating procedures including decisions to subcontract work; to reorganize, consolidate, or

---

[8] See legal principle 12.A.

[9] See legal principle 12.A.

[10] See legal principle 12.B.

relocate operations; to sell all or part of a business or its assets; or a decision to invest in labor saving machinery, etc. (The plurality decision did acknowledge, however, that under the Supreme Court's *Fibreboard* decision, an employer would have to bargain over both the decision and the effect of a decision to subcontract work to be done on premises.) The other two Board members, although agreeing with the plurality opinion's conclusion that the employer had no obligation under the facts of the case to bargain with the union over its decision to consolidate operations, did not agree that "labor costs" should be the controlling factor. Rather, in separate opinions they each proposed somewhat broader but vague standards under which a decision would be subject to bargaining only if the subject is "amenable to resolution" through the bargaining process. Under this approach, an employer would be obligated to bargain over a decision if a factor over which the union has control, such as labor costs, is a significant consideration in the employer's decision so that union assistance or a union concession could make a difference in the decision.

Although only two of the four then-current Board members adopted the narrow "labor costs" test in the *United Technology* case, the Board as a whole applied that test as controlling in later cases. Thus, a Board majority subsequently held that an employer has no obligation to bargain over a decision unless labor costs are the primary or most important factor, that is, the decision must "turn upon" labor costs before an employer has any obligation to bargain over it. This narrow rule would enable an employer to evade any obligation to bargain over a decision to change its operations simply by publicly justifying the decision on other grounds even if labor costs are, in fact, an important factor. However, more recently in *LaPeer Foundry and Machine, Inc.*,[11] the Board lessened the impact of *United Technologies* by ruling that an employer's *decision*

[11] See legal principle 12.C.

to lay off employees for economic reasons is a mandatory subject of bargaining. In *LaPeer* the Board distinguished an employer's decision to lay off employees from a decision to shut down an unprofitable department or to consolidate operations. The Board reasoned that the decision to lay off employees directly affects the employees' terms and conditions of employment and turns on labor costs while, in contrast, the decision to shut down unprofitable departments or to consolidate operations, etc., may result in job losses as only a secondary effect. Also, the decision to lay off employees is amenable to resolution through the collective bargaining process because the union can offer alternatives such as wage reductions or modified work rules as a means for the company to save money without a layoff.

Although the Board concluded in *LaPeer* that an employer must provide notice to and bargain with a union concerning both the decision to lay off bargaining unit employees and the effects thereof, the Board also emphasized that to protect the employer's interest in a quick resolution, negotiations concerning the decision must occur in a timely and speedy fashion and that a union must make a timely request for bargaining once an employer has notified it that a layoff is under consideration. Also the Board stated that *LaPeer* applies only to an economically motivated decision to lay off employees to reduce labor costs during a period of economic difficulty. The decision does not require that an employer bargain over a decision to change the scope and direction of the enterprise, such as to shut down part of a business as in *First National Maintenance Corp.*, or to consolidate facilities as in *United Technologies*. Thus the Board's current approach in *LaPeer Foundry*, while somewhat broader than that applied in *United Technologies* at the height of the Reagan Board, is still restrictive on a union's bargaining rights. The Worker Adjustment and Retraining Notification Act, effective February 4, 1989, which in general requires that employers employing 100 or more employees provide at least sixty days advance notice before a mass layoff or plant closing, does not impose any bargaining obligations. Thus the duty to bargain after notice is still determined under the LMRA under the principles discussed above.

5. Bankruptcy as a Justification for Unilateral Employer Action

In the *Bildisco* decision, the Supreme Court held that an employer in bankruptcy could unilaterally modify or terminate the preexisting collective bargaining agreement before receiving the formal approval of the bankruptcy court to reject the agreement.[12] This decision was widely criticized, and labor was successful in obtaining an amendment to the Bankruptcy code (Title 11, United States Code Section 1113) that requires prior approval of the bankruptcy court before the bankrupt employer (technically called the debtor-in-possession or the trustee) can reject a collective bargaining agreement. The amendment requires that the debtor in possession, or the trustee, first submit its proposed contract modifications to the union for consideration before filing a petition for rejection with the bankruptcy court and provide the union with the relevant information necessary to evaluate the proposal. The debtor in possession or trustee must meet in good faith with the union before the hearing on the employer's application to reject the agreement in an effort to reach mutual agreement on the modifications. The Bankruptcy Code also provides that the proposed modifications must be "necessary" to permit the reorganization of the debtor and assure that all creditors and all of the affected parties (i.e., the employees) are treated fairly and equitably.

There are detailed procedures and time requirements to be followed in a hearing to modify a collective bargaining agreement that must be reviewed by any union involved in bankruptcy proceedings.

[12] See legal principle 11.D.

6. Board Remedies for Unilateral Actions

The Board has strong remedies against an employer who refuses to bargain over a decision over which the employer must bargain. The employer can of course be ordered to bargain with the union over both the decision and the effect as appropriate. The Board can also order the employer to resume the prior operation as it existed before the improper unilateral change if that is at all feasible. If employees have been terminated or laid off as a result of the employer's decision, the employer may be ordered to reinstate the employees to the positions they previously held or, if those positions no longer exist, to substantially equivalent positions with full seniority rights. If work has been improperly transferred to another location so that the employees would have to move in order to resume work, the employer may be required to pay the employees' moving costs or even reasonable retraining costs for employees who decide not to move. To ensure that the employees are made whole, the Board can also order an employer to pay its adversely affected employees backpay whether or not the prior operation is restored from the date of the employer's unilateral action until the employer and the union reach a mutual agreement on the decision and effect, a bona fide impasse is reached, the union fails to begin negotiations with the employer after the employer notifies the union it is willing to bargain, or the union itself fails to bargain in good faith after negotiations begin.

The Board's remedy is more limited if the employer has only failed to meet its obligation to bargain over the effect of a decision. In such a case, the employer is, of course, ordered to bargain with the union over the effect. Also, as an incentive to the employer to bargain in good faith, the Board customarily imposes a limited backpay remedy to compensate the employees for their losses resulting from the employer's failure to bargain beginning five days after the date of the Board's decision ordering bargaining and continuing until the earliest of the following conditions: (1) the date the company and union reach agreement on the effect of the decision; (2) the parties reach a bona fide impasse in bargaining; (3) the union fails to request bargaining within five days of the date of the Board's decision or fails to begin bargaining within five days of the company's notice of its desire to bargain; or (4) the union fails to bargain in good faith. As a further limitation, backpay may not exceed the amount an employee would have earned from the date of the employer's unilateral action to the date when the employee secured equivalent employment elsewhere or the employer offered to bargain, but not less than the employees would have earned in a two-week period at their normal wage rate.

Prior to the Supreme Court's *First National Maintenance* decision, and the Board's subsequent decision in *United Technologies,* it was frequently unclear whether an employer was obligated to bargain over a decision itself or only over the effect. As a tactic, unions usually demanded bargaining over both a decision and the effect. Under *United Technologies,* of course, there are far fewer decisions on which an employer may be obligated to bargain. However, there may still be some tactical advantage to the union to demand bargaining over both the decision and the effect of most employer actions. This will avoid any question of waiver by the union and place at least some pressure on the employer to bargain over a decision to avoid any potential liability even under the current Board doctrine.

7. Arbitration and the NLRB's Role in Unilateral Change Cases: The Collyer Doctrine

As the *C & C Plywood* case noted above points out, it is possible for an employer's unilateral change to be both an unfair labor practice and a contract violation. If the contract contains an arbitration clause, should the arbitrator or the Board interpret the contract? *C & C Plywood* establishes that the Board has the authority to interpret the contract. However, national labor policy also strongly favors arbitration as a means of resolving contractual disputes. How should the respective roles of the arbitrator and the Board be accommodated?

The Board resolved these issues in *Collyer Insulated Wire,* holding that if a collective bargaining agreement provides for arbitration, the Board will defer unfair labor practice charges alleging a unilateral change in violation of Section 8(a)(5), that might also be a contract violation, to arbitration.[13] The Board defers to arbitration even though it has the statutory authority to resolve the issue. This policy is known as the "*Collyer* doctrine."

The Board defers these cases to arbitration because resolution of the contract-interpretation issue will also resolve the unfair labor practice charge. Thus, if the employer's action violates the contract, the employer cannot take unilateral action. The arbitrator's award requiring the employer to rescind the action and restore the prior conditions also remedies any possible unfair labor practice. If the arbitrator decides that the contract permits the employer's action, there is no need for bargaining and no Section 8(a)(5) violation because an employer does not have to bargain if the contract permits unilateral action. Thus, the arbitrator's decision, either way, resolves the unfair labor practice issues as well.

The procedures the Board follows in deferring cases to arbitration and the standards it applies in determining whether to accept an arbitrator's decision on a matter that may also be an unfair labor practice are discussed in Chapter Nine.

8. The Duty to Bargain upon the Contract's Expiration

When a contract expires, the contractual wages, hours, and other terms and conditions of employment remain in effect as established conditions. Conditions that are

---

[13] See legal principle 16.

mandatory bargaining subjects cannot be changed unilaterally by the employer although the agreement has expired. The employer must bargain to impasse before making a change. For instance, an employer cannot unilaterally change the employees' contractual wages or the seniority system after the contract has expired before bargaining to impasse. The employer's bargaining obligation before changing the conditions of employment after a contract expires is basically the same as its bargaining obligation before a contract is executed. A unilateral change without bargaining violates Section 8(a)(5).

As an exception, contractual union security and checkoff clauses expire automatically; employees cannot be required to be union members or pay union dues after the contract expires (see Chapter Ten).

The Board has held that contractually established grievance procedures remain in effect after the contract expires and are subject to unilateral change only after a bargaining impasse is reached. Also a grievance arising before a contract expires is arbitrable even if the request to arbitrate is not made until after the contract expires. At one time, the Board held that there was no duty to arbitrate grievances *arising after* a contract providing for arbitration expired. Currently, however, the Board's view is that if a contract contains a broad arbitration clause and does not contain language to the contrary, there is a presumption that the contractual obligation to arbitrate grievances extends to post-expiration disputes if they are over rights "arising under" the expired contract, that is, the dispute concerns contract rights capable of accruing or vesting to some degree during the life of the contract and ripening or remaining enforceable after the contract expires. This issue is discussed in greater detail in Chapter Nine.

To prevent the employer from making unilateral changes after a contract expires, a union can propose short-term extensions of the contract while bargaining on a new agreement takes place. If the employer agrees, the entire agreement remains in effect and cannot be changed unilaterally. An extension preserves the union security provisions.

Of course, the contractual no-strike clause also remains in effect if the contract is extended. Thus, before striking, the union must wait until the end of an extension period or serve a cancellation notice if the contract is extended indefinitely.

E. THE DUTY TO PROVIDE INFORMATION FOR BARGAINING

1. The Right to Relevant Information

Unions have a broad right to information relevant to the negotiation and administration of the collective bargaining agreement. This obligation is based on the principle that the employer's duty to bargain includes the duty to provide the union with the information it needs to engage in informed bargaining. There cannot be a good-faith bargaining impasse on a subject if the employer has refused to provide the union with relevant information it has requested in order to bargain over the issue.

The employer need not give assistance voluntarily so the union must request the information it wants. The information requested must be relevant to the formulation of the union's bargaining position, contract negotiations, or contract administration. Also, the union is entitled to information needed to evaluate and process a grievance through the grievance procedure to arbitration. For example, if a union is considering a proposal limiting subcontracting, it can request data on company subcontracts. If the union believes contractual overtime provisions have been violated, it can request data on the number and distribution of overtime hours. If there is a grievance as to production-line speed, the union is entitled to the company's time-study data, and may even make its own time study. The employer must give a union representative access to company property for this purpose. If an employee is discharged, the union can request information about the basis of the discharge and the evidence supporting it. However, an employer is not obligated to provide copies of witness statements before the hearing.

The union is entitled to information on the employer's hiring and promotion of minority group bargaining unit employees. However, a union usually is not entitled to a copy of an employer's affirmative action program, if any. A union is entitled to the names of each employee in the bargaining unit, their job classifications, wage rate, and seniority date. These basic data are necessary to begin bargaining. The union can also request the name of each new employee, as hired, in order to enforce the union security provisions of a contract. Technically, a union represents strike replacements; thus, a striking union can request the names of the replacements. However, the Board has held that an employer does not have to release the names if the employer has a reasonable basis for believing that the union will use the list to harass the replacements.

If relevant, the union is also entitled to information pertaining to nonbargaining unit employees. Thus, for example, if the union has reason to believe that employees outside the bargaining unit are performing bargaining unit work it can request information about the work such employees are doing. The union may be entitled to information as to the wages and fringe benefits received by nonunit employees because such information may be relevant to the union's formulation of its own contract proposals. If a union suspects that an employer has improperly established an alter-ego or double-breasted operation to evade the collective bargaining agreement (see discussion later in this chapter), the union may request detailed personnel and financial information to uncover the relationship between the companies.

This list of possible information is far from exhaustive. Basically, the scope of the union's right to information is as broad as the union's need for information on any matter relevant to the bargaining process, contract administration, and the evaluation and processing of grievances.

Although it does not occur often, employers are also entitled to relevant data from the union. If a contract requires that an employer obtain his employees from a union hiring hall, the employer can request data as to the union's ability to refer enough qualified employees to meet the employer's needs such as the list of names and addresses of employees who apply for referral.

2. Limits on the Employer's Duty

There are some limits on the employer's obligation to provide information. The union's request cannot unduly burden the employer. Unions may have to pay for the employer's administrative expenses (such as clerical and copying costs) when gathering large amounts of information. If substantial costs are involved in gathering the requested information, the parties may bargain over the amount the employer may charge the union. If no agreement is reached, the employer may simply permit the union to have access to the records from which the union can reasonably compile the needed information on its own. Also, the employer can require the union to state its reasons for requesting information.

Usually the employer does not have to interpret the data provided to the union or put them in the precise form the union requests. However, if the information requested is computerized or needs explanation to be understood, the employer must put the data in a useable form and give the necessary explanation. In most cases, a union is entitled to a copy of relevant company records. However, if the records are simple and uncomplicated, the employer may only have to allow the union to inspect the records and make notes as to their contents.

a. *Right to Profit Information.* The union is entitled to financial information about company profits only if the employer pleads it is financially unable to pay a requested increase. This is called "pleading poverty." The union is not entitled to financial data just because it would assist it in preparing wage demands for bargaining. The Board is very strict in applying this doctrine. Thus, if an employer indicates that it could afford a certain increase with difficulty but prefers to use its available funds for other purposes, the union would not be entitled to financial information because the employer did not specifically state that it could not afford the increase.

b. Confidential Data. The Supreme Court has indicated that an employer's legitimate interest in the confidentiality of certain information may prevail over the union's need. In *Detroit Edison*, the union requested that the company provide it with a copy of an aptitude test used to determine eligibility for promotions and copies of the test results for those taking the test.[14] The data were needed to prepare a grievance the union was arbitrating over the denial of promotions to certain senior employees. The company denied the union's request for the test on the grounds that the test had to be kept secret. The company did offer to allow a psychologist, selected by the union, to evaluate the test in confidence, but the union rejected this proposal. The employer also denied the union's request for the test results of individual employees because the company had promised employees that it would keep the results confidential. The company did offer to release the test results of any employee who signed a waiver permitting the release.

The Board held that the union was entitled to a copy of the test and the individual employees' test scores. The Supreme Court reversed the Board, holding that the employer did not have to turn over the test directly to the union and that the employer's requirement that the individual employees agree to the release of their scores was reasonable. The Court stated that the bur-

[14] See legal principle 17.A.

den on the union in getting the releases was minimal.

Since the *Detroit Edison* decision, the Board has proceeded carefully on a case-by-case basis in balancing the union's need for relevant information containing personal information about individual employees against the employees' privacy rights. The Board has required that the information provided identify the employees even without individual releases if identification is necessary for the union to use the information in a meaningful way and/or the employees' privacy interests are relatively slight compared to the union's need for the information. For example, co-employees usually know when another employee is disciplined or is absent. Thus, individual employees have only a very slight privacy interest at stake if the union is provided information about the number of times the employee has been absent or disciplined without the employee's consent. However, the reasons for an employee's absence may be personal, so that, depending upon the union's need for the information, the employer might reasonably require that the employee sign a release before that information is provided to the union.

c. Occupational Safety and Health Information. The Board has held that a union is entitled to a broad range of data from the employer pertaining to occupational safety and health, including such items as morbidity and mortality statistics on past and present employees; the generic names of all substances used in the plant and a statement of their known effects; results of clinical and laboratory studies of individual employees taken by the employer; and company statistics on occupational illnesses and accidents related to workers' compensation claims. Usually, however, an employer may remove the name of the individual employee and any references that would identify the individual from any medical information provided. Supplying the union with statistical or aggregate medical data may result in the unavoidable identification of some individual employees' medical information, but the Board has reasoned the union's need for the data, potentially revealing the past effects of the work place environment on the employees, outweighs any minimal intrusion into the employee's privacy.

The Board requires that the parties bargain in good faith regarding the conditions under which needed generic chemical information should be furnished to the union with appropriate safeguards to protect the company's legitimate rights to maintain trade secrets. The Board will impose specific remedies as to the records to be provided and the union's use or distribution of the information only if the parties are unable to agree.

A union has the right to select an outside specialist to enter the employer's facility and make necessary on-site inspections and tests relevant to the administration of a contractual safety clause, a pending grievance, or upcoming negotiations. The union does not have to rely upon the employer's safety data which, intentionally or not, may be biased. The Reagan Board applied a somewhat restrictive rule to determine a union's right to on-site testing, balancing the need for such tests against the employer's private property right. This means that an employer can lawfully deny access if the union could obtain the same information without going on premises. However, in most cases the union should still be able to justify its need for access to the company's property to inspect and test for safety hazards or to verify data provided by the company. The employer may limit union testing to reasonable times and periods and require the union to sign an agreement protecting any company trade secrets (e.g., confidential industrial processes) to which it may have access during the inspection.

F. THE BARGAINING DUTY OF SUCCESSOR EMPLOYERS

Generally, an employer is a successor employer if it takes over the business of another

employer, the predecessor's employees are retained as a majority of the new employer's work force, and the new employer continues operations in the same industry. The takeover may be through a merger or consolidation of two companies, a stock transfer, transfer of assets or any other business combination. In *Burns International Security Services, Inc.,* the Supreme Court held that a successor employer is not bound by the predecessor's collective bargaining agreement and is free to bargain for its own contract.[15] The Court said that ordering a successor employer to adopt the predecessor's contract is contrary to the principle of Section 8(d), which states an employer cannot be compelled to agree to specific contract terms. The successor may, however, be required to recognize and bargain with the incumbent union under the conditions discussed below. A successor employer may also be liable for the unfair labor practices committed by the predecessor provided the successor was aware of the violations at the time it assumed control.

1. Retaining the Prior Work Force

Under *Burns,* a new employer has no obligation to hire the prior employees. The new employer can hire or bring in all new employees if it wishes. However, the employer cannot discriminatorily refuse to retain prior employees because the employees were represented by a union. If the Board finds that the new employer discriminatorily refused to hire the prior employees, it will presume that the prior employees would have been a majority of the new workforce but for the discrimination and that the successor was obligated to bargain with the incumbent union before setting initial terms of employment. This can result in a substantial back pay award to the employees.

Under *Burns,* the new employer is obligated to bargain with the prior incumbent union when the employees represented by it comprise a majority of the new workforce. If the employer hires all the predecessor's

[15] See legal principle 18.A.

employees, it becomes a successor employer obligated to bargain with the incumbent union from the date of hiring. If the employer hires six of ten prior employees and five new employees, the Board presumes that the union continues to represent the six employees. The successor will be required to bargain with the union from the time it is clear that the six employees are a majority of the new workforce. If the new employer retains all ten of the prior employees and brings in twelve new employees as well, the employer is not legally a successor. It has no obligation to bargain with the prior union even though all the old employees are retained because the prior employees are not a majority of the new workforce. If the employer does not retain any of the prior employees it has no bargaining obligation with the incumbent union provided the decision to hire all new employees is not discriminatorily motivated.

In *Fall River Dyeing and Finishing Corp.,* the United States Supreme Court decided an important issue as to the time when a successor employer is obligated to recognize the incumbent union.[16] In that case, the purchasing employer initially started operations on a one-shift basis. It planned to expand ultimately to a second shift. The prior employees constituted a majority of the employees initially working on the first shift, but the company refused to recognize the incumbent union on the grounds that the company had no bargaining obligation until it employed its full workforce. The company started the second shift operation three months later, but it then refused to recognize the union because the prior employees did not constitute a majority of the employees in the expanded two-shift workforce. The Supreme Court affirmed the NLRB's ruling that the employer was obligated to recognize and bargain with the incumbent union as of the date the employer resumed production on the first shift. The Court upheld the NLRB's rule that a successor employer is obligated to

bargain with the incumbent union at such time as the incumbent represents a majority of the employees in a "substantial and representative complement" of employees. The criteria for determining whether a successor employer employs a substantial and representative employee complement are the same as the Board applies in determining whether a newly opened company has a substantial and representative workforce for the purpose of holding a representation election (discussed in Chapter Two). In upholding the Board's successorship rules, the Supreme Court emphasized the importance of permitting employees to be represented by their incumbent bargaining agent as quickly as possible in the unstable situation created by a change in ownership and the need to prevent an employer from exploiting the delay in recognition to undermine the union's support.

2. Remaining in the Same Industry

The principal requirement for successorship is that the prior employees comprise a majority of the new workforce. There is also a secondary requirement that there be substantial continuity of the employing industry. Basically, this requirement is met if the new employer uses substantially the same facilities, equipment, and production process; produces the same or a similar product; or performs the same services or is essentially in the same business. The Board also considers the similarity in the employees' working conditions and supervisors before and after the change in ownership, and whether the employer serves basically the same body of customers and geographic area.

What if an employer sells off part of its existing business to another company? The purchasing company will be a successor if the employees in the portion sold are an appropriate bargaining unit and the old employees constitute the majority of the new workforce. What if there is a time gap between the time the prior company closes down and the successor resumes business?

---

[16] See legal principle 18.B.

In *Fall River Dyeing,* the successor employer was obligated to bargain with the incumbent union even though there was a seven-month gap ("hiatus") between the date the old company closed and the new company resumed operation. Thus, regardless of the time gap, a successor employer may be obligated to bargain with the incumbent union if the two basic requirements for successorship are met: The old employees constitute a majority of the new workforce, and there is substantial continuity in the employing industry.

3. The Successor's Right to Establish Initial Terms of Employment

An employer is usually obligated to bargain with a union before making unilateral changes in wages, hours, or working conditions. Under *Burns,* however, the new employer is not obligated to bargain with the incumbent union until it is clear that the union still represents a majority, a fact that cannot be determined until after the workforce is hired. Thus, the new employer can unilaterally set the initial terms of employment and offer each employee presently working the right to continue under the new terms.

For example, if the employees were making $12.00 an hour, the new employer can unilaterally announce it will retain employees willing to work for $10.00 per hour. The employer is classified as a successor employer obligated to bargain with the incumbent union only if the prior employees are a majority of the workforce hired at the new rate. The employer cannot make further unilateral changes from then on and must bargain with the incumbent union for a new contract.

As an exception, if an employer announces at the time of a takeover that it is keeping the entire workforce so that it is immediately clear that the incumbent union will continue to represent the employees, the employer must bargain with the union from the beginning. It cannot unilaterally set the initial terms of employment.

Note, however, that even if the employer announces it will keep all employees, its only obligation is to negotiate the initial terms of employment. It is still not obligated to assume the existing bargaining agreement. This exception is narrowly applied. For example, if an employer announces it will retain any of the prior employees who agree to its terms, the employer will be able to establish such initial terms unilaterally because the union's majority status is not determined until the employees have hired on at the new rate. Sophisticated employers, even if they want to keep the present workforce, will go through the motions of rehiring employees individually to preserve their right to establish initial terms.

4. The Demand for Recognition

It is important that the incumbent union make a demand for recognition and bargaining from the successor employer. Otherwise, the union may have waived its right to recognition even though the new employer meets the requirements for a successor. In *Fall River Dyeing Corp.,* the Supreme Court upheld the Board's view that once a union demands recognition, the demand remains in effect continuously until the union is recognized. Thus, even if the union's initial demand is premature (i.e., made before the union represents a majority of the employees in a substantial and representative workforce) and the employer lawfully rejects it, the employer must thereafter recognize and bargain with the union when the union's majority status is established even though the union did not make another demand for recognition.

5. The Effect of Successorship Clauses

Before the *Burns* case, contracts frequently contained a successorship clause generally stating that the contract was binding on the employer and any successor. Under *Burns,* general successorship language in a collective bargaining agreement is ineffective and does not bind the successor. The new employer still has the right to employ its own workforce and establish the terms and conditions of employment notwithstanding the clause.

While a general successorship clause is ineffective, a union may bargain for specific protection. The union can negotiate a contract clause under which the predecessor employer agrees that it will not sell or otherwise transfer the business to another employer unless the new employer agrees to assume the existing collective bargaining agreement as part of the transfer agreement. The Board has held that such restrictions are lawful and that a union's demand for such a clause is a mandatory subject of bargaining.

If the predecessor employer attempts to sell the business without requiring the predecessor to assume the collective bargaining agreement, the union can seek an injunction prohibiting the transfer until the contractual provision is fulfilled and can sue the predecessor employer for damages for breach of its contract. Also, the union can picket both the old and new employer to require that they fulfill the terms of the contract.

G. THE BARGAINING OBLIGATION OF ALTER-EGO AND DOUBLE-BREASTED EMPLOYERS

A successor employer must be distinguished from an alter-ego employer. An alter-ego employer is, in fact, the same employer as before, in effect continuing in a disguised form even though the outward appearance or name may have changed. The new company, as the alter-ego of the old, is not only required to recognize and bargain with the incumbent union but is also bound by the existing collective bargaining agreement if any. There are certain factors that the Board and the Courts normally consider in determining whether one company is the alter-ego of another. These factors include whether the two companies have substantially identical management and ownership;

common business purpose; common methods of operation and supervision; common premises and equipment; and common customers. No one factor is controlling, and an employer may be an alter-ego even if one or more of the factors is missing if, on balance, the Board concludes that one employer is a disguised continuance of the other.

It is not necessary that the original company totally cease operations in order for the new company to be an alter-ego bound by the contract. Thus, an employer may purportedly sell part of its business to another company. Both the old company and the new entity may continue to operate as separate corporations. However, if the new company meets the criteria listed above for an alter-ego, it may be required to recognize and bargain with the incumbent union and even to abide by the existing collective bargaining agreement even though the original company is continuing to operate. Evidence that a new company was established to evade an existing collective bargaining relationship is an important factor in determining that one employer is the alter-ego of the other. However, the Board and most courts of appeals have held that one employer may be the alter-ego of another if sufficient factors are present even though the new company was established for a legitimate business reason.

1. The Double-Breasted Operation

Some employers operate two closely related companies, one with a union contract and one without. This is often referred to as a "double-breasted" operation, and is most common in the construction industry. If the union can establish that the nonunion and union employers are alter-egos, the nonunion employer will be bound by the collective bargaining agreement. Sometimes, however, the two employers may not have sufficient common factors. They may, for example, employ different supervisors, operate from separate premises, use separate equipment, and have different customers (one company serving only customers who are unionized, the other serving only nonunion customers).

Although not alter-egos, the two sides of a "double-breasted" employer may still constitute a "single employer" if there is functional integration of operations between the two companies, centralized control of labor relations, common management, and common ownership or financial control. In that case, however, the nonunion company will be bound by the collective bargaining agreement only if its employees would be an "accretion" to the existing bargaining unit based on the traditional "community-of-interest" standards (discussed in Chapter Two). The Board particularly considers whether the two employee groups have common supervision; whether there is frequent interchange of employees and job assignments; and whether the daily operations of the two companies are separate and autonomous. Thus, the Board frequently finds that the union and nonunion sides of a double-breasted employer constitute a single employer but that the two employee work groups are so separate and distinct that separate bargaining units are still appropriate. In contrast, if one employer is the alter-ego of the other, then the alter-ego, as well as the original company if still operating, will be required to recognize and bargain with the union and apply the existing collective bargaining agreement if any to the overall work force.

The AFL-CIO has proposed legislation that would combat double-breasted employer practices in the construction industry by requiring a construction employer to apply the terms of its existing collective bargaining agreement to any other company it establishes in the industry. Also some unions have negotiated contract language requiring the employer to apply the terms of its existing collective bargaining agreement to any other company it establishes so as to prohibit a nonunion double-breasted operation. The legality of such clauses is discussed in Chapter Eight.

2. Joint Employers

An employer may also be liable for certain contractual or legal obligations of another employer if it is classified as a "joint employer." This situation arises when two companies are in fact separate legal entities, but one employer shares responsibility for or codetermines essential terms and conditions of employment for the employees of the other company. For example, a building owner may be a joint employer if it contracts out cleaning maintenance to an independent cleaning contractor but still controls the wages, hours, and working conditions of the cleaning contractor's employees on its premises. The doctrine is important because a joint employer may be liable for any unfair labor practices committed by the primary employer in the course of their joint operations, such as discharging employees for union activity or bad faith bargaining, especially if the joint employer dictates the action. Also the joint employer is not entitled to the protection that the Act affords to neutral "secondary employers" against certain kinds of picketing and boycotts in a labor dispute (discussed in Chapter Seven).

H. THE DUTY TO BARGAIN AND SUCCESSOR UNIONS

1. The Bargaining Rights of Successor Unions

Sometimes two locals of the same international merge during the term of their respective collective bargaining agreements. Or an international union may reassign employees from one local to another. An independent union may vote to affiliate with an international. Or two international unions may merge and the names and numbers of the preexisting locals may be changed to reflect the new designation.

If a local union's internal structure changes as a result of a merger or affiliation change, is the employer still obligated to recognize and bargain with it? This issue arises most frequently when an employer refuses to recognize a union after a structural change and the union files a Section 8(a)(5) refusal to bargain charge, or when a union files a petition to amend its certification (see Chapter One) (to reflect a new name) following a change without holding a new representation election. The Board has held that an employer must continue to recognize a union (and abide by the existing contract, if any, after a merger, a new affiliation, or other structural changes without a representation election) if two basic requirements are met. First, the union members must have had an adequate opportunity to vote on the change. Second, there must be "substantial continuity" in the union before and after the change. For the membership vote to be valid, there must be adequate "due process" safeguards, including notice of the right to vote, an opportunity to discuss the matter, an orderly voting procedure, and reasonable precautions to maintain secrecy. Since the election is an internal union matter, only bargaining unit employees who are members of the union have the right to vote. In determining whether there is substantial continuity in representation, the Board considers the structure and the administration of the union before and after the change; whether the officers remained the same; the local's size and membership; the manner in which contracts are negotiated, ratified, and administered; and the degree of autonomy that the local's membership exercised before and after the change.

In the past, the Board has upheld the bargaining rights of a successor union, despite substantial differences in the administration and structure of the old and new unions, and the loss of local autonomy, as long as the change was approved by the membership in an election conforming to due process. However, the Reagan Board ruled in several cases involving the merger of a small local into a larger one that there was not substantial continuity in the bargaining representative despite the member-

ship's approval because different officers negotiated and administered the contract and the members no longer controlled their own affairs. But the Board has continued to uphold the principle that the merger of a small independent union into a larger local or into an international union does not necessarily create a substantially different entity as long as the members retain substantial authority over collective bargaining matters and continued control over their financial affairs. Unions considering a merger or affiliation should structure the surviving successor organization so that the former members retain the autonomy necessary to meet the Board's requirements.

2. The Successor Union's Right to Assume an Existing Contract

An existing collective bargaining agreement (e.g., one for four years) may not bar a representation election in some cases (see Chapter Two). If an election is held and a new union certified, what is the effect on the existing contract? The Board has held that following an election the newly certified successor union has a choice either to assume the contract for its remaining term or to cancel the existing agreement and negotiate a new one. The employer cannot hold the new union to the existing contract, and is obligated to bargain for a new agreement at the union's request.

I. REMEDIES FOR REFUSAL TO BARGAIN

The Board can adequately remedy some bargaining violations. For example, if a party refuses to sign an agreed-to contract, the Board can order the party to sign the agreement and pay backpay for the period the party failed to abide by the contract's terms. If an employer makes unilateral changes, it can be ordered to reinstate the prior conditions and pay backpay equal to any unilateral reduction in benefits. Unfortunately, the Board's only remedy against bad-faith surface bargaining is to order the employer to bargain in good faith. If an employer is determined to defeat the union it can appeal the Board's decision to the court of appeals, perhaps delaying bargaining for several years. Even if the employer is eventually forced to the bargaining table, the union may have been defeated through delay. Many of the union's original supporters may have quit or been discharged in the meantime. The union may lack the bargaining power to negotiate a successful agreement.

At one time, the Board tried to remedy bad-faith surface bargaining by requiring an employer to sign an agreement incorporating the provisions the employer would have agreed to if the employer had bargained in good faith. However, in *H. K. Porter,* the Supreme Court held that the Board does not have authority to order an employer to accept any specific clause not agreed to.[17] The Court said that Congress intended that the Board regulate the bargaining process, but it could not compel agreement to any specific terms.

Even after this decision, unions continued to argue that the Board should require an employer who bargains in bad faith to pay employees backpay equal to the difference between what the employees would have earned if the employer had bargained in good faith for a contract and the amount the employees actually earned during that period. However, the Board has held that this remedy is beyond its jurisdiction, that basing a remedy on what the employer would have agreed to would be like dictating the terms of the agreement, which *H. K. Porter* prohibited. Thus, legislation is needed to give the Board additional authority to impose more meaningful and effective remedies for bargaining violations.

The Board imposes additional remedies within its power in extreme cases of flagrant refusal to bargain, or if the employer raises frivolous defenses to a refusal to bargain charge, such as ordering the employer to pay the union's legal expenses for the litigation. In *J. P. Stevens,* for example, the Board required the employer to reimburse the union for the additional organizational costs the union incurred because of the employer's flagrant unlawful opposition to its employees' organizational rights.[18] The Board also ordered the employer to pay the union's legal fees and expenses in the litigation before the Board because of the company's deliberate violations of the law and the serious and sustained nature of the violations.

In some cases where bargaining orders have been enforced by a court of appeals, employers have been held in contempt by the court for failure to comply with the court's enforcement order. These remedies are effective in some cases, but not in those instances where an employer is willing to pay the price to defeat the union.

Summary   This chapter considered bargaining rights and responsibilities, focusing on the meaning of good-faith bargaining required by Sections 8(a)(5), 8(b)(3), and 8(d) of the LMRA. Although good faith means bargaining with an intention to reach an agreement, neither party is compelled to agree to a proposal or required to make a concession. Going through the formalities of bargaining with no intention of reaching an agreement is unlawful "surface bargaining." No one factor determines whether a party is engaged in surface bargaining. Good faith is judged by the "totality of conduct."

Bargaining items are either mandatory, permissive, or illegal subjects

---

[17] See legal principle 20.
[18] See legal principle 20.

of bargaining. Both parties are obligated to bargain over mandatory subjects and the union may strike over them. A party may choose, but is not required, to bargain over a permissive subject. A party cannot strike to compel the other party to reach agreement on a permissive subject. Wages, hours, and working conditions are mandatory subjects. Permissive subjects are legal, but not directly related to wages, hours, or working conditions.

There is an irrebuttable presumption of a union's continued majority status for its certification year or for a reasonable period not to exceed one year if the employer voluntarily recognizes the union. The employer may withdraw recognition thereafter if it has good-faith and reasonable doubt, based on objective considerations, as to the union's continued majority status. The duty to bargain arises before, during, and after the negotiation of a contract. In the absence of a contract, an employer must bargain before unilaterally changing any mandatory bargaining condition of employment. There is generally no duty to bargain over items covered by the contract during its term. Thus, if an employer demands wage concessions from a union during the contract term, and threatens to transfer operations to a new location unless the union agrees, the union can refuse to discuss the changes. The employer cannot implement the changes unilaterally, but may lawfully carry out its threat to transfer operations unless the contract prohibits such action. An employer has the duty to bargain before making unilateral changes and conditions not covered by the agreement unless the union has waived that right. After an impasse is reached, the employer can make the changes in accordance with its last offer to the union. Under the *Collyer* doctrine, the Board defers to arbitration most Section 8(a)(5) charges alleging the unilateral change in wages, hours, or working conditions that are also contract violations. The Board defers because the arbitrator's resolution of the contract interpretation issue also resolves the unfair labor practice issue.

The employer also has a duty to bargain with the union after the contract expires. Most contract terms under the expired agreement remain in effect as established conditions of employment. The employer cannot change them unilaterally until bargaining to impasse.

The scope of an employer's duty to bargain over changes in business operations, such as subcontracting, plant transfers, or plant closings, is one of the most controversial areas under Section 8(a)(5). Under the *Fibreboard* decision an employer must bargain over both the decision and the effect of a decision to subcontract bargaining unit work to an independent contractor who performs the same work under similar conditions of employment. This decision has been strictly limited to that situation, and, in general, an employer is obligated to bargain only over the effect of a decision to change the scope and direction of the enterprise, commonly referred to as a basic capital decision. The Board's current view is that an employer may have an obligation to bargain over both the decision and the effect if the decision, such as one to lay off employees to reduce labor costs during a period of economic difficulty, is one amenable to resolution through the collective bargaining process so that union concessions or alternative suggestions may change the decision.

Although the Board has effective remedies against unilateral changes in working conditions, its remedies are inadequate against the employer who intentionally drags out negotiations to undermine the union. Legislative changes are needed to permit financial remedies against these employers.

The union has a broad right to information from the employer relevant to the negotiation and administration of a collective bargaining agreement and to the processing of grievances to arbitration. The information must be relevant and must be requested, and the data must not be unduly burdensome. An employer may impose reasonable restrictions on the union's access to confidential information, and, depending upon the union's need, may require that individual employees consent to the release of personal information. An employer need not provide information about its profits unless it pleads financial inability to pay (pleading poverty).

A successor employer is not required to accept the predecessor's collective bargaining agreement. It is, however, obligated to bargain with the incumbent union if the employees comprise a majority of the new workforce employed in the same industry. In most cases, the successor is able to set the employees' initial terms or conditions of employment even if it subsequently must recognize the union. In contrast, if one employer is the "alter-ego" of the prior employer, it is immediately obligated to recognize the union and is bound by the existing collective bargaining agreement.

Review Questions

1. What are the statutory notice requirements under Section 8(d) if a party desires to terminate or modify a collective bargaining contract?
2. Is it surface bargaining for an employer to reject a union's proposal for a union security clause?
3. Can an employer lawfully "threaten" to shut down its operations unless the union agrees to reduce the wages in effect under the current collective bargaining agreement?
4. How may the consequences of giving late statutory notice differ from giving a late contractual termination notice?
5. Must an employer continue to bargain with the incumbent union after the expiration date of their contract?
6. When is an employer regarded as a successor for purposes of the duty to bargain?
7. What bargaining obligation does an employer have before subcontracting bargaining unit work?
8. Can a successor employer unilaterally set the employees' initial wages and working conditions even if it keeps the prior work force?

9. Can the Board require an employer to sign a contract incorporating a specific term as a remedy for refusing to bargain?

10. Does an employer have to bargain over increased retirement benefits for employees who have already retired?

11. Must an employer bargain over union proposals to pay employees on the union's negotiating committee?

12. What information may the union request from the employer in administering the contract?

(Answers to review questions are at the end of the book.)

Basic Legal Principles

1.A. There is an irrebuttable presumption of a union's continued majority status for its certification year, or for a reasonable period, not to exceed one year, if the employer voluntarily recognizes the union. Thereafter, the employer may withdraw recognition if it has a good-faith and reasonable doubt, based on objective considerations, as to the union's continued majority status. Except in very rare circumstances, an employer cannot withdraw recognition during a contract's term. See *Chemetron Corp.,* 258 NLRB No. 159, 108 LRRM 1202 (1981); *Cowles Publishing Co.,* 280 NLRB No. 105, 123 LRRM 1013 (1986); *Central Soya Co.,* 281 NLRB No. 173, 124 LRRM 1026 (1986) (continuing duty to recognize union); *Royal Coach Lines, Inc.,* 282 NLRB No. 145, 124 LRRM 1246 (1987); *Hajoca Corp.,* 291 NLRB No. 16, 129 LRRM 1296 (1988), enforced, *Hajoca Corp. v. NLRB,* 872 F.2d 1169, 131 LRRM 2447 (3rd Cir. 1989); *Burger Pits, Inc.,* 785 F.2d 796, 121 LRRM 3305 (9th Cir. 1986); *NLRB v. Action Automative,* 853 F.2d 433, 128 LRRM 3239 (6th Cir. 1988); *NLRB v. Creative Food Design,* 852 F.2d 1295, 128 LRRM 3089 (D.C. Cir. 1988). See also *Buckley Broadcasting,* 284 NLRB No. 113, 125 LRRM 1281 (1987) (no presumption that strike replacements favor union). Compare *Curtin Matheson Scientific, Inc. v. NLRB,* 859 F.2d 362, 129 LRRM 2801 (5th Cir. 1988) (applying presumption that large number of strike replacements hired at same time do not support union) with *Bickerstaff Clay Products v. NLRB,* 871 F.2d 980, 131 LRRM 2378 (11th Cir. 1989) (replacements' loyalty determined on case by case basis).

1.B. The filing of a timely rival representation or decertification petition does not require or permit an employer to withdraw from bargaining or to refuse to execute a contract with an incumbent union. *Dresser Industries, Inc.,* 264 NLRB No. 145, 111 LRRM 1430 (1982); *Eastern States Optical Co.,* 275 NLRB No. 58, 119 LRRM 1107 (1985); *Architectural Woodwork Corp.,* 280 NLRB No. 108, 123 LRRM 1319 (1986); *Johns-Manville Sales,* 281 NLRB No. 40, 123 LRRM 1315 (1986); *Atwood & Morrill Co.,* 290 NLRB No. 100, 129 LRRM 1210 (1988).

1.C. In the construction industry, a pre-hire agreement under Section 8(f) is binding for its full term from project to project unless either the employer or employees files a representation election petition and the union loses the election. However, there is no presumption of a union's majority status under a pre-hire agreement and the employer may accordingly withdraw recognition from the union and unilaterally change the terms and conditions of employment established by the contract as soon as it expires. To establish a majority status agreement under Section 9(a) of the Act, a construction union must unequivocally demand majority status recognition and the employer must unequivocally grant such recognition. *John Deklewa & Sons, Inc.*, 282 NLRB No. 184, 124 LRRM 1185 (1987), affirmed 843 F.2d 770, 128 LRRM 2020 (3d Cir. 1988); *W. L. Miller Co.*, 284 NLRB No. 127, 126 LRRM 1100 (1987), enforced 871 F.2d 745, 130 LRRM 3102 (8th Cir. 1989); *Brannan Sand & Gravel Co.*, 289 NLRB No. 128, 128 LRRM 1249 (1988); *J & R Tile, Inc.*, 291 NLRB No. 144, 130 LRRM 1005 (1988); *Mesa Verde Construction Co. v. Laborers*, _____ F.2d _____, 132 LRRM 2461 (9th Cir. 1989). See also *McNeff v. Todd*, 461 U.S. 260, 113 LRRM 2113 (1983); *NLRB v. Iron Workers Local 103 (Higdon Contracting Co.)*, 434 U.S. 335, 97 LRRM 2333 (1978); *CSCAC v. J.L.M. Construction Co.*, 809 F.2d 594, 124 LRRM 2561 (9th Cir. 1987); *Hageman Underground Construction*, 253 NLRB 60, 105 LRRM 1385 (1980).

2. Under Section 8(d) of the Act, a party seeking to terminate or modify a contract must serve a written notice of the proposed termination or modification on the other party at least sixty days before the expiration or modification and provide notice of the dispute to the Federal Mediation and Conciliation Service and to any state agency established to mediate and conciliate labor disputes within thirty days thereafter. The respective notice periods are ninety and sixty days for health care institutions. Neither party may unilaterally change the terms of the contract or engage in a strike or lockout until proper notice is given, but the burden of notifying the FMCS or any state mediation agency rests with the party that gives the initial notice so that the other party is free to terminate or modify the agreement at the end of the initial notice period even if no notice is given to the FMCS. *United Artists Communications, Inc.*, 274 NLRB No. 17, 118 LRRM 1353 (1985), affirmed, *IATSE v. NLRB*, 779 F.2d 552, 121 LRRM 2237 (9th Cir. 1985); *C. E. K. Mechanical Contractors Inc.*, 295 NLRB No. 70, 131 LRRM 1737 (1989). See also *Speedrack Inc.*, 293 NLRB No. 128, 131 LRRM 1347 (1989) (statutory notice requirements apply to bargaining pursuant to a midterm contract reopener provision, so that employer may unilaterally implement its last offer made during such bargaining after impasse has been reached, provided notice requirements have been met, unless contract prohibits such action).

3.A. Bargaining items are either mandatory, permissive, or illegal subjects of bargaining. Both parties are obligated to bargain over mandatory subjects and may strike over them. A party may choose to, but need not, bargain over a permissive subject. A party cannot strike to compel the other party to agree to a permissive subject. *Pistoresi, Nello and Son, Inc.*, 203 NLRB 905, 83 LRRM 1212 (1973); *Allied Chemical and Alkali Workers v. Pittsburgh Plate Glass*, 404 U.S. 157, 78 LRRM 2974 (1971); *Peerless Publications, Inc.*, 283 NLRB No. 54, 124 LRRM 1331 (1987); *Getty*

Refining & Marketing Co., 279 NLRB No. 126, 122 LRRM 1150 (1986); *Colfor, Inc.*, 282 NLRB No. 160, 124 LRRM 1204 (1987) (selection of bargaining committee permissive subject of bargaining); *Communications Workers*, 280 NLRB No. 9, 124 LRRM 1009 (1986) (transcript of arbitration hearing mandatory subject); *Chicago Truck Drivers Union*, 279 NLRB No. 122, 122 LRRM 1100 (1986) (combining separate bargaining units permissive subject); *NLRB v. Pennsylvania Telephone Guild*, 799 F.2d 84, 123 LRRM 2214 (3d Cir. 1986) (recording of grievance sessions permissive subject of bargaining).

3.B. The use of economic force to compel agreement is not inconsistent with good-faith bargaining. *NLRB v. Insurance Agents International Union*, 361 U.S. 477, 45 LRRM 2705 (1960).

4. Withdrawal of pending unfair labor practice charges at the end of a strike is a permissive subject of bargaining. Thus, the parties cannot condition the execution of a contract on such agreement. *Griffin Inns*, 229 NLRB No. 26, 95 LRRM 1072 (1977).

5.A. The implementation of a drug/alcohol testing program for current employees is a mandatory subject of bargaining. *Johnson-Bateman Co.*, 295 NLRB No. 26, 131 LRRM 1393 (1989). But a preemployment drug/alcohol testing program for job applicants is not a mandatory subject. *Star Tribune*, 295 NLRB No. 63, 131 LRRM 1404 (1989).

5.B. A proposal for interest arbitration, in contrast to grievance arbitration, is a permissive subject of bargaining. *Sheet Metal Workers Local 59*, 227 NLRB No. 90, 94 LRRM 1602 (1976); *Plumbers Local 387*, 266 NLRB No. 30, 112 LRRM 1365 (1983). Compare *Sea Bay Manor Home*, 253 NLRB 739, 106 LRRM 1010 (1980) (once entered into, an agreement for interest arbitration is binding).

6. Internal union matters are permissive subjects of bargaining. Thus, an employer cannot insist that the execution of a contract be contingent upon ratification by the union's membership. *NLRB v. Corsicana Cotton Mills*, 178 F.2d 344, 24 LRRM 2494 (5th Cir. 1949); *Houchens Market*, 155 NLRB No. 59, 60 LRRM 1384 (1965); *NLRB v. Cheese Barn, Inc.*, 558 F.2d 526, 95 LRRM 3096 (9th Cir. 1977).

7. Once a union is lawfully recognized, either through a Board certification, a bargaining order, or voluntary recognition, an employer has the duty to bargain to impasse before unilaterally changing any mandatory condition of employment unless the change is permitted by a collective bargaining agreement or the union has waived its bargaining rights. An impasse is reached when the parties, bargaining in good faith, are warranted in assuming that further bargaining would be futile. There is thus no set time the parties must bargain before reaching an impasse. *Milwaukee Spring Div., Illinois Coil Spring Co.*, 268 NLRB No. 87, 115 LRRM 1065 (1984), affirmed *UAW v. NLRB*, 765 F.2d 175, 119 LRRM 2801 (D.C. Cir. 1985); *Teamsters Local 175 v. NLRB*, 788 F.2d 27, 121 LRRM 3433 (D.C. Cir. 1986); *Stecher's Super Markets*, 275 NLRB No. 71, 119 LRRM 1129 (1985); *Schaeff Namco, Inc.*, 280 NLRB No. 150, 123 LRRM

1058 (1986); *American Gypsum Co.*, 285 NLRB No. 16, 128 LRRM 1105 (1987); *Tampa Sheet Metal Co.*, 288 NLRB No. 43, 129 LRRM 1188 (1988); *Southwest Forest Industries v. NLRB*, 841 F.2d 270, 127 LRRM 2913 (9th Cir. 1988); *Sierra Publishing Co.*, 291 NLRB No. 84, 131 LRRM 1377 (1989); *Van Dorn Plastic Machinery v. NLRB*, 881 F.2d 302, 132 LRRM 2200 (6th Cir. 1989).

8. Going through the formalities of bargaining without the intention of reaching an agreement is "surface bargaining," violating Section 8(a)(5) of the Act. No one factor determines whether a party is engaged in illegal surface bargaining versus lawful hard bargaining. Good faith is based on the "totality of conduct." *General Electric Co.*, 150 NLRB No. 36, 57 LRRM 1491 (1964), enforced 418 F.2d 736, 72 LRRM 2530 (2d Cir. 1969); *Winn-Dixie Stores*, 243 NLRB No. 151, 101 LRRM 1534 (1979); *American Thread Co.*, 274 NLRB No. 164, 118 LRRM 1499 (1985); *Boaz Carpet Yarns*, 280 NLRB No. 4, 122 LRRM 1139 (1986); *Reichhold Chemicals, Inc.*, 288 NLRB No. 8, 127 LRRM 1265 (1988); *Cook Brothers*, 288 NLRB No. 46, 128 LRRM 1074 (1988); *Prentice-Hall Inc.*, 290 NLRB No. 79, 129 LRRM 1052 (1988); *Overnite Transportation Co.*, 296 NLRB No. 77, 132 LRRM 1176 (1989).

9. Within limits, employers are permitted to communicate directly with employees during negotiations on the status of bargaining, but cannot bypass the union in an attempt to undermine it. *Safeway Trails Inc.*, 233 NLRB No. 171, 96 LRRM 1614 (1977); *United Technologies*, 274 NLRB No. 163, 118 LRRM 1556 (1985); *Putnam Buick, Inc.*, 280 NLRB No. 101, 122 LRRM 1344 (1986); *Heck's Inc.*, 293 NLRB No. 132, 131 LRRM 1281 (1989) (unlawful to implement unilaterally employee handbook containing anti-union policy).

10.A. There is no duty to bargain during a contract's term over matters covered by it, and the contract cannot be modified during its term without consent, but there is a duty to bargain to impasse before making unilateral changes in mandatory subjects of bargaining not covered by the agreement unless that right has been waived. *NLRB v. C&C Plywood Corp.*, 385 U.S. 421, 64 LRRM 2065 (1967); *Keystone Consolidated Industries*, 237 NLRB No. 91, 99 LRRM 1036 (1978); *Empire Pacific Industries*, 257 NLRB No. 180, 108 LRRM 1091 (1981) (duty to bargain with union over providing benefits to bargaining unit previously granted to nonunit employees); *Milwaukee Spring Div., Illinois Coil Spring Co.* in legal principle 7; *NLRB v. Ford Brothers*, 786 F.2d 232, 121 LRRM 3324 (6th Cir. 1986); *Brown Co.*, 278 NLRB No. 113, 121 LRRM 1250 (1986).

10.B. Although an employer cannot unilaterally change the terms of the contract, it can request that the union agree to midterm concessions because of changed economic circumstances. The union does not have to agree to bargain or to make any concessions, but if the union does not agree the employer may lawfully transfer or relocate work out of the bargaining unit as it proposed unless the contract expressly prohibits such action. *Milwaukee Spring Div.* in legal principle 7; *DeSoto, Inc.*, 278 NLRB No. 114, 121 LRRM 1226 (1986).

11.A. Waiver of the right to bargain over matters not covered by a contract must be clear, but is based on all the facts and circumstances of bargaining that took place. *GTE Automatic Elec. Inc.*, 261 NLRB No. 196, 110 LRRM 1193, (1982); *Rockwell International Corporation*, 260 NLRB No. 153, 109 LRRM 1366 (1982); *National Metalcrafters, Inc.*, 276 NLRB No. 14, 120 LRRM 1080 (1985); *Intersystems Design Corp.*, 278 NLRB No. 111, 121 LRRM 1229 (1986) (no waiver if employer presents union with accomplished fact); *Auto Workers Local 449 v. NLRB*, 802 F.2d 969, 123 LRRM 2677 (7th Cir. 1986); *Stevens Pontiac-GMC, Inc.*, 295 NLRB No. 66, 131 LRRM 1683 (1989) (employer cannot avoid union's bargaining demand by refusing certified mail letter).

11.B. Usually, a contractual "zipper clause" in which a union waives the right to bargain over matters not covered by the contract can be used only as a "shield" to maintain the contractual status quo but not as a "sword" to prevent bargaining over unilateral changes in contractual terms. However, a zipper clause may also permit the employer to make unilateral changes in mandatory subjects of bargaining (conditions of employment) not covered by the contract if it is clear from the bargaining history that the clause was intended to authorize such action. *GTE Automatic Electric, Inc.* in legal principle 11.A. (applying contractual "zipper clause" as a "shield" constituting union waiver of employer's duty to bargain over matters not covered by contract, provided there is no unilateral change in contractual terms); *Electrical Workers Local 1466 v. NLRB*, 795 F.2d 150, 122 LRRM 2948 (D.C. Cir. 1986), affirming 270 NLRB No. 95, 116 LRRM 1148 (1984) (zipper clause applied to permit employer to unilaterally discontinue Christmas bonus).

11.C. A payment such as a Christmas bonus may be considered a mandatory subject of bargaining rather than a gratuity that can be discontinued unilaterally by the employer if the payment has been in effect for a long time, has been given consistently regardless of the employer's economic situation, and if it is based upon an individual employee's pay rate, years of service, or productivity rather than the same for all employees. Compare *Radio Electric Service Co.*, 278 NLRB No. 78, 121 LRRM 1185 (1986) (company violated Act when it unilaterally discontinued long-established Christmas bonus) with *Columbus & Southern Ohio Electric Co.*, 270 NLRB No. 95, 116 LRRM 1148 (1984), affirmed *Electrical Workers Local 1466 v. NLRB*, 795 F.2d 150, 122 LRRM 2948 (D.C. Cir. 1986) (zipper clause applied to permit employer to unilaterally discontinue Christmas bonus). See also *Benchmark Industries, Inc.*, 270 NLRB No. 8, 116 LRRM 1032 (1984) (holiday gift hams can be unilaterally discontinued).

11.D. The bankruptcy code (Title 11, United States Code Section 1113) requires prior approval of the bankruptcy court before a bankrupt employer can reject a collective bargaining agreement. The employer must first submit its proposed contract modifications to the union for consideration and bargain with the union in good faith on the proposed modifications in an effort to reach mutual agreement before the hearing on the employer's application to reject (modify) the agreement. Contract modifications must be "necessary" to permit the reorganization. Compare *Local 807 IBT v. Carey Transportation,* 816 F.2d 82, 125 LRRM 2093 (2d Cir. 1987) (proposed contract changes must be made in good faith and contain necessary, but not absolutely minimal, changes to enable the debtor to reorganize successfully) with *Wheeling-Pittsburgh v. Steelworkers,* 791 F.2d 1074, 122 LRRM 2425 (3d Cir. 1986) (only changes that are essential to permit successful reorganization may be made in contract); *Image Systems, Inc.,* 285 NLRB No. 56, 126 LRRM 1129 (1987). See also *NLRB v. Bildisco & Bildisco,* 465 U.S. 513, 115 LRRM 2805 (1984) (prior decision permitting debtor-in-possession to unilaterally reject contract subject to bankruptcy court's approval overruled by Section 1113 of Bankruptcy Code).

12.A. An employer has no obligation to bargain over *decisions* as to the basic scope and ultimate direction of the enterprise, but must bargain over decisions that are amenable to resolution through the bargaining process. *First National Maintenance Corp. v. NLRB,* 452 U.S. 666, 107 LRRM 2705 (1981); *General Motors Corp.,* 191 NLRB No. 149, 77 LRRM 1537 (1971).

12.B. Currently, the Board basically restricts the duty to bargain over a decision to those in which labor costs are the primary consideration. *United Technologies (Otis Elevator Co.),* 269 NLRB No. 162, 115 LRRM 1281 (1984); *Metropolitan Teletronics,* 279 NLRB No. 134, 122 LRRM 1107 (1986); *Litton Systems, Inc.,* 283 NLRB No. 144, 125 LRRM 1081 (1987); *Pertec Computer Corp.,* 284 NLRB No. 88, 126 LRRM 1134 (1987); *Collateral Control Corp.,* 288 NLRB No. 41, 128 LRRM 1097 (1988); *Storer Cable TV,* 295 NLRB No. 34, 131 LRRM 1769 (1989); *UFCW v. NLRB,* 880 F.2d 1422, 132 LRRM 2104 (D.C. Cir. 1989). Compare *Mid-South Bottling Co.,* 287 NLRB No. 146, 128 LRRM 1101 (1988) (decision to close part of business unlawful because motivated by anti-union animus). But see *Arrow Automotive Industries, Inc. v. NLRB,* 853 F.2d 223, 128 LRRM 3137 (4th Cir. 1988) (employer has no obligation to bargain over decision to close one of its plants under *First National Maintenance* [legal principle 12.A.] even though decision turned on labor costs).

12.C. An employer must bargain over the decision and the effect of a decision to lay off employees to reduce labor costs during a period of economic difficulty because such a decision may be amenable to resolution through the collective bargaining process. However, an employer is only obligated to bargain over the effects of a decision to change the scope and direction of the enterprise even if it results in layoffs. *LaPeer Foundry and Machine, Inc.,* 289 NLRB No. 126, 129 LRRM 1001 (1988). See also *Marriott Corp.,* 264 NLRB No. 178, 111 LRRM 1354 (1982) (pre-Reagan Board analysis of employer's obligation to bargain over both decision and effects applying broader criteria).

13. An employer must bargain over the decision and effect of subcontracting bargaining unit work if the work is still to be done on the

company's premises under similar conditions even though there may be a legitimate economic reason for the decision. *Fibreboard Paper Products Corp. v. NLRB*, 379 U.S. 203, 57 LRRM 2609 (1964); *ACF Industries*, 231 NLRB No. 20, 96 LRRM 1291 (1977); *Donn Products Inc.*, 229 NLRB No. 9, 95 LRRM 1033 (1977). However, the subcontracting must also have demonstrable adverse impact on unit employees. *Westinghouse Electric Corp.*, 150 NLRB No. 136, 58 LRRM 1257 (1965); Compare *United Technologies*, 278 NLRB No. 41, 121 LRRM 1156 (1986). See also *NLRB v. Eltec Corp.*, 870 F.2d 1112, 130 LRRM 3080 (6th Cir. 1989) (employer must bargain over decision to subcontract out parts assembly work because conditions of employment were motivating factor for decision).

14. An employer has the absolute right to close or partially close his business without any bargaining over the decision itself, but is required to bargain over the effect. *Textile Workers Union v. Darlington Mfg. Co.*, 380 U.S. 263, 58 LRRM 2657 (1965); *First National Maintenance Corporation v. NLRB*, 452 U.S. 666, 107 LRRM 2705 (1981) (partial closure).

15.A. On termination, a contract's wages, hours, and other terms and conditions of employment are regarded as established conditions that cannot be changed unilaterally even though the agreement has expired. A union security clause expires automatically. *Industrial Union of Marine Workers v. NLRB*, 320 F.2d 615, 53 LRRM 2878 (3d Cir. 1963); *Trico Products Corp.*, 238 NLRB No. 184, 99 LRRM 1473 (1978); *American Sink Top & Cabinet Co.*, 242 NLRB No. 53, 101 LRRM 1166 (1979); *Hassett Maintenance Corp.*, 260 NLRB No. 135, 109 LRRM 1273 (1982); *NLRB v. Carilli*, 648 F.2d 1206, 107 LRRM 2961 (9th Cir. 1981) (employer must continue to contribute to contractually established fringe benefit funds after contracts' expiration); *Southwestern Steel & Supply, Inc. v. NLRB*, 806 F.2d 1111, 123 LRRM 3290 (D.C. Cir. 1986).

15.B. The contractually established grievance procedures remain in effect after the contract expires subject to change only after a bargaining impasse. Also an employer may be obligated to arbitrate grievances arising after the contract expires if the grievance "arises under" the expired contract, that is, the dispute concerns contract rights accruing or vesting during the contract remaining enforceable after the contract expires. *Nolde Brothers v. Bakery Workers Local 358*, 430 U.S. 243, 94 LRRM 2573 (1977); *Indiana & Michigan Electric Co.*, 284 NLRB No. 7, 125 LRRM 1097 (1987). See Chapter Nine for detailed discussion of this issue.

16. The Board defers to arbitration most Section 8(a)(5) charges alleging a unilateral change in wages, hours, or working conditions that may also be contract violations. *Collyer Insulated Wire*, 192 NLRB No. 150, 77 LRRM 1931 (1971); *Roy Robinson Chevrolet*, 228 NLRB No. 103, 94 LRRM 1474 (1977); *Olin Corp.*, 268 NLRB No. 86, 115 LRRM 1056 (1984).

17.A. Unions have a very broad right to information relevant to the negotiation and administration of a collective bargaining agreement. The information must be relevant and it must be requested. The data must not be unduly burdensome and, under certain circumstances, must not be confidential. *NLRB v. Truitt Mfg. Co.*, 351 U.S. 149, 38 LRRM 2042 (1956); *NLRB v. Acme Industrial Co.*, 385 U.S. 432, 64 LRRM 2069 (1967); *NLRB v. Detroit Edison*, 440 U.S. 301, 100 LRRM 2728 (1979); *Westinghouse Electric Corp*, 239 NLRB No. 19, 99 LRRM 1482 (1978) (civil rights data); *Roadway Express, Inc.*, 275 NLRB No. 156, 120 LRRM 1024 (1985); *Whirlpool Corp.*, 281 NLRB No. 7, 124 LRRM 1138 (1986); *New York Post Corp.*, 283 NLRB No. 60, 124 LRRM 1377 (1987); *United States Postal Service*, 289 NLRB No. 123, 129 LRRM 1169 (1988); *New Jersey Bell Telephone Co.*, 289 NLRB No. 55, 131 LRRM 1315 (1989).

17.B. The union has a broad right to data pertaining to the employees' occupational safety and health including the right to have an outside specialist make necessary on-site inspections and tests. However, depending on the union's need for the information, the employer may require that individual employees authorize the release of personal data and may negotiate reasonable restrictions as to safeguards to protect company trade secrets included in the information provided. *Minnesota Mining & Mfg. Co.*, 261 NLRB No. 2, 109 LRRM 1345 (1982); *Holyoke Water Power Co.*, 273 NLRB No. 168, 118 LRRM 1179 (1985), affirmed 778 F.2d 49, 120 LRRM 3487 (1st Cir. 1985); *Hercules, Inc. v. NLRB*, 833 F.2d 426, 126 LRRM 3187 (2d Cir. 1987).

17.C. An employer need not provide information about profits unless he pleads financial inability to pay a requested increase (pleading poverty). *NLRB v. Truitt Mfg. Co.*, in legal principle 17.A.; *Advertisers Mfg. Co.*, 275 NLRB No. 19, 119 LRRM 1123 (1985).

17.D. An employer is also entitled to relevant data from a union, such as the union's ability to provide enough qualified employees under contractual manning or hiring hall requirements. *NLRB v. Electrical Workers 497*, 795 F.2d 836, 122 LRRM 3259 (9th Cir. 1986).

18.A. A successor employer is not obligated to assume the collective bargaining agreement of the predecessor. Its only obligation is to bargain with the incumbent union if and when the prior employees comprise a majority of the new work force. *NLRB v. Burns International Security Services, Inc.*, 406 US 272, 80 LRRM 2225 (1972); *Golden State Bottling Co. v. NLRB*, 414 U.S. 168, 84 LRRM 2839 (1973) (successor liable for predecessor's unfair labor practices); *Evans Services, Inc. v. NLRB*, 810 F.2d 1089, 124 LRRM 2802 (11th Cir. 1987); *UFCW v. NLRB*, 768 F.2d 1463, 119 LRRM 3473 (1985); *Homosassa Springs Restaurant, Inc.*, 275 NLRB No. 213, 120 LRRM 1051 (1985); *American Press, Inc.*, 280 NLRB No. 109, 123 LRRM 1064 (1986); *State Distributing Co., Inc.*, 282 NLRB No. 151, 124 LRRM 1241 (1987); *U.S. Marine Corp.*, 293 NLRB No. 81, 131 LRRM 1105 (1989).

18.B. The successor employer is obligated to bargain with the incumbent union as soon as the incumbent represents a majority of the employees in a "substantial and representative complement" of employees. This obligation may exist even though there is a gap (a "hiatus") between the time the prior employer closed and the successor resumed operations and the incumbent union's initial demand for recognition was premature. *Fall River Dyeing & Finishing Corp. v. NLRB*, 482 U.S. 27, 125 LRRM 2441 (1987).

18.C. An alter-ego employer, which is a continuation of the old employer in a disguised form, is obligated to recognize the incumbent union and to abide by the existing collective bargaining agreement, if any, for its full term. *NLRB v. DMR Corp.*, 795 F.2d 472, 123 LRRM 2253 (5th Cir. 1986); *NLRB v. Allcoast Transfer, Inc.*, 780 F.2d 576, 121 LRRM 2393 (6th Cir. 1986); *Crest Tankers v. NMU*, 796 F.2d 234, 122 LRRM 3237 (8th Cir. 1986); *Voorhees Painting Co.*, 275 NLRB No. 114, 119 LRRM 1228 (1985); *Continental Radiator*, 283 NLRB No. 34, 124 LRRM 1288 (1987); *Haley & Haley, Inc.*, 289 NLRB No. 87, 128 LRRM 1319 (1988); *C. E. K. Mechanical Contractors Inc.*, 295 NLRB No. 70, 131 LRRM 1737 (1989). In contrast, if an employer operates two closely related (double-breasted) companies, the employer may be obligated to apply its contract to the nonunion side of its operations only if the two work forces are so closely integrated as to constitute a single collective bargaining unit under "community of interest" standards. *South Prairie Construction Co. v. Operating Engineers Local 627*, 425 U.S. 800, 92 LRRM 2507 (1976); *Operating Engineers v. NLRB*, 595 F.2d 844, 100 LRRM 2792 (D.C. Cir. 1979); *Hotel & Restaurant Employees Union*, 282 NLRB No. 139, 124 LRRM 1250 (1987). Compare, as to joint employer status, *Clinton's Ditch Co-op v. NLRB*, 778 F.2d 132, 120 LRRM 3562 (2d Cir. 1985); *NLRB v. Browning Ferris Industries*, 691 F.2d 1117, 111 LRRM 2748 (3d Cir. 1982); *Chesapeake Foods, Inc.*, 287 NLRB No. 43, 127 LRRM 1156 (1987).

19. An employer must recognize a successor union following a merger, a new affiliation, or other structural changes and will remain bound by the existing collective bargaining agreement if the union members have had an adequate opportunity to vote on the change and there is "substantial continuity" in the union before and after the change. Bargaining unit employees who are not union members have no right to vote in the election. The members of the prior union must retain substantial authority over collective bargaining matters and continued control over their financial affairs following the change in order for the new union to have successorship rights. *NLRB v. Financial Institution Employees* 475 U.S. 192, 121 LRRM 2741 (1986); *NLRB v. Insulfab Plastics, Inc.*, 789 F.2d 961, 122 LRRM 2105 (1st Cir. 1986); *Seattle First National Bank*, 290 NLRB No. 72, 129 LRRM 1020 (1988) (on remand from the Supreme Court); *May Department Stores*, 289 NLRB No. 88, 128 LRRM 1299 (1988); *Western Commercial Transport, Inc.*, 288 NLRB No. 27, 127 LRRM 1313 (1988).

20. The Board cannot require an employer or a union to agree to contractual terms to which the party has not agreed as a remedy for bad-faith bargaining. *H. K. Porter Co. v. NLRB*, 397 U.S. 99, 73 LRRM 2561 (1970): *Ex-Cell-O Corp.*, 185 NLRB No. 20, 74 LRRM 1740 (1970); *Barry*

Co., 278 NLRB No. 56, 121 LRRM 1161 (1986). The Board can, however, impose "extraordinary" remedies such as requiring the employer to reimburse the union for its litigation expenses and extra organizing costs caused by the employer's unlawful misconduct, *J. P. Stevens*, 244 NLRB No. 82, 102 LRRM 1039 (1979).

21. A union or individual employer can withdraw from a duly established multi-employer bargaining unit by giving written notice of an intention to withdraw before the date set by the contract for modification or the date agreed upon for the beginning of multi-employer negotiations. The notice must be both timely and unequivocal. Once bargaining has begun, withdrawal is not permitted except by mutual consent or in unusual circumstances. A bargaining impasse is not considered an unusual circumstance. *Bonanno Linen Service, Inc.*, 243 NLRB 1093, 102 LRRM 1001 (1979), affirmed *Bonanno Linen Service Inc. v. NLRB*, 454 U.S. 404, 109 LRRM 2257 (1982); *NLRB v. Dependable Tile Co.*, 774 F.2d 1376, 120 LRRM 2992 (9th Cir. 1985); *Watson-Rummell Electric Co.*, 277 NLRB No. 162, 121 LRRM 1118 (1985); *Jasper Enterprises, Inc.*, 287 NLRB No. 77, 127 LRRM 1192 (1987); *Universal Enterprises*, 291 NLRB No. 103, 131 LRRM 1031 (1988).

Recommended Reading

"A Union's Duty to Furnish Information to an Employer for Purposes of Collective Bargaining," 4 *U. Day. L. Rev.* 257 (1979).

Bosanac, "Expiration of the Collective Bargaining Agreement: Survivability of Terms and Conditions of Employment," 4 *Lab. Lawyer* 715 (1988).

Dannin, "Statutory Subjects and the Duty to Bargain," 39 *Lab. L.J.* 44 (1988).

Delaney and Sockell, "The Mandatory Permissive Distinction and Collective Bargaining Outcomes," 42 *Industrial & Labor Relations Review* 566 (1989).

DiGiovanni, "Surface vs. Hard Bargaining: Tilting Toward Non-intervention," 2 *Lab. Lawyer* 771 (1986).

Mace, "The Supreme Court's Labor Law Successorship Doctrine after *Fall River Dyeing*," 39 *Lab. L.J.* 102 (1988).

McGuire, "Management's Right to Relocate its Plant and to Make Similar Decisions: Recent Developments," 38 *Lab. L.J.* 747 (1987).

Morales, "Presumption of Union's Majority Status in NLRB Cases," 29 *Lab. L.J.* 309 (1978).

Pleasure and Gorman, "Extension of Bargaining Rights and Contracts to Single Employer and Alter Ego Entities in the Construction Industry," *Southwestern Legal Foundation, 30th Annual Institute on Labor Law* (1984).

Wachter and Cohen, "The Law and Economics of Collective Bargaining: An Introduction and Application to the Problems of Subcontracting, Partial Closings and Relocations," 136 *U. Pa. L. Rev.* 1349 (1988).

Willen, "Regulation of Section 8(f) Contract Negotiations after the NLRB's Decision in *Deklewa*," 4 *Lab. Lawyer* 797 (1988).

Zimarowski, "Interpreting Collective Bargaining Agreements: Silence, Ambiguity and NLRA Section 8(d)," 10 *Ind. Rel. L.J.* 465 (1989).

chapter 6

STRIKES, STRIKER RIGHTS, AND LOCKOUTS

The vast majority of all collective bargaining disputes are peacefully resolved. Yet, there are times when bargaining breaks down. On such occasions, employees may resort to their basic traditional right to strike. It is no exaggeration that the freedom of workers to strike, legally exercised, is one of the fundamental distinctions between democratic and totalitarian societies. A lockout is the employer's economic equivalent to a strike. The right to lockout is governed by many of the same principles covering the employee's right to strike.

A. STATUTORY PROTECTION OF THE RIGHT TO STRIKE

A strike is a concerted stoppage of work. While there is a constitutional right of free speech and constitutional protection against involuntary servitude, there is no absolute constitutional right to strike. The right to strike is subject to legislative regulation as embodied in the Labor Management Relations Act.

The Supreme Court has repeatedly stated that there is no federal anti-strike policy. The law recognizes the right of both employers and unions to exercise their economic strength except as limited by statute or their collective bargaining agreement. The Norris-LaGuardia Act, by prohibiting issuance of injunctions in labor disputes, recognizes the legitimacy of the strike weapon.

Five sections of the LMRA expressly deal with the right to strike: Sections 8(b)(4)(B), 13, 502, 8(d), and 8(g).

Section 8(b)(4)(B) regulates secondary picketing and boycotts (see Chapter Seven). A proviso to Section 8(b)(4)(B) states: "Nothing contained in this clause (B) shall be construed to make unlawful, where not otherwise unlawful, any primary strike or any primary picketing."

A primary strike is a strike against the employer with whom a union has its dispute. For example, if the employees of company A are on strike because of a dispute with A, perhaps for a new collective bargaining agreement, the employees are engaged in a primary strike. On the other hand, if the employees of company B stop work in support of the strike at A, the employees of B are engaged in a secondary strike, which is prohibited by Section 8(b)(4)(B). The employees of company A are engaged in a primary strike protected by the Section 8(b)(4)(B) proviso, but the employees of company B are not. The circumstances under which employees of one employer may lawfully stop working in support of a labor dispute elsewhere are discussed in the next chapter.

The second statutory protection of the right to strike is Section 13, which provides:

Nothing in this Act, except as specifically provided for herein, shall be construed so as either to interfere with or impede or diminish in any way the right to strike, or to affect the limitations or qualifications on that right.

The third statutory recognition of the right to strike is Section 502, which states:

Nothing in this Act shall be construed to require an individual employee to render labor or service without his consent, nor shall anything in this Act be construed to make the quitting of his labor by an individual employee an illegal act; nor shall any court issue any process to compel the performance by an individual employee of such labor or service, without his consent; nor shall the quitting of labor by any employee or employees in good faith because of abnormally dangerous conditions for work at the place of employment of such employee or employees be deemed a strike under this Act.

The final sections of the Act dealing with the right to strike are the provisions of Section 8(d), requiring that a party serve notice of its intention to terminate or modify a collective bargaining agreement and prohibiting a strike for the notice period (see Chapter Five), and Section 8(g), requiring that a labor organization give ten-days notice of its intent to engage in a strike, picketing, or other concerted activity at a health care facility. Section 8(g) is unique, because it applies whether or not the union has a collective bargaining agreement with the health care facility. The 8(g) notice requirement is discussed more fully in Chapter Seven.

A strike, as a form of concerted activity, may be protected by Sections 7, 8(a)(1), and 8(a)(3) of the LMRA under the same principles that apply to any form of concerted activity (see Chapter Four). For example, employees engaged in a primary strike against their employer for a new collective bargaining agreement are engaged in protected concerted activity and therefore may not be discharged for striking. In contrast, a strike in breach of a contractual no-strike clause is concerted but unprotected activity. Employees who strike in violation of the Section 8(d) and Section (g) statutory strike notice requirements, or in support of a bargaining demand that is not a mandatory subject of bargaining (see Chapter Five), are engaged in unlawful conduct, and their activity, although concerted, is therefore also unprotected. The employees are subject to discharge and do not have the recall or reinstatement rights of employees engaged in protected conduct under the Act. Section 7 of the Act grants employees the right to engage in concerted activity or to *refrain* from such conduct. Thus, although this chapter concentrates on the rights of employees to engage in strike activities, employees also have the right to refrain from such conduct, that is, the right to cross a union picket line and return to work during a strike. A union's right to discipline members who return to work during a strike is discussed in Chapter Ten.

B. ECONOMIC VERSUS UNFAIR LABOR PRACTICE STRIKES

1. Basic Definitions Applied by the NLRB

Strikes are generally classified as either an unfair labor practice or an economic strike. The distinction between an unfair labor practice and an economic strike is very important because reemployment, voting (see Chapter Two), and other rights of strikers engaged in lawful protected strike activity are determined by the type of strike.

a. Unfair Labor Practice Strikes. An unfair labor practice strike is a strike over an employer's unfair labor practices. A strike protesting an employer's discharge of a union supporter because of union activity is a typical example. A strike protesting the employer's refusal to bargain in good faith is an unfair labor practice strike.

As discussed in Chapter Five, however, the current Board has broadened the scope of permissible employer bargaining tactics to the point that strikes protesting the tactics will seldom be classified as unfair labor practice strikes.

b. Economic Strikes. An economic strike is a strike over an economic issue, such as wages, hours, or working conditions. A strike for a contract is an economic strike as long as an employer is bargaining in good faith. Normally, a strike for recognition is an economic strike except if the employer not only refuses to recognize the union, but also engages in extensive unfair labor practices that undermine the union's majority status. In those cases in which a Board bargaining order is appropriate (see Chapter Three), a strike for recognition may be considered an unfair labor practice strike.

What if a strike is over both an employer's unfair labor practices and an economic dispute? A strike is an unfair labor practice strike if it is in part caused by an unfair labor practice. However, if the unfair labor practice occurs some time before the strike begins, the Board may conclude that the economic dispute is the sole reason for the strike.

2. Recall versus Reinstatement Rights

a. The Right to Replace Economic Strikers. Employees engaged in lawful protected strike activity may not be discharged. However, the Board and the courts have historically distinguished the replacement of a striker from discharge. An employer has the right to continue operations during a strike and to hire replacements for the work. The reinstatement rights of striking employees who have been replaced during a lawful protected strike depend upon whether they are economic or unfair labor practice strikers. An employer may lawfully refuse to reinstate an economic striker who is permanently replaced by the time the

strike has ended (the legal principles for determining whether a replacement is temporary or permanent were discussed in Chapter Two). However, the striker must be placed on a recall list and reinstated as vacancies occur. This list is commonly referred to as *Laidlaw* list, after the NLRB decision establishing the right to be recalled.[1] Employees are frequently recalled to work in seniority order. However, the Board has held that an employer is not obligated to do so. It may, for example, recall the striker who is "best qualified" for a particular opening. An employer's criteria for recall must be consistently applied to all employees, not manipulated to discriminate against employees based on their union or strike activity. An economic striker who is not replaced by a permanent replacement is entitled to reemployment when the strike ends.

Employees must offer to return to work before the employer has any obligation to reinstate them. If an employer and union agree to a contract, the employees offer to return in accordance with the contract's terms. However, if a union simply abandons an unsuccessful strike, the employees' offer to return must be unconditional before the employees have reinstatement rights. For example, what if employees making $10.00 per hour strike for a wage rate of $11.00 per hour, but the employer rejects any increase? If the union offers to return to work if the employer agrees to $10.50 per hour, the offer is not unconditional. The employees must be willing to return to work under the conditions offered by the employer.

The Board will permit an employer and union to negotiate an agreement limiting the recall period for replaced economic strikers as long as the period fixed is not unreasonably short, is not intended to be discriminatory or misused by either party to accomplish a discriminatory objective, is not insisted upon by the employer in order

[1] See legal principle 2.A.

to undermine the status of the union, and is the result of good-faith bargaining. Thus, for example, the Board would not accept such an agreement if a union, weakened by a losing strike, was forced into accepting such a limitation by the employer as a condition for signing a collective bargaining agreement, or if it is apparent that so few vacancies would arise during the shortened recall period that the agreement is intended to deprive the employees of their statutory recall rights.

The Board has held that an employer has an affirmative duty to seek out replaced strikers and notify them when a vacancy occurs. Some employers follow the practice of sending periodic letters to replaced strikers asking whether the striker is still interested in returning to his former employment. If a striker indicates that the striker is no longer interested, the employer may lawfully remove the employee from the recall list. However, the Board has held that an employer cannot require an employee to respond to such an inquiry, and that an employer cannot terminate an employee who does not respond. Some courts of appeals, however, have upheld an employer's right to require that replaced employees periodically reaffirm their interest in returning to work. Of course, if an employee should fail to respond to an employer's request for an updated address, and if the employer is thereafter unable to notify an employee who has moved of a job vacancy, the employee will lose reinstatement rights.

b. Contractual Recall Rights of Economic Strikers. When a strike is over, permanent replacements who are working usually have less seniority than the replaced strikers awaiting reinstatement. If a contract has a provision that layoffs and recalls are in seniority order, can the replaced striker exercise this seniority to return to work? Unfortunately, no. The Board has held that unreinstated economic strikers do not have any contractual right to recall in accordance with provisions governing recall from layoff because replaced employees are not in a layoff status.

What if an employer lays off permanent strike replacements because of lack of work? If the employer's work picks up, who should be recalled: the replacement or the replaced striker with greater seniority with recall rights? In the past, the Board held that it was unlawful for an employer to give recall preference to laid-off permanent replacements over the strikers with greater seniority because such action would discriminate against the strikers in violation of Section 8(a)(3). As a limited exception, an employer was permitted to recall the replacements first in relatively short-term layoffs, such as those resulting from "acts of God" or brief parts or material shortages, in order to maintain stability in the work force. The Reagan Board changed this rule. Currently the layoff of a replacement creates a vacancy only if, based on objective factors, the laid-off permanent replacement has no reasonable expectancy of recall. If the replacement has a reasonable expectancy of recall, then the laid-off replacement is entitled to reinstatement when the work becomes available ahead of the replaced striker. If, however, the replacement had no reasonable expectancy of returning to work when laid off, the layoff would create a vacancy. In that event the replaced striker would be entitled to reinstatement before replacements with less seniority if the employer subsequently expands the workforce.

The Board indicated that the objective factors to use in determining whether a replacement had a reasonable expectancy of recall should include the prior history of the employer in recalling laid-off employees, the employer's future business plans, the reasons for and length of the layoff, and what the employees were told at the time regarding the likelihood of recall. These are basically the same factors used in determining a laid-off employee's right to vote in a representation election (see Chapter Two). Obviously, the Board's current approach will give striker replacements preference for recall in many cases in which replaced strikers would have had preference under the prior rule.

c. *Reinstatement of Unfair Labor Practice Strikers*. An employer can also continue operations during an unfair labor practice strike. But, in contrast to an economic striker, an unfair labor practice striker cannot be permanently replaced. An unfair labor practice striker who unconditionally applies for reinstatement when a strike ends is entitled to reinstatement with full seniority and other benefits to the striker's former job, or if the former job no longer exists, to a substantially equivalent position. If necessary, the employer will be required to discharge the replacements to restore the unfair labor practice strikers to their former or equivalent positions.

The differences between the rights of economic versus unfair labor practice strikers are based on an application of Section 8(a)(3) principles (see Chapter Three) in which the Board balances the adverse effect of employer conduct on employees against the employer's business justification. Permanent replacement obviously has an adverse impact on employees and discourages them from striking. The Board balances this adverse impact against the employer's business justification for hiring permanent replacements, that is, that an employer may not be able to hire enough employees to maintain operations during a strike unless the employer promises them permanent employment. The Board has determined that in an *economic* strike, the employer's need to hire permanent replacements outweighs the adverse impact on the employees so that permanent replacement is lawful under Section 8(a)(3). In contrast, the need to preserve an employee's right to protest an employer's unfair labor practices without the fear of permanent replacement for doing so outweighs the employer's justification in an unfair labor practice strike, so that the permanent replacement of unfair labor practice strikers would violate Section 8(a)(3). It is a violation of Section 8(a)(3) to

discharge either economic or unfair labor practice strikers unless they have engaged in strike misconduct (discussed below) because the significant adverse impact far outweighs any business justification the employer may have for such conduct.

d. *The Five Day Rule*. Normally, the Board allows an employer five days to reemploy strikers after they offer to return to work. This period gives the employer time to make the necessary administrative arrangements. Backpay begins immediately when the strikers offer to return if the employer rejects the offer, unduly delays or ignores the reinstatement offer, or places unlawful conditions on reemployment, such as telling employees they can return to work if they disclaim their union.

3. Conversion to an Unfair Labor Practice Strike

A strike that begins as an economic strike can be coverted into an unfair labor practice strike if an employer commits serious unfair labor practices during the strike that prolong it, such as unlawfully discharging the strikers or engaging in bad-faith bargaining after a strike begins. The strikers become unfair labor practice strikers when the unfair labor practices occur. Thus strikers who were already permanently replaced before then are not entitled to reinstatement, but no additional strikers can be permanently replaced thereafter.

C. LOSS OF RECALL OR REINSTATEMENT RIGHTS

1. Permanent Employment Elsewhere, or a Legitimate Business Reason for Denying Reinstatement

There are certain situations in which either economic or unfair labor practice strikers may lose their recall rights. Unless an employer and union have negotiated a time limit as discussed above, a replaced economic striker's right of recall to the striker's former or substantially equivalent employment continues indefinitely until such time as the employee acquires regular and substantially equivalent permanent employment elsewhere; the employer establishes a legitimate and substantial business reason for failing to offer reinstatement; or the employee declines a bona fide recall notice from the employer. To be bona fide, the offer must be for reinstatement to the employee's former or substantially equivalent employment and without any restrictions such as reduced seniority rights. The employer must give the employee a reasonable time to report back to work after receiving the recall notice.

The employer has the burden of establishing that an employee has obtained regular and substantially equivalent employment elsewhere. That an employee is receiving wages that are as high or even higher than the employee would receive if reinstated by the prior employer does not necessarily mean that the new employment is substantially equivalent. The Board considers a number of factors including the desire and intent of the employee concerned to return to the former employer; whether the fringe benefits and working conditions of the two employers are substantially equivalent; the seniority rights of the employee at the old versus the new employer (an employee may very well want to return to the former job offering greater seniority protection even though the new job pays higher wages); and the location and distance between the new job and the employee's home.

The question of whether an employer has established a legitimate and substantial business reason for not recalling a striker arises most commonly when an employer asserts that the employee's prestrike job has been abolished and that the employee is not qualified for the remaining available work. Thus, for example, an employer may have permanently closed the department in which an employee was working before the strike or converted a job from manual labor to a computerized operation. Even an employee whose job has been abolished has the right to be recalled to other available work unless the employer can establish that the employee does not have the ability to perform the new operation. An employer has the burden of proving that a job has been abolished permanently. The Board looks closely to make sure that an employer has not just discontinued an operation temporarily due to the strike or is not manipulating its operational structure in an attempt to deprive employees of their recall, reinstatement, or voting rights (see Chapter Two).

These principles also apply to the reinstatement rights of unfair labor practice strikers. Thus an employer may deny reinstatement to an unfair labor practice striker who has obtained regular and substantially equivalent permanent employment elsewhere or if the employer has a legitimate and substantial business reason for denying reinstatement.

2. Unprotected or Illegal Conduct or Strike Misconduct

As discussed in Chapter Five, economic strikers who strike without giving the notices required by Section 8(d) of the Act, or strike before the notice period required under Section 8(g) for a strike or picketing against a health care institution has expired, lose their status as employees under the Act and are therefore subject to discharge. (Unfair labor practice strikers do not have to comply with these notice requirements.) The Board and the courts have historically held that Sections 8(a)(1) and (3) only protect an employee engaged in a total strike against the employer. Thus tactics such as quickie or partial strikes, sit-ins, or slowdowns (although concerted activity) are not protected by the Act, and employees engaging in such conduct are subject to discharge. Also, as discussed below, employees who strike in breach of a contractual no-strike clause are engaged in unprotected activity and are therefore subject to discharge.

The Board has long held that employees who engage in misconduct that may cause serious harm to persons or property during an otherwise lawful protected strike may be discharged by their employer and thereby lose their right to recall or reinstatement. This rule applies to both economic and unfair labor practice strikers. The misconduct must be serious because the Board is reluctant to permit the termination of a good employee because of a momentary lapse in the heat of a strike.

The Reagan Board in theory continued to apply the principle that only serious misconduct justifies the discharge of a striker. However, in *Clear Pine Mouldings* the Board in fact substantially weakened the standard.[2] Previously, in the absence of unusual circumstances, strikers who engaged only in oral threats against other employees or persons who crossed the union's picket line without any attempt to carry out the threat were not subject to discharge for their action. The Board reversed this principle in *Clear Pine Mouldings* and held that verbal threats standing alone may constitute serious misconduct justifying the discharge of an employee if the threat tended to coerce or intimidate employees in the exercise of rights protected by the Act (e.g., the right to cross the picket line). In *Clear Pine Mouldings* and subsequent cases applying the decision, the Board has upheld the discharge of strikers who made oral threats against employees crossing the union's picket line even though there was no evidence that the strikes made any attempt to carry out the threat.

Prior Boards have upheld the reinstatement rights of discharged employees even in some cases involving a physical assault on another person if no one was hurt, if the attack was provoked, or even if a striker became momentarily carried away by the heat of strike emotions. The Board referred to such behavior as "anticipated animal exuberance." Since *Clear Pine Mouldings*, the Board has upheld the discharge of employees for conduct such as throwing nails or slashing the tires of vehicles going through

a picket line, throwing rocks, or using grossly offensive language, on the grounds that the conduct tended to coerce or intimidate employees, even though no one was injured or there was little if any property damage. Prior Boards frequently condoned such conduct especially if there were no injuries and the violence was an isolated occurrence.

The Board used to give unfair labor practice strikers greater leeway than economic strikers in strike activity. The Board balanced the provocation of the employer's unfair labor practice against the employee's violent response. In *Clear Pine Mouldings*, the current Board specifically rejected this principle. It stated that it would deny reinstatement and backpay to employees who engaged in strike violence even in unfair labor practice strikes. Similarly, the Board also rejected provocation by the employer or nonstriking employees as a defense. Thus in one case, pickets found nails under their cars apparently thrown by the company's guards and nonstriking employees. The pickets responded by throwing nails on the roadway entering the plant. The Board, stating that "two wrongs do not make a right," upheld the employer's discharge of the strikers for their vandalism.

In strike misconduct cases before the NLRB, the burden is on the employer to show that it had a reasonable and honest belief that the discharged employee engaged in serious strike misconduct. The burden then is on the general counsel to prove that the employee did not engage in the conduct or that the employer treated strikers and nonstrikers who engaged in the same misconduct differently. If the employer was mistaken in concluding that the employee engaged in misconduct, the employee is entitled to reinstatement, even if the employer acted in good faith.

Strike misconduct issues are frequently considered by arbitrators, either because a strike occurred while a collective bargaining agreement was in effect or the parties agree as part of a strike settlement agreement to arbitrate the cases of discharged strikers.

[2] See legal principle 3.B.

Many arbitrators applying a contractual just cause standard still follow the principles that a discharge for strike misconduct is not for just cause if the conduct was isolated, involved only oral threats, if there were no serious injuries or property damage, or if the employee was provoked, etc., even though the Board no longer follows this approach.

3. Conduct of Officers during a Strike

At one time, it was an accepted industrial relations doctrine that a union officer could be held to a higher standard of conduct during a strike because of the officer's position. Employers argued that other employees looked up to the officer for guidance and would engage in misconduct if the officer did. Thus, it was argued, an officer could be discharged for misconduct that would not be serious enough to terminate other employees.

The Board rejected this approach in the *Precision Castings*[3] decision, holding that officers can be held only to the same standards as other employees during a strike. Thus, if an officer has a leadership role in a wildcat strike or engages in strike misconduct, the officer can be disciplined in the same way as any other strike leader or employee who engages in misconduct. But an officer cannot be subjected to greater discipline than other employees committing the same offense. Also, an officer can be disciplined if a contract requires the officer to take affirmative steps to end a strike in breach of contract but the officer fails to take such action.

In the *Metropolitan Edison Co.* case,[4] the United States Supreme Court upheld the *Precision Castings* doctrine in full. The Court agreed with the Board that imposing greater discipline on union officers violated Section 8(a)(3) of the Act because it would deter qualified employees from seeking office. The Court rejected the employer's argument that the officers have an implied duty to uphold the contract. The Court reasoned that permitting an employer to impose greater discipline on officers who were not strike leaders or who had not contractually agreed to take affirmative steps to end a strike would give the employer too much control over the officers and undermine the basic principle of the Act that unions must be free from employer control in conducting their affairs (see discussion in Chapter Four).

D. DISCRIMINATION AGAINST STRIKERS

An employer violates Section 8(a)(3) if it unlawfully discriminates against strikers because of their union activities. An employer may not discriminatorily refuse to reinstate or reemploy strikers merely because of union membership or strike activity.

1. Superseniority for Replacements

The Supreme Court's decision in *Erie Resistor* is the leading case protecting strikers against unlawful discrimination.[5] In this case employees had engaged in a lawful economic strike against their employer for a new contract. The employer began to permanently replace the strikers as it was legally entitled to do. It then announced that it would award twenty additional years of seniority ("superseniority") to strike replacements and strikers who returned to work by a certain date. The employer argued that this incentive was necessary to get replacements to work. After an increasing number of strikers returned to work, in part because of the fear of losing seniority, the union gave up and signed a contract with the employer. The union then filed an unfair labor practice charge that granting of superseniority during the strike was discrimination against the strikers because of

[3] See legal principle 10.
[4] See legal principle 10.

[5] See legal principle 4.A.

their union activities in violation of Section 8(a)(3).

The Supreme Court affirmed the Board's decision that the employer violated the Act. The Court stated that superseniority violated Section 8(a)(3) because it was inherently discriminatory or destructive of the employees' right to engage in concerted activity and that the discriminatory impact outweighed the employer's justification.

2. Vacation Pay and Other Contract Benefits

Following *Erie Resistor,* the Supreme Court held in *Great Dane Trailers, Inc.* that an employer violated Section 8(a)(3) of the Act by denying accrued vacation benefits to striking employees while paying those benefits to employees who returned to work.[6] Based on *Erie Resistor, Great Dane Trailers, Inc.,* and subsequent cases following their principles, an employer cannot grant greater seniority or other special benefits to striker replacements. A striker who returns to work retains pre-strike seniority and cannot be made to start over as a new employee. Also, an employer cannot disqualify an employee for benefits because of strike activity. Time lost because of a strike must be treated the same as any other period of unemployment for purposes of contractual benefits. If employees have certain benefits that accrued before a strike and are payable on a certain day, an employer cannot refuse to pay the benefits because the employees are on strike at the time. Thus, if an employee is entitled to vacation pay when a strike begins, the employer cannot withhold the vacation payment until the strike is over. However, if a contract requires that an employee work a certain number of weeks to receive a vacation, the employer need not count the strike period in meeting the eligibility requirement.

Is an employee on sick or disability leave at the time a strike begins entitled to receive benefits during the strike? At one time the

Board held that an employer could not terminate sickness and disability benefits for employees receiving them when a strike began even if the employee participated in strike activity as long as the employee was disabled for work. Active participation in a strike, such as by picketing, could indicate that the employee is no longer disabled for work, depending upon the nature and extent of the disability, in which case the employer could properly cut off the benefits.

The current Board has adopted a more restrictive approach applying Section 8(a)(3) principles in determining whether employees are entitled to receive certain contractual benefits such as sick-leave pay during a strike. First, the union (actually the general counsel in an unfair labor practice proceeding) must establish that the benefit (e.g., sick leave pay) was accrued at the time of the strike in the sense that it was due and payable on the date on which the employer denied it. If the benefit was due and payable the employer must then establish that it denied or discontinued the benefit based on a nondiscriminatory contract interpretation or past practice that is reasonable and arguably correct. If the employer so justifies the denial of benefits, then the employer's conduct is lawful under Section 8(a)(3) unless there is proof that the employer acted with an actual anti-union intent (animus) in denying benefits, a difficult matter to prove. In applying this new approach, the Board has upheld an employer's right to deny accrued vacation pay to employees if, as a matter of contract or past practice, an employee must be actively at work on a certain day to receive vacation pay for the year and the employees are on strike at the time. The Board has also upheld the denial of sick-leave benefits during a strike if, as a matter of contract or past practice, employees are ineligible for sick-leave pay during periods when no work would be available for them if they were well. Thus, if employees are ineligible for sick pay if they would have been on layoff anyhow, the employer may also deny sick pay to them when no work is

---

[6] See legal principle 4.A.

available due to a strike or lockout. If, however, disabled employees normally continue to receive benefits as long as the employee is disabled until benefits are exhausted, whether or not work is available, then the employer cannot deny such benefits to disabled employees during a strike or lockout.

Questions sometimes arise regarding the status of probationary employees during a strike. An employer cannot terminate probationary employees because of their participation in a lawful strike nor require that they begin their probationary period over again at the end of the strike. Although the strike period does not count in meeting the probationary period, a probationary employee resumes the probationary period from the date when the employee left off.

E. RIGHT TO PAY WHILE ON STRIKE

Employees engaged in an economic strike understand that they are not entitled to pay during the strike. However, employees sometimes erroneously believe that they are entitled to pay if they are engaged in an unfair labor practice strike. That is not so. Because they are withholding their services, employees are not entitled to pay while engaged in either an unfair labor practice or economic strike. As an exception, unfair labor practice strikers and economic strikers who have not been replaced may be entitled to backpay if their employer unlawfully rejects an unconditional offer to return to work.

1. Backpay for Discharged Unfair Labor Practice Strikers

The Board has held that an unfair labor practice striker who is unlawfully discharged is entitled to backpay from the date of the discharge even though the striker does not offer to return to work. Instead, the burden is upon the employer to offer reinstatement. The Board reasons that if an

employee has been discharged, it is senseless to require that the employee request reinstatement to be eligible for backpay. However, if an employer offers reinstatement without attaching any unlawful conditions and the employee refuses and continues to strike, the employee is ineligible for backpay. Also, as is true for any unlawfully discharged employee, the discharged unfair labor practice striker must attempt to reduce losses by seeking employment elsewhere. If the employee spends all the time on the picket line and does not look for work, the employee is not eligible for backpay.

F. STRIKE SETTLEMENT AGREEMENTS

Many strikes end with the execution of a strike settlement agreement covering such matters as reemployment of strikers and payment of fringe benefits for the strike period. It is a good idea to have an express agreement in which the employer waives the right to discipline employees returning to work for strike misconduct or at least agrees to submit strike misconduct disciplinary cases to arbitration. Otherwise, provided that the employer acts with reasonable promptness after a strike is over, the employer can still discharge or discipline employees for misconduct occuring during the strike. The issues of recall rights for replaced economic strikers and waiving discipline for strike misconduct are permissive subjects of bargaining (see Chapter Five). Such agreements are especially important now that the Board, as discussed above, has broadened the circumstances under which an employer may lawfully discharge a striker under the Act for strike misconduct.

In the past, even though an employer announced that strike replacements were permanent, it was common for the employer and union to agree as part of a strike settlement that the replacements would be terminated and that the strikers would return to work. The use of such agreements has been limited by the Supreme Court's decision in *Belknap v. Hale*.[7] In that case, the employer promised replacements that they would be retained at the end of the strike. However, the Company entered into a strike settlement agreement with the union to reinstate a number of the strikers, and the employer discharged the replacements to make way for the returning employees. The Supreme Court held that the discharged replacements had the right to file suit in state court against the employer to recover damages for misrepresentation and breach of the employer's agreement to retain them as employees. The *Belknap* decision obviously limits an employer's ability to take back replaced strikers as part of a settlement if the employer has promised the replacements permanent employment for doing so.

G. SYMPATHY STRIKERS

A sympathy strike is a strike in which employees (whether in a union or not) who have no dispute with their employer, honor a union's picket line. Sympathy strikes usually occur in one of two ways. First, employees with the same employer may respect a picket line established by their co-employees who are in another bargaining unit. For example, clerical employees may respect the picket line established by striking production employees. The clerical employees are sympathy strikers. Second, employees of one employer may honor a picket line established by a union representing employees of another employer. For example, truck drivers employed by one company may refuse to make deliveries to another company across a picket line established by the other company's striking employees.

1. The Protected Status of Sympathy Strikers

Sympathy strikers have the same rights as the employees whose picket line they

[7] See legal principle 2.B.

respect. Thus, employees who honor a picket line established to protest an employer's unfair labor practices have the status of unfair labor practice strikers and they cannot be permanently replaced. Employees who honor an unlawful secondary picket line (see Chapter Seven) are unprotected and are subject to discharge. Employees who honor a picket line established in an economic dispute are considered economic sympathy strikers. They can be temporarily or permanently replaced, as is necessary for their employer to continue operations. However, the economic sympathy striker cannot be discharged for engaging in a lawful sympathy strike.

Suppose an employee of company A refuses to make deliveries across an economic picket line established by company B's employees at B's plant. Company A uses one of its supervisors or another employee to drive across the picket line and make deliveries. Has the sympathy striker been permanently replaced? No. The supervisor or other employee is only a temporary replacement for the employee. The employee cannot be discharged, but is not entitled to receive pay for the time the employee refused to cross the picket line.

Suppose the company has to hire another employee to make the delivery the first employee refuses to make. The employer can hire the new employee as a permanent replacement for the sympathy striker, if that is necessary to maintain operations, just as an employer can hire permanent replacements for economic strikers.

Sometimes a union may be lawfully picketing an employer even though it does not represent any of that employer's employees. For example, a union may picket to protest that an employer's substandard wages are undermining union standards in the area (see Chapter Seven). Such a picket line is known as a "stranger picket line" because the union is a stranger to (does not represent the employees of) the target employer. The Board's position is that employees who honor a lawful stranger picket line have the same rights as any other sympathy striker.

However, one court of appeals has indicated that the rights of sympathy strikers who respect a "stranger" picket line may be more restricted than in other cases. In *Business Services By Manpower*,[8] employees of the temporary employment service refused to cross a picket line at the plant where they were to work established by an outside "stranger" union protesting that work being performed at the plant had been shifted from another plant that was on strike. The employer discharged the employees for violating its rule requiring advance notice if employees are unable to fulfill an assignment they have accepted. The Board held that the employer unlawfully discharged the employees rather than just replacing them on that job. However, the court of appeals reversed the Board decision and upheld the discharges. The court concluded that the employees' interest in honoring the "stranger" picket line was relatively weak because the pickets were not employees of the facility being picketed and the picket signs indicated that the picketing was "informational" only. In contrast, according to the court, the employment service had a strong interest in preserving its reputation for reliability in supplying temporary employees and had clearly informed the employees of the advance notice requirement. Also, unlike the usual case in which employees who respect a stranger picket line may be replaced with little or no disruption of the employer's operations, or with only a harmless delay, the employer in this case could not replace the employees promptly to maintain service because they had not called in ahead of time.

So far, the Board itself has refused to adopt any distinction as to the rights of sympathy strikers depending upon whether the picket line was established by a stranger union. The Board has also held that an employer may not impose a rule requiring that employees notify the employer in advance if they intend to honor a picket line unless the employer can demonstrate a com-

pelling business justification for the rule. The court of appeals decision, although a very troublesome one as to the rights of sympathy strikers, may be viewed as one of those few cases falling within this compelling business justification exception.

Many collective bargaining agreements contain provisions permitting an employee to respect a lawfully established primary picket line established either at the employee's own place of employment or at other facilities where the employee may be required to work. Such clauses commonly state that an employee may not be "disciplined" for honoring such a picket line. However, the Board has held that a contract clause prohibiting "discipline" does not prohibit an employer from permanently replacing sympathy strikers in an economic strike. The Board reasons that *replacing* a striker is not legally the same as *discipline* so that a contract clause prohibiting discipline does not waive the employer's right to replace sympathy strikers permanently in an economic strike. Thus, to protect employees, appropriate contract language should be drafted prohibiting not only the discipline but also the permanent replacement of employees engaged in lawful sympathy action. (Additional legal restrictions on picket line clauses imposed by Section 8(e) of the LMRA are discussed in Chapter Eight.)

2. Concerted Activity Versus Fearful Acts

An employee who honors a picket line is frequently acting alone, but the employee may be engaged in protected concerted activity because the employee is supporting the picket (see Chapter Four). What if an employee refuses to cross a picket line out of fear of physical harm rather than any desire to support the pickets in their cause? At one time, the Board held that an employee who refused to cross a picket line out of fear was not engaged in concerted activity and therefore could be lawfully discharged for refusing to cross. However, the Board has reversed this position and now holds that even employees who refuse to cross a picket line out of fear are engaged in protected concerted activity.

3. Refusal to Handle Struck Goods

An employee who refuses to handle struck work (i.e., work produced by an employer whose employees are on strike) is in effect engaged in a sympathy strike. As in the case of an employee who honors an economic picket line, employees who refuse to handle struck work can be replaced, but cannot be discharged.

There is a major restriction on refusing to handle struck work. Two employers have the legal right to maintain their normal business relationship even though one of them is on strike. Thus, the Board has held that employees are not protected if, out of sympathy for strikers at another plant, they refuse to do their normal work on the product of a struck employer. Employees can be disciplined for refusing to do their normal work, but they can refuse to do work on a product that they would not be doing but for the strike.

For example, suppose a product consists of two components, one produced by company A and one produced by company B. The product is assembled at B's plant. Company A is struck, but continues to operate with replacement employees. Company B's employees cannot refuse to assemble the component produced by company A during the strike. Companies A and B are simply maintaining their normal business relationship and the employees are doing their normal work. But if company A sends the material to company B, and company B orders its employees to make the part company A would have produced except for the strike, the employees can refuse to do the work because they are being asked to do work they would not do if there were no strike. As in the case of sympathy strikers, employees who lawfully refuse to handle struck work have the same protection against permanent replacement as the strikers (economic or unfair labor practice) they are supporting by their action.

Some contracts contain clauses specifically protecting the right of employees to refuse to handle struck work. The legal restrictions on such clauses are discussed in Chapter Eight.

H. CONTRACTUAL RESTRICTIONS ON THE RIGHT TO STRIKE

1. Scope of the No-strike Obligation

As a general rule, the courts interpret a no-strike clause as having the same scope as the contractual arbitration clause so that a union cannot strike over an arbitrable issue. This is known as the doctrine of "coterminous interpretation." Also, employees who strike in violation of the no-strike clause are engaged in unprotected conduct and are therefore subject to discipline.

The legal basis for the "coterminous" doctrine is that the union's no-strike pledge is considered an exchange for the employer's agreement to arbitrate. Thus, logically, the scope of a no-strike clause and an arbitration clause should be the same. However, the parties can expressly negotiate a no-strike clause that either permits the union to strike over certain arbitrable issues or broadly prohibits a union from striking even over nonarbitrable issues. The courts will enforce the contract according to its terms. For example, some contracts permit a union to strike if an employer fails to make payments to fringe benefit funds. The employer's failure to pay the contractual amounts owed is certainly arbitrable, but the union can strike because of the express authority. In general it takes clear language before a court interprets a contract to permit a strike over an arbitrable issue or prohibit a strike over an issue that is not arbitrable. Recently, however, the Board and courts have limited the doctrine of coterminous interpretation as applied to sympathy strikes by holding that a general no-strike clause may prohibit a sympathy strike even though such a strike is not over an arbitrable dispute. This issue is discussed more fully below.

2. Damage Suits for the Breach of a No-strike Obligation

If a union strikes in violation of a no-strike commitment, the employer, in addition to disciplining the employees taking part, can also sue the union under Section 301 of the Labor Management Relations Act to enforce the contract. The employer can file suit without first following (exhausting) the contractual grievance procedure unless that procedure expressly provides for employer grievances or there is a past history of employer grievances. (The procedural requirements for a suit under Section 301 to enforce contractual rights are discussed more fully in Chapter Nine.)

An employer may sue only for its actual, but not punitive, damages in a suit for breach of contract. However, even actual damages for such items as lost production, lost customers resulting from the strike, or continuing overhead costs may be substantial. A union may also be sued for punitive damages if it engages in violent conduct during a strike. Technically in such cases, the employer files a single suit in two counts (parts), one count governed by Section 301 of the Labor Management Relations Act for damages arising out of the contract violation and the other count governed by state law for punitive damages arising out of the violence. This issue is discussed further in Chapter Fourteen.

Although a union can be sued for damages under Section 301, the Supreme Court in the *Carbon Fuel* decision[9] placed important limitations on the scope of a union's liability. In that case, locals of the United Mine Workers engaged in a series of wildcat strikes in alleged breach of a no-strike clause. The employer brought suit for damages against the International Union and its District Councils that had signed the contracts in addition to the locals. The employer

alleged that the International Union and the Councils should be held responsible for the local union wildcat strikes because they had failed to take any affirmative steps to stop the misconduct. The Supreme Court held that neither the International Union nor the District Councils were liable for the contractual breaches. The Court held that these bodies could be responsible only if they had authorized, participated in, or ratified the conduct. The Court also held that there is no statutory obligation to take affirmative action to end a strike that is not so authorized, participated in, or ratified. Of course, a union could contractually agree to take affirmative action to end a wildcat strike, and would be liable for damages if it failed to meet such a contractual commitment.

Since the Supreme Court's decision, the federal courts have applied the same reasoning to damage suits against local unions. Thus, if the members of a local engage in a strike in breach of contract, the local cannot be sued for damages growing out of the strike unless it authorized, participated in, or ratified the strike, or unless it failed to meet a contractual commitment to take steps to end an unauthorized strike. The fact that the local's officers and stewards take part in an unauthorized strike along with the other employees does not necessarily mean that the union will be held liable. However, if union officers or stewards take an active role in a strike once it begins, even though they did not initiate the strike action, the union may be liable on the grounds that it thereby participated in or condoned the strike. Similarly, if a union should distribute picket signs to the strikers, or pay them strike benefits, it may be liable for damages because it "ratified" the unlawful conduct, although the union did not otherwise instigate or participate in the stoppage.

What if all or nearly all the membership of a union participate in an unauthorized work stoppage even though the union, as a body, does not instigate, participate in, or ratify the stoppage? Some employers have argued, under the "mass action" theory,

[9] See legal principle 9.

that the union should be held liable for the concerted activity of its members even though the action is not formally taken in the name of the union. However, since the *Carbon Fuel* decision, the courts have generally rejected this approach and required evidence that the union, as an entity, has either authorized, participated in, or ratified the stoppage.

The Supreme Court has also held that individual union members cannot be sued for the breach of a no-strike clause whether or not the work stoppage is taken as a union action or is a wildcat action by the employees themselves. The only remedy is against the union as an entity. Remember, however, that employees who participate in a work stoppage in breach of contract are subject to discharge for their misconduct even though they cannot be individually sued.

3. Injunctions to Enforce an Express No-strike Obligation (The *Boys Market* Decision)

Although a union's liability for damages for a strike in breach of contract is well established, the question of whether a court can issue an injunction prohibiting a strike in breach of contract was not finally resolved until the Supreme Court's 1970 *Boys Market* decision.[10] Prior to this decision, the Supreme Court had held that Section 4 of the Norris-LaGuardia Act prohibited an injunction against a strike and that damages were the only remedy. Section 4 provided:

No Court of the United States shall have jurisdiction to issue any restraining order or temporary or permanent injunction in any case involving or growing out of any labor dispute to prohibit any person or persons . . . from doing whether singly or in concert, any of the following acts: (a) Ceasing or refusing to perform any work or to remain in any relation of employment; . . . (i) Advising, urging, or otherwise causing or inducing without fraud or violence the acts heretofore specified. . . .

[10] See legal principle 6.

In *Boys Market*, the Court expressly overruled its prior decision. It held that an injunction can be issued against a work stoppage in violation of a no-strike pledge if the strike is over an issue the parties are contractually bound to arbitrate. The Court stated that it was making an exception to Norris-LaGuardia in order to implement the strong congressional preference for resolving industrial disputes through arbitration.

The Court also set down the requirements that must be met before an injunction can be issued, stating:

A District Court entertaining an action . . . may not grant injunctive relief against concerted activity unless and until it decides that the case is one in which an injunction would be appropriate despite the Norris–LaGuardia Act. When a strike is sought to be enjoined because it is over a grievance which both parties are contractually bound to arbitrate, the District Court may issue no injunctive order until it first holds that the contract does have that effect; and the employer should be ordered to arbitrate, as a condition of his obtaining an injunction against the strike. Beyond this, the District Court must, of course, consider whether issuance of an injunction would be warranted under ordinary principles of equity—whether breaches are occurring and will continue, or have been threatened and will be committed; whether they have caused or will cause irreparable injury to the employer; and whether the employer will suffer more from the denial of an injunction than will the union from its issuance.

A suit to enforce a collective bargaining agreement, including the no-strike clause, is usually brought in federal court under Section 301 of the Labor Management Relations Act (see Chapter Nine).

4. Enforcement of an Implied No-strike Clause

A union with a contract containing an arbitration clause, but that does not contain a no-strike clause, might believe that it is free to strike as it wishes. That is not so. The Supreme Court has held that there is an implied obligation not to strike over any issue arbitrable under the arbitration clause. A union that strikes over an arbitrable issue is subject to a damage suit and a court may issue an injunction against the strike as if there were an express no-strike agreement. The union would, of course, be free to strike over any issue that is not subject to arbitration.

I. EXCEPTIONS TO NO-STRIKE CLAUSES

1. Sympathy Strikes

The Supreme Court ruled in *Buffalo Forge* that the courts cannot issue an injunction against a sympathy strike.[11] The Court reasoned that an injunction is permitted under the *Boys Market* decision as an exception to the Norris-LaGuardia Act to uphold the arbitration process as the means to resolve an underlying dispute between the parties as to the meaning or application of their collective bargaining agreement. In contrast, a sympathy strike does not involve an underlying dispute between the contracting employer and the union subject to arbitration under the parties' contract. Therefore, there is no basis for an injunction to uphold the arbitration process, and the Norris–LaGuardia Act restrictions on the issuance of injunctions in a labor dispute apply.

Applying the same reasoning, the Supreme Court held in *Jacksonville Bulk Terminals, Inc.* that a no-strike clause does not prohibit a union from refusing to work as a political protest (in that case the refusal of the longshoremen's union to handle goods bound for the USSR in protest over the Afghanistan invasion), and that such conduct cannot be enjoined because there is no contractual dispute between the employer and the union subject to arbitration.[12] However, as discussed in Chapter Seven, a union engaging in such a boycott may be subject to a damage suit for engaging in a secondary boycott.

Initially after the *Buffalo Forge* decision, most courts also held that a union could not be sued for damages for engaging in a sympathy strike unless the no-strike clause expressly prohibited such actions. The courts generally applied the doctrine of coterminous interpretation, discussed above, under which a union is only prohibited from striking over an arbitrable issue.

More recently, however, the courts' approach to sympathy strikes has gradually shifted to a more restrictive interpretation. Rather than applying a presumption that a no-strike clause does not prohibit sympathy strikes unless it states so expressly, the courts have sought to determine the parties' actual intent under the language of their no-strike clause. Thus, if a contractual no-strike clause is specifically limited to arbitrable issues, or it specifically excludes sympathy strikes from coverage, that express provision will control. If, however, the issue is not specifically covered by the contract, the courts look to other factors such as the placement of the no-strike clause, the bargaining history, and whether sympathy actions have taken place in the past to determine the parties' intent.

If the no-strike clause is contained in the same contract section or article as the arbitration provisions, or if the no-strike clause contains a provision to the effect that neither party will resort to a strike or lockout but will refer all disputes to arbitration, the courts generally conclude that there is a "link" between the arbitration and no-strike clauses, so that the no-strike clause applies only to arbitrable issues. In contrast, if a contractual no-strike clause very broadly prohibits a strike or work stoppage "for any reason," and especially if the no-strike and arbitration provisions are in separate contract articles, the courts have applied the broad language as written to prohibit all strikes including sympathy strikes. If a union has unsuccessfully proposed a specific provision permitting employees to engage in a sympathy strike, the courts regard the

---

[11] See legal principle 6.
[12] See legal principle 6.

proposal as very strong evidence that the existing language bars such conduct. In reviewing the parties' past conduct under the contract language, the courts consider whether a union has successfully engaged in sympathy actions in the past. That employees have not been disciplined is strong evidence that the parties understood that the contract language permits sympathy action.

The NLRB has also changed its position regarding an employee's right to engage in a sympathy strike. Initially, after *Buffalo Forge,* the Board ruled that a broadly worded no-strike clause did not constitute a clear and unmistakable waiver of the employee's right to engage in a sympathy action unless the contract expressly prohibited a sympathy action or extrinsic (outside) evidence (such as the bargaining history) made it clear that such a bar was intended. However, in *Indianapolis Power and Light* the Reagan Board adopted the opposite view.[13] It ruled that a general no-strike clause prohibits a sympathy strike unless the clause specifically permits sympathy strikes as an exception or it is clear from extrinsic evidence that the parties intended to permit sympathy actions. Most courts of appeals reviewing Board decisions applying its new rule generally refused to approve the Board's very broad approach limiting sympathy strikes. These courts reasoned that rather than applying a presumption against sympathy strikes the Board should try to determine the parties' *actual intent*. This is basically the same approach the courts use in damage suit actions as discussed above.

The United States Court of Appeals for the District of Columbia refused to enforce the Board's decision in *Indianapolis Power and Light* and returned the case to the Board for reconsideration. Upon reconsideration, the Board stated that it would modify its position and give greater consideration to the parties' actual intent in negotiating their no-strike clause as determined by the bargaining history and past practice. Although

the Board stated that it was not overruling its earlier decision, the modification broadening the factors it will consider will undoubtedly change the result in many cases. Thus the Board held in its first decision in *Indianapolis Power and Light* that the broad language of the no-strike clause therein waived the employees' right to engage in a sympathy strike. However in its second decision, in which the Board considered the bargaining history as well as the literal language, the Board concluded that the company and the union had consistently disagreed as to whether the existing language prohibited a sympathy strike. Based on the history of this disagreement, the Board reversed its prior decision and ruled that the language did not constitute a waiver of the right to engage in a sympathy strike.

What should a union do then if its collective bargaining agreement does not contain an express sympathy strike provision? Every bargaining situation is, of course, different. However, in general, if the existing no-strike provision is contained in the same section of the agreement as the arbitration clause, or it is otherwise clear that the no-strike obligation is "linked" to arbitrable disputes, or if the bargaining history or past practice supports the union, the union should probably be content with the existing language as is. If a union does decide to seek an express provision permitting the sympathy actions, the union should indicate in bargaining that the proposal is submitted to "clarify" the employees' right to engage in a sympathy action. This may minimize employer arguments that the union's proposal constitutes an admission that the current language does not permit a sympathy action or that an unsuccessful bargaining attempt constitutes a waiver of the employees' rights.

Finally, remember that whether or not a sympathy strike is barred by a no-strike clause, it is still well established under the *Buffalo Forge* decision, discussed above, that even a sympathy strike in breach of contract cannot be enjoined by a federal court because the dispute is not over an arbitrable

---

[13] See legal principle 8.B.

issue. The employer's remedies are limited to a damage suit against the union and disciplinary action against the employees who engaged in the unprotected activity.

2. Unfair Labor Practice Strikes

The Supreme Court has held that a general no-strike clause does not prohibit a strike in protest over an employer's unfair labor practices unless the provision clearly and unmistakably waives the right. The Court reasoned that a no-strike clause is intended to apply to economic disputes between an employer and a union arising under the terms of their collective bargaining agreement and not to waive the union's statutory right to protest employer unfair labor practices. However, the Board has limited the impact of the Court's decision by holding that an employer must commit a serious unfair labor practice before a union can strike notwithstanding a contractual no-strike clause. Also, the unfair labor practice must in fact be the reason for striking or for prolonging a strike, and the union must strike promptly after the occurrence of the unfair labor practice. The Board adopted this policy to prevent a union from seizing upon a minor infraction to justify a strike primarily motivated by economic reasons.

A waiver of the right to strike over an unfair labor practice must be expressly stated in the contract or unmistakably clear from the bargaining history. As discussed above, the Board and the courts have somewhat narrowed the employees' rights to engage in a sympathy strike under a broad no-strike clause. To date, however, the Board and the courts have continued to require a very clear waiver before employees lose the right to engage in an unfair labor practice strike.

3. Safety Dispute Strikes

Many collective bargaining agreements contain a provision allowing an employee to refuse an assignment that the employee in good faith believes is unsafe. As discussed in Chapter Four, the United States Supreme Court held in the *City Disposal Systems* decision that an employee who refuses a job on grounds of safety under such a contractual provision is engaged in protected concerted activity if the employee's refusal is based on a reasonable and honest belief that the employee was being directed to perform a task that the employee could not be required to perform under the contractual safety clause.

In addition to being protected under a contractual safety provision, the refusal to perform an abnormally dangerous job is protected by Section 502 of the Labor Management Relations Act providing:

. . . nor shall the quitting of labor by an employee or employees in good faith because of abnormally dangerous conditions for work at the place of employment of such employee or employees be deemed a strike under this Act.

The Supreme Court held in *Gateway Coal* that a general no-strike clause does not prohibit a strike protected by Section 502.[14] The Court stated that employees who refuse to work because of unsafe conditions, notwithstanding an express or implied no-strike obligation, cannot be disciplined as long as there is ascertainable objective evidence supporting the employee's conclusion that the work is abnormally dangerous. The courts and the Board have held that a strike or other concerted activity over abnormally dangerous conditions is protected under Section 502 even though the employees are wrong about the danger or there is a good-faith disagreement between the employer and the employees as to the danger. The employees' decision must only be reasonably based on ascertainable objective evidence.

Remember that these restrictions on the right to strike over a safety dispute apply only if there is a contractual no-strike commitment. In the absence of an express or implied restriction on the right to strike, or

---

[14] See legal principle 7.

if a contract expressly excludes a safety dispute from the no-strike clause, employees would have the right to engage in a concerted work stoppage over a safety dispute as protected concerted activity under Section 7.

Also, most contractual safety provisions, as noted above, protect an employee's right to refuse a job that is "unsafe." A job may be "unsafe" even though it is not so threatening as to be an "abnormal danger" under Section 502. Thus, contractual safety provisions usually provide employees with greater protection than Section 502, provided, of course, that an employee's refusal to do a job is based on a reasonable and honest belief that the assignment was unsafe under the contractual safety provision.

J. LOCKOUTS

1. Offensive versus Defensive Lockouts

A lockout refers to an employer's action prohibiting its employees from working as a tactic in a labor dispute. A defensive lockout occurs when an employer fears that the employees will strike at a time when the employer is particularly vulnerable (its busy season) and so locks out the employees instead at a time that strengthens its bargaining position. In an offensive lockout, the employer locks out employees in order to put greater economic pressure on a union to adopt the employer's bargaining demands, just as unions strike to put greater pressure on employers.

Unions have argued that any lockout violates Section 8(a)(3) of the Act because it is inherently destructive of an employee's right to engage in union activity (see Chapter Four). At one time, the Board permitted lockouts for defensive purposes only. However, the Supreme Court rejected the limitation on offensive lockouts in the *American Ship Building Co.* case and upheld the employer's right under Section 8(a)(3) to use a lockout either defensively or offensively to

secure more favorable contract terms.[15] The Court basically equated an employer's right to lockout with a union's right to strike, holding that a lockout is permissible unless the Board can prove that there is specific intent under Section 8(a)(3) to discriminate against employees because of their union activities.

Since *American Ship Building Co.*, the Board has generally upheld the right of employers to engage in an offensive lockout. A union can strike at any time after its contract has expired provided that the proper statutory notices have been given, even though no bargaining impasse has been reached. Similarly, an employer can lock out its employees after a contract has expired even before a bargaining impasse has been reached, in support of its bargaining position.

2. Replacement of Locked-Out Employees

The employer's right to continue operations with replacements during a lockout remains a major unresolved issue.

Both the Board and the courts agree that an employer can lock out employees and continue operations using supervisors, temporary replacements, or both whether the lockout is offensive or defensive. The open issue is whether an employer can permanently replace employees whom the employer has locked out. An employer obviously would have very strong bargaining power if it could lock out its employees and then permanently replace them. That places the employees' continued employment totally in the employer's hands. The impact is similar to an employer granting replacements superseniority, which the Supreme Court held unlawful in the *Erie Resistor* case discussed above. For these reasons, unions have argued that employees should not be permitted to permanently replace locked-out employees.

There have been very few reported cases

---

[15] See legal principle 11.

of the permanent replacement of locked-out employees. Apparently most employers avoid the tactic because of its questionable legality. In one case the Board held that an employer violated Section 8(a)(1) and (3) by permanently locking out employees without giving the union prior notice and bargaining with it first. In another case the Board held that an employer who had permanently locked out its employees violated the Act in doing so because it acted with the discriminatory intent to avoid its obligations under a valid and existing collective bargaining agreement and to sever completely its relationship with the union. There may be some situation in which the Board or the courts would uphold the permanent replacement of locked-out employees, but such a case would undoubtedly have to involve very unusual circumstances.

Summary

This chapter covered strikes and strikers' rights, focusing on the statutory protection of the right to strike, the reemployment rights of strikers under the LMRA, and the scope and enforcement of contractual no-strike clauses. While there is no constitutional right to strike, the LMRA affords a statutory basis for the right to engage in a primary strike.

Strikes are generally classified as either an unfair labor practice strike (a strike over an employer's unfair labor practice) or an economic strike (a strike over an economic issue). Whether a union is engaged in an unfair labor practice or economic strike is important because it determines the striker's reemployment rights. In an economic strike, the employer is free to hire permanent replacements for the strikers. Replaced strikers have the right to reinstatement as vacancies occur. In contrast, an unfair labor practice striker cannot be replaced. An unfair labor practice striker who unconditionally offers to return to work is entitled to reinstatement. Both economic and unfair labor practice strikers may lose their reinstatement or recall rights if they obtain substantially equivalent permanent employment elsewhere, their jobs had been permanently abolished and they are not qualified to perform the remaining work, or if they engage in serious strike misconduct.

An employer may violate Section 8(a)(3) if it unlawfully discriminates against strikers because they engaged in a strike. After the termination of a strike, an employer may not discriminatorily refuse to reinstate or reemploy the strikers because of their union membership or concerted activity. Also, the employer cannot discriminate between strikers and nonstrikers on wages, hours, or working conditions such as granting replacements superseniority after the strikers' return to work.

A contractual no-strike clause usually restricts only the right to engage in an economic strike over an arbitrable issue. However, a broadly worded no-strike clause may prohibit a sympathy strike if that intent is established based on the wording, the bargaining history, and the past practice under the language. If a contract provides for arbitration, a no-strike obligation is implied over arbitrable issues even in the absence of an express no-strike clause. In the absence of express wording or very clear intent, a no-strike clause does not prohibit an unfair labor practice strike over an employer's serious unfair labor practices. Sympathy strikers have the same statutory protection as the employees whose strike they respect. Thus, a sympathy striker who refuses to cross a picket line established by economic strikers can be replaced, but not discharged.

In *Boys Market*, the Supreme Court held that the federal courts have jurisdiction to enjoin a strike in violation of an express or implied no-strike clause over an arbitrable issue. In addition to injunctive relief, an employer can lawfully discharge employees who strike in breach of contract and file suit for damages against the union under Section 301 of the Labor Management Relations Act if it instigates, participates in, or ratifies a work stoppage in breach of contract.

In *Buffalo Forge*, the Supreme Court held that the *Boys Market* doctrine did not apply to a sympathy strike because a sympathy strike is not over an arbitrable issue under the parties' contract. Although a sympathy strike cannot be enjoined, an employer might be able to collect damages growing out of such a strike if the court or arbitrator should find that the no-strike clause prohibits a sympathy strike based on either the clause's express wording or the parties' intent.

An employer lockout is the counterpart to a union strike. Generally, an employer may engage in either a defensive or offensive lockout in support of its bargaining position. The Board has held that an employer can lawfully continue operating with temporary replacements. It may be unlawful for an employer to lock out its employees and then permanently replace them, but there is no clear case on the point.

*Review
Questions*

1. Is there a constitutional right to strike?
2. What is the statutory basis of the right to strike?
3. What is an unfair labor practice strike?
4. What is an economic strike?
5. What is the difference in reinstatement rights for economic and unfair labor practice strikers?
6. How do the voting rights of economic and unfair labor practice strikers differ in an NLRB election?
7. How can economic or unfair labor practice strikers lose their reinstatement or recall rights?
8. Are unfair labor practice strikers entitled to lost wages during the term of the strike?
9. What is a sympathy strike?
10. Can a sympathy striker be discharged for engaging in a sympathy strike if the contract contains an express no-strike clause?
11. Can a sympathy striker be permanently replaced?
12. Does a no-strike clause prohibit all strikes during a contract?
13. Under what circumstances will a court imply a contractual obligation not to strike in the absence of an express no-strike clause?
14. What are an employer's judicial remedies against a union's breach of a no-strike clause?

15. Will a federal court enjoin a sympathy strike under Section 301 of the Labor Management Relations Act?

(Answers to review questions are at the end of the book.)

Basic Legal Principles

1. Unfair labor practice strikers are entitled to reinstatement to their former jobs even if the employer has hired replacements. *Tarlas Meat Co.*, 239 NLRB No. 200, 100 LRRM 1210 (1979); *Advance Pattern & Machine Corp.*, 241 NLRB No. 70, 100 LRRM 1537 (1979); *Laredo Coca-Cola Bottling Co.*, 258 NLRB No. 69, 108 LRRM 1271 (1981); *Radio Electric Service Co.*, 278 NLRB No. 78, 121 LRRM 1185 (1986); *NLRB v. Bonanno Linen Service, Inc.*, 782 F.2d 7, 121 LRRM 2400 (1st Cir. 1986); *McCormick-Shires Millwork, Inc.*, 286 NLRB No. 68, 126 LRRM 1283 (1987).

2.A. An employer is entitled to hire permanent replacements for economic strikers and may lawfully refuse to reinstate them. Economic strikers are entitled to recall as vacancies occur. An economic striker who has not been replaced is usually entitled to reinstatement upon an unconditional offer to return to work. *NLRB v. Fleetwood Trailer Co.*, 389 U.S. 375, 66 LRRM 2737 (1967); *NLRB v. Mackay Radio and Telegraph Co.*, 304 US 333, 2 LRRM 610 (1938); *Laidlaw Corp.*, 171 NLRB No. 175, 68 LRRM 1252 (1968); *Southern Fla. Hotel & Motel Assn.*, 245 NLRB No. 49, 102 LRRM 1578 (1979); *Charleston Nursing Ctr.*, 257 NLRB No. 66, 107 LRRM 1533 (1981); *Harrison Ready Mix Concrete, Inc.*, 272 NLRB No. 47, 117 LRRM 1235 (1984), enforcement denied *NLRB v. Harrison Ready Mix Concrete, Inc.*, 770 F.2d 78, 120 LRRM 2077 (6th Cir., 1985); *Lone Star Industries*, 279 NLRB No. 78, 122 LRRM 1162 (1986); *Hansen Brothers Enterprises*, 279 NLRB No. 98, 122 LRRM 1057 (1986).

2.B. An employer and union may negotiate a strike settlement agreement providing for the reinstatement of replaced economic strikers. But the employer may be subject to suit if it discharges replacements it has promised permanent employment. *Belknap v. Hale*, 463 U.S. 491, 113 LRRM 3057 (1983).

3.A. Economic strikers may lose their recall rights and unfair labor practice strikers may lose their right to reinstatement at the end of a strike if they obtain regular and substantially equivalent permanent employment elsewhere; if the employer has a substantial legitimate business justification for denying reemployment (e.g., the employer has permanently abolished the striker's prior job and the striker is not qualified for any other available work); or for serious strike misconduct. *New Galax Mirror Corp.*, 273 NLRB No. 155, 118 LRRM 1519 (1984); *Crystal Linen & Uniform Service, Inc.*, 274 NLRB No. 137, 118 LRRM 1625 (1985); *Salinas Valley Ford Sales*, 279 NLRB No. 89, 122 LRRM 1120 (1986); *John Cuneo, Inc. v. NLRB*, 792 F.2d 1181, 122 LRRM 3063 (D.C. Cir. 1986); *Teamsters Local 162 v. NLRB*, 782 F.2d 839, 121 LRRM 2804 (9th Cir. 1986); *Axelson, Inc.*, 285 NLRB No. 118, 129 LRRM 1344 (1987); *Aztec Bus Lines*, 289 NLRB No. 125, 131

LRRM 1214 (1988); *White Oak Coal Co.*, 295 NLRB No. 64, 131 LRRM 1802 (1988).

3.B. Even verbal threats against employees crossing a picket line may justify the discharge of either unfair labor practice or economic strikers for strike misconduct if the threats tend to coerce or intimidate employees in the exercise of rights protected by the Act, such as the right to cross the union's picket line and return to work. *Clear Pine Mouldings*, 268 NLRB No. 173, 115 LRRM 1113 (1984); *Richmond Recording Corp.*, 280 NLRB No. 77, 124 LRRM 1081 (1986); *Roto-Rooter*, 283 NLRB No. 117, 125 LRRM 1055 (1987); *Tube Craft, Inc.*, 287 NLRB No. 51, 127 LRRM 1234 (1987). But see *Champ Corp.*, 291 NLRB No. 119, 131 LRRM 1555 (1988) (employer cannot discharge strikers for substantially same misconduct it tolerated when committed by employees who did not join in strike).

4.A. An employer cannot discriminate against strikers or hold out inducements, such as superseniority, favoring nonstrikers or replacements over the strikers in order to destroy the right to strike. *NLRB v. Erie Resistor Corp.*, 373 U.S. 221, 53 LRRM 2121 (1963); *NLRB v. Great Dane Trailers Inc.*, 388 U.S. 26, 65 LRRM 2465 (1967); *MCC Pacific Valves*, 244 NLRB 931, 102 LRRM 1183 (1979) (seniority rights for bidding purposes); *Kansas City Power & Light Co. v. NLRB*, 641 F.2d 553, 106 LRRM 2525 (8th Cir. 1981) (discrimination against probationary employees).

4.B. Employees are entitled to receive contract benefits such as vacation and sick-leave pay during a strike if the benefit was accrued (due and payable) on the date the employer denied it and the employer cannot establish that it denied or discontinued the benefit based on a reasonable and arguably correct interpretation of the contract or past practice. *Texaco, Inc.*, 285 NLRB No. 45, 126 LRRM 1001 (1987); *Amoco Oil Co.*, 285 NLRB No. 117, 126 LRRM 1265 (1987); *Bil-Mar Foods, Inc.*, 286 NLRB No. 84, 126 LRRM 1275 (1987); *Texaco Oil Co.*, 287 NLRB No. 91, 127 LRRM 1213 (1987); *Advertisers Mfg. Co.*, 294 NLRB No. 51, 132 LRRM 1024 (1989).

4.C. Once a striker returns to work, the striker's seniority rights are restored, but an economic striker cannot exercise seniority to be reinstated to employment over a permanent replacement. Even if a replacement is laid off, the employer may have the right to recall the replacement to work before the striker with greater seniority if the replacement had a reasonable expectancy of being recalled to work when laid off. *Aqua-Chem, Inc.*, 288 NLRB No. 121, 128 LRRM 1237 (1988).

5.A. A sympathy striker is engaged in protected activity to the same extent as the picket whose picket line is respected. Thus the employer may permanently replace sympathy strikers honoring an economic picket line if replacement is necessary for the employer to continue operations. *Redwing Carriers, Inc.*, 137 NLRB No. 162, 50 LRRM 1440 (1962); *Newbery Energy Corp.*, 227 NLRB No. 58, 94 LRRM 1307 (1976). A contract clause protecting employees from "discipline" for honoring a lawful primary picket line does not prohibit an employer from permanently replacing sympathy strikers in an economic strike because "replacement" is not legally regarded as "discipline." *Butterworth-Manning-Ashmore Mortuary*, 270 NLRB No. 148, 116 LRRM 1193 (1984).

5.B. An employee honoring a stranger picket line (a picket line established by a union that does not represent the employees of the target employer) is a sympathy striker, and, in general, is entitled to protection to the same extent as any other sympathy striker. Compare *Business Services By Manpower*, 784 F.2d 442, 121 LRRM 2827 (2d Cir. 1986) with *Savage Gateway*, 286 NLRB No. 12, 126 LRRM 1296 (1987). See also *Western Stress, Inc.*, 290 NLRB No. 81, 129 LRRM 1299 (1988).

5.C. The refusal of an employee to cross a picket line because of fear of physical harm is regarded as protected concerted activity, the same as an employee who refuses to cross out of respect for the line. *Ashtabula Forge*, 269 NLRB 774, 115 LRRM 1295 (1984).

6. A court can enjoin a strike in violation of a no-strike clause over an arbitrable dispute between the employer and the union. *Boys Markets Inc. v. Retail Clerks, Local 770*, 398 U.S. 235, 74 LRRM 2257 (1970). A sympathy strike cannot be enjoined because it is not over an arbitrable issue. *Buffalo Forge Co., v. Steelworkers*, 428 U.S. 397, 92 LRRM 3032 (1976) *John Morrell & Co. v. Local 304A*, 804 F.2d 457, 123 LRRM 3084 (8th Cir. 1986). See also *Carbon Fuel Co. v. Mine Workers*, 444 U.S. 212, 102 LRRM 3017 (1979) (international union not liable for local strike in breach of contract); *Jacksonville Bulk Terminals, Inc. v. International Longshoremen's Ass'n*, 457 U.S. 702, 110 LRRM 2665 (1982) (no injunction against politically motivated boycott of cargo for USSR).

7. A no-strike obligation is implied if a contract provides for arbitration and the strike is over an arbitrable issue. *Teamster Local 174 v. Lucas Flour Co.*, 369 U.S. 95, 49 LRRM 2717 (1962); *Gateway Coal Co. v. United Mine Workers*, 414 U.S. 368, 85 LRRM 2049 (1974).

8.A. An employee who strikes in violation of a no-strike clause is not engaged in protected concerted activities and can be discharged. *NLRB v. Rockaway News Supply Co.*, 345 U.S. 71, 31 LRRM 2432 (1953); *NLRB v. Lion Oil Co.*, 352 U.S. 282, 39 LRRM 2296 (1957); However, the typical general no-strike clause does not prohibit an unfair labor practice strike or the refusal to work under abnormally dangerous conditions unless the contract expressly so provides or the contractual intent is very clearly established. *Mastro Plastics Corp. v. NLRB*, 350 U.S. 270, 37 LRRM 2587 (1956); *Arlans Dept. Store*, 133 NLRB 802, 48 LRRM 1731 (1961); *Dow Chemical Co.*, 244 NLRB 1060, 102 LRRM 1199 (1979) (serious unfair labor practices justifying strike); *Studio 44, Inc.*, 284 NLRB No. 67, 125 LRRM 1203 (1987); *Gateway Coal Co. v. United Mine Workers* in legal principle 7; *Gary-Hobart Water Corp.*, 210 NLRB 742, 86 LRRM 1210 (1974) enforced, 511 F.2d 284, 88 LRRM 2830 (7th Cir. 1975). See also *Hydrologics*

Inc., 293 NLRB No. 129, 131 LRRM 1350 (1989) (union has right to strike over issues subject to contract reopener clause, provided statutory and contractual notice requirements have been met, unless contractual no-strike clause clearly prohibits such action).

8.B. Whether a no-strike clause prohibits a sympathy strike depends upon the parties' contractual intent as determined by the express wording of the agreement, the relationship between the arbitration and no-strike clauses in the contract (whether the two clauses are "linked"), the parties' bargaining history, and past practice under the no-strike clause. *Indianapolis Power & Light Co.,* 273 NLRB No. 211, 118 LRRM 1201 (1985), enforcement denied and remanded *IBEW Local 1395 v. NLRB,* 797 F.2d 1027, 122 LRRM 3265 (D.C. Cir. 1986), reconsidered and modified 291 NLRB No. 145, 130 LRRM 1001 (1988); *Lear Siegler Inc.,* 293 NLRB No. 48, 130 LRRM 1417 (1989); *Inland Steel Co. v. NLRB,* 719 F.2d 205, 114 LRRM 3414 (7th Cir. 1983); *Arizona Public Service Co.,* 292 NLRB No. 144, 130 LRRM 1385 (1989), on remand from *IBEW Local 387 v. NLRB,* 788 F.2d 1412, 122 LRRM 2304 (9th Cir. 1986); *Electrical Workers Local 803 v. NLRB,* 826 F.2d 1283, 126 LRRM 2065 (3d Cir. 1987).

9. A union is liable for a strike by employees in breach of their collective bargaining agreement only if the union instigates, participates in, or ratifies the work stoppage, or has contractually agreed to take steps to end an unauthorized stoppage. *Carbon Fuel Co. v. Mine Workers,* 444 U.S. 212, 102 LRRM 3017 (1979); *North River Energy Corp. v. United Mine Workers,* 664 F.2d 1184, 109 LRRM 2335 (11th Cir. 1981). Individual employees cannot be sued for participating in a work stoppage in breach of contract, whether or not their union participated in or authorized the strike, but may be subject to discharge or other discipline for participating. *Complete Auto Transit, Inc. v. Reis,* 451 U.S. 401, 107 LRRM 2145 (1981); *Alabama Power Co. v. Local 1333,* 734 F.2d 1464, 116 LRRM 3209 (11th Cir. 1984); *Consolidation Coal Co. v. Local 2216 UMW,* 779 F.2d 1274, 121 LRRM 2156 (7th Cir. 1985). See also *Yellow Bus Lines Inc. v. Local 639,* 883 F.2d 132, 132 LRRM 2164 (D.C. Cir. 1989) (union liability for damages arising out of strike violence under the Racketeer Influenced and Corrupt Organizations Act (RICO)).

10. An employer cannot impose greater discipline on union officers or stewards than on other employees who participate in, but do not instigate, an unauthorized work stoppage solely because of the employees' status as officers or stewards, but may be permitted to impose greater discipline if union officers or stewards have a leading role in the strike or fail to comply with a contractual commitment to prevent or take steps to end an illegal work stoppage. *Metropolitan Edison Co. v. NLRB,* 460 U.S. 693, 112 LRRM 3265 (1983); *Precision Castings Co.,* 233 NLRB 183, 96 LRRM 1540 (1977).

11. Generally, both defensive and offensive employer lockouts are lawful. An employer can engage in an offensive lockout in support of its

bargaining position. *American Ship Building Co. v. NLRB*, 380 U.S. 300, 58 LRRM 2672 (1965). However, an offensive lockout, initiated in part to compel the union to accept the employer's position on a permissive subject of bargaining, is unlawful. *Movers and Warehousemen's Association*, 224 NLRB No. 64, 92 LRRM 1236 (1976), enforced 550 F.2d 962, 94 LRRM 2795 (4th Cir. 1977). See also *Globe Business Furnitiure Inc.*, 290 NLRB No. 94, 130 LRRM 1492 (1988) (lockout unlawful where employer had bargained in bad faith before locking out employees).

12. An employer can continue to operate with temporary replacements during an offensive lockout. The hiring of permanent replacements for locked-out employees is probably prohibited. *NLRB v. Brown*, 380 U.S. 278, 58 LRRM 2663 (1965); *Johns-Manville Products Corp.*, 223 NLRB No. 189, 92 LRRM 1103 (1976), enforcement denied on other grounds 557 F.2d 1126, 96 LRRM 2010 (5th Cir. 1977); *Pankratz Forest Industries*, 269 NLRB No. 10, 115 LRRM 1240 (1984); *Harter Equipment, Inc.*, 280 NLRB No. 71, 122 LRRM 1219 (1986), affirmed *Operating Engineers v. NLRB*, 829, F.2d 458, 126 LRRM 2337 (3d Cir. 1987); *United Chrome Products*, 288 NLRB No. 130, 128 LRRM 1223 (1988); *Boilermakers Local 88 v. NLRB*, 858 F.2d 756, 129 LRRM 2569 (D.C. Cir. 1988). See also *Harter Equipment Inc.*, 293 NLRB No. 79, 131 LRRM 1059 (1989) (locked out employees are eligible to vote in Board conducted representation election, but their replacements are ineligible).

Recommended Reading

"An Employer's Recourse to Wildcat Strikes Includes Fashioning His Own Remedy: §301 Does Not Sanction an Individual Damage Suit," 57 *Notre Dame Lawyer* 598 (1982).

Bartlett, Newman, Mauro, "Strikes in Violation of the Contract: A Management View. A Union View.," 31 *N.Y.U. Conf. Lab.* 64 (1978).

Bosch and Tufano, "Establishing a Uniform Standard for Striker Misconduct in Arbitration Cases," 39 *Lab. L.J.* 629 (1988).

Bulger, "*Boys Markets* Injunctions: A Brief Overview of Injunctions to Prevent Breaches of Collective Bargaining Agreements," 69 *Ill. B. J.* 94 (1980).

"Discriminatory Discipline of Union Representatives for Breach of Their 'Higher Duty' in Illegal Strikes," 1982 *Duke L.J.* 900 (1982)

Erickson, "Forfeiture of Reinstatement Rights through Strike Misconduct," 31 *Lab. L. J.* 602 (1980).

Estreicher, "Strikers and Replacements," 3 *Lab. Lawyer* 897 (1987).

"Sympathy Strikes, Coterminous Interpretation, and the Clear and Unmistakable Waiver Standard: Unweaving the Tangled Web," 1988 *Colum. Bus. L. Rev.* 793 (1988).

chapter 7

PICKETING, BOYCOTTS, AND RELATED ACTIVITY

Effective picketing is a key to an effective strike. Although most employees associate picketing with a strike against their own employer, picketing occurs in other situations as well. Picketing, for example, may be directed against another employer to protest substandard wages it is paying that undercut union wages and benefit levels or against a product produced by a company whose employees are on strike.

The statutory restrictions on the right to engage in picketing are contained in Sections 8(b)(4) and 8(b)(7). There is a limited constitutional right to picket as a matter of free speech. The courts have held that picketing is a form of action, not just speech, and can be regulated. The right to engage in picketing on a labor matter is comprehensively regulated by the LMRA. The Supreme Court has upheld the constitutionality of these provisions. It has further held that a union's right to picket is determined by the LMRA rather than based on constitutional grounds.

A. AN OVERVIEW OF SECTION 8(b)(4)

Section 8(b)(4) is one of the most complex provisions in the LMRA. Its express meaning is so unclear at points that the Supreme Court has held that on some issues, the intent of the provision, rather than the actual wording, must be applied to achieve the statutory purpose. The Board and court decisions emphasize the statutory intent rather than the Act's wording in determining the legality of certain union actions. This chapter concentrates on the restrictions developed by the Supreme Court and Board decisions interpreting the Act rather than analyzing the express wording in detail.

Subsections (A), (B), (C), and (D) of Section 8(b)(4) each prohibit different union conduct. Subsection (A) applies to forcing or requiring an employer to join any labor or employer organization. It also prohibits a union from forcing or requiring an employer to enter into an agreement prohibited by Section 8(e). Section 8(e) pertains to hot cargo agreements (see Chapter Eight). Subsection (B), the so-called secondary boycott or secondary activity provision, prevents a union from forcing or requiring a person to cease dealing with any other person because of the union's dispute with the other person. Subsection (C) prohibits forcing or requiring an employer to recognize or bargain with one union if another union has been certified as the bargaining representative. Subsection (D), which governs jurisdictional disputes, also prohibits forcing or requiring an employer to assign work to one union rather than another (see Chapter Eight).

Section 8(b)(4) contains certain protections for primary picketing. Subsection (B) contains a proviso that "nothing contained in this clause (B) shall be construed to make unlawful, where not otherwise unlawful, any primary strike or primary picketing." Primary picketing, as discussed later in this chapter, is picketing directed against the employer against whom a union has a dispute. There is also a proviso following Subsection (D) that states: "nothing contained in this subsection (b) shall be construed to make unlawful a refusal by any person to enter upon the premises of any employer (other than his own employer), if the employees of such employer are engaged in a strike ratified or approved by a representative of such employees whom such employer is required to recognize under this Act." This section recognizes the right of employees of one employer to honor a primary picket line established by other striking employees.

The first paragraph of Section 8(b)(4) has two clauses. Clause (i) prohibits a union from engaging in a strike or inducing an employee to strike or otherwise refuse to work in order to force an employer into one of the acts prohibited by Subsections (A), (B), (C) or (D). Clause (ii) prohibits a union from threatening, restraining or coercing any person to engage in conduct prohibited by (A), (B), (C) and (D).

Note that (ii) prohibits threats, etc., against any person, not just employees. This section thus prohibits union threats, etc., directly against an employer in order to obtain one of the objects prohibited by Subsections (A), (B), (C), or (D). In contrast, clause (i) prohibits a union even from peacefully inducing or encouraging an employee to engage in a strike or other refusal to work, etc. to force an employer into one of the acts prohibited by Section 8(b)(4). As

discussed below, this distinction between clauses (i) and (ii) has proven to be very important in upholding a union's right to engage in a peaceful consumer boycott against an employer and to make peaceful direct appeals for management support in a labor dispute.

B. THE PRIMARY/SECONDARY PICKETING DISTINCTION

If Section 8(b)(4)(B) were applied literally, it could prevent any picketing. If employees strike and picket their own employer, forcing it to close down, that undoubtedly forces an employer to cease using, selling, or handling the products of another employer or to cease doing business with another employer. However, the last sentence of Section 8(b)(4)(B) contains the proviso protecting the right to engage in primary picketing or a primary strike "not otherwise unlawful." In *Rice Milling* (1951), the Supreme Court had to determine what this proviso meant in relationship to Section 8(b)(4)(B).[1]

1. Traditional Primary Picketing

In *Rice Milling*, the union was picketing an employer for recognition. The Act now contains restrictions on recognition picketing, added in 1959 long after the *Rice Milling* decision (see below), but in 1951 the picketing was lawful. Picketing an employer with whom a union has a direct dispute, as in *Rice Milling*, is traditional primary picketing. As a customer's truck came up to the Rice Milling picket line, the union's pickets approached the truck and asked that the occupants not cross the picket line. Applied literally word for word, the pickets' request violated 8(b)(4)(i), which prohibits employees from inducing or encouraging any employee or any person in the course of his employment to refuse to transport or otherwise handle the goods of any other person.

---

[1] See legal principle 1.

Did this mean that 8(b)(4)(B) prevented the pickets from asking other employees to respect their picket line?

The Supreme Court examined the structure of Section 8(b)(4) and acknowledged that applied literally, the Act prohibited this type of direct appeal. But the Court went on to conclude that Congress had not intended this result. The Court said that the intent of the Act was to preserve the traditional union right of primary picketing. It said the Act's intent was to distinguish between primary and secondary picketing. A union's right to appeal to other employees to honor their picket line is a traditional primary tool. The Court concluded in *Rice Milling* that Congress had not intended to take away that right, therefore upholding the union's right to encourage other employees who approached the primary picket line to honor the line.

In *Rice Milling*, the picketing was primary even though the mill's employees were not on strike. Some employees mistakenly believe that the only kind of primary picket line is that established by employees on strike against their own employer. That is one kind of primary picket line, but it is not the only kind. A primary picket line is any picket line directed against the employer with whom the union has a dispute, even if the employees of that employer are not on strike. Thus, the union in *Rice Milling* had a primary dispute with the mill attempting to achieve recognition even though the employees were not striking. The *Rice Milling* principle on the right of primary pickets to appeal to persons crossing their picket line applies to any primary picket line.

A secondary picket line is a line established against an employer other than the employer with whom the union has a dispute. The purpose is to pressure the secondary employer into taking some action, such as terminating its business relationship with the primary employer, which will in turn pressure the primary employer to resolve its dispute with the picketing union.

The union in *Rice Milling* appealed to the customer's employees as they approached the primary line. What if the union had gone directly to the customer's plant, instead of waiting for the customer to approach the picket line, and had asked the customer's employees not to deliver any goods to the struck plant? At that point, the union would have stepped over the line into prohibited secondary picketing. The union would then be putting direct pressure on the secondary employer, involving the secondary employer in a labor dispute that is not its own. Section 8(b)(4)(B) is intended to prevent such direct pressure on secondary employers. Section 8(b)(4)(B) prevents a union from entangling a so-called "neutral employer" in another employer's labor dispute. The section seeks to isolate a labor dispute to the primary employer and union directly involved.

2. The Primary Object versus Secondary Effect

Another important distinction under 8(b)(4) is the difference between a primary object and a secondary effect. The first paragraph of 8(b)(4) refers to the object of a dispute. Based on this wording, the courts have developed a distinction between the object of picketing and the effect. As long as the object is primary, picketing is lawful even though there may be a secondary effect. Thus, in *Rice Milling*, the primary object was to shut down the picketed employer. There was a secondary effect because the truck driver who was employed by the customer (the secondary employer) refused to cross the picket line and the secondary employer's operations were interfered with. However, since the purpose of the picketing was primary, this secondary effect did not matter.

To be protected, primary picketing must have only a primary object. If picketing has both a primary and secondary object, the picketing is unlawful. For example, if the striking employees of employer A went to the facility of a supplier (employer B) and encouraged B's employees not to cross their picket line, that would violate Section

8(b)(4)(B). Even though the striking employees have a primary object of shutting down primary employer A, the pickets also had the secondary object of enlisting employer B's employees in their support. That entangles employer B in employer A's primary labor dispute in violation of Section 8(b)(4)(B).

Rice Milling dealt with the right of primary pickets to make direct appeals to customers approaching the primary picket line. Subsequent cases have held that primary pickets also have the right, at the primary location, to appeal to suppliers of the primary employer to honor their picket line. Pickets may also appeal to employees of the primary employer and to strike replacements not to cross the line.

Although the Supreme Court has indicated that Section 8(b)(4)(B) should not be applied literally to defeat its purpose, the Court applied a very literal interpretation in its decision in *Allied International, Inc.*[2] holding that the International Longshoremen's Association's action in ordering its members not to load or unload cargo for the Soviet Union, in protest of the Soviet invasion of Afghanistan, constituted a secondary boycott. The Court ruled that Section 8(b)(4)(B) applied even though the boycott was for a political reason, rather than growing out of a labor dispute. The Court also ruled that one of the objects (not just effect) of the boycott was to bring pressure on the importers whose shipments were disrupted. The Court viewed these importers as secondary parties entitled to the Act's protection.

As noted above, if a union engages in lawful primary picketing and employees of other (secondary) employers respect the picket line, the action of the secondary employees is the lawful effect of the primary picketing. Suppose, however, that the union representing the employees of a secondary employer encourages its members to respect the picket line, or even orders its members not to cross the picket line at the risk of

being fined for doing so. In that case, although the primary picketing would still be lawful, the union representing the secondary employees would itself have engaged in secondary conduct violative of Section 8(b)(4) by placing pressure on the secondary employer in support of the dispute between the picketing union and the primary employer, the exact kind of secondary pressure Section 8(b)(4) was intended to prevent. For this reason, a union representing employees of a secondary employer may inform its members of their right to respect a lawful primary picket line (i.e., to engage in a sympathy action unless that right has been waived as discussed in Chapter Six), and the union leadership may even go so far as to state that the officers, as good union members, would not cross the line as a matter of individual choice. However, the union should not go further and "suggest" that its members should honor the line. To avoid violating Section 8(b)(4), the decision to respect the line must be made individually by each union member. Under some circumstances, a union's fine of a member for crossing a picket line may also be unlawful under Section 8(b)(1)(A) of the Act as a restraint of an employee's right under Section 7 to refrain from concerted activities. This issue is discussed fully in Chapter Eleven.

3. Picketing in Breach of Peace

The picketing in *Rice Milling* was violent at times. The Supreme Court held, however, that picketing does not lose its primary status because it is violent. Although violence does not violate Section 8(b)(4)(B), violence directed against employees who refuse to honor the picket line does violate Section 8(b)(1)(A) because the conduct restrains the employee's right under Section 7 to refrain from concerted activity.

Picketing employees have only the moral strength of their picket signs and their power of peaceful persuasion to prevent people from crossing their picket line. Thus, an employer can obtain an injunction in state court against violence, against so-called mass picketing in which large numbers of employees patrol a picket line at one time, or to prevent employees from crowding around or lying in front of vehicles trying to cross the line. A state court may enjoin only conduct that is violent or in breach of the peace. Peaceful picketing, even if unlawful, is subject to the exclusive regulation of the NLRB. This rule involves an application of the "pre-emption doctrine," discussed in detail in Chapter Fourteen, under which conduct that is arguably protected or prohibited by the LMRA is subject to the Board's exclusive jurisdiction except for certain narrow exceptions such as a state court's jurisdiction to prohibit violent conduct.

As discussed in Chapter Six, a federal court can enjoin a strike in breach of a no-strike clause over an arbitrable issue, but the Norris-LaGuardia Act otherwise broadly prohibits federal court injunctions in labor disputes even against violence or other strike misconduct. As discussed above, violence or some other strike misconduct may violate Section 8(b)(1)(A) of the Act. Section 10(j) of the LMRA permits the Board, but not an individual employer, to seek a federal court injunction against conduct violating the Act as an exception to the Norris-La-Guardia Act *after* a complaint has been issued. Thus although the power is not used very often, the Board has authority to seek a federal court injunction against strike misconduct that may violate Section 8(b)(1). Most employers faced with violent or mass picketing file suit for an injunction directly in the state court where the injunction can be (and usually is) quickly granted rather than relying on the Board to seek a federal court injunction after a complaint is issued. (The Norris-LaGuardia Act restrictions apply only to the federal courts.)

Unions frequently attempt to picket or handbill on private property such as in a shopping center during a labor dispute even though such conduct may violate state trespass laws. This right is discussed later in this chapter.

C. COMMON SITUS PICKETING

Rice Milling establishes the basic ground rules of a union's right to picket a primary employer and to appeal to those approaching the picket line at the primary employer's place of business. This is called primary situs picketing. These principles govern picketing at industrial plants, retail stores, etc.

What if striking employees normally work alongside other employees of another employer at the same location, called a common situs? Can the striking employees appeal to the other employees on the common situs to honor their picket line, just as the picketing union in *Rice Milling* could appeal to another employer's driver?

The Supreme Court faced this issue in the *Denver Building Trades* case.[3] That case involved a construction project situs where different construction trades employed by various subcontractors worked. The Construction Trades Council struck the project to protest the use of a nonunion subcontractor. A picket line was established and all the construction trades honored the picket line, shutting down the entire project.

The construction unions argued that the contractors and subcontractors on a construction situs should be treated as a single primary employer because they all perform related work. Therefore, the unions argued, any one union should be permitted to picket the entire project. All employees of a single employer may honor a strike by any of their co-employees as mutual aid and protection except where this right may be waived by a contractual no-strike clause (see Chapter Six). The construction unions argued in *Denver Building Trades* that all employees on a construction project, even though separately employed, should also be permitted to engage in mutual aid and protection.

The Supreme Court rejected the unions' arguments. It held that each employer on a construction situs should be treated as a

---

[3] See legal principle 3.A.

separate employer. Therefore, a union picketing an entire project violates Section 8(b)(4)(B) because the object is to induce employees of other contractors to quit work and involve those secondary employers in another primary employer's dispute. The Court emphasized that shutting down an entire project is a secondary object, not just a secondary effect. The situation was different from *Rice Milling*, because any effect on the customer in *Rice Milling* was a secondary effect of a primary object. The Court stressed that a secondary object need not be the only object of picketing as long as it is an object.

D. RESERVED GATES— THE *MOORE DRY DOCK* STANDARDS

The *Denver Building Trades* case is the basis for the dual-gate system now commonplace in construction industry strikes. If there were only one gate to a construction project, a striking union would have the right to picket it. In that case, the striking union would have only a primary object, publicizing its dispute. If other unions honor the line, that would simply be a secondary effect of the primary object and the picketing would be lawful.

But what if a general contractor puts up separate gates, one reserved for the employees, suppliers, and customers of the primary employer who is the target of the picketing and one or more other gates (the neutral gates) for the employees, suppliers, and customers of all other employers working on the job site. Provided that the reserve and neutral gates are clearly identified as such, and that they are properly established and maintained as discussed below, the picketing union cannot picket at the neutral gates, but is limited to the reserve gate marked for the primary employer's use. If the union pickets at the neutral gates, it is obviously appealing to other employees with the object of encouraging them to quit

work for their employers in support of the picketing union's dispute with the primary employer. Section 8(b)(4)(B) is designed to prevent just this type of secondary pressure. Thus establishing reserve and neutral gates effectively limits a labor dispute to the primary employer.

The rules for picketing at a common situs were set forth by the Board in the *Moore Dry Dock* case in 1950.[4] In the field of labor law, in which change is common, it is unusual, but true, that the rules established in *Moore Dry Dock* remain the governing principles.

In *Moore Dry Dock,* a ship owned by an employer with whom the union had a primary labor dispute was at a dry dock owned by another employer for repairs. The ship owner had an office that the union could have picketed, but the union picketed at the entrance to the dry dock, a secondary situs, instead. The dry dock owner argued that the picketing at the dry dock had a secondary object of inducing the dry dock's employees to honor the picket line and thus embroiling the secondary employer in the union's dispute with the ship owner.

The Board upheld the union's picketing. In doing so, the Board set down four requirements unions must follow in order to picket lawfully at a secondary situs. If a union follows these guidelines, the picketing is presumed to have only a primary object of publicizing the union's dispute with the primary employer. If the secondary employer's employees should honor the picket line, that is considered as only the secondary effect of the lawful picketing. (Remember, however, as discussed above, that the union representing the employees of the secondary employer may itself be engaged in an unlawful secondary boycott if it orders or encourages its members to honor the picket line. The choice must be that of the individual employees.) If, however, a union fails to follow the guidelines, and the employees of a secondary employer honor the picket

[4] See legal principle 4.

line, the picketing is considered to have a secondary object and is thus in violation of Section 8(b)(4)(B). The requirements are:

1. The primary employer must be engaged in its normal business at the common situs.
2. The picket signs of the picketing union must clearly identify the struck employer who is the subject of the dispute.
3. The pickets must be as reasonably close as possible to the situs of the primary employer.
4. The primary employer must be "present" when the picketing occurs.

These rules covering secondary or common situs picketing apply to both industrial and construction unions. They also apply to so-called roving situs cases in which an employer moves from one location to another during the work day, such as a struck employer making deliveries. The rules also apply when the primary employer shares a facility away from its main plant with other employers, such as a common warehouse used by a number of employers.

In most cases, the four requirements are applied strictly to determine the legality of the object. However, both the Board and the courts have emphasized that the requirements are basically evidentiary rules used to determine a union's true object. Thus, as discussed below, even if a union complies in full with the *Moore Dry Dock* requirements in its picketing, but there is other evidence to establish that the picketing was a "signal" for secondary employees to leave a job, then the picketing will be unlawful because of that secondary object despite compliance with the *Moore Dry Dock* standards. In contrast, in some unique situations, such as remotely located primary gates as discussed below, picketing may be upheld as solely primary even though it does not strictly comply with the standards. Each of the four *Moore Dry Dock* requirements will be discussed in turn.

1. Normal Business Operations at the Common Situs

This requirement is easily met, as most employers engage in their normal business operations at a secondary situs. It is normal operations for an employer to purchase supplies or make deliveries at a secondary location. Thus, a picketing union can follow an employer around from supplier to supplier or customer to customer and picket at the secondary premises as long as the other *Moore Dry Dock* standards are met. Having repairs made is also part of an employer's normal operations, so a union may picket a repair facility, as in the *Moore Dry Dock* case.

2. Identifying the Struck Employer

To meet *Moore Dry Dock* standards, picket signs cannot just say the union is on strike. They must identify the struck employer. The purpose of this requirement is to prevent an innocent secondary employer from being involved in a dispute because the picket signs are unclear. Many unions also print "no dispute with any other employer" on their picket signs to make the primary object clear. Note that a striking union picketing at its own primary situs does not have to identify the struck employer. The sign can simply say "on strike."

3. Picketing Reasonably Close to the Primary Employer

This requirement is again designed to limit the scope of the dispute and the picketing impact to employees of the primary employer. If an access road leads to many factories, one of which is the situs of a dispute, the union cannot picket at the entrance to the road under *Moore Dry Dock*. That would be an attempt to interfere with deliveries to other employers and involve them in the dispute. Instead, the union must picket at the entrance to the specific plant.

Furthermore, if striking employees follow a struck employer making deliveries, the employees must picket the gate through which the truck enters the secondary employer's premises in order to be reasonably close to the situs. They cannot picket the entire plant that the struck employer enters because the object of such picketing would be to encourage the secondary employer's employees to cease work, thus entangling the secondary employer in the dispute.

What if the secondary employer's employees on their own cease working, even though the picketing union properly limits its picketing to one gate? The picketing is still lawful, even though the result is a total shutdown of the secondary employer because the shutdown is the effect, but not the object, of the proper primary picketing.

a. Remotely Located Gates. If an employer purposely establishes a separate reserved gate for the primary employer in a remote area of a common situs, such as at the end of a back alley or other area where the public will not see the pickets, must the picketing union limit its picketing to such a location? There is no easy answer. The primary employer does have the right to establish a gate away from that used by other employers to keep neutral employees from being involved in the dispute. If a picketing union ignores the reserve gate and neutral employees honor a picket line established at the neutral gate, there would certainly be a Section 8(b)(4)(B) violation. On the other hand, in several cases the Board and the courts have held that a picketing union has a legitimate right to publicize its dispute to the public and that the union can properly refuse to limit its picketing to the reserve gate if the union cannot legitimately publicize its dispute at that location. However, the location must substantially and unreasonably impair a union's right to convey its message to the public before the union is justified in ignoring the gate.

That the picketing union may not be required to limit its picketing to the gate reserved for the primary employer in a particular case does not necessarily mean, however, that it may station its pickets at the neutral gate. If there is another location away from the neutral gate near the job site where the union could reasonably station its pickets to reach the public, then the union may be required to establish its pickets at

that location. If the union stations its pickets at or near the neutral gate when there is another reasonable location available, the Board would undoubtedly conclude that the true object of the picketing was to appeal to the employees of the secondary employers on the job site which would, of course, violate Section 8(b)(4)(B).

Certainly, a union should not decide lightly to ignore a reserve gate. If a union makes the wrong decision it is not only subject to Board charges, but also, as discussed below, to a damage suit by a secondary employer.

The Board held in one case that a picketing union trailing the truck of a primary employer may follow the truck through a reserve gate established for the picketed employer on a construction project and picket "between the headlights" of the truck even though picketing at this location brought the pickets into much closer contact with the secondary employer's employees than if the pickets had stopped at the reserve gate entrance. However, a court of appeals refused to enforce the Board's decision, and it is doubtful that the Board, as presently constituted, would reach the same result.

b. Mixed-Use Gates. One well recognized exception to the reserve gate doctrine is that the *neutral* gate must in fact be reserved solely for the employees, suppliers, and customers of the secondary employer. If the primary employer or its employees, suppliers, or customers also use the neutral gates (a "mixed use"), the union is entitled to picket all entrances to the job site, not just the reserve gate. The reserve gate cannot be used to divert the union's attention while the primary employer enters elsewhere. However, even if the neutral gates have been "tainted" by mixed use, an employer can reestablish the dual-gate system by insisting that the primary employer and its employees, suppliers, and customers use the gate reserved for them and taking the necessary steps to ensure compliance (e.g., placing guards at the gates to ensure that only the proper employees enter a gate designated for them). If a proper dual-gate system is reestablished in this manner, and the union is notified of the action taken, then the union must once again limit its picketing to the reserve gate, or else its picketing will violate Section 8(b)(4). Also, a violation of a neutral gate may not taint a dual gate system if the violation is isolated or *de minimis* (e.g., minor or sporadic) and the gates are otherwise properly established and maintained.

Although the situation has arisen only rarely, there is some authority to support the position that a dual-gate system may be tainted not only if a primary employer (or its employees, suppliers, or customers) uses a neutral gate, but also if the secondary employer (or its employees, suppliers, or customers) uses the gate reserved for the primary employer. However, it is probable that a neutral employer's use of the reserved gate will "taint" the dual-gate system permitting a union to picket both the reserve and neutral gates only if the neutral employer uses the reserve gate to such an extent that the picketing union can reasonably conclude that the reserve gate system is not in fact being adhered to at all on the job site despite the fact that reserve and neutral gates are supposedly established.

c. Signal Picketing. As noted above, the *Moore Dry Dock* standards are not applied mechanically, and a union's picketing may still violate Section 8(b)(4)(B) if the picketing actually has a secondary object despite technical compliance with the standards.

The most common example of this is so-called "signal picketing." If a striking union informs a union representing secondary employees that it will be picketing a struck truck making deliveries and would appreciate the other union's "cooperation," that is a signal to the other union to stop working when the pickets arrive. If picketing is, in fact, a signal for other employees to stop working, the picketing violates Section 8(b)(4)(B), even though the picket signs are properly worded and the picketing is conducted reasonably close to the primary em-

ployer's location on the common situs, because it would have a secondary object.

Some unions faced with a dual-gate system limit their pickets to the reserve gate, but then station an observer close enough to the neutral gate to make sure that it is not being improperly used by employees, customers, or suppliers of the primary employer. Some employers have argued that an observer is an unlawful "signal" for secondary employees to leave the job, but the Board has upheld a union's right to an observer if the observer is clearly identified as such and there is no evidence of an actual secondary object. Thus, to avoid problems, many unions have an observer wear a special apron stating that the person is an observer only and that there is no dispute with any employer using the gate.

The possibility of a signal picketing violation is one reason why union officers and members engaged in picketing should be extremely cautious in any public statements they make. If a striking union about to engage in *Moore Dry Dock* type picketing makes public statements about expecting other unions to honor its picket line, the union has probably doomed its picket to failure. If other employees walk out, the Board may conclude, based on the statements, that the picketing was a signal although there has been technical compliance with the *Moore Dry Dock* standards.

4. Presence of the Primary Employer

The final requirement under *Moore Dry Dock* is that the primary employer must be present at the secondary situs when the picketing occurs. If an employer works continually at one location, there is no difficulty. A maintenance contractor may work continually doing routine maintenance in a factory. A union in dispute with the contractor can picket continually at the factory. Picketing can take place even if no one from the primary employer's work force is present if the primary employer still has supplies and equipment at the situs. These supplies and equipment constitute the employer's presence for *Moore Dry Dock* purposes.

a. Roving Employers. But what if a primary employer moves from job site to job site or roves to different locations during the work day such as a delivery truck? If the union knows when and where the employer will be, the pickets must move from location to location with the primary employer. Picketing must be limited to the time the primary employer is actually present at the secondary situs and at the proper gate if a dual-gate system is properly established and maintained. However, if the employer tries to evade the pickets or if the union does not know when and where the employer will be next, the union may picket continuously at each location where the primary employer regularly engages in its normal business operations.

If the picketed employer gives the union a schedule of where and when the primary employer will be working, the union can picket only when the employer is present according to its schedule, even if the primary emloyer is scheduled to work at odd hours when no other employees will be present. In such a case, the mere presence of the employer's equipment or supplies on a job site may not be sufficient to permit picketing at the site except when the employer is actually working there. Why have this restriction? Once again, recall the distinction between the primary object and a secondary effect. The Board reasons that if a union pickets only when the employer is present, the union has the primary object of publicizing its dispute. If the union knows that the primary employer will be present at certain times, but pickets even though the employer is not present, the Board reasons that the union has a secondary object of entangling the secondary employer's employees in the dispute.

If an employer provides a union with a schedule, but does not follow it, or tries to evade the union pickets and leave before the pickets arrive, the union is no longer required to picket only when the employer is at a location. The union can then picket permanently at all the places where the employer works.

As an exception to the requirement that the employer be present, a union can continue picketing if the primary employer is briefly gone from the situs. If the primary employees are working at a construction site in the morning, leave for lunch and come back in the afternoon, a union can continue to picket during the lunch break.

b. Employers Ceasing Operations During Picketing. An employer is also considered present if it would be working at the situs, except that the picketing is effectively stopping operations at the situs. Assume there are maintenance employees working for an outside contractor at a manufacturing plant who are permanently stationed at the plant. Since the maintenance contractor has an office elsewhere, the plant is a secondary situs. After maintenance employees strike and establish a picket line at the plant where they regularly work, the maintenance employer shuts down completely because of the strike. If the maintenance contractor ceases all operations at the plant, the employer technically is no longer present at the secondary situs. Still, the Board has upheld the right of employees in such a situation to continue picketing at the plant because the employer would be present, but for the fact that the picketing has effectively closed down operations. The union has a right to continue picketing to assure the continued effectiveness of its strike and also to publicize its dispute.

Similarly, if the employer is working at a number of locations when a strike begins but stops operations because of the strike, the union can picket each location where the employer was working when the strike began if the employer would be working there but for the strike.

Frequently, the struck employer continues to operate, but leaves each location as soon as the pickets arrive. The employer would not leave but for the pickets' arrival that forces the employer to cease operations at the location. In cases where the union's pickets prevent the primary employer from working or the primary employer keeps its employees off a job because the picketing might be effective, the Board has held that the union can continue to picket during the period the primary employer would have been present, but for the effective picketing.

5. Trailing Trucks of the Struck Employer

Although many common situs problems involve construction unions, the same principles also apply to industrial unions. If an industrial plant is on strike, the striking employees can follow the struck employer's trucks and picket in accordance with *Moore Dry Dock* as the trucks make deliveries. The Board has indicated that if the truck enters private property, the pickets should request permission to enter and picket next to the truck. If the secondary employer refuses permission to follow the truck onto the property, the union can picket at the entrance the truck used. Once the truck leaves, the pickets must leave with it.

What if the secondary employees refuse to unload the truck that is being picketed? That is a legal result of picketing that can properly have the object of forcing the struck employer to cease operations entirely. The picketing would be lawful even if the secondary employees refuse to do any work for their employer as long as the truck is present, because the secondary employees' refusal to work is a secondary effect of a valid primary object, as long as the picketing employees follow the *Moore Dry Dock* standards and there is no "signal picketing."

E. SECONDARY EMPLOYERS AT THE PRIMARY SITUS: THE *GENERAL ELECTRIC* RULES

What happens when employees are on strike against their own employer, but the employees of other employers work at the same location? As discussed above, maintenance employees employed by an outside contractor at a factory can picket at the factory provided they follow the *Moore Dry Dock* rules. They cannot picket a properly estab-lished and maintained neutral gate for the factory employees. What about the reverse situation, in which the factory employees strike and establish a picket line? Can they appeal to the outside maintenance employees as they approach the factory as in *Rice Milling?* Can a neutral gate be established for the maintenance employees so that picketing directed at the maintenance employees is thereby prohibited under *Denver Building Trades* and *Moore Dry Dock?* If outside construction employees are building an addition to the plant at the time the factory employees strike, can the factory employees direct their picketing at these outside contractor employees or can a neutral gate be established for them?

The Supreme Court set down the rules under which striking employees can direct their picketing at secondary employees working on the primary situs in the *General Electric* case.[5] In *General Electric,* the company tried to have certain maintenance and new construction work done by outside contractors while the production employees were on strike. The company established separate gates for its own employees and for the employees of the outside contractors to enter the plant. The issue was whether the striking employees could picket the neutral gates established for the outside contractors. The company wanted to apply the principles of *Denver Building Trades* and *Moore Dry Dock* to the industrial plant situation, which would have meant that the striking production union could not picket the neutral gate established for the outside contractors.

The Supreme Court refused to apply *Moore Dry Dock* and *Denver Building Trades* to the industrial plant situation. The Court noted that the General Electric plant employees were picketing their own plant, which was the primary situs of the dispute. *Moore Dry Dock* and *Denver Building Trades* both involved picketing at secondary locations. So, rather than applying these cases, the Court looked to *Rice Milling*, in which

[5] See legal principle 5.

the picketing had occurred at the primary situs, for the controlling principles. However, the Court held that even an industrial union does not have an unlimited right to picket outside employees working at the primary location. The Court held that a union cannot picket a separate gate if:

1. There is a separate gate for the outside employees identified as such.
2. The work of the outside employees is unrelated to normal operations.
3. The work being done by the outside contractors is not work that could be done only during a strike or plant shutdown.

If all *three* requirements are met, the striking union cannot picket at the neutral gate established for the outside employees. Such picketing is secondary picketing in violation of Section 8(b)(4)(B). On the other hand, if there is not a separate gate, if the work of the outside employees is related to normal operations, or if the company is taking advantage of the strike to do work that could be done only while the plant is shut down, the union can picket the gates used by the employees doing that work. The picketing would then be primary activity outside the scope of Section 8(b)(4)(B).

These rules limiting picketing apply only to employees of outside contractors. Striking employees have the right to appeal to co-workers to support a strike for mutual aid and protection even though those employees are not in the bargaining unit (see Chapter Six). Thus, regardless of the work the primary employer's other employees may be doing, the striking employees can picket the gates used by them.

1. Construction Work by Outside Contractors

What if an employer building an addition to the plant during a strike established a separate neutral gate for the construction contractor's employees? New construction is usually considered unrelated to normal operations. If the work could have been done

with the plant open, so that the employer is not taking advantage of a strike to do work that requires a shutdown, a neutral gate established for the construction employees cannot be picketed. But what if a factory has three production lines and during the strike, the employer uses an outside contractor to renovate one of the lines? The employer cannot establish a neutral gate for the employees doing the renovation work because renovating a line is work related to normal operations and the employer would have had to shut down the line to renovate it but for the strike. The union can picket the gate used by the renovation employees even if the striking employees would not have done the work.

What if a struck employer normally does its own construction work with its own employees? If an employer's own construction employees would normally do or have the capability to do the work contracted out during the strike, the union can picket a gate established for the outside employees doing the work. The work is considered related to normal operations.

As in *Moore Dry Dock*, the rules established in the *General Electric* case are not applied mechanically. Thus, if construction employees perform unrelated work, but the striking employees engage in signal picketing so that the construction employees leave although the production employees do not picket the neutral gate, the picketing violates Section 8(b)(4)(B). On the other hand, if there is no prearrangement, and the striking employees properly picket, the picketing is lawful even if the construction employees leave the plant as their own decision; that is a secondary effect of a lawful primary object.

2. Mixed-use Construction Gates

A separate gate for an outside contractor must be strictly limited to the employees of the outside contractor. If a struck employer tries to bring in its own employees or strike replacements through the neutral gate, the gate loses its protected status and can then be picketed continually the same as any other gate.

Striking employees have the right to appeal to their employer's suppliers and customers not to cross their primary picket line. Company supplies, even office supplies, are related to normal operations and separate gates cannot be established for their delivery. However, suppliers of outside contractors are protected to the same extent as the contractor. Thus, if a contractor is doing work unrelated to normal operations, the contractor's suppliers may use the contractor's neutral gate and cannot be picketed.

F. PUBLICITY CAMPAIGNS AND PRODUCT PICKETING

1. Consumer Handbilling and Other Publicity

The right to engage in handbilling and other publicity in a labor dispute is protected by the second proviso following Section 8(b)(4)(D) that states:

That for the purposes of this paragraph (4) only, nothing contained in such paragraph shall be construed to prohibit publicity, other than picketing, for the purpose of truthfully advising the public, including consumers and members of a labor organization, that a product or products are produced by an employer with whom the labor organization has a primary dispute and are distributed by another employer, as long as such publicity does not have an effect of inducing any individual employed by any person other than the primary employer in the course of his employment to refuse to pick up, deliver, or transport any goods, or not to perform any services, at the establishment of the employer engaged in such distribution.

This proviso is part of the 1959 amendments to Section 8(b)(4) aimed at tightening the provisions against secondary boycotts that were first passed in 1948 as part of the Taft-Hartley Act. Until the Supreme Court decision in *Edward J. DeBartolo Corp.* (1988), discussed below, the Board and the courts interpreted the proviso narrowly as an ex-

ception to Section 8(b)(4), permitting publicity for only the specific purposes stated therein.[6] Thus, the proviso was interpreted to mean that a union could pass out a handbill addressed to the public stating that a union had a dispute with primary employer A; that employer B (the secondary neutral employer) continued to distribute or sell A's products; and that the public should not deal with employer B while it continued to distribute A's product. Although the proviso expressly refers only to "products" produced by the primary employer, the Board, with general court approval, held that the proviso should apply to the performance of services as well as to the processing or distribution of physical products. Thus, a union could urge consumers to boycott a company that continued to sell the products distributed by a struck employer or a union representing janitorial employees could urge the public not to deal with a company using a struck janitorial service to clean its building.

The application of the 8(b)(4) publicity proviso as discussed above raised serious questions under the First Amendment to the United States Constitution guaranteeing freedom of speech. It is arguable that any statutory restrictions on publicity urging a peaceful consumer boycott violate the First Amendment so that the proviso would be unconstitutional if it limited the purposes for which a union could engage in a publicity campaign. Restrictions on picketing do not raise such constitutional issues because picketing, as a form of action as well as speech, is subject to regulation. The constitutional issue came to a head in the *DeBartolo* case. In this case, one store within a shopping center owned by DeBartolo was built by a nonunion contractor. The union distributed a handbill urging the public not to shop at any store within the shopping center because the one store had been built by a contractor paying substandard wages and fringe benefits. DeBartolo filed an unfair labor practice charge alleging that this con-

[6] See legal principle 8.A.

sumer boycott of all the stores in the center violated Section 8(b)(4) because it constituted "coercion" within the meaning of Section 8(b)(4)(ii) and was not protected by this proviso. Eight years of litigation including two Supreme Court decisions resulted.

Ultimately, in a 1988 decision, the Supreme Court upheld the handbilling and broadly ruled that peaceful consumer publicity such as handbilling that does not involve picketing is not prohibited by Section 8(b)(4) of the Act. The Court was concerned that there would be a serious constitutional issue of free speech if Section 8(b)(4) was interpreted to prohibit peaceful publicity. As a basic rule of statutory interpretation, if a statute has two possible interpretations, one which would be constitutional and one which would raise serious constitutional issues, a court construes the statute in the way that would clearly be constitutional unless that interpretation is plainly contrary to the statutory intent. The Supreme Court applied this rule in the *DeBartolo* case. To avoid the constitutional issue, the Court concluded that Congress did not intend for publicity such as handbilling to be classified as a threat, coercion, or restraint within the meaning of Section 8(b)(4)(ii). Rather, the Court concluded that handbilling was mere persuasion that the Act did not intend to prohibit at all. The Court reasoned that the proviso was intended only as a clarification that pure publicity was not prohibited by Section 8(b)(4) and that the specific purposes for publicity listed in the proviso were intended only as examples of the kind of publicity permitted rather than a restricted list. The Court thus rejected the argument that the proviso was an exception to Section 8(b)(4) that limited consumer publicity to only the purposes specifically protected by the proviso as the Board and most lower courts had previously interpreted the language.

The very broad basis of the Court's decision in *DeBartolo* clearly establishes that every form of pure publicity urging a consumer boycott of a neutral secondary employer in a labor dispute is outside the scope of Section 8(b)(4), whether the publicity entails handbilling, newspapers, radio or television advertisements, etc., and regardless of the nature of the business relationship between the primary and secondary employers. A handbill or other publicity may request that the consumers stop all dealings with the secondary neutral employer, not just refuse to buy or use the product or service of the target primary employer. Thus, in one case decided by the Board before the final *DeBartolo* Supreme Court decision, the Board ruled that a union violated Section 8(b)(4) when it distributed a handbill urging consumers not to patronize the bank where a struck employer kept its accounts. The Board had held that this handbilling was not protected by the proviso. Now, however, under the *DeBartolo* decision, such a handbill would clearly be lawful.

The *DeBartolo* decision protects only pure publicity. Thus the Court pointed out in *DeBartolo* that the handbilling at issue did not involve violence, picketing, or patrolling tantamount to picketing. Thus, if handbills urging a consumer boycott of a secondary employer are handed out at the same time as picketing is taking place, the handbilling would be subject to Section 8(b)(4). The proviso protects publicity "other than *picketing*" (emphasis added) but the Act does not define what "picketing" is. The Board and the courts have held that "picketing" may be taking place even though no one is carrying a picket sign. Thus, if persons distributing handbills walk back and forth in front of the facility where they are distributing a handbill or otherwise attempt to block persons from entering or leaving, the Board may determine that such conduct, which is usually associated with "picketing," is in fact picketing not protected by the publicity proviso even though only handbills are distributed. Thus, handbillers should avoid such conduct to assure that their activity is protected.

Also, handbilling is outside the scope of Section 8(b)(4) only if it is directed to the public rather than to the employees of a secondary employer. Thus, although Section 8(b)(4)(ii) that was before the Court in *DeBartolo* prohibits only threats, coercion, or restraint, Section 8(b)(4)(i) more broadly prohibits a union from inducing or encouraging any individual employed by any person to engage in a secondary boycott. This language of Section 8(b)(4)(i) prohibits a union from passing out a leaflet to the employees of a secondary employer, such as a supplier, urging that those employees refuse to make deliveries to the primary employer, but under Section 8(b)(4)(ii) as interpreted in *DeBartolo*, the union could distribute a leaflet to the public urging customers not to patronize the supplier as long as it continued to do business with the primary employer.

2. Product Picketing

As noted above, the Section 8(b)(4) publicity proviso protects only pure publicity without any picketing. The Supreme Court dealt with the issue of whether publicity picketing at a secondary location may also be lawful in some circumstances in the *Tree Fruits* case.[7] In *Tree Fruits*, the employees of companies packing Washington State apples were on strike. When grocery stores continued to sell the apples, the employees picketed and handbilled at grocery stores urging consumers not to buy Washington State apples. Neither the picket signs nor the leaflets requested a total boycott of the stores, only that consumers not buy the apples.

The Supreme Court upheld the union's right to picket the product on the grounds that Section 8(b)(4) did not intend to take away this traditional employee right. The Court established the basic principles that handbills may urge a total consumer boycott and that picketing may urge consumers not to buy the specific struck product. Of course, handbills can be limited to the product if that is all the union wants to boycott.

Product picketing and a handbill urging

[7] See legal principle 8.B.

a total boycott cannot be used together even though both the picket signs and the handbills are properly worded. The Board would conclude that the handbills were intended to aid the picketing; and the object of the picketing, used in conjunction with the handbills urging a total boycott, was a total consumer boycott in violation of Section 8(b)(4). The picketing/handbill combined campaign would not be protected by the proviso because it applies to only pure publicity other than picketing. If the handbills only requested that customers boycott the struck product rather than a secondary employer, the handbill and the picketing could take place at the same time. The publicity proviso would not apply because the picketing and handbilling were combined, but the campaign would fall within the *Tree Fruits* doctrine exception for product picketing.

3. Single and Merged Products

What happens if a secondary employer's entire stock consists only of the struck product, so that if a union pickets the struck product, the union is in effect urging a total boycott of the secondary employer? What if in *Tree Fruits*, for example, the union had picketed an apple stand rather than a grocery store selling many items? The Board has held that a union cannot picket a product if the net effect of the picketing is a total boycott. The union, of course, can handbill in that situation, because handbills can urge a total boycott. For example, in one case, refinery workers picketed a gas station that sold only the struck brand of gas. The Board concluded the picketing was unlawful because the product picketing amounted to a call for a total boycott of the station. The Supreme Court affirmed a Board decision applying the merged product doctrine that a union on strike against a real estate title insurance underwriter could not picket independently owned retail title insurance companies that received more than 90 percent of their gross income from selling the struck company's title insurance although the retail companies could sell other insurance.

What if the struck product is so interwoven with the secondary employer's other products that a consumer can stop using the struck product only by engaging in a total boycott of the secondary employer? The Board applies the merged product doctrine. For example, if a striking bakery union pickets a hamburger stand urging customers not to eat struck buns, the employees are, in fact, urging a total boycott. Under the merged product doctrine, the union cannot picket the secondary hamburger stand, although it can handbill since handbills may request a total consumer boycott.

The merged product doctrine has been applied to construction unions picketing to urge consumers not to buy newly constructed homes containing fixtures made by companies with which the union has a dispute. Several courts have held that since fixtures are merged into a home, picketing of the fixtures is actually a request for a total boycott of the home contractors. The courts have accordingly held that the picketing violated Section 8(b)(4). Again, handbills or other publicity urging a boycott would have been lawful.

4. Direct Appeals to Management

Section 8(b)(4)(ii) was intended to protect employers from union pressure. However, this Section does not prohibit a union from inducing or encouraging employers to assist the union. It protects only against threats, etc. Thus the Supreme Court has held that a union can appeal to an employer's discretion not to stock or sell goods involved in a primary labor dispute so long as no threats, etc. are made. The union can even tell the secondary employer that unless certain products are removed the union will handbill the store or picket the product. Those are legal tactics and it is not a threat to tell an employer that the union will take lawful action unless the employer removes the product.

G. THE ALLY DOCTRINE

The reason for the restrictions on secondary picketing is the principle that a neutral secondary employer should not become embroiled in a dispute not of its own making. If the secondary employer is, however, the ally of a primary employer who continues to operate during a strike, the other employer is not neutral. The union may picket a secondary, allied employer to the same extent as it can picket the primary employer.

1. Commonly owned Companies

The mere fact that two companies are owned by the same persons or parent corporation does not automatically make the two companies allies. A union on strike against one corporate subsidiary cannot picket another subsidiary unless there is central management and control over labor relations. For example, employees were on strike against a newspaper in Detroit that also owned a paper in Miami. The Detroit employees established a picket line at the Miami paper. The Board held that the picketing at Miami was unlawful secondary activity in violation of Section 8(b)(4)(B) because each paper had separate control over labor relations at its facility even though they had the same higher ownership.

The situation of separate subsidiaries of the same company must be contrasted to multi-plants of the same employer. A union on strike against an employer at one plant can picket all other plants as well. That is simply a primary appeal to fellow employees for mutual aid.

Although the situation does not arise frequently, two employers may also be allies if they are part of a single integrated enterprise. For example, in the food processing industry, a can manufacturer and food processor may share a common facility. The cans may go directly from the manufacturer to the processing line. If the employees of one of the employers strike, they could picket the entrances that the employees of the other employer use to enter the facility because of the integrated nature of the two companies' operations.

2. Performance of Struck Work

The most common ally situation is that in which one company does the struck work of another. The key to whether one employer has become the ally of another is whether the two are maintaining their normal business relationship or whether the struck employer has shifted work to the other during the strike. Two employers who had a business relationship before a strike are entitled to maintain it during a strike. An employer does not become an ally by maintaining the same business relationship as before.

Suppose employer A manufactured a product for which employer B manufactures a part. The companies had been dealing with each other before a strike. Employer A's employees strike, and A tries to continue operations during the strike. B continues to supply the part. Can union A picket at employer B's plant? No, because all B is doing is maintaining the existing business relationship, which does not make B the ally of A. But what if employer B, to assist employer A, makes an additional part during the strike that A's employees would have made but for their strike? Then B would become A's ally because B is not just maintaining its normal business relationship; it has crossed that point and is assisting A to resist the strike. That makes B an ally of A subject to the same picketing as A.

Although an employer who simply maintains a normal business relationship with a struck employer is not an ally, the employer is not totally immune from picketing. Such an employer can be picketed under the same restricted conditions (*Moore Dry Dock*) as any other secondary employer. For example, employer A's striking employees could picket employer A's truck when it picked up parts at employer B's plant.

3. Need for an Arrangement

The fact that one employer takes over work previously performed by a struck employer before a strike does not make the employers allies unless there has been an agreement or arrangement to shift the work from one struck employer to the other. Suppose employers A and B are competing companies. A is struck so that customers of A, on their own, go to B for the same product. B is doing A's work, but the companies are not allies. There is no agreement between employers A and B for B to help out during the strike. It is simply the customer's choice. On the other hand, what if employer A arranged to have B take care of A's customer needs during the strike? Then there is an arrangement between A and B and they are allies.

Two employers are not necessarily allies just because they first begin dealing with each other during a strike. It is possible for a normal business relationship to start during the strike. For example, a struck employer might obtain a new supplier for a production part during a strike. If the supplier is furnishing a part that would have been furnished by an outside supplier before the strike began, the struck employer and the supplier have a normal business relationship and they are not allies. But if the supplier is furnishing a part that the striking employees would have produced, but for the strike, the two companies may be considered allies.

Although the principle is not altogether clear, some Board cases seem to indicate that an outside employer doing struck work must have notice that a strike is going on in order to be an ally. In most cases the secondary employer's knowledge of the strike can be implied from all the facts, such as if the secondary employer or a supervisor is seen crossing the union's picket line. To avoid any question, however, if a striking union believes that another employer may not know it is doing struck work, the union should consider sending the employer a notice informing the employer of the strike and giving the employer a chance to stop doing business with the struck employer before picketing begins.

H. SUBSTANDARD WAGES PICKETING

Unions have the right to picket an employer who pays its employees substandard wages even though the union does not represent the employees. The Board has held that a union has a legitimate right to oppose substandard wages because they tend to undercut the conditions that the union has negotiated for its members. The Board recognizes that a union may have absolutely no interest in representing the employees of the picketed employer because the employer is too marginal or the employees are uninterested.

A union that is picketing an employer because of its substandard wages has a primary dispute with that employer. What if a union is engaged in substandard picketing against an employer and suppliers refuse to deliver to that employer? That does not violate Section 8(b)(4)(B). Substandard picketing is governed by the same principles that apply to the other forms of primary picketing. It *can* have the effect of inducing other employees to honor the picket line. Thus, if a union is engaged in substandard picketing of an employer working on a common situs, the picketing is lawful provided it conforms to the *Moore Dry Dock* standards.

Substandard wage picketing runs afoul of the Act when the object of the picketing, in fact, is to require the picketed employer to recognize the union and sign a contract. Picketing for recognition is limited by Section 8(b)(7) of the Act. That Section's relationship to substandard wages picketing is discussed more fully below.

I. ORGANIZATIONAL AND RECOGNITIONAL PICKETING

Organizational or recognitional picketing, in which a union pickets for recognition from the employer or to organize the employees, is regulated by Section 8(b)(7). This section applies only to picketing or threats of picketing; it does not prohibit any other conduct such as handbilling. However, as discussed above in regard to consumer handbilling, conduct may be regarded as "picketing" even though no picket signs are used. Thus, although the situation does not arise frequently, if union handbillers walk back and forth in front of a facility much the same way as someone carrying a picket sign would do, the conduct might be considered as picketing within the meaning of Section 8(b)(7).

Section 8(b)(7)(A) prohibits recognitional picketing where the employer has lawfully recognized any other labor organization in accordance with the Act and a question concerning representation (see Chapter Two) may not appropriately be raised. An employer may lawfully recognize a union under the Act voluntarily or following Board certification (see Chapter Five). Thus, Section 8(b)(7)(A) may prohibit recognitional picketing if another union is recognized in either manner.

Section 8(b)(7)(B) prohibits organizational or recognitional picketing if a *valid* Board election has been conducted within the preceding twelve months. Thus if an election is set aside based on union objections, the union would still be able to picket for recognition. Also, even though a union has lost an election, it can still get voluntary recognition from an employer within a year. Voluntary recognition through peaceful persuasion does not violate Section 8(b)(7).

The third type of picketing prohibited under 8(b)(7)(C) is picketing that has been conducted without an election petition being filed within a reasonable period of time not to exceed thirty days from the beginning of the picketing. Remember that this provision applies only to picketing for recognition or organizational purposes under Section 8(b)(7). Picketing for any other purpose, such as protesting an employer's substandard wages, may continue indefinitely. Also, Section 8(b)(7)(C) has been interpreted to apply to only picketing for initial recognition. Thus, for example, if an employer withdraws recognition from a union in bad faith at the termination of a contract, and the union strikes for continued recognition, the picketing would not violate Section 8(b)(7). (A different rule, however, applies to pre-hire agreements in the construction industry as discussed below.)

Note that Section 8(b)(7)(C) applies to picketing beyond a reasonable period not *exceeding* thirty days. Thus, the provision does not necessarily permit a union to picket for recognition for the full thirty days, and, in some cases, the Board has found that picketing for a shorter period without filing an election petition was unreasonable under the circumstances, such as if the picketing was violent or otherwise coercive. Also, the thirty-day period is measured from the beginning of the picketing even though picketing does not occur every day. Thus, for example, if a union pickets an employer on a sporadic basis, the Board may conclude that the separate picketing episodes are part of a single campaign that has extended beyond a reasonable period not to exceed thirty days in violation of Section 8(b)(7)(C). If the union files a representation petition, the union may continue picketing pending the outcome of the Board procedures. If the union wins the election, then it may continue the picketing indefinitely without violating Section 8(b)(7). If the union loses the election, then continued picketing would violate Section 8(b)(7)(B) prohibiting organizational or recognitional picketing if a valid Board election has been conducted within the preceeding twelve months. A union's representation petition must be properly supported by a 30 percent showing of interest of support among the bargaining unit employees (see Chapter One) in order to toll the thirty-day period.

1. Expedited Elections under Section 8(b)(7)(C)

Section 8(b)(7)(C) contains an expedited election procedure. The employer who is being picketed may file a Section 8(b)(7)(C) unfair labor practice charge and an election petition (an RM petition, see Chapter One). The petition must be filed within thirty days from the beginning of the picketing in order for the Board to hold an expedited election. No showing of interest is required. If the regional director concludes that the Section 8(b)(7)(C) charge has merit and the employer has filed a timely representation petition, the regional director directs an expedited election in such unit as the director finds appropriate and certifies the results. The purpose of this section is to enable an employer to get a quick election determining whether a picketing union, in fact, represents a majority of its employees. Thus preelection hearings are not held except in rare instances in which there are novel or complex issues, particularly if they relate to the composition of the bargaining unit. The union does not receive a list of the names and addresses of the bargaining unit employees as in a regularly conducted election (see Chapter One). Note that only an employer has the right to file a representation petition under Section 8(b)(7)(C) without a showing of interest. A union petition must be properly supported with a 30 percent showing. Thus, the union cannot circumvent normal election procedures by picketing for recognition and then filing an unsupported petition for an expedited election.

This expedited election procedure is rarely used. In most cases, the picketing union realizes that it has no chance of winning an expedited election under Section 8(b)(7)(C). Rather than proceed, most unions will enter into a settlement of the charge with the Board, under which the union agrees to cease the picketing and disclaim any interest in representing the employees.

2. The Publicity Proviso to Section 8(b)(7)(C)

a. Secondary Effect of Consumer Picketing. Section 8(b)(7)(C) contains a proviso that:

Nothing in this paragraph (C) shall be construed to prohibit any picketing or other publicity for the purpose of truthfully advising the public (including consumers) that an employer does not employ members of, or have a contract with, a labor organization, unless an effect of such picketing is to induce any individual employed by any other person in the course of his employment, not to pick up, deliver or transport any goods or not perform any services.

This proviso permits recognitional picketing directed at customers to continue beyond thirty days as long as it does not have an effect on any other employees. A union can lawfully picket to encourage customers not to deal with the employer as long as it does not have a contract with the union. As in the publicity proviso to Section 8(b)(4) permitting consumer boycotts, consumer recognitional picketing is not protected if it has a secondary effect on employees. A secondary object is not necessary.

The Board takes the view that a few isolated instances of employees refusing to cross a properly established recognitional picket line directed at consumers does not violate Section 8(b)(7)(C). There must be a pattern to establish the effect. Thus, if a picketed employer receives fifty deliveries a day, and one truck refuses to cross the line, that single incident does not invalidate the picketing. On the other hand, if all fifty truck drivers refuse to cross the picket line, even though the union tells them to cross, the unlawful effect is clear. There is no hard and fast cutoff. Obviously, the more times employees refuse to cross the picket line, the more likely the Board will hold that there is an unlawful effect.

b. Recognitional versus Substandard Wages Picketing. In applying the Section 8(b)(7)(C) proviso, it is important to distinguish between recognitional picketing and substandard wages picketing (discussed above) to protest wages and working conditions below those the union has established. Some employers argued that the Section 8(b)(7)(C) proviso should prohibit substandard wages picketing that has the effect of causing employees other than those employed by the picketed employer to quit work or that interrupts deliveries by suppliers to the picketed employer. The Board rejected this argument. The Board's view, which the courts have upheld, is that the proviso applies only if the union has a recognitional object prohibited by Section 8(b)(7). Substandard wages picketing, which does not have a recognitional object, can continue indefinitely. Also, as for all other protected primary picketing, it can have the effect (but not the object) of interrupting delivery of supplies etc.

c. Pitfalls in Substandard Wages Picketing. Although unions, primarily in the construction field, that engage in substandard wages picketing know the rules, they sometimes fall into innocent traps. Suppose a union establishes a substandard wages picket line. The picketed employer, or perhaps the manager of a construction project where the picketing is occurring, asks one of the pickets what can be done to get the picket line removed. The picket answers that the line would be removed if the picketed employees join the union. This picket has made it appear that the purpose of the picket line is not to protest substandard wages, but to seek recognition. That places the picketing under Section 8(b)(7).

On the other hand, if the picket replies that the union would not be picketing if the employer paid the prevailing wages and benefits level, the picketing could go on indefinitely. The best answer the picket could have given, however, is no answer at all. As a general rule, pickets should be instructed, if questioned, to reply that their picket sign speaks for itself and they should refer all questions to the union office. This approach is true for any type of picketing.

Another mistake unions make is to tell a prime contractor, in response to questions, that a valid substandard wages picket line will be taken down if the offending employer is removed from a project. This statement makes it appear that one object of the picket line is to put pressure on a prime contractor to remove the offending subcontractor from a project. That is unlawful secondary activity in violation of Section 8(b)(4). The union should tell the inquiring employer that the dispute is not with it and there is nothing for it to do. Of course, that is not a very satisfactory answer, but it is the best way for the union to avoid having an innocent remark be the basis of an Section 8(b)(4) charge.

Does the picketing become unlawful if a prime contractor decides on its own to remove the picketed employer from a project? No, because that is the secondary effect of a primary object. But if, rather than the primary contractor's reaching that conclusion on its own, the union suggests removing the subcontractor, that might be considered a secondary object rather than a secondary effect and thus a violation of Section 8(b)(4).

Another requirement for successful substandard wages picketing is that the union must have evidence that an employer is not paying the prevailing wages and benefits before picketing. If the union does not have any evidence that the employer is actually paying less than the area standard, then the Board will probably conclude that the picketing's true object is recognition and Section 8(b)(7) will apply. Also, substandard wages picketing can have the object of requiring an employer to pay a total wage and fringe benefit package equal in value to that contained in the union's contract. However, the picketing cannot have the object of requiring the picketed employer to pay the same wages and pay into the same fringe benefit funds. The employer has the right to divide the total economic package any way it wishes. The Board reasons that picketing to require the employer to pay the exact same union wages and benefits (rather than just requiring the same total figure) is, in fact, picketing for recognition to which Section 8(b)(7) would apply.

3. Picketing to Obtain or Enforce a Pre-hire Contract

As discussed in Chapter Five, a construction industry union may enter into a pre-hire agreement under Section 8(f) of the Act even though the union does not represent a majority of the employees at the time. Under the Board's decision in *John Deklewa & Sons, Inc.* (discussed in detail in Chapter Five), a contractor is bound by a pre-hire agreement until its expiration date, whether or not the union attains majority status among the employees covered by the contract, unless either the employer or the employees file a representation election petition and the union loses the election.

It is well established that picketing to obtain a pre-hire agreement may violate Sections 8(b) 7(A),(B), or (C) as appropriate. The *Deklewa* case did not change this rule. Thus, a construction union may picket to obtain a pre-hire agreement for a reasonable period of time (usually the full thirty days permitted by the statute) without violating Section 8(b)(7)(C) *unless* the employer does not currently employ any employees in the bargaining unit sought. Also, prior to *Deklewa* it was well established that a union could not picket to enforce a pre-hire agreement until it attained majority status under the contract. However, once a union attained majority status, the contract "converted" and the union could picket for continued recognition without violating Section 8(b)(7), the same as any other incumbent union, as discussed above. When the contract expired, the union could also lawfully picket for a new agreement. Now, under *Deklewa*, although a pre-hire agreement cannot be repudiated unilaterally by an employer during its term, the agreement is regarded as a pre-hire contract for its term regardless of the union's majority status. Therefore, if a union pickets for a new or renewed pre-hire agreement after the old agreement expires, the picketing may violate Section 8(b)(7)(C) (if it continues for more than the permitted thirty day period) unless the union has been certified as the exclusive bargaining representative, has been expressly recognized voluntarily by the employer as the majority status representative, or files a timely representation petition as required by Section 8(b) (7)(C). Since a pre-hire agreement is now enforceable for its full term regardless of the union's majority status, it is arguable that picketing to enforce a pre-hire agreement that an employer improperly rescinds in mid-term should be lawful whether or not the union has attained majority status. However, there is no definitive ruling on this issue as of yet.

J. PICKETING OR HANDBILLING ON PRIVATE PROPERTY OR OF A PRIVATE RESIDENCE

A union's right to picket or pass out handbills on private property, such as within a shopping center, is a recurring issue. Property owners argue that they should have the right to exclude pickets or handbillers from their property. Of course, this limits the effectiveness of a union campaign. Customers entering a shopping center parking lot, for example, drive by without paying attention. Thus, unions argue that private property such as a shopping center that is generally open to the public should be treated the same as public property so that pickets should be able to enter a shopping center and picket directly in front of a store with which they have a dispute. This issue was resolved in part by the Supreme Court in *Hugdens v. NLRB*.[8] In *Hugdens*, striking warehouse employees sought to picket their employer's retail outlet in a shopping center mall. The mall owner threatened the pickets with arrest for trespass and the union filed a Section 8(a)(1) unfair labor practice charge against the shopping center owner.

The NLRB held that the pickets had a First Amendment freedom of speech right to picket in the shopping center because the center was generally open to the public. The decision was appealed. The Supreme Court held that the Board erred in applying the constitutional free speech standard because

that standard applies to the government, not to private parties such as a shopping center. The Court stated that a union's right to picket in a shopping center is to be determined solely under the LMRA by applying the general statutory principles on the right to enter private property during a labor dispute (see Chapter Three). That entails balancing the employees' Section 7 rights to picket and publicize their dispute against the center's private property rights "with as little destruction of one as is consistent with the maintenance of the other." The Court remanded the case back to the Board for reconsideration in light of the Court's decision.

In accordance with the Supreme Court decision, the NLRB reconsidered its prior decision in light of the general statutory principles. The Board weighed the shopping center's private property rights against the union's rights and concluded that the striking employees had the right to enter the center and picket in front of their employer's establishment. The Board reasoned that picketing directly in front of the store was a reasonable way for the pickets to reach customers of the struck store and the store's employees. The Board said picketing on the edges of the center would be ineffective because many people do not pay as much attention as they do to a sign directly in front of the store and also dangerous because of the traffic. It also runs the risk that truck drivers will refuse to make deliveries to other employers in the shopping center, not just the struck employer. Picketing directly in front of the struck employer avoids these possibilities. The Board held that these considerations outweighed the private property rights of the center owner. Thus, a property owner or employer violates Section 8(a)(1) under these circumstances if it prohibits the union from engaging in the activity on its property; demands that the union cease the activity or causes the union's pickets or handbillers to be removed from the property; or threatens or causes the arrest of the pickets or handbillers.

Based upon the Supreme Court decision in *Hudgens,* and the subsequent Board decisions applying it, many unions were able

[8] See legal principle 11.

to justify their right to handbill or picket directly in front of the target employer on private property because the property was generally open to the public and the picketing and/or handbilling to publicize the dispute would have been ineffective unless the union entered upon the private property to do so. However, in the 1986 *Fairmount Hotel* decision[9] the then-current Board changed its analytical approach in determining whether a union has the right to enter on private property. The Board stated that prior Boards had given too much weight to the union's effective ability to communicate its message to the public as a factor in determining the right to enter private property. The Board stated that rather than weighing the private property owner's rights against the union's effectiveness in conveying its message, the Board would instead weigh the private property right against "the nature of the Section 7 right" (i.e., the object of the picketing or handbilling that the union was asserting). If in the Board's judgment one of these two interests is greater than the other, then that interest would prevail without regard to whether or not the union had another effective means of communicating its dispute. The existence of effective alternate means for a union to communicate its message to the public would become determinative only in those cases in which the respective claims of the employer and union are relatively equal in strength.

The standards adopted by the Board in *Fairmont Hotel* proved unworkable. In subsequent cases, the Board members disagreed among themselves as to the weight to give to the purpose of the union's picketing or handbilling, the weight of the employer's private property interest, or the relative strength of the union's purpose versus the employer's private property interest. The union's ability to communicate to the public frequently remained the controlling factor in decisions even though the Board intended for it to be of lesser importance under the *Fairmont Hotel* test. Thus, only

two years later, in *Jean Country* the Board overruled *Fairmont Hotel*.[10] The Board stated that it would return to the principles under which the availability of reasonable alternative means to publicize a dispute is a factor to consider in every case. The Board said that the union must establish that it does not have other reasonable means of communicating to the public in order to conduct its campaign on private property, but that a union does not actually have to attempt alternative means first in every case if it is clear, based on objective considerations rather than subjective impressions, that other reasonably effective alternative means are not available. Thus, for example, if it is obvious that union handbillers stationed at the public entrances to a shopping center parking lot that cars enter at high speed could not effectively pass out handbills urging consumers to boycott a store within the shopping center, the union would not have to post the handbillers at the public entrances first to establish that the effort is futile. Rather the union could begin its campaign directly in front of the store.

Under *Hudgens* and *Jean Country*, the purpose of a union's picketing or handbilling campaign is still a factor in determining a union's right to enter private property in a particular case. Thus the Board indicated in a detailed analysis in *Jean Country* that pickets or handbillers may have greater right of access to private property (their conduct has "greater weight") when their activity directly benefits the employees of the target employer, such as during an organizing campaign, in support of a primary strike, or in protest of an employer's unfair labor practices, than when the conduct has a more indirect relationship such as a campaign protesting the substandard wages of another employer. Picketing or handbilling activity directed against the primary employer in a dispute may have greater weight than activity lawfully directed at a secondary employer. The Board indicated that it would also consider the relationship of the target employer to the

---

[9] See legal principle 11.

[10] See legal principle 11.

property and the intended audience for the union's activity. Thus, a union may have a greater right to enter private property when the target employer is the owner or principal tenant of the property than when the property owner is an "innocent bystander" to the dispute. A union may have greater right of access when the target employer is only one of many tenants in a large shopping center than when the target employer is the only tenant and thus readily apparent to anyone entering the property. The factors considered in weighing the private property right include the use to which the property is put; the restrictions, if any, that are imposed on public access to the property; and the property's relative size and openness (e.g., the union would have a greater right to enter a large shopping center generally open to the public than to enter a hospital restricted to employees, patients, and patient visitors).

In determining whether there are reasonable alternative means to publicize the dispute, the Board said it would consider such factors as the desirability of avoiding the involvement of neutrals in the dispute, the safety of the alternative means at public sites, the burden and expense of the alternative means, and the extent to which the exclusive use of other nontrespassory alternatives would dilute the effectiveness of the message. Significantly, the Board stated that it would regard newspaper, radio, or television advertisements as feasible alternative means to direct contact only in exceptional cases because of their greater expense and effort and lower degree of effectiveness.

The Board's approach in *Jean Country* is obviously complex, but the Board's decision emphasized that it would consider the availability of reasonably effective alternative means as especially significant in the balancing process. This should mean, in practical effect, that even a union exercising a relatively weak picketing or handbilling right (e.g., substandard wages picketing not directly benefiting the employees of the target employer) would probably have the right in most cases to conduct its campaign on private property within a shopping cen-

ter or mall. That is so because the union's right, although relatively "weak," would be substantially impaired unless the union could enter the property, while, in contrast, the private property rights of a shopping center or mall that are also relatively weak would suffer little additional impairment if the conduct is permitted. Note that only a party with a private property interest has the right to object to the union's conduct on private property. Thus, for example, if a target store leases space in a shopping center, but the walkway or corridor in front of the store is common property not covered by the lease, the target store cannot object if the union has pickets or handbillers stationed on the private property. Only the private property owner could raise the issue. Also, a private property owner cannot discriminatorily permit other outside groups to use its property but deny a union access. Such disparate treatment is a clear violation of Section 8(a)(1).

Finally, some courts of appeals have been stricter than the Board in requiring evidence in all cases that a union has no reasonable alternative to conducting its campaign on private property. Thus, even in a case in which it might appear obvious under the Board's *Jean Country* standard that a union has no reasonable alternative to entering the property, such as an indoor mall surrounded by large parking lots, it may still be advisable for the union to go through the motion of attempting to picket or handbill on the edges of the property first so that there can be no question as to the futility.

Picketing or handbilling on private property potentially conflicts with state trespass laws. The Supreme Court, in attempting to balance a union's protected right under Section 7 to engage in picketing or handbilling on private property against the state's interest in protecting private property rights, has held that if a property owner demands that a union leave its property, the union must be given a fair opportunity to file an unfair labor practice charge with the NLRB to determine its rights under the Act before the property owner or employer can seek a state court injunction against the union's activity. If the Board rules in the union's favor on the issue under the criteria discussed above, then the union has the right to remain on the property even though the activity would technically constitute trespass under state law. If, however, the Board determines that the activity is not protected (e.g., the General Counsel may dismiss the union's charge or the Board may rule against the union), then the owner or property owner may seek a state court injunction against the union's conduct that constitutes trespass under state law unless the union voluntarily leaves. (The right of state courts to regulate picketing or handbilling, including conduct that would constitute trespass under state law, is discussed more fully in Chapter Fourteen.)

Some unions as a strike tactic have picketed the homes of officials of the struck employer or of employees who cross the union's picket line. There have not been many NLRB or court cases pertaining to the legality of such conduct. However, to date, the general principle that appears to be developing is that peacefully conducted residential picketing is protected by the Act. However, if such picketing against an employer representative is coercive (e.g., is loud, boisterous, violent, or involves an excessive number of pickets), then it would violate Section 8(b)(1)(B) of the Act (prohibiting a union from restraining or coercing an employer in the selection of its bargaining representatives). Such coercive picketing directed against an employee who chose to cross the union's picket line would violate Section 8(b)(1)(A) of the Act (prohibiting a union from restraining or coercing employees in the exercise of their rights protected by Section 7 of the Act). Residential picketing in breach of peace would also be subject to a state court injunction.

Recently, the United States Supreme Court has upheld the constitutional right of states or municipalities to enact laws or ordinances prohibiting residential picketing directed at a specific home. The Court rejected the argument that such laws violate free speech rights protected by the First Amendment to the United States Constitution. Rather, the Court concluded that the state's interest in protecting residential privacy justified such laws. The Court's decision is a narrow one. Thus it indicates that a law may ban residential picketing aimed at a specific household, but not ban all picketing in a residential neighborhood, as that broad restriction would impermissibly limit the free speech right to communicate to the public. Also, the Court has ruled that laws or ordinances restricting residential picketing cannot constitutionally contain exceptions permitting picketing for certain purposes (such as in a labor dispute) because of its content but prohibiting it for other purposes that are not so approved. It is not yet clear whether a constitutionally valid state law or ordinance prohibiting residential picketing could be applied to prohibit picketing that would otherwise be protected under the Labor Management Relations Act. It is arguable that the states should be able to enforce state laws against residential picketing only to the same extent that they may enforce state trespass laws to prohibit picketing on private property in the course of a labor dispute, that is, that the Board must first determine whether the picketing is protected under the Act before the state courts can take jurisdiction.

K. REMEDIES FOR SECTION 8(b)(4) AND 8(b)(7) VIOLATIONS

1. NLRB Remedies

Under Section 10(1), the regional director is required to give priority to charges alleging violations of Section 8(b)(4) or 8(b)(7) over all other charges. In practice, if an 8(b)(4) or 8(b)(7) charge is filed against a union, the regional director will immediately take an affidavit from the charging party. The regional director will then telegraph the charged union requesting it to produce any information it wishes immediately. If the regional director finds reasonable cause to believe that 8(b)(4) or 8(b)(7) have been violated, the regional director will seek an injunction in the federal district court against the picketing until the Board proceedings are completed. Some unions, to avoid an injunction, simply cease their picketing voluntarily and give the regional director a letter with assurances that the picketing will not resume. The regional director usually will not seek an injunction as long as the union abides by the letter. State courts do not have jurisdiction to issue injunctions against picketing that violate Sections 8(b)(4) or 8(b)(7) of the Act as long as the picketing is peaceful. (See discussion of the "pre-emption doctrine," Chapter Fourteen.)

2. Section 303 Damage Suits

The other means of enforcing Section 8(b)(4) is for the injured party to bring a suit under LMRA Section 303, which provides for a private damage suit for violation of Section 8(b)(4). Section 303 is the only section of the Act that allows private damage suits to remedy an unfair labor practice. Note that this section does not apply to Section 8(b)(7) violations.

Section 303 does not allow an injunction against a violation of Section 8(b)(4); injunctions can only be sought by the regional director under Section 10(l). The employer is entitled to recover actual damages resulting from the unlawful secondary activity. Damages might include items such as loss of customer orders, the overhead cost of maintaining a plant that has shut down because of secondary picketing, or the cost of delayed completion of goods or new construction. Some large judgments have been assessed against unions under Section 303. In addition, if picketing violating Section 8(b)(4) is violent, the employer may also sue the union for punitive damages under state law as discussed in Chapter Fourteen.

Section 8(b)(4) and Section 303 are concurrent remedies. This means that the injured employer can both go to the Board under Section 8(b)(4) and file a civil suit under Section 303. The Board and the court independently decide the case before them.

A union can win before the Board, but lose in court, or vice versa. Some courts have held, however, that if a union loses an 8(b)(4) case before the Board, the court will accept the Board's decision about a violation and the union will not be permitted to relitigate the issue in court. Technically, this is called the doctrine of collateral estoppel. In such cases, the only issue in court is the amount of damages. That is one reason why there is a strong incentive for unions to settle Section 8(b)(4) charges without a formal Board decision. However, a union should be cautious to request a nonadmission clause if it agrees to a Board settlement. Otherwise, the settlement might be used as an admission in court that the union engaged in secondary picketing in violation of Section 8(b)(4).

L. SPECIAL REQUIREMENTS FOR PRIMARY PICKETING IN THE HEALTH CARE INDUSTRY

Section 8(g) imposes special restrictions on picketing at any health care institution. A union must give ten days prior written notice to the health care institution and the Federal Mediation and Conciliation Service before engaging in any strike, picketing, or other concerted refusal to work at a health care institution. Under Section 8(d), an employee who strikes or pickets in violation of this provision loses his status as an employee under the Act, and is therefore subject to discharge for the conduct.

Section 8(g) applies only to strikes, picketing, or concerted activity by the hospital's own employees or to an outside union if it has a direct dispute against the institution. Thus, if a construction union is picketing to protest hospital employees' doing certain construction-type work at a substandard wage (e.g., repainting the hospital's walls), the union must give notice. If the union's dispute is with an outside contractor working at the hospital, the union need not give notice.

Although Section 8(g) requires ten-days

written notice to the institution and the Federal Mediation and Conciliation Service before a strike or picketing, the Board has upheld the lawfulness of a strike without such notice if the notice was sent in time to be received on time but was delayed in the mail, as long as the employer had actual notice ten days ahead of time and had time to make preparations. Also, although Section 8(g) literally requires that the employer and union mutually agree in writing to the extension of a strike deadline, the Board has held that a union may unilaterally postpone a strike for a reasonable period. If the time is extended, the union must give the employer at least twelve hours actual notice of the time the strike will begin. Generally, without some special justification, the Board requires that a strike (or picketing) begin within seventy-two hours of the stated starting time in the notice. If the union delays beyond this period, it must give the employer a new ten-day notice. The Board has also indicated that the notice requirement does not apply if an employer engages in flagrant unfair labor practices and the employees strike in protest. This exception is, however, very narrowly applied and a union should be on very firm grounds before risking a strike without notice.

Summary

This chapter considered picketing and boycotts, focusing on the union's right to picket and the restrictions imposed by LMRA, Section 8(b)(4). The important distinctions under Section 8(b)(4) are between primary and secondary objectives and between a secondary object and a secondary effect. A primary object is an action directed against the employer with whom the union has its dispute, even if the employees of the employer are not on strike. A secondary object is directed against an employer other than the one with whom the union has its dispute.

In *Rice Milling*, the Supreme Court held that pickets in a primary dispute can seek to persuade people appearing at the primary line not to cross the line in support of the picket. If any employees of another employer honor the line, that is a secondary effect of a primary object. As long as the object is primary, picketing is lawful even though there may be a secondary effect.

The policy of Section 8(b)(4) is to prevent innocent employers from becoming embroiled in a labor dispute that is not their own. An employer who assists a struck employer to resist a strike becomes an ally, has embroiled himself in the dispute, and may be picketed the same as any other primary employer. However, two employers who maintain a normal business relationship are not allies.

In *Denver Building Trades*, the Supreme Court held that each contractor on a construction situs is a separate entity. Therefore, a union cannot picket an entire project because the picketing would have the secondary object of embroiling the employees of other contractors in the dispute. For this reason, an employer may establish a dual-gate system, with one gate reserved for the employees, suppliers, and customers of the primary target employer and other neutral gates reserved for the other secondary employers on the job. The union must limit its picketing to the neutral gate with rare exceptions if the dual-gate system is properly established and maintained.

Moore Dry Dock establishes the criteria for lawful picketing at a secondary location. Remember, the factors are not always rigidly applied. Thus, a union may violate Section 8(b)(4) if it is engaging in signal picketing even though it is technically meeting the *Moore Dry Dock* standards.

The *General Electric* decision governs picketing at a primary situs (such as an industrial plant) where other employers also work. A union may not picket at a gate reserved for outside employees if (a) there is a separate gate for the outside employees identified as such; (b) the work of the outside employees is unrelated to normal operations; and (c) the work being done by the outside contractors is not work that can be done only during a strike or plant shutdown.

The right to picket in a shopping center is not determined on constitutional free speech grounds. Instead, the Board applies the statutory test of balancing private property rights against the purpose of the union's campaign and the availability of reasonable alternate means to publicize the dispute.

The right to handbill or to engage in publicity other than picketing is protected by the proviso following Section 8(b)(4)(D). Under the *DeBartolo* decision, such publicity can urge a total consumer boycott of a secondary employer. Although the publicity proviso does not protect picketing, the Supreme Court held in *Tree Fruits* that a union can picket at a secondary situs to persuade consumers not to purchase a struck product. However, a union cannot engage in product picketing if the secondary employer handles only that product or picket a merged product because that amounts to a total boycott of the secondary employer. Only handbilling or other nonpicketing publicity is permitted in such cases.

Organizational or recognition picketing is regulated by Section 8(b)(7). Section 8(b)(7) does not apply to substandard wages picketing. Thus, substandard picketing may have the object of stopping deliveries to the picketed employer and may continue indefinitely the same as other primary picketing.

Review Questions

1. Is there a constitutional right to picket?
2. What is the difference between a primary and a secondary picket line?
3. Can a union engage in mass picketing in which a large number of employees patrol the picket line at one time?
4. What is the difference between a primary object and a secondary effect under Section 8(b)(4)?
5. Can picketing lawfully have a mixed primary-secondary object?
6. Would a picket sign that was simply worded "on strike" meet *Moore Dry Dock* standards?
7. Can a union picket during the regular workday if a prime contractor schedules a picketed employer to work only in the evenings when no other employees are present?

8. Can a striking union appeal to employees of the same employer to join a strike even though they are not in a bargaining unit?

9. Can a union picket at a secondary situs to persuade customers not to buy a specific struck product? What additional rights, if any, would the union have against the secondary employer if the union used handbills or other publicity rather than picketing?

10. Is substandard picketing unlawful if it has the effect of inducing other employees to honor the picket line?

11. When may "informational picketing" violate the Act?

12. What remedies does an employer have against unlawful secondary activity under Section 8(b)(4)?

(Answers to review questions are at the end of the book.)

Basic Legal Principles

1. At the primary location primary pickets have the right to appeal directly to customers, suppliers, fellow employees, and striker replacements not to cross the picket line. *NLRB v. International Rice Milling Co.,* 341 U.S. 665, 28 LRRM 2105 (1951); *United Steel Workers v. NLRB,* 376 U.S. 492, 55 LRRM 2698 (1964); *Production Workers,* 283 NLRB No. 56, 124 LRRM 1305 (1987), on remand from *Production Workers 707 v. NLRB,* 793 F.2d 323, 122 LRRM 2877 (D.C. Cir. 1986); *Chipman Freight Services, Inc.,* 843 F.2d 1224, 128 LRRM 2099 (9th Cir. 1988).

2.A. A boycott is permissible under Section 8(b)(4)(B) if it has solely a primary object although there may be a secondary effect. Boycotts that have both a primary and secondary object are illegal. See cases cited in legal principle 1; *International Longshoremen's Assn. v. Allied International, Inc.,* 456 U.S. 212, 110 LRRM 2001 (1982) (politically motivated boycott having secondary object violates Section 8(b)(4)(B)).

2.B. Even if a primary picket line is lawfully established, the union representing secondary employees may violate the Act if it encourages or orders its members to honor the picket line. *Elevator Constructors Union Local 3,* 289 NLRB No. 132, 129 LRRM 1066 (1988).

3.A. A union having a dispute with one construction contractor cannot picket the entire project, because the picketing would have the secondary object of embroiling other employers in the dispute. *NLRB v. Denver Building and Construction Trades Council,* 341 U.S. 675, 28 LRRM 2108 (1951); *Building Trades Council (Markwell & Hartz, Inc.),* 155 NLRB No. 42, 60 LRRM 1296 (1965); *Sheet Metal Workers, Local 80,* 236 NLRB No. 6, 98 LRRM 1223 (1978); *Carpenters District Council of Sacramento,* 244 NLRB No. 139, 102 LRRM 1234 (1979).

3.B. If an employer establishes a dual-gate system, with one gate reserved for the primary employer and other gates reserved for the neutral secondary employers, the union must limit its picketing to the reserved primary gate if it is properly established and maintained. This rule may not apply if the gate is tainted by mixed use, if the gate is remotely located so that the union's right to publicize the dispute is substantially and unreasonably impaired, or if the primary employer seeks to use the dual-gate system as a means to evade the union's picketing. A union may have an observer present at the neutral gate to ensure that the gate is properly maintained if the observer is identified as such and there is no evidence that the observer is stationed at the gate as a signal (a secondary object) for neutral employees to leave the job site. *Electrical Workers Local 501 v. NLRB,* 756 F.2d 888, 118 LRRM 3103 (D.C. Cir. 1985) (remotely located gate); *NLRB v. Carpenters Local 1622,* 786 F.2d 903, 121 LRRM 3539 (9th Cir. 1986); *Carpenters Local 316,* 283 NLRB No. 16, 124 LRRM 1323 (1987); *Operating Engineers Local 12,* 286 NLRB No. 114, 127 LRRM 1122 (1987); *Carpenters Local 33,* 289 NLRB No. 67, 129 LRRM 1035 (1988); enforced, 873 F.2d 316, 131 LRRM 2065 (D.C. Cir. 1989) (remote gate); *Iron Workers Local 433,* 294 NLRB No. 17, 131 LRRM 1305 (1989) and 293 NLRB No. 74, 131 LRRM 1001 (1989); *Mautz & Oren Inc. v. Teamsters Local* 279, 882 F.2d 1117, 131 LRRM 3244 (7th Cir. 1989) (use of primary gate by neutral employer does not taint reserve gate system.)

4. Primary picketing at a secondary location is lawful if (a) the primary employer is engaged in its normal business at the situs; (b) the picket signs identify the primary employer; (c) the picket is as reasonably close to the situs as possible; and (d) the primary employer is "present" when the picketing is occurring. *Sailor's Union of the Pacific (Moore Dry Dock),* 92 NLRB No. 93, 27 LRRM 1108 (1950); *Linbeck Construction Corp. v. NLRB,* 550 F.2d. 311, 94 LRRM 3230 (5th Cir. 1977); *Wire Service Guild Local 221,* 218 NLRB No. 186, 89 LRRM 1397 (1975); *Teamsters Local 83,* 231 NLRB No. 181, 96 LRRM 1165 (1977) (picketing "between headlights" of truck on job site), enforcement denied, *Allied Concrete, Inc. v. NLRB,* 607 F.2d 827 102 LRRM 2508 (9th Cir. 1979). *Local 453 IBEW (Southern Sun Electric Corp.),* 237 NLRB No. 104, 99 LRRM 1076 (1978), enforced, 620 F.2d 170, 104 LRRM 2081 (8th Cir. 1980); *J.F. Hoff Electric Co. v. NLRB,* 642 F.2d 1266, 105 LRRM 2345 (D.C. Cir. 1980). See also *Laborers Local 1253,* 248 NLRB 244, 103 LRRM 1526 (1980) (picketing by construction union at hospital). See also, cases cited, Legal Principle 3.

5. A striking industrial plant union may not picket a gate reserved for outside contractor's employees if (a) there is a separate gate identified as such; (b) the work of the outside employer is unrelated to normal operations; and (c) the work being done by outside contractors is not work that could be done only during a strike or plant shutdown. *Electrical Workers Local 761 v. NLRB (General Electric),* 366 U.S. 667, 48 LRRM 2210 (1961); *NLRB v. Electrical Workers, Local 369,* 528 F.2d 317, 91 LRRM 3006 (6th Cir. 1976).

6. Secondary employers who are allied with the primary employer because they are performing farmed-out struck work, because of common ownership and control, or because of integration of operations are not neutrals. They can be picketed the same as the struck employer. *Graphic Arts Union, Local 277,* 225 NLRB No. 186, 93 LRRM 1113 (1976); *Los*

Angeles Newspaper Guild (Hearst Corp.), 185 NLRB 303, 75 LRRM 1014 (1970), enforced 443 F.2d 1173, 77 LRRM 2895 (9th Cir. 1971); *Television and Radio Artists*, 185 NLRB 593, 75 LRRM 1018 (1970), enforced 462 F.2d 887, 80 LRRM 2001 (D.C. Cir. 1972); *Teamsters, Local 743*, 231 NLRB No. 156, 97 LRRM 1169 (1977); *Teamsters, Local 560*, 248 NLRB No. 156, 104 LRRM 1003 (1980) (union on strike against branch warehouse in New Jersey did not violate Section 8(b)(4) by picketing employer's other branch warehouse in Missouri as branches are essentially part of a single enterprise).

7. Two employers do not become allies if they maintain a normal business relationship during a strike. See cases cited in legal principle 6.

8.A. Peaceful consumer publicity, such as handbilling urging a secondary consumer boycott, is not prohibited by Section 8(b)(4) as long as it does not involve picketing. Thus, for example, a union can handbill at a secondary situs to persuade customers not to deal with an employer who has used or is continuing to use, distribute, sell, or handle, etc., a struck product or service; whose facility was built by a non-union contractor; or who has a business relationship with a struck employer. *DeBartolo Corp. v. NLRB*, 485 U.S. 568, 128 LRRM 2001 (1988); *Boxhorn's Gun Club v. Local 494*, 798 F.2d 1016, 123 LRRM 2139, rehearing denied 123 LRRM 2856 (7th Cir. 1986). Compare *Food and Commercial Workers Local P–9*, 281 NLRB No. 135, 123 LRRM 1225 (1986) (pre-*DeBartolo* decision holding that union could not engage in consumer boycott against bank doing business with struck employer). See also *Storer Communications v. NABET*, 854 F.2d 144, 129 LRRM 2129 (6th Cir. 1988).

8.B. A union can picket a struck product at a secondary location unless the product is the "sole product" distributed by the secondary employer or the product is "merged" into the secondary employer's business, so that a consumer must in effect boycott the secondary employer in order to cease using the product or service. *NLRB v. Fruit and Vegetable Packers, Local 760 (Tree Fruits)*, 377 U.S. 58, 55 LRRM 2961 (1964); *NLRB v. Servette, Inc.*, 377 U.S. 46, 55 LRRM 2957 (1964); *American Bread Co. v. NLRB*, 411 F.2d 147, 71 LRRM 2243 (6th Cir. 1969); *K & K Const. Co. v. NLRB*, 592 F.2d 1228, 100 LRRM 2416 (3d Cir. 1979), denying enforcement to 233 NLRB No. 99, 96 LRRM 1575 (1977); *NLRB v. Retail Clerks, Local 1001*, 447 U.S. 607, 104 LRRM 2567 (1980) (upholding sole-product picketing doctrine).

9.A. Section 8(b)(7)(C) limits only the right to picket for initial recognition, and even picketing for recognition may continue indefinitely if the picketing is addressed solely to the public unless it has the effect of inducing any individual employed by any other person not to pick up, deliver, or transport any goods or not perform any services. *Teamsters Local 544*, 274 NLRB No. 34, 119 LRRM 1052 (1985); *IATSE Local 15*, 275 NLRB No. 105, 119 LRRM 1193 (1985); *Laborers Local 133*, 283 NLRB No. 138, 125 LRRM 1066 (1987); *UFCW Local 23*, 288 NLRB No. 103,

128 LRRM 1119 (1988); *Newspaper & Mail Deliverers,* 289 NLRB No. 68, 128 LRRM 1309 (1988).

9.B. Section 8(b)(7) does not apply to substandard wages picketing that attempts to induce an employer to observe area wage standards. Such picketing may have the object of stopping deliveries to the picketed employer since it is primary picketing. *Claude Everett Construction Co.,* 136 NLRB 321, 49 LRRM 1757 (1962); *Local 399, Carpenters (K & K Construction Co.),* in legal principle 9.A. See also, as to picketing to obtain or enforce a pre-hire agreement, *John Deklewa & Sons, Inc.,* 282 NLRB No. 184, 124 LRRM 1185 (1987); as clarified by *Laborers Local 1184,* 296 NLRB No. 165, 132 LRRM 1273 (1989) (construction union may picket to obtain pre-hire agreement for a reasonable period of time [usually the full thirty day period permitted by the statute] without violating Section 8(b)(7)(C) unless the employer does not currently employ any employees in the bargaining unit sought). See also *NLRB v. Iron Workers, Local 103,* 434 U.S. 335, 97 LRRM 2333 (1978); *Donald Schriver, Inc. v. NLRB,* 635 F.2d 859, 105 LRRM 2818 (D.C. Cir. 1980) (pre-*Deklewa* decisions regarding picketing for or to enforce a pre-hire agreement); *Operating Engineers Local 181* 292 NLRB No. 47, 130 LRRM 1153 (1989); *Operating Engineers Local 18,* 291 NLRB No. 127, 131 LRRM 1223 (1989).

10. A striking union can appeal to a store manager's discretion not to stock a struck product, but cannot appeal to the manager to cease work in support of the strike. *NLRB v. Servette, Inc.* in legal principle 8.B.

11. Unions may lawfully picket or handbill on private property such as within a shopping center if, on balance, the purpose of the union's activity and the lack of reasonable alternate means to publicize the dispute outweigh the private property interests of the employer or property owner. *Hudgens v. NLRB,* 424 U.S. 507, 91 LRRM 2489 (1976); *Fairmont Hotel,* 282 NLRB No. 27, 123 LRRM 1257 (1986); *Jean Country,* 291 NLRB No. 4, 129 LRRM 1201 (1988), overruling *Fairmont Hotel; 40–41 Realty Associates,* 288 NLRB No. 23, 128 LRRM 1001 (1988); *D'Alessandro's Inc.,* 292 NLRB No. 27, 130 LRRM 1089 (1988); *Mountain Country Food Store Inc.,* 292 NLRB No. 100, 130 LRRM 1329 (1989); *Target Stores,* 292 NLRB No. 93, 130 LRRM 1331 (1989); *Hardees Food Systems Inc.,* 294 NLRB No. 48, 131 LRRM 1345 (1989); *Giant Food Stores,* 295 NLRB No. 38, 131 LRRM 1617 (1989); *Little & Co.,* 296 NLRB No. 89, 132 LRRM 1173 (1989) (picketing in office building corridor); *Red Food Stores, Inc.,* 294 NLRB No. 49, 131 LRRM 1362 (1989) (store properly barred handbilling on its property protesting that store had been built by non-union contractor paying substandard wages and benefits).

12. A state or municipality may pass a general statute or ordinance barring picketing against a specific residence but may not ban all picketing in a residential neighborhood. *Frisby v. Schultz,* ＿＿ U.S. ＿＿, 108 S.Ct. 2495 (1988). However, a state court may prohibit picketing or handbilling within the private property of a shopping center only if the Board rules

that the union does not have a protected right under the LMRA to engage in such conduct on the private property, and this same principle may also apply to prohibit a state from applying a general law prohibiting residential picketing to a labor dispute until the NLRB first rules on whether the picketing is protected under the Act. *Sears, Roebuck & Co. v. San Diego Council of Carpenters,* 436 U.S. 180, 98 LRRM 2282 (1978); *Carpenters Local 1098,* 280 NLRB No. 102, 123 LRRM 1002 (1986). See *Howard Gault Co. v. Texas Rural Legal Aid,* 848 F.2d 544, 128 LRRM 2890 (5th Cir. 1988) (limiting power of state to regulate mass picketing).

13. A union having an economic dispute with a health care industry employer must give ten-days written notice of its intent to strike or picket the employer. The union may unilaterally extend the strike deadline for a reasonable period, usually not to exceed seventy-two hours, without giving a new ten-day notice, provided that it gives reasonable notice, usually at least twelve hours, of the actual strike deadline. The ten-day notice requirement does not apply if a union strikes or pickets in protest over a serious unfair labor practice committed by the employer. *Orange Belt District Council of Painters, No. 48,* 243 NLRB 609, 101 LRRM 1457 (1979); *District 1199-E, National Union of Hospital and Health Care Employees,* 243 NLRB 23, 101 LRRM 1346 (1979); *Bio-medical Applications of New Orleans,* 240 NLRB 432, 100 LRRM 1300 (1979).

Recommended Reading

Avery, "Federal Labor Rights and Access to Private Property: The NLRB and the Right to Exclude," 11 *Industrial Relations Law Journal* 145 (1989).

Brinker, Taylor, "Secondary Boycott Maze," 25 *Lab. L.J.* 418 (1974).

Brod, "Through the Window of Legislative History: A View on an Employee's Right to Honor a Stranger Picket Line," 35 *U. Kans. L. Rev.* 9 (1986).

"Determination of Secondary Boycott Violations in Common Situs Picketing during Area Standards Disputes," 59 *Temple L.Q.* 1071 (1986).

Golazeski, "Secondary Boycotts—*Pet, Incorporated,*" 22 *B.C. Law Rev.* 73 (1980).

Modjeska, "Recognition Picketing under the National Labor Relations Act," 35 *U.Fla. L. Rev.* 633 (1983).

Orkin and Tirone, "Consumer Secondary Picketing, *Safeco* and the Limits of Economic Jurisprudence," 40 *Lab. L.J.* 21 (1989).

Pleasure, "Construction Industry Labor Law: *Deklewa, DeBartolo,* and *Boxhorn,*" 10 *Ind. Rel. L.J.* 40 (1988).

chapter 8

UNION REGULATION OF WORK AND THE ANTITRUST LAWS (HOT CARGO AGREEMENTS, JURISDICTIONAL DISPUTES, AND FEATHERBEDDING)

Unions have many legitimate reasons for attempting to regulate work. The historical claim of a fair day's pay for a fair day's work symbolizes labor's claim to negotiate limits on job content and effort. Union efforts to regulate job content and protect work jurisdiction raise issues as to hot cargo clauses, restrictions on subcontracting, jurisdictional disputes, and featherbedding.

Work restrictions affect competition and trade between employers. If a union negotiates a clause with its employer limiting the companies to whom the employer may subcontract work, some companies may be denied business they might otherwise have received. Thus, union efforts to restrict work raise questions about the application of the antitrust laws that are designed to encourage free competition and prohibit restraint on trade.

PART I. HOT CARGO CLAUSES

A. THE PURPOSE AND GENERAL COVERAGE OF SECTION 8(e)

Section 8(e), commonly called the "hot cargo" provision, prohibits agreements between employers and unions "whereby such employer ceases or refrains or agrees to cease or refrain from handling, using, selling, transporting or otherwise dealing in any of the products of any other employer, or to cease doing business with any other person." The section provides that such agreements are void and unenforceable. Section 8(e) was enacted in 1959 as part of the Landrum-Griffin Amendments to the Labor Management Relations Act. Prior to Section 8(e), it was common for employers

and unions to enter into agreements under which employees, such as truck drivers, would not have to pick up or handle goods of any employer whose employees were on strike. The struck work was considered "hot cargo." These hot cargo clauses were, in effect, agreements in which the contracting employer agreed to cease doing business with another employer. Section 8(e) now broadly prohibits such agreements.

Prior to the 1959 amendments, the original Taft–Hartley version of Section 8(b)(4)(A) prohibited a union from coercing an employer into entering into agreements under which the employer agreed to cease dealing with any other person. However, the Act did not prohibit an employer from voluntarily agreeing to cease dealing with another employer who was struck. The

Board held that a union could not coerce an employer into keeping such an agreement, but that the Act did not prohibit an employer's voluntary compliance. Section 8(e) closed this gap by prohibiting even voluntary agreements or voluntary compliance.

Section 8(e) follows the general policy of Section 8(b)(4), limiting a labor dispute to the primary employer and the striking union. Hot cargo clauses were a lawful means of secondary activity that Section 8(e) now prohibits.

Section 8(e) contains a limited exception for the construction industry (discussed more fully below). The garment industry is totally excluded from the provision, based on a congressional concern that the garment industry has many small employers and that hot cargo type agreements have a legitimate function of maintaining wage standards in the industry.

Section 8(e) prohibits hot cargo agreements whether they are express or implied. That means that oral agreements, informal understandings, or vague contractual language that could be applied in an unlawful manner are prohibited.

Section 8(b)(4)(A), as amended in 1959, makes it unlawful to coerce or restrain an employer into entering into an agreement prohibited by Section 8(e). But remember that Section 8(e) voids and even prohibits agreements that an employer makes voluntarily. The Board will seek injunctive relief under Section 10(1) for a violation of Section 8(b)(4)(A) (see Chapter Seven). The employer may also sue for damages under Section 303.

B. THE APPLICATION OF SECTION 8(e) TO PICKET LINE, SUBCONTRACTING, AND SUCCESSORSHIP CLAUSES

Section 8(e) had a specific purpose. Unfortunately the language of the section, as is frequently true in labor legislation, goes much beyond the purpose. There are many types of contract clauses in which an employer agrees not to deal with another employer. For example, an employer's agreement not to subcontract bargaining unit work is an agreement to cease doing business with someone else. Does Section 8(e) prohibit any agreement limiting subcontracting? The Board and the courts, by looking at the intent of Section 8(e), determined which type of agreements are lawful and which are not.

1. Picket Line Clauses

What about a contract clause that protects the right of employees to honor a primary picket line established at the plant of another employer? In effect, the contracting employer has agreed to a provision under which it will not deal with another employer who is on strike. Literally, that agreement is prohibited by Section 8(e). But did Congress, in enacting Section 8(e), intend to prohibit this traditional form of employee mutual assistance? The Board, in determining the legality of picket line clauses, has followed the primary-secondary object distinction (see Chapter Seven). The Board has reasoned that Section 8(e) is intended to prohibit secondary activity. An employee's right to honor another union's primary picket line is a traditional primary right. Thus, the Board has held that a picket line clause that permits employees to honor a primary picket line established at another location is lawful under Section 8(e). However, a clause that permits a union to honor a secondary picket line is unlawful.

What if a contract gave construction union employees the right to walk off a construction job situs whenever pickets appeared? That clause would be unlawful because it might sanction secondary activity such as walking off a job although picketing did not meet the *Moore Dry Dock* standards (see Chapter Seven). A picket line clause permitting employees to honor *any* picket line would be prohibited under Section 8(e) because it might permit employees to honor a secondary picket line. To be lawful, the picket line clause, through appropriate wording, must be expressly limited to primary picketing.

As discussed in Chapter Seven, it is common for construction contractors to establish a dual-gate system when there is picketing at a job site, one gate reserved for the employees of the target primary employer and the other exclusively for employees of neutral employers on the job. A union representing neutral employees would engage in an unlawful secondary boycott under Section 8(b)(4)(B) if it encouraged its members not to work because of the picket line established at the reserve gate. Recently, based on this principle, the Board has held that a contractual picket line clause violates Section 8(e) if it prohibits an employer who is a neutral in a dispute from disciplining its employees who refuse to work at a construction site because of picketing at the primary employer's gate when there is a neutral gate they can use to report to work. The Board reasoned that since it is unlawful secondary activity for a union to encourage neutral employees to support a picket line directed at another employer, it is equally unlawful to accomplish the same secondary result indirectly through a picket line clause that in effect encourages such conduct by prohibiting discipline against employees who honor such a line. This decision applies only when there is a properly established and maintained dual-gate system, but it still partially undercuts what previously appeared to be the well-established right of an employee as a matter of individual choice to refuse to work at a job site where a lawful primary picket line had been established (dual gates or not) even though the union could not encourage the neutral employees as a group to honor the line. It is possible that the courts of appeals or the Supreme Court may not uphold the Board's narrow interpretation of Section 8(e) on this point.

2. Struck Goods Clauses

A struck goods clause protects the right of employees not to handle goods produced

by a struck employer. However, Section 8(e) imposes limits on these clauses similar to those on a picket line clause. Thus, as in the case of a picket line clause, a clause permitting employees to refuse to handle struck goods must be expressly limited to goods produced by an employer struck in a primary dispute so that it does not sanction secondary activity.

There is one additional limitation on a struck goods clause. Two employers have the right to continue their normal business relations during a strike (see Chapter Seven). The Board, applying this policy, has held that a struck goods clause cannot permit an employee to refuse to handle work produced by a struck employer that the employee handled before the strike began as that clause might in effect sanction a secondary boycott in violation of Section 8(e). A struck goods clause can only protect an employee's right to refuse to handle or work on goods that employees engaged in a primary labor dispute would have produced but for the strike, that is, if doing the work would make the two employers allies rather than simply maintain their normal business relationship.

3. Subcontracting clauses

a. Work Preservation Clauses. Any restrictions on subcontracting bargaining unit work are literally an agreement with the contracting employer to cease or refrain from dealing with another employer in violation of Section 8(e). The courts and the Board recognize that Congress did not intend to prohibit all restrictions on subcontracting, but the scope of permissible clauses was not established until the Supreme Court's decision in *National Woodwork*.[1]

In *National Woodwork*, the Carpenters Union collective bargaining agreement prohibited the use of prehung doors. The contract required that all hanging be done

---

[1] See legal principle 1.

on the job site. The purpose of the clause was to preserve this work for the job site carpenters rather than using prefabricated materials produced elsewhere. The company, despite its contractual agreement, decided to use prehung doors and the union refused to install them. The issue was whether the clause prohibiting the use of prehung doors violated Section 8(e). If the clause violated Section 8(e), then the union's refusal to hang the prehung doors in order to force the employer to live up to its agreement violated Section 8(b)(4)(A), which prohibits coercion to enforce an agreement prohibited by Section 8(e).

In *National Woodwork*, the Court relied on the primary-secondary distinction under Section 8(b)(4). The Court stated that Section 8(e) was intended to prohibit agreements having the object of controlling labor relations of another employer. That would be a secondary object. But the Court stated that Section 8(e) does not prohibit clauses that have the primary object of regulating the labor relations between the contracting employer and the union. The purpose of the carpenters' prehung door clause was to preserve bargaining unit work. The Court stated that preserving bargaining unit work was a primary object; therefore, the clause was not prohibited by Section 8(e). Also it was not unlawful under Section 8(b)(4)(A) for the union to refuse to do work that violated its contract. The prehung door clause could possibly cause the prehung door manufacturer to lose business, but that would not make the clause unlawful because the manufacturer's lost business would simply be the secondary effect (not object) of a valid primary restriction.

b. Union Standards and Union Signatory Clauses. Under *National Woodwork*, subcontracting clauses that have the sole object of preserving bargaining unit work do not violate Section 8(e), but subcontracting clauses that go beyond a primary object are void. What if a contract clause prohibited all subcontracting of bargaining unit work?

That would be a valid primary work preservation clause permitted under Section 8(e).

What if the clause permitted subcontracting only to an employer who maintains wages, hours, and fringe benefits equivalent to the economic provisions in the union's contract, referred to as a union standards clause? Union standards clauses are also a lawful work preservation method. They take the economic incentive out of subcontracting by requiring the subcontractor to pay wages and benefits equivalent to those required under the union's contract. Of course, a potential subcontractor might be affected by a union standards clause. A subcontractor might have to increase employees' wages to be eligible for a subcontract. However, that result is considered to be a secondary effect of the union's primary object of preserving unit work.

What if a contract permits subcontracting only to employers whose own employees are represented by a union, a so-called union-signatory clause? Such clauses are unlawful under Section 8(e) except for work done on a construction project (discussed below). The union-signatory clause goes beyond the valid object of preserving unit work. By limiting subcontracts only to union contractors, the clause has a secondary object of influencing the labor relations of the secondary employer. That is the type of secondary object Section 8(e) is intended to prohibit.

c. Requiring Payment of Identical Benefits. Union standards clauses requiring that a subcontractor pay the cash equivalent of union wages and benefits are lawful, but the Board has held that a union cannot require that subcontracts be limited to employers who maintain exactly the same wages, hours, or working conditions. A union cannot dictate the manner in which a subcontractor cuts up the economic pie for its own employees. A clause requiring the subcontractor to provide the same benefits goes beyond the primary object of taking away the employer's economic incentive for subcontracting. It also has the secondary object of dictating the terms of the secondary employer's relationship with its own employees. That violates Section 8(e).

The Supreme Court has held that a union may have a subcontracting clause in its contract providing that, if work is subcontracted, contributions must be paid into the union's pension and health and welfare funds for the employees doing the work as if the work had been done by the bargaining unit employees. Employers argued that the clause violates Section 8(e) because the subcontractor's employees who do the work are not members of the union, are not covered by the pension and health and welfare plans, and will never get any benefits from the contributions. But the Supreme Court upheld the clause as a legitimate work preservation provision designed to take away the economic incentive of subcontracting.

d. Work Expansion Clauses. *National Woodwork* covered a situation in which a union was attempting to preserve bargaining unit work it was performing. What if a union finds that its traditional work is declining due to technological change? As a matter of preservation, the union negotiates an agreement under which the bargaining unit employees perform work that has previously been subcontracted and that the unit employees have not done before. The Board has held that an agreement expanding the unit's work by prohibiting the subcontracting of work the unit has not previously performed violates Section 8(e). The Board reasons that such a clause is not limited to the primary object of preserving work, but also has the secondary object (not just secondary effect) of removing work from another employer. As an exception, unions have the right to reclaim work they are not currently doing, but used to perform. For example, if bargaining unit employees used to do certain maintenance work that is currently subcontracted, the union could lawfully seek a contract clause requiring the

company to once again use bargaining unit employees for the work.

The Supreme Court, in two cases pertaining to contractual provisions negotiated by the International Longshoremen's Association,[2] has stressed the very broad authority that unions have to negotiate work preservation clauses. In these cases, the union negotiated clauses limiting the employers' right to bypass longshoremen's functions by using containerized cargo directly loaded onto or taken off a ship. The contract required that certain of the containers be unloaded and reloaded on the dock by longshoremen. In about 20 percent of the cases, longshoremen loaded and/or unloaded containers even though the same work had already been done by other employees outside the bargaining unit. The Board held that the containerization rules were invalid in part for two reasons: (1) because of their adverse effect on certain trucking companies and warehouses that handled the containerized cargo and, (2) because the bargaining unit work of loading and unloading ship cargo in the traditional manner had been eliminated, so that the union was in essence seeking to acquire new work rather than to preserve existing work. The Supreme Court reversed the Board on both these grounds. First, the Court emphasized that the impact on other employers, no matter how severe, does not matter as long as the agreement is bargained for in the face of a genuine job threat and to preserve rather than enlarge the unit's work. Second, the Court concluded that a work preservation agreement is lawful even though it seeks to preserve work that has been eliminated in the sense that the work is not necessary due to technological innovation.

In upholding the clauses, the Court emphasized that the purpose of the containerized cargo restrictions were solely primary, to preserve bargaining unit work, not tactically calculated to achieve union objec-

[2] See legal principle 1.

tives with another employer that would be unlawful under Section 8(e). The Court stated that when the objective of an agreement is clearly work preservation, it is lawful in the absence of some other evidence of a secondary purpose. The Court also emphasized that one of the basic premises of the LMRA is that the collective bargaining process will result in a better resolution of issues pertaining to technological change than Board or court decisions, and the fact that an agreement is not the most rational or efficient response to the problem does not matter as long as the agreement has solely the primary object of preserving work for the bargaining unit. Remember, that a bargaining unit has lost work does not permit the union to negotiate a contractual provision requiring that bargaining unit employees do certain work performed by another employer that the bargaining unit employees have never done before. Such a provision would be a work expansion or acquisition clause which, as discussed above, is prohibited by Section 8(e). This restriction did not apply to the Longshoremen agreements because the work to be performed was related to work that the bargaining unit employees had traditionally performed. To be lawful under Section 8(e), a work preservation clause must be limited to work related to or functionally equivalent to the bargaining unit's traditional work.

The Section 8(e) limitations on protecting bargaining unit work apply only to subcontracting restrictions affecting other employers. Section 8(e) does not regulate clauses on the division of work among the primary employer's employees. Thus, a union can have a clause prohibiting the performance of bargaining unit work by supervisors or the employer's nonunit employees. The union can seek a clause transferring new work from other employees to the bargaining unit. These clauses are outside the scope of Section 8(e) because they only regulate the primary employer's operations and have no secondary object.

e. The Right-of-Control Test. The principal limitation on work preservation clauses is the so-called right-of-control test. What if a union's contract prohibits use of a certain process, but the contracting employer does not control the work assignment on a project? What if, in *National Woodwork*, for example, the carpenters' contractor had been told by the project developer to use prehung doors and had no choice of material? Could the carpenters, relying on their contract, refuse to hang prehung doors even though their employer had no control over the work? The Board has held that a union cannot refuse to perform work if their employer has no control over the assignment, even though the process used violates the union's collective bargaining agreement. The Board reasons that if the contracting employer has no control over the material or process used, the union's actual dispute is with the party, such as the project developer, who does have control. If the union refuses to do the work for its own employer, the contracting employer at that point becomes the innocent secondary employer in the union's dispute with the employer who has control. The union's refusal to work is coercion of its own employer to pressure the employer who has control. Thus, the Board has concluded that the refusal to do work if the contracting union's employer has no control over the assignment is unlawful secondary activity under Section 8(b)(4)(B). The Board has rejected the union argument that a contracting employer is not an innocent secondary employer if it enters into a contract requiring it to do work or use a process that would violate its own collective bargaining agreement.

The Supreme Court, in *Pipefitters Local 638*, upheld the Board's right-of-control test.[3] In that case, the union's collective bargaining agreement required that certain internal piping work on climate control equipment be done on the job site. This restriction is a valid work preservation clause. The prime contractor required the use of prefabricated material in violation of the union's contract. The pipefitters' sub-

---

[3] See legal principle 3.

contractor agreed to the building contract even though the contract violated the pipe-fitters' collective bargaining agreement. The employees refused to install the prefabricated pipe, just as the carpenters had refused to install the prehung doors in *National Woodwork*. However, the Supreme Court upheld the Board's position applying the right-to-control test. The Supreme Court agreed with the Board that the union's refusal to install the pipe was unlawful secondary activity in violation of Section 8(b)(4)(B) because the union's dispute was with the general contractor who had required the use of prefabricated materials. The union's refusal to install the prefabricated material, even though its use violated the collective bargaining agreement, constituted secondary pressure on the union's own employer directed at the general contractor. Thus, since the pipefitter's employer did not have the right to control the work, the union was prohibited from enforcing the contractual restriction by refusing to do the work.

1. EMPLOYER OPTION TO ABIDE BY THE SUB-CONTRACTING RESTRICTIONS. Although the Board's right-of-control test has been upheld, the Board has indicated that the test will not be applied mechanically. The Supreme Court quoted approvingly from the Board's decision in *George Koch Sons, Inc.*[4] In that case the Board Stated:

The Board has always proceeded with an analysis of (1) whether under all the surrounding circumstances the union's objective was work preservation and then (2) whether the pressures exerted were directed at the right person, i.e., at the primary in the dispute. . . . In following this approach, however, our analysis has not nor will ever be a mechanical one, and, in addition to determining under all the surrounding circumstances whether the union's objective is truly work preservation, we have studied and shall continue to study not only the situation the pressured employer finds himself in but also how

[4] See legal principle 3.

he came to be in that situation. *And if we find the employer is not truly an "unoffending employer" who merits the Act's protections, we shall find no violation in a union's pressures such as occurred here, even though a purely mechanical or surface look at the case might present an appearance of a parallel situation.* [Emphasis added.]

When the Board says it will determine whether the employer is truly unoffending this means that the Board will determine whether the employer did or did not truly have an option of living up to its collective bargaining agreement. What if the subcontractor tells the prime contractor that it has a clause in its collective bargaining agreement prohibiting prefabricated goods and the subcontractor suggests that the prime contractor specify the use of prefabricated goods in order to get around the collective bargaining restrictions? The subcontractor is not truly unoffending. Rather, the primary and subcontractor have engaged in collusion to avoid the subcontractor's collective bargaining agreement. If collusion is proven, the union can lawfully refuse to do the work. But if there is a good-faith arm's-length business transaction in which the primary contractor insists that the subcontractor use materials violating the subcontractor's collective bargaining agreement, the right-of-control test will undoubtedly apply. The union cannot lawfully refuse to do the work.

It is clear that a subcontractor does not have to give up a job because the specifications require that the subcontractor violate its own collective bargaining agreement. Given a choice between living up to its collective bargaining agreement or doing the work as a prime contractor requires, the subcontractor can accept the job and the employees will be required to do the work.

The right-of-control test also applies to the negotiation of work preservation provisions. Thus the Supreme Court emphasized in the *Longshoremen* cases that to be lawful a work preservation clause must not have only the sole object of preserving work traditionally performed by employees, but must also be directed at work assignments that the contracting employer has the power to control. The Court found that the employers who entered into the container agreements with the Longshoremen's Union had such power.

2. LAWFUL MEANS OF ENFORCING THE RESTRICTIONS. Although a union cannot refuse to do the work over which its employer has no control as long as its employer is unoffending, the union may be able to file a grievance or sue to enforce lawful subcontracting restrictions. The union might be able to prove that fewer employees were used on a project because of the contract violation and win backpay for the employees who would have been employed. Refusing to do the work is a form of coercion that violates Section 8(b)(4)(B), but the Board has held that filing a grievance to enforce a contract right is not coercive unless, as a narrow exception, the union does not have a colorable contract claim for the work, that is, the grievance is obviously without merit. In that event, the grievance is regarded as secondary pressure (coercion) on the employer that does not have control to force the employer having control to reassign the work.

Of course, an arbitrator cannot order an employer to abide by an agreement that would violate Section 8(e). Remember, Section 8(e) prohibits all hot cargo agreements whether entered into voluntarily or through coercion. An arbitrator's decision is not coercion, but an employer's actions in abiding by an arbitrator's decision enforcing an unlawful clause in itself violates Section 8(e).

4. Successorship Clauses

Under the Supreme Court's *Burns Detective* decision (see Chapter Five), a successor employer who purchases a business is not obligated to accept the predecessor employer's collective bargaining agreement. The successor's only obligation is to bargain with the incumbent union if it represents a majority of the new workforce. Can a union

negotiate a contract clause in which the employer agrees to sell or transfer its business only to a company that agrees to assume the collective bargaining agreement as a condition of the transaction? Would such a clause require one employer to cease doing business with another employer in violation of section 8(e)? The Board has upheld such clauses as having a legitimate work preservation object. The clause can be enforced by picketing or by an injunction against selling the business in violation of the assumption agreement. If the predecessor employer fails to include the required assumption clause in the sales agreement, the union might also be able to sue or file a grievance against the predecessor employer for damages the employees have suffered, such as lost jobs or reduced wages resulting from the successor employer's failure to accept the existing collective bargaining agreement.

In contrast to successorship clauses applying to the sale or transfer of a business, the Board has held that a clause that limited leasing arrangements only to lessees who agree to assume the union's existing contract with the lessor (e.g., a hotel restaurant leased to an outside operator) is unlawful under Section 8(e). The Board regards such a restriction as tantamount to an unlawful union signatory subcontracting clause. The Board distinguishes a lease from the sale of a business because a lease is not a permanent transfer in which one business entity is substituted for another. Thus, it is possible that the Board may uphold some contractual restrictions on lease arrangements if the lease is long term and the lessor places so few restrictions on the property's use by the lessee that there is, in fact, a "permanent" transfer from one employer to another.

5. The Construction Industry Exception to Section 8(e)

Section 8(e) contains a proviso that:

[N]othing in this subsection (e) shall apply to an agreement between a labor organization and an employer in the construction industry relating to the contracting or subcontracting of work to be done at the site of the construction, alteration, painting, or repair of a building, structure, or other work.

As discussed above, subcontracting clauses generally cannot limit subcontracting to union employers. Such a clause goes beyond preserving unit work and is an attempt to dictate the labor relations policies of another employer. However, the proviso to Section 8(e), as an exception, permits a construction union to negotiate a clause with an employer in the construction industry limiting contracts and subcontracts for work to be done at a construction site to union contractors or to contractors having collective bargaining agreements for job site work with certain unions, such as to AFL-CIO construction unions only. Congress agreed to this exception for the construction industry because the traditional pattern on construction projects is for all contractors to be union. Congress concluded that retention of this practice was necessary to preserve harmony on the job site. Clauses permitted by the construction industry exception may be included in a pre-hire agreement under Section 8(f) of the Act and are a mandatory subject of bargaining (see Chapter Five).

Section 8(e) permits only job-site subcontracting agreements with an employer "in the construction industry," but the Board has held that if an employer is engaged in construction work on a specific job site, it is in the construction industry even though it is not generally or usually involved in the industry. Furthermore, if a property owner acts as its own general contractor for construction work on its premises, then the owner may be regarded as an employer in the construction industry for that work so that a union may lawfully enter into an agreement with the owner limiting work to be done at the construction site to union contractors.

a. Scope of the Exemption.

1. APPLICABILITY TO JOB SITE WORK ONLY. The construction industry proviso applies only to work done on the job site. The *National Woodwork* case pertained to a contract clause prohibiting prefabricated doors, but that clause was not covered by the construction industry proviso because the prefabrication was done off the construction site. On work done off the situs, construction unions are subject to the same restrictions as other unions. Thus, construction unions, as in *National Woodwork*, can have a clause limiting or prohibiting off situs subcontracting as a means of preserving bargaining unit work, but they cannot have a clause limiting off situs subcontracting to union employers. The Board has held that the delivery of materials to a construction site is not "on site" work so that a subcontracting clause limiting the delivery of materials to a job site to union contractors is therefore not permitted by the construction industry proviso to Section 8(e).

A construction union cannot limit use of prefabricated materials to those made by union subcontractors because that would violate Section 8(e). But, a construction union can have a clause requiring that prefabricated materials be installed by a union contractor on the construction situs. That restriction would apply to work done on the construction situs and thus would be within the construction industry exception. An industrial union cannot have a clause requiring that any subcontracted maintenance work in the plant be done by union contractors. That restriction would violate Section 8(e) and there is no exception for industrial unions.

2. THE CONNELL CONSTRUCTION LIMITATION ON THE CONSTRUCTION INDUSTRY EXCEPTION. In the *Connell Construction* case, the Supreme Court placed an additional limitation on the Section 8(e) construction industry proviso.[5] In *Connell*, a pipefitters' local picketed a general contractor to require that the general contractor sign an agreement that all work within the union's jurisdiction would be subcontracted to con-

[5] See legal principle 6.

tractors whose employees were represented by the union. The union did not represent any employees directly employed by the general contractor. The general contractor signed the agreement under protest. It then filed suit against the union under the antitrust laws to invalidate the agreement.

The primary issue in *Connell* was whether the union's attempt to force this agreement on the general contractor violated the antitrust laws (see below). However, one of the union's defenses was that the agreement was valid under the construction industry exception to Section 8(e) because it regulated subcontracting on a construction situs. The union argued that the construction industry proviso controlled over any possible antitrust violation.

The Supreme Court held that Section 8(e) did not protect the union's agreement. First, the Court noted that the union did not seek to represent any of the employees hired by the general contractor. Instead, the union attempted to engage in "top-down organizing" by requiring the general contractor to deal only with subcontractors who recognized the union. The Court said Section 8(e) was intended to prevent this type of top-down activity. Second, the Court noted that the proposed clause was intended to apply to all jobs of the general contractor, even those on which no pipefitters were working. Thus, to the extent that the construction industry exception was intended to prevent hostility on the job site between union and nonunion workers, that purpose was not served by the pipefitters' proposal. The Court held that the Section 8(e) construction industry proviso permitted subcontracts limited to union contractors only as part of an overall collective bargaining agreement, which the union was not seeking in *Connell*, and "possibly to common situs relationships on particular job sites. . . ."

3. POST-CONNELL BOARD DECISIONS. In cases since *Connell*, the Board has followed the Court's basic ruling that a union may seek construction industry agreements limiting job situs subcontracts to union con-

tractors only if the union has a collective bargaining relationship with the signatory employer. Some contractor associations have argued that construction industry clauses are lawful only if limited in application to specific job sites at which both union and nonunion employees are employed. However, the Board has held that, in the context of a collective bargaining relationship, Section 8(e) broadly permits such subcontracting clauses on all job sites. The Supreme Court has upheld the Board's interpretation. The Board has also held that a union seeking to represent an employer's employees may propose such a construction industry agreement as part of its initial contract. The union need not be recognized before making the proposal.

The Board has indicated that it might uphold a construction industry agreement even if there is no collective bargaining relationship between the union and the signatory employer, if the clause is limited to jobs on which employees represented by the union will be working. The purpose is then to prevent the disharmony that results when union and nonunion employees work on the same project. The construction industry proviso was intended to preserve this union right. However, in that case, the restrictions must be limited to the specific jobs on which the union's membership is working. The clause cannot apply generally to all projects as a means of top-down organizing. The clause would probably have to prohibit all nonunion subcontractors, not just those doing work within the union's jurisdiction. Otherwise, the clause would not prevent disharmony, but could be used for top-down organizing that the Supreme Court indicated was impermissible in *Connell*.

b. Enforcement of Construction Industry Proviso Clauses.

1. STRIKING TO ENFORCE A CLAUSE. Assume that a construction union obtains a clause limiting subcontracting on the construction situs to union contractors; but the contractor violates the agreement by hiring

a nonunion subcontractor. May the union stop work on the project until the nonunion contractor leaves the job in accordance with the contract?

The key to understanding the rules on enforcing a construction industry proviso clause is to remember that such a clause has a secondary object to require that contractors be union. The clause would be unlawful under Section 8(e), as in all other industries, except for the express proviso.

Section 8(b)(4)(B) prohibits picketing or other coercive acts with the object of requiring one employer to cease doing business with any other person. Although Section 8(e) contains an exception for the construction industry, it has no exception for Section 8(b)(4)(B) violations. From this, the Board and the courts have reasoned that, since a construction industry clause has a secondary object, it cannot be enforced through picketing, refusal to work, or other self-help measures. Self-help to enforce the clause, requiring that a nonunion subcontractor be removed from a project, would be coercion, forcing the contractor to cease dealing with a nonunion subcontractor. Although the clause would not violate Section 8(e), enforcement in this manner would still violate Section 8(b)(4)(B). Thus, a valid construction industry clause can be enforced only through peaceful means such as a court injunction to force compliance or through arbitration. Enforcement through court procedures or through arbitration is not considered coercion provided that, as discussed above, the union has a colorable contract claim to the work.

Under the same principles, a construction industry clause limiting subcontracts to union contractors violates Section 8(e) if the contract permits any form of self-help for enforcement. Thus, the clause cannot permit the union to cancel the entire collective bargaining agreement, including the no-strike clause, if the employer violates the subcontracting clause or fails to follow an arbitrator's decision enforcing the clause. That would permit self-help to enforce the clause. Enforcement of construction indus-

try subcontracting clauses must be strictly through voluntary compliance, the courts, or arbitration.

At one time, the Board held that if a lawful construction industry subcontracting clause permitted self-help for enforcement, the entire clause was void and unenforceable. The Board's current rule, however, is that although an unlawful self-help provision is void under Section 8(e), the basic underlying subcontracting restrictions remain in effect without the self-help clause and may be enforced through peaceful means. Note that the self-help provisions do not have to be part of the subcontracting clause itself in order for Section 8(e) to be violated. Thus, if a contract contains a construction industry clause and an arbitration clause providing that the union may strike if the employer fails to abide by an arbitrator's decision, Section 8(e) would be violated unless the contract specifically exempts the subcontracting clause from the provision permitting a strike.

In contrast to the restrictions on enforcing a construction industry clause, a primary work preservation clause under *National Woodwork* may be enforced through self-help, provided, of course, the collective bargaining agreement does not contain a no-strike clause. This self-help would not violate Section 8(e), because enforcing the valid work preservation clause is a primary object, although there may be a secondary effect on a subcontractor. The garment industry, of course, has a total exemption from Section 8(e).

2. STRIKING TO OBTAIN A CLAUSE. A union can strike for a valid work preservation clause because the clause has a valid primary object. At one time, the Board held that a union could not strike to obtain a construction industry clause, reasoning that a strike to obtain the clause had a secondary object. The courts of appeals, however, disagreed with the Board's interpretation. Eventually, the Board adopted the courts' view that a construction union can strike to *obtain* a valid construction industry clause, but may

not strike to *enforce* the clause because that would violate Section 8(b)(4)(B).

The legal reasoning for the distinction between obtaining a clause and enforcing it rests on the argument that if a construction union uses self-help to enforce a clause to remove a subcontractor from a job, it has a secondary object directed against the specific subcontractor. On the other hand, if a union strikes to obtain a clause, and there is no subcontractor working at the time, the union's acts are directed solely against its own employer to obtain the clause. So the dispute is primary only.

What if a subcontractor is already working on a project at the time a union strikes to obtain a construction industry clause? The Board's position is that a strike to obtain a clause that would require the contracting employer to terminate or change its relationship with an existing subcontractor on a project violates Section 8(b)(4)(B). One object of the strike is to remove the subcontractor or require that the subcontractor become unionized. If there is an existing nonunion contractor, the union can still strike for a construction industry clause if the clause excludes existing subcontractors from the provision.

c. Restrictions on Alter-Ego Operations.
As discussed in Chapter Five, it is increasingly common, particularly in the construction industry, for union employers to establish a second nonunion company, termed a "double-breasted operation," to enable the employer to bid on both union and nonunion work. Construction unions, to deter this practice, have proposed contract language providing that the contract apply to all on-site bargaining unit construction work that the signatory contractor performs through any other company that the contractor manages or controls, or in which the contractor has majority ownership. As discussed in Chapter Five, two companies may have common ownership but still be regarded as separate legal entities so that a collective bargaining agreement covering the unionized company may not necessarily

apply to the other unless it is an "alter-ego." If two companies are commonly owned, but are not a single employer under the alter-ego doctrine, then requiring the union employer to apply its contract to the other separate legal entity as a condition of performing work, as the unions' proposal would do, is arguably tantamount to an unlawful "union signatory" clause under Section 8(e) just as if the companies were totally unrelated. However, as discussed above, construction unions enjoy a partial exemption from Section 8(e) for work performed on the job site. Thus, construction unions have argued that their proposed anti-double-breasting provision is lawful under the construction industry exception even though it is not limited to the alter-ego employer situation because it applies solely to job site work. This issue is currently before the NLRB for resolution. It may take several more years, and perhaps a Supreme Court decision, before the issue is finally resolved.

PART II. WORK ASSIGNMENT DISPUTES

The Board's role in work assignment disputes, sometimes referred to as jurisdictional disputes, arises under Sections 8(b)(4)(D) and 10(k). Section 8(b)(4)(D) makes it an unfair labor practice to engage in a strike or other coercive activities with an object of "forcing or requiring any employer to assign particular work to employees in a particular labor organization or in a particular trade, craft, or class, rather than to employees in another labor organization or in another trade, craft, or class, unless the employer is failing to conform to an order or certification of the Board determining the bargaining representative for employees performing such work." Section 10(k) empowers the Board to resolve a work assignment dispute under certain circumstances.

A. VOLUNTARY AGREEMENTS TO RESOLVE JURISDICTIONAL DISPUTES

Jurisdictional disputes occur in both craft and industrial union settings. One craft union on a project may assert that work belongs to it rather than to another craft. Each of two industrial unions representing competing bargaining units in a plant may each claim that certain work should be assigned to it rather than the other unit. Under Section 10(k), if the Board has reasonable cause to believe that Section 8(b)(4)(D) is being violated, the Board determines the merits of the dispute and assigns the work unless the parties have a voluntary means of adjusting the matter. The Board will not determine the dispute if the parties produce evidence within ten days after a Section 8(b)(4)(D) charge has been filed that they have either resolved the dispute themselves or have agreed upon a method for voluntarily resolving it. A contractual agreement to arbitrate the dispute is an agreed-upon method. Some unions are parties to national or local agreements establishing joint boards or arbitration procedures to resolve jurisdictional disputes. These agreements may constitute an agreed-upon method under Section 8(b)(4)(D). The parties do not actually have to resolve the dispute within ten days, but need agree upon only the method of resolution.

All parties must be bound by a voluntary means of adjustment for the Board to defer to it. For example, if two craft unions are bound to a national agreement to resolve jurisdictional disputes between them, but the employer is not a party to the agreement, there is no agreed-upon method. The Board will proceed under Section 10(k). If an employer has a contract containing an arbitration clause with one competing union, but not with the other, there is no agreed-upon method. Even if the employer has separate contracts with both unions that contain arbitration clauses, the contracts probably do not provide for tripartite arbitration (two unions and the employer taking part in the same arbitration proceedings). The Board has held that separate agreements to arbitrate with each union are not an agreed-upon method of resolving a dispute unless the parties agree to a tripartite procedure in which they are all bound by the result.

If the board has notice of an agreed-upon method of resolving the dispute within ten days, the Board will hold the case until the proceedings are completed. If the parties comply with the award, the Section 8(b)(4)(D) charge will be dismissed.

B. COERCIVE ACTIVITY TO TRIGGER A SECTION 10(k) PROCEEDING

Unions sometimes erroneously believe that the Board can resolve every jurisdictional dispute. The Board has jurisdiction to resolve a dispute under Section 10(k) only if one of the competing unions is charged with violating Section 8(b)(4)(D). That means that one of the competing unions must engage in a strike, the threat of a strike, or other coercive activity to have the work assigned to it. Peaceful persuasion by the union on the employer to assign the work to the union does not violate Section 8(b)(4)(D). Furthermore, filing or threatening to file a grievance over the assignment of disputed work is not regarded as coercion under Section 8(b)(4)(D) and does not trigger a Section 10(k) proceeding if the union has a colorable claim to the work under its contract, even if the employer does not control the assignment. Sometimes a union may continue to process a grievance claiming certain work even though Section 10(k) proceedings are pending. That is not unlawful if the grievance is at least arguably meritorious. However, in the event of a conflict between an NLRB and an arbitrator's decision assigning work, the NLRB determination would control. The union cannot file another grievance claiming the work contrary to the Board's determination.

Sometimes an employer having control of certain work at the time it enters into a collective bargaining agreement subcontracts the work in violation of its agreement. In that case, the union can file a grievance against the employer for its contract violation even though the union representing the employees of the subcontractor also claims the work. The Board may award the work to the subcontractor's employees in a Section 10(k) proceeding based on the criteria it uses for making such a determination (discussed below) even though the union has a meritorious claim to the work under its contract. In that event, the union cannot pursue a grievance seeking the return of the work itself contrary to the Board determination, but an arbitrator can still award monetary damages for the contract breach.

The Board does not have to find an actual violation of Section 8(b)(4)(D) in order to assert jurisdiction under Section 10(k). The Board will proceed if it has reasonable cause to believe that Section 8(b)(4)(D) has been violated. That standard is not difficult to meet. Although a contract may contain a no-strike clause, a union may still tell an employer that it will strike if the employer assigns certain work to another union. Although the union may not intend to carry out the threat, the strike threat is sufficient for the Board to find reasonable cause to believe that Section 8(b)(4)(D) has been violated.

Suppose an employer testifies that a union has threatened to strike to have certain work assigned to it and union witnesses deny the accusation. Can the Board make a Section 10(k) determination when the testimony as to the threat is in direct conflict? Yes, because the Board only has to find reasonable cause to believe that Section 8(b)(4)(D) has been violated in order to proceed under Section 10(k). The Board does not have to make credibility findings in a Section 10(k) hearing. Thus, if the employer testifies about a threat, even though the union denies it, there may still be reasonable cause to believe Section 8(b)(4)(D) has been violated.

C. THE NEED FOR TWO COMPETING EMPLOYEE GROUPS

The Board has held that Section 8(b)(4)(D) applies only if there are at least two competing groups for the disputed work. The section is intended to protect an employer from conflicting pressure, not just pressure from one union, regardless of how strong the pressure may be. Assume that one union represents production employees in a plant and another union represents maintenance employees. The employer assigns certain work to the production employees that the maintenance union regards as its work. The maintenance employees threaten to strike unless the employer reassigns the work to them. Is that threat a possible violation of Section 8(b)(4)(D) to which Section 10(k) will apply? Not necessarily. If the production union does not claim the work, then there are not two competing claims. The dispute is only between the employer and the maintenance union. Thus, Section 8(b)(4)(D) is not violated. If the production union, however, claims the work and if either of the competing unions threatens to strike or engage in other coercive conduct if the work is not assigned to it, Section 8(b)(4)(D) has been violated. The threat may be made by either union, the one doing the work or the one claiming it. A jurisdictional dispute can involve only one union if the employer assigns disputed work to unorganized employees. The Board assumes that these employees want the work and the employer represents their interests. What if one of the unions disclaims or renounces its demand for the disputed work? Usually, in that event, the Board will dismiss the charge and not proceed with a Section 10(k) hearing unless there is evidence that the disclaimer was made as a ruse to avoid an NLRB determination.

Section 10(k) proceedings are intended to resolve work assignment disputes, not issues about which union should represent the employees doing the work. If the Board concludes that, rather than seeking certain work for its bargaining unit, a union is actually attempting to add additional employees to the unit as an organizing method, the Board will not proceed under Section 10(k). The union must follow representation case procedures by petitioning for an election or filing a clarification petition to add the additional employees to the existing unit.

Also, the Board has held that Section 10(k) is not intended to resolve a dispute as to the preservation of bargaining unit work that is essentially between the union and the employer rather than between rival groups, and the employer created the dispute by its unilateral action in assigning the work rather than being willing to assign the work to either group. For example, suppose that an employer contracts out certain work. The union representing the contractor's employees alleges that the subcontract violates contractual restrictions on subcontracting and files a grievance, but the union representing the employees of the subcontractor threatens to strike if the work is reassigned back to the employees of the contracting employer. Technically, Section 8(b)(4)(D) could apply to this dispute, because two unions are competing for the work, and one of the competing unions has threatened to strike. However, the Board may refuse to proceed under Section 10(k) in this case because the basic underlying dispute is between the contracting employer and its union as to the scope of the subcontracting provision and the union acted to preserve bargaining unit work. Also, the employer created the dispute by its own unilateral action in contracting out the work rather than being willing to assign the work to either group of employees to end the dispute. In such cases, the Board emphasizes that the employer is not the "innocent" employer Section 10(k) is intended to protect, and that the employer itself could have

ended the dispute by canceling its subcontract had it chosen to do so.

The Board applies the exception for collective bargaining disputes very narrowly. Thus, to fall within the exception, the sole object of the union asserting a contractual right to certain work must be to preserve that work for the bargaining unit, not gain new or additional work. Also a jurisdictional dispute may exist under Section 10(k) even though, as is frequently the case, the employer favors assigning the work to one group over the other. The critical issue is whether the dispute is essentially between the employer and one union as to the meaning of its collective bargaining agreement or whether there is a genuine dispute between two competing groups with the employer in the middle even though it may favor one group over the other.

D. FACTORS USED IN ASSIGNING DISPUTED WORK

The Supreme Court, in the *CBS* case,[6] held that Section 10(k) requires that the Board make a positive award of disputed work in cases falling under Section 8(b)(4)(D). The Board usually considers certain factors in awarding work: (1) the skills and work involved; (2) certifications by the Board; (3) company and industry practice; (4) agreements between unions and between employers and unions; (5) awards of arbitrators, joint boards, and the AFL-CIO in the same or related cases; (6) the assignment made by the employer; and (7) the efficient operation of the employer's business.

Usually a Board decision awarding work in a Section 10(k) proceeding applies only to the specific work in dispute at the job site where the dispute arose. However, the Board may issue a broad areawide award if the evidence establishes that there is a continuing dispute throughout the area over the work that is likely to recur and the union charged with a Section 8(b)(4)(D) violation

[6] See legal principle 8.A.

in the current case has a "proclivity" (likelihood based upon its past conduct) to engage in unlawful conduct in order to obtain work similar to that in dispute.

E. THE CRITICAL IMPORTANCE OF THE EMPLOYER'S ASSIGNMENT

Although the Board states that it considers all factors, the controlling factor in almost every case is the employer's assignment. In well over 90 percent of all cases, the Board awards disputed work to the union to which the employer had assigned the work. The employer's own estimate of efficient operations is the next most significant factor. The other factors seldom turn out to be controlling. The only time the employer's assignment might not control is if the assignment clearly violates a collective bargaining agreement, but that is rare. Frequently, both unions have a contractual claim to work based upon the jurisdictional clauses of their respective collective bargaining agreements. In that case, neither contract controls. But if one union clearly has a contractual right to the work, which the employer's assignment violates, the Board will probably enforce the contract. Remember, however, that the Board is not bound by the contract. If the other factors considered have greater weight in the particular case the Board can assign the work to another union, despite what appears to be a clear contractual right.

The great weight the Board places on the employer's assignment has important tactical consequences. First, if an employer is about to make an assignment of disputed work, it is important for the union to approach the employer before the assignment is made and convince the employer to assign the work to it. If the employer makes the initial assignment to the other union, the union that did not receive the assignment has little chance of success at the Board. Second, a union that did not receive the assignment, but still claims the work, should do its utmost to avoid Section 10(k) pro-

ceedings. The union should avoid any statements that can be considered a threat in violation of Section 8(b)(4)(D). A union that believes it has a strong contractual claim to work that an employer has assigned to another union has a far better chance in arbitration than before the Board. If there is no threat in violation of Section 8(b)(4)(D), the union can proceed with arbitration and hope to attain a favorable award. If a threat is made, however, the Board will assert jurisdiction under Section 10(k). In that case, the union may consider disclaiming the work currently in dispute in the hope that the employer may assign the work to it in the future rather than participating in a futile Section 10(k) hearing or, as discussed above, the union may decide to proceed with the grievance if it is based on a colorable contract claim even though the Board is also proceeding under Section 10(k). However, the Board's assignment would prevail over any conflicting arbitrator's decision.

The Section 8(b)(4)(D) charge giving rise to a Section 10(k) hearing remains pending during the proceeding. When the Board issues its award assigning the work, the unions must notify the Board whether they will comply with the decision. If so, the Board dismisses the charge. If a union desires to contest the award, it notifies the Board that it will not comply. In that event, the Board will proceed with a hearing on the Section 8(b)(4)(D) complaint as in any other case. The union may then appeal the final Board decision in the unfair labor practice case including its determination in the Section 10(k) proceeding to the appropriate court of appeals. Such appeals are very rare. In a few cases, reviewing courts have held that the Board erred in concluding that Section 8(b)(4)(D) was violated (e.g., that there were not two groups competing for the work or that the dispute was actually over work preservation rather than a jurisdictional dispute between two competing unions). However, unless the appealing union prevails on such a technical point, it is very unlikely that a court of appeals will reverse the Board's determination assigning the work because of the very broad discretion that the Board has under Section 10(k).

PART III. FEATHERBEDDING

Section 8(b)(6) makes it an unfair labor practice for a union "to cause or attempt to cause an employer to pay or deliver or agree to pay or deliver any money or other thing of value, in the nature of an exaction, for services which are not performed or not to be performed." This provision is referred to as the antifeatherbedding provision of the Act.

A. REQUIRING UNNECESSARY WORK

Suppose a piece of equipment can be maintained by one employee, but a union insists that two employees be used. That would commonly be regarded as featherbedding because two employees are doing work that one could do. But insisting that more employees be used than are necessary does not violate Section 8(b)(6). That issue was resolved by the Supreme Court in *American Newspaper Publishers Assn.*[7] In that case, ads produced by outside agencies came to the newspaper ready to print, but the printers insisted that they make a copy of the same work, called bogus work. This was a way of preserving bargaining unit work. The copy prepared by the outside agency, not the bogus copy, was used in the advertisement.

The Supreme Court held that the union's demand to do the unnecessary bogus type work did not violate Section 8(b)(6). The bogus type requirement was featherbedding in the sense that the work was clearly unnecessary. But the Supreme Court held that the union's insistence on doing the bogus type work did not violate Section 8(b)(6) because the work was actually done, even though it was unnecessary. The Section makes it a violation to cause an employer to

pay money for services that are not performed or not to be performed. The Court reasoned that the Section did not make it unlawful to require payment for services rendered even though they are unnecessary. It only prohibited pay for work that employees did not do or were not going to do. The Court noted that the original statutory proposal leading to Section 8(b)(6) had broadly prohibited featherbedding, but the actual language agreed to was much narrower. In light of the legislative history, the Court refused to apply the section beyond the express wording.

B. EMPLOYEES' WILLINGNESS TO DO UNNECESSARY WORK

The Court's narrow application of Section 8(b)(6) was reaffirmed in *Gamble Enterprises, Inc.*[8] In that case, the Musician's Union refused to permit out-of-town orchestras to appear in a theater unless the theater agreed to employ local musicians for a number of independent performances, depending upon the number of traveling orchestra appearances. The theater signed an agreement to use the local orchestras. The local orchestras were available to play; however, the theater had no need for the local orchestras and did not use them. The Supreme Court held that this agreement did not violate Section 8(b)(6) because the local musicians were willing to play even though the employer decided not to use them.

PART IV. UNIONS AND THE ANTITRUST LAWS

Limits on subcontracting, work preservation clauses, jurisdictional claims, and restrictive work rules lessen or prevent competition between employers. For example, a subcontracting clause or a union's insistence on its jurisdictional rights may prevent an employer from bidding on a job or force two

---

[7] See legal principle 10.

[8] See legal principle 10.

employers to terminate their business relationship. That reduces competition. As a union organizes more employees in an industry and achieves uniformity in wages and benefits, wages are removed as a means of competition. These are legitimate goals of collective bargaining, but they conflict with the goals of the antitrust laws to prevent restraint on trade and encourage competition. The history of Congress and the Supreme Court in reconciling the conflicting policies of the antitrust laws and collective bargaining is long and intricate, as described below.

A. THE SHERMAN ANTITRUST ACT

In 1890 Congress passed the Sherman Act that was designed to curtail the monopolistic practices of certain businesses. Section 1 of the Act makes illegal every contract, combination, or conspiracy to restrain trade, fix prices, or limit competition. Section 2 provides that every person who monopolizes or conspires with others to monopolize trade or commerce is guilty of a misdemeanor and could be punished by fine or imprisonment. A person injured by activity illegal under the Sherman Act is entitled to monetary damages up to three times the amount of the actual damages.

The early federal court decisions took the position that the Sherman Act applied to all classes of people and all types of combinations, including labor unions. The courts held that union activities that physically interrupted the free flow of trade or tended to create business monopolies were illegal. They also held that a combination of employees to obtain a raise in wages was itself a prohibited monopoly. Injunctions were often issued to stop union activity even if no violation of the Sherman Act was charged.

B. THE CLAYTON ACT

The Clayton Act of 1914 expanded the general coverage of the antitrust laws, but also limited the application of the antitrust laws to unions. It states, in part, that the labor of human beings is not a commodity or an article of commerce, and that nothing contained in the antitrust laws should be interpreted to forbid the existence and operation of labor organizations instituted for the purpose of mutual help, or to forbid or restrain individual members of such organizations from lawfully carrying out their legitimate objectives. The Act also provides that neither unions nor their members should be held or construed to be illegal combinations or conspiracies in restraint of trade under the antitrust laws. The Clayton Act recognizes a union's right to remove wages as a competitive factor.

The Supreme Court did not interpret the Clayton Act as a total exemption of labor unions from the antitrust laws. In several cases, it decided that secondary boycotts against dealers who sold goods manufactured by employers with whom a union had a labor dispute violated the antitrust laws. The Court stated that the Clayton Act exemption applied only to union activities directed against the employee's immediate employer.

C. THE NORRIS-LAGUARDIA ACT

Congress did not agree with the Supreme Court interpretation of the Clayton Act. In 1932, Congress enacted the Norris-La-Guardia Act that greatly broadened the meaning of the term "labor dispute." The Act defines labor dispute to include "any controversy concerning terms or conditions of employment, or concerning the association or representation of persons in negotiating, fixing, maintaining, changing, or seeking to arrange terms or conditions of employment, regardless of whether or not the disputants stand in the proximate relation of employer and employee." This meant that a secondary boycott could still be a labor dispute contrary to the Supreme Court decisions interpreting the Clayton

Act. The Act further restricted the use of injunctions against labor activities.

Norris-LaGuardia specifically provides that the following acts are not considered unlawful combinations or conspiracies: (1) ceasing or refusing to perform any work or to remain in any relation of employment; (2) becoming or remaining a member of any labor organization; (3) giving publicity to any labor dispute by any method not involving fraud or violence; and (4) assembling peaceably to act or to organize to act in promotion of their interests in a labor dispute.

The Sherman, Clayton, and Norris-LaGuardia Acts are still in effect. The best way to understand labor's current coverage under the antitrust laws is to examine some of the major cases decided by the Supreme Court since the Norris-LaGuardia Act was enacted.

D. THE CURRENT BASIC RULE: UNIONS ACTING ALONE IN THEIR OWN SELF-INTEREST

1. The Hutcheson Decision

In *United States v. Hutcheson* (1941), the Court first considered the interrelationship of the Sherman, Clayton, and Norris-LaGuardia Acts.[9] In that case, the carpenters and machinists unions at an Anheuser-Busch plant had a jurisdictional dispute over certain work. After Anheuser-Busch awarded the work to the machinists, the carpenters struck against Anheuser-Busch and against two construction companies who were building facilities for Anheuser-Busch and a tenant on land adjacent to the plant. The union also picketed Anheuser-Busch and the tenant and urged that its members and others boycott Anheuser-Busch beer.

The federal government filed criminal charges against the leaders of the carpenters' union alleging that the union's actions constituted a combination and conspiracy in restraint of trade in violation of the Sherman Act. The Supreme Court held that the acts did not violate the antitrust laws. It ruled that the jurisdictional dispute was a "labor dispute" as defined by the Norris-LaGuardia Act. The Court stated that the union could picket the contractors and the tenant, even though they were not directly involved in the dispute. The Court also ruled that the carpenters' actions, including the members' refusal to work, the peaceful picketing, and the boycott were protected by the Clayton and Norris-LaGuardia Acts. The Court stated that as long as a union engages in such activities only to promote its own self-interest and does not combine with nonlabor groups, it is exempt from the Sherman Act.

Hutcheson was decided before the Taft-Hartley Act enacted Section 8(b)(4) abolishing most secondary boycotts (see Chapter Seven). Thus, although the union conduct in *Hutcheson* would still not violate the antitrust laws, at least part of the tactics would be unlawful under Section 8(b)(4)(B).

2. The Allen-Bradley Decision

The principle that a union loses its antitrust exemption if it combines with a nonlabor group was applied several years later by the Supreme Court in *Allen-Bradley*.[10] In *Allen-Bradley*, a local union representing both production and construction electrical workers in New York City decided that the best way to increase the wages and employment opportunities of its members was to promote the sale of goods produced by local manufacturers who employed its members. To accomplish this, the union waged an aggressive campaign, using strikes and boycotts, to obtain closed shop agreements with all local electrical equipment manufacturers and contractors. Under these agreements, construction contractors were obligated to purchase equipment from only those manufacturers who also had closed shop agreements with the local. Manufacturers, in

[9] See legal principle 11.

[10] See legal principle 11.

turn, were obligated to confine their New York City sales to contractors employing local union members. Over time these individual agreements expanded into industrywide understandings that concerned not only conditions of employment, but also the price of goods and market control. Agencies were set up composed of representatives of the union, the manufacturers, and the contractors to boycott local manufacturers who did not abide by the terms of the understanding to bar equipment manufactured outside New York City from the New York City market.

A lawsuit seeking to enjoin these activities as antitrust violations was filed by manufacturers of electrical equipment who produced their goods outside New York City. These manufacturers could not bargain with the union because the local's jurisdiction was limited to the city. As a result of the understandings between the local and the electrical contractors, these manufacturers were excluded from the New York City market. The Supreme Court ruled that the union had violated the antitrust laws. It stated that the union, acting alone, would not have violated the antitrust laws by entering into bargaining agreements in which the employer agreed not to buy goods manufactured by companies that did not employ union members. However, the Court held that the union lost its exemption in this case because it did not act alone. Instead, it participated in a combination with business interests. The Court stated:

We may assume that such an agreement standing alone would not have violated the Sherman Act. But it did not stand alone. It was but one element in a far larger program in which contractors and manufacturers united with one another to monopolize all the business in New York City, to bar all other businessmen from the area, and to charge the public prices above a competitive level. It is true that victory of the union in its disputes, even had the union acted alone, might have added to the costs of goods, or might have resulted in individual refusals of all of their employers to buy electrical equipment not made

by Local No. 3. So far as the union might have achieved this result acting alone, it would have been the natural consequence of labor union activities exempted by the Clayton Act from the coverage of the Sherman Act. But when the unions participated with a combination of businessmen who had complete power to eliminate all competition among themselves and to prevent all competition from others, a situation was created not included within the exemptions of the Clayton and Norris-LaGuardia Acts.

E. MULTI-EMPLOYER AGREEMENTS AND THE ANTITRUST LAWS (THE *PENNINGTON* AND *JEWEL TEA* DECISIONS)

The *Allen-Bradley* decision establishes that the same labor union activities may or may not violate the antitrust laws, depending upon whether the union acts alone or in combination with business groups. This principle was further illustrated in two later cases decided by the Supreme Court on the same day: *United Mine Workers v. Pennington* and *Meat Cutters v. Jewel Tea.*

In the *Pennington* case, the United Mine Workers negotiated a collective bargaining agreement with a multi-employer association of large coal operators in which these operators agreed to pay union members increased wages and fringe benefits.[11] The union then sought to have smaller coal companies sign the same agreement. One of the smaller operators signed the agreement, but then failed to make required payments into the pension fund. The fund's trustees sued for the delinquent contributions. The small operator then filed a countersuit against the union alleging that the union and the large coal operators had conspired to restrain trade in violation of the Sherman Act. The company alleged that the union had agreed with the multi-employer association to demand the same wage and benefit package from the smaller coal companies, regardless of their ability to pay. The company further alleged that the pur-

[11] See legal principle 11.

pose of the agreement was to drive the small operators out of business. The jury awarded damages to the small operator against the union and the union appealed.

In *Jewel Tea*, the butchers' union contract in Chicago for many years had contained a provision restricting the marketing hours for fresh meat from 9:00 A.M. through 6:00 P.M. when the union's members were present.[12] The union wanted this restriction to limit the working hours of its members.

During negotiations, a number of employers, including Jewel Tea, proposed changes in the restriction. The union rejected the changes. Finally, a number of employers, including a multi-employer association, agreed to the contract provision; however, Jewel Tea continued to resist. It finally signed the contract containing the restriction only after being threatened with a strike if it refused. Jewel Tea then filed suit against the union and the multi-employer association seeking to invalidate the marketing hour restriction on the grounds that it violated the antitrust laws. It contended that the union and the association had conspired to restrain the sale of meat.

In *Pennington*, the Supreme Court reversed the judgment against the union because of certain erroneous trial court instructions to the jury. The Court, however, stated that the union would have violated the antitrust law if the union had *agreed* with the large coal operators to impose the contractual terms on the smaller operators in order to eliminate the smaller operators as competition. The Court again emphasized that the union might legally be able to obtain the same result if, on its own, it sought to require the smaller employers to sign the same contract. The Court also stated that multi-employer contracts in themselves do not violate the antitrust laws. Unions act unlawfully only if they attempt to impose the multi-employer association contract on other employers in accordance with an agreement with the multi-employers.

12 See legal principle 11.

In *Jewel Tea*, the Court found that there was no evidence of any agreement between the union and the multi-employer association to impose the hours restriction on all other employers. The union acted alone following its own longstanding policy concerning the working hours of its members. The Court noted that the hours provision was a restraint on trade, but further stated that working hours are a legitimate subject for collective bargaining. The prohibition on selling meat when no butchers were present was a means of enforcing the hours restriction and protecting bargaining unit work when the butchers were not present. Thus, the restricted marketing hours provision was exempt from the antitrust laws.

F. UNION ANTITRUST VIOLATIONS IN THE ABSENCE OF A BARGAINING RELATIONSHIP (THE *CONNELL CONSTRUCTION* CASE)

The latest Supreme Court case concerning labor's exemption from the antitrust laws is the *Connell Construction* case (previously discussed in this chapter under hot cargo clauses). In *Connell*, the plumbers union sought an agreement from Connell that it would subcontract plumbing work only to firms whose employees were represented by the union. The clause was a means of putting pressure on nonunion plumbing contractors to recognize the union. It was also a restraint on trade to the extent that it limited Connell's choice of subcontractors. The union contended that the agreement was exempt from the antitrust laws because it acted solely on its own behalf and not in combination with any employer.

The Supreme Court held that the union's attempt to impose the clause on Connell was not exempt from the antitrust laws. The Court noted that labor's antitrust exemption came from two sources: (1) the statutory exemptions of the Clayton and Norris-LaGuardia Acts providing that labor unions are not combinations or conspiracies in restraint of trade and exempting specific union activities such as secondary boycotts and picketing from the antitrust laws and (2) the nonstatutory exemption derived from the congressional policy favoring collective bargaining on wages, hours, and other terms and conditions of employment even though competition may be reduced. The Court said that *Jewel Tea* was an example of the nonstatutory exemption applied to collective bargaining. The Court stressed that a union entering into an agreement with an employer may be protected by the nonstatutory exemption because of the strong labor policy favoring the association of employees to eliminate competition over wages and working conditions. The Court stated that this policy could not be achieved unless the courts tolerated the lessened business competition that resulted from it. But the Court emphasized that the nonstatutory exemption would not apply if a union and a nonlabor party agreed to restrain competition in a business market as in the *Allen-Bradley* case discussed above.

The Court stressed in *Connell* that the contractor and the union did not have a collective bargaining relationship. The union did not represent or seek to represent Connell's own employees. Thus, the nonstatutory exemption, derived from the policy favoring collective bargaining, did not apply. Furthermore, the Court said that the construction industry proviso to Section 8(e) did not apply in the absence of a collective bargaining relationship and that Section 8(e) did not sanction the top-down organizing the union was attempting.

The Supreme Court then analyzed the effect the agreement between Connell and the union would have on the construction industry in the area. It found that the agreement had the potential of reducing competition of mechanical subcontracting work by excluding nonunion subcontractors from the market. Also, the union's contract with its multi-employer association contained a "most favored nation" clause. This meant that no other subcontractor could enter into a collective bargaining agreement with the union that contained more competitive terms. Taking all these factors into consideration, the Court concluded that the union's proposed clause, in the absence of a bargaining relationship between the union and Connell, was not exempt from the antitrust laws.

The *Connell* decision is significant because there was no evidence of any conspiracy or improper agreement between the union and any employers. The union was acting solely in its own behalf. Prior cases had exempted unions acting solely on their own from the antitrust laws. The Court indicated, however that the agreement the union sought might not have violated the antitrust laws if the union and Connell had a bargaining relationship because the nonstatutory exemption for collective bargaining agreements might have applied.

Since the *Connell* case, a number of non-union contractors in the construction industry have filed suits against construction unions, or jointly against a union and the employers or employer association with which the union bargains, alleging that contractual agreements to limit job-site construction work to union contractors violate the antitrust laws. The decisions considering these suits in light of *Connell* are legally complex and frequently entail detailed analysis of specific fact situations. However, although the issues are not yet fully resolved, certain key principles appear to be emerging. First, that a subcontracting restriction is valid under Section 8(e) does not necessarily shield the provision from the antitrust laws if in fact there is an underlying agreement between a union and a nonlabor party to restrain competition in a business market and the clause is used to carry out that conspiracy or scheme to eliminate competition. Second, a subcontracting restriction that is lawful under Section 8(e) *will* be protected by the nonstatutory exemption for collective bargaining agreements unless there is evidence beyond the natural anticompetitive effect of such a clause that the union entered into the agreement with an employer as part of an underlying conspiracy to reduce competition. The clause alone cannot be the basis of an antitrust claim. Also, even if an agreement does not fall within the labor exemption from the antitrust laws, there would still be no antitrust violation unless, in fact, the agreement is an unreasonable restraint on trade. In some markets, the unionized segment of an industry may be so small that even an agreement that is not shielded by the labor exemption would not have sufficient impact on competition to constitute an unreasonable restraint on trade. Such a determination entails a detailed factual analysis of the nature of the restraint, the businesses affected, and the impact under general antitrust law principles that would apply to any agreement in restraint of trade.

Finally, although some employers have attempted to use the antitrust laws against unions, it does not appear that unions will be able to use the laws as an effective weapon against nonunion contractors. Thus, in one case a union brought suit against a multi-employer association alleging that the association, in violation of the antitrust laws, was coercing association members and non-member employers that employed union labor to deal with nonunion firms. The Supreme Court held that the union did not constitute an "injured party" within the meaning of the antitrust laws and therefore had no legal right (standing) to bring such a suit. Presumably such a suit could be brought by the contractors who suffered an economic loss as a result of the alleged coercion.

Summary

This chapter covered a union's right to regulate work content and the application of the antitrust laws to such attempts. Besides the antitrust laws, union efforts to regulate work are subject to LMRA Section 8(e) prohibiting "hot cargo" agreements, Section 8(b)(4)(D) pertaining to jurisdictional disputes, and Section 8(b)(6) pertaining to "featherbedding" practices.

The courts and the Board recognize that Section 8(e) was not intended to prohibit all restrictions on subcontracting. There are two general categories of subcontracting clauses: work preservation clauses and union signatory clauses. Work preservation clauses are lawful in both the construction field and other industries. Work preservation clauses can lawfully prohibit all subcontracts or impose restrictions that remove the economic incentive for subcontracting. Work preservation clauses cannot go beyond the objective of preserving work and seek to control the labor relations of another employer. A work preservation clause may seek to reclaim work, but not to acquire new work. A union can strike to obtain a work preservation clause and to enforce the contract absent a no-strike clause.

A union signatory clause is lawful only in the construction industry for work done on the construction situs. A construction union can usually strike to obtain a construction industry union signatory clause unless there is a subcontractor already working on a project who would be forced to leave if the clause were applied. However, once a clause is adopted, the union cannot use self-help to enforce it. The clause can be enforced only through peaceful means, which might be either arbitration or court action. The primary limitation on enforcing work preservation clauses is the right-of-control test, under which a contractor may avoid compliance with a valid clause because the contractor does not have control over the work. Clauses protecting an employee's right to respect a picket line or to refuse to handle struck work are also lawful under Section 8(e) if they apply only to primary activity. In addition, a struck work clause may not permit an employee to refuse to handle work that is part of the normal business relationship between the primary and secondary employer rather than work shifted to the secondary employer that would have been produced by the striking employees but for the strike.

Section 10(k) empowers the Board to determine the merits of a jurisdictional dispute if the Board has reasonable cause to believe that Section 8(b)(4)(D) has been violated. Although the Board supposedly considers a number of factors in its determination, the work assignment made by the employer is the controlling factor in almost every case.

The Supreme Court has narrowly applied Section 8(b)(6) by holding that a union's insistence on doing unnecessary work does not violate the section if the work is actually done, or if employees are willing to do the work, but the employer chooses not to have it done.

Although union efforts to control wages and working conditions may limit and/or restrict competition, Congress partially exempted unions from the antitrust laws in the Clayton Act and prevented injunctions against alleged secondary boycotts in the Norris-LaGuardia Act. Based on these statutes and the policy favoring collective bargaining, the Supreme Court has held that a union's collective bargaining activities are exempt from the antitrust laws as long as the union acts to promote its own self-interest and does not combine with nonlabor groups. In *Connell Construction*, however, the Court applied the antitrust laws to a union acting in its own behalf. There the union sought a clause requiring the contractor to restrict subcontractors to employers that recognize the union. This clause was not exempt from the antitrust laws because there was no collective bargaining relationship between the contractor and the union and the clause was viewed as an attempt at "top-down organizing." In general, a subcontracting restriction that is lawful under Section 8(e) will probably be exempt from the antitrust laws unless there is evidence that the union entered into the agreement with an employer as part of an underlying conspiracy to reduce competition.

Review Questions

1. What is the statutory intent of Section 8(e)?
2. Would a picket line clause permitting employees to honor *any* picket line be lawful under Section 8(e)?
3. Is a clause stating that employees cannot be disciplined for refusing to handle goods produced by a struck employer lawful under Section 8(e)?
4. Is a union signatory clause (permitting subcontracting only to employers whose own employees are represented by a union) lawful?
5. Is a clause limiting subcontracts to employers who pay the same benefits as the contracting employer lawful?

6. Can a union contractually require a successor employer to assume an existing collective bargaining agreement even though the law does not require it?

7. What is the construction industry exception to Section 8(e)?

8. Can a primary work preservation clause be enforced through self-help?

9. Does the NLRB have authority to resolve all jurisdictional disputes under Section 10(k)?

10. What is the most important factor the Board applies in making work assignments?

11. Can a union bargain to impasse for a manning requirement that would result in "make work"?

12. Can a labor union negotiate a contract prohibiting a store from engaging in Sunday sales?

13. Does multi-employer bargaining violate the antitrust laws?

(Answers to review questions are at the end of the book).

Basic Legal Principles

1. A subcontracting clause preserving bargaining unit work or re-claiming lost work has a primary object and does not violate Section 8(e) even if the work is no longer technologically necessary. The work must be related to or functionally equivalent to the bargaining unit's traditional work. *National Woodwork Manufacturers Assn. v. NLRB*, 386 U.S. 612, 64 LRRM 2801 (1967); *NLRB v. International Longshoreman's Association*, 447 U.S. 490, 1054 LRRM 2552 (1980) (restrictions on containerized cargo may be valid work preservation provision); *NLRB v. International Long-shoremen's Association*, 473 U.S. 61, 119 LRRM 2915 (1985); *International Longshoremen's Association*, 278 NLRB No. 20, 121 LRRM 1216 (1986) (on remand from the Supreme Court), enforced in part *California Cartage Co. v. NLRB*, 822 F.2d 1203, 126 LRRM 2566 (D.C. Cir. 1987); *ILWU Local 13*, 295 NLRB No. 74, 132 LRRM 1102 (1989).

2. A union may negotiate a clause protecting the right of employees to respect a picket line or to refuse to handle struck work provided that the clauses are limited to primary strikes and picketing and that the struck work clause does not permit employees to disrupt an established business relationship between the primary and secondary employer. *Bricklayers Local 2*, 224 NLRB 1021, 92 LRRM 1347 (1976), enforced, 562 F.2d 775, 95 LRRM 3310 (D.C. Cir. 1977); *Lithographers Local 78*, 130 NLRB, 47 LRRM 1380 (1961); enforced in part 301 F.2d 20, 49 LRRM 2869 (5th Cir. 1962); *Teamsters Local 467*, 265 NLRB 1679, 112 LRRM 1231 (1982); *Painters Local 829 v. NLRB*, 762 F.2d 1027, 119 LRRM 2675 (D.C. Cir. 1985); *Teamsters Local 25 v. NLRB*, 831 F.2d 1149, 126 LRRM 2886 (1st Cir. 1987); *Elevator Constructors Local No. 3*, 289 NLRB No. 132, 129 LRRM 1066 (1988).

3. A union cannot use self-help to enforce a work preservation clause if the primary employer does not have the legal right to control the

disputed work. *NLRB v. Plumbers, Local 638*, 429 U.S. 507, 94 LRRM 2628 (1977); *IBEW Local 501 v. NLRB*, 566 F.2d 348, 96 LRRM 2940 (D.C. Cir. 1977), enforcing *IBEW Local 501*, 216 NLRB 417, 88 LRRM 1220 (1975); *George Koch Sons, Inc.* 201 NLRB No. 7, 82 LRRM 1113 (1973).

4. Except in the construction industry (as to job-site work) or the garment industry (which is totally exempt from Section 8(e)), an employer cannot expressly or by implication agree to subcontract only to union employers. *Machinists District 9*, 134 NLRB 1354, 49 LRRM 1321 (1961); *Bakery Wagon Drivers and Salesmen, Local 484*, 137 NLRB 987, 50 LRRM 1289 (1962); *Sheet Metal Workers Local 91*, 294 NLRB No. 61, 131 LRRM 1609 (1989).

5.A. Union standards subcontracting clauses are lawful under Section 8(e). *Teamsters Local 107*, 159 NLRB 84, 62 LRRM 1224 (1966); *Orange Belt District Council of Painters, No. 48 v. NLRB*, 328 F.2d 534, 55 LRRM 2293 (D.C. Cir. 1964); *In re Bituminous Coal Wage Agreements*, 756 F.2d 284, 119 LRRM 3148 (3rd Cir. 1985); *NLRB v. Teamsters Local 525*, 773 F.2d 921, 120 LRRM 2651 (7th Cir. 1985); *Teamsters Local 89*, 254 NLRB No. 93, 106 LRRM 1177 (1981). But see *Associated General Contractors*, 227 NLRB No. 27, 94 LRRM 1210 (1976); and *Chicago District Council of Carpenters*, 275 NLRB No. 51, 119 LRRM 1114 (1985) (clause cannot require payment of identical benefits); *Virginia Sprinkler Co. Inc. v. Local 699*, 868 F.2d 116, 131 LRRM 2147 (4th Cir. 1989).

5.B. A clause permitting an employer to sell or transfer its business only to another employer who agrees to assume the existing collective bargaining agreement as a condition of the transaction serves a legitimate work preservation object and is therefore lawful under Section 8(e). *Teamsters Local 814*, 225 NLRB 609, 93 LRRM 1344 (1976); *United Mine Workers*, 231 NLRB 573, 96 LRRM 1083 (1977), enforced, 639 F.2d 545, 104 LRRM 3144 (10th Cir. 1980). Compare *Chicago Bartenders Union*, 248 NLRB No. 83, 103 LRRM 1429 (1980) (contract cannot require lessee to assume agreement as condition of lease). On construction unions' contractual right to limit alter-ego and/or double-breasted operations on a construction situs, see *Painters and Allied Trades District Council 51*, Case No. 5–CC–1036 et al., Administrative Law Judge Recommended Decision, (1986) (Board decision pending).

6. A construction industry proviso clause limiting subcontracting on a construction situs to union contractors is lawful if the agreement is made in the context of a collective bargaining relationship between the employer and the union or is to prevent the union members from having to work with nonunion employees on the same project. *Connell Construction Co. v. Plumbers and Steamfitters, Local 100*, 421 U.S. 616, 89 LRRM 2401 (1975); *Carpenters Local 944*, 239 NLRB No. 40, 99 LRRM 1580 (1978); *Woelke and Romero Framing Inc. v. NLRB*, 456 U.S. 645, 110 LRRM 2377 (1982); *Donald Schriver, Inc. v. NLRB*, 635 F.2d 859, 105 LRRM 2818 (D.C. Cir. 1980); *Pacific Northwest Chapter, Associated Builders v. NLRB*, 654 F.2d 1301,

107 LRRM 2065 (9th Cir. 1981), as modified, 699 F.2d 488, 112 LRRM 3177 (9th Cir. 1983); *Laborers Local 210 v. AGC*, 844 F.2d 69, 128 LRRM 2060 (2d Cir. 1988); *Ironworkers District Council Pacific Northwest*, 292 NLRB No. 53, 131 LRRM 1726 (1989).

7. A union may usually strike or picket to compel an employer in the construction industry to execute a construction industry proviso subcontracting clause. However, such a clause cannot be enforced by self-help, but only through peaceful persuasion, arbitration if the union has a colorable contract claim, or court action. *Los Angeles Building and Construction Trades Council*, 214 NLRB No. 86, 87 LRRM 1424 (1974); *Operating Engineers Local 701*, 239 NLRB No. 43, 99 LRRM 1589 (1978); *Donald Schriver, Inc. v. NLRB*, 635 F.2d 859, 105 LRRM 2818 (D.C. Cir. 1980); *Plumbers District Council*, 277 NLRB No. 128, 121 LRRM 1057 (1985) (provision for self-help not enforceable but does not void entire subcontracting provision).

8.A. Section 10(k) requires the Board to make an affirmative assignment of disputed work in cases falling within the provision. This determination would prevail over a conflicting arbitrator's decision. *NLRB v. Broadcast Engineers Local 1212 (Columbia Broadcasting System)*, 364 U.S. 573, 47 LRRM 2332 (1961); *Carey v. Westinghouse*, 375 U.S. 261, 55 LRRM 2042 (1963); *ILWU Local 32 v. Pacific Maritime Assn.*, 773 F.2d 1012, 120 LRRM 2881 (9th Cir. 1985).

8.B. Section 10(k) does not apply if all parties are bound to an agreed-upon method to resolve their dispute, unless at least two employee groups (unions) claim the work and at least one engages in coercive conduct in support of its claim, or if the dispute is actually over the preservation of bargaining unit work rather than work assignments. *ILWU Local 62-B v. NLRB*, 781 F.2d 919, 121 LRRM 2719 (D.C. Cir. 1986); *Operating Engineers Local 150 v. NLRB*, 755 F.2d 78, 118 LRRM 2909 (7th Cir. 1985); *Golden Grain Macaroni*, 275 NLRB No. 162, 119 LRRM 1242 (1985); *ILA Local 799*, 280 NLRB No. 24, 122 LRRM 1278 (1986); *Teamsters Local 578*, 280 NLRB No. 95, 123 LRRM 1074 (1986); *Laborers Local 1*, 285 NLRB No. 75, 127 LRRM 1099 (1987); *Massachusetts Laborers District Council*, 290 NLRB No. 40, 129 LRRM 1095 (1988). Regarding filing or processing grievance as coercion within the meaning of Section 10(k), see *Carpenters Local 33*, 289 NLRB No. 167, 129 LRRM 1311 (1988); *ILWU Local 7*, 291 NLRB No. 13, 130 LRRM 1033 (1988); *International Longshoremen's Associaton v. NLRB*, ____ F.2d ____, 132 LRRM 2556 (D.C. Cir. 1989).

9. The determination of jurisdictional disputes under Section 10(k) is based upon a balancing of "all relevant factors" including (1) certifications and collective bargaining agreements, (2) efficiency and economy of operation, (3) skills and work involved, (4) area and industry practice, and (5) employer's practice and preference. *Machinists, Lodge No. 1743*, 135 NLRB No. 139, 49 LRRM 1684 (1962); *Typographical Union 48*, 230 NLRB

No. 113, 95 LRRM 1361 (1977); *Stage Employees Locals 27 and 48*, 227 NLRB No. 8, 94 LRRM 1050 (1976); *Hanford Trades Council*, 227 NLRB No. 145, 95 LRRM 1007 (1977); *Laborers' Local 449*, 260 NLRB No. 112, 109 LRRM 1210 (1982); *Mine Workers Union*, 280 NLRB No. 68, 123 LRRM 1052 (1986).

10. A union can insist upon "make work" for its members, provided some actual work is performed, without violating Section 8(b)(6) even though the work may neither be necessary nor desired by the employer. *American Newspaper Publishers Assn. v. NLRB*, 345 U.S. 100, 31 LRRM 2422 (1953); *NLRB v. Gamble Enterprises*, 345 U.S. 117, 31 LRRM 2428 (1953).

11. A union is generally exempt from the antitrust laws if it is acting alone on a collective bargaining matter in its own self-interest. *United States v. Hutcheson*, 312 U.S. 219, 7 LRRM 267 (1941); *Allen Bradley Co. v. IBEW Local 3*, 325 U.S. 797, 16 LRRM 798 (1945); *United Mine Workers v. Pennington*, 381 U.S. 657, 59 LRRM 2369 (1965); *Amalgamated Meat Cutters Local 189 v. Jewel Tea Co.*, 381 U.S. 676, 59 LRRM 2376 (1965). The antitrust exemption does not apply if a union seeks an anticompetitive restriction from an employer with whom the union does not have or seek a collective bargaining relationship. See *Connell Construction Co. v. Plumbers* in legal principle 6. However, a subcontracting restriction that is lawful under Section 8(e) is probably exempt from the antitrust laws unless there is evidence that the union entered into the agreement with an employer as part of an underlying conspiracy to reduce competition. Contrast *Sun-Land Nurseries v. Laborers*, 793 F.2d 1110, 122 LRRM 2921 (9th Cir. 1986) and *Local 210 Laborers v. AGC of America, N.Y.S. Chapter*, 844 F.2d 69, 128 LRRM 2060 (2nd Cir. 1988) with *Altemose Construction Co. v. Building and Construction Trades Council of Philadelphia*, 751 F.2d 653, 118 LRRM 2276 (3d Cir. 1985). See also *Adams Construction Co. v. Georgia Power*, 733 F.2d 853, 116 LRRM 2553 (11th Cir. 1984).

Recommended Reading   Altman, "Antitrust: A New Tool for Organized Labor?" 131 *U. Pa. L. Rev.* 127 (1982).

Antoine, "*Connell (Connell Constr. Co v. Plumbers Local 100)*, Anti-trust Law at the Expense of Labor Law." 62 *Va. L. Rev.* 603 (1976).

Gifford, "Redefining the Antitrust Labor Exemption," 72 *Minn. L. Rev.* 1379 (June 1988).

Leslie, "Role of the NLRB and the Courts in Resolving Union Jurisdictional Disputes," 76 *Colum. L. Rev.* 1470 (1975).

McKinney, "The Work Preservation Doctrine: Judicial Stability or Instability," 39 *Lab. L.J.* 828 (1988).

"NLRB Primary Jurisdiction and Hot Cargo Issues Arising in Sec. 301(a) Actions," 48 *Univ. of Chicago L. Rev.* 992 (1981).

chapter 9

ENFORCEMENT OF COLLECTIVE BARGAINING AGREEMENTS AND THE DUTY TO ARBITRATE

Section 301(a) of the Labor Management Relations Act provides that suits for violation of contracts between an employer and a union or between unions may be brought in any district court of the United States. Section 301 permits either an employer or a union to enforce the terms of a collective bargaining agreement. Suits to enjoin a strike in violation of a collective bargaining agreement and for damages are brought under Sectin 301 (see Chapter Six). Suits brought by a union to enforce an employer's agreement to pay fringe benefit contributions, or to collect union dues that have not been forwarded to the union under a dues checkoff clause, are other examples of Section 301 suits.

Today, everyone accepts the idea that a collective bargaining agreement is an enforceable agreement in federal court. But before Section 301 was enacted as part of the Taft-Hartley Act, the only law governing collective bargaining agreements was state common law enforced by the state courts. There were many difficulties in enforcing collective bargaining agreements under state law. Section 301 has ended these problems by establishing uniform federal requirements for the enforcement of agreements.

Section 301 applies not only to contracts between an employer and a union, but also to agreements between unions. This provision permits the enforcement of no-raiding agreements between unions.

Most collective bargaining agreements contain provisions for final and binding arbitration of contract disputes. Federal law developed under Section 301 has established that agreements to arbitrate are binding and that both the employer and the union are bound by an arbitrator's decision.

A. UNION AND EMPLOYEE RIGHTS TO FILE SECTION 301 ACTIONS

Although Section 301 authorizes suits for the enforcement of a contract, the section does not state who can bring such a suit. For a long time, it was unclear whether suits to enforce a contract were to be brought by the union or individual union members. Initially, the Supreme Court took the position that a union could file suit under Section 301 only to enforce "union rights" such as the contract's arbitration, checkoff, or union security clauses, but could not sue to enforce rights that were "uniquely personal" to individual employees, such as seniority rights or pay matters. The Court later changed its position. Currently, a union can bring suit to enforce all terms of a collective bargaining agreement, whether a particular dispute pertains to a union right or an individual employee's rights.

Although the union may bring suit to enforce the contract, individual employees may also bring suit under some circumstances. If a contract has a grievance procedure, but does not provide for final and binding arbitration, either the affected employee or the union can bring suit to enforce a contractual right after the available grievance procedures have been exhausted. The employee's right to sue, however, is restricted. The Supreme Court has held that an employee is bound by a union's settlement of a case in the grievance procedure, including a union decision to drop the matter. The employee cannot sue to enforce alleged contractual rights contrary to the union's resolution of the dispute, unless the union's action violated its duty of fair representation (see Chapter Twelve).

B. SUITS BETWEEN A UNION AND A MEMBER

Section 301 provides for suits to enforce contracts between labor organizations so that, for example, one union may sue another to enforce a no-raiding agreement between them. Also, an international union constitution is a contract between the international union and its locals and is therefore regarded as a contract between labor organizations under Section 301. Thus, either the international or the local, as appropriate, may sue the other in federal court under Section 301 to enforce provisions of the international constitution. For example, if the international constitution permits the international executive board to merge locals involuntarily under certain circumstances and a local resists a merger within

the international union's constitutional authority, the international union can bring suit in federal court to compel the merger.

At one time most courts held that an individual member could not sue either a local or the international union in federal court to enforce the international constitution. More recently, however, the courts that have considered this issue have held that since the international constitution is a contract within the meaning of Section 301, an individual member may sue either the international union or a local in federal court to enforce a provision of the international constitution.

In contrast, although a local union's constitution and bylaws are considered a contract between the local and the member (see Chapter Ten), they are not a contract between a union and an employer or between two unions. Therefore, a suit between a local and a member to enforce the local's constitution and bylaws cannot be brought in federal court under Section 301, but only in a state court applying state law. A member's suit alleging a union's violation of the duty of fair representation is based on the underlying collective bargaining agreement that has allegedly been violated. Thus, a fair representation suit may be brought in federal court under Section 301 even though the suit is between the member and the local union.

C. JURISDICTIONAL AND PROCEDURAL REQUIREMENTS OF A SECTION 301 SUIT

There are very few limitations on the right to sue under Section 301. The basic requirement is that the union represent employees in an industry affecting commerce, basically the same broad jurisdictional standard as for the NLRB (see Chapter One). Almost every business purchases goods or material either directly or indirectly from businesses in other states or sends goods across a state line. Thus, the commerce requirement is easily met. Only the smallest employers are not covered under Section 301. Of course, Section 301 actions cannot be brought by or against employers or unions that are not covered by the Labor Management Relations Act. Thus, Section 301 does not apply to a collective bargaining agreement between a governmental agency and a public employee union. Section 301(b) provides that a suit to enforce contracts can be brought without regard to the amount in controversy or the residency of the parties.

1. Suits by or against the Union as an Entity

Under Section 301(b) suits may be brought by or against the union as an entity. Before Section 301 was enacted, it was frequently necessary to sue union members directly and individually in order to enforce a collective bargaining agreement. This procedure was necessary because a union is an unincorporated association at common law (see Chapter Ten) and cannot be sued as an entity. Congress wanted to make it easier to enforce collective bargaining agreements, and thus provided in Section 301 that a union can be sued as an entity. Section 301 also provides that any judgment against a union under Section 301 is enforceable only against union assets, not against individual members or their assets. Prior to Section 301, if an employer successfully sued individual union members for breach of contract, money owed on the judgment could be collected from each union member. The trade-off for permitting a union to be sued as an entity in federal courts, thus making it much easier to enforce contracts, was that any judgment entered could be collected only from union assets. This means, for example, as discussed in Chapter Six, that union members are not individually liable for damages if they strike in violation of a contractual no-strike clause.

Sometimes a suit can be filed in federal court, but state law determines the parties' legal rights. For example, if a plaintiff and defendant involved in litigation (such as an auto accident) are residents of different states, the suit can be filed in federal court if the amount in controversy exceeds $50,000. This is called "diversity" jurisdiction. Usually the law of the state where the incident giving rise to this suit occurred governs. Laws on a particular subject may vary between states. Therefore the law applied by the federal courts in such cases also varies depending upon the applicable state's law.

Does state or federal law apply in a suit brought under Section 301? The Act itself does not say, but the Supreme Court has held that the courts are to apply federal law so that there is uniformity in the law governing enforcement of contracts under Section 301. Thus, all federal courts apply the same principles discussed in this chapter regardless of where the court is located or the state where the dispute arose. The courts have in effect developed a federal common (judge-made) law on the enforcement of labor contracts. This is a unique situation. Usually, federal courts apply either detailed federal statutes or state law, but not federal common law principles. The United States Arbitration Act (U.S.A.A.) regulates arbitration under certain commercial contracts. The Supreme Court has held that the U.S.A.A. does not apply to arbitration under a collective bargaining agreement, but that the courts may properly consider the procedures set forth in that act as guidance in labor arbitration cases.

There are a few Section 301 matters not covered by federal law. The principal one is the statute of limitations. Section 301 does not say how long a party has to bring suit to enforce a contract. As a general principle, the federal courts apply state law to procedural matters not covered by federal law. Thus, in general the length of time for bringing suit under Section 301 equals the length of time that a suit for breach of contract may be brought in the state where the contract was made. The time varies widely from state to state. However, as discussed more fully below, some courts are now applying a shorter limitations period for suits to compel arbitration under a collective bargaining agreement or to enforce an arbitrator's award, and there is a six-month limitations period for filing suit against a union for breach of its duty of fair representation (see Chapter Twelve). Some courts are also applying this six-month period to suits brought by an individual member under Section 301 against an international or local union to enforce the international constitution.

The Supreme Court has held that suits to enforce collective bargaining agreements can also be brought in the state courts, but that the state courts must apply the federal law. Through a legal procedure called "removal," the defendant in a state suit to enforce a collective bargaining agreement can transfer the case to the federal courts. Many unions exercise their right to remove state court suits to the federal courts because they believe that federal judges are more familiar with the governing principles. The vast majority of suits are initially brought in federal courts.

D. ENFORCEMENT OF AGREEMENTS TO ARBITRATE AND ARBITRATION AWARDS: THE "STEELWORKERS TRILOGY"

The great majority of all collective bargaining agreements provide for final and binding arbitration of disputes that arise under the contract. Arbitration has taken the place of court action to enforce contractual rights that would be brought under Section 301. Initially, following enactment of Section 301, it was unclear whether the section authorized the federal courts to enforce a contractual agreement to arbitrate. Under the law in many states at the time, agreements to arbitrate were not enforceable. The state courts took the view that parties are free to go directly into court on a dispute even though they have agreed to arbitration. Some employers argued that the federal courts should apply the state law principles.

The Supreme Court resolved this issue in the *Lincoln Mills* decision.[1] The Court pointed to Sections 201(b) and 203(d) of the Labor Management Relations Act, which favor arbitration as the desirable method for the peaceful resolution of industrial disputes. The Court reasoned that since national labor policy favors arbitration to resolve industrial disputes, the courts should specifically enforce agreements to arbitrate. As a result of this decision, agreements to arbitrate are enforceable under Section 301 in the federal courts and state courts.

Although *Lincoln Mills* established that a grievance arbitration provision in a collective bargaining agreement can be enforced, many questions remained about the subjects covered by the duty to arbitrate and the scope of the court's power to enforce an arbitrator's award. The issues were resolved several years later in three landmark decisions issued at the same time known as the "Steelworkers Trilogy."

1. Enforcement of Agreements to Arbitrate: The *Warrior and Gulf Navigation* Decision

The first case in the trilogy was *United Steelworkers v. Warrior and Gulf Navigation Co.*[2] In that case, the employees filed a grievance challenging the company's right to lay off employees and use an outside contractor for their work. The collective bargaining agreement between the employer and the union provided for arbitration, but it also contained a provision excluding matters that were strictly a function of management from the arbitration process.

The employer and union did not resolve the grievance and the union requested arbitration. The employer refused to arbitrate on the grounds that contracting out is a function of management and therefore not subject to arbitration. The union sued in

---

[1] See legal principle 1.

[2] See legal principle 3.

federal district court under Section 301 to compel arbitration. The district court agreed with the employer's provision that the use of outside contractors is a management function under the collective bargaining agreement. Also, no specific clause of the contract prohibited subcontracting. The court refused to order arbitration because the conract was clear and there was nothing to arbitrate. The case was appealed to the appropriate court of appeals and then to the United States Supreme Court.

a. The Need for an Agreement to Arbitrate.
The Supreme Court reversed the ruling of the lower courts and held that the matter of contracting out should be arbitrated. The court noted initially that arbitration is a matter of contract and that a party cannot be required to arbitrate any dispute that it has not agreed to arbitrate. But, because national labor policy favors arbitration to resolve labor disputes, a court should determine only whether the party that refuses to arbitrate a grievance has agreed to arbitrate the matter in dispute. The Court stated that a party should be required to arbitrate a dispute if a collective bargaining agreement provides for arbitration, *unless it can be stated with positive assurance that the arbitration clause of the collective bargaining agreement does not apply to the particular dispute.* The Court emphasized that any doubts about whether the parties have agreed to arbitrate a particular matter should be resolved in favor of arbitration.

Applying these principles, the Court, in *Warrior and Gulf,* limited its inquiry to whether the employer had agreed to arbitrate the subcontracting dispute. The Court noted that the arbitration clause applied to any difference between the parties. The dispute over contracting out, the Court reasoned, was such a difference, and was therefore arbitrable.

b. Court Consideration of the Dispute's Merits. But what if, as the district court concluded, the employer had the contractual right to subcontract as it had? Should an employer be required to arbitrate a dis-

pute when its actions were correct under the contract? The Supreme Court rejected this approach to determining arbitrability. The Court stressed that the courts are to decide only whether the parties have agreed to arbitrate the dispute, not consider the dispute's merits. Thus, the lower courts in *Warrior* had been wrong in deciding that contracting out was a function of management excluded from arbitration. That approach improperly interjected the courts into the merits of the dispute.

The Supreme Court strongly stressed the role of the arbitrator and that arbitration is not limited to the express terms of the agreement. Rather, the arbitrator may also consider the practices of the parties. The Court stated:

The labor arbitrator's source of law is not confined to the express provisions of the contract, as the industrial common law—the practices of the industry and the shop—is equally a part of the collective bargaining agreement although not expressed in it. The labor arbitrator is usually chosen because of the parties' confidence in his knowledge of the common law of the shop and their trust in his personal judgment to bring to bear considerations which are not expressed in the contract as criteria for judgment. The parties expect that his judgment of a particular grievance will reflect not only what the contract says but, insofar as the collective bargaining agreement permits, such factors as the effect upon productivity of a particular result, its consequence to the morale of the shop, his judgment whether tensions will be heightened or diminished. For the parties' objective in using the arbitration process is primarily to further their common goal of uninterrupted production under the agreement, to make the agreement serve specialized needs. The ablest judge cannot be expected to bring the same experience and competence to bear upon the determination of a grievance, because he cannot be similarly informed.

That a dispute is not arbitrable does not necessarily mean that a union has no recourse. If the union believes that the contract was violated, but the dispute is not arbitrable, the union can bring suit directly under Section 301 to enforce its contract rights. For example, some contracts provide only for arbitration of disciplinary actions. In such a case, the union could file suit over any other alleged contract violation. Also, the scope of the no-strike clause is generally the same as the scope of a contract's arbitration clause. Thus if a dispute is not arbitrable, the union may be able to strike over the issue (see Chapter Six).

2. The American Manufacturing Decision

The second trilogy case is *United Steelworkers v. American Manufacturing Co.*[3] In that case, the collective bargaining agreement provided for arbitration of any disputes between the parties "as to the meaning, interpretation and application of the provisions of this agreement." The contract also reserved to management the power to suspend or discipline any employee for cause and provided that promotions would be made on the principle of seniority where ability and efficiency were equal. An employee who left work due to an occupational injury settled a claim for workmen's compensation benefits against the company on the basis of a 25 percent permanent partial disability. The union filed a grievance that the employee was entitled to return to his job by virtue of the seniority provisions in the collective bargaining agreement.

The company refused to arbitrate the grievance and the union brought suit in district court under Section 301 to compel arbitration. The district court and the court of appeals ruled in the employer's favor on the grounds that the grievance was without merit and therefore not subject to arbitration. The Supreme Court reversed the lower courts. As in *Warrior and Gulf*, the Court stated that the courts have no business weighing the merits of a grievance in determining whether to order arbitration, but that their sole function is to determine whether the parties have agreed to arbitrate

the matter. Since the parties in *American Manufacturing* had agreed to arbitrate any dispute arising under the contract, the Court ruled that the grievance should be arbitrated. The Court strongly stated:

The function of the court is very limited when the parties have agreed to submit all questions of contract interpretation to the arbitrator. It is then confined to ascertaining whether the party seeking arbitration is making a claim which on its face is governed by the contract. Whether the moving party is right or wrong is a question of contract interpretation for the arbitrator. In these circumstances the moving party should not be deprived of the arbitrator's judgment, when it was his judgment and all that it connotes that was bargained for.

The courts therefore have no business weighing the merits of the grievance considering whether there is equity in a particular claim, or determining whether there is particular language in the written instrument which will support the claim. The agreement is to submit all grievances to arbitration, not merely those the court will deem meritorious. The processing of even frivolous claims may have therapeutic values of which those who are not a part of the plant environment may be quite unaware.

Most recently, in *AT&T Technologies, Inc.* the Supreme Court strongly reaffirmed the principles of the Steelworkers Trilogy.[4] The Court listed four guiding principles in enforcing the duty to arbitrate:

1. Arbitration is a matter of contract so that a party cannot be required to arbitrate a dispute that it has not agreed to arbitrate.
2. Whether the parties have contractually agreed to arbitration is to be decided by a court, not by an arbitrator, unless the contract clearly leaves this issue to the arbitrator.
3. A court cannot rule on the potential merits of a grievance in determining arbitrability even if the claim appears frivolous to the court.
4. If a contract contains an arbitration clause, there is a presumption of arbitrability and an order to arbitrate should not be denied unless the court concludes with positive assurance

[3] See legal principle 3.

[4] See legal principle 3.

that the arbitration clause is not susceptible to an interpretation covering the dispute.

3. Enforcement of an Arbitrator's Award: The *Enterprise Wheel* Decision

Both *Warrior and Gulf* and *American Manufacturing* dealt with enforcement of agreements to arbitrate. The third case of the steelworkers trilogy, *United Steelworkers v. Enterprise Wheel and Car Corp.*, pertained to the enforcement of an arbitrator's award.[5] In *Enterprise Wheel*, a group of employees staged a wildcat strike to protest an employee's discharge. The union advised the employees to return to work, but the employer refused to allow them back. The union filed a grievance. Although the collective bargaining agreement provided for binding arbitration of any differences over the meaning and application of the agreement, the employer refused to arbitrate. The union then successfully brought suit under Section 301 to compel arbitration. The arbitrator found that although the employee's conduct was improper, the facts warranted, at most, a ten-day suspension for each employee. The collective bargaining agreement had expired after the employees' discharge, but before the arbitrator's decision. The arbitrator rejected the company's contention that expiration of the agreement barred reinstatement of the employees. He awarded the employees reinstatement with backpay, minus the period of a ten-day suspension and such sums as the employees received from interim employment.

The employer refused to comply with the arbitrator's award, and the union brought suit under Section 301 in the district court to enforce it. The district court ordered the employer to comply, but the court of appeals reversed the decision on the grounds that the employees had no contractual right to reinstatement or to backpay for any time subsequent to the expiration of the contract.

[5] See legal principle 3.

The Supreme Court reversed the court of appeals.

The Supreme Court stated that an arbitrator's decision must be enforced by the courts so long as it "draws its essence" from the collective bargaining agreement, even though the court may disagree with the decision. The Court stated it was unclear whether the arbitrator in *Enterprise* had based his award, allowing backpay even though the collective bargaining agreement had expired, on an interpretation of federal labor law statutes or on the contract. The Court said the award would not be enforceable if the decision was based solely upon the law, but would be enforceable if it was based upon the arbitrator's interpretation of the contract. Moreover, the Court held that the award had to be enforced even though it was ambiguous. The Court stated:

[A]n arbitrator is confined to interpretation and application of the collective bargaining agreement; he does not sit to dispense his own brand of industrial justice. He may of course look for guidance from many sources, yet his award is legitimate only so long as it draws its essence from the collective bargaining agreement. When the arbitrator's words manifest an infidelity to this obligation, courts have no choice but to refuse enforcement of the award.

The opinion of the arbitrator in this case, as it bears upon the award of back pay beyond the date of the agreement's expiration and reinstatement is ambiguous. It may be read as based solely upon the arbitrator's view of the requirements of enacted legislation, which would mean that he exceeded the scope of his submission. Or it may be read as embodying a construction of the agreement itself, perhaps with the arbitrator looking to "the law" for help in determining the sense of the agreement. A mere ambiguity in the opinion accompanying an award which permits the inference that the arbitrator may have exceeded his authority, is not a reason for refusing to enforce the award. Arbitrators have no obligation to the court to give their reasons for an award. To require opinions free of ambiguity may lead arbitrators to play it safe by writing no supporting opinions. This would be undesirable for a well-reasoned opinion tends to engender confidence in the integrity of the process and aids in clarifying the underlying agreement.

Moreover, we see no reason to assume that this arbitrator has abused the trust the parties confided in him, and has not stayed within the areas marked out for his consideration. It is not apparent that he went beyond the submission. The Court of Appeals opinion refusing to enforce the reinstatement and partial back pay portions of the award was not based upon any finding that the arbitrator did not premise his award on his construction of the contract. It merely disagreed with the arbitrator's construction of it.

The Supreme Court further stated:

As we . . . emphasized, the question of interpretation of the collective bargaining agreement is a question for the arbitrator. It is the arbitrator's construction which was bargained for; and so far as the arbitrator's decision concerns construction of the contract, the courts have no business overruling him because their interpretation of the contract is different from his.

Suppose a collective bargaining agreement provides that promotions are to be based on seniority provided the senior employee has sufficient ability for the job. The union grieves that the employer violated the collective bargaining agreement by promoting a junior employee. If the arbitrator sustains the grievance with no explanation and orders the company to assign the job to the senior employee, the award is enforceable. Applying *Enterprise Wheel*, a court will assume that the arbitrator based the decision on the contract and will order the employer to comply.

What if the arbitrator states that the employer had the contractual right to promote the junior employee, because the senior employee lacked the ability, but the arbitrator still orders the company to award the job to the senior employee on the grounds that the employee can learn the job? In that case, a court would probably not enforce the arbitrator's decision as the arbitrator would be erroneously dispensing the arbitrator's own brand of industrial justice rather than drawing the essence of the decision from the contract.

Since the *Enterprise Wheel* decision was issued in 1960, the courts of appeals have generally applied very narrow grounds for setting aside an arbitrator's decision. Some of the circuits tend to examine the decisions more closely than others to determine whether a decision "draws its essence" from the collective bargaining agreement, but all the courts recognize that a decision must be enforced, even if it is clearly erroneous, as long as it is based on the arbitrator's interpretation of the contract. Various courts have stated that an award may be set aside if it is a gross mistake, if the findings are insupportable in the record, or if the decision is irrational. These are each slightly different standards, but each is a very narrow exception under which an arbitrator's decision is upheld in almost every case. As a practical matter, the standard of review applied by the appellate courts under the "Trilogy" cases has been so narrow that most employers or unions do not attempt to have an unfavorable decision set aside regardless of how erroneous it may appear to be. This finality, of course, is what the parties to the collective bargaining agreement intended when they provided for final and binding arbitration.

Recently in the *Misco* decision the United States Supreme Court has strongly reaffirmed the Steelworkers Trilogy principles as to the narrow scope of judicial review.[6] The Court stated:

Because the parties have contracted to have disputes settled by an arbitrator chosen by them rather than by a judge, it is the arbitrator's view of the facts and of the meaning of the contract that they have agreed to accept. Courts thus do not sit to hear claims of factual or legal error by an arbitrator as an appellate court does in reviewing decisions of lower courts. To resolve disputes about the application of a collective bargaining agreement, an arbitrator must find facts and a court may not reject those findings simply because it disagrees with them. The same is true of the arbitrator's interpretation of the contract. The arbitrator may not ignore the plain language of the contract; but the parties having authorized the arbitrator to give meaning to the

---

[6] See legal principle 4.

language of the agreement, a court should not reject an award on the grounds that the arbitrator misread the contract. . . . So, too, where it is contemplated that the arbitrator will determine remedies for contract violations that he finds, courts have no authority to disagree with his honest judgment in that regard. If the courts were free to intervene on these grounds, the speedy resolution of grievances by private mechanisms would be greatly undermined. . . . As long as the arbitrator is even arguably construing or applying the contract and acting within the scope of his authority, that a court is convinced he committed serious error does not suffice to overturn his decision. Of course, decisions procured by the parties through fraud or through the arbitrator's dishonesty need not be enforced.

a. Violation of Public Policy as a Basis for Setting Aside an Award.

Some employers have sought to have arbitration awards reinstating an employee to employment set aside on the grounds that reinstatement would violate "public policy." The scope of a "public policy" exception to an arbitrator's broad authority was before the United States Supreme Court in the *Misco* case. In *Misco*, the employer discharged an employee for violation of a company rule against having illegal drugs on the plant premises. The arbitrator held that the discharge was not for just cause and ordered the company to reinstate the discharged employee with backpay and full seniority. The company filed suit to vacate the award on the grounds that reinstating the employee who had allegedly possessed marijuana on the plant premises was contrary to public policy against the operation of dangerous machinery by persons under the influence of drugs or alcohol. Both the federal district court and the court of appeals ruled that the arbitrator's award should be set aside on public policy grounds. However, the United States Supreme Court, in a unanimous decision, reversed the lower courts and upheld the arbitrator's award. The Court said that an award can be set aside on public policy grounds only if the contract as interpreted would "violate some explicit public policy that is well defined and dominant, and is to be ascertained by reference to the laws and

legal precedent and not from general considerations of supposed public interest." The Court emphasized that the violation of such a policy, if established, must be clearly shown before an award may be set aside. The Court found no well-defined dominant public policy against the operation of dangerous machinery while under the influence of drugs. The Court stated that while that was a matter of common sense, such general considerations of supposed public interest are not sufficient to set aside an arbitrator's award.

In *Misco* the Court also reaffirmed the principle established in the Trilogy decisions that arbitrators have very broad authority to determine the appropriate remedies for a contract violation unless the contract expressly limits the arbitrator's authority to do so. Thus, the Court noted that if the arbitrator in *Misco* had found that the employee had possessed drugs on company property but still imposed a lesser penalty than discharge because the arbitrator believed that the employee would not use them on the job, the court of appeals could not set aside the award because of its own view that public policy in regard to plant safety was threatened. Suppose, however, that a contract specifically provides for discharge as the penalty for an employee possessing drugs on company property. In that case, if an arbitrator found that an employee had possessed drugs, the arbitrator could not impose a lesser penalty than that provided by the contract. Otherwise, the arbitrator would be improperly dispensing the arbitrator's own brand of industrial justice and the decision would not "draw its essence" from the contract. The decision could be set aside by a reviewing court.

Another generally well-recognized limitation on an arbitrator's authority to determine the remedy is that an arbitrator can award only compensatory rather than punitive damages as the remedy for a contract violation. To be compensatory, there must be a causal relationship between the violation and the loss claimed by the employee. As a general rule an award that exceeds the monetary loss that an employee suffers as a result of a contract violation is regarded as punitive. Basically, punitive damages can be awarded only if the contract expressly provides for them. Note, however, that damages for emotional distress are not necessarily punitive. Thus, if a union proves that an employer acted maliciously in discharging an employee, an arbitrator may have authority to award damages to the employee for the resulting emotional distress causally related to the employer's action. Such damages would be regarded as compensatory rather than punitive. An arbitrator's authority to award damages for such items as emotional distress would be narrowly limited to employer actions taken maliciously in bad faith. A court would almost certainly conclude that an arbitrator has no authority to award such damages in the typical case in which an arbitrator simply finds that disciplinary action was not for just cause but there is no evidence of any underlying malice or bad faith.

4. The Arbitrator's Authority over the Conduct of a Hearing

Unless the arbitrator's authority is expressly limited by the contract, the arbitrator has very broad authority over the conduct of an arbitration hearing including the order of witnesses, the examination and cross examination of witnesses, and the introduction of evidence. An arbitrator need not comply with the formal rules of evidence that apply in court or administrative proceedings such as NLRB cases. Thus, an arbitrator's award cannot be set aside for any defect in the hearing as long as the hearing meets the fundamental requirements of fairness, including notice of the hearing, the right to be heard, and an impartial decision (right or wrong). Also, although the situation rarely if ever occurs, the award must be free of fraud or corruption. In *Misco*, the Supreme Court indicated that even if an arbitrator errs in refusing to consider certain evidence, the arbitrator's decision may be set aside only if the error

was in bad faith or so gross as to amount to affirmative misconduct. These are the standards set forth in the United States Arbitration Act which, as discussed above, the courts sometimes use for guidance in determining the scope of an arbitrator's authority in labor arbitration proceedings. Certainly, such bad faith or a gross error would be very infrequent occurrences.

The Supreme Court also emphasized in *Misco* that even if an arbitrator's award is properly set aside, a reviewing court, as a rule, should still not settle the merits of the dispute according to its own judgment of the appropriate award, as that would improperly substitute a judicial determination for an arbitrator's decision. Instead, the Court said that a reviewing court should simply vacate the award, leaving open the possibility of further proceedings as permitted under the collective bargaining agreement, or remand the case to the arbitrator for reconsideration or even a rehearing in light of the court's decision.

5. The Arbitrator's Authority to Modify or Clarify An Award

Sometimes the parties disagree as to the meaning of an arbitrator's decision or as to the implementation of the award, such as the amount of backpay owed a successful grievant. Frequently, the parties agree in such cases to resubmit the dispute to the arbitrator for clarification. With possible rare exception such as a mathematical mistake, an arbitrator has no power to reconsider a decision or to modify, clarify, or interpret the award after it is issued unless the parties mutually so agree or unless the contract grants the arbitrator the authority. This is known as the doctrine of "functus officio" (a "completed act"). What can a union do if a dispute arises over the meaning or application of an arbitrator's decision, but the employer refuses to resubmit the matter to the arbitrator? There are two choices. First, the union can file a new grievance over the dispute that would ultimately proceed to arbitration like any other grievance. Second, the union may file suit in federal court to enforce the award. The court may order the employer to comply with the award or, if the award is unclear or ambiguous, the court may remand the matter to the arbitrator for clarification or modification as necessary. The courts have the authority to order such a reconsideration even though, under the doctrine of functus officio, an arbitrator cannot take such action on the arbitrator's own authority without the parties' mutual consent. Court proceedings are, of course, complex, time consuming, and expensive. The parties should therefore consider including a provision in their contractual arbitration clause authorizing an arbitrator to retain jurisdiction for a stated period to clarify the decision if so requested by one of the parties.

6. Time Limits on a Suit to Compel Arbitration or to Enforce an Award

As discussed above, Section 301 does not specify the time limit for filing a suit to enforce contractual rights, and the federal courts therefore look to the analogous (comparable) state law governing suits to enforce contract rights or to the United States Arbitration Act for guidance as to the applicable limitations period. Many states have adopted the Uniform Arbitration Act, a model act applicable to commercial arbitration, that provides that an appeal of an arbitration award must be made within ninety days after the award is mailed to the parties. Some state laws, however, establish a different time limit. Section 9 of the United States Arbitration Act requires that a suit to vacate, modify, or correct an arbitrator's decision be filed within three months after the award is filed or delivered to the parties. Thus, federal courts considering the issue have ruled virtually uniformly that the losing party in a labor arbitration case, subject to federal court jurisdiction under Section 301, must file a suit to modify, clarify, or vacate the arbitrator's decision within the time allowed under the state law for appealing an arbitrator's decision in a commercial arbitration case.

Ninety days is the most common period, but there may still be some variance depending upon the law of the state.

Most states do not have a specific law establishing a limitations period for a suit to *compel* arbitration. It is arguable that such a suit may be brought within the general time limit for enforcing any right based on a written contract, which might be two years, five years, or even longer depending on the state. However, the federal courts that have considered this issue to date have held that, as a matter of federal labor policy, suits to compel arbitration should be promptly filed. Thus, the rule that is gaining wide acceptance by the federal courts is that a suit to compel arbitration must be brought within six months from the date the other party refuses a demand for arbitration.

Many state laws do not establish a specific time limit for suits to *enforce* an award. Thus, most federal courts that have considered the issue have held that the proper limitations period for filing a suit to enforce an award is the general limitations period to enforce a written contract right. As noted above, this period varies from state to state, but is typically in the range of two to five years or longer. Several courts have also held that if a party that refused to comply with an arbitrator's decision does not file suit to modify, clarify, or vacate the award within the time limit for filing such a suit (most commonly ninety days), and the other party subsequently files suit for enforcement of the award after that deadline, the party opposing the award cannot raise any reason for refusing to comply with the award as a defense to the suit that it could have raised if it had filed a timely suit to have the award vacated, etc. The courts apply this rule so that a party disagreeing with an arbitrator's decision will take prompt action to have that decision vacated, etc. What if a collective bargaining agreement does not provide for arbitration? How long would a union have to file a suit over a breach of the collective bargaining agreement? In that case, the general state limitations period for enforcing a written contract right would prevail, not the shorter period for filing suit to compel arbitration.

E. EXPIRATION OF THE DUTY TO ARBITRATE

As discussed above, the duty to arbitrate is a matter of contract, and a party cannot be compelled to arbitrate a dispute unless it has contractually agreed to do so. It is therefore arguable that once a contract containing an arbitration clause expires, the duty to arbitrate expires as well. However, the courts have long recognized that there is a duty to arbitrate disputes that arise while a contract is in effect even if the grievance is not filed or the request to arbitrate is not made until after the contract's expiration. Furthermore, more recently in *Nolde v. Bakery Workers*, the Supreme Court held that, under some circumstances, there is a duty to arbitrate disputes that arise after the contract expires.[7] In that case the employer and the union were parties to a collective bargaining agreement that called for arbitration of any grievance. The contract provided for severance pay on termination of employment for all employees having three or more years of active service. The employer closed the plant and terminated all the employees three days after the contract expired. The union filed a grievance for the severance pay on the grounds that the severance pay clause still applied to a shutdown occurring after the contract expired. The company refused to arbitrate on the grounds that the dispute did not arise until after the contract's expiration date.

The union brought suit under Section 301 to compel arbitration. The case reached the Supreme Court, which held that the dispute was arbitrable, even though the dispute arose after the contract's expiration, because the issue was the continued application of the severance pay clause. There was, therefore, a dispute as to the contract's

[7] See legal principle 12.

meaning and application that was arbitrable. The court stated that there is a presumption that postexpiration grievances pertaining to the continued applicability of a contract provision are arbitrable unless negated expressly or by clear implication. The Court noted that the contract in question did not expressly provide that postexpiration date grievances were not arbitrable and that the dispute had arisen only a few days after the expiration.

Note that the Supreme Court did not consider the merits of the union's claim to severance pay based on the expired contract. The Court only concluded that the dispute was arbitrable. Thus, even though a dispute arising after a contract expires may be arbitrable, it is quite possible, depending upon the issue and the contractual language, that an arbitrator will still conclude on the merits that a specific contract right did not survive after the expiration.

The basic principle that has developed under *Nolde* as applied by the courts of appeals is that a grievance occurring after a contract's expiration date is arbitrable only if the grievance involves rights that vested or accrued at least in part during the life of the contract or that relate to events which occurred at least in part during the term of the contract. Thus, disputes as to severance pay or vacation pay arising after a contract's expiration are arbitrable because they are arguably based on work performed and rights accrued under the contract. If an employee is discharged after a contract expires based in part on conduct occurring during the agreement (e.g., long-term poor attendance), or if an employer decides to close a plant because of circumstances that initially arose during the contract term, a grievance challenging the company's action would probably be arbitrable because it relates to events occurring at least in part while the agreement was still in effect. Also, although there is no clearly established outer limit, the courts have held that a dispute must occur within a "reasonable period" after a contract's expiration in order to be arbitrable under the theory that it "arose under" the contract. The courts have emphasized, however, that an employer cannot evade arbitration by holding back an action that would violate the contract until a few days after the contract's expiration. *Nolde* was intended, in part, to prevent just such conduct.

Sometimes a dispute exists as to whether a contract is in effect at the time an employer takes certain action. For example, a collective bargaining agreement may require that the parties give timely notice of their intent to terminate the agreement and provide that the contract remains in effect if timely notice is not given. A union may argue that an employer's notice was defective (e.g., not mailed on time) so that the contract was still in effect when the employer took some action, such as subcontracting work prohibited by the contract. The courts have generally held that a dispute as to whether or not a contract has expired is for the arbitrator, not for a court, to decide.

The National Labor Relations Board may also become involved in issues as to the duty to arbitrate grievances arising after the contract has expired. As discussed in Chapter Five, Sections 8(a)(5) and 8(d) of the Act generally prohibit an employer from unilaterally changing the terms and conditions of employment established by a contract when the agreement expires until the employer first bargains with the union over the proposed changes to a good-faith impasse. Prior to the *Nolde* decision the Board has held as an exception to this rule that a contract's grievance and arbitration procedures terminated when the contract expired so that an employer had no duty to follow the contractual grievance procedures as to disputes that arose after the expiration date or to arbitrate such disputes.

After the *Nolde* decision, the Board changed its position. The board's current rule is that the contractual *grievance procedure* remains in effect until the parties bargain to a good-faith impasse on proposed changes. As to the duty to *arbitrate*, the Board adopted a position similar to that of the court of appeals: An employer is obligated to arbitrate only those postexpiration date grievances that concern contract rights capable of accruing or vesting to some extent during the life of a contract and ripening or remaining enforceable after the contract expires. Under this principle, the Board has held that an employer did not have to arbitrate disputes arising under expired contracts pertaining to such issues as safe working conditions, overtime distribution and premium pay, the contractual just cause requirement, and seniority rights for promotion. The Board has, however, required an employer to arbitrate postcontract grievances on severance pay issues.

The Board has not yet developed a clear position as to whether an employer may be required to arbitrate a postexpiration grievance pertaining to seniority in a layoff. In one case, in which recall rights were based solely on seniority, the Board held that seniority rights arguably survived the contract's expiration so that a grievance challenging the employer's failure to recall employees in seniority order was arbitrable. But in another case in which recall rights were based on aptitude and ability as well as seniority, the Board held that an employer was not obligated to arbitrate a grievance challenging a layoff occurring after the contract had expired.

F. PROCEDURAL DEFENSES TO ARBITRATION

1. Late Grievances

Other than the defense that a matter is not covered by the arbitration clause, the most common employer defense against arbitration is that a particular grievance was not filed within the time limits specified in the collective bargaining agreement or not processed within the time limits imposed between grievance steps.

The Supreme Court has held that a court should order arbitration even though a grievance was filed late. The court reasons that procedural defenses such as timeliness pertain to the merits of a grievance and accordingly should be decided by the arbitrator, not a court. Of course, a court order requiring arbitration of a late grievance does not mean that the union will prevail before the arbitrator. It is up to the arbitrator to decide whether the grievance was untimely, and if it was, whether there are circumstances for which the time limits should not be applied (e.g., that the time limits had not been strictly followed in past cases or that the employer had actual notice in time that a grievance was to be filed even though it was not formally filed until later).

Suppose that an arbitrator decides that the late filing of a grievance is excusable and rules in the union's favor on the merits of the dispute. If the employer refuses to comply with the award, a court will enforce the decision, right or wrong, as long as it is based on the arbitrator's interpretation of the contract's procedural requirements, that is, the decision draws its "essence" from the agreement, the same standard applied in reviewing an arbitrator's decision on the merits of a dispute.

2. Equitable Defenses to Arbitration

Employers sometimes argue that there are reasons why it would be unfair (inequitable) to permit a union to arbitrate a grievance even though the time limits have not expired. These are called equitable defenses. For example, what if an employer subcontracts work and the union does not file a grievance? The employer subcontracts the same work again. This time the union files a grievance claiming that the subcontracting violates the collective bargaining agreement and seeks backpay for the lost work. The employer can argue that it is inequitable for the union to arbitrate the validity of the second subcontract because the employer would not have subcontracted the work in dispute if the union had protested the first time. Arbitrators may deny a grievance based upon such equitable defenses regardless of the contractual merits of the union's claim.

The Supreme Court has held that equitable defenses should be treated the same as procedural defenses. If the subject of a dispute is covered by the arbitration clause, the court must order arbitration regardless of possible equitable defenses. The arbitrator decides whether an equitable defense has merit, just as the arbitrator decides timeliness issues.

Employers sometimes argue that if a union breaches a contractual no-strike clause by engaging in a wildcat strike, the employer has the right to terminate the agreement in full. That means the employer could discharge the employees or change the contract's terms and that its actions could not be arbitrated. The Supreme Court has held, however, that a breach of a no-strike clause does not relieve the employer of its duty to arbitrate. Of course, an arbitrator is free to consider what effect, if any, the union's breach of its no-strike clause has on the employer's contractual obligations.

G. EMPLOYER'S DUTY TO GRIEVE OVER A UNION BREACH OF CONTRACT

What happens if the union violates the contract? Can the employer sue the union for breach of contract or must the employer submit its claim to arbitration?

The Supreme Court has held that an employer must exhaust (complete) the grievance procedures, including arbitration, before filing suit, unless it is clear that the employer has no contractual right to file a grievance. Most contracts provide that a union or an employee may file a grievance, but say nothing about the employer's right to file a grievance. If the contract is silent, the employer is not required to arbitrate its claim before filing a suit against the union. If, however, the contract provides that the employer may file grievances or if the employer has filed grievances as a matter of past practice, the employer must arbitrate. Of course, if the union strikes in violation of a no-strike clause, the employer can file suit to enjoin the strike even though the contract provides for employer grievances. But if the employer seeks money damages, as well as an injunction, and the contract allows employer grievances, the employer must arbitrate the damage issues.

H. TRIPARTITE ARBITRATION

An arbitration hearing in which an employer and two unions participate is called tripartite arbitration. The usual arbitration hearing between the employer and a single union is called bilateral arbitration. What if an employer has contracts with two unions and each claims that certain work belongs to it under its agreement? If both contracts provide for arbitration, then both unions have the right to arbitrate their respective claims in a bilateral hearing. However, since arbitration is a matter of contract, neither union can be compelled to participate in a tripartite arbitration hearing unless the contract provides for it.

If an employer separately arbitrates each union's claim to the disputed work, the employer might end up with two conflicting awards. Both unions might have their grievances sustained and be awarded the work. What can the employer do? Can it refuse to arbitrate with one union?

The Supreme Court decided in *Carey v. Westinghouse* that an employer can be required to arbitrate with only one of the competing unions despite the possible conflict.[8] The court said that arbitration should be ordered because the possibility that two arbitrators' awards might conflict is speculative. The Court would not presume that the awards would conflict or that the arbitrators could not frame their awards to avoid conflict. Also, the Court said that arbitration might prove beneficial even if conflict did result because the arbitrators might still point out ways of resolving the dispute.

Although a union can compel an employer to proceed with bilateral arbitration

under *Carey*, there have been a few cases in which the courts have ordered two unions involved in a jurisdictional dispute with their employer to arbitrate their claims in a tripartite arbitration proceeding provided both union contracts provide for arbitration. That is, however, still an uncommon procedure.

I. ARBITRATION OF SUCCESSORSHIP RIGHTS

Under the Supreme Court's *Burns Detective* decision, a successor employer normally has no obligation to assume the collective bargaining agreement of the prior employer (see Chapter Five). The successor's only obligation is to bargain with the incumbent union if and when the former employees represented by the union constitute a majority of the new work force. If a successor employer voluntarily assumes the existing contract, it is bound by the entire agreement, including the duty to arbitrate. But if the employer does not assume the contract, does it have any obligations under the prior agreement?

In *John Wiley and Sons v. Livingston*, the Supreme Court held that a successor employer is obligated to arbitrate the extent of its obligations under a prior collective bargaining agreement.[9] In that case, a small publishing company merged into a larger company and the small company ceased to exist. The successor retained a majority of the prior work force. The prior union brought suit to compel arbitration as to the successor's obligations under the prior contract. The Court did not rule that the successor employer had any specific liability under the old contract; it ruled only that the successor is obligated to arbitrate the question. Following the usual rules, the Court did not consider the merits of the union's claim.

Wiley was decided before the decision in *Burns Detective* that a successor employer is

---

[8] See legal principle 8.

[9] See legal principle 9.

not bound by its predecessor's agreement. In the *Howard Johnson* case, decided after *Burns*, Howard Johnson purchased the assets of a motel.[10] Howard Johnson continued to operate the facility as a motel, but only nine out of forty-five employees had worked for the prior owner, who had employed fifty-three employees. The Supreme Court held that Howard Johnson was not required to arbitrate the question of its liability under the prior owner's collective bargaining agreement. The Court noted that, in contrast to *Wiley*, the prior motel company still existed even though the motel in question had been sold to Howard Johnson. Also, Howard Johnson had not kept the former employees. The Court also reasoned that since the prior motel owner was still in operation, the union can look to the predecessor for contractual damages, if any, growing out of the motel's sale to Howard Johnson. Apparently, the *Wiley* decision requiring arbitration can still apply if a predecessor employer has ceased all operations and the former employees are a majority of the successor employer's work force. However, since *Burns Detective* has established that a successor employer is not obligated to assume a prior contract, the practical usefulness of arbitration is questionable. A court might require a successor employer to arbitrate, but the arbitrator might decide, based on *Burns*, that the successor employer has no contractual obligations except those expressly assumed.

Assume that a contract contains strong successorship language specifically requiring that a successor employer assume the collective bargaining agreement as a condition of any sale or transfer of the company's assets, but that the contracting employer sells the company to another employer shortly after the contract expires without complying with the successorship provision. If the union files a grievance alleging that the sale violated the expired collective bargaining agreement, would the

contracting employer be required to arbitrate the grievance? The courts that have considered this issue have ordered arbitration under the principles of the *Nolde* case discussed above as to the arbitrability of grievances arising after the contract expires.

J. INJUNCTIONS PENDING ARBITRATION

Virtually every union grievance protests some unilateral employer action that the union alleges violates the parties' agreement. A few collective bargaining agreements contain "status quo" provisions under which an employer's unilateral act is suspended, once the union files a grievance, until such time as an arbitrator upholds the action taken. However, under most contracts the employer's unilateral action remains in effect until an arbitrator sustains the union's grievance, rescinds the employer's action, and requires an appropriate remedy. Of course, arbitration takes time. Can a union seek a "status quo" injunction requiring the employer, pending arbitration, to maintain the conditions existing before the employer's alleged breach of contract?

The primary difficulty in obtaining a status quo injunction is that, as discussed in Chapter Six in regard to injunctions against union strikes in breach of a no-strike clause, the Norris-LaGuardia Act prohibits a federal court from issuing an injunction in a labor dispute, and a grievance over an alleged contract violation is a labor dispute. However, a few court decisions have upheld the union's right to a status quo injunction pending arbitration if an arbitrator's decision sustaining the grievance would be futile unless the status quo is maintained in the meantime. The injunction is issued in aid of the arbitration process, just as an injunction against a strike in breach of contract over an arbitrable dispute is issued to preserve the effectiveness of the arbitration remedy. For example, courts have issued

[10] See legal principle 9.

injunctions if an employer attempts to relocate a plant in breach of contractual provisions prohibiting or limiting relocation, reasoning that once a plant is shut down and relocated at a new location, the plant could probably not be reopened at the original location even if the arbitrator sustains the grievance. Thus, the injunction is issued to maintain the status quo.

Remember that injunctions to maintain the status quo may be granted only if the dispute is over an arbitrable issue on which the union has filed a grievance. Also, as in all injunction proceedings, the union must prove irreparable harm before an injunction will be issued. In the usual grievance, such as over an improper promotion, layoff, or discharge, there is no irreparable harm to the employee, because the arbitrator can reinstate the employee to the proper position and award full backpay. The employee's inconvenience in working in the wrong job, or being without work while his grievance is pending, is insufficient to justify an injunction.

Some unions opposing the unilateral adoption of drug testing programs by an employer have sought a temporary injunction against the program pending the arbitrator's resolution of the union's grievance challenging the program. These attempts have met with mixed results. In a few cases courts have issued injunctions against drug testing programs pending an arbitrator's decision on the grounds that irreparable harm will result to an employee's privacy rights and to an employee's reputation resulting from a possibly false positive test result. Other courts, however, have denied interim injunctions against drug testing programs. These courts have reasoned that an injunction is permitted only if arbitration of the underlying dispute would be futile unless the injunction is issued, and that drug testing programs do not fall within this narrow exception. Thus, status quo injunctions, although an important remedy in critical situations, will undoubtedly be issued in only a few instances.

K. INTEREST ARBITRATION

The principles previously discussed primarily pertain to grievances arising under the terms of an existing collective bargaining agreement, called "grievance arbitration." There is another type of arbitration known as "interest arbitration." Interest arbitration is arbitration of unresolved bargaining issues on a new or amended agreement. An arbitrator determines the terms of the agreement rather than interpreting the agreement the parties have reached, as in grievance arbitration. A contract clause providing that the contract may be opened at midterm for the purpose of bargaining on wages, and that the matter should be submitted to arbitration if the parties are unable to reach mutual agreement on an increase, is an example of interest arbitration.

The NLRB has held that interest arbitration is a permissive, rather than a mandatory, subject of bargaining. (See Chapter Five for a discussion of the distinction between mandatory and permissive subjects of bargaining.) Therefore, a party cannot bargain to impasse over a proposal for interest arbitration and a union cannot strike to obtain an interest arbitration clause.

Some early court decisions held that a provision requiring interest arbitration is not enforceable under Section 301. Those cases were decided, however, before the Steelworkers trilogy decisions discussed above. The cases since the Trilogy have held that a provision requiring interest arbitration is binding and enforceable under Section 301. Furthermore, under the *Nolde* doctrine, a party may be required to engage in interest arbitration required by a collective bargaining agreement even if the request for such arbitration is made after the contract has expired. However, an agreement to engage in interest arbitration must be expressly spelled out in the contract. A general arbitration clause requiring the arbitration of any dispute arising under the contract applies only to grievance arbitrations. Such a clause does not obligate the party to engage in interest arbitration of new or amended contract terms. In addition, although there have not been many decisions on the issue, it appears that if a party is compelled to take part in interest arbitration for a successor collective bargaining agreement, the arbitrator cannot require that the new agreement again contain an interest arbitration provision, that is, an employer cannot be held to collective bargaining agreements in perpetuity through successive contracts providing for interest arbitration.

L. ARBITRATION AND THE NLRB

1. The Concurrent Role of the Board and the Arbitrator

Under Section 10(a) of the LMRA, the NLRB is empowered to prevent all unfair labor practices. This power cannot be affected by an agreement that the parties may have about adjusting their disputes.

A contract violation is not necessarily an unfair labor practice. At the time the Taft-Hartley Act was under consideration, a proposal was made to make the breach of a contract by either an employer or a union an unfair labor practice. The proposal was rejected and Section 301 was enacted instead. Thus, the Board has no jurisdiction to determine typical employer-union disputes as to a contract's meaning or application. However, the Board has held that the total repudiation of an agreement by either an employer or a union is an unfair labor practice in violation of the duty of good-faith bargaining.

Although the Board does not have general jurisdiction to enforce contracts, some specific contract breaches may also be unfair labor practices. If a union officer is discharged, the employer's action may violate the just cause provisions of the contract and may also be an unfair labor practice if it is in retaliation for the officer's union activities.

Although Section 10(a) establishes the Board's paramount authority, federal labor policy also favors the resolution of disputes through arbitration. The courts and the Board have developed principles balancing the Board's authority with the policy favoring arbitration.

The Supreme Court has held that an arbitrator has authority to resolve a contract dispute even though the facts may also allege an unfair labor practice. Thus, a court can order arbitration of a contract dispute that might also involve an unfair labor practice (such as a discharge of a union officer), applying the same principles that apply to any other case arising under a contract arbitration clause. On the other hand, the Board has authority to remedy unfair labor practices even though there may also be a contract violation. The Supreme Court held in *C & C Plywood* (see Chapter Five) that the Board, not just the arbitrator, has authority to interpret a contract if that is necessary to determine whether an unfair labor practice has occurred.

Often there is no conflict between a Board and an arbitrator's decision. Consider the case of the union officer who was discharged. An arbitrator might decide that the officer was not discharged for cause under the contract, even though the Board might conclude that the discharge was not an unfair labor practice. These decisions do not conflict, because the Board's decision that the employee was not discharged for union activity is not inconsistent with the arbitrator's decision that the discharge was not for cause. The Board's only concern is whether the discharge was for union activity. If the Board concludes that the discharge was not for union activity, it has no authority to determine whether the discharge was for cause under the contract.

What if the arbitrator decides that the discharge was for cause, but the Board decides that the discharge was unlawful? Then the arbitrator and the Board's decision are inconsistent. Under Section 10(a), the Board's decision prevails and the employee would be reinstated.

2. The *Spielberg* Doctrine: Deferral to an Arbitrator's Award

It is in the interest of both the Board and the arbitration process that conflict between arbitrators and the Board be held to a minimum. Industrial peace is not furthered by the same matter being processed before both an arbitrator and the Board. The Board has developed two doctrines limiting the circumstances under which it will decide the merits of an unfair labor practice charge that may also be a contract violation subject to arbitration. The *Spielberg* doctrine governs the circumstances under which the Board will accept a prior arbitration award on an issue that may also be an unfair labor practice.[11] The *Collyer* doctrine governs the circumstances under which the Board will require the parties to arbitrate a dispute before proceeding to the Board.[12]

The Board does not defer to arbitration on representation issues (see Chapter Two), such as the unit placement of disputed employees or whether an existing contract should cover employees in a newly acquired facility. The Board regards representation issues as being within its expertise rather than an arbitrator's. The parties may arbitrate such issues under their contract if they so desire, but the Board does not require that such disputes be arbitrated and is not bound by the arbitrator's decision.

The question of Board deferral to an arbitrator's award frequently arises in cases in which an employee is allegedly discharged without just cause and in violation of Section 8(a)(3) for engaging in concerted activity (see Chapter Four). Another frequent case is that in which an employer's action, such as subcontracting, allegedly violates the collective bargaining agreement and is also a unilateral change in working conditions violating Section 8(a)(5) (see Chapter Five). The Board will not defer to arbitration in Section 8(a)(4) cases (alleged retaliation against an employee for filing an unfair labor practice charge or testifying in Board proceedings).

a. The* Spielberg *Requirements: The Fair Hearing Requirement. The *Spielberg* doctrine, named after the principal case, establishes four requirements that must be met before the Board accepts an arbitrator's decision without a full retrial. First, the arbitration proceedings must be fair and regular so that the employee receives a fair hearing as in a Board proceeding. The Board will consider, for example, whether the grievant was present and permitted to present evidence at the arbitration hearing. Most arbitration hearings are less formal than Board hearings, and such informality is not grounds for refusing to defer as long as the hearing was fair. The Board will not defer to a decision if it is apparent that the union is so hostile to the employee-grievant that the employee's interests were not adequately represented. In that case, the Board will hold a hearing.

b. Binding Arbitration. Second, arbitration of the matter must be mandatory and binding on the parties. If arbitration is voluntary or if one of the parties is free to disregard the arbitrator's decision, the Board will not defer to the award, even if the proceedings were conducted properly.

c. Consistency with Board Policies. Third, the arbitrator's decision must not be repugnant to the Act. This means that the arbitrator's decision cannot be contrary to principles established by the Board, thus depriving an employee of rights guaranteed by the LMRA. Currently, under the most recent restatement of the *Spielberg* doctrine in *Olin Corporation*, the Board regards an arbitrator's decision as repugnant to the Act only if it is "palpably wrong," that is, the decision is not susceptible to an interpretation consistent with the Act.[13] Suppose that an employee is discharged for distributing literature on the employee's own time in a nonwork area, a statutory right under the LMRA. If an arbitrator upholds the dis-

---

[11] See legal principle 10.

[12] See legal principle 11.

[13] See legal principle 10.

charge, the Board will not accept the arbitrator's decision because it is repugnant to the employee's statutory right to distribute literature. The employee will receive a full evidentiary hearing before the Board.

The Board distinguishes between a possible factual error in an arbitrator's decision and an error on a governing legal principle. Suppose in the prior example the arbitrator finds that the employee has, in fact, distributed literature on company time in a work area. That is not a statutory right. If the arbitrator holds that there was just cause for discharge based on this factual determination, the Board will accept the arbitrator's award, provided that the other requirements for deferral (a fair hearing, etc.) are met. The arbitrator's factual determinations, even if in error, are not repugnant to the Act. If an arbitrator's factual decision, however, is clearly erroneous and thus deprives an employee of his statutory rights, the Board will not defer to the arbitrator's award.

d. Consideration of the Unfair Labor Practice Issues. The fourth requirement of the *Spielberg* doctrine is that the arbitrator must consider the unfair labor practice issue for the Board to defer to the decision. The application of this requirement has changed several times with changes in the Board's membership. At times, the Board has required that the unfair labor practice issue must be both presented to and expressly considered by the arbitrator. Under this approach, if a union filed a charge that an employee allegedly discharged for drug abuse was discharged for union activity, the Board would not defer to an arbitrator's award upholding the discharge if the only issue submitted to the arbitrator pertained to the alleged drug abuse and no mention was made of the employee's participation in union activities, or if the arbitrator did not expressly consider the unfair labor practice issue in the decision. At other times, the Board has deferred to an arbitrator's decision if (1) the contractual issue is factually parallel to the unfair labor practice charge

and (2) the arbitrator is presented generally with the facts relevant to resolving the unfair labor practice matter, even if the unfair labor practice issue is not specifically presented to and expressly considered by the arbitrator. The Board ruled most recently in the *Olin Corporation* case, that it will follow the "factually parallel" test, and that the party opposing deferral to an arbitrator's decision has the burden to establish that the deferral standards have not been met. In the past, the Board required the party favoring deferral to prove that the requirements for deferral have been met.

The "factually parallel" test is more likely to deprive an employee of statutorily protected rights in a specific case than the alternate test requiring that the unfair labor practice issue be both presented to and considered by the arbitrator. Indeed, at least one court of appeals has refused to enforce a Board decision applying the factually parallel test as set forth in *Olin* on the grounds that it gives up too much of the Board's statutory responsibility to protect individual employee rights. Ultimately, given the importance of the deferral standards and the Board's shifting position on the issue, the matter may have to be resolved by the Supreme Court.

If all four *Spielberg* requirements are met, the Board will accept an arbitrator's award and not relitigate the same issues. If any of the factors are not met, the Board will not defer and will hold a hearing as in any other unfair labor practice case. What if an employer refuses to comply with an arbitrator's decision favorable to the union? It is arguable that in that event the Board should proceed with the unfair labor practice case. However, the Board has not adopted this approach. It still defers to the arbitration process, and the union must seek judicial enforcement of the award.

3. Requiring Arbitration Before Board Proceedings: The *Collyer* Doctrine

The *Spielberg* doctrine pertains to deferral to an arbitrator's award. But if the union does not request arbitration, but goes directly to the Board, should the Board proceed or require the parties to arbitrate their dispute? The Board's approach to this issue is known as the *Collyer* doctrine.

In *Collyer*, the union alleged that an employer had made certain unilateral changes in wages and working conditions in violation of Section 8(a)(5). The employer argued that the contract and past practice authorized the changes so that there was no need to bargain with the union first. An employer has no duty to bargain before making unilateral changes the contact permits (see Chapter Five). In *Collyer*, the Board held that if the determination of a Section 8(a)(5) violation depends upon interpreting the contract and the contract provides for arbitration, the Board will require the parties to arbitrate their dispute before proceeding to the Board.

Although *Collyer* entailed an alleged employer unilateral action violating Section 8(a)(5), the Board quickly expanded the doctrine to cover virtually any case in which the actions that give rise to an unfair labor practice charge are also a contract violation subject to arbitration. Thus, if a union filed a charge that an employee was discharged for union activity in violation of Sections 8(a)(1) and 8(a)(3), but the discharge might also have violated the contractual just cause provision, the Board required the union to arbitrate the dispute. Following a change in Board membership, however, the Board reversed its position and returned to the original doctrine under which the Board deferred only to cases of alleged unilateral action violating Section 8(a)(5). Most recently, however, in the *United Technologies* case, the Board again ruled that it would apply the *Collyer* doctrine broadly to Section 8(a)(1), 8(a)(3), and 8(a)(5) cases.[14] This is obviously an issue on which the Board, with further changes in its membership, could change its position once again.

What if the union files a grievance on a matter on which the Board does not require arbitration under the *Collyer* doctrine, but then files an unfair labor practice charge as well. Under the *Dubo* doctrine[15] (named after the case establishing the principle), the Board will defer the case to arbitration, and will not proceed with the unfair labor practice charge while arbitration is pending. However, if the union withdraws the grievance, and the dispute is not one in which deferral is required under *Collyer*, the Board will proceed with the unfair labor practice charge. The *Dubo* doctrine is not very important when, as at present, the *Collyer* doctrine is broadly applied to Section 8(a)(1), (3), and (5) cases, but the doctrine will be important again if the Board should return to a narrow application of *Collyer* to Section 8(a)(5) cases only.

4. Procedure in Cases Deferred to Arbitration

The Board's procedure in cases that still fall within the *Collyer* or *Dubo* doctrines is to make a preliminary determination on whether a charge may have merit. If the charge lacks merit, it is dismissed outright. Remember, even though the Board might conclude that there is no statutory violation, there might still be a contractual one. If the Board determines that a charge may have merit, it will defer the charge to arbitration, but retain jurisdiction while arbitration is proceeding. In that way, the six-month limit for filing a charge does not expire. If the charging party is dissatisfied with the arbitrator's decision, it may request that the Board reassert jurisdiction. The Board will consider whether to accept the arbitrator's decision under the *Spielberg* doctrine. If the *Spielberg* criteria are met, the Board dismisses the unfair labor practice charge. If the criteria are not met, the Board reasserts its jurisdiction and considers the charge on the merits. The filing of a grievance does not toll the six-month period for filing an unfair labor practice charge. Therefore, most unions in a case involving both unfair labor practice and contract violations file an unfair labor practice charge even though it

[14] See legal principle 11.

[15] See legal principle 11.

will be deferred to arbitration in order to meet the statutory time limit and preserve the possibility of review under the *Spielberg* standards. Otherwise, the limitations period might pass before the arbitrator ruled.

Remember that most cases involving the *Spielberg* or *Dubo* doctrines do not actually reach the Board. If an unfair labor practice charge is filed prior to arbitration the regional director decides whether the case falls within the *Collyer* or *Dubo* doctrines or whether a complaint should be issued leading ultimately to a trial and a Board decision. Similarly, the regional director decides whether an arbitrator's decision meets the *Spielberg* standards or a complaint should be issued.

5. Exceptions to the *Collyer* Doctrine

There are few exceptions to the *Collyer* doctrine as presently applied. The most important is that the employer must be willing to arbitrate a dispute on the merits before the Board will defer it to arbitration. If a union files an unfair labor practice charge, and the employer maintains that the dispute is not arbitrable, the Board will not defer. Similarly, if a union files an untimely grievance and the employer raises a procedural defense, the Board does not defer to arbitration. If the employer delays arbitration proceedings, the Board reasserts jurisdiction and proceeds. Also, if an employer essentially has repudiated the agreement, the Board does not defer to arbitration. Finally, remember that the *Collyer* doctrine applies only if the collective bargaining agreement provides for binding arbitration. Since, as discussed above, arbitration is a matter of contract, the Board will not order arbitration if the contract does not provide for it.

Summary   This chapter considered the enforcement of collective bargaining agreements under Section 301 of the Labor Management Relations Act. Section 301 permits either an employer or a union to enforce the terms of a contract against the other. Individual employees may also bring suit under some circumstances.

Suits under Section 301 can be brought by or against the union as an entity in federal court. Suits to enforce contracts can also be brought in state courts, but the state courts must apply federal law so that uniformity in enforcing agreements, a prime goal of Section 301, is maintained. Employer suits against unions for damages and/or injunctive relief growing out of a strike and breach of contract are brought under Section 301.

Before an employer can sue the union for breach of contract, the employer must first exhaust the contractual arbitration provisions unless it is clear that the employer has no contractual right to file a grievance.

The *Lincoln Mills* decision established that a grievance arbitration provision in a collective bargaining agreement can be enforced under Section 301, an important change from state law under which a party could take a matter to court notwithstanding an agreement to arbitrate. In the landmark "Steelworkers Trilogy," the Court held that the parties should be required to arbitrate a dispute subject to arbitration under their contract unless it can be stated with positive assurance that the arbitration clause of the collective bargaining agreement does not apply to the particular dispute. Doubts are to be resolved in favor of arbitration, and the courts cannot consider the merits of a dispute in determining its arbitrability. An arbitrator's decision must be enforced by a court as long as it draws its essence from the collective bargaining agreement even though the court may disagree with the arbitrator's decision. Under the *Misco* decision, an arbitrator's decision may be set aside on the grounds that it violates "public policy" only if it would violate an explicit public policy that is well defined and dominant, not on general considerations of supposed public interest.

Procedural or equitable defenses to arbitration pertain to the merits of a grievance and must be decided by the arbitrator, not by a court. Thus a court must order arbitration if a dispute is covered by the contract even though the grievance is filed late. The arbitrator decides whether the grievance is untimely or, if it is, whether there is some special circumstance for which the time limit should not be applied. Unless expressly limited by the contract, the arbitrator has very broad authority on procedural and evidentiary issues arising during the hearing. However, under the doctrine of functus officio, an arbitrator has no power to modify or clarify his award after it is issued unless the parties mutually agree or the contract grants the arbitrator such authority.

An arbitrator has authority to resolve a contract dispute even though the facts may also allege an unfair labor practice. Under the *Spielberg* doctrine, the Board, to avoid conflict, will accept an arbitrator's decision meeting its standards rendered on an issue that may also be an unfair labor practice.

Under the *Collyer* doctrine as currently applied, if a contract provides for arbitration, the Board requires the parties to arbitrate cases alleging that an employer's unilateral action violates the contract and Sections 8(a)(1), (3), or (5) of the Act. The Board reviews an arbitrator's decision in cases deferred to arbitration under the *Spielberg* standards requiring that the employee involved receives a fair hearing, that the arbitrator's decision be consistent with Board policies, and that the arbitrator consider the unfair labor practice issue. However, at present the Board will defer to an arbitrator's decision even if the arbitrator did not expressly consider the unfair labor practice issues if the contractual and statutory issues are factually parallel and the arbitrator was presented generally with the facts relevant to resolving the unfair labor practice.

Review Questions

1. Does Section 301 apply only to contracts between an employer and a union?
2. Can an employee sue a local union for violation of the local's bylaws under Section 301?
3. Does Section 301 apply to a collective bargaining agreement between a governmental agency and a public employee union?
4. Is a dispute that arises after a contract has expired arbitrable?
5. Can an individual employee bring a suit to enforce contract rights contrary to a union's settlement of a grievance?
6. How long does a party have to bring a suit under Section 301?

7. What is the federal standard for enforcing an agreement to arbitrate?

8. To what extent can the courts consider the merits of a dispute in determining its arbitrability?

9. What is the importance of the *Warrior and Gulf* decision?

10. Must a court enforce an arbitrator's decision that is clearly wrong?

11. Is an employer required to arbitrate a claim for damages growing out of a union's breach of a no-strike clause?

12. What is the difference between grievance and interest arbitration?

13. Which decision will prevail if there are any inconsistent decisions by an arbitrator and the NLRB over a matter that is both an alleged contract violation and an unfair labor practice?

14. Is there any advantage for a union to file an unfair labor practice charge over a matter that the Board will defer to arbitration anyway?

(Answers to review questions are at the end of the book.)

Basic Legal Principles

1. Suits brought under Section 301 to enforce a collective bargaining agreement can be brought in federal or state court, but federal law governs in either court in determining the merits. Only the union as an entity is liable for damages against it. *Textile Workers Union v. Lincoln Mills*, 353 U.S. 448, 40 LRRM 2113 (1957); *Smith v. Evening News Assn.*, 371 U.S. 195, 51 LRRM 2646 (1962); *Atkinson v. Sinclair Refining Co.*, 370 U.S. 238, 50 LRRM 2433 (1962); *Plumbers v. Plumbers Local 334*, 452 U.S. 615, 107 LRRM 2715 (1981). (International constitution is enforceable contract under Section 301); *Local 367 v. Graham County Electric*, 783 F.2d 897, 121 LRRM 2924 (9th Cir. 1986); *Lewis v. Teamsters Local 771*, 826 F.2d 1310, 126 LRRM 2030 (3d Cir. 1987); *Mack Truck v. Auto Workers*, 856 F.2d 579, 129 LRRM 2338 (3d Cir. 1988); *Groves v. Ring Screw Works*, 882 F.2d 1081, 132 LRRM 2306 (6th Cir. 1989) (individual suits by members to enforce contract).

2. Since Section 301 does not specify the time limit for filing a suit to enforce contractual rights thereunder, the federal courts look to the analogous state law or to the United States Arbitration Act for guidance. In general, a suit to modify, clarify, or vacate an arbitrator's award must be filed within the state law time limit for appealing an arbitrator's decision, most commonly ninety days. A suit to compel arbitration must be brought within six months from the date the other party refuses a demand for arbitration, but a suit to enforce an award may be brought within the state limitations period for filing a suit on any contract right, typically in the range of two to five years or longer. *CWA v. Western Electric Co.*, 860 F.2d 1137, 129 LRRM 2933 (1st Cir. 1988) (six months to compel arbitration); *Teamsters Local 174 v. Trick & Murray*, 828 F.2d 1418, 126 LRRM 2736 (9th Cir. 1987) (six months to compel arbitration); *Occidental Chemical Corp. v. ICWU*, 853 F.2d 1310, 128 LRRM 3161 (6th Cir. 1988) (ninety days to file suit to vacate award); *Pension Fund v. Domas Mechanical*,

778 F.2d 1266, 121 LRRM 2146 (7th Cir. 1985); *Smith v. Kerrville Bus Co.,* 748 F.2d 1049, 118 LRRM 2164 (5th Cir. 1984); *Teamsters Local 579 v. B&M Transit Inc.,* 882 F.2d 274, 132 LRRM 2255 (7th Cir. 1989.)

3. Under the "Steelworkers Trilogy," (1) the function of a court is limited to determining whether the party seeking arbitration has a claim which, on its face, is governed by the contract; (2) doubts on the coverage of the arbitration clause should be resolved in favor of arbitration; (3) courts cannot consider the merits of a dispute in determining arbitrability; and (4) an arbitrator's award must be enforced if it draws its essence from the collective bargaining agreement even though a court may disagree with the result. *Steelworkers v. Warrior & Gulf Navigation Co.,* 363 U.S. 574, 46 LRRM 2416 (1960); *Steelworkers v. American Manufacturing Co.,* 363 U.S. 564, 46 LRRM 2414 (1960); *United Steelworkers v. Enterprise Wheel & Car Corp.,* 363 U.S. 593, 46 LRRM 2423 (1960); *AT&T Technologies v. CWA,* 475 U.S. 643, 121 LRRM 3329 (1986); *Local 261 v. Great Northern Paper Co.,* 765 F.2d 295, 119 LRRM 3082 (1st Cir. 1985); *Dobbs, Inc. v. Teamsters Local 614,* 813 F.2d 85, 124 LRRM 2827 (6th Cir. 1987); *Grigoleit Co. v. Local 270,* 769 F.2d 434, 119 LRRM 3585 (7th Cir. 1985); *Roadmaster v. Laborers Local 504,* 851 F.2d 886, 129 LRRM 2449 (7th Cir. 1988); *McGraw Edison v. Local 1104 IUOE,* 767 F.2d 485, 119 LRRM 3403 (8th Cir. 1985); *Local 206 v. R. K. Burner Sheet Metal, Inc.,* 859 F.2d 758, 129 LRRM 2866 (9th Cir. 1988) (enforcement of interest arbitration award).

4. An arbitrator's award may be set aside on public policy grounds only if it violates some explicit public policy that is well defined and dominant, not just general considerations of supposed public policy. Arbitrators also have very broad authority to determine the appropriate remedy for a contract violation unless the contract expressly limits the authority; but, in general, punitive damages can be awarded only if the contract expressly provides for them. *United Paperworkers Union v. Misco,* 484 U.S. 29, 126 LRRM 3113 (1987); *W. R. Grace & Co. v. Rubber Workers Local 759,* 461 U.S. 757, 113 LRRM 2641 (1983); *Postal Workers v. Postal Service,* 789, F.2d 1, 122 LRRM 2094 (D.C. Cir. 1986); *Foley Co. v. Electrical Workers Local 639,* 789 F.2d 1421, 122 LRRM 2471 (9th Cir. 1986) (no punitive damages); *S. D. Warren Co. v. Local 1069,* 846 F.2d 827, 128 LRRM 2432 (1st Cir. 1988); *Daniel Construction Co. v. Local 257 IBEW,* 856 F.2d 1174, 129 LRRM 2429 (8th Cir. 1988).

5. Courts determine whether a particular dispute is subject to arbitration, but procedural defenses, such as timeliness and equitable defenses, are determined by the arbitrator. *John Wiley & Sons, Inc. v. Livingston,* 376 U.S. 543, 55 LRRM 2769 (1964); *Operating Engineers Local 150 v. Flair Builders,* 406 U.S. 487, 80 LRRM 2441 (1972); *Franklin Electric Co. v. UAW,* ___F.2d___, 132 LRRM 2457 (8th Cir. 1989).

6. The arbitrator has broad authority, unless expressly limited by the contract, over the conduct of a hearing and any evidentiary issues which may arise. However, an arbitrator has no power to reconsider a decision

or to modify, clarify, or interpret an award after it is issued unless the contract grants such authority or the parties mutually agree that the arbitrator may do so. If a suit is filed under Section 301 to enforce or set aside an award, the court has authority to remand the matter to the arbitrator for clarification or modification even though the arbitrator cannot do so on the arbitrator's own authority. *United Paper Workers Union v. Misco* in legal principle 4; *Electrical Workers v. N.E. Telephone Co.*, 628 F.2d 644, 105 LRRM 2211 (1st Cir. 1980); *Teamsters Local 115 v. Desoto, Inc.*, 725 F.2d 931, 115 LRRM 2449 (3d Cir. 1984); *Ethyl Corp. v. Steelworkers*, 768 F.2d 180, 119 LRRM 3566 (7th Cir. 1985); *Local P–9 v. George A. Hormel & Co.*, 776 F.2d 1393, 120 LRRM 3283 (8th Cir. 1985); *Sunshine Mining Co. v. Steelworkers*, 823 F.2d 1289, 124 LRRM 3198 (9th Cir. 1987).

7. A court may enforce an agreement to arbitrate, even though a contract violation is also an unfair labor practice, but the Board's decision prevails in case of conflict between a Board and arbitrator's decision. *Carey v. Westinghouse Electric Corp.*, 375 U.S. 261, 55 LRRM 2042 (1964); *Local 4-23 v. American Petofina Co.*, 759 F.2d 512, 119 LRRM 2395 (5th Cir. 1985).

8. An employer can be required to arbitrate a work assignment dispute with only one of two competing unions although both claim the same work under their respective collective bargaining agreements. *Carey v. Westinghouse Electric Corp.*, in legal principle 7.

9. A successor employer may be required to arbitrate the extent to which the successor incurred any obligation under its predecessor's collective bargaining agreement. Since the *Burns Detective* decision, however, it is unlikely that the union would prevail on the merits of any such claim. Compare *John Wiley & Sons, Inc. v. Livingston* in legal principle 5 with *Howard Johnson Co. v. Hotel & Restaurant Employees Detroit Local Joint Board*, 417 U.S. 249, 86 LRRM 2449 (1974).

10. The Board will defer to an arbitrator's decision if (1) the arbitration proceeding is fair and regular; (2) the arbitration proceeding is final and binding on the parties; (3) the award is not repugnant to the policies of the Act; and (4) the arbitrator considered the unfair labor practice issue. At present, the Board will defer to an arbitrator's decision even if the arbitrator does not expressly consider the unfair labor practice issue as long as the contractual and unfair labor practice issues are factually parallel and the arbitrator is presented generally with the facts relevant to resolving the unfair labor practice. *Spielberg Mfg. Co.*, 112 NLRB No. 1080, 36 LRRM 1152 (1955). Compare *Olin Corp.*, 268 NLRB No. 86, 115 LRRM 1056 (1984) (applying factually parallel test) with *Propoco, Inc.*, 263 NLRB No. 34, 110 LRRM 1496 (1982) and *Suburban Motor Freight*, 247 NLRB 146, 103 LRRM 1113 (1980) (arbitrator must actually consider the unfair labor practice issue). Contrast *NLRB v. Aces Mechanical Corp.*, 837 F.2d 570, 127 LRRM 2513 (2d Cir. 1988) (upholding factually parallel test) with *Taylor v. NLRB*, 786 F.2d 1516, 122 LRRM 2084 (11th Cir. 1986)

(Olin deferral standards impermissibly broad deferral of statutory authority to arbitration). See also *J & H Rainwear*, 273 NLRB No. 78, 118 LRRM 1074 (1984) (deferring to arbitration even though employer refused to comply with award); *Garland Coal & Mining Co.*, 276 NLRB No. 102, 120 LRRM 1159 (1985); *Manitowoc Engineering Co.*, 291 NLRB No. 122, 130 LRRM 1072 (1988).

11. If the contract provides for arbitration and a contract violation may also violate Sections 8(a)(1), (3), or (5), or 8(b)(1)(A) or (2) of the Act, the Board defers the unfair labor practice charge to arbitration. The arbitrator's award is subject to review under the *Spielberg* standards (legal principle 10). The Board will not defer to arbitration if the employer is unwilling to arbitrate the dispute on its merits, for example, the employer alleges that the dispute is not arbitrable or that the grievance was untimely. *Collyer Insulated Wire*, 192 NLRB 837, 77 LRRM 1931 (1971). Compare *United Technologies Corp.*, 268 NLRB No. 83, 115 LRRM 1049 (1984) (current broad deferral policy) with *General American Transportation Co.*, 228 NLRB 808, 94 LRRM 1483 (1977) (narrow deferral to Secton 8(a)(5) allegations only). See *Consolidated Freightways Corp.*, 288 NLRB No. 144, 128 LRRM 1198 (1988); *NLRB v. Paper Manufacturers Co.*, 786 F.2d 163, 121 LRRM 3278 (3d Cir. 1986) (no deferral in representation cases). Compare *Dubo Mfg. Co.*, 142 NLRB 812, 53 LRRM 1158 (1963) (Board will defer to arbitration procedure [in cases in which deferral not required under *Collyer*] as long as charging party continues to process the grievance).

12. There is a presumption that grievances arising after a contract expires are arbitrable if they pertain to the continued applicability of a contractual provision after the expiration date (e.g., contractual severance pay if a facility closes several days after the contract expires). This presumption can be negated by express contract language or by clear implication. As a general rule, a grievance occurring after an expiration date is arbitrable only if the grievance involves rights that vested or accrued at least in part while the contract was in effect or that relate to events that occurred at least in part during the contract term. *Nolde Brothers Inc. v. Bakery & Confectionery Worker Union Local 358*, 430 U.S. 243, 94 LRRM 2753 (1977); *Teamsters Local 238 v. C.R.S.T., Inc.*, 795 F.2d 1400, 122 LRRM 2993 (8th Cir. 1986); *Local 2 v. Chicago Tribune*, 794 F.2d 1222, 123 LRRM 2488 (7th Cir. 1986); *Local 174 v. Hebrew National Kosher Foods, Inc.*, 818 F.2d 283, 125 LRRM 2486 (2d Cir. 1987); *Local 70 v. Interstate Distributor Co.*, 832 F.2d 507, 126 LRRM 3127 (9th Cir. 1987); *Indiana & Michigan Electric Co.*, 284 NLRB No. 7, 125 LRRM 1097 (1987); *Uppco Inc.*, 288 NLRB No. 98, 128 LRRM 1129 (1988); *IBEW Local 113*, 132 LRRM 1297, 296 NLRB No. 144 (1989) (enforcement of agreement for interest arbitration).

13. Employers may be required to exhaust contractual remedies before bringing suit against the union for breach of contract. A union's breach of the no-strike clause does not release the employer from its

obligation to arbitrate. *Packinghouse Workers Local 721 v. Needham Packing Co.*, 376 U.S. 247, 55 LRRM 2580 (1964); *Lehigh Portland Cement v. Cement Workers*, 849 F.2d 820, 128 LRRM 2766 (3d Cir. 1988).

14. A Court may enter an injunction to require an employer to maintain the status quo pending arbitration of a contractual dispute if necessary to preserve the effectiveness of the arbitrator's remedy, and the union would otherwise suffer irreparable harm for which a monetary remedy could not provide complete relief. Compare *Machinists Local Lodge 1266 v. Panoramic Corp.*, 668 F.2d 276, 109 LRRM 2169 (7th Cir. 1981) (granting status quo injunction to prohibit sale of company's assets) with *Postal Workers v. Bolger*, 621 F.2d. 615, 104 LRRM 2341 (4th Cir. 1980) (denying injunction to prohibit transfer of employees pending arbitration of dispute as to shift merger). Regarding injunctions against unilaterally implemented drug testing program pending arbitration, see *Utility Workers Local 246 v. Southern California Edison*, 852 F.2d 1083, 129 LRRM 2077 (9th Cir. 1988) (denying injunction); *IBEW Local 1900 v. Pepco*, 634 F.Supp. 642, 121 LRRM 3278 (D.C. Dist. Ct. 1986) (denying injunction); *Local 2-286 v. Amoco Oil Co.*, ___F.2d___, 132 LRRM 2533 (10th Cir. 1989) (granting injunction).

Recommended Reading

Bush, "The Nature of the Deferral Problem Involving Section 8(a)(1) and 8(a)(3) Charges," 39 *Lab. L.J.* 131 (1988).

Dunsford, "The Judicial Doctrine of Public Policy: *Misco* Reviewed," 4 *Lab. Lawyer* 669 (1988).

Edwards, "Arbitration as an Alternative in Equal Employment Disputes," 33 *Arb. J.* 22 (1978).

Henkel and Kelly, "Deferral to Arbitration After *Olin*: Has the NLRB Gone Too Far?" 43 *Wash. & Lee L. Rev.* 37 (1986).

Hogler, "Just Cause, Judicial Review, and Industrial Justice: An Arbitral Critique," 40 *Lab. L. J.* 281 (1989).

Meltzer, "After the Labor Arbitration Award: The Public Policy Defense," 10 *Ind. Rel. L.J.* 241 (1988).

Parker, "Judicial Review of Labor Arbitration Awards: *Misco* and its Impact on the Public Policy Exception," 4 *Lab. Laywer* 683 (1988).

Rudyk, "The Relationship between Federal Sector Arbitration and the MSPB," 37 *Lab. L.J.* 372 (1986).

St. Antoine, "Current Issues in Arbitration Law," 10 *Ind. Rel. L.J.* 2 (1988).

Wayland, Stephens, and Franklin, "*Misco:* Its Impact on Arbitration Awards," 39 *Lab. L.J.* 813 (1988).

Werner and Holtzman, "Clarification of Arbitration Awards," 3 Lab. Lawyer 183 (1987).

chapter 10

UNION MEMBERSHIP
AND UNION SECURITY

This chapter includes a discussion of the internal relationship between a union and its own members, including the nature of the legal relationship, the right to union membership, required union membership (union security agreements), and related matters.

A. THE UNION AS AN UNINCORPORATED ASSOCIATION

1. The Labor Union at Common Law

To understand the legal relationship between the union and its members, it is necessary to understand what a union is. Of course, a union is an organization that engages in collective bargaining, but there is a common law legal definition of a union that is important to understand. Common law is the law gradually developed over the years by judges through decisions handed down in individual cases, in contrast to statutory law such as the Labor Management Relations Act, passed by a legislative body. For example, most of the legal principles governing the right to own, buy, and sell real estate are based on the common law. In contrast, worker's compensation law is statutory.

Under common law, a union is regarded as an unincorporated association, as is a partnership, another form of unincorporated association. A labor organization, as an unincorporated association, is simply a combination of members. It has no legal existence apart from its members. A corporation is different. It is a legal entity, legally separate from the stockholders. The officers or shareholders of a corporation may change, but the corporation continues to exist. A corporation sues and is sued in its corporate name. It is not necessary to sue the officers or the shareholders to enforce a corporation's legal obligations. In contrast, an unincorporated association cannot sue or be sued as an entity because it has no separate legal existence apart from its members. It is necessary to sue the individual members to enforce the association's legal obligations.

Because it is not practical to sue individually all the members of a large union, the law allows large unincorporated groups to sue or be sued as a class. A representative group, usually a union's officers, can file suit or can be sued on behalf of all the members as a class. The decision is binding on all members of the class as if they had been sued individually.

Under the common law, every member of a union was individually liable for a judgment rendered against the association in a class action. The personal assets of each and every union member could be attached to pay a judgment against a union. Of course, there were limitations. Most states restricted property that could be seized to collect the judgment. In many cases employers with judgments against union members as a class found collection procedures so cumbersome that they either did not bother to collect or compromised their claim to avoid the problem.

2. The Union under Federal Law

The legal status of a union has changed under federal law. Section 301 of the LMRA, pertaining to suits for the enforcement of contracts, specifically provides that a labor organization may sue or be sued as an entity in federal court, but a judgment against a union is only enforceable against the union's assets, not against individual union members (see Chapter Nine).

Section 303, which pertains to private damage suits against unions for engaging in secondary boycotts (see Chapter Seven), provides that the procedures of Section 301 are to be followed under Section 303, thus permitting a union to be sued as an entity under Section 303.

In addition to the specific statutory authority under Sections 301 and 303, the Supreme Court has held that a union may sue or be sued as an entity in the federal courts in any action involving application of a federal law to a union. For example, a union may be sued as an entity for alleged violations of the federal antitrust laws (see Chapter Eight), even though these laws do not specifically authorize such suits.

3. The Continued Applicability of State Law to Unions

The common law rule that a union is an unincorporated association still has practical importance. Many union matters are not regulated by federal law. A union's right to own real estate involves continued application of the old common law rules. In most states an unincorporated association cannot hold real estate in its own name. How does a union own its hall? Technically, each union member can individually own a portion. But that is a practical impossibility. Every time a member left, the member would have to deed back the portion. To avoid these problems most unions establish a separate building corporation that owns the hall. Alternately, a union can establish a separate real estate trust and union members can serve as trustees to hold title to the union's property. Some states now permit unincorporated associations to own real estate in their own name so that these technicalities are no longer necessary.

4. Federal Court Application of Common Law Rules

Sometimes the federal courts have a case that involves a union in which state rather than federal law applies. Suppose a union in one state contracts to purchase office equipment from a supplier in another state. A dispute arises and the union refuses to pay for the equipment. The federal courts have jurisdiction to decide cases in which the parties to a suit are from different states and the amount involved in the suit exceeds $50,000, even though there is no federal law involved. The federal court applies the relevant state law in deciding the case. This is called diversity jurisdiction.

The federal courts still apply the old common law rule governing unions as unincorporated associations in diversity jurisdiction cases. Thus, the supplier in the example must bring suit against the union members as a class, not against the union as an entity as it could if a federal law were involved. There is a requirement in federal court diversity cases that there be complete diversity between the parties. That means that none of the defendants can reside in the same state as the plaintiff. What if a union located in New Jersey has members who live in both New York and New Jersey? A New York supplier cannot file a diversity suit in the federal courts against the New Jersey union on a state law claim because some of the defendant union members live in the same state as the plaintiff supplier. There would not be complete diversity. So, the common law rule covering the union as an unincorporated association still applies and has importance today. Remember, these rules apply only to common law actions brought in federal courts. Suits based on federal labor laws can be brought directly against the union as an entity.

B. THE CONTRACTUAL RELATIONSHIP BETWEEN A UNION AND ITS MEMBERS

If a union is an unincorporated association composed of its membership, how are the rights and responsibilities of the members determined? The courts have traditionally held that the relationship between a union and its members is contractual. The union's constitution and bylaws are the contract. The individual, by becoming a union member, becomes contractually bound by the constitution and bylaws.

Suppose a union's bylaws provide that dues are $25 a month. If a member refuses to pay, can the union collect the dues in court, even though the member personally voted against the increase? Yes, because by becoming a union member, the member became contractually bound to pay the dues provided in the bylaws. Suppose the bylaws provide that if a member is sued for delinquent dues, the member must pay the union's attorney's fees for collecting the amount owed. Normally under our court system, each side in a suit must pay their own attorney fees unless a statute (such as certain civil rights statutes) provides that the winning side is entitled to an attorney's fee from the loser. However, a union can collect its attorney's fees from the member who is being sued for delinquent dues because the member is contractually bound to pay the union's legal fees in accordance with the bylaw provision.

The common-law principle that a union member is bound by the constitution and bylaws as a contract has been modified to an extent by the Labor Management Relations Act and the Labor-Management Reporting and Disclosure Act. These statutes guarantee members certain rights that the bylaws cannot change but still give unions great leeway in internal regulation through their constitution and bylaws (see Chapter Eleven).

If a union wants to enforce a bylaw provision or collect a fine in court against a member, the suit must be filed in the state court because the union is enforcing its bylaws as a matter of state contract law. Since enforcing a bylaw is a common law rather than a federal statutory right, the union has to file suit through its members as a class except in those few states that have adopted statutes permitting unions to file suit as an entity. The union officers can be named as the plaintiffs representing the entire membership.

C. THE RIGHT TO UNION MEMBERSHIP

Since a union was regarded as a private association at common law, the courts held that a union had the right to admit whomever it wished as members, the same as a fraternal organization or a social club. A union had no obligation to admit all employees to membership.

Except to the extent that federal or state law prohibits discrimination in selecting members (see Chapter Thirteen), unions still have the common law right as a private association to determine eligibility for membership. Congress recognized a union's right to establish its own membership requirements in LMRA Section 8(b)(1)(A), providing that nothing in that section should impair the right of a labor organization to prescribe its own rules with respect to the acquisition or retention of union membership. There are many reasons for which a union can still choose to exclude certain persons. Some international union constitutions prohibit a person from joining one local of the international if that person still owes a debt to another local. That is a valid restriction that a union has the right to impose as a private organization.

D. REQUIRED UNION MEMBERSHIP

1. Statutory Provisions on Union Security Clauses

Section 8(a)(3) permits a company and a union to negotiate an agreement requiring union membership as a condition of employment on or after the thirtieth day following the beginning of employment or the effective date of the contract, whichever comes later. Under Section 8(f), an agreement can require union membership in the construction industry after the seventh day of employment. Contract provisions requiring union membership are commonly called union security clauses. Section 8(a)(3) prohibits an employer from discharging an employee because of membership or nonmembership in the union except if the employee has refused to pay uniformly required initiation fees and dues and initiation fee under a union security clause. Section 8(b)(2) prohibits a union from requesting an employee's discharge for nonmembership except for failure to tender the periodic dues and initiation fee required under a union security clause.

Under Section 19 of the LMRA, as amended effective December 24, 1980, any employee who is a member of and adheres to established and traditional tenets or teachings of a bona fide religion, body, or sect that has historically held conscientious objections to joining or financially supporting a union cannot be required to join or financially support the union as a condition of employment. However, under Section 19, an employer and union may contrac-

tually agree that an employee who has such religious objections may be required to pay a sum equal to the union's periodic dues and initiation fee to a nonreligious, nonlabor charity chosen by the employee from a list of at least three such funds designated in the contract. If the contract does not designate the fund, then the employee may choose any such fund. As an important limitation, Section 19 also provides that an employee holding conscientious objections to joining or supporting a union, who requests a union to use the grievance-arbitration procedure on his behalf, may be required to pay a charge to the union for the reasonable costs for using such procedures. Title VII of the Civil Rights Act of 1964, as amended, may also require a union to make a "reasonable accommodation" for an employee who has a religious objection to joining a labor organization (see discussion in Chapter Thirteen).

2. Types of Union Security Clauses

Section 8(a)(3) specifically authorizes contracts requiring union membership after thirty days of employment. A thirty-day provision is the most common form of union security clause, but it is not the only kind. There are three basic kinds of union security clauses: (1) the union shop clause, (2) the maintenance of membership clause, and (3) the agency shop clause. Although Section 8(a)(3) expressly refers to only the thirty-day union shop agreement, the Supreme Court has held that the lesser varieties of union security, such as maintenance of membership or agency shop, are also permitted. Prior to the Taft-Hartley Act, which enacted Section 8(a)(3), closed shops were permitted. A closed shop provision, which Section 8(a)(3) abolished, required that an employee be a union member in order to be hired for a job.

A union shop clause is one that requires that an employee become a union member on or after thirty days of employment or after the seventh day in the construction industry. Of course, a collective bargaining agreement can provide for a longer employment period than the statutory minimum, but it cannot require a shorter period. Remember that, as discussed above, employees with religious objections to joining a union have the right to pay the equivalent of the initiation fee and dues to a charity instead.

Under a maintenance of membership clause, each employee who is a union member on the effective date of the contract must remain a member, but the initial decision to join is voluntary. Maintenance of membership clauses frequently contain an escape provision allowing an employee to resign membership during a specified period before the contract's termination date. Membership is automatically renewed for anyone who does not resign during this period.

Sometimes a contract combines maintenance of membership and union shop provisions. A clause may state that employees already employed on the contract's effective date will not be required to join the union, but must remain members once they do join. All newly hired employees will be required to join the union after thirty days. This combination occurs most frequently when a union organizes a new employer and the employer objects to requiring "old and faithful employees" to join the union.

An agency shop is a contract provision under which employees do not have to join the union but are required to pay a service fee instead. This type of provision is becoming especially popular among public-employee unions in states that prohibit compulsory membership for governmental employees. The Supreme Court has upheld the constitutionality of agency shop clauses applied to state public employees if the state law permits such a clause.

All forms of union security clauses under the LMRA must provide for the minimum applicable thirty- or seven-day grace period.

a. Union Security and Probationary Periods.
What if a collective bargaining agreement has a ninety-day probationary period during which the employer can discharge

employees without just cause? Can a union have a union security clause requiring employees to join the union in thirty days, even though the employee is still subject to discharge? Yes, because there is no necessary correlation between a probationary period and union membership. Although probationary employees may be subjected to discharge, they are covered by other contractual provisions. A union has the duty to represent these employees whether or not they are union members. Thus, it is not unreasonable to require probationary employees to join. Some unions may, however, conclude, on balance, that it is too burdensome administratively to take in employees as members before their probationary period is over.

3. The Financial Core Member

Although Section 8(a)(3) refers to mandatory union membership, the Supreme Court held in *General Motors* that an employee cannot actually be required to join the union, but only to pay the initiation fee and monthly dues.[1] The Court reached this conclusion based upon the language of Sections 8(a)(3) and 8(b)(2) that an employee can be discharged only for failure to *tender* dues and the initiation fee. The Court reasoned that if an employee is willing to tender the initiation fee and dues the employee cannot be discharged even though the employee refuses to become a full member. A person who pays the initiation fee and dues but refuses to become a full member is called a "financial core member." Contracts may legally use the typical union security clause language requiring membership, but only financial core membership can be enforced through discharge. The result is similar to an agency shop provision that requires that an employee pay only a "service fee."

A financial core member is not bound by the union's constitution and bylaws and is not subject to union discipline. Such em-

---

[1] See legal principle 1.

ployees are covered by the collective bargaining agreement and have all contractual rights, but they have no right to participate in the union. Thus only full union members can vote on the ratification of collective bargaining agreements. Only members can vote for union officers or union policies, or have the right to vote in a union merger or affiliation election (see Chapter Five).

4. Dues Required of a Financial Core Member: The Collective Bargaining Functions Test

A union's dues income may lawfully be used for many purposes: from collective bargaining to certain kinds of community and political action; from social events to sponsoring youth athletic leagues. The dues of a full union member may be used for any such lawful purpose that has been duly authorized pursuant to the union's constitution and bylaws, and a member must pay the union's full dues to remain a member in good standing. Following the *General Motors* decision establishing the concept of a "financial core" member, the Board and most courts that considered the issue interpreted Section 8(a)(3) to mean that a financial core member, although not required to join the union, could be required to pay the full amount of the union's regular periodic dues. However, the Supreme Court, in the landmark decision of *Communications Workers v. Beck*,[2] reached the opposite conclusion. The Court held that a financial core member cannot be required to pay a union's full dues as a condition of employment under a union security clause, but, rather, can be required to pay only that proportion of the dues used to support expenditures necessarily or reasonably incurred by the union for collective bargaining functions. The Court defined collective bargaining functions as including bargaining, contract administration, and grievance adjustment functions for the employees *in the bargaining unit.*

The Court said in *Beck* that it would apply the same interpretation to Sections 8(a)(3) and 8(b)(2) of the Labor Management Relations Act permitting agreements requiring union membership as a condition of employment as it applied to the similarly worded provision of the Railway Labor Act (Section 2, Eleventh of that Act). The Court had first held in *Machinists v. Street*[3] in 1981 that the Railway Labor Act (RLA) provision permitting agreements requiring union membership as a condition of employment only required that a financial core member provide financial support to the union's collective bargaining activities including contract administration and grievance adjustment. Thus, the Court specifically held in *Street* that a financial core member cannot be required to financially support a union's political activities. Under the *Beck* decision, the ruling in the *Street* and subsequent cases arising under the Railway Labor Act as to the scope of a financial core member's financial obligations are fully applicable to unions under the Labor Management Relations Act.

A union can charge an employee who does not wish to join the union under a union security clause full dues unless the member objects. Upon objection, the dues must be reduced to that percent of the union's dues used for collective bargaining functions. Thus, if dues are $20.00 a month, and 80 percent of that amount, determined as discussed below, is used for collective bargaining functions, the objecting member is entitled to a 20 percent reduction to $16.00 a month. The percentages of course, will vary among unions and may also vary from year to year within a union. An objecting financial core member can be "charged" for collective bargaining functions in the sense that the objecting member's dues can be used for those functions and they are included in determining the percentage of union dues the objecting member may be required to pay as a condition of employment.

---

[2] See legal principle 1.

[3] See legal principle 1.

In *Ellis v. Brotherhood of Railway Clerks*,[4] a 1984 Supreme Court decision interpreting the RLA, the Court clarified the criteria for determining the activities that a financial core member may be required to support as a condition of employment under a union security clause. Since the *Beck* decision, these same principles would now apply to the LMRA as well. The Court considered five specific expenses: union conventions; union social activities; union publications; litigation; and organizing. In reviewing these expenses, the Court stated:

The test must be whether the challenged expenditures are necessarily or reasonably incurred for the purpose of performing the duties of an exclusive representative of the employees in dealing with the employer on labor-management issues. Under this standard, objecting employees may be compelled to pay their fair share of not only the direct costs of negotiating and administering a collective bargaining contract and of settling grievances and disputes, but also the expenses of activities or undertakings normally or reasonably employed to implement or effectuate the duties of the union as exclusive representative of the employees in the bargaining unit.

Applying this standard, the Court held that the dues of objecting employees can be used to defray the costs of the union's national convention. The Court stated that a union, in order to carry out its collective bargaining functions, must be able to maintain its corporate or associational existence, must elect officers to manage and carry on its affairs, and may consult its members on overall bargaining goals and policies. The Court also held that the dues money paid by the nonmembers can be used for the union's social activities because those activities bring about harmonious working relationships, promote closer ties among employees, and create a more pleasant environment for union members. However, the Court noted that these social activities

were formally open to nonmember employees. Thus, if social activities are not open to all bargaining unit employees, nonmembers may not be required to contribute toward them. The Court upheld the basic right of a union to use the dues of nonmembers for the cost of union publications that report on the union's activities. However, the Court held that a protesting nonmember's dues cannot be used to support that percentage of the union's publications that report on activities that the protesting nonmember cannot be required to support. Thus, for example, a protesting nonmember cannot be required to support the union's political activities. Therefore, the percentage of a union's newspaper (calculated by the percentage of lines so used) devoted to political activities cannot be charged to the nonmember. The same cost adjustment would have to be made for any other activity reported in the paper that the nonmember could not be required to support.

As to litigation expenses, the Court concluded that the dues of an objecting nonmember can be used only for the litigation expenses that relate to that employee's bargaining unit such as litigation incident to negotiating and administering the contract or any other litigation before agencies or courts that concerns the bargaining unit employees and is normally conducted by an exclusive bargaining representative. Litigation that is not of direct concern to the bargaining unit cannot be so charged even if it would benefit the union membership as a whole. This would mean, for example, that the union's arbitration costs arising from disputes under a contract other than the one covering the objecting nonmember cannot be included in determining the objector's dues.

The Court held in *Ellis* that a union's expenses for organizing efforts cannot be charged to the nonmember. The Court reasoned that organizing costs are not directed at the bargaining unit, but rather on employees outside the unit. The Court stated that an objecting nonmember can be required to pay only the member's share of

---

[4] See legal principle 1.

the expenses incurred in representing the member and related activities. Of course, unions recognize that organizing new employees benefits the employees who are already represented, not only because it increases the union's income but also because it reduces the number of nonunion competitors paying substandard wages that may limit the union's bargaining power. However, the Supreme Court rejected this argument as a reason for requiring the objecting nonmember to support organizing activities. The Court concluded that the relationship between organizing and benefits for the bargaining unit was too indirect to charge the objecting nonmember. The Court also indicated that expenses incurred to recruit new union members within the bargaining unit itself (internal "union building") cannot be charged to objecting nonmembers.

Remember, the use of union funds contributed by full members for purposes other than collective bargaining functions is lawful, and a union may have a perfectly valid reason for the expenditure (e.g., lobbying for the passage of safety legislation). Thus, that one union may spend a lower proportion of its dues money than another on collective bargaining functions does not imply in any way that the union with the lower percentage is not properly representing its members.

Of course, the activities specifically approved by the Court in *Ellis* are not the only ones that are related to collective bargaining functions and thus chargeable to an objecting employee. They were simply the activities that happened to be challenged in *Ellis*. Many other functions would meet the criteria established by the Court. For example, a union's overhead expenses for maintaining its offices and the wages and benefits for the union's officers and staff would be chargeable as necessarily or reasonably incurred to perform the union's collective bargaining functions. However an objecting nonmember may be chargeable only for the proportion of the union's office overhead

and staff expenses attributable to collective bargaining functions as defined by the Court.

The *Beck* case began as a fair representation suit (see Chapter Twelve) in which certain employees alleged that the union had violated its duty of fair representation by requiring them to pay "dues" under a union security clause used for purposes to which they objected. The employees did not have to file an unfair labor practice charge with the NLRB challenging the dues because, as discussed in Chapter Twelve, both the federal courts and the Board have jurisdiction over alleged fair representation violations. Although the *Beck* decision did not involve the NLRB, the Board will undoubtedly be involved in cases determining the dues required of a financial core member. Thus, if a union demands the payment of dues that an employee alleges are being used for purposes other than collective bargaining functions over the employee's objection, or demands that an employer discharge an employee for refusing to pay such dues, the employee may file Section 8(a)(3) and 8(b)(2) charges, as appropriate, with the Board on the grounds that the amount in dispute cannot be required as a condition of employment from a financial core member. The employee may also file a Section 8(b)(1)(A) charge that the union's conduct violates its duty of fair representation. The Board would then determine whether the fees in dispute are for a collective bargaining function; whether, as discussed below, the union properly considered the employee's protest; and/or whether the union used proper procedures in determining the proportion of its dues the employee could be required to pay as a condition of employment.

a. Procedures for Processing and Resolving a Dues Protest. Although the Supreme Court has clearly stated in several cases that the burden is on the employee to object before the union has any obligation to reduce an employee's dues to the financial core minimum, the cases to date do not clearly indicate whether a union has a duty to inform an employee subject to a union security clause of the right to object. As discussed below, the NLRB requires that a union give an employee clear notice of the employee's obligation under a union security clause before requesting the employer to discharge an employee for failure to comply. It is thus possible that the Board or the courts will rule that a union also is obligated to notify every new employee when hired of the right to request financial core status or, at a minimum, notify an employee who initially refuses to pay the union's full initiation fees and dues of the right to financial core status before requesting the employee's discharge. Until this issue is resolved, unions should carefully consider giving such notice in order to avoid potentially large liability if an employee who is discharged without such notice subsequently alleges that he or she would have been willing to be a financial core member if offered that option.

If an employee does object to paying full membership dues as a condition of employment, the union must promptly determine the amount owed for collective bargaining functions and provide the objector with an adequate explanation for the determination. Even a potential objector, upon request, must be furnished the financial information needed to verify the union's calculation of the amount payable before filing a formal objection. A union need not provide nonmembers with an exhaustive and detailed list of all of its expenditures, but must make adequate disclosure including the major categories of expenses as well as verification by an independent auditor. The Supreme Court has emphasized in several cases that the burden is on the union to substantiate the proportion of its dues used for collective bargaining functions, not on the objecting member to establish the proportion used for other nonchargeable purposes. The Court has recognized however, that there cannot be absolute precision

in calculating the charges to nonmembers and that, for example, a union may calculate the fee on the basis of its expenses during the preceding year.

1. REBATE ARRANGEMENTS. Some unions subject to the Railway Labor Act followed the practice of requiring an objecting member to pay the full amount of the monthly dues and then periodically giving the member a rebate for the nonchargeable portion. However, in the *Ellis* decision, the Supreme Court specifically ruled that rebate systems are improper because they would permit a union to have full use of an objecting member's dues for a period of time that could be used for purposes other than collective bargaining functions. The Court said that a union cannot commit a dissenter's funds to "improper" uses even temporarily. The same rule would undoubtedly apply under the LMRA.

2. USE OF A NEUTRAL DECISION MAKER. In *AFT Local 1 v. Hudson*,[5] involving an agency shop fee for public employees, the Court also stated that if a member objects to paying full dues, the union must provide a reasonably prompt decision by an *impartial decision maker* such as an arbitrator to determine the amount. The neutral must be either mutually agreed to by the union and the objecting member or selected using the services of a person or agency providing arbitrators, such as the Federal Mediation and Conciliation Service, the American Arbitration Association, or a state mediation agency, provided that the union does not have an unrestricted choice of the arbitrator. The Court emphasized that an appropriately justified advance reduction in dues (i.e., not just a rebate) and a prompt decision on a challenge are absolute requirements to collect union dues from an objecting member.

In the *Hudson* case, there was no independent governmental agency such as the NLRB to determine the amount the union

---

[5] See legal principle 1.

could charge a financial core member. Thus the Court imposed the requirement of an outside neutral decision maker. In contrast, the NLRB has authority under the Act to determine such questions. Thus, as discussed above, a financial core member who objects to the union's fees can file a charge that the amounts violate Sections 8(a)(3), 8(b)(1)(A), and 8(b)(2) of the Act. Thus, it is possible that unions subject to the Board's jurisdiction will not have to use a neutral outside party to decide fee dispute issues since any determination a union makes would be subject to scrutiny by the NLRB. Neither the Board nor the courts have ruled on this issue to date. However, unions subject to the LMRA would undoubtedly still have to meet the other requirements discussed in this chapter such as providing employees with financial information needed to verify the amount spent on collective bargaining functions, promptly ruling on any challenge to the amount charged, and (as discussed below) placing any amount reasonably in dispute in escrow pending a final determination. Even if not required, some unions may decide to establish internal union procedures to resolve dues challenges culminating in a determination by an impartial decision maker. Should the Board or the courts defer to such a procedure or to a neutral's determination as the Board does to arbitration when an alleged unfair labor practice also involves a contract violation (see Chapter Nine)? There are strong reasons for deferring, but the Board and the courts have not yet ruled on this issue.

3. ESCROW ARRANGEMENTS. In *Hudson* the Court also considered escrow arrangements under which an objecting member's dues in dispute are held in a separate account to which the union does not have access until the amount payable is impartially determined. The Court stated that 100 percent of the amount in dispute need not be placed in escrow until the issue is resolved. Rather, a union is entitled to collect and use that proportion of a member's dues "that no dissenter could reasonably challenge." The

Court emphasized that a union must carefully justify the limited escrow on the basis of an independent audit breaking down expenditures, and the escrow figure itself must be independently verified. Only the amounts reasonably in dispute may be placed in escrow while a challenge is pending. Thus if a certain percentage of dues is undisputedly used for purposes other than collective bargaining functions, the objecting member would not have to pay that proportion of the dues at all. The dissenting member would have to pay the verified proportion of the dues used for collective bargaining functions that could not be reasonably challenged, and the remaining amount could be placed in escrow. Although *Hudson* is a public employment case, these principles probably also apply to unions subject to the LMRA.

In *Hudson*, the Court referred to the use of a certified public accountant (CPA) to determine the dues breakdown. It is not clear whether the Court referred to a CPA as an example of an acceptable person, so that someone else with comparable ability could be used, or whether a CPA must be used for the union's determination to be acceptable. In any event, especially considering the uncertainty, a union would be well advised to use a CPA to reduce the possibility that its determination will be successfully challenged. Also, although the law is not entirely clear on the point, it appears that the escrow funds should be held in an interest bearing account so that the objecting member will not suffer any loss if any part of the amount held in escrow must be refunded to the objector.

There are a number of important procedural issues as to financial core dues determinations on which neither the courts nor the Board have definitively ruled. These include:

1. How often may an individual financial core member request a redetermination of the required dues? (Probably not more than once per union fiscal year.)
2. Once a financial core dues determination has

been duly made in one case by an outside neutral person or by the Board, is that determination binding on all employees in the bargaining unit for the year at issue, or can other employees still protest the amount and be entitled to a hearing as well?

3. If several members challenge the dues required of financial core members, is each employee entitled to a separate determination or can the cases be consolidated?

4. Can the union establish an "open window" period each year for filing dues protests and require employees to pay full dues unless a protest is timely filed?

Any union facing these issues should check for the latest ruling in this developing area of the law.

b. Dues versus Assessments or Fines. Prior to the *Beck* decision, the Board, in interpreting Sections 8(a)(3) and 8(b)(2), held that a financial core member's only obligation was to pay a union's dues, but not an assessment. Dues are defined as payments used to meet the union's general and current obligations. The payments must be regular, periodic, and uniform. Payments used for a special purpose, especially if required only for a limited time, are regarded as assessments that a financial core member cannot be required to pay. For example, if a union passed a special assessment for repairs to the union's office, a financial core member could not be required to pay the amount as a condition of employment and cannot be discharged under the union security clause for refusing to pay. The *Beck* decision, limiting an objecting member's dues obligation to collective bargaining functions, will undoubtedly reduce the number of cases in which the distinction between dues and assessments will be important in determining a financial core member's obligations, but there may still be some situations in which a financial core member may not be required to pay a particular fee regardless of its relationship to collective bargaining functions because it would constitute an assessment rather than dues.

The purpose of a payment rather than the label placed on it determines its classification by the Board. Thus the union may call a payment dues, but the payment may legally be an assessment because it is used for a special purpose, etc. In contrast, a payment termed an assessment may legally be classified as dues because it is used to meet current general obligations, etc. All employees may be required to pay an assessment legally classified as dues and used for a collective bargaining function as a condition of continued employment under a union security clause.

Remember that this distinction between dues and assessments applies only to a financial core member. Any employee who wishes to be a full union member enjoying all the privileges of membership must pay an assessment provided it is duly passed in accordance with a union's bylaws and also in accordance with Section 101(a)(3) of the Labor Management Reporting and Disclosure Act that requires reasonable notice and a secret ballot in most instances. A full union member who refuses to pay the assessment can be sued in state court to collect the amount owed or internal union discipline can be imposed. The member cannot be discharged, however, because the only grounds for discharge permitted by Sections 8(a)(3) and 8(b)(2) are failure to pay the initiation fee or dues (i.e., be a financial core member).

A union fine is not classified as dues and a union bylaw that states that a fine is treated as dues is not enforceable. Thus, an employee cannot be discharged for failure to pay a fine. The Board has held that if a contract contains a union security clause, a union bylaw provision requiring that a member pay any fines owed to the union, before any amounts paid are credited to the member's dues obligations, violates Section 8(b)(1) of the Act and is void as applied to members covered by the contractual union security clause. A full member, however, may be suspended or expelled for failure to pay a lawful fine and a fine can be collected in court (see Chapter Eleven). Remember that the term "dues" when referring in this chapter to the dues required by a union security clause or to the discharge of an employee for failure to pay dues, means the amount that can be required of a financial core member to support collective bargaining functions.

5. Excessive or Discriminatory Dues

Section 8(b)(5) makes it an unfair labor practice for a union to require employees covered by a union security agreement to pay a membership fee in an amount that the Board finds excessive or discriminatory under all the circumstances. The section requires the Board to consider, among other relevant factors, the practices and customs of labor organizations in the particular industry and the wages currently paid to the affected employees.

There are very few reported cases involving Section 8(b)(5). This section does not prohibit classes of membership. Thus, a union that represents employees with different skills, in different industries, or at different pay levels, can divide its membership into classes or divisions. There can be different dues structures for each classification it represents. This arrangement would not violate Section 8(b)(5) as long as the union has a reasonable basis for the distinction.

The Board has held that a union does not violate Section 8(b)(5) by establishing two reinstatement fees; one for employees who leave the union in good standing and another higher rate for members expelled from the union for failure to pay their dues who subsequently seek reinstatement. The Board stated that the different reinstatement fees were not adopted for a discriminatory purpose and were based upon a reasonable classification.

6. Union Dues Rebates and Attendance Incentives

Section 8(b)(2) provides that required dues be uniform, and Section 101(a)(5) of the Labor-Management Reporting and Disclosure Act (see Chapter Eleven) requires that a member have a hearing before being disciplined for any reason other than nonpayment of dues. What if a union adopts a dues schedule under which dues are $20 a month, but are reduced to $15 a month if the member attends the union's monthly meeting? Is the reduction, in effect a $5 fine on members who do not attend a weekly meeting? If so, it cannot be imposed without a hearing.

The courts have held that this kind of dues reduction is an incentive to attend meetings, not a fine for failure to attend. Similarly, courts have upheld union policies reducing dues if they are paid by a certain date early in the month as a legitimate incentive to get dues in early, not a fine against those who do pay late in the month. Also, since all members have an equal right to the reduction by meeting the uniformly applied requirements, the reduction does not violate the Section 8(b)(2) uniformity requirement. An employee who does not come to union meetings or pay the dues by the established cutoff date may be required to pay the full amount. The employee may be discharged under the union security clause if the employee fails or refuses to pay.

7. Late Payment of Union Dues

If a collective bargaining agreement contains a union security clause, can an employee be discharged for paying the required dues after the date established in the constitution and bylaws? An employee who has signed a checkoff form authorizing the employer to deduct the initiation fee and dues and forward them to the union cannot be discharged. It is the union's responsibility to make sure the employer deducts the proper amount and forwards it on time. But if the collective bargaining agreement does not provide for checkoff, or if an employee has not signed a checkoff form, the employee is obligated to get the dues in on time.

Any policy on discharging employees for late payment must be uniformly applied to all employees. If a union bylaw or practice allows a grace period for late payments or permits an employee to pay a reinstatement fee to regain membership, all employees must have the same grace period or be permitted to regain membership in the same way. If the union makes exceptions in hardship cases (perhaps an employee has extra medical bills to pay), the hardship rules must be applied to all employees in the same situation. There are also certain notice requirements a union must meet before an employee can be discharged (see below).

If a union has been lax in enforcing a dues payment deadline, it cannot suddenly begin enforcing the rule strictly. The union must give employees fair notice of its intention. But if a union has a hard and fast rule requiring payment on time with no exceptions and no excuses, that rule can be enforced and an employee can be discharged for late payment in accordance with the union security clause of the collective bargaining agreement.

8. Effect of a Union's Rejection or Explusion of an Employee on Continued Employment

Suppose an employee who applies for membership is rejected by the union for a valid nondiscriminatory purpose. Can the union then have the employee discharged for failure to be a member as required by a union security clause? No, the union cannot have it both ways. If the union rejects an employee for membership, the employee is not subject to discharge and cannot even be charged the fee required of a financial core member. The union would violate Section 8(b)(2) by requesting that an employee be discharged under those circumstances and the employer would violate Section 8(a)(3) by discharging the employee. The employee would become a legal "free rider."

Section 8(a)(3) prohibits an employer from discriminating against (discharging) an employee for nonmembership in a labor organization pursuant to a union security agreement if the employer has reasonable grounds for believing membership is not available to the employee on the same terms and conditions generally applicable to other members or that the employee was denied membership for reasons other than the employee's failure to *tender* the uniformly required periodic dues and initiation fee. "To tender" means to offer the initiation fee and dues. Thus, if an employee offers to pay the initiation fee and dues to be a member, but the union rejects the employee, the employer cannot discharge the employee, because the tender was made. If the employee does not tender the dues and initiation fee (or at least the financial core minimum as discussed above), then the employee can be discharged. Of course, the law does not require meaningless acts. If a union has advised an employee that the employee will not be admitted, the employee does not even have to offer to pay and the employee cannot be discharged for failing to make the tender.

If a member is expelled from full membership for refusing to tender the periodic dues and initiation fee, then the employee can be required to pay the fee required of a financial core member as a condition of continued employment under a union security clause. The employee can be discharged for refusing to pay the fee. If an employee is willing to be a full union member and pay full dues and is thus expelled for some other reason (which may be perfectly lawful under the union's constitution and bylaws), the employee cannot be charged a fee and would become a legal free rider the same as an employee rejected for membership.

The rejected or expelled member is not entitled to participate in union affairs, but is entitled to all collective bargaining benefits including the right to have grievances adjusted by the union.

9. Application of Union Security Clauses to Supervisors and Transferred Employees

A union cannot require that supervisors pay dues, although it is customary and not unlawful for first line supervisors to remain union members in many industries. Contracts frequently contain provisions permitting supervisors to return to the bargaining unit with full seniority. The Board has held that, in most cases, supervisors returning to the unit must be given the full thirty-day grace period under Section 8(a)(3) to rejoin the union. However, in *A. O. Smith Corp.*, the Board upheld a contract clause requiring supervisors to rejoin the union immediately.[6] In that case, supervisors frequently shuttled back and forth from supervisory to bargaining unit positions. The Board stated that the critical factor in determining whether a supervisor may be required to pay union dues immediately is whether an employee who becomes a supervisor has a reasonable expectation of returning soon to the bargaining unit. If an employee anticipates frequent transfer from employee status to supervisor and back to employee, depending upon production factors, etc., then the union may require that the employee resume paying union dues immediately each time he or she returns to the bargaining unit. But, if an employee who becomes a supervisor does not have a reasonable expectation of returning frequently to the bargaining unit, the supervisor cannot be required to resume membership payments immediately upon return. The supervisor then is entitled to the thirty-day grace period afforded a new employee.

The Board had also held that a union can negotiate a clause permitting employees transferred out of the unit to other jobs or to supervision to retain or continue to accrue seniority rights in the bargaining unit, provided the employee remains a union member and continues to pay dues while employed out of the unit. The Board reasoned that the employee can be required to pay

[6] See legal principle 6.A.

dues because the employee is receiving a benefit to which the employee would not otherwise be entitled. Recently, however, the Board reversed its position and held that such clauses are unlawful under Section 8(a)(3) of the Act because they unlawfully discriminate in favor of union members and encourage employees to engage in union activity, the payment of union dues, while they are not being represented by the union.

10. Effect of Contract Expiration on a Union Security Clause

If a contract containing a union security clause expires and the parties immediately enter into a new contract without any break in coverage that also contains a union security clause, the current employees have a continuing obligation to remain union members (or at least maintain financial core membership). There is no new statutory grace period. What if, however, there is a time gap between the expiration of the old contract and a new agreement? Some contract provisions remain in effect as a condition of employment after a contract expires until a bargaining impasse is reached (see Chapter Five). That is not true of a union security clause, which expires immediately unless the parties agree to extend the contract beyond its expiration date. This means that union members can resign from the union after a contract containing a union security clause has expired. In that way (as discussed in Chapter Eleven) employees who wish to do so can cross a union's picket line without being disciplined. However, if the union subsequently negotiates a contract containing a union security clause, the employees who resigned can be required to rejoin. They must pay the same reinitiation fee required of any other employee who resigns and returns. They cannot be charged a higher fee; that would violate the Section 8(b)(2) requirement that initiation fees and dues be uniformly required of all employees. Furthermore, even if the new contract is retroactive to the expiration date of the prior agreement, an employee cannot be required to pay dues for the period when there was actually no contract in effect as a condition of continued employment.

What if the union refuses to take the employee back or requires that the employee pay a fine before being readmitted? Under those circumstances, the employee is not obligated to tender the initiation fees and dues and becomes a legal free rider.

11. Union Deauthorization Elections

A union deauthorization election (referred to as a UD election) nullifies the union security clause of a collective bargaining agreement. A union deauthorization election is sometimes confused with a union decertification election (an RD petition). The two are very different. A decertification election is one to revoke the representation rights of a union. A UD election is to revoke only the contractual union security clause. If a union loses a decertification petition, it no longer represents the employees. If the union loses a union deauthorization election, it still represents the employees, but the union security clause cannot be enforced. Decertification procedures are based on Section 9(c)(1)(A), whereas deauthorization procedures are based on Section 9(e)(1). The election procedures are those followed in all representation cases (see Chapters One and Two).

a. Majority Vote Requirement for Union Deauthorization. As in other representation matters, a union deauthorization petition must be supported by a 30 percent showing of interest of bargaining unit employees. A deauthorization election, however, is different in one respect. A representation or decertification election is determined by a majority of the eligible employees voting. But a deauthorization election requires a majority of all employees in the bargaining unit. Thus, if there are ten employees in the unit, six votes are needed to deauthorize the union security clause.

b. Dues Obligation During Deauthorization Proceedings. Questions sometimes arise about whether employees must continue to pay union dues while a UD petition is pending. The Board's view is that employees are obligated to continue paying dues until the Board certifies the results of a deauthorization election revoking the union security clause. The same rule applies to decertification petitions. The Board has held that a union may continue to enforce a union security clause after a decertification petition is filed until the results of the decertification petition are certified. This means that, if a union loses a decertification or deauthorization election but files objections to the election, the union can continue to enforce the union security clause until the objections are ruled on and the results certified.

E. ENFORCEMENT OF A UNION SECURITY CLAUSE

1. Notice of the Union Security Requirement

The most important point to remember in enforcing a union security clause is that responsibility for lawful enforcement lies completely with the union. The Board has held that a union is obligated to notify the employees that their collective bargaining agreement has a union security clause requiring union membership by a specific date and that the employee can be discharged is for failure to pay initiation fees and dues as required. The Board refers to this requirement as the union's fiduciary obligation. A fiduciary obligation is the obligation owed by a person in a position of trust and confidence. So, the Board has established a very high standard for unions to meet.

What if the employer tells the employees when they are hired that they have to join the union at the specified time? Can the union later discharge an employee who fails to join as required by a union security clause? No. There are numerous Board cases that stress that an employer's notice to the employee is insufficient. If the union wants to enforce a union security clause, it must notify the employee of the obligation.

A union may prepare a letter welcoming each new employee and informing the employee of the employee's contractual obligation to join the union. Politely, but clearly, the union should make sure that the employee understands the employee is subject to discharge if the employee does not join. This letter can be given to the employee directly by the shop steward or union officer or can be mailed to the employee's home. The union should keep a record so that, if necessary, the union can prove that an employee had notice. Unless the union can prove notice, an employee cannot be discharged for failure to comply with a union security clause.

A union has wide discretion in determining its dues policies. But the policy, once determined, must be applied equally to all employees and all employees must have notice of it. Thus, the union's notice to the employee must specifically tell the employee the amount the employee is obligated to pay, the due date for payment, whom and where to pay, installment payment procedures, if any, and grace periods for late payment, if available. The notice must also inform the employee of the availablity of dues checkoff and how to obtain checkoff forms. The Board has held that a union must accept a dues payment in cash; it cannot insist upon a check or money order.

2. Notice of a Delinquency

If an employee, despite notice of the union security obligation, fails to join the union or subsequently falls behind in dues payments, the union must send the employee a discharge warning letter. This second notice must remind the employee of the union security obligation and state the amount the employee owes, how the amount was determined, the months for which the dues are owed, and to whom, where, and by what final date the amounts must be paid. The employee must once again be reminded of the availability of installment payments and of dues checkoff, if any. The employee must be given a reasonable time to pay the amounts owed. That, of course, depends on the amount. The notice must specifically tell the employee that unless the necessary payment is made by a certain date or satisfactory arrangements are made for payment by a certain day, the employee will be discharged.

The Board has repeatedly emphasized that the union has a fiduciary duty to make sure that the employee has actual notice of the delinquency and possible discharge. Posting a delinquency notice on a plant bulletin board, for example, is not sufficient, even if the employee regularly passes by the board. If an employee is sent a letter there must be proof, such as a certified mail-return receipt, that the letter was received. If an employee denies receiving the letter, the Board will not uphold the discharge in the absence of proof. The union can also personally hand the notice to the employee and have the employee initial a copy. As a rare exception, the Board may uphold the discharge of an employee who has not received formal notice from the union if the employee has actual notice from another source (e.g., the employer) and the employee is obviously avoiding notice from the union, such as rejecting certified letters.

Remember that, although a union security clause may lawfully refer to joining the union and most employees, in fact, join, an employee's only obligation is to become a financial core member and pay that proportion of the union's dues used for collective bargaining functions. Thus, if an employee refuses to join the union but is willing to become a financial core member, the employee cannot be discharged. Also, if an employee objects to paying dues used for noncollective bargaining functions, the union can require as a condition of employment only that the objecting member pay the proportion of the dues used for collective bargaining functions properly determined as discussed above. As previously discussed in regard to the *Beck* decision, it is possible that the Board and the courts may rule that a union's discharge warning notice to a delinquent member must specifically advise the employee of the right to financial core status, and a union should carefully consider advising an employee who has refused to join of this right before requesting the employee's discharge.

3. Consequences of Late Notice

What if a union does not give an employee notice of the dues obligation until several months after the employee is hired? Can the union require the employee to pay the past due amounts or has the union forfeited that right? The Board applies a rule of reason in such cases. If a union fails to notify an employee for a reasonably short period of time, the union can give proper notice and can collect the amounts owed retroactively for the entire period provided the employee is given reasonable time to pay. There is no hard and fast rule on the period for which a union may retroactively collect dues. It depends on the facts and circumstances. Certainly the longer it waits, the harder it is for a union to justify retroactive payments.

What if the employee actually knows the dues obligation because the employer or other bargaining unit employees tell the employee about it? That is not enough. The union has the duty to give notice, and notice from another source does not relieve it of the responsibility.

4. Strict Adherence to the Board's Standards

The Board strictly enforces the requirements that a union give an employee proper notice of a union security obligation and of a delinquency before requesting the employee's discharge. But, the Board has upheld such discharges in many cases when the union has properly fulfilled these requirements. A union can even refuse an employee's offer to pay what is owed after the last date stated for payment in the notice, provided that all employees are treated in the same fashion. Unions get into avoidable problems when they attempt to take shortcuts to speed up the process, such as not making sure that the employee has actual personal notice of the delinquency before requesting the employee's discharge.

Mistakes in enforcing a union security clause can be costly to the union. Thus, if a union unlawfully requests the discharge of an employee, and the employer complies with the request without knowing that proper procedures were violated, the union is required to make the employee whole for all losses of wages and benefits suffered by the employee as a result of the union's unlawful conduct until the employee is either reinstated by the employer to his or her former or substantially equivalent employment or until the employee obtains substantially equivalent employment elsewhere. If the employer is aware that the union's request is unlawful, but still complies with it, then both the union and the employer are liable for the employee's losses. The union, however, still has the primary liability to pay the employee's loss if it instigated the action. However, if the employer is also liable, the union's financial liability terminates five days after it gives notice to the employer that it has no objection to the employee's reemployment. The employer remains liable until it offers the employee reemployment.

F. RESIGNATION FROM THE UNION

Some union constitutions have historically contained provisions limiting a member's right to resign from the union, such as prohibiting a resignation immediately before or during a strike, while the member owed any debt to the union, or while internal union charges are pending against the member. Some unions required that a member give notice a specified period in advance before a resignation was effective. Issues regarding the right to resign frequently arose during a strike when a member attempted to resign to avoid union discipline for crossing a picket line and returning to work. The Board's membership and the courts were deeply divided over whether any union restrictions on the right to resign during a strike violated Section 8(b)(1)(A) of the Act because they coerced employees in the exercise of their right to refrain from concerted activity under Section 7 of the Act (i.e., the right not to strike and return to work) or whether union restrictions were permitted by the proviso to Section 8(b)(1) preserving a union's right to prescribe its own rules in regard to the acquisition or retention of membership.

Ultimately, in *Patternmakers League*,[7] a case involving resignation during a strike, the United States Supreme Court held that any restrictions on the right to resign violated Section 8(b)(1)(A). The Court reasoned that under Section 8(a)(3) of the Act membership in a union is voluntary (i.e., an employee may be required to pay a union's initiation fees and dues but not actually join the union) and that any restriction on the right to resign was contrary to this principle of voluntary unionism. The Court concluded that the proviso to Section 8(b)(1)(A) protected only a union's right to determine the rules for admission or expulsion from the union, but not rules restricting the right to resign. Although *Patternmakers League* involved only restrictions on the right to resign during a strike, the ruling has been broadly applied in subsequent cases to invalidate other restrictions as well, such as rules prohibiting resignation without prior notice, while a member owes a debt to the union, or while internal union charges are pending. Considering the very broad reasoning of the *Patternmakers League* decision, it is highly unlikely that any union restrictions on the right to resign are lawful. Remember, however, that if a member resigns while a lawful union security clause is in effect, the member will still be obligated to pay the union's initiation fees and dues, that is, to remain a financial core member. Also, as discussed

[7] See legal principle 5.

below, if a member has signed a checkoff authorization for the payment of the union's initiation fee and monthly dues, that authorization, depending upon its precise wording, may remain in effect even after the member has resigned.

A member's resignation is effective when received by the union. Thus, if a member hands a letter of resignation directly to a union officer, the resignation is effective immediately. What if the union's constitution or bylaws provide that a resignation must be turned into a specific union officer, delivered personally to the union's office, or be approved by the union's executive board to be effective? Under the *Patternmakers League* decision such restrictions would be void, and the resignation would be in effect immediately. However, if a member gives a letter of resignation to another employee to deliver to the union, or uses some other messenger, the resignation would not be effective until actually received. If a member crosses the union's picket line before the resignation is received, the member is subject to union discipline based on the conduct occurring before the resignation is so effective. Thus, for example, if a member mails a resignation letter to the union and then crosses the picket line on the date of mailing before the resignation is received, the member would be subject to union discipline.

The Board applies certain presumptions as to the receipt of a resignation. Thus, if a member submits a resignation by mail, the Board presumes that it was received by the union in the regular course of the mails, normally the next business day, unless the union can prove that it was actually received on a later date. If a resignation is received either directly or by mail by a union on the same day that a member crosses the picket line, the Board presumes absent evidence to the contrary that the resignation was received and thus in effect one hour before the employee crossed the line, so that the employee was not subject to union discipline at the time of crossing. If a union has a night deposit box for use when its office is closed, a resignation is effective when placed in the box even though a union officer may not actually pick up the resignation until some time later. A union may not delay the effective date of a resignation by attempting to evade service. Thus, if a letter of resignation is delivered to the union's office, the resignation is effective immediately even though a union officer refuses to open the envelope. Similarly, a union officer cannot refuse to accept a letter that is handed to the officer, attempt to avoid a member looking for the officer to submit a resignation, or not go to the post office to pick up mail that the officer believes may be a resignation. In such cases, a resignation is effective when it would have been received in due course but for the attempted evasion. Finally, if a union advises a member, contrary to law, that the member cannot resign so that a member believes that submitting a resignation would be futile, the member is excused from even attempting to resign and cannot be disciplined for returning to work.

G. RIGHT-TO-WORK LAWS

So called "right-to-work" laws are authorized by Section 14(b) of the LMRA, providing: "Nothing in this Act shall be construed as authorizing the execution or application of agreements requiring membership in a labor organization as a condition of employment in any State or Territory in which such execution or application is prohibited by State or Territorial law."

Most right-to-work laws prohibit all forms of union security, but they do not have to. Under Section 14(b) a state may prohibit all forms of union security, or may permit some forms of union security, but prohibit others. At one time Indiana had a right-to-work law that it has since repealed. The Indiana Supreme Court held that an agency shop was permissible under the law.

An employee who normally works in a state that does not have a right-to-work law can be required to join the union (or at least be a financial core member) under a union

security clause even if the employer's home office is in a right-to-work state or the employee was initially hired in a right-to-work state.

An employee in a right-to-work state who formally joins a union is bound by the constitution and bylaws of the union, as is a member in any other state. If a member does not pay dues, the member can be expelled from membership and/or sued in the state court for the amount owed. The employee cannot be discharged for not paying the dues because a right-to-work law prohibits conditioning employment upon the payment of union dues or initiation fees.

Under the duty of fair representation (see Chapter Twelve), a union must represent all employees fairly whether or not the employee is a union member. A union security clause insures that employees bear their fair share of the union's costs. In contrast, in right-to-work states, or under contracts that do not contain a union security clause, some employees are free riders on the coattails of the other employees who do contribute. This is one of the strongest arguments against right-to-work laws.

H. CONTRACTUAL CHECKOFF PROVISIONS

1. Termination and Renewal

Section 302(c)(4) permits an employee to sign a written statement authorizing the employer to deduct the employee's initiation fee and monthly dues from the employee's wages and forward them to the union. This is commonly referred to as union dues checkoff. An employer's agreement to checkoff initiation fees and dues as authorized (a contractual "checkoff clause") is a mandatory subject of bargaining (see Chapter Five). A checkoff card may also authorize the deduction of union assessments as well as dues. An employee's decision to sign a checkoff authorization must be voluntary. Thus, a union cannot require that an employee sign a checkoff card to pay the initiation fee and dues required under a union security clause. The employee must have the option of paying the amounts personally if so desired.

The checkoff form can be irrevocable for up to a year or until the expiration date of the collective bargaining agreement, whichever occurs first. The form may provide for automatic renewal if the employee does not revoke the checkoff within a specified period before its expiration. The Board has held that if the checkoff form does not expressly provide for revocation, the checkoff authorization is revocable at any time. The union cannot required that a special form provided by the union be used for revocation. Any written notice is sufficient as long as it is timely. Also, if a contract contains a union security clause and an employee signs a checkoff card, the employee may revoke a checkoff authorization at any time if the union security clause is deauthorized notwithstanding any restrictions set forth in the checkoff form.

The Board has held that a checkoff authorization may lawfully remain in effect in the periods between collective bargaining agreements if the form expressly so provides. Otherwise, the authorization remains in effect only during the contract's term. What if a member resigns from the union during a period when the checkoff form by its terms is irrevocable? Does the checkoff authorization remain in effect? The Board's view is that resignation from a union does not automatically terminate a checkoff authorization as a matter of law and that whether the checkoff remains in effect depends upon the wording of the authorization form. The Board, however, strictly construes a card's wording. Thus, if a checkoff authorization refers only to union membership and/or only to the deduction of union initiation fee and dues, the Board regards the form as binding only if the employee is a member, so that the form is revocable as soon as the employee resigns from membership. In contrast, if the authorization form is broadly worded, authorizing not only the deduction of union fees

and dues but also an amount equivalent to the initiation fee and dues for nonmembers (i.e., the amount payable by a financial core member), then the form would remain in effect as to the amount that is still subject to collection for the duration of the authorization period even if the member resigns. Several courts of appeals have criticized the Board's rule as too narrow. These courts have reasoned that even a checkoff authorization that refers only to membership should remain in effect for its full term if a member voluntarily resigns as long as the union is ready and willing to retain the employee as a member. Of course, a union may avoid problems even under the Board's narrow approach by properly drafting a checkoff authorization form so that it applies not only to union members but also to the initiation fees and dues of an employee who does not join or who resigns.

That a member has properly revoked a union authorization form does not mean that the person has resigned from the union as well. Thus, the employee will remain a union member until the employee specifically resigns from the union. Finally, as noted above, even if an employee resigns from the union and properly revokes a checkoff authorization form, the employee may still be required to remain as a financial core member as long as there is a valid union security clause in effect.

2. Consequences of Late Payment to the Union

What is the status of an employee who signs a checkoff form if the initiation fees and dues are not deducted or if the employer deducts the proper amounts but fails to forward them to the union? The courts and Board have held that signing a checkoff form is equivalent to tendering dues. The employee is a member in good standing even if the funds are not forwarded to the union and cannot be discharged. It is the union's responsibility to insure compliance with the checkoff provision. Section 401(e) of the Labor-Management Reporting and

Disclosure Act, which governs election procedures, specifically provides:

No member whose dues have been withheld by his employer for payment to such organization pursuant to his voluntary authorization provided for in a collective bargaining agreement shall be declared ineligible to vote or be a candidate for office in such organization by reason of alleged delay or default in the payment of dues.

What if a union requires that a member be in good standing for a certain number of months before an election to hold office, defining good standing as having paid dues by the tenth day of each month? If an employee has executed a checkoff form and the employer pays the union late, the employee will still be in good standing. On the other hand, if an employee who has not executed a checkoff form pays late, the employee is bound by the bylaw provision and will not be in good standing. An employee who pays individually is responsible for paying on time and bears the consequences of late payment.

Employees sometimes confuse the checkoff concept with union security clauses. A contract can have a checkoff clause whether or not it contains a union security clause. Furthermore, right-to-work states cannot prohibit checkoff clauses because checkoff is not a form of union security.

I. HIRING HALLS

Some people regard an exclusive hiring hall, in which all employees are referred to employment through the union, as a form of union security. It is not. An exclusive hiring hall has to serve everyone, whether a union member or not. Since hiring halls are not a form of union security, they cannot be prohibited or regulated in right-to-work states.

The Board has set strict standards for a union operating an exclusive hiring hall.

There must be specific objective standards for determining the order in which employees are referred for employment that cannot be arbitrary or discriminate in favor of union members (subject to a limited exception for the construction industry discussed below). The failure to have objective standards or to apply them properly violates Section 8(b)(1)(A) on the theory that such broad discretionary power in the union's control would encourage employees to join the union or to be a "good union member" in order to be referred to employment. (See Chapter Four for a discussion of these underlying legal principles.)

The Board holds a union to a high "fiduciary" standard in administering hiring hall procedures. Thus a union also violates its duty of fair representation under Section 8(b)(1)(A) (see Chapter Twelve) if it fails to adopt objective nondiscriminatory standards or deviates from the established standards without proper justification. In addition, an employer violates Section 8(a)(3) of the Act by contractually agreeing to hiring hall provisions that are arbitrary or discriminatory or by acquiescing in union referral practices that are arbitrary or discriminatory in practice even if the contractual hiring hall provisions are lawful on their face.

A hiring hall may base referral preference on seniority determined by years of employment in the industry or even on employment within the bargaining unit. Technically, such requirements do not favor union members because nonmembers may also have experience in the industry or in the bargaining unit. Rules basing referral on the length of time that an employee has been on layoff or on the order in which employees sign the out-of-work list are also reasonable objective standards. Referrals may be based on an employee's qualifications for a specific job as long as the qualifications are objective and the qualification standards are not administered in an arbitrary or discriminatory manner. In contrast, presence in the hiring hall when a call comes in cannot be the sole factor for referrals because of the very broad discretion it gives the union in selecting the specific employees to be referred.

Although a union must refer nonmembers in a nondiscriminatory manner, a union is entitled to charge nonmembers a reasonable fee, based on the cost of operating the hiring hall, for using the hiring hall's services. Obviously, this charge could not be more than the cost of union membership.

Employees utilizing the hiring hall must have notice of the standards the union is applying in its operation and advance notice of any changes to the established procedures. However, there is no absolute requirement that the referral procedures be posted as long as the employees in fact have notice of them. Also, a union is obligated to provide employees using the hiring hall with information upon their request as to the employee's place on the referral list, the employees who have been referred to employment before the employee, and the criteria the union applied in making those referrals. As discussed in Chapter Five, the union is also obligated to provide an employer who is party to a contract providing for an exclusive hiring hall with information that the employer needs upon request to ascertain that the hiring hall is being operated in compliance with contractual and legal requirements.

Section 8(f) of the Labor Management Relations Act establishes certain special rules for the operation of a hiring hall in the construction industry. Under Section 8(f), a construction industry hiring hall can base referral priority on length of service with a specific employer; with employers within a multi-employer association; or with employers who, although not association members, agree to be bound by the multi-employer contract while performing work within the union's geographic jurisdiction. This provides construction unions with greater flexibility in hiring hall criteria than unions in other industries may have. However, except for the specific Section 8(f) provisions, construction unions are subject to the same high standards in the administration of a hiring hall that other unions must follow.

The Board has upheld a construction union's right to require that the first employee referred to a new job site be the steward selected by the union. The Board regards this as a reasonable requirement to insure that the contract is complied with. This is similar to the right of an industrial union to require that shop stewards be given preference for work on a certain shift or on overtime to ensure that someone is present to enforce the collective bargaining agreement (see Chapter Four).

If an employer and union agree to hiring hall procedures that are unlawful on their face (e.g., because there are no objective standards or the provisions unlawfully discriminate in favor of union members), the Board regards both the union and the employer as equally guilty of the violation (jointly and severally liable) and may seek backpay for any employees discriminatorily denied employment from either the union or the employer, although, in practice, each party usually pays one-half the total. In the past, if a contractual hiring hall provision was lawful on its face, but the union administered the hiring hall in an unlawful manner, the Board still held the employer jointly and severally liable with the union on the theory that the employer must be strictly responsible if it delegates the hiring process to a union by agreeing to a hiring hall referral system. Recently, however, the Board changed this rule. Now, if a hiring hall provision is lawful on its face, an employer will not be liable if the union administers the referral system unlawfully unless the employer knew or should have known of the union's actions.

Summary   This chapter covered union membership and union security, focusing on the internal relationship between a union and its members. At common law, a union is an unincorporated association, simply a combination of its members. It has no legal existence apart from its members and cannot sue or be sued as an entity. The LMRA Section 301 specifically provides that a labor organization may sue or be sued as an entity in federal court to enforce a contract. The old common law rules still apply, however, on the many aspects of unions not governed by federal law.

The courts have traditionally held that the relationship between the union and its members is contractual. The constitution and bylaws of the union are the contract. A union that wants to enforce a bylaw provision against a member must file such a suit as a class action in the state courts. Such a suit over an internal union matter is not governed by federal law.

Section 8(a)(3) permits a company and a union to negotiate an agreement requiring union membership as a condition of employment on or after the thirtieth day following the beginning of employment or the effective date of the contract, whichever comes later. Under Section 8(f) membership can be required after seven days in the construction industry. Although the statute refers to membership, an employee can be required to be only a "financial core member" who pays that proportion of the union's dues used for collective bargaining functions. Such an employee is entitled to the same representation and contract benefits as anyone else, but is not entitled to participate in internal union matters such as elections of union officers or voting on a contract. There is a distinction between the union's internal right to discipline members and the right to have an employee discharged for nonmembership. The union can fine or even expel a member for violating the union's bylaws or policies. But an employee cannot be discharged except for failure to pay the dues required of a financial core member.

If the union rejects or expels an employee who is willing to be a full union member, the employee cannot even be required to pay the financial core minimum and would become a legal free rider. An employee has the right to resign from the union at any time without any restrictions, but an employee who resigns can be required to be a financial core member and can be discharged for refusing to pay that proportion of the dues used for collective bargaining functions.

The critical point in enforcing a union security clause is that responsibility for proper enforcement lies completely with the union. The union has a fiduciary obligation to give employees detailed information of their obligation under a union security clause. Employees who are delinquent must be given a specific warning that they are delinquent and will be discharged. Union attempts to short circuit this procedure may result in an invalid discharge and a substantial backpay liability. But a union that establishes proper procedures and applies them uniformly can strictly enforce a union security clause. The burden is on the employee to request financial core status. However, the law is not yet settled as to whether a union must advise an employee of the right to financial core membership status before requesting the employee's discharge under a union security agreement.

Hiring halls and contractual checkoff provisions are not forms of union security. They are permitted even if a contract does not have a union security clause and also in a right-to-work state. A checkoff authorization form can remain in effect for its full term even if the employee resigns from the union if the form so provides. An exclusive hiring hall has to serve all employees whether they are union members or not. There must be specific objective nondiscriminatory standards for determining the referral order. However, the Board has upheld the right of unions to refer a union steward first to a new job site. This is a reasonable requirement to insure that the employer complies with the contract.

Review Questions

1. What is a union at common law?
2. Can a union be sued in its own name as an entity under the common law?
3. Can an employee be required to join a union as a condition of employment under a union security clause.
4. Can a financial core member's dues be used to support a union's lobbying efforts for better occupational safety and health laws?
5. How are the internal union rights and responsibilities of union members determined?
6. If a union rejects an employee who is willing to join the union as required by a union security clause, can the union have the employee discharged for failure to be a union member?
7. Can a union require that an expelled member continue paying periodic dues, as a kind of service charge, since the employee still has all contractual benefits?
8. Why would an employee be willing to pay the union's initiation fee and dues, or at least the financial core minimum, but not want to become a full member?
9. Does a union security clause remain in effect as a condition of employment after the contract expires?
10. What can be done in a right-to-work state if a voluntary member does not pay the required dues?
11. Can a union's dues checkoff form be irrevocable?
12. What is the effect of a member's resignation on a checkoff authorization?
13. Can an exclusive hiring hall give preference in referrals to union members?
14. Can an employee be discharged for late payment of union dues?
15. Can the union require that all debts owed to it be paid before a member resigns from membership?
16. If the union fails to notify an employee of a dues delinquency, but the employee has actual notice from the employer of the amount

owed, can the union require the discharge of the employee for failing to comply with a union security clause?

(Answers to review questions are at the end of the book.)

Basic Legal Principles

1. Althought the Labor Management Relations Act refers to requiring union membership, or the payment of the union's initiation fee and dues, as a condition of employment, only financial core membership under which an employee pays the union's initiation fee and dues without actually becoming a union member can be required under a union security clause. If a financial core member objects to paying the union's full initiation fee and dues, the employee can be required to pay only that proportion of the fee and dues used for collective bargaining functions including bargaining, contract administration, and grievance adjustment functions pertaining to that employee's bargaining unit. *NLRB v. General Motors Corp.*, 373 U.S. 734, 53 LRRM 2313 (1963); *Plumbers Local 141 v. NLRB*, 675 F.2d 1257, 110 LRRM 2027 (D.C. Cir. 1982) (service fees prohibited under applicable state right-to-work law); *Communications Workers v. Beck*, 108 S.Ct. 2641, 128 LRRM 2729 (1988); *International Association of Machinists v. Street*, 367 U.S. 740, 48 LRRM 2345 (1961); *Ellis v. Railway Clerks*, 466 U.S. 435, 116 LRRM 2001 (1984); *American Federation of Teachers (Chicago Teachers Union Local 1) v. Hudson*, 475 U.S. 292, 121 LRRM 2793 (1986); *Crawford v. Airline Pilots Assn.*, 870 F.2d 155, 130 LRRM 2932 (4th Cir. 1989).

2. If an employee objects to paying full dues, the union must promptly reduce the employee's dues to the financial core minimum. A rebate system under which the employee pays the full amount and the excess portion is ultimately refunded at periodic intervals is not permitted. Until a final determination is made, the employee can be required to pay only that proportion of the dues that cannot be reasonably disputed. Any portion that is subject to reasonable dispute may be placed in an escrow account until the determination is made by an impartial person or agency. *American Federation of Teachers (Chicago Teachers Union Local 1) v. Hudson* in legal principle 1.

3. If the union rejects an employee as a member or expels the employee from membership for any reason, and the employee was willing to be a full union member, the union cannot require the employee to pay the dues required of a financial core member as a condition of employment under a union security clause and cannot request that the employer discharge the employee. An employee can be discharged only if the employee voluntarily resigns from or refuses to join the union and refuses to pay that proportion of the union's initiation fee and dues lawfully required of a financial core member. *H. C. Macaulay Foundry Co. v. NLRB*, 543 F.2d 1198, 95 LRRM 2581 (9th Cir. 1977); *Pen & Pencil Workers*, 91 NLRB No. 155, 26 LRRM 1583 (1950).

4. A union cannot require an employer to discharge an employee

covered by a union security agreement for failure to pay fines or assessments. Assessments are payment to a special fund or for a special purpose. *Painters Local 1627*, 233 NLRB No. 118, 97 LRRM 1010 (1977); *Longshoremen Local 13*, 228 NLRB No. 174, 96 LRRM 1450 (1977); *Pittsburgh Press Co.*, 241 NLRB No. 99, 100 LRRM 1542 (1979); *Elevator Constructors Local 8 v. NLRB*, 665 F.2d. 376, 108 LRRM 2322 (D.C. Cir. 1981); *Furriers Joint Council*, 280 NLRB No. 107, 123 LRRM 1105 (1986); *Plumbers Local 314*, 295 NLRB No. 49, 131 LRRM 1532 (1989); *Pacific N.W. Newspaper Guild v. NLRB*, 877 F.2d 998, 131 LRRM 2924 (D.C. Cir. 1989).

5. An employee has the absolute right to resign from the union at any time and cannot be disciplined for conduct occurring after the resignation is effective. Any restrictions on the right to resign in a union's constitution and bylaws, such as advance notice or that no debt be owed to the union, are void and unenforceable. A resignation is effective when it is received by the union unless the union tries to evade receipt in which case the resignation is effective when tendered. *Pattern Makers League v. NLRB*, 473 U.S. 95, 119 LRRM 2928 (1985); *Teamsters Local 439*, 281 NLRB No. 164, 123 LRRM 1228 (1986), enforced 837 F.2d 888, 127 LRRM 2581 (9th Cir. 1988); *Communications Workers Local 9201*, 275 NLRB No. 214, 120 LRRM 1063 (1985); *Carpenters District Council, Seattle*, 277 NLRB No. 19, 120 LRRM 1327 (1985); *OCAW Local 1-591*, 283 NLRB No. 10, 124 LRRM 1223 (1987); *Machinists Lodge 1233*, 284 NLRB No. 132, 126 LRRM 1008 (1987); *NLRB v. Sheet Metal Workers Local 73*, 840 F.2d. 501, 127 LRRM 2801 (7th Cir. 1988); *NLRB v. Hotel Employees Local 54*, ____F.2d____, 132 LRRM, 2625 (3rd Cir. 1989).

6.A. Supervisors returning to the bargaining unit are generally treated as new employees with thirty days to join the union for union security purposes. However, supervisors who shuttle between supervisory and bargaining unit positions may be required to rejoin the union immediately if there is a reasonable expectation of their returning to the unit when they became supervisors. *Electrical Workers Local 399*, 200 NLRB 1050, 82 LRRM 1077 (1972), enforced 499 F.2d 56, 86 LRRM 2826 (7th Cir. 1974); *A. O. Smith Corp.*, 227 NLRB No. 116, 94 LRRM 1115 (1977).

6.B. A union cannot require that an employee pay union dues while working out of the bargaining unit or as a supervisor as a condition of retaining or continuing to accrue bargaining unit seniority. *Manitowoc Engineering Co.*, 291 NLRB No. 122, 130 LRRM 1072 (1988).

7. A union cannot request the discharge of an employee for failure to comply with a union security clause unless the union first informs the delinquent employee in writing of the employee's obligation under the clause and the delinquency. The notice must state the amount owed; the months for which owed or the method of calculating the amount; the payment procedures, including reasonable time to pay; and the last day the employee can pay the amount owed before being dis-

charged. Employees who have religious objections to joining or supporting a union may also be exempt from a union security clause. *Boilermakers Local 732*, 239 NLRB No. 69, 99 LRRM 1706 (1978); *District 9, Machinists*, 237 NLRB No. 207, 99 LRRM 1133 (1978); *Teamsters Local 122*, 203 NLRB No. 157, 83 LRRM 1235 (1973), enforced 509 F.2d 1160, 87 LRRM 3274 (1st Cir. 1974); *Sheet Metal Workers Local 355*, 254 NLRB 773, 106 LRRM 1137 (1981) (remedy against union for unlawful discharge). See also *AMF, Inc.*, 247 NLRB No. 45, 103 LRRM 1122 (1980) (employee who tendered his dues in cash cannot be discharged for failure to pay by check or money order); *SEIU Local 32B-32J*, 289 NLRB No. 83, 128 LRRM 1333 (1988); *CWA Local 9509*, 295 NLRB No. 27, 131 LRRM 1500 (1989).

8. A union security clause terminates automatically at the expiration of the collective bargaining agreement, and members are thereafter free to resign from the union or to cease paying the amounts required of a financial core member until a new contract including a union security provision is agreed to. *Trico Products Corp.*, 238 NLRB No. 184, 99 LRRM 1473 (1978); *Auto Workers Local 1756*, 240 NLRB No. 13, 100 LRRM 1208 (1979); *Kaiser Foundation*, 258 NLRB No. 4, 108 LRRM 1093 (1981) (dues cannot be retroactively required for period contract was not actually in effect).

9. Checkoff authorizations that do not expressly contain any limitation on their revocation are revocable at will. *Trico Products Corp.*, 238 NLRB 1306, 99 LRRM 1473 (1978); *Cameron Iron Works, Inc.*, 235 NLRB 287, 97 LRRM 1516 (1978); *Peninsula Ship Builders Assn. v. NLRB*, 663 F.2d 488, 108 LRRM 2400 (4th Cir. 1981) (no special form required for revocation). However, if properly worded, a checkoff authorization may remain in effect according to its terms between contracts or even after a member has resigned from the union. Compare *NLRB v. U.S. Postal Service*, 827 F.2d 548, 126 LRRM 2277 (9th Cir. 1987) with *NLRB v. U.S. Postal Service*, 833 F.2d 1195, 126 LRRM 3137 (6th Cir. 1987); *Transit Union Local 1222*, 285 NLRB No. 131, 129 LRRM 1077 (1987); *Machinists Local 2045*, 268 NLRB 635, 115 LRRM 1092 (1984). See also *Communications Workers, Local 1101*, 281 NLRB No. 64, 124 LRRM 1207 (1986) (employee cannot be required to sign dues checkoff form as sole means of paying required dues).

10. An exclusive hiring hall must base referrals on specific objective standards that cannot be arbitrary or discriminate in favor of union members. However, preference based on length of service in the industry (not length of union membership) is lawful if the procedure is not discriminatorily applied. *NLRB v. Laborers Local 534*, 778 F.2d 284, 121 LRRM 2073 (6th Cir. 1985); *Operating Engineers Local 450*, 267 NLRB No. 132, 114 LRRM 1201 (1983); *Teamsters Local 328*, 274 NLRB No. 160, 119 LRRM 1103 (1985); *Iron Workers Local 505*, 275 NLRB No. 159, 119 LRRM 1241 (1985); *Boilermakers Local 374*, 284 NLRB No. 140, 127 LRRM 1047

(1987); *Wolf Trap Foundation*, 287 NLRB No. 103, 127 LRRM 1129 (1988); *Cell-Crete Corp.*, 288 NLRB No. 32, 128 LRRM 1035 (1988); *Tenn-Tom Constructors*, 291 NLRB No. 40, 131 LRRM 1467 (1989): *Iron Workers Local 373*, 295 NLRB No. 71, 132 LRRM 1008 (1989); *Teamsters Local 896*, 296 NLRB No. 132, 132 LRRM 1212 (1989).

11. A union with an exclusive hiring hall can legally insist that the first employee referred to a job be a shop steward to insure compliance with the collective bargaining agreement. *Teamsters Local 959*, 239 NLRB No. 193, 100 LRRM 1160 (1979); *Sachs Electric Co.*, 248 NLRB No. 92, 104 LRRM 1070 (1980); *Plumbers Local 520*, 282 NLRB No. 167, 124 LRRM 1281 (1987). But see *Paintsmiths, Inc. v. NLRB*, 620 F.2d 1326, 104 LRRM 2368 (8th Cir. 1980) (burden on union to show substantial justification for removing employee from job when wrongfully hired by employer before referral of steward).

Recommended Reading

"A Union's Right to Control Strike-Period Resignations," 85 *Colum. L. Rev.* 339 (1985).

Moreland and Stapp, "Primer on Hiring Halls in the Construction Industry," 37 *Lab. L.J.* 817 (1986).

"Political Contributions and Tax-Exempt Status for Labor Organizations," 1974 *Wash. U.L.Q.* 139 (1974).

Smith and Drotning, "Fair Share Fees: Theory, Law and Implementation," 39 *Lab. L.J.* 464 (1988).

"Union Dues Checkoff as a Subject in Labor-Management Negotiations: Good Faith Bargaining and NLRB Remedies," 39 *Fordham L. Rev.* 299 (1970).

Volz and Costa, "A Public Employee's 'Fair Share' of Union Dues," 40 *Lab. L.J.* 131 (1989).

Wilhoit and Gibson, "Can a State Right to Work Law Prohibit the Union Operated Hiring Hall?," 26 *Lab. L.J.* 301 (1975).

Zipp, G. A., "Rights and Responsibilities of Parties to a Union Security Agreement," 33 *Lab. L.J.* 202 (1982).

chapter 11

RIGHTS AND RESPONSIBILITIES OF UNION MEMBERS

The rights and responsibilities of union members to the union are governed by the Landrum-Griffin Act, formally the Labor-Management Reporting and Disclosure Act of 1959 (LMRDA). It is the basic federal legislation pertaining to individual rights of union members. The most important section of the law covering individual rights is Title I, entitled the "Bill of Rights of Members of Labor Organizations."

A. AN OVERVIEW OF THE "BILL OF RIGHTS" FOR UNION MEMBERS

Section 101(a)(1) of the LMRDA gives every union member equal rights. It states: "Every member of a labor organization shall have equal rights and privileges within such organization to nominate candidates, to vote in elections or referendums of the labor organization, to attend membership meetings, and to participate in the deliberations and voting upon the business of such meetings, subject to reasonable rules and regulations in such organization's constitution and bylaws."

1. Section 101(a)(1): The Meaning of Equal Rights

Section 101(a)(1) does not grant any specific rights, nor does it require that a union grant its members any specific rights. It simply requires that every member have an equal chance to exercise the rights established by the union's constitution and by-laws. Some candidates for union office have filed suits challenging union requirements for holding office such as attending a certain percentage of the union's meetings. They have alleged that, in violation of Section 101(a)(1), the restrictions deny members the equal right to nominate candidates of their choice. The courts have uniformly rejected these suits, holding that the equal rights provision of Section 101(a)(1) does not apply, because all members have an *equal right* to nominate those who are eligible. The result would be different if some members were barred from the nominations meeting; then, some members would have the right to nominate while others would have no right at all. That would violate Section 101(a)(1).

What if a union's constitution permits all business to be conducted by the union's executive board, and provides that general membership meetings are to be called only at the discretion of the executive board? Can a member file suit under Section

101(a)(1) of the LMRDA to compel the union to hold regular meetings? One court of appeals has held that Section 101(a)(1) does not require that a union hold membership meetings, only that all members receive equal treatment when meetings are held. In contrast, suppose that the only office of a union covering a large geographic area is located in the largest city in the area but that it is difficult, if not impossible, for members residing in outlying regions to attend membership meetings at the union hall because of the distance and their work schedules. In that case, the same court of appeals held that the union was obligated either to hold regional meetings that the outlying members could attend or to provide for voting by mail. The Court reasoned that since the union's members did have the right to vote on certain matters, Section 101(a)(1) required that all members have an equal right to vote on those issues. Restricting the right to vote only to members who could be present at the union's office was an unreasonable restriction on the equal right of the members to vote considering the large geographic area the union served.

Can a union establish membership divisions and restrict voting on matters affecting a division, such as ratification of a collective bargaining agreement, only to division members? Yes, that is a lawful, reasonable regulation permitted by Section 101(a)(1) even though not all union members can vote on the issue. The other members would have an equal right to vote on matters affecting their divisions.

2. Section 101(a)(3): Dues Increases

Section 101(a)(3) regulates the procedure for enacting or increasing union dues, initiation fees, and assessments. The most important requirements are that a dues increase must be passed by a *secret* vote and that there must be reasonable notice of the intention to vote. The notice must specifically state that a *vote* will be taken. A notice that dues will be the subject of a meeting that does not indicate that a vote will be taken is insufficient.

It is a common misconception that the only way a local union can increase its dues is by a vote of the local's members. That is incorrect. Under Section 101(a)(3)(B), local dues can be increased by action at an international convention or by a secret ballot referendum of the entire international membership.

Section 101(a)(4) governs a member's rights to sue the union. A union cannot bar its members from suing it, but it can require a member to exhaust reasonable internal union remedies for up to, but not beyond, four months before filing suit. Section 101(a)(5) provides procedural safeguards to insure a fair hearing in internal union disciplinary proceedings. Sections 101(a)(4) and (5) are discussed fully below.

3. Section 101(b): The Primacy of the LMRDA over the Union's Bylaws

Finally, Section 101(b) states: "Any provision of the constitution and bylaws of any labor organization which is inconsistent with the provisions of this section shall be of no force or effect." This is a very important section. Sometimes a union leader, if told that some particular union practice does not meet Landrum-Griffin requirements, replies that the practice is permitted by the union's constitution and bylaws. The answer to that is clear. The union's constitution and bylaws cannot conflict with the law's requirements. A union's constitution and bylaws are a contract and are binding on the members, except in those areas governed by federal law (see Chapter Ten). In those areas (such as Landrum-Griffin Title I rights), the federal law prevails over inconsistent union provisions.

Section 102 deals with civil enforcement of Title I and establishes a member's rights to file suit to enforce the Bill of Rights. Title 1 is unique. Most of the Landrum-Griffin Act is enforced by the Department of Labor, but Title I is enforced by individual members going directly to court, subject to internal exhaustion requirements under Section 101(a)(4) (see below).

Section 103, "Retention of Rights," insures that the law does not take away any rights. Thus, if a union's constitution and bylaws establish a higher standard of conduct on a specific matter than the law requires, the union cannot apply the lower legal standard; the higher union standard must prevail. Also, state laws continue to apply where applicable. A few states have detailed laws governing internal union activities and individual member rights. Union members may continue to exercise their rights under state law as well as Landrum-Griffin.

Under Section 104 every employee has a right to a copy of the collective bargaining agreement covering the employee. Section 105 requires every labor organization to inform its members concerning the provisions of the LMRDA. These are simple requirements routinely complied with.

B. COVERAGE OF THE LABOR-MANAGEMENT REPORTING AND DISCLOSURE ACT

1. Definition of a Union Member

Who is covered by the law? Section 101(a) grants rights to every *member* of a labor organization. The limitation on rights to union members is different from the Labor Management Relations Act, which covers all "employees" (see Chapter One). Thus, a bargaining unit employee who is not a member has no rights under Landrum-Griffin. If the union's bylaws require a vote to ratify collective bargaining agreements, all union members in the bargaining unit have an equal right to vote on the contract, but nonmember employees have no such right under Landrum-Griffin.

Section 3(o) states: "Member, or member in good standing when used in reference to a labor organization, includes *any person who has fulfilled the requirements for membership* in such organization, and who neither has

voluntarily withdrawn from membership nor has been expelled or suspended from membership after appropriate proceedings . . ." (emphasis added). Suppose a union requires that a person take an oath before becoming a member. Is it possible that a person can be a "member" covered by Landrum-Griffin even before taking the oath if the person meets all other union requirements? What if, for example, an employee has applied for membership and tendered the initiation fees, but has yet to attend the membership initiation ceremony? Section 3(o) defines a member as someone who has *fulfilled the requirements of membership*. The law does not require that the person be *admitted* to membership to be classified as a member. The important factor is whether the remaining requirements to become a formal member are simple administrative acts. An initiation ceremony is an administrative act. If an employee has been employed for thirty days and has fulfilled all the requirements for membership except to be formally initiated, the courts would probably say that the employee is a member for purposes of the rights guaranteed under Landrum-Griffin.

Issues sometimes arise as to the membership rights of members who are either retired or on layoff. Many unions have bylaw provisions that limit the right to vote to members who are actively at work. The courts have upheld such restrictions as a reasonable rule under Section 101(a)(1) on the theory that, since the union's purpose is to represent and protect the members' employment rights, it is reasonable to restrict decision-making authority to members who are employed rather than laid off or retired. However, in one case, a union negotiated a contract revision that would have restricted the recall rights of employees on layoff. Under the union's constitution, employees who were on layoff were not permitted to pay union dues and were therefore not in good standing. The union therefore prohibited the laid-off employees from voting on the proposal. Only the employees who were actively at work, who would benefit from the contract change at the expense of the laid-off employees, were permitted to vote. Although the laid-off employees were not members in good standing, they had not been formally expelled or suspended from membership. Under these circumstances, a court concluded that the union's constitutional provision limiting the right to vote to members in good standing was unreasonable and that the employees on layoff were entitled to vote. The Court did note, however, that a union rule limiting the right to participate in union affairs to members in good standing is generally a reasonable restriction. The rule was invalid in this case only because of the unique circumstances under which employees on layoff were barred from paying their dues, even on a voluntary basis, and thus prohibited from voting on issues of importance to them.

2. Arbitrary Denial of Admission

The definition of member is very carefully drafted. Its purpose is to prevent a union from arbitrarily denying membership to people who meet all the requirements for membership. Historically, some unions restricted their *membership* to only a few of the employees they represented. Since only union members could vote, relatively few persons could control the destiny of many. The definition of member was intended to prevent these restrictions. Now if an employee meets the requirements for membership but the union arbitrarily denies it, the employee is classified as a member under the LMRDA and entitled to the rights that the Statute grants to members. The employee would have the same right as other members to vote on union contracts, for example. Note, however, that the Act does not regulate requirements for union membership; that is still an internal union matter.

There is a distinction between someone who voluntarily chooses not to become a member and someone who is denied membership. The statutory definition is designed to provide membership rights to employees who seek membership but are arbitrarily denied it. If membership is open, but persons choose not to join, they are not entitled to the member rights the LMRDA protects.

3. Membership Votes for Admission

What if a union requires a membership vote before an applicant is admitted to membership? When is an applicant who has fulfilled all membership requirements except the vote considered a member under the LMRDA? Some courts have held that a person is not a member as defined in Section 3(o) until voted in. Thus, a person who is brought up for membership and rejected would not be classified as a member because all the requirements for membership would not have been met. However, if a union arbitrarily refused to bring a person's name up for consideration, the person would probably be classified as a member under the statute. This area of the law has not been fully developed by the courts. The definition of a member must be applied in light of the Act's intent to prevent a union from arbitrarily denying membership to people who meet the requirements and want to join and enjoy the benefits of membership.

4. Rights of Officers under the LMRDA

Title I of the LMRDA refers to the rights of union members, but it does not expressly refer to the rights of officers or the right to hold office. Under Section 101(a)(5), a union member cannot be disciplined for exercising the right to free speech, etc. under Title I. What if a union president removes a lower union officer (or business representative) from a position because the officer opposes the president's policies. Does removing the officer from the position constitute retaliatory *discipline* against the officer violating the right as a union member to free speech?

This issue was considered by the Supreme Court in the *Finnegan* decision.[1] In that

[1] See legal principle 9.

case, the challenger for the position of union president won over the incumbent. The union's business agents had openly supported the incumbent for reelection. The union's bylaws permitted the union president to appoint and remove business agents. When the challenger took office as president, he immediately removed the former business agents, on the grounds that they were loyal to the former president and would be unable to follow and implement the new president's policies and programs. The business agents filed suit under the LMRDA alleging that their removal constituted unlawful discipline in retaliation for the exercise of their rights, as union members, to support the candidate of their choice. The Supreme Court, in a strongly worded decision, upheld the right of the new president to remove the former business agents. The Court concluded that the removal of an officer does not constitute discipline as long as the officer's rights or status as a member are not impaired (e.g., the officer cannot be expelled or suspended from membership). The Court stated that the LMRDA does not restrict the freedom of an elected union leader to choose a staff with compatible views. The Court said it was leaving two issues regarding removal from office open for further consideration in an appropriate case: (1) whether removal might violate Title I if it were part of a "purposeful and deliberate attempt to suppress dissent within the union" as distinct from an officer's right to choose a compatible staff; and (2) whether an officer can be removed from a nonpolicy-making, nonconfidential position.

The Supreme Court subsequently held in *Sheet Metal Workers v. Lynn*[2] that the *Finnegan* decision applies only to the removal of appointed officers, and that the removal of elected union officers for the exercise of rights protected by Title I of the LMRDA is unlawful. The Court reasoned that permitting a duly elected union officer to appoint a compatible staff to carry out the

[2] See legal principle 9.

officer's policies furthered the Title I goal of democratic unionism, but that the removal of an elected officer for exercising protected free speech rights under Title I would have the opposite effect; it would chill elected officers and the employees who voted for them in the exercise of their rights. In addition to the Supreme Court's ruling limiting *Finnegan* to appointed officers, several courts of appeals have also held that an officer cannot be removed from office if the removal is part of a purposeful and deliberate attempt to suppress dissent within the union, one of the issues that the Supreme Court left open in the *Finnegan* decision.

Finally, remember also that, as discussed above, a union must follow its own constitution and bylaws if they establish a higher standard than the LMRDA. Thus, while the LMRDA would not prohibit the removal of an appointed officer in most cases, as long as the officer's rights as a member are not affected, the union's constitution or bylaws may restrict the grounds for removal, or require a hearing before removal. If so, those provisions would be binding on the union.

5. Election Procedures: Title I versus Title IV

Other than establishing an equal right for all members to nominate and vote, Title I does not regulate internal union election procedures. Union elections are regulated by Title IV. Most of its provisions are administrative and it is a matter of reading the requirements and following them.

a. Major Provisions of Title IV. A local union must elect officers at least once every three years by secret ballot (Section 401(b)). The union must mail a notice of the election to each member to his last known home address at least fifteen days before the election (Section 401(e)). A union, upon a candidate's request, must distribute the candidate's campaign literature to all union members in good standing at the candidate's expense. A candidate is entitled to inspect a list of persons required to be members pursuant to a union security clause once within the 30 days prior to the election. The right to inspect is important because Title I of the LMRDA does not require that a union's membership list be open or provided to a member on request. (If however, a union violates one of the specific rights of members under Title I, then a court, in an appropriate case, may order a union to make its membership list available as part of the remedy to cure the violation.) A union is prohibited from discriminating between candidates with respect to distribution of literature and the inspection of membership lists (Section 401(c)). Union funds cannot be used to promote anyone's candidacy (Section 401(g)). Section 401(e) requires that all members be given a reasonable opportunity to nominate candidates. Every member in good standing must be eligible to be a candidate and hold office subject to Section 504 (prohibiting certain persons from holding office) and reasonable uniformly imposed qualifications for office.

Whether a given eligibility requirement is reasonable depends in part upon the percentage of the union's membership who are excluded from holding office by the rule's application. Thus, for example, the Supreme Court has upheld the Department of Labor's position that a rule requiring a member to attend a certain number of union meetings before the nominations date to be eligible for office is invalid, because most members would not meet the eligibility requirement and the rule would prevent a member from deciding at the last moment to run for union office. Another court has upheld the Department of Labor's position that a union bylaw provision designating that certain union executive board positions be held by minority group members is invalid because the provision denies nonminority group members the right to hold the reserved positions. But in another case, a court rejected the Department of Labor's position against a rule requiring that a member's dues be paid on time with certain

limited exceptions for a specified period before an election date to be eligible to run for office. The Court said there was no proof that the rule unreasonably restricted the number of members who were eligible for office and the union in fact had a history of vigorously contested elections.

The United States Department of Labor publishes a pamphlet entitled "Electing Union Officers" that covers nomination and election procedures in detail. This pamphlet is must reading for all candidates for union office and anyone who oversees an election.

b. Title IV as the Exclusive Remedy for Election Challenges. The courts have held that Title IV, not Title I, protects the right to run for office. Title IV is also the exclusive federal remedy for challenging election irregularities. Section 403 preserves a limited state court remedy to enforce a union's constitution and bylaws on elections before an election is held, but provides that Title IV is the exclusive remedy for challenging an election that has been held.

There are important procedural distinctions between Titles I and IV. An individual must bring his or her own suit to enforce rights guaranteed under Title I. In contrast, the Department of Labor enforces Title IV through individual complaints filed with it. The Department of Labor investigates the complaint and files suit if it determines that there is probable cause to believe that Title IV has been violated. The member cannot file suit directly individually. However, if the Department of Labor files suit, the member is permitted to intervene in the case. If the Secretary of Labor refuses to file suit, a member may file suit to compel the Secretary to proceed on the case. However, a court may order the Secretary to proceed only if the Secretary's decision not to file suit was arbitrary or capricious, a very difficult standard to prove. Complaints under Title IV may challenge an election only after the election is held, not before. A federal court injunction cannot be used to prevent an election from being held.

Why did Congress structure the law so

that an action challenging election irregularities can be brought only under Title IV after the election, but not under Title I beforehand? Congress preferred the risk of an improper election to the risks of delayed elections because it did not want elections to be delayed for years. If a member were to get an injunction against an election, who would be the union officers in the meantime? Do the officers hold over after their terms expire or not? No one can be sure. It might be years before a contested election was resolved in the courts. Congress wanted to avoid any instability that would hamper the legitimate operations of the union.

C. THE MEMBER'S RIGHT OF FREE SPEECH

1. The "Absolute" Free Speech Right

Suppose a union member accuses the union president of using union funds for personal use. The member, a political opponent of the president, makes the charge at the union meeting in the hope that it will arouse union opposition to the president. The charge is false and would constitute slander in court. Can the union president bring charges under the union's constitution against the opponent for attacking the president's character? Can the member be fined, suspended, or perhaps expelled for the slanderous remarks? No. Under LMRDA, Section 101(a)(2) a member has virtually an *absolute* right of free speech. The member's statements may be outrageous and totally unfounded, and might be considered as slanderous in a court action—that does not matter. Subject to certain limited exceptions discussed below, this right to meet, assemble, and speak freely with other members without any union imposed restrictions or discipline applies not only to union meetings but elsewhere as well, such as at work or at a private meeting at someone's home to discuss union matters.

A union may violate Section 101(a) by failing to keep proper order in a union meeting, so that a member is unable to present a viewpoint effectively. Thus, courts have upheld monetary damage awards against unions and union officers if union officers who oppose a member's position fail to keep order in the meeting when the member tries to speak, refuse to recognize the member at union meetings to speak although the member's request is in order, or publicly ridicule the member before the membership to apply peer-group pressure on the member to cease the opposition. A union cannot retaliate against a member for exercising the right of free speech, such as by refusing to refer a member for employment. Obviously, physical abuse or intimidation of a member would be a violation.

2. Common Law Remedies against False Statements

Although a member cannot be disciplined by the union for what the member says, a member who has been falsely accused may personally bring a civil suit for libel or slander. Libel is a written falsehood; slander is a spoken falsehood. Libel and slander are jointly referred to as defamation. However, the courts have treated a union officer as a "public figure" for the purpose of winning a defamation suit. The Supreme Court has held that if a false statement is made about a politician or "public figure," the public figure cannot successfully sue for defamation unless the person proves not only that the statement was false, but also that the statement was malicious. Malice means that (1) a person knows a statement is false but makes it anyway or (2) a person does not know whether a serious accusation is true or not, but makes the statement anyhow without trying to verify it (technically termed intentional disregard of the truth). These same two requirements apply to defamatory accusations against a union officer. Thus, if a union officer is defamed by a member, the officer must prove not only that the statement is false, but also that it is malicious.

Even if a statement is defamatory and made with malice, in which case the member might be subject to successful suit by the officer, the member still is not subject to internal union discipline. The statutory right to free speech applies even though the statements are defamatory.

3. Exceptions to Membership Free Speech

There are some exceptions to a member's free speech. Section 101(a)(2) has a proviso stating: "*Provided*, that nothing herein shall be construed to impair the right of a labor organization to adopt and enforce reasonable rules as to the responsibility of every member toward the organization as an institution and to his refraining from conduct that would interfere with the performance of its legal or contractual obligations.

a. Dual Unionism. The exception permitting a union to enforce reasonable rules on the responsibility of every member toward the organization applies to dual unionism. Dual unionism means supporting another union, such as advocating that the members leave their union and join another. A union can, for example, prohibit a member from standing up at a union meeting and urging everybody to join another union. That would be a reasonable rule governing the responsibility of the member to the organization as an institution.

The free speech exceptions are narrowly applied. If a member at a union meeting severely criticizes the union's operations, even without good reason, but does not advocate any other union in its place, the criticism is protected free speech. A union cannot prevent criticism on the grounds that it violates the member's responsibility to the organization as an institution. The law regards criticism as beneficial. A member can be stopped only if the member steps over the line from criticism to advocating another union.

There are some unexpected twists in the law on dual unionism. If a member files a decertification petition, the member is subject to union discipline. The NLRB has held,

however, that a member can be expelled from the union as discipline for filing a decertification petition, but cannot be fined. Why the distinction? Isn't expulsion more severe than a fine? The reason for expulsion instead of a fine is to minimize the conflict between the individual's statutory right under the LMRA to file a decertification petition and the union's right to protect its existence as the employees' representative. If a member is so hostile that the member seeks to decertify the union, the union should be able to protect itself by expelling that person. On the other hand, expelling the member, in context, is not a great penalty because obviously the person is not interested in the union. A monetary fine is, therefore, a greater penalty than expulsion. That is why, in resolving the conflicting interests of the union and the member, the Board has held that it is lawful to expel, but not fine a member for filing a decertification petition.

b. Interference with Legal or Contractual Obligations. The second exception to a members' free speech right is that a union can prevent conduct that interferes with the performance of its legal or contractual obligations. Under this exception, a union, for example, can discipline participants in a wildcat strike. If members engage in a wildcat strike, the union may, under some circumstances, be sued for breach of its no-strike clause (see Chapter Six) Thus, a union can prevent its members from interfering with the union's performance of its legal or contractual obligations by engaging in a strike, a slowdown, or other unlawful conduct. The union can prohibit discussion of illegal conduct at its meetings and can fine members for advocating or participating in such conduct.

Although the union has the right to discipline a member under the limited freedom of speech exceptions, the member is entitled to a hearing first under Section 101(a)(5) (Safeguards against Improper Discipline). A hearing is necessary before a member can be disciplined for any reason except failure to pay dues. There are no other exceptions regardless of how flagrant a violation may be or how clear the evidence. Congress apparently did not require a hearing before disciplining a member for failure to pay dues because there is not a factual issue and to prevent a person from enjoying the benefits of union membership without paying for them pending a hearing.

D. UNION'S DISCIPLINARY AUTHORITY OVER ITS MEMBERS

1. Union's Authority to Establish Grounds for Discipline

At common law the union, as a private unincorporated association, had a virtually unlimited right to fine or discipline its members, subject only to whatever limitations on discipline or procedural requirements were established by its own constitution and bylaws. Under the "contract theory" (see Chapter Ten), the constitution and bylaws formed a contract binding upon all the members.

Even under Landrum-Griffin, the union still retains broad authority over its members. A union cannot discipline a member without a hearing, except for nonpayment of dues. A union cannot discipline a member for exercising any of the rights protected under the Bill of Rights. Furthermore, as discussed below, a union cannot discipline members for exercising certain rights protected under the Labor Management Relations Act. But, it cannot be overemphasized that these restrictions have limited scope. Congress intended for most discipline to remain solely an internal union matter. To a great extent, unions still have the right to decide what actions to prohibit and what discipline to impose.

The Supreme Court has held that a union has the right, through its trial board, to determine whether its constitution and bylaws have been violated. A court cannot substitute its judgment for the union's. The Supreme Court stated that if a member appeals discipline to court, the court must uphold the union's decision on discipline as long as it is supported by some credible evidence. Also, the grounds for discipline do not have to be spelled out in detail in the union's constitution and bylaws. The Supreme Court's decision recognizes Congress's intent that unions regulate their own affairs. Of course, the courts will more closely scrutinize a union's actions that appear to impinge upon statutorily protected rights.

2. Discipline for Crossing a Picket Line

A union's right to discipline its members for crossing a picket line is a recurring issue under Title I of the LMRDA and also under the Labor Management Relations Act. Generally, under Title I of the LMRDA, unions have the right to fine or otherwise discipline members for crossing a lawfully authorized picket line established by the union, provided of course that the member receives a fair hearing on the charges as discussed below. (See Chapter Seven discussing permissible picketing and the right to honor picket lines, etc.) A member's duty to respect a picket line established by the member's union is a responsibility of the member to the union as an institution, and is one of the exceptions to membership free speech.

As discussed in Chapter Six, employees have the right under Section 7 of the LMRA to engage in concerted activity such as a strike or to refrain from such conduct. Some persons thus argued that a union violated Section 8(b)(1)(A) of the LMRA by disciplining members who refused to join in a lawful union strike. In *Allis-Chalmers Mfg. Co.*, the Supreme Court rejected this argument.[3] The Court extensively reviewed the LMRA legislative history and concluded that Congress had not intended to interfere in the union's traditional power to maintain control and unity over members during such a strike. However, union discipline may still

---

[3] See legal principle 13.

violate Section 8(b)(1)(A) if it is imposed on a member for refusing to engage in unprotected activity (see Chapter Four) such as striking in breach of a contractual no-strike clause or honoring an unlawful picket line. The Board has reasoned that an employee can be disciplined by the employer for such conduct, and a union cannot, by threat of disciplinary action, place an employee in the middle, subject to lawful employer discipline if the member supports the union or union discipline if the member refuses to do so. Also, as discussed in Chapter Seven, a union cannot *require* a member to honor a lawful picket line established by another union against another employer. An employee has the right as an individual under Section 7 of the LMRA to honor a primary picket line, but a union would be engaged in a secondary boycott in violation of Section 8(b)(4) of the Act if it compelled its members to honor the line.

The Supreme Court and the NLRB have held, in a series of cases, that if a member resigns from the union, even after a strike has begun, the member cannot be disciplined for any strike conduct occurring after the effective date of the resignation. As discussed in Chapter Ten, a resignation is generally effective at the time received.

Some unions have enacted constitutional or bylaw provisions prohibiting a member from resigning during or immediately before a strike. However, under the *Pattern-makers League* decision (discussed in Chapter Ten), any such restrictions violate Section 8(b)(1)(A) of the Act and are void. A member has the absolute right to resign from the union at any time and return to work. The Board has held that if a member does resign, the union has the right in return to suspend or expel the employee formally from membership so that the employee is prohibited from becoming a member again after the strike is over. Remember, however, as discussed in Chapter Ten, if a contract contains a lawful union security clause and the union rejects an employee as a member, that employee becomes a legal "free-rider."

Thus, if an employee who resigned from membership during a strike is barred from rejoining, that employee would become a free rider if the poststrike contract contains a union security clause. In contrast, if the employee who resigned is eligible for readmission but refuses to reapply, the employee can at least be required to pay the amount required of a financial core member and can be discharged under a union security clause for refusing to do so.

3. Discipline of Supervisors

Questions frequently arise about a union's right to fine supervisors who are union members. The laws do not prohibit supervisors from remaining in a union if they wish, and it is especially common in craft unions for supervisors to retain membership. However, a union, through its constitution and bylaws, need not allow supervisors to be members. Furthermore, employers can require that supervisors resign from their union. The NLRB has held that an employer can lawfully discharge a supervisor who refuses to resign because a supervisor has no statutory right to engage in union activity.

a. Crossing the Union's Picket Line. If a supervisor is a union member, but continues to work during a strike, can the union discipline the supervisor for crossing the picket line and continuing to work? As is frequently the case in legal questions, it depends on the facts. If a supervisor crosses the line but does only supervisory work, the supervisor cannot be disciplined by the union. This rule is based on Section 8(b)(1)(B) that makes it an unfair labor practice for a labor organization to restrain or coerce an employer in selecting its representative for the purpose of collective bargaining or the adjustment of grievances. The NLRB's view is that if a supervisor is just doing supervisory functions during a strike, the supervisor cannot be disciplined by the union for crossing the picket line.

The discipline would have an intimidating effect on the supervisor and thus interfere in the employer's selection of its representative for bargaining or adjusting grievances in violation of Section 8(b)(1)(B).

b. Doing Bargaining Unit Work During a Strike. In contrast, under the Supreme Court's decision in *Florida Power and Light*, a supervisor can be fined for doing bargaining unit work during a strike.[4] The Court reasoned that discipline of a member who is a supervisor violates Section 8(b)(1)(B) only if it may adversely affect the supervisor's duties in adjusting grievances or serving as a collective bargaining representative for the employer. Therefore, discipline for performing bargaining unit work during a strike is lawful because it is not based on the supervisor's performance of duties protected by Section 8(b)(1)(B).

The Board's membership has been split through the years on the proper implementation of the *Florida Power and Light* decision. Some Board members have argued that a supervisor/member may be disciplined for crossing the union's picket line and doing any bargaining unit work during the strike. Other members have argued that a supervisor/member can be fined only if the supervisor performs more bargaining unit work during a strike than the supervisor performed before the strike. The current majority view that the Board is now applying is that a supervisor/member may be disciplined for crossing the union's picket line and doing more than a "minimal" amount of bargaining unit or struck work. Eventually, because of the continued uncertainty, the Supreme Court may have to resolve this issue.

c. Supervisor Conduct in Administering the Collective Bargaining Agreement. Suppose a supervisor who is also a union member assigns work out of the bargaining unit in direct violation of a contractual restriction. Can the union discipline the supervisor

for this violation? No. The Board, as upheld by the Supreme Court, has ruled that administering and interpreting the contract (whether the supervisor is right or wrong) falls under Section 8(b)(1)(B) because these functions are closely related to collective bargaining.

For a while, the Board applied Section 8(b)(1)(B) very broadly to bar virtually any union attempt to discipline supervisors/members by applying the so-called "reservoir doctrine." Under this doctrine the Board reasoned that all supervisors constitute a reservoir of persons who might eventually engage in collective bargaining or the adjustment of grievances for their employer. Thus any union discipline of a supervisor-member, even one not currently performing Section 8(b)(1)(B) duties, might have a chilling effect on the supervisors when they performed such duties in the future or discourage members from accepting supervisory positions. In the *Electrical Workers Local 340* case,[5] the Supreme Court rejected the Board's reservoir doctrine on the grounds that the doctrine was contrary to the wording of Section 8(b)(1)(B) that prohibits union discipline only against supervisors actually involved in grievance adjustment or collective bargaining (including contract administration and interpretation). The Court stated that the possibility that discipline imposed for some other reason might have an adverse effect on the performance of Section 8(b)(1)(B) duties in the future was too speculative to constitute a violation of the Act. The Court also noted that an employer may easily protect itself against the possibility of divided loyalty by requiring, as it has the right to do, that a supervisor resign from the union.

4. Union Discipline to Maintain Production Limits

Suppose a union, to protect declining jobs, sets a production quota on the number

---

[4] See legal principle 11.

[5] See legal principle 12.

of units that its members can produce a day and prohibits employees from working overtime. Can a union fine a member for failure to follow these restrictions? Under the Supreme Court's decision in *Scofield v. NLRB*, a union can maintain production quotas and enforce them through membership fines[6] if the quota is not inconsistent with terms of the collective bargaining agreement.

In *Scofield*, the contract provided for piece work. The union limited the number of units any employee-member could put out in a day. If the employee-member put out more units, the employee was prohibited from collecting additional pay so there was no incentive to produce more. The union enforced the rule through fines. The Supreme Court held that the production restriction was lawful and could be enforced by a fine. The quota did not violate the collective bargaining agreement because the contract did not prohibit the employees from stopping production when they reached the point established by the union. Also, the union never refused to bargain with the company about the quota. Thus, the union was not compelling its members to engage in unlawful conduct.

The Court noted that under LMRA Section 8(b)(1)(A), a union is "free to enforce a properly adopted rule that reflects a legitimate union interest, impairs no policy Congress has imbedded in the labor laws, and is reasonably enforced against union members who are free to leave and escape the rule." The Court's reference to the member's freedom to leave the union is based upon the concept of the "financial core" member (see Chapter Ten). The Court generally has stressed, in cases involving a union's right to fine members, that any member can avoid union discipline altogether even if there is a union security clause in the collective bargaining agreement, by resigning from the union and becoming a financial core member.

[6] See legal principle 14.

Some contracts require mandatory overtime, while others make overtime voluntary. If overtime is voluntary under a contract, can a union, as a means to encourage the employer to hire more employees, enforce a union rule prohibiting employees from working overtime? Such a rule is probably lawful under the *Scofield* decision because it does not violate the collective bargaining agreement. (However, the concerted refusal of employees to work voluntary overtime in protest over some employer action, rather than filing a grievance over the matter, may violate a contractual no strike clause, and subject the employees to disciplinary action for obeying the rule. In that event the rule would not be enforceable by the union.) In contrast, if the contract makes overtime mandatory, the union cannot enforce a rule against accepting overtime contrary to the agreement because the employees could be disciplined by their employer for refusing the overtime, and the union would be violating its duty of good-faith bargaining by attempting unilaterally to impose a voluntary overtime rule in violation of the contract (see Chapter Five). Furthermore, just as a union cannot discipline an employee for refusing to engage in unprotected strike activity, discussed above, a union also violates Section 8(b)(1)(A) if it places a member in the middle of a union work rule dispute with the employer, facing employer discipline for following the union's rule or union discipline for obeying the employer's contrary order.

5. Discipline for Filing an NLRB Charge

A member can be expelled for filing a decertification petition; however, the Board has held that a member has an absolute right to file an unfair labor practice charge against the union or to testify in Board proceedings against the union regardless of the merit of the charge and cannot be expelled or disciplined in any way for doing so.

E. REQUIRED PROCEDURES FOR IMPOSING INTERNAL DISCIPLINE

The procedures that a union must follow in disciplining a member are listed in LMRDA Section 101(a)(5). The language is broad: "No member of any labor organization may be fined, suspended, expelled, or otherwise disciplined except for nonpayment of dues by such organization or by any officer thereof unless such member has been (A) served with written specific charges; (B) given a reasonable time to prepare his defense; (C) afforded a full and fair hearing."

1. Written Specific Charges

The first requirement of Section 101(a)(5) is that a member be served with written *specific* charges. Suppose that a member violates a union bylaw by crossing a primary picket line during a strike. Can the union simply serve the member with a charge that the member violated the union's bylaws without stating the reasons? No, that would violate the requirement for a *specific* charge; the union must tell the member specifically what the member did. The charge should state that the member violated the article by crossing the union's picket line and returning to work beginning on a certain day and continuing thereafter.

2. Reasonable Time to Prepare

Section 101(a)(5) requires that the member be given a reasonable time to prepare a defense. This is a very straightforward requirement. If a union serves notice on the member one day before the hearing day, the union is not giving reasonable time. Is two days reasonable or two weeks? There is no definite answer. It depends on the nature of the charge, the availability of witnesses, and the complexities of the case.

3. A Full and Fair Hearing

Finally, Section 101(a)(5) requires that the member be afforded a full and fair hearing. A full and fair hearing does not require that a lawyer be present. The courts have held that, since discipline is fundamentally an internal union matter, union trial boards are properly composed of lay union members. The hearing need meet only basic due process requirements. Due process, in our democratic society, contains the common-sense precepts that a defendant must be permitted to face the accuser, the decision must be based on evidence presented at the hearing, and the defendant must be permitted to cross-examine the witnesses and present evidence and witnesses in the member's own defense. Of course, a union's bylaws may go farther than minimum due process. They may allow a member to have a lawyer or be assisted by co-union member, even though the statute does not require it.

a. Composition of the Trial Board. As a matter of due process, a member who brings a charge should not sit on the trial board. Beyond that, however, any union member, as permitted by the bylaws, can be appointed a trial board member. The trial board determines the guilt or innocence and penalty for an accused member. There is no need for an independent outside person to be the judge. Frequently, the union executive board sits as the trial board. This is permissible, except that a board member who is personally involved in a matter should not sit as a board member in that case.

The only other restriction on the trial board membership is that the trial board cannot be stacked against the defendant member. A trial board composed of political opponents of the accused is highly suspect. Nor can the board be composed of persons who have prejudged the matter.

b. Applying the Rules of Evidence. Courts have fairly strict rules for court proceedings covering the type of evidence that can be admitted at a trial, the form evidence must take, and the weight it can be given. These rules do not apply to internal union procedures.

The Supreme Court has held that the courts must uphold a union's disciplinary decision if it is supported by some credible evidence. A court will not reverse a union's decision just because the trial was not conducted the way the court would have conducted it. The union's trial procedures need meet only basic due process standards for a full and fair hearing.

The right to cross-examine witnesses and the right to confront your accusers are fundamental rights required to meet the full and fair hearing requirement of Section 101(a)(5). If a member is denied these rights, the discipline is set aside.

Except for these basic rights of fair notice, reasonable time to prepare, and a full and fair hearing, there are no other statutory requirements for discipline. This once again emphasizes how much leeway unions have in their internal disciplinary proceedings.

F. CONTROL OVER THE AMOUNT OF UNION FINES OF MEMBERS

The amount of a union's fine is not controlled by federal law. Some persons had argued that an excessive fine against a union member for crossing the union's picket line and returning to work violates Section 8(b)(1)(A) because it coerces an employee in the exercise of the right to refrain from union activity. The Supreme Court rejected this argument in *NLRB v. Boeing Co.*[7] In *Boeing*, an employee crossed the union's picket line and returned to work without resigning from the union. He was subject to union discipline and fined $450. The union sued the member in state court to collect the fine and the employee filed a charge with the NLRB alleging the fine was unreasonable. The Board dismissed the complaint and the employee appealed. The Supreme Court held that the NLRB had no authority to regulate the amount of a fine. The Court stated: "While 'unreasonable'

[7] See legal principle 15.

fines may be more coercive that 'reasonable' fines, all fines are coercive to a greater or lesser degree. The underlying basis [is] not that reasonable fines were noncoercive under the language of Section 8(b)(1)(A) of the Act, but was instead that those provisions were not intended by Congress to apply to the imposition by the union of fines not affecting the employer-employee relationship and not otherwise prohibited by the Act."

What did the Supreme Court mean when it said the Act did not apply to fines not affecting the employer-employee relationship? It meant that a member cannot be discharged for refusing to pay a fine. Discharging an employee for failure to pay a fine would violate LMRA Sections 8(a)(3) and 8(b)(2) (see Chapter Ten). However, court action to enforce a fine does not violate the LMRA, provided, of course, that the fine was imposed for a lawful reason. (Remember for example, a union cannot fine a member for filing a decertification petition although the union can expel the member for doing so.)

There are limits on the amount of a union fine. The Supreme Court stated in *Boeing* that the state court in which the suit is pending has authority to determine whether the fine is reasonable. The Supreme Court stated: "Issues as to the reasonableness or unreasonableness of such fines must be decided upon the basis of the law of contracts, voluntary associations, or such other principles of law as may be applied in a forum competent to adjudicate the issue. Under our holding, state courts will be wholly free to apply state law to such issues at the suit of either the union or the member fined."

G. MEMBERSHIP SUITS AGAINST UNIONS: THE EXHAUSTION REQUIREMENT

Members have the right under LMRDA, Section 102, to sue their union for violation of their Title I rights. However, most union constitutions restrict a member's right to sue the union. Unions customarily establish internal dispute procedures, including provisions for appealing an adverse local decision to the international president, the international executive board, and even to the international convention. The constitution usually requires a member to exhaust (complete) these internal remedies before filing suit. It can take many months, perhaps a year or more, to exhaust internal union remedies. Many unions do not even hold international conventions every year.

Section 101(a)(4) limits a union's right to restrict suits by members. The section provides that a member *may* be required to exhaust reasonable hearing procedures not to exceed four months within the union before instituting legal or administrative proceedings against the union or any of its officers. This is a compromise between the union's right to require use of internal procedures and the member's right against unreasonable delay.

However, some courts have interpreted Section 101(a)(4) as governing a court's right to require exhaustion of internal union remedies, rather than authorizing a union to impose bylaw restrictions on a member's right to file suit without first attempting internal union procedures. Thus, it may be unlawful under Section 101(a)(4) for a union to fine or otherwise discipline a member for filing suit without first attempting internal union procedures, although a court, as discussed below, may, at its own discretion, impose an exhaustion requirement for a reasonable period not to exceed four months.

1. Court Restrictions on the Exhaustion Requirement and Time Limits for Filing Suit

The use of the word "may" in Section 101(a)(4) is significant. This means that the four-month exhaustion requirement is discretionary with the courts. If a member files a suit before the period is up, a court can waive the requirement for good cause. The most common exception to the exhaustion requirement is if a member's appeal within the union would be futile. For example, if a union member files a charge against an action of the international president and the internal appeal is to the international president, the likelihood of the member succeeding within the union is very slim. So, a court in such a case will probably conclude it is futile to wait four months and will permit an immediate suit.

As another exception, courts have held that a member does not have to exhaust internal union remedies if the member is clearly right in a claim. This exception may be applied if the member's claim pertains to a statutory right that clearly has been violated. Also, exhaustion may not be required if internal union remedies are unclear or inadequate. Although there are ways of avoiding the exhaustion requirement, a member is probably better off pursuing internal union remedies in most cases. The courts do not lightly disregard the exhaustion requirement. After all, federal labor policy strongly favors resolving union disputes within the union. Also, courts sometimes rule that they will not set aside disciplinary action based on grounds that the member had not raised with the union during the course of internal proceedings. This approach is in accord with the policy favoring internal resolution of disputes. Thus, a member who goes into court without even attempting to pursue internal remedies may be more limited in the arguments the court will consider. Finally, unions try to handle as many of their problems as possible internally. A member who has a union's best interests in mind, even though engaged in a dispute with it, might well consider exhausting internal remedies first in the hope that public litigation can be avoided.

The Supreme Court has ruled that the time period that a member has to file suit alleging a violation of Title I rights is the same period that a person has to file suit over a personal injury claim in the state where the violation occurred. This period, of course, varies from state to state. The Court specifically rejected the argument that a member should have only six months to file a suit, the time limit permitted for filing an unfair labor practice charge or filing a suit over the violation of the duty of fair representation (see Chapter Twelve).

2. NLRB Restrictions on Exhaustion

The four-month exhaustion requirement does not apply at all to NLRB proceedings.

The Board has held that a union member has the right to file an NLRB charge immediately without attempting to exhaust internal remedies. The Board bases this rule on LMRA Section 10(a), establishing the Board as the agency to prevent unfair labor practices and stating that the Board's authority cannot be affected by any other means of adjustment or prevention. As discussed above, a member cannot be disciplined in any way for filing an NLRB charge.

Summary

This chapter considered internal union matters primarily regulated by the Labor-Management Reporting and Disclosure Act, focusing on Section 101, known as the Bill of Rights. Under the Bill of Rights, members have virtually an unlimited statutory right, with only narrow exceptions, to criticize an officer or union policy. The union can enforce a member's responsibility as a member to the organization (e.g., prohibit dual unionism), and members may be prohibited from encouraging actions, such as wildcat strikes, that interfere with the union's legal obligations. However, the LMRDA does not protect a member's right to hold an appointive union office. Thus a subordinate may be removed from an appointed office for opposing the policies of the elected union leader as long as the subordinate's right to speak out as a member is not impaired or the member is not removed as part of a scheme to suppress dissent within the union.

Despite the statutory restrictions, most aspects of the relationship between a union and its members are still internal matters. As long as no federally protected rights are infringed, the union has broad authority to determine the actions for which it will impose discipline and the penalties. Thus, a union can fine its members for crossing a lawfully established picket line or for violating a union imposed work restriction that does not violate the terms of a collective bargaining agreement. Similarly, the union decides whether its rules have been broken subject only to limited judicial review. The basic reason for which the Supreme Court has upheld such broad union disciplinary authority is that a member is always free at any time to resign as a member and thus avoid all union discipline for conduct occurring after the resignation is effective.

Discipline can be imposed only following a full and fair hearing with reasonable notice of the specific charge. No hearing is necessary to discipline a member for failure to pay dues. A fair hearing entails the right to present evidence in one's defense, confront one's accusers, and cross-examine them.

As long as fair procedures are followed and the discipline does not infringe on a federally protected right, federal law does not govern the amount of a fine. However, if a union sues in the state courts to enforce a fine, the member may raise the reasonableness of the fine as a defense.

Review Questions

1. What rights does Section 101(a)(1) of the Labor-Management Reporting and Disclosure Act (LMRDA) guarantee to union members?
2. Must a person be formally admitted to union membership in order to be protected under the LMRDA?
3. Can a union fine members who return to work during a duly approved lawful strike?
4. Can a member be disciplined by the union for slandering a union officer at a meeting?
5. What grounds for discipline does the LMRDA permit?
6. Can the union discipline a supervisor who has remained a union member?
7. What are the statutory requirements for a hearing before discipline is imposed?
8. What are the basic due process requirements with which a union disciplinary hearing must comply?
9. How much may a union fine a member?
10. Must a union member exhaust internal union remedies before suing the union?

(Answers to review questions are at the end of the book.)

Basic Legal Principles

1. A person is considered to be a union member under the LMRDA if the person has fulfilled all requirements for membership, even though he or she may not be formally admitted. In some cases, if a membership vote is required, a person will not be considered a member until voted in. *Axelrod v. Stoltz*, 391 F.2d 549, 67 LRRM 2764 (3d Cir. 1968); *Alvey v. General Electric Co.*, 622 F.2d 1279, 104 LRRM 2838 (7th Cir. 1980) (laid-off members).

2. A union's constitution and bylaws may provide a member with more rights than the LMRDA requires, but a statutory violation cannot be excused or waived on the grounds that the union constitution and bylaws permitted the action taken. *Pignotti v. Sheet Metal Workers International Association*, 477 F.2d 825, 83 LRRM 2081 (8th Cir. 1973).

3. A member has an absolute right of free speech under the LMRDA except for the statutory exceptions for reasonable rules on the conduct of union meetings, the individual's responsibility to the union as an institution, and conduct interfering with the union's legal or contractual obligations. Free speech includes the right to make critical or even false statements about the union or its officers without discipline. *Hall v. Cole*, 412, U.S. 1,

83 LRRM 2177 (1973); *Salshandler v. Caputo*, 316 F.2d 445, 52 LRRM 2908 (2d Cir. 1963); *Fulton Lodge No. 2, International Association of Machinists v. Nix*, 415 F.2d 212, 71 LRRM 3124 (5th Cir. 1969); *Giordani v. Upholsterers International Union*, 403 F.2d 85, 69 LRRM 2548 (2d Cir. 1968); *King v. Grand Lodge International Association of Machinists*, 335 F.2d 340, 56 LRRM 2639 (9th Cir. 1964); *Wood v. Dennis*, 489 F.2d 849, 84 LRRM 2662 (7th Cir. 1973); *International Brotherhood of Boilermakers v. Rafferty*, 348 F.2d 307, 59 LRRM 2821 (9th Cir. 1965); *Parker v. Steelworkers Local 1466*, 642 F.2d 104, 106 LRRM 3038 (5th Cir. 1981); *Steelworkers v. Sadlowski*, 457 U.S. 102, 110 LRRM 2609 (1982); *Petramale v. Laborers Local 117*, 847 F.2d 1009, 128 LRRM 2461 (2d Cir. 1988); *Ferguson v. Iron Workers*, 854 F.2d 1169, 129 LRRM 2131 (9th Cir. 1988) (upholding discipline for dual unionism); *Guidry v. Operating Engineers Local 406*, 882 F.2d 929, 132 LRRM 2563 (5th Cir. 1989).

4. Except for the nonpayment of the union initiation fee and dues, a member must be afforded a hearing before being disciplined, regardless of how clear the member's violation of a policy may be. *Figueroa v. National Maritime Union*, 342 F.2d. 400, 58 LRRM 2619 (2d Cir. 1965).

5. Although Title I of the LMRDA requires that all members have an equal right to nominate officers, Title I does not regulate union election procedures or requirements for holding office. Election procedures are governed by Title IV of the Act as the exclusive remedy, which is administered by the Department of Labor. *Calhoon v. Harvey*, 379 U.S. 134, 57 LRRM 2561 (1964); *Schonfeld v. Penza*, 477 F.2d 899, 83 LRRM 2020 (2d Cir. 1973); *Crowley v. Teamsters Local 82*, 679 F.2d 978, 110 LRRM 2445 (1st Cir. 1982). Any restrictions on the right to hold office must not unreasonably restrict the right under Title IV for every member in good standing to be eligible to be a candidate and to hold office. *Steelworkers Local 3489 v. Usery*, 429 U.S. 305, 94 LRRM 2203 (1977) (meeting attendance requirement unreasonable); *Donovan v. Illinois Education Association*, 667 F.2d 638, 109 LRRM 2310 (7th Cir. 1982) (unreasonable to restrict specified number of union executive board positions to members of minority groups); *Shelley v. Brock*, 793 F.2d 1368, 122 LRRM 3005 (D.C. Cir. 1986); *Brock v. Masters, Mates & Pilots*, 842 F.2d 70, 127 LRRM 3070 (4th Cir. 1988) (requirement that dues be paid on time for twenty-four-month period preceding election reasonable under the circumstances).

6. LMRDA Title I requires that members have an equal right to vote on matters on which the union's constitution and bylaws require a vote, but the law does not specify the matters on which a vote must be taken. *Christopher v. Safeway Stores, Inc.*, 644 F.2d 467, 107 LRRM 2554 (5th Cir. 1981); *American Postal Workers Union, Local 6885 v. American Postal Workers Union*, 665 F.2d 1096, 108 LRRM 2105 (D.C. Cir. 1981) (burden on international union to have reasonable justification for requiring membership ratification of national contracts but no membership ratifi-

cation for members covered only by local agreements). Compare *McGinnis v. Teamsters Local 710,* 774 F.2d 196, 120 LRRM 2641 (7th Cir. 1985) (union holding meetings only at headquarters must make arrangements for additional meeting locations or mail ballots for members residing in outlying areas) with *Grant v. Chicago Truck Drivers Union,* 806 F.2d 114, 123 LRRM 3065 (7th Cir. 1986) (no requirement to hold membershp meetings); *Carothers v. Presser,* 636 F.2d 817, 122 LRRM 3273 (D.C. Cir. 1986) and related case 818 F.2d 926, 125 LRRM 2225 (D.C. Cir. 1987); *Zamora v. Hotel Employees Local 11,* 817 F.2d 566, 125 LRRM 2538 (9th Cir. 1987) (union must have translator at meetings so that Spanish speaking members can participate equally with other members in proceedings). *Millwright Local 1079 v. United Brotherhood of Carpenters,* 878 F.2d 960, 131 LRRM 3138 (6th Cir. 1989).

7. Application of the LMRDA's four-month exhaustion requirement before a member may file suit against the union is discretionary with the courts. An immediate suit may be allowed for such reasons as exhaustion is futile, the member's statutory rights have been clearly violated, or internal union remedies are unclear or inadequate. *NLRB v. Industrial Union of Marine and Shipbuilding Workers,* 391 U.S. 418, 68 LRRM 2257 (1968); *Detroy v. American Guild of Variety Artists,* 286 F.2d 75, 47 LRRM 2452 (2d Cir. 1961); *Fruit and Vegetable Packers v. Morley,* 378 F.2d 738, 65 LRRM 2424 (9th Cir. 1967); *Mallick v. Electrical Workers,* 644 F.2d 228, 106 LRRM 2738 (3d Cir. 1981) (union cannot discpline member for failure to exhaust internal remedies before filing suit); *Guidry v. Operating Engineers Local 406,* in legal principle 3. See also *Reed v. United Transportation Union,* 109 S.Ct. 621, 130 LRRM 2137 (1989) (limitations period for filing suit over alleged violation of LMRDA Title I rights is same as that permitted under state law for filing personal injury suit).

8. A union is free to determine the grounds for disciplining a member and the penalty as long as the discipline does not infringe upon statutorily protected rights or affect the member's employer-employee relationship and the member receives a fair and full hearing. The union's decision as to whether a violation has occurred need only be supported by some credible evidence. *International Brotherhood of Boilermakers v. Hardeman,* 401 U.S. 233, 76 LRRM 2542 (1971); *Rosario v. ILGWU Local 10,* 605 F.2d 1228, 101 LRRM 2958 (2d Cir. 1979) (due process requires verbatim record of union disciplinary proceedings); *Myers v. Theatrical Stage Employees, Local 44,* 667 F.2d 817, 109 LRRM 2799 (9th Cir. 1982); *Molders Local 164 v. NLRB,* 765 F.2d 858, 119 LRRM 3311 (9th Cir. 1985) (member cannot be disciplined for refusing to participate in unlawful strike); *Murphy v. Operating Engineers Local 18,* 774 F.2d 114, 120 LRRM 2837 (6th Cir. 1985) (fair hearing requirement); *Gustafson v. Train Dispatchers Assn.* 788 F.2d 1284, 122 LRRM 2199 (7th Cir. 1986); *NLRB v. Operating Engineers Local 139,* 796 F.2d 985, 123 LRRM 2021 (7th Cir. 1986); *Carpenters Local*

720 v. NLRB, 798 F.2d 781, 123 LRRM 2299 (5th Cir. 1986); *Mayle v. Laborers Local 1015*, 866 F.2d 144, 130 LRRM 2798 (1989).

9. An elected union officer may remove appointed subordinates who oppose the officer's policies as long as the subordinate's rights or status as a member are not impaired and the removal is not part of a scheme to suppress dissent within the union. Elected officers cannot be removed for exercising the free speech right under Title I of the LMRDA to oppose union policies, as such removal would chill the elected officers and the employees who voted for them in the exercise of their rights. *Finnegan v. Leu*, 456 U.S. 431, 110 LRRM 2321 (1982); *Sheet Metal Workers v. Lynn*, 109 S.Ct. 639, 130 LRRM 2193 (1989); *Cotter v. Owens*, 753 F.2d 223, 118 LRRM 2451 (2d Cir. 1985); *Witmeyer v. BRAC*, 779 F.2d 206, 121 LRRM 2049 (4th Cir. 1985); *John v. Kay*, 860 F.2d 529, 129 LRRM 2760 (2d Cir. 1988) (no discipline or retaliation against union officer as part of scheme to suppress dissent within the union); *Franza v. Teamsters Local 671*, 869 F.2d 41, 130 LRRM 2944 (2nd Cir. 1989).

10. A member may be expelled from membership for filing a decertification petition with the NLRB, but may not be fined or otherwise disciplined for such activity. *Tawas Tube Products, Inc.*, 151 NLRB No. 9, 58 LRRM 1330 (1965); *Molders Local 125*, 178 NLRB No. 25, 72 LRRM 1049 (1969). A member may not be expelled or disciplined in any way for filing an NLRB unfair labor practice charge against the union. *NLRB v. Industrial Union of Marine Workers*, 391 U.S. 418, 68 LRRM 2257 (1968); *International Assn. of Iron Workers*, 277 NLRB No. 99, 121 LRRM 1001 (1985); *Roofers Local 81*, 294 NLRB No. 20, 131 LRRM 1450 (1989).

11. A union may fine supervisors who are union members for crossing its picket line and doing bargaining unit work. *Florida Power and Light Company v. IBEW Local 641*, 471 U.S. 790, 86 LRRM 2689 (1974). The Board's majority opinion is that a supervisor may be fined for doing more than a minimal amount of bargaining unit work during the strike. *IUOE Local 501*, 287 NLRB No. 68, 127 LRRM 1201 (1987), enforced 806 F.2d 1405, 124 LRRM 2272 (9th Cir. 1986); *Rasmussen v. NLRB*, 875 F.2d 1390, 131 LRRM 2557 (9th Cir. 1989).

12. A union cannot fine a supervisor for matters pertaining to the supervisor's function as the employer's representative for bargaining, contract administration, or grievance adjustments. *American Broadcasting Cos. Inc. v. Writers Guild*, 437 U.S. 411, 98 LRRM 2705 (1978); *NLRB v. Electrical Workers Local 340*, 481 U.S. 573, 125 LRRM 2305 (1987); *Carpenters District Council of Dayton*, 296 NLRB No. 67, 132 LRRM 1153 (1989).

13. A union may fine members for crossing its lawful picket line unless they have effectively resigned from the union before crossing. *NLRB v. Allis-Chalmers Mfg. Co.*, 388 U.S. 175, 65 LRRM 2449 (1967); *NLRB v. Textile Workers Granite State Joint Board*, 409 U.S. 213, 81 LRRM 2853 (1972); *Booster Lodge 405, IAM v. NLRB*, 412 U.S. 84, 83 LRRM 2189

(1973); *Pattern Makers League v. NLRB*, 473 U.S. 95, 119 LRRM 2928 (1985): *UFCW Local 81*, 284 NLRB No. 131, 125 LRRM 1257 (1987); *Distillery Workers Local 186*; 296 NLRB No. 72, 132 LRRM 1129 (1989); *UFCW Local 1439*, 293 NLRB No. 4, 130 LRRM 1387 (1987).

14. A union may fine members for violating union-imposed work restrictions as long as the rules do not otherwise violate the law or the collective bargaining agreement. *Scofield v. NLRB*, 394 U.S. 423, 70 LRRM 3105 (1969); *Orange County Carpenters*, 242 NLRB No. 75, 101 LRRM 1173 (1979); *GAIU Local 13–B*, 252 NLRB 936, 105 LRRM 1416 (1980); *Paper Workers Local 5*, 294 NLRB No. 84, 131 LRRM 1545 (1989).

15. As long as a fine of a member is for a lawful purpose, the amount of the fine is not regulated by federal law. *NLRB v. Boeing Co.*, 412 U.S. 67, 83 LRRM 2183 (1973); *NLRB v. Operating Engineers Local 319*, 796 F.2d 985, 123 LRRM 2021 (7th Cir. 1986).

16. The alleged refusal by individual union officers to refer a member for employment through the union's hiring hall as a "personal vendetta" against the member for supporting a political rival does not constitute discipline within the meaning of LMRDA Section 101(a)(5) as the provision only applies to punishment or penalties authorized by the union as a collective entity to enforce its rules, not to retaliation by individual officers acting on their own in a specific case. The suspension of job referrals could constitute "discipline" if it were imposed as a sentence on an individual by a union in order to punish a violation of union rules. *Breininger v. Sheet Metal Workers*, ____ U.S. ____, 132 LRRM ____ (Sup.Ct. 1989).

Recommended
Reading

Abraham, "Individual Autonomy and Collective Empowerment in Labor Law: Union Membership Resignations and Strikebreaking in the New Economy," 63 *N.Y.U.L. Rev.* 1268 (1988).

"Current Issues in Union Democracy Law," 4 *Hofstra Lab. L.J.* 217 (1987).

"Free Speech and Union Newspapers: Internal Democracy and Title I Rights," 20 *Harv. C.R. & C.L. L. Rev* 485 (1985).

"Into the Mire of Uncertainty: Union Disciplinary Fines and NLRA Section 8(b)(1)(A)," 84 *W. Va. L. Rev.*, 411 (1982).

Levy, "Electing Union Officers and the LMRDA," 5 *Cardozo L. Rev.* 737 (1984).

"Substantive and Procedural Due Process in Union Disciplinary Proceedings," 3 *U. San Francisco L. Rev.* 389 (1969).

"Title I and Union Democracy," 12 *N.Y.U. Rev. L. & Soc. Change* 449 (1983–1984).

"Union Officials and the Labor Bill of Rights," 57 *Fordham L. Rev.* 601 (1989).

chapter 12

THE DUTY OF FAIR REPRESENTATION

The duty of fair representation is becoming increasingly important to unions as they negotiate collective bargaining agreements, administer contracts, and resolve grievances. Almost every union member has heard of the duty of fair representation, but there are many misunderstandings about the doctrine.

A. THE DEVELOPMENT OF THE FAIR REPRESENTATION DOCTRINE

1. The Steele Decision

The fair representation doctrine began with *Steele v. Louisville & Nashville Railroad*, a 1944 Supreme Court decision concerning racial discrimination by a union.[1] The union had been certified under the Railway Labor Act to represent a bargaining unit of railway firemen. A majority of the work force was white, but there was a substantial black minority. The union, however, excluded blacks from membership. The case predated the Civil Rights Act that prohibits race discrimination in membership. The union proposed contract changes that would have ultimately excluded all blacks from fireman positions. A black bargaining unit employee brought suit to have the agreement between the employer and the union voided.

The Supreme Court held that the union had to represent all employees in the bargaining unit fairly, even if they were not union members. The Railway Labor Act provides that a union is the exclusive bargaining representative of all employees in a bargaining unit. The Court said this right to exclusive representation imposed the duty to represent all employees fairly.

2. Early Developments under the Labor Management Relations Act

Unions under the Labor Management Relations Act also have the right to exclusive representation (see Chapter Four). Accordingly, the Supreme Court held in *Ford Motor Company v. Huffman* (1953) that unions governed by the LMRA also have the duty to represent all bargaining unit employees fairly.[2] In *Huffman*, the Court upheld the union's right to negotiate a seniority clause giving certain seniority preferences to veterans. In *Miranda Fuel* (1962), the NLRB ruled that a union's violation of its duty of

---

[1] See legal principle 1.

[2] See legal principle 1.

fair representation is an unfair labor practice.[3] The Board reasoned that Section 7 of the Act guarantees employees the right to engage in collecting bargaining, and that right includes the right to be represented fairly by the exclusive bargaining representative. Thus, the Board concluded that, by failing to represent all employees fairly, a union violates Section 8(b)(1)(A) (prohibiting interference with Section 7 rights).

3. Full Development of the Doctrine: The *Vaca* Decision

Although the fair representation doctrine began with the *Steele* decision, the doctrine was not fully developed until the Supreme Court's decision in *Vaca v. Sipes* (1967).[4] In *Vaca*, an employee had been discharged because of poor health. The employee claimed he was able to do his job and filed a grievance. The union processed the grievance through the prearbitration steps of the grievance procedure. At the union's expense, the employee went to a doctor for examination, but the examination was unfavorable. The union tried to convince the employer to give the employee light work, but the employer refused. The union then decided to drop the grievance.

The employee filed suit against the union in the state court, alleging that the union had arbitrarily and capriciously dropped his grievance. A jury awarded the employee $10,000 in damages. The case was appealed to the state supreme court that upheld the jury verdict. The state court reasoned that there was sufficient evidence for the jury to conclude that the employee was able to work and that the union had made the wrong decision in not arbitrating the grievance. The case was appealed to the United States Supreme Court.

The Supreme Court reversed the state court decision. The Court said that the actual issue in the case was whether the union had violated its duty of fair representation in dropping the employee's grievance. A union breaches its duty of fair representation if it represents an employee arbitrarily, discriminatorily, or in bad faith. Arbitrarily means making a decision without reason or at whim. The Supreme Court said the state court had incorrectly based the union's liability on whether the union was right or wrong in its decision. The Court indicated that it did not matter whether a union was right or wrong, only whether a union had acted arbitrarily, discriminatorily, or in bad faith in dropping a grievance. The Court concluded that the union had not acted arbitrarily and had met the fair representation standard in this case.

B. UNION DISCRETION TO ARBITRATE

The *Vaca* decision clearly establishes that a union does not have to take every grievance to arbitration. A union has the right to settle or to drop a grievance even though the grievance may have merit, as long as its decision does not violate the union's duty of fair representation. The Court stated:

A breach of the statutory duty of fair representation occurs only when a union's conduct toward a member of the collective bargaining unit is arbitrary, discriminatory, or in bad faith. There has been considerable debate over the extent of this duty in the context of a union's enforcement of the grievance and arbitration procedures in a collective bargaining agreement. . . . Some have suggested that every individual employee should have the right to have his grievance taken to arbitration. Others have urged that the Union be given substantial discretion to decide whether a grievance should be taken to arbitration, subject only to the duty to refrain from patently wrongful conduct such as racial discrimination or personal hostility.

Though we accept the proposition that a union may not arbitrarily ignore a meritorious grievance or process it in perfunctory fashion, we do not agree that the individual employee has an absolute right to have his grievance taken to arbitration regardless of the provisions of the

---

[3] See legal principle 2.
[4] See legal principle 4.A.

applicable collective bargaining agreement. In providing for a grievance and arbitration procedure which gives the union discretion to supervise the grievance machinery and to invoke arbitration, the employer and the union contemplate that each will endeavor in good faith to settle grievances short of arbitration. Through this settlement process, frivolous grievances are ended prior to the most costly and time-consuming step in the grievance procedures. Moreover, both sides are assured that similar complaints will be treated consistently, and major problem areas in the interpretation of the collective bargaining contract can be isolated and perhaps resolved. And finally, the settlement process furthers the interest of the union as statutory agent and as coauthor of the bargaining agreement in representing the employees in the enforcement of that agreement. . . .

If a union's decision that a particular grievance lacks sufficient merit to justify arbitration would constitute a breach of the duty of fair representation because a judge or jury later found the grievance meritorious, the union's incentive to settle such grievances short of arbitration would be seriously reduced. The dampening effect on the entire grievance procedure of this reduction of the union's freedom to settle claims in good faith would surely be substantial. Since the union's statutory duty of fair representation protects the individual employee from arbitrary abuses of the settlement device by providing him with recourse against both employer . . . and union, this severe limitation on the power to settle grievances is neither necessary nor desirable. . . .

C. PERFUNCTORY PROCESSING AS A VIOLATION OF FAIR REPRESENTATION: THE *HINES* DECISION

The Supreme Court briefly noted in *Vaca* that perfunctory processing of a grievance could violate the duty of fair representation. Perfunctory means acting in a superficial or cursory manner without care or interest. This aspect of the doctrine was clearly inapplicable to the union's conduct in *Vaca*. However, the Court directly faced the issue of perfunctory processing in *Hines v. Anchor*

Motor Freight, Inc.[5] In *Hines*, the employer discovered that certain drivers had turned in expense vouchers for motel rooms that, according to motel records, were higher than the amount the drivers had actually paid for the rooms. The employer, concluding that the drivers had pocketed the difference, discharged them. The drivers maintained that they had paid the full amount for the rooms. They told the union that the motel clerk must have altered the motel's records and embezzled money from the motel. The union business agent told the drivers that he would check with the motel, but he never did. The union processed the drivers' case to arbitration. The drivers continued to maintain their innocence, but the arbitration board upheld the discharge.

The employees sued the union for breach of fair representation and the employer for breach of contract in the same suit, on the theory that their discharges had violated the just cause provision of the contract. During pretrial proceedings, the motel clerk admitted that he had stolen the money and that the drivers were innocent, as they had claimed. The employer argued that the arbitration board's decision was final and binding, even though the employees could now prove their innocence. The Supreme Court stated that normally an arbitrator's decision, right or wrong, is final and binding on the employees. However, the Court held that an arbitrator's decision is not binding on the employees if the union violates its duty of fair representation in processing the case. The Court concluded that the union had violated its duty because it had handled the grievances in a perfunctory manner by failing to check out the employees' defense that the motel clerk was guilty.

1. Perfunctory Processing versus Mistake

The Supreme Court emphasized in *Hines* that the union had not violated its duty of fair representation just because the employ-

[5] See legal principle 3.

ees could prove their innocence. The *Vaca* decision had already established that a right/wrong test is not the basis for determining whether or not a union has violated its duty of fair representation.

Thus, the employees in *Hines* had to prove more than bad judgment or a poor investigation by the union. The court said that the grievance process could not be expected to be error free. The employees had to prove perfunctory treatment. What if the union had checked out the drivers' claims that the clerk was guilty by contacting the motel, but the clerk had not admitted his guilt? Then, the union's handling of the grievance would not have been perfunctory and the employees would have been bound by the arbitrator's decision.

The *Hines* case requires that a union investigate the merits when a grievance is filed; it cannot simply go through the motions. A union's decision whether to proceed, drop, or settle a grievance must be based on a consideration of the grievance's merits, and the advantages or disadvantages of proceeding. A grievance cannot be treated as a casual matter or processed as a matter of form without any interest or true consideration of its merits. As long as a union gives a grievance the consideration it deserves and does not deal arbitrarily, discriminatorily, or in bad faith with employees, the union's decision (right or wrong) does not violate the duty of fair representation.

The United States Court of Appeals for the Seventh Circuit, which covers Illinois, Indiana, and Wisconsin, has narrowly ruled that a union violates the duty of fair representation only if it engages in "intentional misconduct," which that Court defines as sabotaging a possibly meritorious grievance because of personal animosity toward the employee, or because the employee is a member of some racial or other minority group or is not a union member. Other courts of appeals, however, have not followed the Seventh Circuit approach, and it is generally well established that a union may violate its duty of fair representation even if it did not engage in intentional misconduct directed against the employee.

2. Practical Steps to Avoid a Fair Representation Suit

A union should keep employees informed on the status of their grievance. Some fair representation suits are filed just because the employee is unaware of the union's efforts in the employee's behalf. Unions win most of these cases, but only after considerable time and expense. If a union drops a grievance, the employee should be advised of the union's decision and its reasons. The union should give the employee the opportunity to present additional evidence or arguments in the employee's behalf. In this way, the union can avoid being accused of treating the grievance in an arbitrary or perfunctory way.

A union is not required to process a grievance every time an employee complains that his or her contract rights have been violated. The facts of a grievance or the contract's language may be such that the grievance is clearly without merit, or a prior grievance may have already raised and answered the same issue. However, a union that does not file a grievance because it apparently lacks merit runs the risk of being accused of perfunctory treatment. After all, the union in *Hines* may have thought it was a waste of time to check with the motel. In most cases, the better practice is to file a grievance for an employee, investigate the facts as necessary, and then withdraw the grievance with notice to the employee if it lacks merit.

D. UNION NEGLIGENCE AS A VIOLATION OF FAIR REPRESENTATION

The Supreme Court's decision in *Hines* as to the perfunctory processing of a grievance has raised questions whether a union violates its duty of fair representation if it handles a grievance negligently, such as by missing the contractual deadline for filing a grievance.

Shortly after the *Hines* decision, several federal district courts indicated that a union's negligent processing of a grievance could violate the duty. More recently, however, the courts of appeals that have considered the issue have generally held that simple or ordinary negligence by a union in the processing of a grievance is not a violation. These courts have indicated that there must be some intentional misconduct on the part of a union, above mere negligence, before a union violates the duty of fair representation. Thus, most courts would conclude that missing a filing deadline, although negligent conduct, does not violate the duty of fair representation. However, one court of appeals has stated that, as a narrow exception, a union may violate the duty of fair representation if it negligently fails to perform a ministerial (administratively routine) act, such as filing a grievance on time and an employee loses the right to challenge an employer's action on an important matter (such as the employee's discharge) solely because of the union's failure. Another court of appeals has held that the "inept handling" of a grievance may violate the duty of fair representation. In that case, the union failed to notice a contract provision directly on point supporting an employee's grievance and the union withdrew a grievance it should have pursued. Also, of course, acts such as missing a filing deadline or overlooking a relevant contract provision may be part of an overall pattern of perfunctory treatment for which a union is liable regardless of negligence. (A busy union representative who accidentally enters the wrong filing deadline date in the union's calendar may be only negligent, but the representative who sets a grievance aside because it initially appears to lack merit and misses the deadline before even investigating the grievance may be liable for perfunctory processing.) Eventually, because of the somewhat differing standards applied by the courts of appeals, the Supreme Court

may have to decide whether the duty of fair representation applies only to intentional misconduct by a union or whether some degree of negligence may be a violation regardless of the union's intent.

E. APPLICATIONS OF THE FAIR REPRESENTATION DOCTRINE

The duty of fair representation applies to the negotiation and administration of the collective bargaining agreement, as well as to processing grievances.

1. Fair Representation in the Negotiation Process

A union that is negotiating a contract must make decisions that favor some bargaining unit employees over others. The union must decide whether to press for higher wages (helping younger workers) or for higher pension benefits (helping older workers). Should a union favor a strict seniority system or one that considers skill and ability? Which decision must a union make to comply with its duty of fair representation? Either decision may fulfill the union's duty. Remember, the duty of fair representation is not based on whether a union's decision is right or wrong, but only on whether the union acts arbitrarily, capriciously, discriminatorily, or in a perfunctory manner. Thus, as long as a union makes a considered choice, weighing the advantages and disadvantages and the relative impact, its duty is fulfilled.

The union's duty of fair representation also includes the duty of a fair explanation of the terms of contractual agreements to be voted on by the membership. Thus, there have been several cases in which unions have entered into agreements with employers on controversial matters, such as seniority rights, which would benefit some employees, but which would be harmful to others. The union leadership, fearing that the agreement might not be approved if the agreement were fully understood, did not fully explain the agreement, or its impact, to the union membership before the vote was taken. The courts have held that such intentional misrepresentation violates the duty of fair representation.

2. Fair Representation during Contract Administration

The union's duty of fair representation also arises in the course of contract administration. The union must decide whether certain employer acts violate the contract. Unforeseen situations may arise, requiring contract changes or side agreements. Again, a union may make agreements with the employer that adversely affect certain employees as long as the union's decision is not arbitrary, discriminatory, in bad faith, or made in a perfunctory manner.

Many union decisions in administering a contract or processing grievances involve conflicting claims or rights of bargaining unit employees. Two employees may bid for a promotion, and the employee who is rejected may file a grievance alleging that the selection of the other employee violated the collective bargaining agreement. Which employee should the union support? Two employees may be discharged for fighting, and each may allege that the other started the fight. Which employee should the union believe? In either case, the union's obligation is to make a reasoned decision based on an investigation of the facts and the contract language. A union taking this approach would meet its duty of fair representation regardless of which employee it supported or whether its decision was "right" or "wrong."

Suppose an employer with two plants represented by the same union decides to close one plant and transfer its employees to the remaining facility. Should the employees of the two work forces be dovetailed into a single seniority list or should the employees of the closed facility be placed at the bottom of the list? There are arguments favoring both approaches, but the union can agree to either method as long as the decision is not arbitrary, etc. without violating its duty of fair representation.

3. Fair Representation at the Arbitration Hearing

The courts that have considered the issue have uniformly held that a union is not obligated to use an attorney in arbitration proceedings and may use its own officials to present its case. However, if a union uses an attorney on occasion, the decision to use an attorney in a particular case must not be arbitrary, discriminatory, or in bad faith. For example, a union would violate the duty of fair representation if it used an attorney only when the grievant is a union member. What if an employee asks to have the employee's own attorney at an arbitration hearing either in place of or to assist the union representative or attorney? The Union has no duty to allow the employee's own attorney at the hearing even at the employee's own cost. The union controls the grievance process, and the grievant's own attorney may unnecessarily complicate or even impair the arbitration hearing. Of course, a union may decide, on balance, to permit the employee's own attorney at the hearing along with the union's attorney or arbitration representative. Such action may reassure a member who has questions about the union's representation. Even then, however, the union representative would remain in charge and have ultimate decision-making power.

What if the union representative at an arbitration hearing does a poor job of representing the employee, such as making procedural errors or failing to cross-examine company witnesses properly? Of course, many experienced union arbitration representatives are very capable, but the courts, recognizing that a union usually has no obligation at all to provide an attorney in arbitration hearings, have held that a union representative cannot be held to the standards that an attorney must meet. Thus, even if the union's arbitration representative does a poor or ineffective job, there is no violation of the duty of fair representation unless the representative acted in an arbitrary, discriminatory, bad-faith, or perfunctory manner in presenting the grievance. If a union loses an arbitration case, must the union appeal the adverse decision to court if the grievant requests it? The courts have held that a union has no obligation to appeal, especially in light of the very narrow grounds for which an arbitrator's decision may be reversed by a court (see Chapter Nine). Under some very unusual set of facts, a union's decision not to appeal an adverse arbitrator's award might be arbitrary, discriminatory, in bad faith, or perfunctory, but that would be very rare.

4. Acts Initiated by Union Hostility

The duty of fair representation occasionally arises in cases of outright union hostility against a particular employee. The union must separate its internal relationship with an individual as a union member from its relationship with the individual as a bargaining unit employee. Regardless of differences on internal union policies, a union cannot retaliate against an employee in employment. Thus, a union cannot treat an employee arbitrarily, discriminatorily, or in bad faith on the job because of an internal union dispute. The employee is entitled to the same treatment as any other bargaining unit employee. Thus, a union may violate its duty of fair representation if (for arbitrary, discriminatory, or bad-faith reasons) it encourages an employer to discharge an employee, refuses to process the employee's grievances, or refers the employee to less desirable jobs.

The Board has held that a union cannot charge a nonunion employee for processing the employee's grievances if other bargaining unit employees are not subject to the same charge. The charge would violate the union's duty of fair representation.

F. REMEDIES FOR A BREACH OF THE DUTY OF FAIR REPRESENTATION

Both the NLRB and the courts have jurisdiction over an alleged violation of the duty of fair representation. A suit would be brought under Section 301 of the Labor Management Relations Act (see Chapter Nine for discussion of Section 301 procedures).

1. NLRB Remedies

The NLRB applies the same criteria as the courts, including the perfunctory treatment standard, in determining whether a union has breached its duty of fair representation. The Board does not regard union negligence as a breach of its duty under the LMRA. Remember that a charge must be filed with the Board within six months of the alleged violation.

If the Board finds that a union has breached its duty, the Board may order the union to process a grievance through the grievance procedure, including arbitration, if warranted, and permit the employee to be represented at the arbitration hearing by an attorney of the employee's own choice at the union's expense. If an employee suffers lost pay because of an employer's action (such as a lost promotion or a discharge) and the employee's grievance over the action is time-barred because the union fails to process the grievance in accordance with its duty of fair representation, the Board may order the union to pay the employee backpay for the lost earnings. The union's backpay liability may continue until such time as the union secures consideration of the grievance by the employer, even though the grievance is technically time-barred, and thereafter pursues the grievance in good faith with due diligence, or the employee is reinstated by the employer or obtains substantially equivalent employment elsewhere.

The Board has held that if the General Counsel in an unfair labor practice proceeding establishes that the union has violated its duty of fair representation in processing a grievance that was clearly not frivolous, the aggrieved employee will be entitled to backpay or other relief to make the employee whole unless the union establishes that the grievance lacked merit. However, this "make-whole" remedy is applied only if the union has failed or has attempted and been unable to have the employer consider the grievance on its merit. This procedure is known as a "provisional make-whole" remedy. The union has a choice of litigating the merits of the employee's grievance at either the hearing or at the compliance stage (see Chapter One for a discussion of these NLRB procedures). Some courts of appeals, contrary to the Board, have held that the burden of proof must be on the General Counsel to prove that a grievance has merit before the Board can issue a make-whole remedy, not on the union to prove that it did not. Thus, this issue as to the burden of proof, although it arises in only a relatively few cases, remains unresolved.

2. Judicial Remedies

a. Exhausting Contractual Remedies. Ordinarily, an employee is required to exhaust all contractual remedies before filing suit under Section 301. Furthermore, as the Supreme Court indicated in *Hines*, an employee is bound by a union's decision to withdraw or settle a grievance, or by an arbitrator's decision upholding the employer's action, and cannot successfully sue the employer unless the union violated its duty of fair representation in processing the matter. This means that an employee may lose a suit, even though the employee's contractual rights were violated, because the union did not violate its duty. The Supreme Court recognized that this rule means that some employees can lose out on meritorious claims, but felt that the need for finality in the decision-making process and the importance of employer-union discretion in resolving grievances outweigh that risk.

If a suit is filed, the court must decide two issues: First, whether the union has violated its duty of fair representation and second, whether the employer's actions violated the collective bargaining agreement. If the court concludes that the union has not violated its duty of fair representation, the suit is dismissed because the employer has no liability unless the union violated its duty. If the court concludes that the union violated its duty, the court then decides whether the employer breached the contract. The employee can lose even though the union has violated its duty if the court concludes that the employer did not violate the contract notwithstanding the union's breach.

Usually, the employee files a single suit against both the union and the employer alleging the employer's breach of contract and the union's breach of its duty of fair representation. Even if the employee brings suit against only the union or the employer, the employee to prevail must still prove that the employer breached the contract *and* that the union violated its duty of fair representation.

b. Procedural Requirements for Suit

TIME LIMITS FOR SUITS. The Supreme Court ruled in the *DelCostello* decision[6] that an employee has six months from the date a union allegedly breached its duty of fair representation to file a fair representation suit against the union and/or the employer. This is the same period allowed for filing an unfair labor practice charge with the National Labor Relations Board.

The six-month period for filing suit begins on the date the employee either knew or should have known of the acts giving rise to the violation. Thus, if a union improperly drops an employee's grievance, the six-month period would run from the date the union *notifies* the employee of its decision. If the union does not notify the employee, the period would run from the date that the employee, with due diligence (e.g., calling the union at reasonable intervals to check on the matter), would have found out

---

[6] See legal principle 8.A.

about the union's action. If a union enters into an agreement with an employer violating the union's duty of fair representation, such as arbitrarily agreeing to modify an employee's seniority rights, but the agreement is not implemented until a later date, the affected employee would have six months from the effective date to file suit even though the agreement itself was made at an earlier date. The limitations period runs from the *final act* giving rise to the violation, either the union's alleged violation of its duty or the employer's alleged breach of contract, whichever occurs later. Sometimes, if a union processes a grievance in a perfunctory manner and loses as a result (e.g., by missing a grievance deadline or overlooking key evidence), the employee may be unaware of the violation until the employee receives a copy of the arbitrator's decision. In such a case, the employee's time limit for filing a suit would run from the date the employee received a copy of the adverse decision. The limitations period for filing suit continues to run (is not *tolled*) even though an NLRB charge has been filed.

EXHAUSTING INTERNAL UNION REMEDIES. The Supreme Court held in *Clayton v. United Automobile Workers* that an employee need not exhaust internal union remedies before filing a fair representation suit against either the union or the employer if the internal union appeals procedure cannot result in reactivation of the employee's grievance or an award of the complete relief sought in the suit.[7] In the *Clayton* case, the employee alleged that the union had violated its duty of fair representation by arbitrarily refusing to process his grievance past the third step of the grievance procedure to arbitration and that his discharge was not for cause. He sued the employer for reinstatement to his job and sought monetary damages from both the employer and the union. By the time the employee learned of the union's decision to drop his grievance, the contractual time limit for requesting arbitration

[7] See legal principle 8.B.

had expired. Thus, even if the employee had appealed the union's decision internally within the union, and the union changed its decision, it would have been contractually too late to proceed with arbitration. Since the internal union procedures could not provide the employee with the complete relief he sought, including reinstatement, the Supreme Court concluded that exhaustion was not required.

Under *Clayton*, if an employee is seeking only monetary damages for an alleged breach of the union's duty of fair representation, but not seeking reinstatement, exhaustion of internal union remedies would be required if they could result in the employee's receiving the amount claimed. Also, some collective bargaining agreements now provide that a union can reactivate a grievance if an employee appeals the union's decision to drop a grievance, and the union concludes on appeal that the grievance has merit. If the contract permits the reactivation of a grievance, the employee may be required to exhaust internal union procedures to appeal the decision dropping the grievance before filing suit. However, as discussed in Chapter Eleven, the requirement of exhausting internal union remedies is always discretionary with a court. A court can permit a suit to proceed without exhaustion for proper cause, such as if the pursuit of internal remedies would be futile. The courts that have considered the issue have concluded that if a member attempts to exhaust internal union remedies first, the limitations period for filing suit is suspended (tolled) while those procedures are pending even if the remedies are, or turn out to be, futile.

c. Damages in a Fair Representation Suit. Most lower court decisions following the *Vaca* case held that if an employer wrongfully discharged or took some other adverse action against an employee in breach of contract, and the union violated its duty of fair representation in processing the employee's grievance to arbitration, the employer was still liable for the full amount of the employee's backpay and lost benefits because the employer's breach of contract was the initial cause for the employee's damages. The union was held liable for only the additional costs the employee incurred in enforcing the employee's contractual rights as a result of the union's violation, usually limited to the employee's attorney fees, court costs, and litigation expenses. However, contrary to this approach, the Supreme Court held in the *Bowen* decision that if a union violates its duty, the employee's damages are to be apportioned between the employer and the union, and that a union may be liable for part of the employee's lost wages and benefits depending upon the extent to which the union's actions increased the loss.[8]

The district court decision in *Bowen* held that the employer therein was liable for only the employee's damages between the date of the employee's wrongful discharge and the date that an arbitrator would have probably ruled in the employee's favor if the grievance had been duly processed by the union. The union was held liable for the employee's additional losses between the time that the arbitrator would have ruled and the date that the district court ruled in the employee's favor. Most grievances are processed to arbitration within a year, but it may take several years for a court decision. Thus, this formula would frequently result in the union paying a greater amount in damages than the employer (as the union did in the *Bowen* case) even though the employer's own contract violation instigated the employee's loss. The only issue that the Supreme Court decided in *Bowen* was that a union can be liable for a portion of the damages. The Court did not specifically approve the formula that the District Court had applied, or consider such questions as whether the relative fault of the employer or union should be considered in apportioning damages, but the basic formula applied by the district court in *Bowen* has become the general rule applied by the courts in apportioning damages.

In a few cases, a union has initiated the employer's contract violation. For example, a union may improperly insist that an employee be discharged and the employer may comply with the request. In that case, if the union's request violates its duty of fair representation, the union may bear the primary financial responsibility for the employee's lost wages and benefits, not just be liable for its proportionate share of the damages.

PUNITIVE DAMAGES. The Supreme Court held in *Electric Workers v. Foust* that punitive damages cannot be awarded against a union that violates its duty of fair representation in processing a grievance.[9] An employee is entitled to recover only his actual losses caused by the breach. The Court reasoned that the possibility of punitive damages would improperly curtail unions in their broad discretion needed to handle grievances and "thus disrupt the responsible decision making essential to peaceful labor relations." Presumably, therefore, punitive damages cannot be assessed against a union for acts growing out of the negotiation or administration of an agreement.

Summary   The duty of fair representation is derived from the authority of a union to be the exclusive representative of a bargaining unit. Since a union is the exclusive representative, with all the authority that implies, a union cannot act arbitrarily, discriminatorily, or in bad faith toward the employees it represents. Also, the union cannot treat its members in a perfunctory manner. Most courts have concluded that negligent acts do not violate the duty except possibly under very narrow exceptions. In some cases, however, the line between perfunctory acts and negligent acts may be difficult to draw.

[8] See legal principle 5.

[9] See legal principle 5.

The union's duty of fair representation applies to the negotiation process, contract administration, and the grievance procedure. A union may properly make decisions favoring the interest of some employees over others as long as its decision does not violate its fair representation duty. Errors in judgment do not violate the duty of fair representation.

A union is not obligated to arbitrate all grievances. It may drop or settle a grievance as long as the decision is not arbitrary, discriminatory, in bad faith, or made in a perfunctory manner. An employee is bound by the settlement or an adverse arbitrator's decision unless the union violated its duty of fair representation in processing the grievance.

The duty of fair representation can be enforced by the NLRB in an unfair labor practice proceeding or by the courts in an action under Section 301 for breach of contract. Suits under Section 301 are usually brought against the union for violation of its duty of fair representation and against the employer for breach of contract. If a court determines that the union breached its duty, an employee is not bound by a grievance settlement or even by an adverse arbitrator's decision. The court then determines whether the employer's actions violated the contract. Technically, it is possible for a union to have violated its duty of fair representation in handling a grievance, but for the employer not to have violated the contract. Suit must be filed within six months from the date an employee either knew or should have known of the acts giving rise to the violation.

The employee's damages in a Section 301 suit are apportioned between the employer and the union. The employer is liable for the damages caused by its breach of contract. The union may be held liable for any additional damages beyond the date that an arbitrator would have ruled in the employee's favor but for the union's breach of its duty. Damages in a fair representation case are limited to the employee's actual losses.

Review Questions

1. What is the basis for imposing the duty of fair representation on a union?
2. What are the basic requirements for meeting the duty of fair representation?
3. Does a breach of the duty of fair representation violate the LMRA?
4. Is an employee bound by an arbitrator's decision upholding a discharge?
5. If a union drops a discharge grievance and the employee subsequently discovers additional evidence proving that the discharge was not for just cause, can the employee successfully sue the employer for breach of contract?
6. Does federal or state law govern a court action for violation of the duty of fair representation?
7. Can a union lawfully negotiate a change in a contract's seniority

system from one basing promotion strictly on seniority to one considering both seniority and ability?

8. Is a mere error in judgment a violation of the duty of fair representation?

9. Who is responsible for an employee's damages in a successful suit growing out of a union's violation of its fair representation duty and an employer's breach of contract?

10. Has a union violated its duty of fair representation if an employee handed a grievance to a union business representative in time, but the representative failed to file it with the employer until the contractual time limit for filing had expired?

(Answers to review questions are at the end of the book.)

Basic Legal Principles

1. A union's duty of fair representation under both the Railway Labor Act and the Labor Management Relations Act is derived from the union's right of exclusive representation under those statutes. *Steele v. Louisville & N.R.R.*, 323 U.S. 192, 15 LRRM 708 (1944); *Ford Motor Co. v. Huffman*, 345 U.S. 330, 31 LRRM 2548 (1953).

2. A union's failure to represent employees fairly is an unfair labor practice in violation of Sections 8(b)(1)(A) and 8(b)(2) of the LMRA. *Miranda Fuel Co.*, 140 NLRB 181, 51 LRRM 1584 (1962); *Glass Bottle Blowers Assoc.*, 240 NLRB 324, 100 LRRM 1294 (1979); *Printing & Graphic Communications, Local 4*, 249 NLRB 88, 104 LRRM 1050 (1980); *Rubber Workers Local 250*, 290 NLRB No. 90, 129 LRRM 1129 (1988) (NLRB provisional backpay remedy if union fails or has attempted and been unable to have employer consider grievance on its merits). See also *Platemakers Union No. 4 v. NLRB*, 794 F.2d 420, 122 LRRM 300 (9th Cir. 1986).

3. In a suit under Section 301, an arbitrator's award sustaining a discharge may be set aside in an action against the employer for wrongful discharge only if the union breached its fair representation duty in the arbitration proceedings. *Hines v. Anchor Motor Freight, Inc.*, 424 U.S. 554, 91 LRRM 2481 (1976); *Hardee v. North Carolina Allstate Services, Inc.*, 537 F.2d 1255, 92 LRRM 3342 (4th Cir. 1976).

4.A. A breach of the union's statutory duty occurs if the union's actions or decisions are arbitrary, discriminatory, in bad faith, or perfunctory. As a general rule, mere errors in judgment are not a breach of the duty. *Vaca v. Sipes*, 386 U.S. 171, 64 LRRM 2369 (1967); *Hughes v. Teamsters Local 683*, 554 F.2d 365, 95 LRRM 2652 (9th Cir. 1977); *Russom v. Sears, Roebuck & Co.*, 558 F.2d 439, 95 LRRM 2914 (8th Cir. 1977); *Teamsters Local 355*, 229 NLRB 1319, 95 LRRM 1232 (1977); *Landry v. Cooper/T. Smith Stevedoring Co.*, 880 F.2d 846 (5th Cir. 1989).

4.B. Ordinarily, a union's negligence in processing a grievance is not a violation of the duty of fair representation. *Riley v. Letter Carriers'*

Local 380, 668 F.2d 224, 109 LRRM 2772 (3d Cir. 1981); *Hoffman v. Lonza, Inc.*, 658 F.2d 519, 108 LRRM 2311 (7th Cir. 1981); *Stevens v. Teamsters Local 600*, 794 F.2d 376, 122 LRRM 3040 (8th Cir. 1986). But see *Milstead v. Teamsters Local 957*, 580 F.2d 232, 99 LRRM 2150 (6th Cir. 1978) (inept handling of a grievance may violate the union's duty of fair representation) and *Eichelberger v. NLRB*, 765 F.2d 851, 119 LRRM 3333 (9th Cir. 1985) (negligence may be a violation if the employee's interest at stake is high and union fails to perform a ministerial act extinguishing the right). Compare *Camacho v. Ritz-Carlton Water Tower*, 786 F.2d 242, 121 LRRM 2801 (7th Cir. 1986) (intentional or discriminatory misconduct required for fair representation violation). See also *Merk v. Jewel Companies*, 848 F.2d 761, 128 LRRM 2608 (7th Cir. 1988) (no duty owed to retired members no longer having employee status).

5. Damages against a union in a fair representation suit are limited to an employee's actual damages. Punitive damages cannot be awarded. *Electrical Workers v. Foust*, 442 U.S. 42, 101 LRRM 2365 (1979); *Baskin v. Hawley*, 807 F.2d 1120, 124 LRRM 2152 (2d Cir. 1986). Damages are apportioned between the employer and the union. The union may be liable for the amount the employee's damages have been increased due to the union's wrongful conduct. Damages may include lost wages and benefits beyond the date an arbitrator would have ruled in the employee's favor but for the union's breach. *Bowen v. United States Postal Service*, 459 U.S. 212, 112 LRRM 2281 (1983).

6. A union is not obligated to arbitrate a grievance that is filed as long as the union's decision not to proceed does not violate its duty of fair representation. *Vaca v. Sipes* in legal principle 4.A.; *Hines v. Anchor Motor Freight, Inc.* in legal principle 3; *Moore v. Bechtel Power Corp.*, 840 F.2d 634, 127 LRRM 3023 (9th Cir. 1988); *Bonds v. Coca-Cola Co.*, 806 F.2d 1324, 123 LRRM 3284 (7th Cir. 1986) (union not obligated to appeal adverse arbitrator's decision); *Landry v. Cooper/T. Smith Stevedoring Co.*, in legal principle 4A.

7. A union may negotiate contract terms or enter into grievance settlements that favor some employees over others as long as the union's decisions are not arbitrary, discriminatory, in bad faith, or perfunctory. *Ford Motor Co. v. Huffman* in legal principle 1; *Humphrey v. Moore*, 375 U.S. 335, 55 LRRM 2031 (1964). See also *Farmer v. Ara Services, Inc.*, 660 F.2d 1096, 108 LRRM 2145 (6th Cir. 1981) (union violated duty of fair representation by failing to adequately explain impact of agreement with employer prior to membership vote); *ACRI v. Machinists Lodge 115*, 781 F.2d 1393, 121 LRRM 2679 (9th Cir. 1986).

8.A. An employee has six months to file a suit arising out of an alleged violation of the duty of fair representation from the date the employee either knew or should have known of the acts giving rise to the violation. The limitations period runs from the final act giving rise to the suit, either the union's alleged violation of its duty or the employer's alleged breach of contract, whichever occurs later. *DelCostello v. Teamsters*, 462 U.S. 151, 113 LRRM 2737 (1983); *West v. Conrail*, 481 U.S. 35, 124 LRRM 3137 (1987); *EATZ v. IBEW DME Unit Local 3*, 794 F.2d 29, 122 LRRM 2953 (2d Cir. 1986); *Hersh v. Allen Products Co.*, 789 F.2d 230, 122 LRRM 2730 (3d Cir. 1986); *Galindo v. Stoody Co.*, 793 F.2d 1502, 123 LRRM 2705 (9th Cir. 1986); *Proudfoot v. Seafarers Union*, 779 F.2d 1559, 121 LRRM 2392 (11th Cir. 1986). See also *Arriaga-Zayas v. ILGWU Puerto Rico Council*, 835 F.2d 11, 127 LRRM 2031 (1st Cir. 1987) (no tolling of limitations period while pursuing NLRB remedies).

8.B. An employee is not obligated to exhaust internal union remedies before filing suit unless the union has authority to reactivate the grievance or award the employee the complete relief sought in his Section 301 suit. *Clayton v. United Automobile Workers*, 451 U.S. 679, 107 LRRM 2385 (1981); *Wozniak v. Auto Workers*, 842 F.2d 633, 128 LRRM 2264 (2d Cir. 1988).

9. A union has no duty to use an attorney in arbitration proceedings nor to permit an employee to use the employee's own attorney. A union is not liable for errors its representative allegedly commits at a hearing unless the representative acted in an arbitrary, discriminatory, bad-faith, or perfunctory manner. *Castelli v. Douglas Aircraft Co.*, 752 F.2d 1480, 118 LRRM 2717 (9th Cir. 1985); *Hellums v. Quaker Oats Co.*, 760 F.2d 202, 119 LRRM 2200 (8th Cir. 1985) (union may maintain neutrality at hearing between two employees discharged for fighting at work); *Valentin v. Postal Service*, 787 F.2d 748, 122 LRRM 2033 (1st Cir. 1986); *Stevens v. Teamsters Local 600*, 794 F.2d 376, 122 LRRM 3040 (8th Cir. 1986); *Hotel Employees Local 64*, 278 NLRB No. 112, 121 LRRM 1283 (1986).

10. The alleged refusal of a union maintaining a hiring hall to refer an employee to jobs in retaliation because the employee opposed the union's leadership may violate the duty of fair representation and is subject to suit under LMRA Section 301 even though no employer breach of contract is alleged. The filing of an unfair labor practice charge with the National Labor Relations Board is not the exclusive remedy for such an alleged violation. *Breininger v. Sheet Metal Workers*, ___ U.S. ___, 132 LRRM ___ (Sup.Ct. 1989).

Recommended Reading

Goldberg, "The Duty of Fair Representation: What the Courts Do in Fact," 34 *Buffalo L. Rev.* 89 (1985).

Hill, "Union's Duty to Process Discrimination Claims," 32 *Arb. J.* 180 (1977).

Jacobs, "Fair Representation and Binding Arbitration," 28 *Lab. L.J.* 369 (1977).

Levine and Hollander, "Union's Duty of Fair Representation in Contract Administration," 7 *Emp. Rel. L.J.* 193 (1981).

Tidewell, "Major Issues in the Duty of Fair Representation Cases Since 1977," 62 *U. Det. L. Rev.* 383 (1985).

Weinstock, "The Union's Duty to Represent Conscientious Objectors," 3 *Lab. Law.* 163 (1987).

chapter 13

UNIONS AND EQUAL EMPLOYMENT OPPORTUNITY

Unions have been in the forefront of legislative efforts to eliminate discrimination and to support equal employment opportunity. Unions enforce the rights of employees to job equality by filing discrimination charges with the Equal Employment Opportunity Commission, negotiating contract clauses eliminating discriminatory practices, and arbitrating issues of job discrimination. Unions are classified as employers in relation to their own employees (secretaries, etc.), and thus have an obligation to comply with fair employment practices like any other employer. Unions are prohibited from discriminating in union membership. They also have a legal duty to ensure that employees are not discriminated against on the job. A union may be joined as a defendant in a civil rights case with the employer if the employer engages in unlawful discrimination that the union either encourages or does not actively oppose. Unions that operate a hiring hall or apprenticeship programs are required to recruit, refer persons to employment, and operate their apprenticeship programs without discrimination.

Civil rights litigation has become so complex that a discussion of civil rights tends to emphasize "do's and don'ts" for avoiding litigation. The cases discussed in this chapter tend to emphasize the problems that remain rather than the progress that has been made. Although there may be disagreement on some issues within the labor movement, organized labor has been and continues to be fundamentally committed to the goal of equal employment opportunity.

A. AN OVERVIEW OF THE STATUTORY REMEDIES AGAINST DISCRIMINATION

1. Title VII, Civil Rights Act of 1964

a. Employers and Unions Covered Under the Act. Title VII of the Civil Rights Act of 1964, as amended in 1972, commonly re-ferred to simply as Title VII (reproduced in the appendix), is the basic statute regulating equal employment opportunity. The other titles of the Act deal with equal rights in housing and education.

Section 701(b) defines the term "employer" as a person who employs at least fifteen employees in twenty or more calendar weeks of the current or preceding year.

Section 701(a) broadly defines a "person" to include individuals, corporations, labor unions, partnerships, trusts, and governmental units, etc. Thus, essentially every form of business organization is covered by the Act. State and local governmental units are covered by the definition of employer. Section 717 of the Act establishes a separate procedure for discrimination claims against federal agencies. This section provides for enforcement by the Civil Service Commission, but a Presidential Reorganization Order has reassigned this function to the Equal Employment Opportunity Commission (EEOC).

If an employer employs at least fifteen employees for more than twenty weeks in the year, the employer is subject to the Act for the balance of that year and the next year even if the work force falls below the fifteen-employee minimum. The requirement that an employer have at least fifteen employees to be covered by Title VII is high compared to the Labor Management Relations Act. The NLRB asserts jurisdiction over employers who have only two employees. To hold down the number of cases, the Board, however, has also established monetary jurisdictional standards that an employer must meet before the Board will assert jurisdiction over the employer (see Chapter One). The Equal Employment Opportunity Commission has no such requirement. Most states also have anti-discrimination laws similar to Title VII which cover smaller employers.

Note that under Section 701(b), only employers engaged in an industry affecting commerce are covered by the Act. This is the same broad statutory coverage the NLRB has under the LMRA (see Chapter One).

Sections 701(d) and (e) establish the coverage of labor unions under Title VII. Basically, every union that operates a hiring hall, regardless of the number of members, is covered by the Act. All other unions having at least fifteen members are covered if they either are a certified bargaining agent

under the National Labor Relations Act or the Railway Labor Act or if the union has been voluntarily recognized as the bargaining representative by an employer engaged in an industry affecting commerce even though the union is not certified.

RELIGIOUS DISCRIMINATION. Section 701(j) is an important provision covering religious discrimination. It requires that an employer make reasonable accommodation to the employee's religious beliefs as long as there is no undue hardship to the employer's business (discussed more fully below). Section 702 exempts religious organizations from the Act, permitting them to hire persons of their faith to carry out the organization's activities. There is a related exemption under Section 703(e) permitting schools of a particular religion to employ employees of that religion.

b. Prohibited Discrimination. Section 703 is the heart of Title VII. Section 703(a) broadly prohibits an employer from discriminating on the basis of a person's race, color, religion, sex, or national origin. Section 703(b) prohibits discrimination by an employment agency.

Section 703(c) broadly prohibits discrimination by a union on the basis of race, color, religion, sex, or national origin in union membership or job referrals. A union is prohibited from limiting, segregating, or classifying its members, or applicants for membership in any way that would deprive or affect a person's employment opportunities or employee status. Unions are prohibited from causing or attempting to cause an employer to discriminate against a person in violation of the Act.

Section 703(d) prohibits discrimination by employers, unions, or joint apprenticeship training programs in apprenticeship or other training programs.

Section 703 does not prohibit all types of discrimination: only discrimination based upon race, color, religion, sex, or national origin. Persons protected by the Act are referred to as members of a protected group or class. Persons discriminated against are referred to as discriminatees. An employer can lawfully discriminate against blonds or left-handed people because the law does not prohibit such discrimination. Section 703 does not prohibit age discrimination, but discrimination against people forty and over is prohibited by the Age Discrimination in Employment Act (discussed more fully below).

BONA FIDE OCCUPATIONAL QUALIFICATIONS (BFOQ). Section 703(e) contains an exception permitting discrimination in religion, sex, or national origin if religion, sex, or national origin is a bona fide occupational qualification (BFOQ). This section, the subject of considerable litigation in sex discrimination, is considered more fully below.The Age Discrimination in Employment Act contains a similar exception. Section 703(e) does not list race as a BFOQ; thus, race can never be a bona fide occupational qualification.

SENIORITY AND TESTING. Section 703(h) deals with the important issues of seniority and testing. This section permits the operation of a bona fide seniority system even though it results in different standards of compensation, different conditions, or privileges of employment between employees, as long as the differences are not the result of an intention to discriminate on the basis of race, sex, religion, or national origin. The section also permits the use of professionally developed ability tests that are "not designed, intended or used to discriminate." The relationship between seniority and the perpetuation of past discrimination, and the lawful use of tests under Section 703(h) are discussed below.

Section 703(j) provides that an employer is not required to grant preferential treatment because of an individual's race, color, religion, sex, national origin, or an imbalance in the work force. This section is important in reverse discrimination and affirmative action programs.

Section 704(a) protects persons against retaliation for opposing unlawful employ-ment practices; for filing a charge with the Equal Employment Opportunity Commission (EEOC); or for testifying, assisting, or participating in any manner in an investigation, procedure, or hearing under Title VII. Section 704(b) prohibits any advertisement for employment indicating a preference based on race, religion, national origin, or sex except where religion, national origin, or sex is a BFOQ.

c. Establishment and Powers of the Equal Employment Opportunity Commission. Sections 705(a), 706, and 707 establish the Equal Employment Opportunity Commission and the procedures to enforce Title VII. The EEOC is composed of five members appointed by the president for five years, one member designated chairman by the president. The commission also has a general counsel appointed by the president for four years. The EEOC is organized into districts.

The role of the EEOC and its general counsel is very different from the role of the NLRB and its general counsel (see Chapter One). Under the Labor Management Relations Act, the general counsel of the NLRB prosecutes unfair labor practice cases before the Board. The Board decides whether the LMRA has been violated and issues appropriate remedial orders.

In contrast, the EEOC only investigates unlawful employment practice charges to determine whether there is reasonable cause to believe the Act has been violated. If the EEOC finds reasonable cause, it attempts to eliminate the practice by conciliation. There is no trial before the EEOC as there is before an administrative law judge in the case of the NLRB. If conciliation fails, either the EEOC, the attorney general, or the complaining party can bring suit in federal court to enforce Title VII rights. The EEOC's general counsel, through his legal staff, litigates cases for the EEOC and provides general legal assistance and advice to the agency. Currently, attorneys assigned to the EEOC's district offices assist the agency's investigators in determining whether unlawful employment practice charges have merit.

Section 706(e) establishes the time limits for filing a discrimination charge with the EEOC, discussed in detail in Part E of this Chapter.

d. Effect on State Laws. Under Section 708, state laws regulating employment discrimination remain in effect. State law, however, cannot permit an act prohibited by federal law. This provision has invalidated so-called "protective legislation," formerly adopted in many states, limiting the hours that women could work or even the jobs they could hold. Some states, however, have stronger laws against employment discrimination than those contained in Title VII. Under Section 708, an employer or union is bound by the higher state standard.

Sections 709 and 710 establish the investigatory powers of the EEOC. Section 709(c) permits the EEOC to establish, as it has done, detailed recordkeeping requirements for employers and unions.

e. EEOC Procedural Guidelines. Section 713(a) permits the EEOC to establish procedural regulations. Some agencies are authorized to establish substantive regulations governing the conduct of people who are subject to the Act the agency administers. The Federal Communications Commission and the Security and Exchange Commission, for example, issue detailed substantive regulations. The EEOC was not given this authority; however, it does issue "guidelines" on what it regards as lawful or unlawful conduct under Title VII. There are detailed guidelines, for example, on testing as a means of employee selection, sex discrimination, and religious discrimination. Technically, these guidelines are only the EEOC's opinion on permissible conduct and they are not binding on a court, an employer, or a union. However, the Supreme Court has held that the guidelines are still entitled to "great deference" in interpreting the Act. Furthermore, an employer or union may raise good faith reliance on an EEOC guideline or opinion as a defense in a suit against it under Title VII.

2. Other Remedies against Employment Discrimination: The Civil Rights Acts of 1866 and 1871

Besides Title VII, two other statutes are important in enforcing equal employment: the Civil Rights Acts of 1866 and 1871. These laws, known as the Reconstruction Civil Rights Acts, were passed by Congress to give effect to the Thirteenth and Fourteenth Amendments of the Constitution that abolished slavery and provided equal protection of the laws for all citizens of the United States. They are now contained in Title 42 of the United States Code, Sections 1981 and 1983 (abbreviated 42 U.S.C. §§1981 and 1983). These provisions are discussed in part G below.

a. Federal Contractor Compliance Programs. In addition to the Civil Rights Acts, federal Executive Orders (issued by the president) prohibit employers with federal contracts from discriminating against their employees and require employers to adopt affirmative action programs for minority hiring. Detailed clauses prohibiting discrimination are part of standard government contracts. An employer may be barred from government contracts for failure to comply with these requirements. Each federal agency has an office responsible for insuring contractor compliance. The programs are centrally administered by the Department of Labor, Office of Contract Compliance.

The State and Local Fiscal Assistance Act prohibited governmental bodies that receive federal revenue sharing funds for their programs from engaging in discrimination in such programs based on race, color. national origin, sex, religion, age, and handicap. The Supreme Court held that only particular programs that received federal funds had to comply with civil rights laws, but the recently enacted Civil Rights Restoration Act overturned that decision, and requires that recipients of federal funds must comply with civil rights laws in all areas of operation.

B. THE BASIC CATEGORIES OF UNLAWFUL DISCRIMINATION: DISPARATE TREATMENT AND DISPARATE IMPACT

The courts have divided unlawful discriminatory conduct into two basic categories: disparate (different) treatment and disparate impact. Disparate treatment, as the name implies, means that an employer treats a person differently because of the person's race, national origin, sex, or religion. Disparate treatment is intentional discrimination. An employer's refusal to hire or promote an employee because of race, etc., is an example of disparate treatment. However, the concept of disparate treatment applies not only to such matters as discrimination in hiring, promotion, or termination, but also to any other form of disparate treatment on account of an employee's race, etc., including harassment on the job. Thus, in *Goodman v. Lukens Steel Co.*, the Supreme Court held certain unions liable under Title VII and Section 1981 (discussed more fully in the text below) because they refused to process grievances alleging that the employer engaged in racial discrimination in administering the contract.[1] The unions allegedly refused to process such complaints because they antagonized the employer and made it more difficult to settle the underlying contractual issues. However, the Court concluded that the unions' systematic refusal to process grievances involving racial discrimination amounted to disparate treatment of black employees.

Disparate impact means that an employer engages in an employment practice or policy that has a greater adverse impact (effect) on the members of a protected group under Title VII than on other employees, regardless of the employer's intent. For example,

an employer's requirement that a certain job be filled by a person with a college education would have a disparate impact on blacks because fewer blacks have college educations than whites. Under some circumstances, this educational requirement might violate Title VII because of the consequences, even though the employer adopted the requirement in good faith without any discriminatory intent.

1. Disparate Treatment Discrimination

The leading case pertaining to disparate treatment discrimination is *McDonnell Douglas Corp. v. Green.*[2] Employee Green, a black male and civil rights activist, worked as a mechanic until he was laid off in the course of a general reduction in the company's work force. While on layoff, Green engaged in protests that the general hiring practices of the company were racially motivated. As part of this protest, Green and others illegally stalled their cars on the main roads leading to the company's plant to block access to the plant during the morning shift change. Shortly thereafter the company advertised for mechanics, a job for which Green was qualified. Green applied for the job, but was not reemployed because of the stall-in.

a. Proving a Prima Facie Case of Disparate Treatment. Green filed a charge with the EEOC that the company had refused to hire him because of his race and his civil rights activities. The case ultimately reached the Supreme Court. The Court set down four factors that a person must prove to establish a "prima facie" case of discrimination based on disparate treatment. The term prima facie case means that the person bringing the suit (the plaintiff) has presented enough evidence at a trial for a court to conclude (infer) that the person was unlawfully discriminated against. The four factors that a plaintiff must prove are:

---

[1] See legal principle 1.A.

[2] See legal principle 1.A.

1. The person belongs to a protected group under Title VII.
2. The person applied for and was qualified for a job for which the employer was seeking applicants.
3. The person was rejected despite being qualified.
4. After the person was rejected, the position was filled by a white person or remained open and the employer continued to seek applications from others with the rejected applicant's qualifications.

The Court held the Green had proven a prima facie case because (1) he was black and therefore a member of a group protected under Title VII; (2) he was qualified for the job; (3) he was rejected despite being qualified; and (4) the company continued to seek persons with Green's abilities after Green was rejected.

b. Legitimate Employer Reasons for Rejecting the Individual.

A person will not necessarily win a discrimination suit because a prima facie case of discrimination has been proven. Instead, the Supreme Court stated that the employer then has the burden to rebut the presumption of discrimination by producing evidence that the plaintiff was rejected, or someone else was preferred, for a legitimate, nondiscriminatory reason. Later Supreme Court decisions applying *McDonnell Douglas* have made it clear that the employer does not have to *prove* that it acted for nondiscriminatory reasons in order to rebut the prima facie case, but only set forth clearly (articulate), through the introduction of admissible evidence, the reasons for the plaintiff's rejection. For example, suppose one black and one white applicant apply for the same job. Both persons are qualified for the job, but the employer selects the white applicant because the white applicant is supposedly better qualified for the position. The rejection of the black applicant who is qualified for the position would raise a prima facie case of discrimination. The employer would then have the burden of explaining clearly the nondiscriminatory reasons for its actions, but it would not have to prove that the white applicant is in fact better qualified than the black. The Court has also held that an employer's hiring procedures need not be the best method to maximize hiring of minority employees so long as the hiring decisions are based on legitimate nondiscriminatory considerations.

c. Employer Pretext for Discriminatory Actions.

Even if the employer successfully articulates a legitimate nondiscriminatory reason for its actions, the case is not necessarily over. The employee can still prevail if the employee proves that the employer's supposed lawful reason was not the true reason (a pretext), and that the employee was in fact discharged or otherwise treated in a disparate manner for discriminatory reasons. Thus, in *McDonnell Douglas* the Court stated that Green's stall-in tactics would be a legitimate reason for discharging Green, refuting the prima facie case, but the Court indicated that Green might still prevail if he could prove that white employees engaged in misconduct comparable to his, but that the white employees were not discharged, or that the employer based Green's discharge on his legitimate civil rights activities. The Court stated that the manner in which Green had been treated in his prior period of employment and the employer's general policies and practices regarding minority employment could also be considered in determining whether the company's lawful reason (Green's stall-in) was a pretext for unlawful discrimination. Proving pretext under Title VII is very similar to proving pretext in cases of unlawful discharge for union activity under the Labor Management Relations Act (see Chapter Four).

Thus, determining whether an employer has unlawfully discriminated against a person by disparate treatment involves what the Supreme Court refers to as a scheme of proof with three evidentiary stages. The employee has the initial burden of proving a prima facie case under the four *McDonnell Douglas* criteria. If the employee establishes a prima facie case, the employer may rebut the inference of discrimination by setting forth a nondiscriminatory reason for its actions. If so, the burden is on the employee to prove that the reason given is a pretext and that the employee was in fact subject to unlawful discrimination.

d. Dual Motives for an Employer's Action.

What if an employer has both a lawful and an unlawful motive for taking an action against an employee, such as discharging an employee in part for poor work performance but also because of the employee's race? The Supreme Court has held that the employee has the burden in such a "mixed-motive" case to prove that race played a motivating part (was one of the reasons) in an employment decision. The burden is then on the employer to prove that it would have made the same decision even if race had not been a factor. This is essentially the same approach that the National Labor Relations Board applies under the "Wright Line" test for determining whether an employer with a dual motive has unlawfully discriminated against an employee for union activity in violation of LMRA Section 8(a)(3) (see Chapter Four).

e. Application of the Basic Disparate Treatment Criteria.

Although *McDonnell Douglas* involved alleged race discrimination, the same order and burden of proof are applied in all disparate treatment discrimination cases against a protected group including those based on religion, national origin, sex, and age. The principles apply not only to refusals to hire, as in *McDonnell Douglas*, but to any other alleged disparate treatment, such as discriminatory layoffs, the denial of a promotion, or a discharge.

The Supreme Court has indicated that although *McDonnell Douglas* establishes the basic procedural and proof requirements in disparate treatment discrimination cases, the four factors listed in that case are not to be applied rigidly or mechanically. The Court said that the case's approach is simply a sensible orderly way to evaluate the evidence in a case.

For example, the fourth requirement stated in *McDonnell Douglas* is that a position remain open after the complaining party was rejected for it and that the employer continue to seek applicants of the complainant's qualifications after he or she was rejected. What if an employer withdraws a job without filling the position at all because the only qualified applicants were members of a minority group?

If the employer could not prove a legitimate reason for its action, a court undoubtedly would find that the employer had violated Title VII under these circumstances, even though all the requirements for a prima facie case under *McDonnell Douglas* were not met.

2. Disparate Impact Discrimination

a. The Adverse Consequences Test: The Griggs Decision.

The basic principles in disparate impact discrimination cases were established by the Supreme Court in *Griggs v. Duke Power Co.*[3] In *Griggs*, the employer required that job applicants for any job other than basic labor be a high school graduate and have a satisfactory score on two professionally recognized general aptitude tests. The tests did not measure the ability to learn or perform a particular job. These two job requirements had a disproportionate impact on blacks because a lower percentage of blacks than whites had a high school education and passed the tests. A suit was filed to have the requirements abolished. The employer argued that the high school graduation and test requirements were lawful because they were not adopted with an intent to discriminate. The employer also argued that the tests were lawful under Section 703(h) that permitted the use of professionally developed aptitude tests.

The Supreme Court held that both the high school graduation requirement and the tests violated Title VII. The Court stated that a specific intent to discriminate was not

---

[3] See legal principle 3.A.

needed for conduct to violate Title VII, but that Congress required:

[T]he removal of artificial, arbitrary, and unnecessary barriers to employment when the barriers operate invidiously to discriminate on the basis of racial or other impermissible classification. . . . The Act proscribes not only overt discrimination, but also practices that are fair in form, but discriminatory in operation.

The Court held that an employer must prove business necessity for an employment practice, such as the high school graduation requirement, which operates to exclude blacks from employment. Title VII prohibits an employment practice that operates to exclude blacks or any other protected group if the practice is not related to job performance. The burden is on the employer to prove job relatedness.

The Court concluded in *Griggs* that neither the general intelligence tests nor the high school graduation requirement had a proven relationship to successful performance on the job. To the contrary, the evidence showed that employees hired before the company adopted these requirements performed satisfactorily even though they were not all high school graduates or had passed the tests. The Court rejected the employer's argument that it acted in good faith, finding that Title VII was directed at the *consequences* of employment practices, not the motivation. The Court held that the provision of Section 703(h) permitting the use of professionally developed tests only applied if the test was job related.

Although *Griggs* involved testing and educational requirements, the case's principles have been applied to any employment practice or policy that has a disparate impact on a protected group. Courts have invalidated employer rules providing for the discharge of employees for excessive garnishments. These rules have had a disproportionate impact on blacks and employers have been unable to demonstrate business necessity for the rules. The employer's minor inconvenience in processing garnishments is insufficient to justify the adverse consequences.

b. Proof Required in Disparate Impact Cases: The* Wards Cove Packing Company *Decision. In *Wards Cove Packing Co. v. Atonio,* a controversial 1989 Supreme Court decision, the Court set forth its current standards for proving unlawful disparate impact discrimination.[4] In that case, skilled positions in the employer's cannery were predominantly filled by white workers but the unskilled positions were filled primarily by nonwhites. The court of appeals held that the nonwhite employees had made out a prima facie case of disparate impact discrimination based on statistics showing a high percentage of nonwhite workers in the unskilled jobs and a low percentage of nonwhite workers in the skilled positions. However, the Supreme Court held that a prima facie case of disparate impact could not be based solely on these statistics. Rather, the Court stated that the employees also must identify the particular employment practices that created the disparate impact and specifically show that each challenged practice has a significant disparate impact on employment opportunities.

The Court further stated in *Wards Cove* that if the employees establish a prima facie case of disparate impact, the employer then has the burden of *producing evidence* of a *business justification* for its employment practice. This burden is similar to the burden an employer has in a disparate treatment case, discussed above, to set forth a nondiscriminatory reason for its actions. Although the Court did not expressly state in *Wards Cove* that it was overruling or modifying the *Griggs* decision, *Wards Cove* appears to modify *Griggs* in several important ways. First, *Griggs* appeared to place the burden of *proof* on an employer to rebut a prima facie case of disparate impact discrimination. In contrast, *Wards Cove* only requires that the employer produce evidence of a business justification for an employment practice, but the ultimate burden of proof remains on

---

[4] See legal principle 3.B.

the employees. Second, the *Griggs* decision appeared to require business *necessity* for an employment practice having a disparate impact, but *Wards Cove* only requires that the employer produce evidence of a business *justification* (not necessity) for the practice. The Court stated in this regard that the practice must serve a legitimate employment goal of the employer but need not be "essential" or "indispensable." This standard appears to be far less stringent than that previously established in *Griggs*.

Even if an employer produces evidence of a business justification for its employment practice, the employees may still prevail in an disparate impact case if they establish that there are other tests or selection devices which would also serve the employer's legitimate needs but without the undesirable disparate impact on a protected group. The Court stated in *Wards Cove* that such evidence of an alternative method would prove that the employer's justification is a pretext for unlawful discrimination. However, the Court also indicated that the alternative methods proposed by the employees must be equally effective as the employer's procedure in achieving the employer's legitimate employment goals including such factors as the cost or other burdens of the proposed alternative. The Court cautioned that judges "should proceed with care before mandating that an employer must adopt a plaintiff's alternate selection or hiring practice in response to a Title VII suit."

The basic concept of disparate impact discrimination still remains in effect under the *Wards Cove Packing Co.* decision, but, as a practical matter, the decision will undoubtedly make it more difficult for employees to prevail in such cases.

c. Use of Statistics in Proving Disparate Impact. As in *Griggs* and *Wards Cove Packing Co.*, statistics are frequently used in proving the disparate impact of employment policies or practices. Statistics may also be relevant in determining whether a particular act of apparent disparate treatment is part of an overall general pattern of discrimination.

Statistics, of course, work both ways. Thus an employer can also use statistics of an overall proportionate work force to refute allegations that a particular employee was denied employment, or otherwise treated differently, because of race. However, as discussed more fully below, that an employer's work force is statistically proportionate is not a defense to unlawful discrimination against any individual member of a protected group. The Supreme Court has also cautioned that statistics are not irrefutable and that their usefulness varies from case to case. They can be rebutted by showing there is an error in the statistics themselves, or that the statistics, while correct, are being used to make improper comparisons.

The *Wards Cove Packing Co.* decision has clarified the use of statistics in disparate impact cases. In *Wards Cove,* the court of appeals relied solely on statistics showing a high percentage of nonwhite workers in the unskilled jobs and a low percentage of nonwhites in the high-skilled jobs to establish a prima facie case. However, the Supreme Court stated that the proper comparison was between the racial composition of the high-skilled jobs at issue and the racial composition of the qualified population for the job in the relevant labor market. (The labor market may vary depending upon the employer's size and the required job skills. For some employers, or for some technical positions, the labor market may consist of an entire metropolitan area or even the entire United States. For some small employers, such as a neighborhood convenience store, the labor market may only be the area where the store is located.) If labor market statistics are difficult to determine, then the Court said other statistics such as comparing the percentage of qualified minority group members who apply with the percentage of minority group members who are hired may be used instead, unless qualified minority group applicants were deterred from applying for jobs due to discriminatory practices by the employer. Figures comparing an employer's minority group employment with figures for the general population may be used if they accurately reflect the pool of qualified applicants. The Court stated that basing a finding of discrimination solely on racial imbalance alone in one segment of an employer's workforce might lead to the use of numerical quotas in the workplace which the Court had rejected in the past.

What if an employer requires that employees pass a test that is not job related, but there is not a disproportionate impact on members of a protected group? The percentage of blacks in the work force, for example, may be the same as the percentage of blacks in the relevant labor market; or the same percentage of black and white applicants may pass the test even though it is not job related. The purpose of Title VII is to prevent practices or policies that have adverse consequences on protected groups. Thus, if an employment policy or practice has no adverse consequences, the employer can retain the requirement. Job relatedness is an issue only if the plaintiff establishes a prima facie case of discrimination by proving a disproportionate impact.

d. Perpetuation of Past Discrimination.

Sometimes practices appear neutral at face value but are in fact discriminatory because they perpetuate (prolong the effect of) past discrimination. An employer may establish a line of promotion with a number of steps from trainee to journeyman status in a particular classification and require that an employee work for a specified period in the lower classification before being promoted to the highest position. Normally, that is a permissible requirement. But, consider the situation in which an employer previously discriminatorily barred members of a protected group from the job classification. What if the employer ceases its discriminatory practices, but still requires the minority employees to work their way up each step of the classification in the specified time. Under those circumstances, requiring experience in the lower jobs first would perpetuate the prior discrimination because the victims of the discrimination (the discriminatees) might already have been in the top

classification but for the prior discrimination. The Supreme Court held in *Griggs* that practices that perpetuate past discrimination in this fashion violate Title VII because of their discriminatory impact.

e. Testing Requirements and Disparate Impact.

The use of tests in making employment decisions, whether for hiring, promotion, or other purposes, has been a recurring issue under Title VII. Under Section 703(h), an ability test can be used if it is professionally developed and is not designed, intended, or used to discriminate. The Supreme Court indicated in *Griggs* that tests that have a disproportionate impact on a protected group must be job related to be lawful under Section 703(h).

Since 1966, the EEOC has periodically issued detailed guidelines for determining whether a test is job related. The Supreme Court has indicated courts should give great deference to these guidelines when determining whether a test with disparate impact violates Title VII. In *Albemarle Paper Co. v. Moody*,[5] the Court relied heavily on the guidelines in ruling that the employer's tests for promotion to skilled jobs violated Title VII because of the disparate impact on black employees. The Court upheld the guidelines' basic principle that a test must be predictive of success on a specific job in order to be job related. There must be a correlation between performance on the test and performance on the job.

The employer in *Albermarle* attempted to validate its test by comparing test results with employee performance on a higher level job in each skilled classification promotion series, not on the entry-level positions in which employees would start. The Court upheld the EEOC guidelines position that tests should generally be validated by comparing test results with employee performance on a job at or near the entry level, unless the job progression structure and seniority system are such that new employees will probably progress to a higher level

---

[5] See legal principle 5.

within a reasonable period of time in the great majority of cases. Tests must be validated at or near the entry level if progress is not nearly automatic or if the time span before promotion is such that the higher level job might change in the meantime or the employee's own potential for the higher job could be significantly changed. There was no evidence in *Albermarle* that employees progressed automatically or rapidly to the higher level jobs. Thus, the Court held the tests were invalid under Title VII because they improperly measured success at the higher level jobs rather than at the entry level.

f. The Bottom Line Concept: The Uniform Testing Guidelines.

A major issue under Title VII is whether an employer has complied with Title VII if the proportion of protected group employees in the overall work force is representative although some aspects of the employer's practices are discriminatory. What if an employer uses an employment test that proportionately fewer blacks pass, but the employer hires a higher percentage of the blacks who do pass so that the employer's overall work force is proportionate? If the test is not job related, some individual black applicants may have been discriminatorily denied employment under the *Griggs'* principles because of the test even though the employer ends up with a proportionate work force. Some persons have argued that any individual member of a protected group denied a job because of a test or any other employment practice that does not meet Title VII requirements has a claim under Title VII, even though the employer's overall work force is proportionate. On the other hand, employers argue that only the "bottom line" should matter and that employers should be judged on the overall impact of their employment policies, not on each individual component practice or policy. Thus, these employers argue, a proportionate work force should be sufficient to comply with Title VII even though a particular practice, such as a test,

might have a disproportionate impact on a protected group.

In 1978, the Equal Employment Opportunity Commission, the Department of Labor, the Department of Justice, and the United States Civil Service Commission, the four agencies having primary federal responsibility in the civil rights field, adopted "Uniform Guidelines on Employee Selection Procedures" that still remain in effect. These guidelines pertain to the use of tests in making employment decisions. They are especially important because these agencies had previously disagreed among themselves on certain issues pertaining to tests. Remember, these guidelines are not necessarily binding on either an employer or a union. They do, however, set forth the agencies' interpretation of the law and, under prior Supreme Court decisions, are entitled to great deference by a court.

The guidelines adopt the bottom-line concept by providing that employment tests need not be validated for job relatedness if the employer's overall selection procedures are such that the selection rate for any race, sex, or ethnic group is not less than four-fifths (80 percent) of the group with the highest selection rate. The agencies regard the four-fifths as a "rule of thumb" for determining whether an employer's practices have a disproportionate impact. For example, if an employer hires 90 percent of the white applicants for employment (the highest selection rate), the employer must hire at least 72 percent of all black applicants (80 percent of 90 percent) in order for the employer's "bottom-line" results to indicate that the employer's overall selection processes do not have a disproportionate impact. If the selection rate for any protected group is less than 80 percent of the selection rate for the highest group, the agencies will find that the employer's employment practices have adverse consequences. In that event, each employment practice, including the test, must be validated for job relatedness. If, however, the four-fifths figure is reached, the agencies look only at the "bottom line" and do not require validation. The guidelines do not require comparison of minority subgroups, such as white males versus black females.

That an employer meets the four-fifths rule of thumb does not necessarily mean that it is not discriminating. Thus, the guidelines emphasize, an individual can still bring a discrimination charge against an employer meeting the four-fifths requirement if the employee can prove that the employee was discriminatorily denied employment based on a specific employment practice or policy, even though the employer's overall statistics meet the bottom-line standard.

The Uniform Guidelines contain a number of exceptions under which the four-fifths rule would not apply. Thus, regardless of meeting the four-fifths requirement, an employer cannot engage in a practice that perpetuates past discrimination against current employees. Furthermore, an employer cannot maintain an employment practice, such as maintaining a policy against hiring employees with an arrest record, that either the courts or an administrative agency have found is not job related under similar circumstances.

The Supreme Court established in *Connecticut v. Teal,*[6] that the "bottom line" of an employer's hiring practices will not excuse discrimination against individual employees. In that case, the state of Connecticut used a test that was not proven to be job related to determine eligibility for promotion to certain supervisory positions. A higher percentage of whites than blacks passed the test, and only those who passed were on the eligibility list. However, a higher percentage of those blacks who did pass were ultimately selected for promotion. The final result was that 22.9 percent of all black applicants who applied for the promotion were selected, while only 13.5 percent of the white applicants were selected. Certain black applicants who had failed the test sued the state on the grounds that the test dis-

criminated against them. The state asserted that even if the test was discriminatory (because of its disproportionate impact and because it was not proven to be job related), the "bottom line" of its hiring practices, in which a greater percentage of black than white applicants were promoted, was a complete defense to the charge. The Supreme Court, in a strongly worded decision, rejected the state's defense. The Court stated that the primary focus of Title VII is on the protection of individual employees rather than the protection of a minority group as a whole, and that Title VII guarantees each minority group member the opportunity to compete equally with members of the majority group on the basis of job-related criteria.

VALIDATION METHODS. The Uniform Guidelines continue the basic policy of the prior EEOC Guidelines that a test must be professionally validated to show a clear relationship between selection procedures and performance on the job. A selection procedure, however, must be validated only if it has a disparate impact. The Uniform Guidelines further require that an employer, as part of a validation study, investigate whether there are alternative selection procedures that would meet its legitimate needs, but that would have less adverse impact on a protected group.

A test can be validated in one of three ways. First, the test can correlate to performance on the job. Second, the test can correlate with success in an important element of the job (typing abilities for a secretary). Third, the test can be validated by demonstrating a correlation with an important trait needed for success on the job, such as traits needed for success as a salesperson.

The Uniform Guidelines contain standards and documentation requirements for validating tests using each of the three basic methods. The guidelines are technical and many pages long. Because there are detailed requirements and exceptions that a book of

---

[6] See legal principle 3.C.

this nature cannot cover, the Uniform Guidelines themselves must be consulted to determine their application to a particular situation.

C. SPECIAL PROBLEMS OF SEX DISCRIMINATION

1. Sexual Stereotypes

Unlawful discrimination because of sex also generally falls into either the disparate treatment or disparate impact categories. Additionally, women have also faced the problem of sexual stereotyping under which employers assume that women are only suited for, or only want to do, certain work. The courts have uniformly held that an employer cannot reject a woman for a job because of a sexual stereotype (e.g., that women are not capable of heavy manual labor). Under Title VII, each woman must be judged on her individual capabilities.

a. Height and Weight Restrictions. There has been considerable litigation over height and weight restrictions on jobs because of the disproportionate impact on women. Many such requirements have been invalidated under Title VII because employers have been unable to prove the need for an arbitrary cutoff on height or weight to do a particular job. Again, the basic principle of Title VII is that each applicant must be judged by her own ability to do a particular job, not by arbitrarily established standards.

b. Different Social, Behavioral, or Moral Standards for Men and Women. An employer cannot limit jobs requiring travel to men on the assumption that married women do not want to travel or that a single woman traveling alone may create a poor image for the company, because the employer would be basing its decision on a stereotyped assumption about the work and social roles of women.

Similarly, women cannot be denied employment on the basis of different moral standards than those that apply to men.

Depending upon the job, employers may be able to consider moral and ethical standards in determining whether to hire a person, but the same standards must be applied to men and women. Also, an employer cannot apply different standards of acceptable behavior on the job for men and women, such as approving certain business tactics as "aggressive" in a man while criticizing similar conduct as "too pushy" for a woman based on a stereotyped perception of femininity.

2. Grooming Standards

Grooming standards are an exception to the usual rule that an employer cannot apply different rules to men and women. The courts have upheld rules requiring short hair for male employees, but allowing women to have any length of hair. The courts have concluded that such rules do not deny employment opportunities and that hair length is "peripheral" (not of concern) to the Civil Rights Act. However, an employer must prove business necessity if a grooming standard, such as a rule forbidding certain hairstyles, has a disproportionate impact on a particular race.

Although different grooming standards for men and women do not violate Title VII, disciplining an employee for failure to meet a particular grooming standard might still violate the just cause provisions of a collective bargaining agreement. For example, if an employer discharged an employee because of hair length, an arbitrator might decide that the hair-length rule was unreasonable, unless justified for safety or public relations reasons, and that the employee could not be disciplined for violating it.

3. Fringe Benefit Contributions for Men and Women

Many fringe benefit plans are funded solely by employer contributions. Other plans require that the employees contribute a percentage of their salary to a plan as well. Such plans are called contributory plans.

The Supreme Court held in *City of Los Angeles v. Manhart* that an employer cannot require women to pay a higher percentage than male employees as their share in a contributory plan.[7] Employers argued that women could be required to pay more into a pension plan than men because women live longer and would therefore receive greater pension benefits upon retirement. But the Supreme Court reasoned that Title VII requires that employees be treated as individuals and not have their rights determined by assumptions based on their sex as a group. The Court stated that since there is no way to determine whether a particular woman would live longer than a particular man, an individual woman cannot be required to pay more than a man. Therefore, an employer must contribute equal amounts to fringe benefit funds for men and women.

Although the *Manhart* case pertained to pension plans, the same reasoning applies to any fringe benefit plan. Thus, an employer cannot require either men or women to pay in more to a health and welfare plan on the assumption that employees of one sex, as a group, are absent or ill more often than the other.

The Court subsequently held in *Arizona Governing Committee for Tax Deferral Annuity and Deferred Compensation Plans v. Norris*,[8] that Title VII also prohibits an employer from offering women lower monthly retirement benefits than men who have made the same contributions. The Court specifically rejected the employer's contention that its plan did not discriminate on the basis of sex because women as a class would receive approximately the same amount in benefits as men because of their longer life expectancy. However, the Court held that its decision would not apply retroactively to employees who were already retired.

4. The Equal Pay Act

In addition to Title VII, women employees are also protected by the Equal Pay Act,

[7] See legal principle 8.

[8] See legal principle 8.

which requires an employer to pay women the same as a man for doing the same work. This Act predated Title VII and prohibits the once common practice of paying women less for doing the same job based on the theory that a married man needed a greater salary to support his family. This Act does not prohibit disparate treatment other than prohibiting paying women less for the same work.

Of course, Title VII also prohibits paying women less for performing the same job as a male employee. However, the Equal Pay Act is part of the Fair Labor Standards Act, commonly known as the Wage-Hour Law. The Fair Labor Standards Act has a two-year limitations period for filing suit in court rather than the basic 180 days allowed under Title VII for filing a charge with the EEOC. Thus, it might be possible to remedy an equal pay violation under the Equal Pay Act after the time for filing a charge under Title VII has expired. Also, the Equal Pay Act permits an employee to collect not only the amount of back pay owed, but also an additional sum as damages equal to the amount of the pay owed. The amount is at the court's discretion. Thus, an employee may receive a greater back pay award under the Equal Pay Act than under Title VII. Sometimes a suit may be brought under both Title VII and the Equal Pay Act if both provisions have been violated. That can be done by filing a charge with the EEOC, waiting six months while the charge is processed (as discussed below), and then filing suit in federal court under both statutes. The Equal Pay Act provides for enforcement through the Department of Labor, but a Presidential Reorganization Order has transferred enforcement to the EEOC.

5. Bona Fide Occupational Qualifications

An employer may use sex as an employment qualification if it is a BFOQ under Section 703(e), although the courts have emphasized that this is a narrow exception. Sex can be a BFOQ only if an employer has a reasonable factual basis for believing that all or substantially all of the excluded group (women) would be unable to perform a job. A distinction based on a stereotyped assumption on male or female roles is not valid.

The Supreme Court upheld the state of Alabama's right to limit "contact" prison guards in an all male prison to men because the prisoners were poorly controlled and the women's sex might incite unrest and even attacks upon them. The Court emphasized, however, that its decision was narrowly based on the specific facts at that prison. In the same decision, the Court still held that Alabama's general height and weight requirements for prison guards were unlawfully discriminatory against women because the requirements excluded 44 percent of all women from consideration for prison guard positions.

6. State Protective Laws

State protective laws for women limited the right of women to work overtime or to engage in certain occupations. These laws originally had good motives. They were designed to protect women, but they were based on sexual stereotypes of a woman's role and work ability. The laws frequently worked against women because employers refused to hire them for certain jobs because of the restrictions.

The EEOC, with court approval, has held that the existence of a state protective law cannot justify an employer's refusal to hire or promote a woman to a certain position. Furthermore, once a woman is hired, she is subject to the same working conditions as any other employee. Under Section 708, the provisions of Title VII prevail over the state legislation.

7. Pregnancy Benefits

Pregnancy benefits were a much debated issue under Title VII. The Supreme Court held in 1976 that Title VII did not prohibit an employer from excluding pregnancy

benefits from a hospitalization plan. This decision raised many questions, such as whether pregnant women were entitled to sick leave if their pregnancy disabled them for work or whether pregnant women who went on pregnancy leave could continue to accumulate seniority under the same conditions as a male employee on sick leave.

These issues were resolved by the Pregnancy Disability Act amendment to Title VII, effective October 31, 1978. The pregnancy amendment broadened the definition of sex discrimination in Title VII to include discrimination on the basis of pregnancy, childbirth, or related medical conditions. Under this amendment, women disabled due to pregnancy must be treated the same as to their conditions of employment, including fringe benefits, as any other person disabled for work for any other reason. Thus, a woman cannot be discharged because she is pregnant. A woman who is able to work, although pregnant, cannot be required to take sick leave at a certain time. A woman on leave due to her pregnancy can continue to accumulate seniority and is entitled to reinstatement under the same conditions as any other temporarily disabled employee.

A pregnant woman disabled for work is entitled to the same disability benefits as a worker disabled for any other reason. Hospitalization plans must cover the cost of hospitalization for pregnancy, childbirth, and related medical conditions. As an exception, however, the amendment states that employers are not required to pay health insurance benefits for abortion except where the life of the mother would be in danger if the fetus were carried to term or where "medical complications" have arisen from an abortion. An employer, however, can provide such benefits voluntarily or if a collective bargaining agreement requires them.

If an employer does not provide disability or paid sick leave to other employees, it does not need to for pregnant workers. The law as amended only requires the employer to treat pregnancy and childbirth the same as other disabilities under fringe benefit plans.

An employer is not required to provide disability payments to a pregnant worker who asks for time off unless she is disabled for work because of her condition. Similarly, after a woman gives birth, she is entitled to benefits while she is disabled for work. If a woman is able to work, however, but chooses to stay off longer to be with her newborn child, she is not entitled to continued benefits while she voluntarily stays off work. A woman who wishes to remain off work longer than medically necessary is entitled to personal leave under the same conditions as any other employee who receives such leave.

8. Emerging Issues—Sexual Harassment, Reproductive Hazards Discrimination, and Comparable Worth

a. Sexual Harassment. Prevention of sexual harassment against female employees on the job, a longstanding problem which has only recently received much public attention, is of increasing importance in Title VII litigation. It is well established that an employer violates Title VII by conditioning concrete employment benefits such as a promotion on sexual favors. The courts refer to this as "quid pro quo" harassment. However, there was some disagreement among the courts as to whether harassment that created a hostile working environment without directly causing a tangible economic loss was also unlawful. The Supreme Court resolved this issue as to a hostile work environment in *Meritor Savings Bank v. Vinson.*[9] In *Meritor*, employee Vinson, a female who had worked at a bank for four years, was discharged for excessive use of sick leave. After her discharge, Vinson brought a Title VII action claiming that during her four years of employment at the bank she was subjected to sexual harassment by a vice president of the bank. Vinson claimed, among other things, that she submitted to

her supervisor's repeated sexual demands out of fear of losing her job.

The Supreme Court held that sexual harassment of an employee can constitute unlawful sex discrimination under Title VII if the harassment is so severe or pervasive as to alter the conditions of the victim's employment and create an abusive working environment. Such harassment may be actionable even if the sex-related conduct was, as in Vinson's case, "voluntary" in the sense that the victim was not forced to participate against her will. The advances need only be unwelcome. However, the Court also held that a plaintiff's alleged sexually provocative speech or dress can be considered in determining whether a plaintiff found particular sexual advances unwelcome. The Court stated that such evidence was relevant in accordance with the EEOC guidelines which emphasize that whether there has been sexual harassment is to be determined by the "totality of the circumstances, such as the nature of the sexual advances and the context in which the alleged incidents occur." However, the Court also stressed that a district court must exercise control in determining exactly what background evidence to admit in a sexual harassment case so as to avoid unfair prejudice against a plaintiff because of her background.

In general, an employer is liable for sexual harassment of an employee by co-workers only if the employer knew or should have known of the conduct but failed to take prompt remedial steps. (An employer "should know" of conduct if it is so blatant or pervasive that the employer would be aware of it through reasonably diligent inquiry.) However, another important issue in sexual harassment cases resolved in part in *Meritor* is whether an employer should be automatically (per se) liable for harassment by a supervisor in all cases or liable only if the employer knew or should have known of the harassment, as in the case of harassment by co-workers. The courts and the EEOC generally agree that in cases of "quid pro quo" harassment, an employer is automatically liable if a supervisor acting in

[9] See legal principle 9.

the course of the supervisor's authority makes or threatens to make an employment decision affecting an employee, such as a promotion, because of the employee's gender. However, courts were divided on the liability issue in hostile environment cases. Some courts held that an employer is per se liable if a supervisor creates a hostile environment, but other courts ruled that an employer is liable in such a case only if it knew or should have known of the conduct. In *Meritor* the Supreme Court held that an employer should not be held liable automatically in a hostile environment harassment case, but the Court refused to set definite standards for determining when an employer should be liable. The Court stated only that the EEOC and the courts should look to "agency" principles for guidance. The law of "agency" holds a principal [an employer] liable for acts of its agents [supervisors] taken in the course of their employment or within their apparent authority, or for acts an employer ratifies or condones. Since *Meritor*, the EEOC and most courts considering the issue to date have taken the position that an employer is liable for hostile environment discrimination only if the employer knew or should have known of the harassment and failed thereafter to take prompt remedial action. Also the EEOC's position is that an employer may be liable for in effect condoning harassment if it fails to establish an express policy against harassment and an effective complaint procedure to remedy a violation.

Another important issue not resolved in *Meritor* is whether an employee must attempt to use an employer's internal grievance procedure to resolve a hostile environment sexual harassment claim in order to have a valid claim under Title VII. Thus, in *Meritor*, the bank argued that it had a policy against discrimination and that the plaintiff's claim should have been barred because she failed to invoke that procedure. The Supreme Court rejected this argument under the specific facts of the case because the bank's policy did not specifically cover sexual harassment. Also, the bank's procedure required individuals to complain first to their supervisor, which in this case was the alleged harasser. The Court stated that the bank's argument would have been stronger if its procedure had been "better calculated" to encourage victims of sexual harassment to come forward. Since *Meritor*, the EEOC's position is that if an employer establishes an express policy against hostile environment sexual harassment and an effective complaint procedure for violations, an employer will not be liable to an employee for alleged sex harassment if an employee fails to use the available procedure, unless the employer in fact knew or should have known of the harassment and failed to take corrective action. The relatively few court cases on this point to date seem to be following a similar approach. There will undoubtedly be further litigation to determine the extent and the circumstances under which employers will be liable for sexual harassment by supervisory and non-supervisory employees and the extent to which an employee is obligated to use an employer's internal grievance procedures to rectify complaints before the employer can be held responsible.

b. Reproductive Hazards and Pregnancy Discrimination. Some employers have prohibited women from holding jobs exposing them to chemicals that may impair their ability to have children or damage a fetus before birth. In contrast, men are seldom barred from holding jobs that may impair their fertility, and there is concern that such exclusions of women may become a new form of sexual stereotyping, blocking women from promotions and higher-paying positions. In 1988 the EEOC issued a policy statement concerning employer fetal protection policies under Title VII. The EEOC stated that the validity of an employer's policy depends upon whether there is a substantial risk of harm to an employee's offspring through exposure to a reproductive fetal hazard in the workplace, whether the harm takes place through the exposure of employees of one sex but not the other, and whether the employer's policy effectively eliminates the risk of fetal or reproductive harm. The policy must be justified by objective scientific evidence and neutrally designed to protect all employees' offspring from workplace hazards. If there is substantial evidence that a reproductive or fetal hazard affects only employees of one sex, then that sex may be excluded from the workplace but only to the extent necessary to protect employees' offspring from the hazard. Thus, an employer may not exclude women from a job if there are reasonable alternative means (such as protective shields) that will protect offspring and have a less discriminatory impact on women. To date, most courts have followed the same basic approach as that advocated by the EEOC in determining the lawfulness of an employer's reproductive or fetal protection policy.

c. Comparable Worth. Some women's groups and unions have urged the adoption of the theory of "comparable worth" as an additional basis for determining sex discrimination against women. Under this theory, sex discrimination could be proven by establishing that certain jobs, some traditionally held by men and others by women, are of the same relative importance ("worth") to an employer, but that the jobs traditionally held by men receive higher compensation. The inference would be that pay scales for the lower-paying jobs are discriminatorily held down because they are occupied by women. To date none of the courts of appeals that have considered the issue have accepted the theory. The courts have either found that certain specific employment practices discriminate against women based on disparate impact or disparate treatment or have refused to apply the theory, reasoning that there is no proven way of determining the relative importance of two different jobs.

For example, in *AFSCME v. State of Washington*, the district court held that the state of Washington engaged in sex discrimination in violation of Title VII because it paid its female employees less than their male counterparts holding positions of "comparable worth."[10] The United States Court of Appeals for the Ninth Circuit overruled the district court's decision. The appellate court rejected the comparable worth theory as an independent basis for establishing a Title VII violation. It held that a complainant must either prove disparate impact or disparate treatment to establish a Title VII violation.

The EEOC has not issued guidelines on comparable worth, and suits raising the issue have dwindled. However, unions have been in the forefront in successfully using comparable worth as an argument for raising the wages of women in some traditionally female jobs. Furthermore, some states have voluntarily changed their pay practices when statistical studies have indicated a disparity in wages between jobs of comparable worth. Thus, the doctrine seems to be gaining some acceptance despite its lack of success in the courts.

D. RELIGIOUS AND AGE DISCRIMINATION

The basic theories of disparate treatment and disparate impact also apply to religion or age discrimination cases. An employee cannot be individually subjected to disparate treatment because of religion or age as determined under the *McDonnell Douglas v. Green* criteria. Also, an employer cannot adopt an employment practice or policy that discriminates because of its disparate impact on employees of a particular age or religion as determined under the *Griggs* standards.

The provision of Title VII prohibiting religious discrimination and the Age Discrimination in Employment Act both contain exceptions permitting religion or age to be bona fide occupational qualifications. The courts use the same criteria in deter-

---

[10] See legal principle 6.

mining whether a person's religion or age is a BFOQ as they use for determining whether a person's sex is a BFOQ for a job; that is, an employer must have a reasonable factual basis to believe that all or substantially all of a group is unable to perform a job before excluding them.

1. Religious Discrimination: The Reasonable Accommodation Test

The principal issue in religious discrimination arises under the provision of Section 701(j) requiring an employer to make reasonable accommodation to an employee's religious observances or practices that do not entail undue hardship on the employer's business. How far must an employer go in accommodating the religious beliefs of an employee? This issue was considered by the Supreme Court in *Trans World Airlines v. Hardison.*[11] Hardison was a member of a religious group whose Sabbath was from Friday night sundown to Saturday night sundown. Hardison refused to work on Saturdays. The collective bargaining agreement required that the lowest seniority employees do weekend work unless a higher seniority employee volunteers to work instead. Because of his low seniority date, Hardison was frequently required to work Saturday, but he refused because of his religious beliefs and was discharged. He filed a charge with the EEOC alleging that he had been discriminated against because of his religion, and the case ultimately reached the Supreme Court.

Hardison argued that the religious accommodation provisions of Section 701(j) required that TWA either find a supervisor to do Hardison's work or else TWA should require another employee, whose religious beliefs did not prohibit Saturday work, to do the work instead. Hardison argued that another employee should be required to work even though that employee might have higher seniority and requiring the other

employee to work would violate the contract's seniority provisions.

The Supreme Court rejected Hardison's argument. It held that an employer does not have to violate the terms of a contractual seniority clause in order to accommodate an employee's religious beliefs. The Court did emphasize, however, that the TWA seniority system was a bona fide system that was not designed or intended to discriminate against employees because of their religious beliefs. If a seniority clause were designed to discriminate, its application would not be protected under Title VII.

As to Hardison's other arguments that TWA could have used supervisory personnel or could have offered employees premium pay to work on Saturday, the Court pointed out that both alternatives involved costs to TWA, either through lost efficiency in other jobs or in higher wages. The Court stated that requiring TWA to bear more than a de minimis cost to give Hardison Saturdays off would be an undue hardship under Section 701(j) that the company was not required to bear.

Thus, under the *Hardison* decision, an employer does not have to change its seniority system or compel an employee to work at a time when the employee would be off in order to accommodate the religious beliefs of another employee. Furthermore, an employer does not have to make any work changes that would involve more than a de minimis expense to it. Of course, the *Hardison* opinion does not permit an employer to sit back and do nothing if an employee requests time off for religious reasons. In Hardison's case, no other employee was available to fill Hardison's position without violating the contract's seniority clause or entailing extra cost to the company.

In *Ansonia Board of Education v. Philbrook*, the Supreme Court appears to have granted employers greater latitude in the area of reasonable accommodation than was previously thought to be the case.[12] In *Ansonia*, a school board's collective bargaining con-

---

[11] See legal principle 16.

[12] See legal principle 16.

tract permitted teachers to use three days annual leave to observe religious holidays. The school board also allowed three additional days of leave for personal reasons, but not for religious purposes. A teacher who belonged to the Worldwide Church of God argued that he should be allowed to use his three additional personal leave days for religious observance. In the alternative, he suggested that he would pay the cost of a substitute and receive full pay for the additional days of religious observance. The school board rejected both proposals. The court of appeals held that the school board had to accept the employee's proposed accommodation unless it would result in undue hardship to the employer. The Supreme Court rejected the appellate court's ruling and held that once an employer offers an accommodation to an employee's religion that is "reasonable" it has complied with Title VII. Furthermore, the Court held that undue hardship is only at issue in Title VII cases where an employer claims that it is unable to offer any reasonable accommodation without such hardship.

Thus, the Court's ruling in *Ansonia* makes clear that an employee is entitled to a reasonable religious accommodation, but not a perfect accommodation. Although the Court did not spell out the standards for determining reasonable religious accommodation, the decision allows employers a great deal of leeway to make accommodations that fit their own needs.

2. Donations to Charitable Organizations in Lieu of Union Membership Dues

Section 19 of the Labor Management Relations Act allows employees who are members of a religion that has historically held objections to unions to make contributions to a charity in lieu of union dues. However, Section 701(j) of Title VII has been interpreted more broadly than Section 19 to apply to employees who sincerely hold religious objections to unions as an individual even though they are not members of a religious organization that holds such ob-

jections. Thus, for example, in one case, a bargaining unit employee objected to union membership based on religious beliefs that were personal, rather than based on membership in an organized religion. The union requested that the employee be discharged because she refused to pay union dues, but the company refused on the grounds that discharging her would violate Section 701(j) of Title VII. The court of appeals held that Section 19 of the LMRA did not supersede Section 701(j) and that an employee with personal religious objections to joining a union should also have the option of donating an equivalent amount to a nonreligious charity in lieu of paying the dues.

3. Age Discrimination

The Age Discrimination in Employment Act (ADEA) prohibits discrimination on account of age against individuals who are at least forty years of age. (The Act contains exceptions that will be discussed fully below.) The Act applies to employers, unions, employment agencies, state government employees, and federal government employees. Originally, the ADEA did not apply to state and federal government employees. However, in 1974 the Act was amended to include such employees. The ADEA was originally enforced by the Department of Labor, but enforcement authority was transferred to the EEOC by a Presidential Reorganization Order effective July 1, 1979.

Essentially, the ADEA prohibits the same discriminatory conduct because of a person's age that Title VII prohibits because of race, religion, national origin, or sex; and the courts basically apply the same disparate treatment/disparate impact analysis applied under Title VII. Thus, the Act prohibits age discrimination against individuals who are at least age forty in hiring, discharge, and conditions of employment. Classifications based on age, which would deprive a person of employment opportunities or otherwise adversely affect such individual's status as an employee, are prohibited. A union is prohibited from discriminating in membership and job referrals on account of age. Nor can a union classify its members by age in any way that deprives an individual of employment opportunities or adversely affects such individual's status as an employee. The Department of Labor's position was that apprenticeship programs do not violate the ADEA by imposing age eligibility limitations on admission to apprenticeship training. However, there has been a continuing controversy within the EEOC as to whether apprenticeship training should be subject to the ADEA. The agency's current position is that bona fide apprenticeship programs are not subject to the ADEA.

As enacted in 1967, the ADEA only applied up to age sixty-five. In 1978 the age limit was raised to age seventy which meant, for example, that employees age seventy and over could be required to retire even though they were fit for work. In 1987, the age cap of seventy was removed. An employee cannot be required to retire at any age subject to several exceptions. Thus, employees engaged in bona fide high policy-making functions, who are entitled to an immediate annual retirement benefit from a pension, profit sharing, savings, or deferred compensation plan, or any combination of such plans, that in the aggregate equals at least $44,000, can be retired at age sixty-five. Employees at institutions of higher learning who are serving under a contract of unlimited tenure can be retired at age seventy. State and local firefighters and law enforcement officers can also be denied employment and/or be retired under an exception which allows such action to be taken pursuant to applicable state and local laws that set ages for hiring and retirement. These exemptions for tenured employees, firefighters, and police expire on December 31, 1993, unless reenacted by Congress.

An employee can also be forced to retire if age is a bona fide occupational requirement (BFOQ). However, in *Western Airlines v. Criswell*, the Supreme Court held that the BFOQ exception is extremely narrow.[13] In

Western Airlines, two pilots, who wished to avoid retirement under the FAA's mandatory age-sixty retirement rule for pilots, applied for reassignment as flight engineers. The employer denied both requests on the grounds that both employees were members of the company's retirement plan that required mandatory retirement at age sixty. A third employee, who was a career flight attendant, was retired after he reached age sixty for the same reason. The company argued that safety concerns made retirement at age sixty a bona fide occupational qualification for flight engineers. In rejecting the company's argument, the Supreme Court supported the consistent views of the EEOC and Department of Labor that an age restriction is a bona fide occupational requirement *only* if the age restriction is "reasonably necessary" to further an overriding interest in public safety and the employer establishes that (1) a factual basis exists for believing that all or substantially all persons over the age limit would be unable to perform the duties of the job in question safely or efficiently, or (2) dealing with older employees on an individual basis would be impossible or highly impractical.

The Court found that the company did not have an objective basis for supporting its position that flight engineers had to be held to the same standards as pilots. Furthermore, in rejecting Western's arguments, the Court stated that the BFOQ standard in the statute is "reasonable necessity," not "reasonableness," as the airline argued. Thus, the *Western Airlines* decision makes clear that employers will not easily be able to rely on the BFOQ exception to force employees to retire at an early age.

The 1986 amendments to the Act prohibit employers from establishing or maintaining an employee pension benefit plan that, in the case of a defined benefit plan, permits or requires the cessation of benefit accrual or a reduction in benefit accrual because of age. Such amendments further prohibit the cessation or reduction of contributions to defined contribution plans be-

---

[13] See legal principle 17.

cause of age. However, plans may lawfully limit the years of service or participation taken into account for determining benefits. Furthermore, seniority systems and employee benefit plans cannot require the involuntary retirement of an employee who has reached at least forty years of age. The ADEA was also recently amended to require employers to provide group health coverage to employees age sixty-five and older under the same terms as younger employees. In recent years, some employers have offered early retirement incentives to employees, but only if such employees signed a waiver stating that they would not file an age discrimination claim. Questions arose as to whether such waivers were truly "voluntary" or whether they were "coerced." To clarify this issue, the ADEA was amended effective in 1989 to provide that such waivers must be knowing and voluntary, cannot contain releases of future rights or claims, and cannot be in exchange for employment benefits to which an employee is otherwise entitled.

a. ADEA Procedures. A charge alleging violations of the ADEA must be filed with the EEOC within 180 days of the alleged unlawful practice. A suit to enforce the ADEA can be filed in federal court either by the EEOC or the individual. But an individual must wait sixty days after filing a charge with the EEOC before filing suit.

If a state has a law prohibiting age discrimination, no suit can be filed unless the complaining party has filed a charge with the state agency and waits at least sixty days unless the state proceedings are terminated before the sixty days are up. If a state law prohibits age discrimination, the 180-day requirement for filing a charge under the ADEA is extended to 300 days after the alleged unlawful employment practice occurs, or to within 30 days after the individual receives notice that the state proceedings have been terminated, whichever is earlier. However, a person can proceed under the ADEA sixty days after filing a charge with the appropriate state agency even if state proceedings are not completed.

There was a question about whether an employee forfeits the right to relief under the ADEA by failing to file a timely charge with a state agency. The Supreme Court resolved this issue in a rather unique way. The Court held that the employee must file the charge with the state agency even though it is untimely. After waiting the required sixty days, even though the state agency may be powerless to act, the employee can then proceed with his case under the ADEA.

E. TITLE VII PROCESSING REQUIREMENTS AND SUIT PROCEDURES

1. Filing the Charge

Under Section 706(e), a charge must be filed with the EEOC within 180 days after the occurrence of an alleged discriminatory act violating Title VII. (As discussed below, this period may be extended up to 300 days in states having a state civil rights enforcement law and agency.) Under Section 706(b), a charge may be filed by or on behalf of a person claiming to be aggrieved (damaged by an unlawful act). This permits a union to file a charge on behalf of its members who may have been discriminated against. A charge may also be filed by a member of the Commission itself.

A charge is filed in one of the EEOC's district or area offices that have the necessary forms and can provide assistance. The EEOC must serve a notice of the charge on the charged party within ten days after filing.

a. Continuing Violations. The filing time for a charge may be longer than 180 (300) days if it alleges a "continuing violation." A continuing violation, as the name indicates, is one that occurs over time rather than being a single isolated occurrence. For example, if a black employee receives lower wages or is forced to work under more difficult working conditions than white employees, those conditions are a continuing violation. However, decisions not to hire or promote a particular person or to discharge an employee are considered single occurrences. A charge must be filed within the required number of days from the occurrence.

What if an employee is discriminatorily laid off, but does not file a charge with the EEOC over the layoff and is then recalled to work more than 180 days after the layoff? Can the employee still file a timely charge with the EEOC within 180 days after being recalled on the grounds that the earlier discriminatory layoff resulted in the employee being recalled later or having lower seniority than the employee should have had? No, the charge must be filed within the required period after the original occurrence or no action can be taken under Title VII regardless of the later consequences. Similarly, if a seniority system is allegedly discriminatory, an employee must file a charge within the required time from the date the system was initially adopted, not from the subsequent date that the system in fact adversely affects the employee, such as the date the employee is laid off under a seniority system in effect for many years. The adoption of the alleged discriminatory system is not considered a continuing violation.

It is not always easy to determine whether a particular violation of Title VII should be classified by a court as a single occurrence or a continuing violation. Therefore, the best procedure is to file a charge within 180 days of the initial occurrence in every case.

2. Deferral to State Civil Rights Agencies

Under Section 706(c), if an alleged unfair employment practice occurs in a state that has both a law prohibiting the alleged practice and an agency to enforce the law, the charging party is required to file a charge with the state agency and wait sixty days before filing a charge with the EEOC. The EEOC, however, has adopted a procedure under which charges can be filed directly with it after which the EEOC defers the charge to the state agency. If the state agency has not resolved the matter within sixty days, the EEOC reasserts its own jurisdiction and proceeds. In some states, the state agency routinely waives its jurisdiction over cases deferred to it, and the EEOC reasserts jurisdiction immediately.

Under Section 706(e) only 180 days are allowed to file a charge in states that do not have fair employment practice agencies more than one-year old. However, the Supreme Court, in interpreting Sections 706(c) and (e) has held that in states that do have fair employment agencies, a timely charge may be filed with the EEOC within 240 days of the alleged discriminatory act. This allows for the sixty-day deferral period to a state agency under 706(c) within the 300 day maximum period for the EEOC to reassert jurisdiction. An employee who files a discrimination charge with the EEOC that is untimely under state law is nonetheless entitled to the extended 300 day filing period of Section 706(e) in states that have fair employment practices agencies if the employee filed the charge within 240 days of the alleged discriminatory act. Even if a charge is not filed within 240 days of the alleged discriminatory act, the charge may still be timely filed with the EEOC if the state or local agency terminates its proceedings or waives its jurisdiction before 300 days.

3. Investigation and Conciliation

Under Section 706(b), the EEOC investigates a charge filed with it to determine whether there is "reasonable cause" to believe that the statute has been violated. If the EEOC determines that there is not reasonable cause, the charge is dismissed and the charging party is so notified. That is not necessarily the end of the matter, however. Even though the EEOC has found no reasonable cause, the charging party still has the statutory right to file suit in federal court against the parties named in the charge. This suit must be filed within ninety days from the date the charging party receives notice that the charge has been dismissed. This notice is referred to as a "right-to-sue letter."

If the EEOC finds a reasonable cause to believe there is a violation, it must attempt to eliminate the practice by "conference, conciliation, and persuasion." Section 706(b) provides that nothing said or done during or as part of conciliation procedures may be made public by the Commission, its officers, or employees or used as evidence in any subsequent proceedings.

4. EEOC Authority to Broaden an Investigation

Most charges are filed by charging parties only in their own behalf. That is true even though the individual may be complaining of an act or an employment policy or procedure that also adversely affects other members of the same minority group. Although individuals may have filed a charge in their own behalf only, the EEOC has authority to broaden the charge to include the class (group) of persons who face the same discriminatory situation. For example, if an employee files a charge that a hiring test discriminated against the employee as a black, the EEOC can broaden the charge to include the class of all black employees. The EEOC can also broaden the charge to include unlawful acts or policies that the charging party did not allege as a violation so long as the additional acts are reasonably related to, or grow out of, the initial charge. Courts permit such broadening on the theory that charging parties frequently do not know their legal rights or know all the facts of an occurrence at the time they file a charge.

Sometimes an employee will file a charge only against the employer, but the remedy for an alleged discriminatory practice may require the employer to change an employment policy or practice contained in a collective bargaining agreement. If the union is not a party to the charge, it is not bound by any agreement the employer makes with the EEOC. However the EEOC's current policy is to seek a union's voluntary cooperation before adding it as a charged party. Also, the EEOC's position, which the courts have approved, is that a union violates Title VII if it does not fairly represent minority group employees and does not actively seek to eliminate discriminatory practices against them.

5. EEOC versus Private Suits under Title VII

a. Authority to Bring Suit. If the EEOC determines that there is reasonable cause to believe that Title VII has been violated and conciliation fails, further proceedings depend upon whether the charge is against a private employer or union or a governmental agency subject to the Act.

If the charge is against a private party, the EEOC has authority to file suit itself in federal court against the charged party. If the EEOC decides not to file suit, it can notify the charging party that conciliation has failed and that the EEOC is not bringing suit, but that the charging party has the right to do so. The charging party then has the right to bring suit within ninety days after receiving the right-to-sue notice. If a charging party does not have an attorney, the Act permits a federal court to appoint one. If the charged party is a state or local government body subject to the Act and conciliation fails, the EEOC refers the case to the United States Attorney General. The EEOC does not have authority to file suit against governmental agencies. The Attorney General's office decides whether to file suit on behalf of the United States in federal court against the governmental body. If the Attorney General decides not to file suit, he notifies the charging party of the right to sue within ninety days after receiving the notice.

6. Time Requirements for Filing Suit

a. Requesting a Right-to-Sue Letter. Prior to the 1972 amendments, charging parties had to sit by helplessly while the EEOC processed their case until they finally received a right-to-sue letter notifying them that their charge had been dismissed or that conciliation efforts had failed. The charging party could take no action until the EEOC sent this letter. The 1972 amendments to Section 706(f)(1) permit a charging party to bring suit on its own 180 days after the charge has been filed with the EEOC by requesting a right-to-sue letter from the EEOC or the Attorney General if the charge is against a governmental agency. The charging party can request the right-to-sue letter even though the agency has not completed its investigation or conciliation efforts; thus, the charging party no longer must wait until the EEOC acts. The EEOC or the Attorney General, as appropriate, however, has the exclusive right to file suit during the first 180 days. The charging party cannot file suit on his or her own behalf during that period. If the agency does file suit, the charging party is permitted to intervene in the action. Similarly, if the charging party files a suit after 180 days, the EEOC or the Attorney General can intervene in the suit.

Remember, the ninety-day statutory period for filing a suit under Title VII starts from the date the charging party receives a right-to-sue letter. Therefore, even though a charge has been filed for more than 180 days, the charging party should not request a right-to-sue letter unless the party is ready to file suit. In practice, attorneys will often prepare their case in advance. After the suit is prepared, the charging party will request a right-to-sue letter and the suit can be filed immediately after the letter is received without any difficulty.

During its early years especially, the EEOC committed many procedural errors in processing charges under the Act. Some defendants in civil rights cases urged that meritorious claims should be barred because of administrative error in enforcing the Act by the EEOC. The Supreme Court, however, held in *McDonnell Douglas Corp. v. Green*, that there are only two basic procedural requirements that the charging party

must meet to file suit. First, the charging party must file a timely charge with the EEOC within 180 days of the alleged unlawful employment practice (or up to 300 days in states having a fair employment practice agency more than one year old, as discussed above). Second, the charging party must file suit within ninety days after receiving the right-to-sue letter. So long as these two requirements are met, a court has jurisdiction over a suit despite what other procedural irregularities may have occurred. The courts have reasoned that charging parties, most of whom are initially not represented by attorneys, should not be held responsible for errors made by the EEOC.

The Supreme Court has held that the time limits for filing a timely charge with the EEOC are subject to waiver if the employer does not raise the issue, and that the limits are also subject to the legal doctrines of estoppel and equitable tolling. This means, for example, that if the aggrieved person is in some way misled by the defendant as to the true facts of an occurrence, or the facts are intentionally hidden, the defendant may be prevented ("estopped") from raising the limitations period as a defense if the person discovers the true situation after the time limit has expired and files a late charge, because the defendant's own wrong doing contributed to the late filing. Similarly, if the aggrieved person complains about a discriminatory act at the time but is in some way misled by the defendant, or even by a governmental agency, as to his or her legal rights or procedures to be followed in filing a claim, and therefore does not file on time or follow proper procedures, the aggrieved person may be able to file a Title VII action even though the time limits have expired. The time for filing a charge could be "tolled" from the date the employee complained but was misled as to his or her rights or proper procedures to follow. For this reason, it is advisable in some cases for an aggrieved person to file a charge with the EEOC even though the charge appears to be untimely. However, a court has discretion in applying these exceptions, and the burden is on the charging party to prove their applicability in a specific case. Thus it is preferrable to file a charge promptly within the statutory time limits.

7. Trial Procedures

If a suit is filed by either the charging party, the EEOC, or the Attorney General, the suit can include any unlawful practices reasonably related to or growing out of the charge. Also, even if the original charge is filed only by an employee on an individual basis, the suit can be filed as a "class action" on behalf of the charging party and all other persons in the same situation. Class action suits can result in very broad remedies against the defendants, including revision of hiring and promotion policies and sizeable back pay awards.

Trial procedures can, of course, be very complex, especially in class action suits against a large employer or union. Most suits brought under Title VII follow the basic format established by *McDonnell Douglas v. Green* in cases of disparate treatment or *Griggs* in cases of disparate impact. It is common in complicated class action suits, to divide the trial into two portions. First, the court determines whether the defendant has engaged in unlawful discrimination. If the court concludes that the Act has been violated, a second hearing is held to determine the damages and the appropriate remedies.

F. REMEDIES UNDER TITLE VII AND THE EQUAL PROTECTION CLAUSE OF THE FOURTEENTH AMENDMENT

1. Broad Judicial Discretion in Framing Remedies

Under Section 706(g), if a court finds that the defendant has or is "intentionally" engaging in unlawful employment practices, the court can enjoin the defendant from engaging in those practices and "order such affirmative action as may be appropriate" including reinstating or hiring employees with or without backpay. The backpay liability cannot be longer than two years prior to the date the charge was filed. As with NLRB proceedings, interim earnings are deduced from the backpay. Also, a person who has lost work because of a discriminatory act must look for employment with reasonable diligence.

The requirement that a court find that a defendant has "intentionally" engaged in discrimination before ordering any remedy is of no practical significance. The word "intentional" has been given the broadest possible legal meaning. An act is intentional under Title VII if a party intends the logical or foreseeable consequences of an act, even though the party acted in good faith. Thus, a court would find that an employer or union intentionally engaged in discrimination under Section 706(g) in any case in which a plaintiff proved a prima facie case of either disparate treatment or disparate impact. The Supreme Court has stressed that Section 706(g) is intended to give the courts power to eliminate the past, present, and future effects of discrimination.

2. Backpay as a Remedy

Section 706(g) indicates that a court has discretion in awarding victims of discrimination ("discriminatees") backpay. The Supreme Court, however, has held that since Title VII is a remedial statute designed to make discriminatees whole, backpay should normally be awarded by a court whenever it finds that a person has incurred lost pay because of a discriminatory act. The Supreme Court has stated that circumstances must be very unusual to deny backpay. Interim earnings are deducted from any backpay award.

a. Backpay in Class Actions. Once discrimination is proven in a class action suit, there is a presumption that each member of the class was similarly discriminated against. Thus, if a class action is filed challenging hiring practices and a court concludes that the employer's practices violated the Act, there is a presumption that each individual member of the class who applied for and was denied employment was discriminated against. This means that each member of the class is presumably entitled to backpay. The employer has the burden of proving that a particular individual was not discriminated against and is thus not entitled to backpay. The employer also must prove that a particular person would not have been hired even if the company had not engaged in discriminatory hiring practices. Similarly, if a court finds that an employer engaged in discriminatory promotion policies, there is a presumption that each member of the class who was denied a promotion was discriminated against.

b. Backpay for Nonapplicants. An individual can be entitled to backpay even if such employee never applied for employment. The Supreme Court has held that such a person may be entitled to backpay if he or she did not apply for a job because the employer's discriminatory practices made it clear that it would have been futile to apply. The Court has stressed, however, that a person who had never applied has a heavy burden of proving that he or she would have applied but for the employer's discriminatory practices.

c. Backpay against Unions. Although the primary burden of damages is usually on the employer, unions also have potential liability in cases in which they are a defendant. The union may be a defendant because it actively encouraged an employer to discriminate, or it violated its duty of fair representation by not actively opposing discriminatory practices. The union may also be a defendant if it has discriminated in the operation of a hiring hall or union membership. Section 706(g) specifically authorizes a court to require that backpay be paid by the employer, employment agency, or labor organization responsible for the unlawful employment practice. A union's backpay liability is usually slight if the employer

is responsible for an unlawful employment practice and the union's only failure is not taking sufficient action to end the practice. However, a union faces greater potential liability if it actively encourages the employer's actions or is itself responsible for the unlawful conduct.

3. Injunctive and Affirmative Action Relief to Remedy Discrimination

a. Employer Affirmative Action. In virtually every case in which a court finds that there has been discrimination, it issues an injunction order enjoining the discriminatory practices cease and reinstating or promoting the person discriminatorily denied employment, denied a promotion, or discharged. However, courts frequently order much broader remedies as required both to eliminate past discrimination and prevent future discrimination. Section 706(g) specifically authorizes a court to require such affirmative action as may be appropriate. Furthermore, affirmative action programs have been ordered by courts based on the equal protection clause of the Fourteenth Amendment to the United States Constitution in cases of discrimination by public employers.

To remedy past discrimination, courts may require that an affirmative action program be established to recruit and train minority group members. Courts may also require that a specified percentage of minority group members be hired or promoted or that a specified ratio of white to black employees be maintained until there is proportionate work force. Thus, in *U.S. v. Paradise*, the Supreme Court upheld a lower court order requiring a one black for one white promotion ratio for state troopers to eliminate discrimination that violated the equal protection clause of the Fourteenth Amendment.[14] In upholding this goal, the Court stressed that there had been long-term discrimination against the hiring of blacks in the position of state troopers.

[14] See legal principle 12.B.

However, it should be noted that in *Paradise*, (as well as in other recent Supreme Court cases) the Court cautioned that it would not always look favorably on quotas to effectuate affirmative action. Rather, the Court favors flexible, temporary quota plans that are imposed only until an employer implements its own plan, or in the case of a voluntarily adopted plan, until goals are met. *Paradise* was a case involving public employees (state troopers) rather than private employees and was made based on an interpretation of the equal protection clause of the Fourteenth Amendment rather than an interpretation of Title VII. Although the Supreme Court does not apply the exact same standards to affirmative action programs arising under Title VII (as opposed to the equal protection clause of the Constitution) or private employees (as opposed to public employees), it is probable that the court would have reached the same decision in *Paradise* if the case involved private employees and had arisen under Title VII.

As a further means of affirmative action, a court can adjust an employee's seniority date to the employee's "rightful place" on a seniority list as if the employee had not been discriminated against. If minority group members lack the background or training to be eligible for certain jobs, a court may require that special training programs be established. A court may also require that minority group members who were previously discriminatorily denied higher paying jobs be processed through the training program and be advanced from step to step as quickly as possible, rather than wait the usual number of years.

b. Union Affirmative Action. A union can also be ordered to take affirmative action to recruit minority group members as union members if membership has been discriminatorily denied previously. If an apprenticeship program has discriminated against minority group members, the apprenticeship program may also be required to take affirmative action to recruit and train more minority group members. If a union has

discriminated in the operation of a hiring hall, it may be required to give some minority group members preference in referrals to make up for past discrimination, to revise the referral system to prevent future discrimination, to refer a certain percentage of minority group members to jobs, or to maintain a specified referral ratio of minority group members to other union members.

Recently, in *Local 28, Sheet Metal Workers v. EEOC*, the Supreme Court decided a case involving the issue of whether a court can order a union to give race conscious relief to benefit individuals who are not the identified victims of unlawful discrimination.[15] In *Sheet Metal Workers*, the union had resisted state and federal directives for almost twenty years to end its discrimination against blacks and Hispanics seeking membership in the union. A district court finally imposed a 29 percent minority membership goal on the union based on the number of nonwhites in the labor pool. The Supreme Court affirmed the lower court's membership goal on the ground that the union's discrimination was "egregious" (flagrant). In so holding, the Court noted that 706(g) provides that no court shall require a remedy for an individual who is not the actual victim of discrimination. However, the Court held that the section does not prohibit a court from ordering race conscious relief benefitting nondiscriminatees as a remedy for past discrimination in certain circumstances. The Court stated that such relief may be appropriate where an employer or union has engaged in persistent or "egregious" discrimination, or where necessary to eradicate the effects of past pervasive discrimination. Accordingly, because of the union's history of past pervasive discrimination and its resistance for many years to eradicating discrimination, the Supreme Court held that the membership goal was warranted.

In upholding the membership goal, the Court mentioned principles that it has

[15] See legal principle 12.B.

stressed in several other decisions concerning affirmative action; first, that the membership goal was a temporary measure; and second, the membership goal did not "unnecessarily trammel" on the rights of white workers in the sense that no individuals were laid off and the goal did not discriminate in any way against existing members.

The remedies mentioned here are merely examples of a court's broad discretion. Each remedial order is tailored to the specific facts of the prior discrimination and the actions necessary to eliminate past and prevent future discrimination.

c. Remedies Displacing Current Employees.

Can a court order that a discriminatee be placed in the job that the discriminatee would have had but for the discrimination, even if another employee must be removed from the position? This is a difficult problem. After all, the employee occupying the position did not cause the discrimination against the other employee. Is it right to remove an innocent employee from a job to remedy the discrimination against the other? The Supreme Court, although recognizing the difficulties, has indicated that it is proper, if necessary, to remove one employee in order to place a discriminatee in the job the discriminatee would have held but for the discrimination. The Court noted that the NLRB routinely orders that employees who have been discharged for union activities be reinstated to their former positions even though reinstatement may mean the discharge of the replacement. The Court also noted that seniority rights are subject to change, either due to statutory requirements or by negotiations between an employer and a union, subject, of course, to the union's duty of fair representation.

Of course, a court may have some discretion to limit the impact of its remedy on innocent employees. For example, a court might order that discriminatees be placed in the appropriate jobs as vacancies occur, rather than replacing the present employees.

Of course, a court's remedy cannot defeat the statutory purpose of Title VII to eliminate both past and future discrimination. Thus, whether a court can postpone a discriminatee's advancement to a higher position might depend upon the number of discriminatees entitled to higher positions and the number of job vacancies anticipated within a reasonable period of time. If necessary, a court can, and perhaps must, require that the discriminatees be placed in the appropriate positions immediately, even if it means that other employees must be removed.

d. Consent Decrees.

Recently, the Supreme Court has ruled in decisions involving consent decrees as a means of achieving affirmative action. (A consent decree is one in which two or more parties voluntarily agree to a course of action that the Court approves, rather than a court imposed remedy.) In *Local 93 Firefighters v. Cleveland*, the Court upheld a consent decree providing for racial preference in hiring, assignment, and promotion within the Cleveland Fire Department.[16] As discussed above, Section 706(g), although interpreted narrowly, precludes a court from ordering race conscious relief to individuals who are not the actual victims of discrimination except in particularly egregious cases. The issue before the Court was whether Section 706(g) prevents the entry of a consent decree that benefits individuals who are not the actual victims of discrimination. A divided court upheld the consent decree. The Court reasoned that a consent decree is not imposed by a court, but rather is actually an agreement of the parties to undertake a course of action. Such mutual agreement binds the parties, rather than a court order. Accordingly, parties are free to enter into consent decrees that courts themselves could not order to benefit nondiscriminatees. However, the Court cautioned that parties cannot voluntarily agree to take action pursuant to a consent decree which violates Title VII or any other law. For example, in *Firefighters*

---

[16] See legal principle 12.C.

Local Union No. 1784 v. Stotts, the Supreme Court struck down a consent decree because it conflicted with Title VII.[17] In *Stotts*, the Supreme Court held that black employees of the Memphis Fire Department hired pursuant to a consent decree were not entitled to be retained by the fire department during a layoff in preference to white employees with greater seniority. In striking down the consent decree, the Court stated that Title VII protects bona fide seniority systems and it is inappropriate to deny an innocent employee the benefits of the employee's seniority in order to provide a remedy in a pattern and practice suit. The Court also subsequently held in *Martin v. Wilks* that employees who were not parties in a case culminating in a consent decree are not bound by the decree and thus have the right to file a suit if they allege that employment actions taken pursuant to the consent decree impermissibly discriminate against them.[18]

4. Revision of a Seniority System as a Remedy

a. Discrimination after Title VII's Effective Date. In *Franks v. Bowman Transportation Co., Inc.*, the Supreme Court held that an individual who is discriminatorily denied employment is entitled to full seniority rights retroactively to the date such individual should have been hired. This is referred to as "rightful place seniority." The discriminatee is entitled to rightful place seniority even though it places the individual ahead of other innocent employees who were not responsible for the discrimination. The Court held that rightful place seniority should be granted routinely to discriminatees, just as they are routinely awarded backpay, unless there is an unusual adverse impact arising from facts and circumstances not generally found in Title VII cases. That is rare.

In *Franks*, the employer's discrimination took place after the effective date of Title VII. In *T.I.M.E.-D.C., Inc. v. United States*, the Supreme Court faced a situation in which discrimination had occurred both before and after the effective date of Title VII.[19] The employer had engaged in a pattern and practice of employment discrimination against blacks and Spanish-surnamed Americans in which only whites were employed in the higher paying over-the-road truck driver jobs. The minority group employees were limited to other lower-paying jobs. An employee's seniority for purposes of benefits, such as vacations and pensions, was based on the date of hire with the company. An employee's seniority for competitive purposes, such as job bidding, layoff, and recall, however, was based upon service as an over-the-road truck driver. This system perpetuated the effects of prior discrimination because a discriminatee who was finally hired as an over-the-road truck driver obviously would have less seniority than the discriminatee would have had, but for the employer's prior discriminatory refusal to hire such discriminatee. The union was a defendant in the suit, charged with having agreed with the employer to create and maintain this seniority system.

One of the primary issues in *T.I.M.E.-D.C., Inc.*, was whether the seniority system had to be revised so it would not perpetuate the effects of the past discrimination against the black and the Spanish-surnamed employees. The Supreme Court had a straightforward remedy for the discrimination taking place after Title VII's effective date: Employees who had been discriminated against after the effective date were entitled to full rightful place seniority under the *Franks v. Bowman* decision.

b. Discrimination before Title VII's Effective Date. For employees who were discriminated against before Title VII's effective date, the Supreme Court looked to the provisions of Section 703(h) under which a "bona fide" seniority or merit system is

---

[17] See legal principle 12.C.
[18] See legal principle 12.C.

[19] See legal principle 4.

lawful under the Act as long as differences created by the system are not the result of an "intention to discriminate" because of race, color, religion, sex, or national origin. The Court, considering the legislative history of Section 703(h), concluded that the unmistakable purpose of the provision was that the routine application of a bona fide seniority system is not unlawful under Title VII. The Court concluded that Congress had intended for seniority rights accumulated before the effective date of Title VII to remain in effect even though the employer had engaged in discrimination prior to the passage of the Act and the system therefore perpetuated the effects of pre-Act discrimination.

Thus, in *T.I.M.E.-D.C.* the Court ruled that the persons who suffered discrimination only before the effective date of Title VII were not entitled to any relief. Employees who suffered discrimination after the effective date were entitled to relief, in the form of rightful place seniority, back to the date of the discrimination against them, but no earlier than the effective date of Title VII. Since these employees would receive full seniority rights through the application of rightful place seniority, there was no need to revise the seniority system.

As an exception, the Supreme Court indicated that a seniority system could be revised, notwithstanding the provisions of Section 703(h), if the seniority system itself was racially discriminatory or had its inception in racial discrimination. If an employer maintained separate seniority lists for black and white employees before Title VII's effective date, the seniority system has its inception in racial discrimination and a court could revise such a system because it would not be bona fide under Section 703(h). On the other hand, if a seniority system, as in *T.I.M.E.-D.C.*, was not discriminatory in its inception, but is discriminatory in impact because of the employer's hiring policies, the seniority system itself would not be revised. Employees who had been subject

to discrimination, however, would still get full relief through rightful place seniority. The Court has also ruled that the provision of Section 703(h) protecting bona fide seniority systems apply whether a seniority system was adopted before or after the effective date of the Act.

5. Attorney's Fees to the Prevailing Party

Section 706(k) permits the court to award an attorney's fee to the prevailing party. Technically, this means that if the defendants win, the court can require that the plaintiff pay their attorney's fee.

The courts have held, however, that a prevailing defendant is entitled to an attorney's fee only if the plaintiff's claim is clearly frivolous and without merit. Thus, even an employee with a questionable claim who loses should not be required to pay the opposing party's attorney's fee.

G. THE RECONSTRUCTION CIVIL RIGHTS STATUTES

1. Coverage under Sections 1981 and 1983

Besides proceeding under Title VII, a discriminatee may file suit under the Reconstruction Civil Rights Statutes (42 U.S.C. Sections 1981 and 1983). Section 1981 provides that all persons shall have the same right to make and enforce contracts and to full and equal benefit of all laws and proceedings for the security of persons and property as are enjoyed by white citizens. Section 1981 prohibits racial discrimination by a private (nongovernmental) employer or union and by state or local governmental bodies, but it does not prohibit sex discrimination. The Supreme Court has held that "race" within the meaning of Section 1981 is not limited to identifiable racial groups, that is, Negroes, Caucasians, and Mongolians, but also protects national or ethnic groups (e.g., Hispanics). Section 1983 prohibits state and local governmental officials from depriving any person of any rights, privileges, or immunities secured by the Constitution and laws. Section 1983 thus prohibits both race and sex discrimination by state officials or by local governmental officials or bodies, but does not apply to federal agencies. Title VII is the exclusive remedy against sex discrimination by a private employer or union and against discrimination by federal agencies.

Sections 1981 and 1983 only prohibit purposeful (intentional) discrimination. Thus, these statutes do not apply to cases of disparate impact discrimination in which the courts, applying Title VII standards discussed above, have held that impact alone without regard to intent is sufficient for a violation. The burden of proof to establish a violation of Section 1981 or 1983 is the same as that required to prove a disparate treatment violation of Title VII under the *McDonnell Douglas v. Green* standards discussed above.

In *Patterson v. McLean Credit Union* the Supreme Court significantly limited the scope of Section 1981.[20] Previously, most courts had concluded that Section 1981 prohibited intentional racial discrimination or harassment to the same extent as Title VII. However, Section 1981 literally only prohibits discrimination in the making or enforcement of contracts. Based on this statutory language, the Supreme Court ruled in *Patterson* that Section 1981 only prohibits racial discrimination in the initial formation of a contract and discriminatory conduct which impairs the right to enforce contractual obligations through the legal process. Thus, the Court indicated that Section 1981 would prohibit the refusal to hire a person because of the person's race or hiring the person under discriminatory terms, but that Section 1981 does not apply to discriminatory conduct after the contrac-

---

[20] See legal principle 14.B.

tual relationship has been established, such as racial harassment. Title VII is the exclusive remedy for other types of discrimination. Under this narrow interpretation, the discharge of an employee because of the employee's race, although violating Title VII, apparently may not violate Section 1981. This issue is currently in litigation.

The Court also indicated in *Patterson* that the denial of a promotion because of race would violate Section 1981 only if the promotion would establish a new and distinct relationship between the employer and the employee equivalent to a new contract. Thus, the denial of a promotion because of an employee's race under the promotion provisions of a typical collective bargaining agreement would probably not violate Section 1981 because such a promotion does not establish a new contractual relationship. However, the Court specifically reaffirmed in *Patterson* that a labor union would be liable under Section 1981 if it discriminated in the processing of grievances because of an employee's race because that action would impair the enforcement of contractual rights through the legal process to which Section 1981 specifically applies.

2. Procedures and Remedies

Sections 1981 and 1983 are enforced directly by the discriminatees by filing suit in federal court. The sections are separate independent remedies from Title VII. Thus, it is not necessary to file a charge with the EEOC and exhaust Title VII procedures before filing suit under Sections 1981 or 1983 as appropriate. Sections 1981 and 1983 do not contain express limitation periods. However, the Supreme Court has held that the applicable limitation period for a suit should be the same as that applied in personal injury actions. This period varies from state to state, but in any event would be longer than under Title VII. Thus, a discriminatee who has waited too long to file a charge under Title VII might still be able to proceed under Section 1981 or Section 1983 if either section applies to the discrimination in question.

Sections 1981 and 1983 do not specify the remedies for their violation. The courts have generally held that an individual is entitled to the same remedies under both statutes as under Title VII. The prevailing party (plaintiff or defendant) is entitled to attorney's fees as under Title VII. However, there are some differences between the remedies awarded by the courts in Title VII cases and Section 1981 and Section 1983 cases. The two-year limitations on backpay under Title VII does not apply to Sections 1981 and 1983. A court can award punitive damages under Section 1981 and Section 1983 if an employer or union has engaged in willful discriminatory conduct. In contrast, punitive damages are not allowed under Title VII. Courts have also awarded compensatory damages for emotional distress under Section 1981. However, the Eleventh Amendment to the United States Constitution has been interpreted to mean that federal courts can only give injunctive or other affirmative relief against violations of Sections 1981 or 1983 by a state, state agency, or state official, but not monetary damages for a past violation. (But state officials can still be sued as individuals.) This restriction on damages does not apply to discriminatory acts by municipal or other local government bodies or officials, nor to discrimination by private employers or unions under Section 1981.

A common procedure in civil rights litigation is for the discriminatee to file a timely charge with the EEOC, wait the required six months, request a right-to-sue letter from the EEOC, and then file suit under both Title VII and Sections 1981 or 1983 as appropriate. The limitations period for filing suit under either Sections 1981 or 1983 continues to run even after a charge has been filed under Title VII. Thus, in states where the time limitation for filing suit is relatively short, the discriminatee must be careful to file suit in time even though the EEOC charge is still being proc-

essed. There are other complex technical principles and procedures applicable to Section 1981 and 1983 litigation beyond the purview of this book.

H. THE ROLE OF ARBITRATION IN ELIMINATING DISCRIMINATION

There is often an overlap between an alleged civil rights violation and a contract violation. A collective bargaining agreement may expressly prohibit discrimination on account of race, religion, national origin, sex, or age. Or, a person may allege that he or she was discharged, denied a promotion, or otherwise denied a contractual benefit, because of race, etc.

1. Arbitration and Title VII as Concurrent Remedies

The Supreme Court has held that Title VII and arbitration are concurrent remedies. Thus, if an employer's discriminatory act violates both Title VII and a collective bargaining agreement, the discriminatee, the union, or both can file an EEOC charge and a grievance leading to arbitration.

The Supreme Court has held that filing a grievance does not toll the time for filing an EEOC charge. Rather the period for filing a charge begins on the day of the discriminatory act and continues to run while a grievance is being processed. Therefore, an employee or union may not be able to wait until the grievance-arbitration procedures are completed before filing a charge with the EEOC. In order to protect the individual's Title VII rights, the charge must be filed, even though the grievance-arbitration procedures may ultimately turn out in the employee's favor.

2. Weight Accorded an Arbitrator's Decision

If an arbitrator rules in the employee's favor within the six-month period for filing an EEOC charge, there is no need to file a charge or to file suit under 42 U.S.C. 1981 or 1983. But what if the arbitrator rules against the employee before the filing period has expired, or only provides partial relief to the employee? Can the union or the employee still file a charge with the EEOC and proceed under Title VII, or is the arbitrator's decision binding? In *Gardner-Denver*, the Supreme Court held that an employee can proceed under Title VII even though the employee lost in arbitration.[21] The Court held that an employee does not waive rights under Title VII by arbitrating such claims first.

The NLRB often defers to an arbitrator's award, which meets its standards for deferral under the *Spielberg* decision, even though the Board might have reached a different result in the case (see Chapter Nine). The Supreme Court, however, held in *Gardner-Denver* that the federal courts should not defer to an arbitrator's award under Title VII and that an employee is entitled to a full court hearing. The Court stated that Congress intended for the federal courts to resolve discrimination cases, noting that an arbitrator's duty is to follow the contract even though in some cases the contract might be in conflict with Title VII rights. Title VII also involves statutory issues to which courts are accustomed rather than contract rights or past practices that are the typical issues for arbitration. The Supreme Court, however, did say that an arbitrator's award can be admitted into evidence and "accorded such weight as the court deems appropriate."

Of course, an employee's grievance alleging discrimination should be evaluated and processed by a union in accordance with the duty of fair representation, the same as any other grievance. A union does not have to arbitrate a grievance that lacks merit just because it alleges discrimination.

I. THE NLRB'S ROLE IN ELIMINATING DISCRIMINATION

The NLRB also has an important role in enforcing the federal policy against discrimination. The Board has held that a union violates its duty of fair representation by treating employees arbitrarily, discriminatorily, or in bad faith because of their race, sex, or religion. The Board has held that a union cannot arbitrarily refuse to process an employee's grievance because it relates to a discrimination issue that the employee could take to the EEOC. Such a grievance must be processed and evaluated the same as any other grievance.

1. Certification Revocation as a Remedy against Union Discrimination

The NLRB held in *Handy Andy* that it would revoke the certification of a union that engages in racial or sexual discrimination against bargaining unit employees.[22] The Board will certify a union regardless of its past record of discrimination. If a union discriminates against bargaining unit employees after being certified, either an employee or the employer can file an unfair labor practice charge against the union. The employer, however, must continue to recognize and bargain with the union while charge is pending. If the Board finds that the union is engaging in discriminatory conduct, it can either order the union to take appropriate steps to remedy the situation or it can revoke the union's certification.

J. REVERSE DISCRIMINATION AND VOLUNTARY AFFIRMATIVE ACTION PROGRAMS

1. Reverse Discrimination

In *McDonald v. Sante Fe Trail Transportation Company*, the Supreme Court held that

---

[21] See legal principle 15.

[22] See legal principle 18.

Title VII and 42 U.S.C. 1981 prohibit reverse discrimination against white employees.[23] In that case, two white employees alleged that a black employee and the two white employees were jointly charged with stealing certain merchandise from a company shipment. The employer discharged the two white employees, but retained the black employee. The two white employees filed a grievance over their discharge, but the union did not pursue it to arbitration. The employees then filed charges with the EEOC. After receiving right-to-sue letters, the white employees filed a timely action against both the employer and the union in federal court under both Title VII and 42 U.S.C. 1981. The employees alleged that the union had failed to represent them properly because it had either not opposed or had joined in the employer's discriminatory discharge. The lower federal court dismissed the employees' suit. The Supreme Court reversed the lower federal courts and held that both Title VII and 42 U.S.C. 1981 prohibit discrimination against white persons as well as blacks. The Court did not consider the merits of the white employees' charges that they had been discriminated against, but held only that if the charges were true, the acts violated both Title VII and 42 U.S.C. 1981.

2. Affirmative Action Programs

The *McDonald* decision raised questions as to whether an employer, union, or both, can voluntarily adopt an affirmative action program to hire and train additional minority group employees. Some argue that such programs are reverse discrimination against those excluded from the program. The legality of affirmative action programs under Title VII, however, has been upheld by the Supreme Court beginning with *Kaiser Aluminum Corporation v. Weber.*[24]

In *Kaiser*, the employer and union voluntarily adopted an affirmative action program to train black workers for the employer's craft work forces at each of its plants. The craft work forces were almost exclusively white. At the plant in question, less than 2 percent of the craft employees were black although blacks made up 39 percent of the available local work force. The affirmative action program required that at least 50 percent of craft trainees be black until the percentage of black skilled craft workers approximated the percentage of blacks in the local labor force.

Weber was denied admission to the craft training program although he had greater seniority than one of the black employees who was admitted. He filed a charge under Title VII alleging that his rejection constituted unlawful reverse discrimination. The charge was processed under Title VII and ultimately reached the Supreme Court.

The Supreme Court upheld the legality of the affirmative action program and held that Weber's rejection did not constitute reverse discrimination. The Court noted that the employer-union plan was voluntarily adopted to eliminate traditional patterns of racial segregation. The Court extensively examined the legislative history of Title VII and concluded that one of the Act's primary purposes was to eliminate such traditional patterns as existed at the Kaiser plant. The Court noted that Section 703(j) provides that no employer can be *required* to grant preferential treatment to any person because of race, color, religion, sex, or national origin because of an imbalance that might exist in the work force for that group. The Court said, however, that although Section 703(j) did not "require" an employer to correct a racial imbalance, the Section did not prevent an employer, union, or both from voluntarily undertaking an affirmative effort to correct a racial imbalance. The Court concluded that Congress did not intend to forbid all voluntary race conscious affirmative action.

The Court's decision, narrowly based on the specific facts of the Kaiser affirmative action program, emphasized that it was

[23] See legal principle 13.
[24] See legal principle 13.

merely holding that Title VII does not prevent all private voluntary race conscious affirmative action programs. It indicated that some affirmative action programs might result in impermissible discrimination, but held that the challenged Kaiser affirmative action plan fell on the permissible side of the line. The Court noted that Kaiser's plan did not require the discharge of white workers and their replacement by new black employees. Furthermore, the plan did not create an absolute bar to the advancement of white employees because half of those trained in the program are white. Additionally, the plan was a temporary measure that would end as soon as the percentage of black skilled craft employees at the plant approximated the percentage of blacks in the local labor force.

Prior to the Court's decision in *Kaiser,* some had argued that an affirmative action program could be voluntarily adopted only if an employer, union, or both were facing a civil rights suit if they did not adopt a program or were potentially liable under Title VII because a disproportionate work force raised questions of disparate treatment or impact discrimination. The Supreme Court, however, did not rely on that argument for approving affirmative action programs; instead, it broadly approved the general right to establish voluntary programs.

In a recent decision, *Johnson v. Transportation Agency,*[25] the Supreme Court reaffirmed and broadened several of the principles it enunciated in *Kaiser.* In *Johnson,* a county agency employed 238 men but no women as skilled craft workers. The county developed a plan whereby the race or sex of a qualified applicant could be taken into account in filling positions in which women or minority group members had been significantly underrepresented. The plan sought a statistically measurable yearly improvement in hiring, training, and promotion of minorities and women in all job classifications. The long-term goal of the plan was to have positions filled by minority and female workers based on their representation in the area work force.

A male employee challenged the plan under Title VII after the county promoted a female employee over him to a road dispatcher position despite the fact that he scored two points higher on an eligibility interview and was recommended by the panel conducting the final interviews. In upholding the plan, the Court largely relied on the language of *Kaiser* and held that the standards for private sector affirmative action programs apply to the public sector as well. That is, as in *Kaiser,* the Court noted the plan did not unnecessarily trammel the rights of male white workers. Rather, the plan merely allowed for race or sex be taken into account in filling positions and did not require the discharge of male workers. The Court also emphasized, as it did in *Kaiser,* that the plan was a flexible, temporary measure to obtain a balanced workforce rather than a fixed quota plan.

Although the Supreme Court has upheld preferential hiring as part of an affirmative action plan, the Court has been unwilling to date to allow special protection against layoffs for minority workers in preference to nonminority workers with greater seniority as a way to eradicate discrimination. Thus, in *Wygant v. Jackson Board of Education,* a provision in a collective bargaining agreement protected minority group members by providing that the percentage of minorities laid off in case of layoffs would not be greater than the percentage of minorities currently employed.[26] The Supreme Court held that this plan violated the equal protection clause of the Fourteenth Amendment. The Court stated that race conscious remedial action is constitutional only if the government organization implementing the plan has a compelling interest in remedying past discrimination and the plan is narrowly tailored to promote that interest. Under this test, the Court stated that general "societal" discrimination is not enough to create a

---

[25] See legal principle 13.

[26] See legal principle 13.

compelling interest justifying an affirmative action remedy. The past discrimination must relate to the particular government employer instituting an affirmative action plan. Furthermore, in striking down the plan, the Court stated that although hiring goals may be a burden on innocent parties, such goals are not as intrusive and do not impose the kind of injury that layoffs impose because loss of a potential job is not as damaging as loss of an existing one. As noted above, *Wygant* involved a constitutional challenge to an affirmative action program adopted by a governmental agency rather than a suit under Title VII. However, the Court would probably follow a similar approach in analyzing a challenge to an affirmative action program arising under Title VII.

There will undoubtedly be further litigation on the scope of permissible or impermissible affirmative action programs. It is clear, however, that such a program may be voluntarily adopted by a private or public employer, a union, or both an employer and a union even if the parties are not potentially liable under Title VII or do not face a law suit if they do not adopt such a program. Furthermore, it is clear that the Court has been more willing to uphold plans that deal with hiring, promotions, and/or training than programs that displace workers from current positions and/or upset bona fide seniority systems.

Summary

This chapter considered equal employment opportunity, focusing on Title VII of the Civil Rights Act of 1964. Title VII prohibits discrimination by employers and unions based on race, color, religion, sex, or national origin. Unions may find themselves on either side in civil rights litigation. They frequently process civil rights claims for their own members. Unions, however, are sometimes the defendants in such cases either because they have joined in or did not actively oppose an employer's discrimination or because the union itself discriminated in membership or job referrals. Unions are classified as employers under Title VII as to their own employees.

There are two basic categories of discrimination under Title VII: disparate treatment and disparate impact. Disparate treatment is intentional discrimination. Disparate impact pertains to the consequences of an act regardless of the intent. Under *McDonnell Douglas v. Green*, the plaintiff in a disparate treatment case must first prove a prima facie case of discriminatory intent. The employer can refute this case by articulating a legitimate nondiscriminatory reason for its actions. The plaintiff must then prove that the employer's reason is a pretext for discriminatory action.

Under *Griggs v. Duke Power Co.* as modified by *Wards Cove Packing Co. v. Atonio*, evidence of adverse consequences to a protected group is prima facie evidence of disparate impact discrimination. However, the plaintiff must identify the specific employment policy or practice that causes the disparate impact. Although statistics establishing that an employer has a disproportionate workforce may be relevant evidence, such statistics are insufficient in themselves to establish a prima facie case. The employer may rebut the plaintiff's evidence by producing evidence of a business justification for the employment practice or policy in question.

If the employer asserts a justification, the plaintiff can still prevail under Title VII if it proves that there are alternate means meeting the employer's legitimate needs that do not have the same adverse consequences. Under either the disparate treatment or disparate impact analysis, the ultimate burden of proof to establish unlawful discrimination remains with the plaintiff. Remember, there is no need to prove necessity for any employer policy or practice regardless of how unreasonable or irrational it may seem to be, as long as it does not have adverse consequences on a protected group.

Current employment policies or practices that perpetuate past discrimination may be unlawful under Title VII because of their disparate impact. The Supreme Court, however, has held that an employee is not entitled to retroactive seniority beyond the effective date of Title VII because of the provisions of Section 703(h) protecting the operation of a bona fide seniority system. A discriminatee, however, is entitled to rightful place seniority from the date of the discriminatory act as far back as the effective date of the Act.

Sexual stereotyping and sexual harassment are among the principal problems in sex discrimination. An employer cannot simply assume that women are only suited for or wish to hold certain jobs or have different performance or behavioral standards for men and women. Nor can an employer establish job requirements that have an adverse impact on women unless the employer can prove the business justification for the requirements. There is a narrow exception for bona fide occupational requirements, but the employer must prove a reasonable factual basis for concluding that all or substantially all women cannot do a specific job. Under Title VII, as amended, pregnant employees must be treated the same as any other employee. If a woman is disabled during her pregnancy or following the birth of her child, she is entitled to the same benefits as any other disabled employee and must be covered by the employer's hospitalization plan, if any.

An employer must make reasonable accommodations to the religious beliefs of its employees as long as there is no undue hardship to the employer's business, but an employer need not necessarily accept the employee's proposed accommodation as long as the employer's proposed method is reasonable. But an employer is not required to violate the seniority rights of other employees to accommodate an employee's religious requirements and is not required to incur more than a *de minimis* expense.

Actions under Title VII begin with the filing of a charge with the Equal Employment Opportunity Commission. A charge must be filed within 180 days of the alleged discriminatory act. However, this period may be extended up to 300 days in some cases in states having fair employment practice agencies even if the charge is untimely under state law. The EEOC investigates to determine whether there is reasonable cause to believe the statute has been violated. If so, the EEOC attempts conciliation. If that fails, either the EEOC, the Attorney General, in the case of discrimination by a state or local governmental body, or the charging party may file suit to enforce the discriminatee's Title VII rights.

The charging party can file suit under Title VII even if the EEOC finds no reasonable cause to believe that the statute has been violated. The charging party can request a right-to-sue letter from the EEOC if the agency has not acted within 180 days from the date the charge was filed. There are two basic jurisdictional requirements for filing a suit in federal court under Title VII: filing a timely charge with the EEOC and filing suit within 90 days from the date the charging party receives the right-to-sue letter. However, these time periods may be waived and are subject to the doctrines of estoppel and equitable tolling, which may permit a suit to be filed even though the time limits have expired. Although the charge may have been filed by an individual, alleging a narrow violation, the suit can be brought as a class action that includes all persons subject to the same discrimination. The suit can also include additional discriminatory acts and practices reasonably related to but beyond those originally alleged in the charge.

A court's remedial power under Title VII is very broad. It can issue an injunction requiring that discriminatory practices cease and can require that corrective steps be taken, including affirmative action to prevent discrimination in the future. Except in very unusual circumstances courts must also award the discriminatees back pay and rightful place seniority to which they are entitled as a result of past discriminatory acts.

A federal court has a clear statutory right to require an employer, union, or both to take affirmative action to eliminate past and future discrimination. The Supreme Court has also upheld the right of employers and unions to establish affirmative action programs voluntarily and of courts to approve consent decrees including affirmative action requirements. Although the Court has approved plans granting protected group members preference for hiring and promotions under certain circumstances, it has not approved programs giving protected group members preferences in a layoff over other employees with greater seniority. Also the Court has indicated that employees who are not parties to a consent decree may challenge the legality of any employer action taken pursuant to the decree which discriminates against them.

In addition to Title VII, victims of discrimination can also bring suit under the Reconstruction Civil Rights Acts, 42 U.S.C. 1981 and 1983. Suits under these sections are independent remedies and can be brought directly in the federal courts without exhausting Title VII remedies. Section 1981 prohibits certain racial discrimination in the making or enforcement of contract rights by either private sector employers, state or local governmental bodies, or by unions, while Section 1983 prohibits both race and sex discrimination by state and local governmental bodies. Sections 1981 and 1983 only prohibit intentional discrimination but not disparate impact discrimination as under Title VII.

An employee also has remedies against discrimination by a union under the LMRA if the union violates its duty of fair representation by discriminating against the employee because of race or sex, etc. A union has a statutory obligation to fairly represent the interests of minority employees; if it fails to meet its obligation, its certification may be revoked in appropriate cases.

Finally, an employee may also arbitrate issues of discrimination arising under a collective bargaining agreement. An employee, however, is not required to arbitrate such cases and may proceed directly to the EEOC or into court under 42 U.S.C. 1981 and 1983 as appropriate. Arbitration and Title VII procedures are separate independent remedies. An employee is not bound by an unfavorable arbitrator's award and may proceed with a Title VII action even though an arbitrator has upheld an employer's action. The federal court will make an independent determination on whether Title VII rights have been violated, giving the arbitrator's award such consideration as the court deems warranted. Because arbitration and Title VII are separate remedies, the time limit for filing a charge with the EEOC continues to run while a grievance is being processed. Thus, an employee and union must be careful to file a charge on time with the EEOC even though they are fairly confident of a favorable arbitrator's award.

Review Questions

1. How many members must a union have to be covered by Title VII of the Civil Rights Act?
2. What groups are protected against discrimination by Title VII?
3. What are the two basic categories of unlawful discrimination?
4. Can an employer violate Title VII even if the employer articulates a legitimate nondiscriminatory reason for rejecting a protected group member for a job?
5. Can an employment practice violate Title VII even though the employer had no discriminatory intent in adopting the practice?
6. Must an employment practice (such as a test) be job related to be lawful under Title VII?
7. Can an employer's employment practices violate Title VII even if its overall work force has a proportionate number of protected group members?
8. Can an employer lawfully bar women from jobs requiring heavy lifting because the work would be too difficult for women to do?
9. How long a leave of absence must an employer allow a woman after she gives birth to a child?
10. Must an employer allow an employee time off because of the employee's religious holiday?
11. At what age may an employer require an employee to retire involuntarily?

12. What are the basic requirements that must be met before an individual can file a federal court suit under Title VII?

13. Can an employee file suit under Title VII even though the EEOC does not find reasonable cause to believe the statute has been violated?

14. What remedies may a court require of an employer or union to eliminate unlawful discrimination?

15. Can an employer lawfully offer women lower monthly retirement benefits than men pursuant to a retirement plan when the women have made the same contributions to such plans as men?

16. Would a black employee who failed to file a timely charge against an employer, union, or both under Title VII have any other remedy against the alleged unlawful discrimination?

17. Can an employee proceed with a charge under Title VII even though an arbitrator has ruled against the employee on the discrimination issue?

18. After receiving an unfavorable arbitrator's decision, how long does an employee have to file a timely charge under Title VII with the EEOC?

19. Will the NLRB certify a union with a past history of racial or sex discrimination against bargaining unit employees?

20. Can an employer and union voluntarily adopt an affirmative action program that prefers black or female employees for certain positions over other employees with higher seniority?

(Answer to review questions are at the end of the book.)

Basic Legal Principles

1.A. An individual may establish a prima facie case of disparate treatment discrimination by proving (1) that the person belongs to a protected group under Title VII; (2) that the person applied for and was qualified for a job for which the employer was seeking applicants; (3) that despite being qualified, the person was rejected; and (4) that after the person was rejected, the position remained open and the employer continued to seek applications from persons of the rejected applicant's qualifications. *McDonnell Douglas v. Green*, 411 U.S. 792, 5 FEP Cases 965 (1973): These criteria, however, only set the general framework for proving a prima facie case and are not to be followed mechanically. *Furnco Construction Corp. v. Waters*, 438 U.S. 567, 17 FEP Cases 1062 (1978). See also, *Goodman v. Lukens Steel*, 482 U.S. 656, 44 FEP Cases 1 (1987).

1.B. If an employer has both a lawful and unlawful discriminatory motive for taking action against an employee (a "mixed-motive" case), the employee has the burden to prove that the unlawful reason, such as the employee's race, played a motivating factor in the decision. The burden is then on the employer to prove that it would have made the same decision anyhow. *Price Waterhouse v. Hopkins*, 109 S.Ct. 1775, 49 FEP Cases 954 (1989).

2. An employer may refute a prima facia case of disparate treatment discrimination by articulating a legitimate nondiscriminatory reason for the action taken. The employer, however, does not have to prove it used the best method to maximize hiring minority employees. *Furnco Construction Corp. v. Waters* in legal principle 1.A. The employer need only produce evidence that the employee was rejected or someone else was preferred for a legitimate nondiscriminatory reason, not prove that it acted for the reason given. *Texas Department of Community Affairs v. Burdine*, 450 U.S. 248, 25 FEP Cases 113 (1981).

3.A. An employment policy that is neutral on its face may be unlawful under Title VII if it has a disparate impact on a protected group regardless of the employer's intent. *Griggs v. Duke Power Co.*, 401 U.S. 424, 3 FEP Cases 175 (1971).

3.B. A prima facie case of disparate impact discrimination may not rest solely on statistics of disproportionate representation of protected group members in an employer's work force. Rather, the employees must identify the particular employment practices that created the disparate impact. The employer may refute the prima facie case by producing evidence of a business justification for its employment practice, but the employees may still prevail if they establish that there are other practices or procedures which would also serve the employer's legitimate needs without the undesirable disparate impact. *Wards Cove Packing Co. v. Atonio*, 109 S.Ct. 2115, 49 FEP Cases 1519 (1989). *Allen v. Seidman*, ____ F.2d ____, 50 FEP Cases 607 (7th Cir. 1989); *Lowe v. Commack Union School District*, ____ F.2d ____, 50 FEP Cases 1400 (2d Cir. 1989) (age discrimination).

3.C. An employment policy that discriminates against an individual member of a protected group may be unlawful under Title VII although the "bottom line" of the employer's overall personnel policies result in an apparently nondiscriminatory work force. *Connecticut v. Teal*, 457 U.S. 440, 29 FEP Cases 1 (1982). See also *Bibbs v. Block*, 778 F.2d 1318, 39 FEP Cases 970 (8th Cir. 1985).

4. Current neutral employment practices that perpetuate past discrimination are unlawful under Title VII. *Griggs v. Duke Power Co.* in legal principle 3.A. However, a bona fide seniority system is lawful under Title VII and does not have to be revised, even though it may perpetuate pre-Title VII discrimination, unless the seniority system had a discriminatory intent in its inception. *T.I.M.E.-D.C., Inc. v. United States*, 431 U.S. 324, 14 FEP Cases 1514 (1977); *American Tobacco Co. v. Patterson*, 456 U.S. 63, 28 FEP Cases 713 (1982). (Section 703(h) exemption for seniority systems applies to systems adopted before or after the effective date of Title VII.) See also *Firefighters Local Union v. Stotts*, 467 U.S. 561, 34 FEP Cases 1702 (1984).

5. A test that has a disparate impact on a protected group is unlawful under Title VII unless it is job related and there is no alternative method

of providing the employer with qualified employees with less disparate impact. *Albemarle Paper Co. v. Moody*, 422 U.S. 405, 10 FEP Cases 1181 (1975). See also *Gillespie v. State of Wisconsin*, 771 F.2d 1035, 38 FEP Cases 1487 (7th Cir. 1985).

6. Under the theory of "comparable worth," sex discrimination could be proven by establishing that certain jobs, some traditionally held by men and others by women, are of the same relative importance ("worth") to an employer but that the jobs traditionally held by men receive higher compensation, the inference being that pay scales for the lower-paying jobs are discriminatorily held down because they are occupied by women. See *AFSCME v. State of Washington*, 770 F.2d 1401, 38 FEP Cases 1353 (9th Cir. 1985); *Lemons v. City & County of Denver*, 620 F.2d 228, 22 FEP Cases 959 (10th Cir. 1980).

7. An employer may violate Title VII by limiting jobs to employees of one sex because of a stereotyped assumption as to the appropriate jobs or behavior for men and women. Jobs may be lawfully restricted by sex only if sex is a bona fide occupational qualification, which means that all or substantially all of the excluded sex would be unable to perform the task. *Price Waterhouse v. Hopkins*, in Legal Principle 1.B.; *Dothard v. Rawlinson*, 433 U.S. 321, 15 FEP Cases 10 (1977) (height and weight restrictions that have disparate impact on women are unlawful under Title VII unless they are justified by "business necessity"); *Southern Bell Telephone and Telegraph Co.*, 408 F.2d 228, 1 FEP Cases 656 (5th Cir. 1969). See also *UAW v. Johnson Controls Inc.*, ___ F.2d ___, 50 FEP Cases 1627 (7th Cir. 1989) (fetal protection policies).

8. An employer must contribute the same amounts to fringe benefit funds for individual male and female employees regardless of general assumptions about the life span or illness rate of men or women as a group. *City of Los Angeles v. Manhart*, 435 U.S. 702, 17 FEP Cases 395 (1978). An employer is in violation of Title VII if it offers women lower monthly retirement benefits than men pursuant to a retirement plan when such women have made the same contributions as men despite the fact that women, as a class, live longer than men. *Arizona Governing Committee for Tax Deferral Annuity v. Norris*, 463 U.S. 1073, 32 FEP Cases 233 (1983). The *Norris* decision does not apply retroactively to employees who retired before such decision. *Florida v. Hughlen Long Corp.*, 805 F.2d 1542, 42 FEP Cases 1058 (11th Cir. 1986).

9. Sexual harassment of an employee can constitute unlawful sex discrimination under Title VII if the harassment is so severe or pervasive as to alter the condition of the victim's employment and create an abusive or "hostile" working environment. *Meritor Savings Bank v. Vinson*, 477 U.S. 57, 40 FEP Cases 1822 (1986). See *Huddleston v. Roger Dean Chevrolet*, 845 F.2d 900, 46 FEP Cases 1361 (11th Cir. 1988). See also *Powell v. Missouri Highway & Transportation Dept.*, 822 F.2d 798, 45 FEP Cases 1747 (8th Cir. 1987); *Hamilton v. Rodgers*, 783 F.2d 1306, 40 FEP Cases 453 (1986).

10. An individual alleging age discrimination must file a charge with the appropriate state agency, if any, before filing suit in federal court. But an employee can proceed with a federal court suit under the Age Discrimination in Employment Act after waiting the required sixty days even though the time for filing a charge with the state agency has already expired. *Oscar Mayer & Co. v. Evans*, 441 U.S. 750, 19 FEP Cases 1167 (1979); *Chapman v. City of Detroit*, 808 F.2d 459, 42 FEP Cases 1016 (6th Cir. 1986). See also *Public Employees Retirement System v. Betts*, 109 S.Ct. 2854, 50 FEP Cases 104 (1989) (employee challenging a benefit plan provision as a subterfuge to evade the ADEA must prove the discriminatory plan provision was intended to serve the purpose of discriminating in some nonfringe-benefit aspect of the employment relationship).

11. The basic jurisdictional requirements for filing suit under Title VII are that a charge must be filed with the EEOC within 180 days of the initial occurrence of the alleged discriminatory act, unless the act is a continuing violation, and that the suit must be filed within 90 days after receiving the right-to-sue letter from the EEOC. *McDonnell Douglas v. Green* in legal principle 1.A. Acts such as a discriminatory refusal to hire an employee, an unlawful discharge, or the denial of a promotion are considered as single occurrences, rather than a continuing violation. Thus a challenge to a seniority provision must be filed within the applicable limitations period from the date the provision was adopted, not from the subsequent date that the provision is adversely applied to the employee. *Lorance v. AT&T Technologies, Inc.*, 109 S.Ct. 2261, 49 FEP Cases 1656 (1989). *United Airlines v. Evans*, 431 U.S. 553, 14 FEP Cases 1510 (1977). A timely complaint can be filed with the EEOC within 240 days of the discriminatory act in a state having a fair employment practices agency over one year old or even up to 300 days in some cases if the state or local agency terminates its proceedings or waives its jurisdiction before this extended limitations period is reached. *EEOC v. Commercial Office Products Co.*, 486 U.S. 107, 46 FEP Cases 1265 (1988); *Mohasco Corp. v. Silver*, 447 U.S. 807, 23 FEP Cases 1 (1980); *Green v. L.A. Supt. of Schools*, 883 F.2d 1472, 50 FEP Cases 1233 (9th Cir. 1989); *Malhotra v. Cotter & Co.*, 885 F.2d 1305, 50 FEP Cases 1474 (7th Cir. 1989).

12.A. Federal courts have broad power to remedy unlawful discrimination including orders to hire or reinstate employees, requiring backpay, and requiring such affirmative action programs as necessary to eliminate past and prohibit future discrimination. *Griggs v. Duke Power Co.* in legal principle 3; *Albemarle Paper Co. v. Moody* in legal principle 5; *Franks v. Bowman Transportation Co., Inc.*, 424 U.S. 747, 12 FEP Cases 549 (1976); *T.I.M.E.–D.C., Inc. v. United States* in legal principle 4 (back pay for nonapplicants).

12.B. A court may order relief benefitting nondiscriminatees if the employer or union has engaged in persistent or "egregious" discrimination or if it is necessary to eliminate the effect of past pervasive discrimination.

U.S. v. Paradise, 480 U.S. 149, 43 FEP Cases 1 (1987). *Local 28, Sheet Metal Workers v. EEOC*, 478 U.S. 385, 41 FEP Cases 107 (1986).

12.C. Parties may also enter into voluntary consent decrees establishing affirmative action programs which a court approves rather than imposes. *Local 93 Firefighters Union v. Cleveland*, 478 U.S. 501, 41 FEP Cases 139 (1986). However, courts will not allow parties to voluntarily agree to remedies that violate Title VII. *Firefighters Local Union v. Stotts*, in Legal Principle 4. Further, employees who are not parties to a consent decree may file suit if they allege that employment actions taken pursuant to the decree discriminate against them. *Martin v. Wilks*, 109 S.Ct. 2180, 49 FEP Cases 1641 (1989).

13. Title VII, and 42 U.S.C. Sections 1981 and 1983 prohibit reverse discrimination against white employees. *McDonald v. Santa Fe Trail Transportation Co.*, 427 U.S. 273, 12 FEP Cases 1577 (1976). However, an employer may voluntarily adopt an affirmative action program to end traditional patterns of segregation even though the program may grant preference to members of a protected group over other employees. *Kaiser Aluminum and Chemical Corp. v. Weber*, 443 U.S. 193, 20 FEP Cases 1 (1979); *Johnson v. Transportation Agency*, 480 U.S. 616, 43 FEP Cases 411 (1987). But the Supreme Court has not allowed preferential retention of minority employees in a layoff over nonminority employees with greater seniority. *Wygant v. Jackson Board of Education*, 476 U.S. 267, 40 FEP Cases 1321 (1986). See also *Firefighters Local Union v. Stotts*, in Legal Principle 4.

14.A. Title 42 United States Code Section 1981 (prohibiting certain forms of racial discrimination by private employers, by state or local governmental bodies, and by unions) and Section 1983 (prohibiting race or sex discrimination by state or local governmental bodies) are independent remedies against discrimination in addition to Title VII. Thus, an individual does not have to exhaust Title VII procedures before filing suit under either Sections 1981 or 1983 as appropriate, and can proceed under those sections even though the time for filing a charge under Title VII has expired. *McDonald v. Santa Fe Trail Transportation Co.*, in legal principle 13; *Johnson v. Railway Express Agency*, 421 U.S. 454, 10 FEP Cases 817 (1975). The Supreme Court has held that the applicable statute of limitations for both Section 1981 and 1983 actions is the same as the state limitations period for a personal injury action. *Wilson v. Garcia*, 471 U.S. 261 (1985); *Goodman v. Lukens Steel Co.*, 482 U.S. 656, 44 FEP Cases 1 (1987); *Will v. Michigan Department of State Police*, 109 S.Ct. 2304, 49 FEP Cases 1664 (1989); *Jett v. Dallas Independent School District*, 109 S.Ct. 2702, 50 FEP Cases 27 (1989).

14.B. Section 1981 only prohibits racial discrimination in the initial formation of a contract such as the refusal of an employer to hire an employee because of race or conduct which discriminatorily impairs the right to enforce contractual obligations such as a union's refusal to process a grievance because of an employee's race. This Section does not apply to discriminatory conduct after the contractual relationship has been established, such as racial harassment. *Patterson v. McLean Credit Union*, 109 S.Ct. 2363, 49 FEP Cases 1814 (1989); *Goodman v. Lukens Steel Co.*, 482 U.S. 656, 44 FEP Cases 1 (1987). *Overby v. Chevron USA*, 884 F.2d 470, 50 FEP Cases 1211 (9th Cir. 1989). See also *St. Francis College v. Al-Khazraji*, 481 U.S. 604, 43 FEP Cases 1305 (1987) ("race" within the meaning of Section 1981 is not limited to identifiable racial groups, that is, Negroes, Caucasians, and Mongolians, but also protects ethnic groups [e.g., Hispanics]).

14.C. Discriminatory intent rather than discriminatory impact alone is required to establish a violation of Sections 1981 and 1983. *Patterson v. McLean Credit Union*, in legal principle 14.B.; *Washington v. Davis*, 426 U.S. 229, 12 FEP Cases 1415 (1976); *General Building Contractors Assn. Inc. v. Pennsylvania*, 458 U.S. 375, 29 FEP Cases 139 (1982).

15. Arbitration is a separate independent remedy against discrimination in addition to Title VII. However, an employee is not required to exhaust contractual grievance procedures before proceeding under Title VII, and filing a grievance does not toll the time for filing a timely charge under Title VII. Courts do not defer to an arbitrator's award on a matter that may also violate Title VII. *Alexander v. Gardner-Denver Co.*, 415 U.S. 36, 7 FEP Cases 81 (1974); *Electrical Workers Local 790 v. Robbins and Myers, Inc.*, 429 U.S. 229, 13 FEP Cases 1813 (1976).

16. An employer is required to make a reasonable accommodation, but not necessarily the "most" reasonable accommodation to the religious beliefs of its employees. *Ansonia Board of Education v. Philbrook*, 479 U.S. 60, 42 FEP Cases 359 (1986). An employer is not required to violate the seniority provisions of a collective bargaining agreement or to incur more than a de minimis expense to accommodate an employee's religious beliefs. *Trans World Airlines v. Hardison*, 432 U.S. 63, 14 FEP Cases 1697 (1977). See also *Hudson v. Western Airlines*, 851 F.2d 261, 47 FEP Cases 295 (9th Cir. 1988); *Eversley v. M. Bank, Dallas*, 843 F.2d 172, 46 FEP Cases 1126 (5th Cir. 1988). See also *Machinists Lodge 751 v. Boeing*, 833 F.2d 165, 126 LRRM 3303 (9th Cir. 1987) (relationship of LMRA Section 19 to Title VII regarding accommodation of employee with religious objection to union membership).

17. An employer cannot require an employee to retire at any age subject to certain exceptions. Some employees engaged in bona fide high policy-making functions can be retired at age sixty-five. Until December 31, 1993, certain tenured employees at institutions of higher learning can be retired at age seventy and state and local firefighters and law enforcement officers can be denied employment and/or be retired pursuant to applicable state and local laws that set ages for hiring and retirement. An employee can also be retired if age is a BFOQ. However, the BFOQ exception is extremely narrow. *Western Airlines v. Criswell*, 472 U.S. 400, 37 FEP Cases 1829 (1985).

18. The National Labor Relations Board may revoke the certification of a union that engages in racial or sex discrimination against bargaining unit employees after it is certified. *Handy Andy, Inc.*, 228 NLRB No. 59, 94 LRRM 1354 (1977).

Recommended Reading

Allotta and Farley, "The Appropriate Test in Determining Union Liability in Employment Discrimination Cases," 5 *Lab. Lawyer* 27 (1989).

Bennett-Alexander, "Can Sex Be Considered in Promotion Determinations?" 39 *Lab. L.J.* 232 (1988).

Blumrosen, "Individual Worker-Employer Arbitration Under Title VII," 31 *N.Y.U. Conf. Lab.* 329 (1978).

Bor, "Fetal Protection Policies and Title VII," 2 *Lab. Law.* 683 (1986).

Brierton, "Religious Discrimination in the Workplace: Who's Accommodating Whom?" 39 *Lab. L.J.* 299 (1988).

"Comparable Worth: Issue for the 80's" (United States Commission on Civil Rights, Vols. 1 and 2, June 6–7, 1984).

"Cost of Growing Old: Business Necessity and the Age Discrimination in Employment Act," 88 *Yale L.J.* 565 (1979).

"Disparate Impact and Disparate Treatment: The Prima Facie Case under Title VII," 32 *Ark. L. Rev.* 571 (1978).

"*Dothard v. Rawlinson:* A Method of Analysis for Future BFOQ Cases," 16 *Urban L.J.* 361 (1979).

Fagot-Diaz, "Employment Discrimination against AIDS Victims: Rights and Remedies Under the Rehabilitation Act of 1973," 39 *Lab. L.J.* 148 (1988).

Hembacher, "Fetal Protection Policies: Reasonable Protection or Unreasonable Limitation on Female Employees," 11 *Industral Relat. L.J.* 32 (1989).

Johnson, "The Legal Use of Racial Quotas and Gender Preferences by Public and Private Employers," 40 *Lab. L.J.* 419 (1989).

"Layoffs and Equal Employment: Retroactive Seniority as a Remedy under Title VII," 10 *U.C.D.L. Rev.* 115 (1977).

Richards, "Handicap Discrimination in Employment: The Rehabilitation Act of 1973," 39 *Ark. L. Rev.* 1 (1985).

"Seniority System Exemption in Title VII: *International Brotherhood of Teamsters v. United States,* and Seniority System Violations under Title VII: A Requirement of Discriminatory Intent," 42 *Albany L. Rev.* 279 (1978) (discusses T.I.M.E.-D.C. Case).

"Sexual Harassment in the Workplace: Employer Liability for a Sexually Hostile Environment," 66 *Wash. U.L.Q.* 91 (1988).

Shoben, "Differential Pass-Fail Rates in Employment Testing: Statistical Proof Under Title VII," 91 *Harv. L. Rev.* 793 (1978).

Sobol and Ellard, "Measures of Employment Discrimination: A Statistical Alternative to the Four-Fifth's Rule," 10 *Industrial Relat. L.J.* 381 (1988).

Vaugh, D. H. "Employment Quotas, Discrimination or Affirmative Action," 7 *Emp. Rel. L.J.* 552 (1982).

Volz and Breitenbach, "Comparable Worth and the Union's Duty of Fair Representation," 10 *Emp. Rel. L.J.* 30 (1984).

chapter 14

FEDERAL-STATE RELATIONSHIPS
IN LABOR RELATIONS

Most aspects of the labor-management relationship and some aspects of the union-member relationship are subject to extensive federal regulation. Some matters, however, are not covered by federal law. Most relationships between unions and their members, which are governed by the union's constitution and bylaws, are enforced solely by state courts (see Chapters Ten and Eleven). Also, the states retain power to prohibit violent conduct in strikes. Some states even have comprehensive state statutes containing many of the same provisions found in the LMRA or the LMRDA.

If both federal and state agencies attempt to regulate labor relations, there is potential for conflict. Acts may be lawful under federal law and unlawful under state law or vice versa. A federal and state statute might contain similar language, but the NLRB and the state agency might interpret the provisions differently or reach different factual conclusions. A balance of power has been drawn between federal and state regulation of labor relations based on two fundamental doctrines: preemption and primary jurisdiction. Preemption is the doctrine under which federal law preempts, or supersedes, state law. Primary jurisdiction is the doctrine used in determining whether particular conduct governed by federal law is regulated by the NLRB, the federal courts, or by both the courts and the Board.

A. THE PREEMPTION DOCTRINE

Congress has constitutional authority (U.S. Const. Art. I, Sec. 8) to regulate exclusively any conduct affecting commerce. This means that federal law may supersede (preempt) state law on the subject. Congress has discretion when it passes federal legislation under the commerce power to determine the extent to which the federal statute preempts or permits state regulation of the same subject. The constitutional basis of federal labor law legislation is the commerce power. Thus, Congress has the power to regulate exclusively all labor matters affecting commerce. The commerce power was previously discussed in Chapter One in relation to the jurisdiction of the National Labor Relations Board.

Sometimes, federal legislation contains a provision stating whether the law is to be the exclusive remedy, or whether, and to what extent, the states are free to regulate the same conduct. Section 103 of the LMRDA expressly provides that state remedies remain as to matters covered by Title

I of that statute (The Bill of Rights). Section 603 of the LMRDA provides that nothing in the Act limits the responsibility of a union under any other federal or state law except as expressly provided in the statute. LMRDA Section 403 is such an express limitation. It makes Title IV (election proceedings) the exclusive remedy for challenging an election. Under Section 708 of the Civil Rights Act of 1964, as amended, the Act does not preempt state law, except to the extent that state law requires or permits an act federal law prohibits. In contrast, Section 514(A) of the Employee Retirement Income Security Act (ERISA) provides that that Act supersedes state law except for state laws regulating insurance or securities.

To what extent did Congress intend for the LMRA to preempt state law over labor management relations? Unfortunately—in contrast to the other statutes indicated above—Congress did not expressly spell out the limits of permissible state regulation. Thus, the Supreme Court has had to define the limits on a case-by-case basis.

1. Arguably Protected or Prohibited Conduct

The basic rule governing state regulation of labor relations was established by the Supreme Court's 1959 decision in *San Diego Building Trades Council v. Garmon*.[1] In *Garmon*, a union engaged in picketing that was probably unlawful secondary activity under Section 8(b)(4). The employer brought suit for damages and an injunction in the California state courts. The California court held that the picketing violated California's state law and awarded the employer damages. The union appealed to the United States Supreme Court on the grounds that the conduct in question was preempted by federal law. The Court held that the matter

was preempted and that the state courts did not have jurisdiction.

Acts permitted by the LMRA are called protected acts. Acts that the statute makes an unfair labor practice are called prohibited acts. Primary picketing is protected, whereas secondary boycotts are prohibited. The Supreme Court recognized in *Garmon* that although the LMRA does not expressly provide for the preemption of state law, the Act was intended to establish uniform federal regulation. The Court, therefore, concluded that the LMRA preempts state law over matters regulated by the statute. The Court emphasized that preemption applied whether the union's conduct was lawful (protected) or unlawful (prohibited) under the federal law. The Court stated the guiding principle that is still applied:

When it is clear or may fairly be assumed that the activities which a State purports to regulate are protected by Section 7 of the Taft-Hartley Act, or constitute an unfair labor practice under Section 8, due regard for the federal enactment requires that state jurisdiction must yield. To leave the States free to regulate conduct so plainly within the central aim of federal regulation involves too great a danger of conflict between power asserted by Congress and requirements imposed by state law. Nor has it mattered whether the States have acted through laws of broad general application rather than laws specifically directed towards the governance of industrial relations. Regardless of the mode adopted, to allow the States to control conduct which is the subject of national regulation would create potential frustration of national purposes . . . It is not for us to decide whether the National Labor Relations Board would have, or should have, decided these questions in the same manner. *When an activity is arguably subject to Section 7 or Section 8 of the Act, the States as well as the federal courts must defer to the exclusive competence of the National Labor Relations Board if the danger of state interference with national policy is to be averted.* (emphasis added).

Thus, under *Garmon*, if conduct is arguably protected or prohibited by the LMRA, federal law preempts. The NLRB has primary jurisdiction to enforce the provisions.

---

[1] See legal principle 1.

State courts or state administrative agencies cannot act. Even if the state law is similar to the federal law, only federal law and procedures apply to conduct that is preempted. Thus, subject to certain narrow exceptions discussed below, a state court cannot issue an injunction against peaceful picketing by a union even if the picketing is in violation of both the Labor Management Relations Act and/or a state law.

The Court has held that the LMRA preempts the state courts or state law even if the remedies available under state law, such as punitive damages for an unlawful act, are different than those available under the LMRA. For example, the state of Wisconsin enacted a law prohibiting state procurement agents from purchasing products from employers found to have violated the Labor Management Relations Act in three separate cases within a five-year period. The Supreme Court held that this statute was preempted because it conflicted with the National Labor Relations Board's authority to regulate industrial relations including remedying violations of the Act.

2. Union Security Matters

Although *Garmon* pertains to state regulation of picketing, the principles apply to any conduct arguably protected or prohibited. Thus, in the Supreme Court's *Lockridge* decision, an employee sued a union for damages in an Idaho state court alleging that he had been wrongfully discharged under a union security clause pursuant to the union's request.[2] The employee maintained that he had paid his dues in time under the union's bylaws and should not have been discharged. The Idaho court awarded the employee over $32,000 in damages. The Supreme Court reversed the Idaho decision, holding that the action was preempted. The Court noted that LMRA Sections 8(a)(3) and 8(b)(2) regulate discharge of an employee under a union se-

curity clause. The Court stated that the union's conduct in requiring that the employee be discharged was either arguably protected or prohibited under the LMRA. Therefore, preemption applied. It did not matter that the state court might have afforded a different remedy than the NLRB.

3. State Labor Standards Legislation

Many states have enacted legislation regulating labor standards such as limits on the number of consecutive hours that employees can work without a break or the prompt payment of wages owed to employees who have been discharged. Recently in the *Metropolitan Life Insurance* and *Fort Halifax Packing Co.* cases[3] the Supreme Court upheld the states' power to enact minimum labor standards. Thus, in *Metropolitan Life* the Court upheld a state law requiring that minimum mental health benefits be provided under certain health insurance policies, and in *Fort Halifax* the Court upheld a law requiring that severance pay be paid to employees in the event of a plant closing. These laws were challenged by employers on the grounds that they interfered with the LMRA's policy that conditions of employment be determined through the free play of the collective bargaining process. The Supreme Court noted, however, that neither law directly regulated the conduct of either the employer or of the union in bargaining nor forced either party to give up the use of any of its economic weapons such as the right to strike, lockout, or picket, etc. The Court further stated that the LMRA is concerned with ensuring an equitable bargaining process rather than with the substantive terms of a collective bargaining agreement, so that state laws establishing certain minimum standards thus neither encourage nor discourage the collective bargaining process that the statute regulates.

[2] See legal principle 7.

[3] See legal principle 5.

B. FEDERAL COURT EXCEPTIONS TO THE BOARD'S PRIMARY JURISDICTION

The only exceptions to the NLRB's primary jurisdiction at the federal level are under LMRA Sections 301 and 303. Section 301 grants the federal courts jurisdiction to enforce collective bargaining agreements (see Chapter Nine). Section 303 authorizes federal court damage suits arising out of unlawful secondary activity prohibited by Section 8(b)(4) (see Chapter Seven). The Supreme Court has held that the federal courts have jurisdiction to enforce collective bargaining agreements, including awarding damages, even though an alleged breach of contract may also be an unfair labor practice. The courts also have jurisdiction under Section 301 to enforce the union's duty of fair representation (see Chapter Twelve), although the Board has also held that a violation of the duty of fair representation is an unfair labor practice. These are areas of concurrent federal court-NLRB jurisdiction.

C. STATE COURT EXCEPTIONS TO THE PREEMPTION DOCTRINE

1. Violent Conduct

The primary exception to federal preemption is that the states still have jurisdiction over traditional areas of state concern that do not impede upon matters regulated by the LMRA. States have the authority to regulate violent conduct, including intimidation and picket line violence. States may even regulate peaceful picketing that interferes with people entering or leaving a struck facility. State courts can prohibit mass picketing at a plant during a strike and regulate threatened or actual destruction of property. These powers are retained as part of the state's traditional control over disturbance of the peace. State courts or state labor agencies as appropriate can enjoin such strike misconduct and award damages against unions that engage in it.

2. Regulation of Libel and Slander

State authority over libel and slander suits is another example of continued state jurisdiction over traditional areas of state concern. In *Linn v. United Plant Guard Workers*, a supervisor sued a union for damages because the union had allegedly made untrue statements about him during a union organizing campaign.[4] The union argued that the matter was preempted because the statements were either arguably protected or prohibited under Board rules as to permissible election propaganda.

The Supreme Court refused to apply the preemption doctrine. The Court viewed the regulation of libel and slander (jointly referred to as defamation) as a traditional area of state concern. Also, the LMRA does not regulate libel and slander. However, the Court recognized the danger that a state court might assess damages for statements that the Board might find permissible campaign propaganda. To lessen the possibility that state courts will interfere with permissible campaign tactics, the Supreme Court held in *Linn* that a person can prevail in a defamation suit arising out of a labor relations matter only if the person proves that a false statement was made with malice. This means that the person making the statement knew it was false or made a serious allegation without checking whether it was true or false—called reckless disregard of the truth. Also, the Court held that the plaintiff must prove actual damages to obtain a monetary award. Damages cannot be presumed. In this way, the Court hoped to balance the traditional state concern in prohibiting libel and slander against the federal interest in regulating labor relations.

---

[4] See legal principle 2.

3. Picketing on Private Property

In *Sears, Roebuck & Co.*,[5] the Supreme Court slightly modified the preemption doctrine when applied to picketing or handbilling on private property. In *Sears*, the company had a dispute with a union because certain carpentry work was done by employees not dispatched from the union hall. The union established a peaceful picket line on sidewalks around the Sears store on Sears's property. Sears asked the union to remove the pickets to public property, but the union refused. The company then sought a state court injunction against the trespass to require that the pickets remain on public property. The court issued an injunction despite the union's argument that the dispute was preempted.

Under *Garmon*, the union's picket line at Sears may arguably have been protected or prohibited activity. The object of the picketing was unclear. The union argued that the purpose was to advertise the employer's substandard wages, which would be lawful primary activity. Arguably, the picketing might have been for recognition or to have the work reassigned to employees represented by the union. In that event, the picketing was prohibited activity. Although the union picket line at Sears arguably was either protected or prohibited activity, and unions have the right under the *Hudgens* decision to enter private property in the course of a labor dispute in some cases (see Chapter Seven), the Supreme Court still upheld the state court injunction. The reasons for the Court's decision were twofold. First, the Court noted that control over trespassing is a traditional area of state concern, similar to the state's right to prevent violence or property damage, which are not preempted. Second, the Court emphasized that Sears did not have a means of bringing the trespassing issue before the NLRB. If Sears had filed a charge with the Board, the Board would decide only

whether the picketing was primary or secondary. But if the Board held that the picketing was primary, the Board would not be concerned about the location. Thus, Sears could not obtain a NLRB order requiring the union to leave the property if the Board held the picketing was primary.

The Supreme Court pointed out that the union had the opportunity to present the issue directly to the Board. When Sears asked the union to leave the property, the union could have filed a charge with the Board against Sears alleging it had a statutory right, applying the *Hudgens* doctrine, to picket on Sears' property. The Board could have then decided the issue. However, the union did not exercise its right to go to the Board, but simply continued to picket. Thus, the Supreme Court reasoned that the only way that Sears could resolve the picketing issue was by a state court action.

Under *Sears*, an employer must demand that a union leave the employer's property and give the union a fair chance to file an unfair labor practice charge to determine its rights before the employer can seek an injunction. Thus, if a union is faced with such a demand, it should promptly file an NLRB charge. A state court would then be powerless to act, and the picketing (or handbilling) can continue until the Board rules. If the union's charge is dismissed or the Board rules that the union has no right under the Act to publicize its dispute on private property under the facts of the case, the state court would then have jurisdiction to issue an injunction against the conduct if it violated state trespass laws.

D. PREEMPTION OF CONDUCT NOT REGULATED BY FEDERAL LAW

Not all conduct arising during a labor-management dispute is regulated by federal law. Federal law does not prohibit unions from engaging in quickie strikes during bargaining in support of their bargaining demands

---

[5] See legal principle 4.

(see Chapter Five). On the other hand, activities such as quickie strikes, sit-down strikes, or slowdowns, are not protected by federal law and employees may be discharged for such conduct.

The states may not be able to regulate certain conduct even though it is neither protected nor prohibited by federal law. The Supreme Court has held it is necessary to consider why Congress chose not to regulate the conduct. Congress might have intended for the conduct to be totally unregulated. In that case, the conduct cannot be regulated by the federal courts or by state courts or agencies. Or, Congress might have intended that the matter be left to the states because the conduct is not considered of federal concern.

The Supreme Court has consistently held that internal union matters not regulated by federal law are subject to state regulation because Congress has not intended for these matters to be totally unregulated. In contrast, the Supreme Court held in *Machinists Lodge 76 v. Wisconsin Employment Relations Commission* that a state cannot prohibit a union from ordering its members not to work any overtime in support of the union's bargaining demands.[6] This conduct is neither protected nor prohibited by federal law, and the Court held that Congress intended for the conduct to be totally unregulated. Because the union's conduct was peaceful, it did not fall under the exception for traditional state regulation of violent conduct. Thus, union self-help activities, such as quickie strikes, are not subject to regulation by either federal or state law. Such activity is simply a test of economic strength between an employer and a union.

The Supreme Court's decision in *Golden State Transit Corp. v. Los Angeles*[7] demonstrates the importance that the Court places on the free play of economic forces in resolving labor disputes. In that case, the City of Los Angeles refused to renew a taxicab operating franchise until the employer resolved its labor dispute with its drivers who were then on strike for a collective bargaining agreement. The Court ruled that the city's insistence on settling the strike interfered with the underlying policy of the Labor Management Relations Act that recognizes the parties' right to use economic force in the resolution of bargaining disputes and that does not compel either party to reach an agreement. Thus, the City's action interfered with the congressional intent that the conduct be unregulated.

The Court's decision in *Golden State* should be contrasted to its decision in *Belknap v. Hale*.[8] In *Belknap*, the employer promised economic strike replacements (see Chapter Six) permanent employment at the end of a strike. However, the company subsequently entered into a strike settlement agreement with the union to reinstate a number of the strikers. The employer discharged the replacements to make way for the returning strikers and the replacements filed suit in state court against the employer to recover damages for misrepresentation and breach of contract. The employer argued that the suit should be preempted because it would interfere with the federal policy giving the parties "free play" in the choice of their economic weapons during a strike. The case reached the Supreme Court, which ruled that the suit was not preempted for two principal reasons: (1) because any questions regarding the rights and status of the strikers and their replacements under the Labor Management Relations Act were totally separate from any issues as to the replacements' rights under state law if the employer breached a promise to retain them; and (2) because the state had a substantial interest in prohibiting misrepresentation and breach of contract. The Court concluded that enforcement of an employer's promise of permanent employment would not interfere with the Congressional policy upholding economic force in a labor dispute. In the Court's view,

[6] See legal principle 3.
[7] See legal principle 3.

[8] See legal principle 3.

if an employer voluntarily relinquishes its rights by promising replacements permanent employment, it is bound by that promise.

E. EMPLOYERS NOT SUBJECT TO THE BOARD'S JURISDICTION

The LMRA applies only to employers whose activities affect commerce (see Chapter One). The operations of some very small employers may not affect commerce and are not subject to federal regulation. Preemption does not apply to these employers; they are subject to state law.

1. Failure to Meet Board Jurisdictional Standards

An employer whose business meets the statutory requirement of affecting commerce may still not meet the discretionary monetary standards the Board has established for asserting jurisdiction (see Chapter One). Initially, the Supreme Court held that if an employer met the statutory standard of affecting commerce, but failed to meet the Board's discretionary standards, a dispute involving that employer was still preempted and not subject to state regulation. This meant that a dispute might not be regulated by either federal or state law creating a jurisdictional "no man's land."

To remedy this situation, in 1959, Congress enacted Section 14(c) of the LMRA that allows the states to take jurisdiction over a labor dispute and to apply state law if the Board declines jurisdiction over it.

Although a few states have employment relations boards to regulate conduct that is not preempted, most do not. Most state laws are very outmoded. Because most disputes are preempted, the states courts have had very few cases in which to develop comprehensive principles. Most state private sector labor law is based on court decisions from the 1940s or early 1950s before the preemption doctrine was fully developed.

F. SECTIONS 301, 303 AND FEDERAL ANTITRUST PREEMPTION OF STATE REGULATION

Sections 301 and 303 provide federal court remedies to enforce collective bargaining agreements and award damages for unlawful secondary activity. Both Sections 301 and 303 preempt state regulation over the matters covered by those statutes. State courts have jurisdiction over suits to enforce collective bargaining agreements, or for damages against secondary boycotts, but the state courts must apply the federal law (see Chapter Nine). The Supreme Court has held that Sections 301 and 303 only permit an employer to collect actual damages, such as lost profits, growing out of a violation. Punitive damages are not permitted. Since state courts must apply the federal law, an employer can collect only actual damages even though the suit is brought in a state court. As an exception, the Supreme Court has held that Section 303 does not preempt state regulation over violent conduct occurring during a secondary boycott. Thus an employer can recover actual damages resulting from a secondary boycott under Section 303 and punitive damages under state law if there is violent conduct.

The Supreme Court has applied the same principles to the antitrust laws that it has applied to Sections 301 and 303. Thus, the federal antitrust laws (see Chapter Eight) preempt state antitrust regulation of labor relations except to the extent that violent conduct is involved.

G. PREEMPTION OF EMPLOYEE CIVIL SUITS BY THE GRIEVANCE PROCEDURE

In recent years some employees have sought to circumvent the grievance procedure and bring a suit directly against the employer by alleging an employer action that might breach the collective bargaining agreement also violates state law. Thus, some employees have filed suits alleging that they were wrongfully discharged under state law rather than pursuing a grievance that their discharge was not for just cause under the collective bargaining agreement. In *Allis-Chalmers Corp. v. Lueck*[9] the Supreme Court narrowly limited the circumstances under which such a suit may be brought. In that case, an employee filed suit for monetary damages against his employer in state court alleging that the employer had repeatedly and in bad faith delayed paying the employee sick-leave benefits to which the employee was entitled under the collective bargaining agreement. Although the collective bargaining agreement provided for arbitration, the employee did not file a grievance. The Supreme Court held that the employee did not have the right to file a state court suit, but rather was required to utilize the grievance procedures as the exclusive remedy.

In holding that the employee was limited to the grievance procedure, the Court emphasized in *Lueck* that arbitration must be the exclusive remedy for resolving contractual disputes. An arbitrator, not a court, must decide whether the employer violated the collective bargaining agreement or acted in bad faith by delaying payments to the employee. Thus the matter was preempted by Section 301 of the Labor Management Relations Act under which federal law controls the meaning and application of collective bargaining agreements and the grievance/arbitration procedure is the exclusive remedy for resolving contract disputes when the contract so provides.

The Court did indicate in *Lueck* that an employee covered by a collective bargaining agreement might still be able to bring a state court law suit based on a state law that establishes rights and obligations independent of a labor contract. This exception was subsequently applied in *Lingle v. Norge Div. of Magic Chef*[10] in which the Court upheld an employee's right to file a state court

damage suit against the employer for discharging her for filing a worker's compensation claim. The Court reasoned that a court would not have to interpret the contractual just cause provision to resolve the claim even though the employer's conduct might also violate the contract and an arbitrator would consider the same factual issues as a court. The Court also regarded the state's interest in protecting employees against retaliatory discharge for filing a worker's compensation claim as similar to a minimum labor standard that was upheld in the *Fort Halifax Packing* case discussed above.

Under *Lueck* and *Lingle*, an employee cannot circumvent the grievance/arbitration provisions in the typical discharge case involving the interpretation of a contractual just cause provision by filing a state court suit under some theory of wrongful discharge or unjust treatment. Such a suit would be preempted because it involves construing the just cause provision to establish the claim regardless of the theory that is used to evade the contractual provisions. Similarly, some employees covered by collective bargaining agreements have filed suits against their employer challenging employee drug-testing programs on the grounds that the programs violate the right of privacy. The courts have held that such suits are preempted by the grievance procedure under Section 301 because the employer's right to test requires consideration and interpretation of a collective bargaining agreement.

In a few cases, employees injured at work have filed suit against the union alleging it was negligent in enforcing contractual safety provisions. In *Electrical Workers v. Hechler*,[11] the Supreme Court held that, as in the *Lueck* case, such claims are preempted by Section 301 of the Labor Management Relations Act because they are based on the meaning and application of the collective bargaining agreement. Thus the union cannot be sued for negligence under state law, but only for

---

[9] See legal principle 11.A.
[10] See legal principle 11.A.

[11] See legal principle 11.B.

breach of contract under federal law. The Court also indicated that the employee's suit cannot be based on an alleged breach of a duty owed by the union directly to the employee. Rather, the union may be liable only if it contractually agreed with the employer to assume or take responsibility for certain safety conditions on the job. If so, the employee can sue the union for damages resulting from the union's breach of its contractual obligation to the employer. This is technically called a "third party beneficiary suit," in which the third party (the employee) brings suit arising from the breach of a contractual provision (the contractual safety clause) negotiated by two other parties (the employer and the union) for the third party's benefit. The Court emphasized that ordinarily the employer, not a union, is responsible for providing a safe workplace and that the union can be held liable only if the contract in fact places that express or implied duty on the union.

Of course, an employee may also file a suit alleging that the union violated its duty of fair representation in improperly enforcing a contractual safety provision against the employer. However, as discussed in Chapter Twelve, a union violates that duty only if it acts arbitrarily, discriminatorily, in bad faith, or in a perfunctory manner in enforcing the contract. Negligence probably is not a violation. In contrast, in the *Hechler* situation, a union may be liable regardless of its good faith, etc. Although *Hechler* potentially exposes unions to substantial liability, very few contracts place the duty to maintain safety on the union rather than on the employer, and any implication of such responsibility should be avoidable by proper contract drafting without any reduction in contractual safety standards.

Summary   This chapter considered federal-state relationships in labor relations focusing on two fundamental concepts: the doctrines of preemption and primary jurisdiction. Preemption is the doctrine under which federal labor law preempts, or supersedes, state law. Primary jurisdiction is the doctrine determining whether particular conduct, preempted by federal law, is to be regulated by the NLRB, the courts, or by both the courts and the Board.

The Supreme Court has held that if conduct is arguably protected or prohibited by the LMRA, federal law preempts state law and state courts or administrative agencies cannot act. Furthermore, the NLRB, as the agency established to administer the Act, has primary jurisdiction over the federal courts to enforce the provision.

Preemption does not apply if an employer is not covered by the Act; that is, if the employer's operations do not affect commerce or if the employer fails to meet the applicable Board monetary jurisdictional standards. The states may still regulate disputes outside the Board's jurisdiction.

The only exceptions to the NLRB's primary jurisdiction at the federal level are Section 301 (pertaining to the enforcement of contracts) and Section 303 (pertaining to damages growing out of secondary boycotts) of the LMRA. The federal courts, under Section 301, and the NLRB have concurrent jurisdiction if a breach of contract is also an unfair labor practice and to enforce the duty of fair representation. Section 301 and Section 303 preempt state law over the matters these provisions regulate.

States, however, retain jurisdiction over traditional areas of state concern that do not impede upon actions regulated by the LMRA. States have authority to regulate violent conduct of any type, including picketing and may even regulate peaceful picketing that interferes with entering or leaving a struck facility. Most internal union matters are still subject to state regulation. The LMRDA expressly provides for concurrent jurisdiction over most matters covered by that Act.

Libel and slander actions growing out of a labor dispute are also not preempted because the Court views defamation as a traditional area of state concern and the LMRA does not regulate it. To avoid conflict, however, the Court held that the party would have to prove malice before prevailing in a defamation suit. Also, an employee covered by a collective bargaining agreement may still be able to file a suit based on a state law establishing rights and obligations independent of the contract as long as the court does not have to interpret the contract to resolve the claim.

Sears, Roebuck & Co. appears to have modified slightly the preemption doctrine. The Court upheld the right of a state court to enjoin a union from picketing in a private shopping center even though the union's dispute was either arguably protected or prohibited activity. The Court emphasized that control over trespass is a traditional area of state concern, similar to the state's right to prevent violence or property damages that are not preempted. The Court also stressed that Sears did not have a means of bringing the trespass issue before the Board.

The *Sears* decision does not mean that an employer can seek a state court injunction whenever a union pickets or handbills on private property. A union must be given a fair opportunity to present the dispute to the NLRB before the employer can seek a state court injunction.

Congress has intended that certain acts, such as work slowdowns or quickie strikes, must be totally unregulated. Neither the federal nor the state agencies have jurisdiction to regulate such conduct as long as it is peaceful.

Review Questions

1. What is the difference between the doctrines of preemption and primary jurisdiction?
2. What conduct does the LMRA preempt?
3. What conduct possibly subject to the LMRA can the state courts still regulate?
4. If the Board decides that an act is unlawful, can the states assess penalties in addition to the NLRB's relief?
5. If a union unlawfully pickets to encourage a total boycott of a store selling struck products, can the store owner obtain a state court injunction?
6. What are the exceptions to the NLRB's primary jurisdiction at the federal level?
7. If certain conduct is neither protected nor prohibited by federal law, are the states free to regulate it?
8. Are internal union matters subject to state regulation?

9. Can the states regulate any employers whose activities affect commerce?

10. Are libel suits preempted?

11. Can a state court assess punitive damages if a union engages in an unlawful secondary boycott?

12. Are suits to enforce collective bargaining agreements preempted?

13. If an employee covered by a collective bargaining agreement is discharged, can the employee sue the employer in state court for damages rather than pursuing the contractual grievance procedure? (Answers to review questions are at the end of the book.)

Basic Legal Principles

1. Conduct that is arguably protected by LMRA Section 7 or prohibited by Section 8 is preempted by federal law and is subject to the primary jurisdiction of the NLRB. *San Diego Building Trades Council v. Garmon*, 359 U.S. 236, 43 LRRM 2838 (1959).

2. A defamatory statement during the course of a labor dispute can be the basis of a state court libel suit only if the statement was made with malice. *Linn v. Plant Guards*, 383 U.S. 53, 61 LRRM 2345 (1966).

3. Federal preemption applies to conduct, such as slowdowns, which Congress intended to be totally unregulated by either federal or state agencies, but "controlled by the free play of economic forces." *Machinists Lodge 76 v. Wisconsin Employment Relations Commission*, 427 U.S. 132, 92 LRRM 2881 (1976). Contrast *Golden State Transit Corp. v. Los Angeles*, 459 U.S. 1105, 121 LRRM 3233 (1986) (municipality may not refuse to renew taxi franchise until employer resolved labor dispute) with *Belknap v. Hale*, 463 U.S. 491, 113 LRRM 3057 (1983) (suit by discharged strike replacements for misrepresentation and breach of contract not preempted). See also *Wisconsin Dept. of Industry v. Gould*, 475 U.S. 282, 121 LRRM 2737 (1986) (LMRA preempts state law prohibiting state from doing business with any employer judicially found to have violated the Act on three separate occasions within a five-year period).

4. As an exception to preemption, state courts may be permitted to issue injunctions against pickets who are trespassing on private property, even if the pickets' conduct is arguably protected or prohibited, if the property owner is unable to present the issue of the picketing's validity to the NLRB, and the union fails to do so although having the opportunity. *Sears, Roebuck & Co. v. Carpenters*, 436 U.S. 180, 98 LRRM 2282 (1978).

5. States have the power to regulate conduct that is violent or causes or threatens to cause injury to persons or property and to establish minimum labor standards. These are traditional areas of state concern that the Act does not preempt. *UAW v. Russell*, 356 U.S. 634, 42 LRRM 2142 (1958); *San Diego Building Trades Council v. Garmon* in legal principle 1; *Metropolitan Life Ins. Co. v. Massachusetts*, 471 U.S. 724, 119 LRRM 2569 (1985); *Fort Halifax Packing Co. v. Coyne*, 482 U.S. 1, 125 LRRM 2455 (1987).

6. State court jurisdiction is not preempted in cases in which a union member sues his union for intentional infliction of emotional distress (intimidation) that no reasonable person could be expected to endure because the conduct is similar to violent conduct traditionally regulated by the state. *Farmer v. Carpenters, Local 25*, 430 U.S. 290, 94 LRRM 2759 (1977).

7. Regulation of purely internal union affairs is not preempted. *Int'l Asso. of Machinists v. Gonzales*, 356 U.S. 617, 42 LRRM 2135 (1958); *Motor Coach Employees v. Lockridge*, 403 U.S. 274, 77 LRRM, 2501 (1971).

8. Federal and state courts have concurrent jurisdiction under Section 301 to enforce collective bargaining agreements, even though the conduct involved may also be arguably protected or prohibited by the Act. However, the state courts must apply federal law. *Textile Workers Union v. Lincoln Mills*, 353 U.S. 448, 40 LRRM 2113 (1957); *Vaca v. Sipes*, 386 U.S. 171, 64 LRRM 2369 (1967).

9. Section 303 preempts civil damage suits for secondary boycotts. Such suits may be brought in federal or state court, but federal law prevails in either court. *Teamsters Local 20 v. Morton*, 377 U.S. 252, 56 LRRM 2225 (1964).

10. The NLRB may seek a federal court injunction to prohibit a state court from improperly issuing an injunction against peaceful picketing in a preempted matter if the state court action is interfering with the Board's administration of the Act. *NLRB v. Nash-Finch Co.*, 404 U.S. 138, 78 LRRM 2967 (1971). The Board may also enjoin an employer suit filed against employees for exercising rights protected under the Act (e.g., filing a slander suit against employees for statements made during the course of a representation election campaign) if the suit lacks a reasonable basis (was meritless) and was filed with a retaliatory intent. *NLRB v. Bill Johnson's Restaurants*, 461 U.S. 731, 113 LRRM 2647 (1983); *Bill Johnson's Restaurants*, 290 NLRB No. 5, 129 LRRM 1105 (1988).

11.A. Under Section 301 of the LMRA, the grievance/arbitration procedure is the exclusive remedy for resolving contract disputes when the contract so provides, but an employee may file a state court suit based on a state law that establishes rights and obligations independent of the contract and that does not require interpretation of the contract to resolve the claim. Contrast *Allis-Chalmers Corp. v. Lueck*, 471 U.S. 202, 118 LRRM 3345 (1985) (employee's state court suit alleging that employer acted in bad faith by denying and delaying payment of sick leave benefits preempted) with *Lingle v. Norge Div. of Magic Chef*, 108 S.Ct. 1877, 128 LRRM 2521 (1988) (employee's claim that she was discharged for filing a worker's compensation claim not preempted as there was no need to interpret the collective bargaining agreement to resolve the claim). See *Hanks v. General Motors Corp.*, 859 F.2d 67, 129 LRRM 2715 (8th Cir. 1988); *Curl v. General Telephone*, 861 F.2d 171, 129 LRRM 3067 (8th Cir. 1988); *Local 246 v. Southern California Edison*, 852 F.2d 1083, 128 LRRM

2317 (9th Cir. 1988) (union's claim that company testing policy violates California constitutional rights to privacy and freedom from unreasonable search and seizures is preempted by Section 301); *Newberry v. Pacific Racing Assn.*, 854 F.2d 1142, 129 LRRM 2047 (9th Cir. 1988).

11.B. An employee's suit that a union acted negligently in failing to enforce contractual safety provisions is preempted by Section 301 so that the union cannot be sued for negligence under state law. However, the union can be sued under Section 301 if it contractually agreed with the employer to assume or take responsibility for certain safety conditions on the job and the employee was injured as a result of the union's breach of this duty to the employer. *Electrical Workers v. Hechler*, 481 U.S. 851, 125 LRRM 2353 (1987).

Recommended Reading

Benke, "Apparent Reformation of Garmon: Its Effect On the Federal Preemption of Concerted Trespassory Union Activity," 9 *U. Tol. L. Rev.* 793 (1978).

"Federal Preemption: Pension and Retirement Plans," 17 *Duquesne L. Rev.* 189 (1979).

Gomez, "Preemption and Preclusion of Employee Common Law Rights by Federal and State Statutes," 11 *Industrial Relat. L.J.* 45 (1989).

Gregory, "Labor Preemption Doctrine: Hamiltonian Renaissance or Last Hurrah?" 27 *Wm. & Mary L. Rev.* 507 (1986).

Kosanovich, "Inching Through the Maze: Recent Developments in Preemption under the NLRA and the Impact of *Caterpillar, Hechler* and others," 4 *Lab. Law.* 225 (1988).

"NLRA Preemption and State Law Actions for Wrongful Discharge in Violation of Public Policy," 19 *U. Mich. J.L. Ref.* 441 (1986).

ANSWERS TO REVIEW QUESTIONS

CHAPTER 1
FEDERAL REGULATION
OF LABOR-MANAGEMENT
REGULATIONS

1. The Norris-LaGuardia Act removed the jurisdiction of the federal judges to issue injunctions in labor disputes regardless of the strike's purpose. The law prevented judges from enjoining a strike because they did not approve of its goals or methods.

2. The Taft-Hartley Act was intended to strike what Congress regarded as a better balance between labor and management. The original NLRA established employee rights and restricted employer acts. Taft-Hartley also established union unfair labor practices.

3. The Board acts as a judge in unfair labor practice cases. It hears only cases in which a complaint has been filed alleging a violation of Section 8. The general counsel serves as the prosecutor. The general counsel, or more commonly the regional director acting on the general counsel's behalf, decides whether a charge filed with the agency has merit. If so, the general counsel issues a complaint that may lead to a trial before an administrative law judge and ultimately to a Board decision. The NLRB also administers elections under Section 9, but the general counsel's authority is limited to the unfair labor practice portions of the Act.

4. In addition to the statutory jurisdictional requirements of affecting commerce, the Board has established additional monetary standards that an employer must meet before the Board will accept jurisdiction over a dispute even though the employer's operations affect commerce.

5. The first step in an unfair labor practice case is the filing of a charge. The Board has no self-enforcement powers. Therefore, even if an unfair labor practice has been committed, the Board can take no action until someone files a charge with it.

6. Anyone can file a charge: an employer, an employee, or a union.

7. A charge must be filed within six months of the date of the alleged unfair labor practice. Sometimes a violation is a continuing act, so that a charge can be filed within six months from the last date the act was committed. However, most charges must be filed within six months from the initial occurrence, such as the date of a discharge.

8. The purpose of a representation hearing is to resolve any disputed issues as to the appropriateness of a bargaining unit, the employees to be included or excluded in the unit, and the election procedures.

9. The Board requires a 30 percent showing of interest of employee support in the appropriate bargaining unit before proceeding with a representation election. The

showing of interest is usually made through signed recognition cards.

10. In most cases the regional director's decision must be appealed by filing a request for review. There are limited grounds for review and granting review is discretionary with the Board.

CHAPTER 2
THE COLLECTIVE BARGAINING UNIT

1. Community of interest refers to what employees have in common, such as skills, interrelated functions, common supervision, and the same working conditions. The more the employees have in common the more likely it is that the Board will find that they have a distinct community of interest and are an appropriate unit for bargaining.

2. Yes. In most cases a workforce could be divided into a number of appropriate units. An election could be held in any of them. The unit does not have to be the best or most appropriate.

3. No. The Board has held that a bargaining unit must have a minimum of two employees because one person cannot engage in collective bargaining. However, this rule does not prevent an employer from voluntarily recognizing a union as the representative for a single employee.

4. A professional employee performs work of a predominantly intellectual nature that is not standardized. The work must require the use of discretion and independent judgment and knowledge of an advanced type in a field of science or learning customarily acquired in an institution of higher learning.

5. No. The function an employee performs, not a title, controls. A person whose job is crowd control is not a guard despite the title. Similarly, classification as a supervisor is based on duties, not a supervisory title.

6. Agricultural laborers, domestics in the service of a family or person in their home, people employed by a parent or spouse, independent contractors, and supervisors are excluded from the definition of employee.

7. An independent contractor is generally distinguished from an employee based on the amount of control the employer exercises over how a person works. The more control an employer exercises over the work, the more likely it is that the individual will be classified as an employee.

8. Yes. Authority to hire or fire are only two of the twelve separate factors under the Act by which a person may be classified as a supervisor. Even effective authority to recommend supervisory action is sufficient for classification as a supervisor.

9. Yes. Seasonal employees can be included in a bargaining unit of regular full-time employees if they have a reasonable expectation of returning each season. Similarly, probationary employees are included in a bargaining unit if they have a reasonable expectation of completing their probationary period and being permanently employed.

10. The contract bar doctrine establishes the periods for filing representation petitions during or at the termination of a collective bargaining agreement.

11. Unfair labor practice strikers are eligible to vote indefinitely as long as they do not obtain permanent employment elsewhere or are not discharged for strike misconduct.

12. The insulated period is the sixty-day period before the termination of a contract when no representation petition may be filed so that the parties may bargain for a contract without interference. The open period is the ninety- to sixty-day period before expiration when a timely petition may be filed. If no contract is agreed to during the insulated period, a petition may be timely filed again after the contract's expiration.

In the health care industry, the open period is 120-to-90 days before the expiration date of the prior collective bargaining agreement.

CHAPTER 3
UNION ORGANIZING RIGHTS AND EMPLOYER RESPONSE

1. No. An employer has an absolute right to a Board-conducted election. But if the employer voluntarily verifies the union's majority status, it has waived its right to an election and must bargain with the union.

2. The two types are a single-purpose card and a dual-purpose card. The single-purpose card states that its purpose is to authorize the union to represent the employee signing the card. The dual-purpose card states it is for recognition and an election.

3. No. The Board requires clear evidence that a union represented a majority of the employees before it will order an employer to bargain with a union that has lost an election. Dual-purpose cards are inadequate because the employee may have signed a card just to get an election, not because the employee supported the union.

4. Yes. A card cannot be more than a year old to be counted as part of the 30 percent "showing of interest" the Board requires. The Board will not accept undated cards.

5. The Board will not count a single-purpose card in determining the union's majority status if the employee signing the card was told its only purpose was for an election.

6. Yes. Handing out recognition cards is considered to be oral solicitation, not distribution of literature. Oral solicitation can take place in working areas, but only on an employee's own time. Literature can be distributed in nonwork areas only.

7. Yes, but unions cannot restrict the offer of free membership to employees who sign recognition cards before the election. Free membership must be allowed for a reasonable time after the election as well as before.

8. No. An employer could discharge an employee for engaging in political activity in violation of a plant rule forbidding it. In contrast, an employer cannot discipline an employee for campaigning for a union in accordance with the Board's rules covering the time and place for such activity because it is a statutorily protected right.

9. At one time the Board applied a strict rule that an employer prediction about an adverse effect within the employer's control was an unlawful threat not protected by the employer free speech provisions of Section 8(c). Under that rule, the employer's prediction of a layoff would be unlawful because it is within the employer's control. However, the current Board permits an employer to present its views regarding the "economic realities of unionization" as long as the employer's predictions are supported by "objective fact." Under that rule, the employer's predictions of a layoff may be lawful.

10. An employer may give benefit increases during an election campaign if the benefit increase was planned before the election. But an employer cannot increase benefits that were not already planned. Similarly, an employer cannot refuse to give employees an increase they would have received but for an election campaign.

11. Yes, because elections are judged on the totality of a party's conduct. Thus an isolated unfair labor practice (e.g., one unlawful threat in an otherwise proper employer campaign) might not be grounds for setting aside the election.

12. The union has seven days after the election to file objections. To be grounds for setting aside an election, the misconduct must occur after the union files its petition. The Board will not issue a bargaining order following an election based on employer unfair labor practices unless the election is also set aside based on timely objections. Thus, it is important to file objections on time.

CHAPTER 4
PROTECTION OF THE EMPLOYEE'S RIGHT TO UNION REPRESENTATION

1. Section 8(a)(1) protects concerted activity whether through a union, through informal groups or through spontaneous employee protest.

2. Once a union is either lawfully recognized voluntarily or certified as a bargaining agent by the NLRB, the employer is prohibited from dealing with any other employee representative about wages, hours, or other terms and conditions of employment. That is the right of exclusive representation.

3. Intent can be proven either by direct evidence of an employer's anti-union animus, or the intent can be inferred from the natural consequences of an employer's actions. Courts divide the consequences into those that are inherently destructive of an employee's rights versus those of a lesser impact. If an act is inherently destructive, it may be unlawful regardless of the employer's business justification. If the conduct is of lesser impact and the employer asserts a legitimate business justification for the act, the conduct is unlawful only if there is proof that the employer in fact acted with an anti-union motivation.

4. An employer has the free speech right under Section 8(c) to state a preference for one union over another. However, it is unlawful under Sections 8(a)(1) and (3) for an employer to couple statements favoring one union with threats of adverse consequences if the other union wins.

5. The purpose is twofold: (1) to maintain arm's-length bargaining between the employer and the union and (2) to prevent a union from becoming dependent on the employer's assistance and thus subject to employer pressure. Therefore, some employer assistance to a union may be lawful if there is an arm's-length relationship between the employer and the union, the assistance would not undermine the independence of the union, and serves a legitimate collective bargaining function.

6. Ordinarily a steward cannot be disciplined for insubordinate remarks made during a grievance or bargaining session. However, a steward may be disciplined for threatening physical harm to an employer or for certain disparaging remarks made in the presence of other employees.

7. Yes. Such clauses lawfully insure that there will be a steward present to enforce the contract under all working conditions. However, superseniority must be limited to union officers who perform stewardlike functions in administering the collective bargaining agreement and whose presence is needed on the job, or in a particular department or shift, etc., to perform their duties.

8. Section 8(f) expressly allows prehire agreements in the construction industry. This exception was made because construction jobs are frequently of short duration and employers look to the construction unions for their employees.

9. Yes. An employee acting alone asserting a contractual right is engaged in concerted activity if the employee's statement or action is based on a reasonable and honest belief that the employee is being, or has been asked to perform a task that the employee is not required to perform under the collective bargaining agreement. Under some circumstances, however, conduct may be unprotected even though concerted such as if an employee refuses an improper job assignment in violation of the broadly worded no-strike clause.

10. The employee is entitled to a steward if the investigation is focused on the employee and the employee reasonably believes that he or she may be facing discipline.

11. The employer can either stop the meeting, offer to continue only if the employee waives the right to representation, or call in the shop steward and continue the investigation in the steward's presence.

12. The discharge may still be unlawful if the purported bona fide reason is a pre-

text or if the employee's union activities are a substantial motivating factor in the employer's decision.

CHAPTER 5
THE DUTY TO BARGAIN

1. The party desiring to terminate or modify a contract must serve a written notice upon the other party of the proposed termination or modification at least sixty days prior to the contract's expiration date and notify the Federal Mediation and Conciliation Service of the dispute within thirty days thereafter. The required notices must be sent respectively ninety and sixty days before a contract's expiration in the health care industry. The notices may be sent earlier than the required date. If one party sends the required sixty- to ninety-day notice to terminate or modify a contract, then the other party is free to terminate or modify the contract after the expiration of the notice period even though neither party gave the required notice to the Federal Mediation and Conciliation Service.

2. Not necessarily. An employer is not obligated to agree to any specific contract term. However, failure to agree to a union security clause may be considered in evaluating an employer's overall good-faith intent to reach an agreement.

3. Yes. The employer can lawfully threaten to shut down plant operations unless the union agrees to midterm concessions unless the contract prohibits the unilateral change or the employer is motivated by unlawful anti-union animus rather than by legitimate economic reasons.

4. If a union fails to meet contractual notice requirements to terminate the contract, the contract may renew itself in accordance with its terms. In that event, the employer has no duty to bargain during the renewal period. The union cannot strike if the contract as renewed contains a no-strike clause, even though the union may have met the statutory notice requirements. A contract is not extended for failure to give statutory notice, but only for failure to give contractual notice.

5. Yes. Normally there is a presumption that the incumbent union continues to have majority status at the termination of a contract. The employer can withdraw recognition only if it has a good-faith doubt of the union's continued majority status based on objective considerations. In the construction industry only, under the *Deklewa* decision, an employer party to a pre-hire agreement can withdraw recognition from the union and unilaterally change the terms and conditions of employment as soon as the pre-hire agreement expires.

6. An employer is a successor obligated to bargain with the incumbent union if the prior employees compose a majority of the successor's work force in the same industry.

7. An employer is obligated to bargain over the decision to subcontract work that involves a change in the scope and direction of the enterprise only if the work is still to be done on the company's premises under similar conditions. Also, the employer may be obligated to bargain over the decision as well as the effect if the decision was made to reduce labor costs during a period of economic difficulty rather than a decision to change the scope and direction of the enterprise.

8. Yes. Normally a successor has no obligation to bargain with the incumbent union until after the successor has individually rehired the present employees at the wages and working conditions unilaterally established. The union's continued majority is not proven until then. As an exception, the successor is required to bargain on initial terms, but not accept the prior contract, if it announces an intention to keep all former employees.

9. The Board can order an employer to sign a contract incorporating a term that the employer has agreed to. However, the Board has no authority to require any party to accept a term not agreed to, even if the party has been engaged in bad-faith bargaining.

10. No. Bargaining for increased retire-

ment benefits for employees who have already retired is a permissive subject of bargaining.

11. Yes. Pay for employees on the union's negotiating committee pertains to wages and is therefore a mandatory subject of bargaining.

12. The union is broadly entitled to any information relevant to administering the contract, insuring the employer's compliance, evaluating grievances, and processing grievances to arbitration. The employer may not be required to produce information to the union in a form that is unduly burdensome, or if, for proper cause, the data is confidential and denial is not unduly burdensome.

CHAPTER 6
STRIKES, STRIKER RIGHTS, AND LOCKOUTS

1. No. The right to strike has never been afforded an unqualified constitutional protection.

2. Section 13 of the LMRA protects the right to strike except as limited by the Act. The proviso to Section 8(b)(4)(B) protects the right to engage in a primary strike or primary picketing not otherwise unlawful. Section 502 protects the right to refuse work that is abnormally dangerous. Sections 7, 8(a)(1), and (3) protect the right to strike as a form of concerted activity.

3. An unfair labor practice strike is a strike over an employer's unfair labor practice, such as the discharge of a union adherent because of union activity.

4. An economic strike is a strike over an economic issue, such as wages, fringe benefits, or working conditions.

5. An unfair labor practice striker cannot be replaced permanently and is entitled to reinstatement upon an unconditional offer to return to work. An economic striker can be permanently replaced. A replaced economic striker is not entitled to immediate reinstatement, but is entitled to recall as vacancies occur.

6. Economic strikers who have been permanently replaced are eligible to vote in a representation election held within twelve months of the commencement of the strike. Their replacements are also eligible. Unfair labor practice strikers and economic strikers who have not been replaced are entitled to vote indefinitely. Temporary replacements are ineligible to vote.

7. Strikers lose their right to reinstatement or recall if they find permanent employment elsewhere or if their job has been permanently abolished and they are not qualified to do the remaining work. There is a presumption that employment during a strike is only temporary. Employees who engage in serious misconduct during a strike can be lawfully discharged.

8. Neither unfair labor practice nor economic strikers are entitled to wages during a strike regardless of the reason because they are withholding their services unless the employer unlawfully rejects their unconditional offer to return to work.

9. A sympathy strike is one in which employees respect another union's picket line although not directly involved in the dispute.

10. Whether a general no-strike clause prohibits a sympathy strike depends upon its express wording and the contractual intent. Thus, an employee may be discharged for engaging in a sympathy strike in violation of a general no-strike clause if it is clear from the bargaining history or past practice that the clause was intended to prohibit sympathy action.

11. If it is necessary to continue operations, an employer can permanently replace, but not discipline, sympathy strikers who are respecting an economic strike picket line.

12. No. A no-strike clause normally prohibits only economic strikes. It does not prohibit strikes over serious unfair labor practices or the refusal to perform abnormally dangerous work. Whether a clause prohibits a sympathy strike depends upon the wording and the underlying contractual intent.

13. The courts will imply a no-strike obligation if a contract contains an arbitration clause and the strike is over an arbitrable issue.

14. A court can award an employer damages for a union's breach of a contractual no-strike clause and enjoin a strike over an arbitrable issue provided that the employer is willing to arbitrate the dispute.

15. No. A federal court has no jurisdiction to enjoin a sympathy strike because it is not over an arbitrable dispute. However, if a sympathy strike does violate the contract, the employer may be able to collect damages even though the strike is not enjoinable.

CHAPTER 7
PICKETING, BOYCOTTS, AND RELATED ACTIVITY

1. There is a limited constitutional right to picket as a matter of free speech. However, picketing is a form of action, not just speech, and can therefore be regulated.

2. A primary picket line is directed against the employer with whom the union has a dispute. A secondary picket line is directed against an employer other than the one with whom the union has its dispute.

3. No. Picketing employees have only the moral strength of their picket signs and their power of peaceful persuasion to prevent persons from crossing. An employer could obtain a state court injunction against mass picketing.

4. Section 8(b)(4) refers to the object of a dispute. From this, the courts have developed a distinction between the object of picketing and its effect. If the object is primary, (i.e., directed against the employer with whom the union has its dispute), the picketing is lawful even though there may be a secondary effect.

5. No. Picketing is unlawful if it has both a primary and secondary object. Picketing can, however, have a primary object with a secondary effect.

6. A union picketing at its own plant can have signs that simply state "on strike" with-

out identifying the picketed employer. However, in the *Moore Dry Dock* secondary situs situation, the union must identify the employer with whom it has its dispute.

7. No. The picketing union must limit its picketing to the scheduled time as long as the primary employer keeps the schedule. The secondary employer can legally limit the picketing's impact in this manner.

8. Yes. An appeal to co-workers is for mutual aid and protection, which is a primary object. The rules set forth in *Moore Dry Dock, Denver Building Trades,* and *General Electric* apply only to a union's appeal to employees of other employers.

9. Yes. A union's right to picket a struck product is not restricted by Section 8(b)(4), unless the object of the picketing is a total boycott of the employer handling the struck products as in the case of a sole or "merged" product. If the union engages solely in handbilling or publicity other than picketing, it can urge a total consumer boycott of a secondary employer without the restrictions applicable to picketing.

10. No. Substandard picketing is primary picketing. It can lawfully have the effect (but not the object) of inducing other employees to honor a picket line.

11. The picketing may be unlawful if it has a recognition object and does not meet the requirements of Section 8(b)(7).

12. The employer may file a charge under Section 8(b)(4) and also file suit for damages under Section 303. Section 303 is the only section of the law that allows private damage suits to remedy an unfair labor practice.

CHAPTER 8
UNION REGULATION OF WORK AND THE ANTITRUST LAWS

1. Section 8(e) follows the general policy of Section 8(b)(4) limiting a labor dispute to the primary employer and the striking union.

2. The clause would be unlawful because it might permit employees to honor a sec-

ondary picket line. A picket line clause must be limited to primary picketing under Section 8(e).

3. No. A clause worded that broadly would violate Section 8(e). A struck work clause must be limited to a primary strike and must permit two employers to maintain a normal business relationship during a strike.

4. Such clauses are unlawful under Section 8(e) except for job site work in the construction industry because they go beyond the valid object of preserving unit work and have the secondary object of influencing the labor relations of a secondary employer.

5. No. A union standards clause permitting subcontracting only to an employer who maintains the equivalent total in wages, hours, and fringe benefits is lawful, but requiring a subcontractor to maintain exactly the same pay package has the secondary object of dictating the subcontractor's labor policies and would be unlawful except for job-site construction work.

6. Yes. A contract clause in which an employer agrees it will not sell its business except to someone who assumes the collective bargaining contract does not violate Section 8(e).

7. The construction industry proviso permits a construction union to negotiate a clause limiting the contracting and subcontracting of work to be done on the construction site to union contractors. Construction unions are subject to the same restrictions as any other union for off situs subcontracting clauses.

8. Yes, provided that a no-strike clause does not prohibit it. Self-help usually does not violate Section 8(e) because enforcing a valid work preservation clause is a primary object even though there may be a secondary effect on a subcontractor. As an exception, self-help may violate Section 8(e) if the contracting employer does not have the "right to control" the disputed work.

9. No. The Board has jurisdiction under Section 10(k) only if the Board has reasonable cause to believe that one of the com-

peting unions has engaged in a coercive act violating Section 8(b)(4)(D). If the unions exert peaceful persuasion on the employer or request arbitration, Section 8(b)(4)(D) is not violated and Section 10(k) does not come into play.

10. The employer's assignment and preference are by far the most important factors.

11. Yes. "Make work" does not violate the Section 8(b)(6) "featherbedding" restrictions, and manning requirements are a mandatory bargaining subject.

12. Yes. Such a clause does not violate the antitrust laws if the union seeks the clause in the union's own self-interest and not in combination with any employers.

13. No. Multi-employer bargaining can violate the antitrust laws only if the union seeks to impose the same contract on other employers pursuant to an agreement with the multi-employer association to do so.

CHAPTER 9
ENFORCEMENT OF COLLECTIVE BARGAINING AGREEMENTS AND THE DUTY TO ARBITRATE

1. No. Section 301 also applies to contracts between unions such as no-raiding pacts and an international union's constitution that is a contract between the international and a union member.

2. No. A local union's bylaws are considered a contract between the union and the member. That is not one of the contracts enforceable under Section 301.

3. No. Section 301 actions cannot be brought by or against employers or unions not covered by the LMRA.

4. A dispute arising after a collective bargaining agreement has expired may be arbitrable if it pertains to rights that vested or accrued at least in part during the contract or that relate to events that occurred at least in part during the term of the agreement.

5. Generally, an employee cannot sue to enforce alleged contract rights contrary to

a settlement. The only exception is if the settlement is made in violation of the union's duty of fair representation.

6. Section 301 does not specify a time limit for filing suit. However, in general most federal courts are enforcing a six-month limitation period from the date the other party refuses to arbitrate to file a suit to compel arbitration and ninety days to file suit to modify, clarify, or vacate an arbitrator's decision, although that period may vary from state to state. The limitations period for filing a suit to enforce an award is the period that the state allows to enforce a written contract right, typically in the range of two to five years or longer.

7. A federal or state court must order arbitration if a collective bargaining agreement provides for arbitration unless it can be stated with positive assurance that the contract's arbitration clause does not apply to the particular dispute. Any doubts should be resolved in favor of arbitration.

8. The merits of a dispute are irrelevant and cannot be considered by a court in determining arbitrability.

9. *Warrior* emphasized that federal labor policy favors arbitration rather than litigation or strikes as a means of resolving industrial disputes. The decision affirmed the right of arbitrators to apply past practice as well as the express provisions of the contract. Finally, *Warrior* established that arbitration is a matter of contract and that the courts determine arbitrability.

10. Yes. Whether a decision is right or wrong does not matter as long as the arbitrator based the decision on the arbitrator's interpretation of the contract. As a narrow exception, an award may be set aside if it violates an explicit public policy that is well defined and dominant, not just general considerations of supposed public interest.

11. The employer must exhaust the contractual provisions for arbitration before filing suit unless it is clear that the employer has no right to file grievances. Many contracts permit only union or employee grievances.

12. Grievance arbitration pertains to a dispute arising under an existing collective bargaining agreement. Interest arbitration is over new contract terms. The arbitrator determines the contents rather than interpreting the agreement the parties have reached.

13. Under LMRA Section 10(a), the Board's decision would prevail. However, under the *Spielberg* doctrine, the Board will sometimes defer to an arbitrator's award meeting its standards even though the Board might not have reached the same result.

14. Yes. If a union waits until after the arbitrator rules before filing a charge, the six-month limit for filing may have already passed. Also, if the union files a charge that the Board defers to arbitration, the arbitrator is more likely to face and determine the unfair labor practice issue.

CHAPTER 10
UNION MEMBERSHIP AND UNION SECURITY

1. At common law a union is an unincorporated association, a combination of its members with no separate legal existence.

2. In most states a union, as an unincorporated association, cannot sue or be sued in its own name as an entity. Large unincorporated groups, however, can sue or be sued as a class. Federal statutes (such as LMRA Sections 301 and 303) expressly permit a union to sue or be sued as an entity in federal court and the Supreme Court has further held that a union may be sued as an entity in federal court for violation of any federal statute.

3. No. Although the LMRA refers to union membership as a condition of employment, the Supreme Court has held that an employee can only be required to be a financial core member and, upon request, can be required to pay only that proportion of a union's dues used for collective bargaining functions.

4. No. Collective bargaining functions

are limited to bargaining, contract administration, and grievance adjustment for employees in the bargaining unit. Lobbying may be just as important to a union in a particular case and benefit all employees, but a financial core member cannot be required to support the activity as a condition of employment.

5. The relationship between the union and its members is contractual. The union's bylaws, as a contract, determine the members' rights and responsibilities.

6. No. If the union rejects an employee who is willing to tender the initiation fees and dues for membership, then the employee becomes a legal free rider.

7. No. If an employee is willing to be a full union member, but the union rejects or expels the employee as a member, the union security clause cannot be enforced against the employee. The employee becomes a legal free rider.

8. An employee who simply pays the minimum financial core dues required as a condition of employment is not bound by the union's bylaws and is not subject to discipline by the union.

9. The clause expires immediately unless the parties agree to keep the contract in effect. This means that employees have the right to resign or to stop paying dues as a condition of employment as soon as the contract expires.

10. An employee in a right-to-work state who formally joins the union is bound by the constitution and bylaws of the union the same as a member in any other state. An employee who does not pay the required dues can be expelled from membership and/or sued in the state court for the amount owed.

11. A checkoff form can be irrevocable for up to a year or until the expiration date of the collective bargaining agreement, whichever occurs first. The form may provide for automatic renewal if the employee does not revoke the checkoff within a specified period before its expiration.

12. Resignation does not automatically terminate a checkoff authorization by operation of law. Thus the authorization may remain in effect if the language so provides.

13. No. An exclusive hiring hall must have specific objective standards that cannot be arbitrary or discriminate in favor of union members. Sometimes, however, a nondiscriminatory requirement, such as experience in the industry, may discriminate in practical effect because union members are those with experience, but such a requirement is lawful because, at least in theory, nonmembers may also have industry experience.

14. An employee who has signed a checkoff form cannot be discharged because it is the union's obligation to make sure the employer deducts the proper amount and forwards it to the union. But if the collective bargaining agreement does not provide for checkoff or if an employee has decided to pay directly, the employee is obligated to pay on time and can be discharged for being late provided all employees are required to meet the same time limit and the union has fulfilled its fiduciary notice requirements.

15. No. The union cannot place any restrictions on a member's right to resign. However, a lawful debt can be collected in state court if it accrued while the employee was a member.

16. No. The union has a fiduciary obligation to give actual notice unless, as a narrow exception, an employee with knowledge is obviously evading service of notice by the union.

CHAPTER 11
RIGHTS AND RESPONSIBILITIES OF UNION MEMBERS

1. Section 101(a)(1) does not guarantee any specific rights. Instead, it requires that whatever rights are established by a union's constitution or its bylaws be shared equally by all members.

2. No. The LMRDA defines a member as a person who has fulfilled the requirements for membership, although in some

cases, that person may not have been formally admitted by the union.

3. Yes. A member who returns to work can be fined because returning violates the responsibility of the member to the union as an institution. However, a member who resigns cannot be disciplined for any conduct occurring after the resignation is effective.

4. No. A member has a virtually unlimited right to say whatever he or she wants at a union meeting, even if the statements are untrue, subject only to reasonable rules to preserve order at the meeting. As *narrow* exceptions, a member may be prohibited from making comments contrary to the members' responsibility toward the union as an institution or that would interfere with the union's legal or contractual obligations.

5. The LMRDA does not specify the grounds for discipline. It only prohibits discipline for the exercise of statutorily protected rights and establishes minimum requirements for a hearing before discipline is imposed. Other than that, the grounds for discipline and the procedures are internal union matters. The Act does not require a hearing before disciplining a member for failure to pay the union's initiation fee or dues.

6. Yes. Provided that the discipline does not impair the supervisor's functioning as the employer's representative for purposes of bargaining, contract administration, or grievance adjustments.

7. Under LMRDA Section 101(a)(5), the member must be served with written specific charges, given a reasonable time to prepare a defense, and afforded a full and fair hearing.

8. Due process requires that the accused member face his or her accuser, that the decision be based on evidence presented at the hearing, and that the accused be permitted to cross-examine the witnesses. A union need not follow the formal rules that a court would apply. The member is not entitled to have a lawyer present.

9. Federal law does not regulate the amount of a fine. The amount is purely an internal union matter subject to state law. Generally, a fine may be any amount that is reasonable under all the facts and circumstances.

10. LMRDA Section 101(a)(4) provides that a member may be required to exhaust reasonable internal appeal procedures for up to four months. However, application of this exhaustion requirement is discretionary with the courts. A court may not require exhaustion if it appears internal procedures would be futile or there is a clear statutory violation.

CHAPTER 12
THE DUTY OF FAIR REPRESENTATION

1. The duty of fair representation is implied from the union's right to exclusive representation under Section 9 of the LMRA.

2. A union meets its duty of fair representation as long as its decisions and actions are not arbitrary, discriminatory, in bad faith, or perfunctory.

3. Yes. There is no specific provision of the LMRA that makes a violation of the fair representation duty an unfair labor practice, but the Board has implied the duty under Sections 7 and 8(b)(1)(A).

4. Ordinarily an employee is bound by an arbitrator's decision unless the union has violated its duty of fair representation in processing the employee's grievance to arbitration.

5. The employee cannot successfully sue the employer unless the union violated its duty of fair representation. The employee must prove that the union did not discover the evidence proving the employee's innocence because the union violated its duty of fair representation. If the employee cannot prove that the union violated its duty, it is irrelevant that the employee was in fact wrongly discharged.

6. Suits for violation of the union's duty of fair representation are governed by Section 301 of the LMRA. Federal law princi-

ples developed under Section 301 determine whether a union has violated its duty of fair representation whether the suit is filed in state or federal court.

7. Yes. A union can change the seniority system, even though the change favors one employee group over another, as long as the union's decision does not violate its duty of fair representation.

8. No. The duty of fair representation does not permit second guessing by either a court or the Board. Errors in judgment, or even the fact that a union made the wrong decision, do not violate the duty of fair representation.

9. The damages are apportioned between the employer and the union. The employer is liable for the damages caused by its breach of contract; the union is liable for any additional damages beyond the date that an arbitrator would have ruled in the employee's favor but for the union's breach of its duty. This may actually result in the union having a greater liability than the employer even though the employer's breach of contract is the underlying cause of the suit.

10. Most courts have ruled that a union does not violate the duty of fair representation if its representative negligently fails to file a grievance on time. However, the failure to file a grievance may be evidence of perfunctory processing that along with other evidence of disinterest may constitute a violation.

CHAPTER 13
UNIONS AND EQUAL
EMPLOYMENT OPPORTUNITY

1. Usually a union must have fifteen or more members to be covered by Title VII. However, a union that maintains or operates a hiring hall is covered by the Act regardless of its size.

2. Title VII prohibits discrimination because of an individual's race, color, religion, sex, or national origin. A person discriminated against for any of these reasons is a

member of a protected group. Thus, the Act prohibits reverse discrimination against white persons because of their race as well as discrimination against blacks. Title VII does not prohibit age discrimination, but age discrimination is prohibited by the Age Discrimination in Employment Act.

3. The two basic categories of unlawful discrimination are disparate treatment discrimination and disparate impact discrimination.

4. Yes. An employer may still violate Title VII even if it articulates a legitimate nondiscriminatory reason for rejecting a protected group member, if the person can prove that the reason given is a pretext, and that the person was in fact discriminatorily denied employment.

5. Yes. Specific intent to discriminate is not needed to violate Title VII. Rather, a practice or policy that has a disparate impact on a protected group may be a violation. However, a practice having disparate impact may be lawful under Title VII if the employer produces evidence of a justification for the practice and the plaintiffs do not establish that there are alternative means available that can meet the employer's legitimate needs without the same disproportionate impact. Note that specific intent is a necessary element of both a Section 1981 or 1983 claim.

6. No. An employment practice does not have to be job related under Title VII unless it has a disproportionate impact on the members of a protected group. So long as there is no disproportionate impact, an employer can set any job requirements it wishes, even if they are clearly not job related.

7. Yes. A specific employment practice can violate Title VII even though the employer's overall work force has a proportionate number of protected group employees. Federal agencies, at their discretion, might not take action against an employer whose overall employment practices result in a proportionate work force, but that does not prevent an individual from proving that he or she was discriminatorily denied em-

ployment in a specific case either because of disparate treatment or disparate impact discrimination.

8. No. Barring women from heavy jobs is unlawful under Title VII because the bar is based upon a stereotyped assumption of a woman's role. A person can be barred from a job only if sex is a bona fide occupational qualification.

9. Title VII, as amended by the Pregnancy Disability Agreement, does not specify the number of months of leave an employer must allow a woman. Rather, an employer must allow a woman, disabled for work due to pregnancy or childbirth, the same number of months off it would allow a disabled male employee.

10. Not necessarily in all cases. An employer must make a reasonable accommodation to an employee's religious observances or practices but not necessarily the "most reasonable" accommodation. An employer need not make an accommodation that entails undue economic hardship or one that incurs more than a de minimis expense. Furthermore, an employer need not infringe on one employee's seniority rights to accommodate another employee's religious practices.

11. An employer cannot require an employee to retire at any age subject to several exceptions. Thus some employees engaged in bona fide high policy-making functions can be retired at age sixty-five. An employee can also be retired if age is a BFOQ. However, the BFOQ exception is extremely narrow.

12. The basic requirements are that a timely charge must be filed with the EEOC within 180 days of the occurrence of the alleged unlawful employment practice (or up to 200 days in a state having a fair employment practices agency over one year old) and that the suit must be filed within 90 days after receiving notice of the right to sue from the EEOC. Also, an individual cannot request a right to sue notice from the EEOC until 180 days after the charge has been filed. These time restrictions are subject to the doctrines of waiver, estoppel, and equitable tolling.

13. Yes. An employee may file suit under Title VII within ninety days after receiving a right-to-sue notice whether or not the EEOC found reasonable cause to believe the statue has been violated.

14. A federal court has broad discretion to impose whatever remedies are necessary to overcome the effect of past discrimination and bar future discrimination. The court's remedies include backpay, rightful place seniority, and affirmative action programs. However, a court cannot order relief to individuals who are not the actual victims of discrimination except in particularly egregious circumstances.

15. No. Title VII requires that women receive the same amount in monthly retirement benefits as men when they have made the same contributions as men, despite the longer life expectancy of women as a class.

16. A black employee who fails to file a timely charge under Title VII could still file suit under 42 U.S.C. 1981 or 1983 as appropriate. These statutes are separate independent remedies from Title VII. A female employee who fails to file a timely charge under Title VII against either a private employer or union has no other remedy; however, she can still file suit under 42 U.S.C. 1983 against discrimination by a state or local governmental body employer.

17. Yes. An employee who has lost an arbitration case can still proceed under Title VII and is entitled to a full hearing on the Title VII claim. A court is not bound by an arbitrator's decision on a Title VII issue. The court may given an arbitrator's award such weight as it deserves, keeping in mind that Congress intended for the courts to make the final decision on Title VII violations.

18. A charge must be filed under Title VII within the required time (180 or up to 300 days, as appropriate) after the *occurrence* of a discriminatory act, not after receiving the arbitrator's award. Filing a grievance does not toll this requirement. Thus, an

employee may not be able to wait for the arbitrator's decision before filing a charge with the EEOC, or the time may pass in the meantime.

19. The Board will certify a union that has engaged in past discrimination regardless of its past record, but it may revoke the certification of a union that engages in such discrimination after it is certified.

20. Title VII prohibits reverse discrimination against white and/or male employees. However, many voluntary affirmative action programs adopted by an employer, a union, or both to remedy traditional patterns of discrimination are lawful under Title VII. Although the Supreme Court has upheld preferential hiring as part of a voluntary affirmative action plan, the Court has not approved preference against layoffs for minority workers over nonminority employees with greater seniority.

CHAPTER 14
FEDERAL-STATE RELATIONSHIPS IN LABOR RELATIONS

1. Preemption is the doctrine used to determine whether federal labor law supersedes state law on a certain matter. Primary jurisdiction is the doctrine used in determining whether a particular matter that is preempted by federal law is to be regulated by the NLRB, the courts, or both the courts and the Board.

2. The LMRA preempts conduct that is arguably protected or prohibited by the Act.

3. State courts can continue to regulate traditional areas of state concern that do not impede activities regulated by the LMRA, such as violent conduct or trespass.

4. No. The states are powerless to act even though the state remedies might be different. Congress intended for the LMRA to preempt not only the conduct, but the remedies as well.

5. No. Since the picketing is either pro-

tected or prohibited by the LMRA, the preemption doctrine applies. A state court cannot enjoin the picketing as long as it is peaceful.

6. The exceptions to the NLRB's primary jurisdiction are LMRA Section 301 (pertaining to enforcement of contracts) and Section 303 (pertaining to damage suits for secondary boycotts).

7. Not always. It is possible that Congress intended that conduct such as sit-down strikes be totally unregulated by either state or federal agencies.

8. Yes. Most internal union matters are subject to extensive state regulation. The LMRDA expressly provides for continued state regulation over most matters covered by that statute.

9. Yes. The states can regulate employers whose activities affect commerce if the employer is not subject to the LMRA or if it fails to meet the Board's monetary standards.

10. No. Libel suits are not preempted, but the Supreme Court requires that a party prove malice in order to recover in a libel suit growing out of a labor dispute.

11. No. Section 303 preempts state regulation over secondary boycotts. Such suits can be filed in the state courts, but the states must apply federal law. Punitive damages are not allowed for peaceful secondary boycotts.

12. Yes. Suits to enforce contracts are governed by federal law even though such suits may be filed in the state courts. The NLRB and courts have concurrent jurisdiction over unfair labor practices that may also be contract violations.

13. Ordinarily the contractual grievance procedure is the exclusive remedy for challenging an employee's discharge. However, as an exception, an employee may be able to bring a state court lawsuit based on a state law establishing rights and obligations independent of the contract if a court does not have to interpret the contract to resolve the claim.

STATUTORY APPENDICES

Text of Labor Management Relations Act, 1947, as Amended by Public Laws 86-257, 1959,* and 93-360, 1974**

[Public Law 101—80th Congress]

DEFINITIONS

SEC. 2. When used in this Act—

(1) The term "person" includes one or more individuals, labor organizations, partnerships, associations, corporations, legal representatives, trustees, trustees in bankruptcy, or receivers.

(2) The term "employer" includes any person acting as an agent of an employer, directly or indirectly, but shall not include the United States or any wholly owned Government corporation, or any Federal Reserve Bank, or any State or political subdivision thereof,** or any person subject to the Railway Labor Act, as amended from time to time, or any labor organization (other than when acting as an employer), or anyone acting in the capacity of officer or agent of such labor organization.

(3) The term "employee" shall include any employee, and shall not be limited to the employees of a particular employer, unless the Act explicitly states otherwise, and shall include any individual whose work has ceased as a consequence of, or in connection with, any current labor dispute or because of any unfair labor practice, and who has not obtained any other regular and substantially equivalent employment, but shall not include any individual employed as an agricultural laborer, or in the domestic service of any family or person at his home, or any individual employed by his parent or spouse, or any individual having the status of an independent contractor, or any individual employed as a supervisor, or any individual employed by an employer subject to the Railway Labor Act, as amended from time to time, or by any other person who is not an employer as herein defined.

(4) The term "representatives" includes any individual or labor organization.

(5) The term "labor organization" means any organization of any kind, or any agency or employee representation committee or plan, in which employees participate and which exists for the purpose, in whole or in part, of dealing with employers concerning grievances, labor disputes, wages, rates of pay, hours of employment, or conditions of work.

(6) The term "commerce" means trade, traffic, commerce, transportation, or communication among the several States, or between the District of Columbia or any Territory of the United States and any State or other Territory, or between any foreign country and any State, Territory, or the District of Columbia, or within the District of Columbia or any Territory, or between points in the same State but through any other State or any Territory or the District of Columbia or any foreign country.

(7) The term "affecting commerce" means in commerce, or burdening or obstructing commerce or the free flow of commerce, or having led or tending to lead to a labor dispute burdening or obstructing commerce or the free flow of commerce.

(8) The term "unfair labor practice" means any unfair labor practice listed in section 8.

(9) The term "labor dispute" includes any controversy concerning terms, tenure or conditions of employment, or concerning the association or representation of persons in negotiating, fixing, maintaining, changing, or seeking to arrange terms or conditions of employment, regardless of whether the disputants stand in the proximate relation of employer and employee.

(10) The term "National Labor Relations Board" means the National Labor Relations Board provided for in section 3 of this Act.

(11) The term "supervisor" means any individual having authority, in the interest of the employer, to hire, transfer, suspend, lay off, recall, promote, discharge, assign, reward, or discipline other employees, or responsibly to direct them, or to adjust their grievances, or effectively to recommend such action, if in connection with the foregoing the exercise of such authority is not of a merely routine or clerical nature, but requires the use of independent judgment.

(12) The term "professional employee" means—

(a) any employee engaged in work (i) predominantly intellectual and varied in character as opposed to routine mental, manual, mechanical, or physical work; (ii) involving the consistent exercise of discretion and judgment in its performance; (iii) of such a character that the output produced or the result accomplished cannot be standardized in relation to a given period of time; (iv) requiring knowledge of an advanced type in a field of science or learning customarily acquired by a prolonged course of specialized intellectual instruction and study in an institution of higher learning or a hospital, as distinguished from a general academic education or from an apprenticeship or from training in the performance of routine mental, manual, or physical processes; or

(b) any employee, who (i) has completed the courses of specialized intellectual instruction and study described in clause (iv) of paragraph (a), and (ii) is performing related work under the supervision of a professional person to qualify himself to become a professional employee as defined in paragraph (a).

(13) In determining whether any person is acting as an "agent" of another person so as to make such other person responsible for his acts, the question of whether the specific acts performed were actually authorized or subsequently ratified shall not be controlling.

***(14) The term "health care institution" shall include any hospital, convalescent hospital, health maintenance organization, health clinic, nursing home, extended care facility, or other institution devoted to the care of sick, infirm, or aged person.

NATIONAL LABOR RELATIONS BOARD

SEC. 3. (a) The National Labor Relations Board (hereinafter called the "Board") created by this Act prior to its amendment by the Labor Management Relations Act, 1947, is hereby continued as an agency of the United States, except that the Board shall consist of five instead of three members, appointed by the President by and with the advice and consent of the Senate. Of the two additional members so provided for, one shall be appointed for a term of five years and the

---

*Pursuant to Public Law 93-360, 93d Cong. S. 3203, 88 Stat. 305. Sec. 2(2) is amended by deleting the phrase "or any corporation or association operating a hospital, if no part of the net earnings inures to the benefit of any private shareholder or individual,".

**Pursuant to Public Law 93-360, 93d Cong. S. 3203, 88 Stat. 395. Sec. 2 is amended by adding subsection 14.

other for a term of two years. Their successors, and the successors of the other members, shall be appointed for terms of five years each, excepting that any individual chosen to fill a vacancy shall be appointed only for the unexpired term of the member whom he shall succeed. The President shall designate one member to serve as Chairman of the Board. Any member of the Board may be removed by the President, upon notice and hearing, for neglect of duty or malfeasance in office, but for no other cause.

(b) The Board is authorized to delegate to any group of three or more members any or all of the powers which it may itself exercise. The Board is also authorized to delegate to its regional directors its powers under section 9 to determine the unit appropriate for the purpose of collective bargaining, to investigate and provide for appropriate hearings, and determine whether a question of representation exists, and to direct an election or take a secret ballot under subsection (c) or (e) of section 9 and certify the results thereof, except that upon the filing of a request therefor with the Board by any interested person, the Board may review any action of a regional director delegated to him under this paragraph, but such a review shall not, unless specifically ordered by the Board, operate as a stay of any action taken by the regional director. A vacancy in the Board shall not impair the right of the remaining members to exercise all of the powers of the Board, and three members of the Board shall, at all times, constitute a quorum of the Board, except that two members shall constitute a quorum of any group designated pursuant to the first sentence hereof. The Board shall have an official seal which shall be judicially noticed.

(c) The Board shall at the close of each fiscal year make a report in writing to Congress and to the President stating in detail the cases it has heard, the decisions it has rendered, the names, salaries, and duties of all employees and officers in the employ or under the supervision of the Board, and an account of all moneys it has disbursed.

(d) There shall be a General Counsel of the Board who shall be appointed by the President, by and with the advice and consent of the Senate, for a term of four years. The General Counsel of the Board shall exercise general supervision over all attorneys employed by the Board (other than trial examiners and legal assistants to Board members) and over the officers and employees in the regional offices. He shall have final authority, on behalf of the Board, in respect of the investigation of charges and issuance of complaints under section 10, and in respect of the prosecution of such complaints before the Board, and shall have such other duties as the Board may prescribe or as may be provided by law. In case of a vacancy in the office of the General Counsel the President is authorized to designate the officer or employee who shall act as General Counsel during such vacancy, but no person or persons so designated shall so act (1) for more than forty days when the Congress is in session unless a nomination to fill such vacancy shall have been submitted to the Senate, or (2) after the adjournment *sine die* of the session of the Senate in which such nomination was submitted.

SEC. 4. (a) Each member of the Board and the General Counsel of the Board shall receive a salary of $12,000* a year, shall be eligible for reappointment, and shall not engage in any other business, vocation, or employment. The Board shall appoint an executive secretary, and such attorneys, examiners, and regional directors, and such other employees as it may from time to time find necessary for the proper performance of its duties. The Board may not employ any attorneys for the purpose of reviewing transcripts of hearings or preparing drafts of opinions except that any attorney employed for assignment as a legal assistant to any Board member may for such Board member review such transcripts and prepare such drafts. No trial examiner's report shall be reviewed, either before or after its publication, by any

person other than a member of the Board or his legal assistant, and no trial examiner shall advise or consult with the Board with respect to exceptions taken to his findings, rulings, or recommendations. The Board may establish or utilize such regional, local, or other agencies, and utilize such voluntary and uncompensated services, as may from time to time be needed. Attorneys appointed under this section may, at the direction of the Board, appear for and represent the Board in any case in court. Nothing in this Act shall be construed to authorize the Board to appoint individuals for the purpose of conciliation or mediation, or for economic analysis.

RIGHTS OF EMPLOYEES

SEC. 7. Employees shall have the right to self-organization, to form, join, or assist labor organizations, to bargain collectively through representatives of their own choosing, and to engage in other concerted activities for the purpose of collective bargaining or other mutual aid or protection, and shall also have the right to refrain from any or all of such activities except to the extent that such right may be affected by an agreement requiring membership in a labor organization as a condition of employment as authorized in section 8(a)(3).

UNFAIR LABOR PRACTICES

SEC. 8. (a) It shall be an unfair labor practice for an employer—

(1) to interfere with, restrain, or coerce employees in the exercise of the rights guaranteed in section 7;

(2) to dominate or interfere with the formation or administration of any labor organization or contribute financial or other support to it: *Provided,* That subject to rules and regulations made and published by the Board pursuant to section 6, an employer shall not be prohibited from permitting employees to confer with him during working hours without loss of time or pay;

(3) by discrimination in regard to hire or tenure of employment or any term or condition of employment to encourage or discourage membership in any labor organization: *Provided,* That nothing in this Act, or in any other statute of the United States, shall preclude an employer from making an agreement with a labor organization (not established, maintained, or assisted by any action defined in section 8(a) of this Act as an unfair labor practice) to require as a condition of employment membership therein on or after the thirtieth day following the beginning of such employment or the effective date of such agreement, whichever is the later, (i) if such labor organization is the representative of the employees as provided in section 9(a), in the appropriate collective-bargaining unit covered by such agreement when made, and (ii) unless following an election held as provided in section 9(e) within one year preceding the effective date of such agreement, the Board shall have certified that at least a majority of the employees eligible to vote in such election have voted to rescind the authority of such labor organization to make such an agreement: *Provided further,* That no employer shall justify any discrimination against an employee for nonmembership in a labor organization (A) if he has reasonable grounds for believing that such membership was not available to the employee on the same terms and conditions generally applicable to other members, or (B) if he has reasonable grounds for believing that membership was denied or terminated

*Pursuant to Public Law 90–206, 90th Cong., 81 Stat. 644, approved Dec. 16, 1967, and in accordance with Sec. 225(f)(ii) thereof, effective in 1969, the salary of the Chairman of the Board shall be $40,000 per year and the salaries of the General Counsel and each Board member shall be $38,000 per year.

for reasons other than the failure of the employee to tender the periodic dues and the initiation fees uniformly required as a condition of acquiring or retaining membership;

(4) to discharge or otherwise discriminate against an employee because he has filed charges or given testimony under this Act;

(5) to refuse to bargain collectively with the representatives of his employees, subject to the provisions of section 9(a).

(b) It shall be an unfair labor practice for a labor organization or its agents—

(1) to restrain or coerce (A) employees in the exercise of the rights guaranteed in section 7: *Provided,* That this paragraph shall not impair the right of a labor organization to prescribe its own rules with respect to the acquisition or retention of membership therein; or (B) an employer in the selection of his representatives for the purposes of collective bargaining or the adjustment of grievances;

(2) to cause or attempt to cause an employer to discriminate against an employee in violation of subsection (a)(3) or to discriminate against an employee with respect to whom membership in such organization has been denied or terminated on some ground other than his failure to tender the periodic dues and the initiation fees uniformly required as a condition of acquiring or retaining membership;

(3) to refuse to bargain collectively with an employer, provided it is the representative of his employees subject to the provisions of section 9(a);

(4) (i) to engage in, or to induce or encourage any individual employed by any person engaged in commerce or in an industry affecting commerce to engage in, a strike or a refusal in the course of his employment to use, manufacture, process, transport, or otherwise handle or work on any goods, articles, materials, or commodities or to perform any services; or (ii) to threaten, coerce, or restrain any person engaged in commerce or in an industry affecting commerce, where in either case an object thereof is:

(A) forcing or requiring any employer or self-employed person to join any labor or employer organization or to enter into any agreement which is prohibited by section 8(e);

(B) forcing or requiring any person to cease using, selling, handling, transporting, or otherwise dealing in the products of any other producer, processor, or manufacturer, or to cease doing business with any other person, or forcing or requiring any other employer to recognize or bargain with a labor organization as the representative of his employees unless such labor organization has been certified as the representative of such employees under the provisions of section 9: *Provided,* That nothing contained in this clause (B) shall be construed to make unlawful, where not otherwise unlawful, any primary strike or primary picketing;

(C) forcing or requiring any employer to recognize or bargain with a particular labor organization as the representative of his employees if another labor organization has been certified as the representative of such employees under the provisions of section 9;

(D) forcing or requiring any employer to assign particular work to employees in a particular labor organization or in a particular trade, craft, or class rather than to employees in another labor organization or in another trade, craft, or class, unless such employer is failing to conform to an order or certification of the Board determining the bargaining representative for employees performing such work:

Provided, That nothing contained in this subsection (b) shall be construed to make unlawful a refusal by any person to enter upon the premises of any employer (other than his own employer), if the employees of such employer are engaged in a strike ratified or approved by a representative of such employees whom such employer is required to recognize under this Act: *Provided further,* That for the purposes of this paragraph (4) only, nothing contained in such paragraph shall be construed to prohibit publicity, other than picketing, for the purpose of truthfully advising the public, including consumers and members of a labor organization, that a product or products are produced by an employer with whom the labor organization has a primary dispute and are distributed by another employer, as long as such publicity does not have an effect of inducing any individual employed by any person other than the primary employer in the course of his employment to refuse to pick up, deliver, or transport any goods, or not to perform any services, at the establishment of the employer engaged in such distribution;

(5) to require of employees covered by an agreement authorized under subsection (a)(3) the payment, as a condition precedent to becoming a member of such organization, of a fee in an amount which the Board finds excessive or discriminatory under all the circumstances. In making such a finding, the Board shall consider, among other relevant factors, the practices and customs of labor organizations in the particular industry, and the wages currently paid to the employees affected;

(6) to cause or attempt to cause an employer to pay or deliver or agree to pay or deliver any money or other thing of value, in the nature of an exaction, for services which are not performed or not to be performed; and

(7) to picket or cause to be picketed, or threaten to picket or cause to be picketed, any employer where an object thereof is forcing or requiring an employer to recognize or bargain with a labor organization as the representative of his employees, or forcing or requiring the employees of an employer to accept or select such labor organization as their collective bargaining representative, unless such labor organization is currently certified as the representative of such employees:

(A) where the employer has lawfully recognized in accordance with this Act any other labor organization and a question concerning representation may not appropriately be raised under section 9(c) of this Act,

(B) where within the preceding twelve months a valid election under section 9(c) of this Act has been conducted, or

(C) where such picketing has been conducted without a petition under section 9(c) being filed within a reasonable period of time not to exceed thirty days from the commencement of such picketing: *Provided, That* when such a petition has been filed the Board shall forthwith, without regard to the provisions of section 9(c)(1) or the absence of a showing of a substantial interest on the part of the labor organization, direct an election in such unit as the Board finds to be appropriate and shall certify the results thereof: *Provided further,* That nothing in this subparagraph (C) shall be construed to prohibit any picketing or other publicity for the purpose of truthfully advising the public (including consumers) that an employer does not employ members of, or have a contract with, a labor organization, unless an effect of such picketing is to induce any individual employed by any other person in the course of his employment, not to pick up, deliver or transport any goods or not to perform any services.

Nothing in this paragraph (7) shall be construed to permit any act which would otherwise be an unfair labor practice under this section 8(b).

(c) The expressing of any views, argument, or opinion, or the dissemination thereof, whether in written, printed, graphic, or visual form, shall not constitute or be evidence of an unfair labor practice under any of the provisions of this Act, if such expression contains no threat of reprisal or force or promise of benefit.

(d) For the purposes of this section, to bargain collectively is the performance of the mutual obligation of the employer and the representative of the employees to meet at reasonable times and confer in good faith with respect to wages, hours, and other terms and conditions of employment, or the negotiation of an agreement, or any question arising thereunder, and the execution of a written contract incorporating any agreement reached if requested by either party, but such obligation does not compel either party to agree to a proposal or require the making of a concession: *Provided,* That where there is in effect a collective-bargaining contract covering employees in an industry affecting commerce, the duty to bargain collectively shall also mean that no party to such contract shall terminate or modify such contract, unless the party desiring such termination or modification—

(1) serves a written notice upon the other party to the contract of the proposed termination or modification sixty days prior to the expiration date thereof, or in the event such contract contains no expiration date, sixty days prior to the time it is proposed to make such termination or modification;

(2) offers to meet and confer with the other party for the purpose of negotiating a new contract or a contract containing the proposed modifications;

(3) notifies the Federal Mediation and Conciliation Service within thirty days after such notice of the existence of a dispute, and simultaneously therewith notifies any State or Territorial agency established to mediate and conciliate disputes within the State or Territory where the dispute occurred, provided no agreement has been reached by that time; and

(4) continues in full force and effect, without resorting to strike or lockout, all the terms and conditions of the existing contract for a period of sixty days after such notice is given or until the expiration date of such contract, whichever occurs later:

The duties imposed upon employers, employees, and labor organizations by paragraphs (2), (3), and (4) shall become inapplicable upon an intervening certification of the Board, under which the labor organization or individual, which is a party to the contract, has been superseded as or ceased to be the representative of the employees subject to the provisions of section 9(a), and the duties so imposed shall not be construed as requiring either party to discuss or agree to any modification of the terms and conditions contained in a contract for a fixed period, if such modification is to become effective before such terms and conditions can be reopened under the provisions of the contract. Any employee who engages in a strike within **any notice period specified in this subsection **, or who engages in any strike within the appropriate period specified in subsection (g) of this section shall lose his status as an employee of the employer engaged in the particular labor dispute, for the purposes of sections 8, 9, and 10 of this Act, as amended, but such loss of status for such employee shall terminate if and when he is reemployed by such employer. **Whenever the collective bargaining involves employees of a health care institution, the provisions of this section 8(d) shall be modified as follows:

(A) The notice of section 8(d)(1) shall be ninety days; the notice of section 8(d)(3) shall be sixty days; and the contract period of section 8(d)(4) shall be ninety days;

(B) Where the bargaining is for an initial agreement following certification or recognition, at least thirty days' notice of the existence of a dispute shall be given by the labor organization to the agencies set forth in section 8(d)(3).

(C) After notice is given to the Federal Mediation and Conciliation Service under either clause (A) or (B) of this sentence, the Service shall promptly communicate with the parties and use its best efforts, by mediation and conciliation, to bring them to agreement. The parties shall participate fully and promptly in such meetings as may be undertaken by the Service for the purpose of aiding in a settlement of the dispute.

(e) It shall be an unfair labor practice for any labor organization and any employer to enter into any contract or agreement, express or implied, whereby such employer ceases or refrains or agrees to cease or refrain from handling, using, selling, transporting or otherwise dealing in any of the products of any other employer, or to cease doing business with any other person, and any contract or agreement entered into heretofore or hereafter containing such an agreement shall be to such extent unenforceable and void: *Provided,* That nothing in this subsection (e) shall apply to an agreement between a labor organization and an employer in the construction industry relating to the contracting or subcontracting of work to be done at the site of the construction, alteration, painting, or repair of a building, structure, or other work: *Provided further,* That for the purposes of this subsection (e) and section 8(b)(4) (B) the terms "any employer", "any person engaged in commerce or in industry affecting commerce", and "any person" when used in relation to the terms "any other producer, processor, or manufacturer", "any other employer", or "any other person" shall not include persons in the relation of a jobber, manufacturer, contractor, or subcontractor working on the goods or premises of the jobber or manufacturer or performing parts of an integrated process of production in the apparel and clothing industry: *Provided further,* That nothing in this Act shall prohibit the enforcement of any agreement which is within the foregoing exception.

(f) It shall not be an unfair labor practice under subsections (a) and (b) of this section for an employer engaged primarily in the building and construction industry to make an agreement covering employees engaged (or who, upon their employment, will be engaged) in the building and construction industry with a labor organization of which building and construction employees are members (not established, maintained, or assisted by any action defined in section 8(a) of this Act as an unfair labor practice) because (1) the majority status of such labor organization has not been established under the provisions of section 9 of this Act prior to the making of such agreement, or (2) such agreement requires as a condition of employment, membership in such labor organization after the seventh day following the beginning of such employment or the effective date of the agreement, whichever is later, or (3) such agreement requires the employer to notify such labor organization of opportunities for employment with such employer, or gives such labor organization an opportunity to refer qualified applicants for such employment, or (4) such agreement specifies minimum training or experience qualifications for employment or provides for priority in opportunities for employment based upon length of service with such employer, in the industry or in the particular geographical area: *Provided,* That nothing in this

---

**Pursuant to Public Law 93–360, 93d Cong., S. 3203, 88 Stat. 396, the last sentence of Sec. 8(d) is amended by striking the words "the sixty day" and inserting the words "any notice" and by inserting before the words "shall lose" the phrase ", or who engages in any strike within the appropriate period specified in subsection (g) of this section." In addition, the end of paragraph Sec. 8(d) is amended by adding a new sentence "Whenever the collective bargaining . . . aiding in a settlement of the dispute."

subsection shall set aside the final proviso to section 8(a)(3) of this Act: *Provided further,* That any agreement which would be invalid, but for clause (1) of this subsection, shall not be a bar to a petition filed pursuant to section 9(c) or 9(e).*

**(g) A labor organization before engaging in any strike, picketing, or other concerted refusal to work at any health care institution shall, not less than ten days prior to such action, notify the institution in writing and the Federal Mediation and Conciliation Service of that intention, except that in the case of bargaining for an initial agreement following certification or recognition the notice required by this subsection shall not be given until the expiration of the period specified in clause (B) of the last sentence of section 8(d) of this Act. The notice shall state the date and time that such action will commence. The notice, once given, may be extended by the written agreement of both parties.

REPRESENTATIVES AND ELECTIONS

SEC. 9. (a) Representatives designated or selected for the purposes of collective bargaining by the majority of the employees in a unit appropriate for such purposes, shall be the exclusive representatives of all the employees in such unit for the purposes of collective bargaining in respect to rates of pay, wages, hours of employment, or other conditions of employment: *Provided,* That any individual employee or a group of employees shall have the right at any time to present grievances to their employer and to have such grievances adjusted, without the intervention of the bargaining representative, as long as the adjustment is not inconsistent with the terms of a collective-bargaining contract or agreement then in effect: *Provided further,* That the bargaining representative has been given opportunity to be present at such adjustment.

(b) The Board shall decide in each case whether, in order to assure to employees the fullest freedom in exercising the rights guaranteed by this Act, the unit appropriate for the purposes of collective bargaining shall be the employer unit, craft unit, plant unit, or subdivision thereof: *Provided,* That the Board shall not (1) decide that any unit is appropriate for such purposes if such unit includes both professional employees and employees who are not professional employees unless a majority of such professional employees vote for inclusion in such unit; or (2) decide that any craft unit is inappropriate for such purposes on the ground that a different unit has been established by a prior Board determination, unless a majority of the employees in the proposed craft unit vote against separate representation or (3) decide that any unit is appropriate for such purposes if it includes, together with other employees, any individual employed as a guard to enforce against employees and other persons rules to protect property of the employer or to protect the safety of persons on the employer's premises; but no labor organization shall be certified as the representative of employees in a bargaining unit of guards if such organization admits to membership, or is affiliated directly or indirectly with an organization which admits to membership, employees other than guards.

*Sec. 8(f) is inserted in the Act by subsec. (a) of Sec. 705 of Public Law 86-257. Sec. 705(b) provides:

Nothing contained in the amendment made by subsection (a) shall be construed as authorizing the execution or application of agreements requiring membership in a labor organization as a condition of employment in any State or Territory in which such execution or application is prohibited by State or Territorial Law.

**Pursuant to Public Law 93-360, 93d Cong., S. 3203, 88 Stat. 396, Sec. 8 is amended by adding subsection (g).

(c)(1) Wherever a petition shall have been filed, in accordance with such regulations as may be prescribed by the Board—

(A) by an employee or group of employees or any individual or labor organization acting in their behalf alleging that a substantial number of employees (i) wish to be represented for collective bargaining and that their employer declines to recognize their representative as the representative defined in section 9(a), or (ii) assert that the individual or labor organization, which has been certified or is being currently recognized by their employer as the bargaining representative, is no longer a representative as defined in section 9(a); or

(B) by an employer, alleging that one or more individuals or labor organizations have presented to him a claim to be recognized as the representative defined in section 9(a):

the Board shall investigate such petition and if it has reasonable cause to believe that a question of representation affecting commerce exists shall provide for an appropriate hearing upon due notice. Such hearing may be conducted by an officer or employee of the regional office, who shall not make any recommendations with respect thereto. If the Board finds upon the record of such hearing that such a question of representation exists, it shall direct an election by secret ballot and shall certify the results thereof.

(2) In determining whether or not a question of representation affecting commerce exists, the same regulations and rules of decision shall apply irrespective of the identity of the persons filing the petition or the kind of relief sought and in no case shall the Board deny a labor organization a place on the ballot by reason of an order with respect to such labor organization or its predecessor not issued in conformity with section 10(c).

(3) No election shall be directed in any bargaining unit or any subdivision within which, in the preceding twelve-month period, a valid election shall have been held. Employees engaged in an economic strike who are not entitled to reinstatement shall be eligible to vote under such regulations as the Board shall find are consistent with the purposes and provisions of this Act in any election conducted within twelve months after the commencement of the strike. In any election when none of the choices on the ballot receives a majority, a run-off shall be conducted, the ballot providing for a selection between the two choices receiving the largest and second largest number of valid votes cast in the election.

(4) Nothing in this section shall be construed to prohibit the waiving of hearings by stipulation for the purpose of a consent election in conformity with regulations and rules of decision of the Board.

(5) In determining whether a unit is appropriate for the purposes specified in subsection (b) the extent to which the employees have organized shall not be controlling.

(d) Whenever an order of the Board made pursuant to section 10(c) is based in whole or in part upon facts certified following an investigation pursuant to subsection (c) of this section and there is a petition for the enforcement or review of such order, such certification and the record of such investigation shall be included in the transcript of the entire record required to be filed under section 10(e) or 10(f), and thereupon the decree of the court enforcing, modifying, or setting aside in whole or in part the order of the Board shall be made and entered upon the pleadings, testimony, and proceedings set forth in such transcript.

(e)(1) Upon the filing with the Board, by 30 per centum or more of the employees in a bargaining unit covered by an agreement between their employer and a labor organization made pursuant to section 8(a)(3), of a petition alleging they desire that such authority be rescinded, the Board shall take a secret ballot of the employees in such unit and certify the results thereof to such labor organization and to the employer.

(2) No election shall be conducted pursuant to this subsection in any bargaining unit or any subdivision within which, in the preceding twelve-month period, a valid election shall have been held.

PREVENTION OF UNFAIR LABOR PRACTICES

SEC. 10. (a) The Board is empowered, as hereinafter provided, to prevent any person from engaging in any unfair labor practice (listed in section 8) affecting commerce. This power shall not be affected by any other means of adjustment or prevention that has been or may be established by agreement, law, or otherwise: *Provided,* That the Board is empowered by agreement with any agency of any State or Territory to cede to such agency jurisdiction over any cases in any industry (other than mining, manufacturing, communications, and transportation except where predominantly local in character) even though such cases may involve labor disputes affecting commerce, unless the provision of the State or Territorial statute applicable to the determination of such cases by such agency is inconsistent with the corresponding provision of this Act or has received a construction inconsistent therewith.

(b) Whenever it is charged that any person has engaged in or is engaging in any such unfair labor practice, the Board, or any agent or agency designated by the Board for such purposes, shall have power to issue and cause to be served upon such person a complaint stating the charges in that respect, and containing a notice of hearing before the Board or a member thereof, or before a designated agent or agency, at a place therein fixed, not less than five days after the serving of said complaint: *Provided,* That no complaint shall issue based upon any unfair labor practice occurring more than six months prior to the filing of the charge with the Board and the service of a copy thereof upon the person against whom such charge is made, unless the person aggrieved thereby was prevented from filing such charge by reason of service in the armed forces, in which event the six-month period shall be computed from the day of his discharge. Any such complaint may be amended by the member, agent, or agency conducting the hearing or the Board in its discretion at any time prior to the issuance of an order based thereon. The person so complained of shall have the right to file an answer to the original or amended complaint and to appear in person or otherwise and give testimony at the place and time fixed in the complaint. In the discretion of the member, agent, or agency conducting the hearing or the Board, any other person may be allowed to intervene in the said proceeding and to present testimony. Any such proceeding shall, so far as practicable, be conducted in accordance with the rules of evidence applicable in the district courts of the United States under the rules of civil procedure for the district courts of the United States, adopted by the Supreme Court of the United States pursuant to the Act of June 19, 1934 (U. S. C., title 28, secs. 723-B, 723-C).

(c) The testimony taken by such member, agent, or agency or the Board shall be reduced to writing and filed with the Board. Thereafter, in its discretion, the Board upon notice may take further testimony or hear argument. If upon the preponderance of the testimony taken the Board shall be of the opinion that any person named in the complaint has engaged in or is engaging in any such unfair labor practice, then the Board shall state its findings of fact and shall issue and cause to be served on such person an order requiring such person to cease and desist from such unfair labor practice, and to take such affirmative action including reinstatement of employees with or without back pay, as will effectuate the policies of this Act: *Provided,* That where an order directs reinstatement of an employee,

back pay may be required of the employer or labor organization, as the case may be, responsible for the discrimination suffered by him: *And provided further,* That in determining whether a complaint shall issue alleging a violation of section 8(a)(1) or section 8(a)(2), and in deciding such cases, the same regulations and rules of decision shall apply irrespective of whether or not the labor organization affected is affiliated with a labor organization national or international in scope. Such order may further require such person to make reports from time to time showing the extent to which it has complied with the order. If upon the preponderance of the testimony taken the Board shall not be of the opinion that the person named in the complaint has engaged in or is engaging in any such unfair labor practice, then the Board shall state its findings of fact and shall issue an order dismissing the said complaint. No order of the Board shall require the reinstatement of any individual as an employee who has been suspended or discharged, or the payment to him of any back pay, if such individual was suspended or discharged for cause. In case the evidence is presented before a member of the Board, or before an examiner or examiners thereof, such member, or such examiner or examiners, as the case may be, shall issue and cause to be served on the parties to the proceeding a proposed report, together with a recommended order, which shall be filed with the Board, and if no exceptions are filed within twenty days after service thereof upon such parties, or within such further period as the Board may authorize, such recommended order shall become the order of the Board and become effective as therein prescribed.

(d) Until the record in a case shall have been filed in a court, as hereinafter provided, the Board may at any time, upon reasonable notice and in such manner as it shall deem proper, modify or set aside, in whole or in part, any finding or order made or issued by it.

(e) The Board shall have power to petition any court of appeals of the United States, or if all the courts of appeals to which application may be made are in vacation, any district court of the United States, within any circuit or district, respectively, wherein the unfair labor practice in question occurred or wherein such person resides or transacts business, for the enforcement of such order and for appropriate temporary relief or.restraining order, and shall file in the court the record in the proceedings, as provided in section 2112 of title 28, United States Code. Upon the filing of such petition, the court shall cause notice thereof to be served upon such person, and thereupon shall have jurisdiction of the proceeding and of the question determined therein, and shall have power to grant such temporary relief or restraining order as it deems just and proper, and to make and enter a decree enforcing, modifying, and enforcing as so modified, or setting aside in whole or in part the order of the Board. No objection that has not been urged before the Board, its member, agent, or agency, shall be considered by the court, unless the failure or neglect to urge such objection shall be excused because of extraordinary circumstances. The findings of the Board with respect to questions of fact if supported by substantial evidence on the record considered as a whole shall be conclusive. If either party shall apply to the court for leave to adduce additional evidence and shall show to the satisfaction of the court that such additional evidence is material and that there were reasonable grounds for the failure to adduce such evidence in the hearing before the Board, its member, agent, or agency, the court may order such additional evidence to be taken before the Board, its member, agent, or agency, and to be made a part of the record. The Board may modify its findings as to the facts, or make new findings, by reason of additional evidence so taken and filed, and it shall file such modified or new findings, which findings with respect to questions of fact if supported by substantial evidence on the record considered as a whole shall be conclusive, and shall file its recommendations, if any, for the modification or setting aside of its original order. Upon the filing of the record with it the jurisdiction of the court shall be exclusive and its judgment and decree shall be final, except that the same shall be subject to review by the appropriate United States court of appeals if application was made to the district court as hereinabove provided, and by the Supreme Court of the United States upon writ of certiorari or certification as provided in section 1254 of title 28.

(f) Any person aggrieved by a final order of the Board granting or denying in whole or in part the relief sought may obtain a review of such order in any circuit court of appeals of the United States in the circuit wherein the unfair labor practice in question was alleged to have been engaged in or wherein such person resides or transacts business, or in the United States Court of Appeals for the District of Columbia, by filing in such court a written petition praying that the order of the Board be modified or set aside. A copy of such petition shall be forthwith transmitted by the clerk of the court to the Board, and thereupon the aggrieved party shall file in the court the record in the proceeding, certified by the Board, as provided in section 2112 of title 28, United States Code. Upon the filing of such petition, the court shall proceed in the same manner as in the case of an application by the Board under subsection (e) of this section, and shall have the same jurisdiction to grant to the Board such temporary relief or restraining order as it deems just and proper, and in like manner to make and enter a decree enforcing, modifying, and enforcing as so modified, or setting aside in whole or in part the order of the Board; the findings of the Board with respect to questions of fact if supported by substantial evidence on the record considered as a whole shall in like manner be conclusive.

(g) The commencement of proceedings under subsection (e) or (f) of this section shall not, unless specifically ordered by the court, operate as a stay of the Board's order.

(h) When granting appropriate temporary relief or a restraining order, or making and entering a decree enforcing, modifying, and enforcing as so modified, or setting aside in whole or in part an order of the Board, as provided in this section, the jurisdiction of courts sitting in equity shall not be limited by the Act entitled "An Act to amend the Judicial Code and to define and limit the jurisdiction of courts sitting in equity, and for other purposes," approved March 23, 1932 (U.S.C., Supp. VII, title 29, secs. 101-115).

(i) Petitions filed under this Act shall be heard expeditiously, and if possible within ten days after they have been docketed.

(j) The Board shall have power, upon issuance of a complaint as provided in subsection (b) charging that any person has engaged in or is engaging in an unfair labor practice, to petition any district court of the United States (including the District Court of the United States for the District of Columbia), within any district wherein the unfair labor practice in question is alleged to have occurred or wherein such person resides or transacts business, for appropriate temporary relief or restraining order. Upon the filing of any such petition the court shall cause notice thereof to be served upon such person, and thereupon shall have jurisdiction to grant to the Board such temporary relief or restraining order as it deems just and proper.

(k) Whenever it is charged that any person has engaged in an unfair labor practice within the meaning of paragraph (4)(D) of section 8(b), the Board is empowered and directed to hear and determine the dispute out of which such unfair labor practice shall have arisen, unless, within ten days after notice that such charge has been filed, the parties to such dispute submit to the Board satisfactory evidence that they have adjusted, or agreed upon methods for the voluntary adjustment, of the dispute. Upon compliance by the parties to the dispute with the decision of the Board or upon such voluntary adjustment of the dispute, such charge shall be dismissed.

(l) Whenever it is charged that any person has engaged in an unfair labor practice within the meaning of paragraph (4) (A), (B), or (C) of section 8(b), or section 8(e) or section 8(b)(7), the preliminary investigation of such charge shall be made forthwith and given priority over all other cases except cases of like character in the office where it is filed or to which it is referred. If, after such investigation, the officer or regional attorney to whom the matter may be referred has reasonable cause to believe such charge is true and that a complaint should issue, he shall, on behalf of the Board. petition any district court of the United States (including the District Court of the United States for the District of Columbia) within any district where the unfair labor practice in question has occurred, is alleged to have occurred, or wherein such person resides or transacts business, for appropriate injunctive relief pending the final adjudication of the Board with respect to such matter. Upon the filing of any such petition the district court shall have jurisdiction to grant such injunctive relief or temporary restraining order as it deems just and proper, notwithstanding any other provision of law: *Provided further,* That no temporary restraining order shall be issued without notice unless a petition alleges that substantial and irreparable injury to the charging party will be unavoidable and such temporary restraining order shall be effective for no longer than five days and will become void at the expiration of such period: *Provided further,* That such officer or regional attorney shall not apply for any restraining order under section 8(b)(7) if a charge against the employer under section 8(a)(2) has been filed and after the preliminary investigation, he has reasonable cause to believe that such charge is true and that a complaint should issue. Upon filing of any such petition the courts shall cause notice thereof to be served upon any person involved in the charge and such person, including the charging party, shall be given an opportunity to appear by counsel and present any relevant testimony: *Provided further,* That for the purposes of this subsection district courts shall be deemed to have jurisdiction of a labor organization (1) in the district in which such organization maintains its principal office, or (2) in any district in which its duly authorized officers or agents are engaged in promoting or protecting the interests of employee members. The service of legal process upon such officer, or agent shall constitute service upon the labor organization and make such organizations a party to the suit. In situations where such relief is appropriate the procedure specified herein shall apply to charges with respect to section 8(b)(4)(D).

(m) Whenever it is charged that any person has engaged in an unfair labor practice within the meaning of subsection (a)(3) or (b)(2) of section 8, such charge shall be given priority over all other cases except cases of like character in the office where it is filed or to which it is referred and cases given priority under subsection (l).

LIMITATIONS

SEC. 13. Nothing in this Act, except as specifically provided for herein, shall be construed so as either to interfere with or impede or diminish in any way the right to strike, or to affect the limitations or qualifications on that right.

SEC. 14. (a) Nothing herein shall prohibit any individual employed as a supervisor from becoming or remaining a member of a labor organization, but no employer subject to this Act shall be compelled to deem individuals defined herein as supervisors as employees for the purpose of any law, either national or local, relating to collective bargaining.

444

(b) Nothing in this Act shall be construed as authorizing the execution or application of agreements requiring membership in a labor organization as a condition of employment in any State or Territory in which such execution or application is prohibited by State or Territorial law.

(c)(1) The Board, in its discretion, may, by rule of decision or by published rules adopted pursuant to the Administrative Procedure Act, decline to assert jurisdiction over any labor dispute involving any class or category of employers, where, in the opinion of the Board, the effect of such labor dispute on commerce is not sufficiently substantial to warrant the exercise of its jurisdiction: *Provided,* That the Board shall not decline to assert jurisdiction over any labor dispute over which it would assert jurisdiction under the standards prevailing upon August 1, 1959.

(2) Nothing in this Act shall be deemed to prevent or bar any agency or the courts of any State or Territory (including the Commonwealth of Puerto Rico, Guam, and the Virgin Islands), from assuming and asserting jurisdiction over labor disputes over which the Board declines, pursuant to paragraph (1) of this subsection, to assert jurisdiction.

SEC. 15. Wherever the application of the provisions of section 272 of chapter 10 of the Act entitled "An Act to establish a uniform system of bankruptcy throughout the United States," approved July 1, 1898, and Acts amendatory thereof and supplementary thereto (U.S.C., title 11, sec. 672), conflicts with the application of the provisions of this Act, this Act shall prevail: *Provided,* That in any situation where the provisions of this Act cannot be validly enforced, the provisions of such other Acts shall remain in full force and effect.

INDIVIDUALS WITH RELIGIOUS CONVICTIONS

SEC. 19 Any employee who is a member of and adheres to established and traditional tenets or teachings of a bona fide religion, body, or sect which has historically held conscientious objections to joining or financially supporting labor organizations shall not be required to join or financially support any labor organization as a condition of employment; except that such employee may be required in a contract between such employees' employer and a labor organization in lieu of periodic dues and initiation fees, to pay sums equal to such dues an initiation fees to a nonreligious, nonlabor organization charitable fund exempt from taxation under section 501(c)(3) of title 26 of the Internal Revenue Code, chosen by such employee from a list of at least three such funds, designated in such contract or if the contract fails to designate such funds, then to any such fund chosen by the employee. If such employee who holds conscientious objections pursuant to this section requests the labor organization to sue the grievance-arbitration procedure on the employee's behalf, the labor organization is authorized to charge the employee for the reasonable cost of using such procedure.

TITLE II—CONCILIATION OF LABOR DISPUTES IN INDUSTRIES AFFECTING COMMERCE; NATIONAL EMERGENCIES

SEC. 201. **That it is the policy of the United States that—**

(a) **sound and stable industrial peace and the advancement of the general welfare, health, and safety of the Nation and of the best interest of employers and employees can most satisfactorily be secured by the settlement of issues**

between employers and employees through the processes of conference and collective bargaining between employers and the representatives of their employees;

(b) the settlement of issues between employers and employees through collective bargaining may be advanced by making available full and adequate governmental facilities for conciliation, mediation, and voluntary arbitration to aid and encourage employers and the representatives of their employees to reach and maintain agreements concerning rates of pay, hours, and working conditions, and to make all reasonable efforts to settle their differences by mutual agreement reached through conferences and collective bargaining or by such methods as may be provided for in any applicable agreement for the settlement of disputes; and

(c) certain controversies which arise between parties to collective-bargaining agreements may be avoided or minimized by making available full and adequate governmental facilities for furnishing assistance to employers and the representatives of their employees in formulating for inclusion within such agreements provision for adequate notice of any proposed changes in the terms of such agreements, for the final adjustment of grievances or questions regarding the application or interpretation of such agreements, and other provisions designed to prevent the subsequent arising of such controversies.

SEC. 202. (a) There is hereby created an independent agency to be known as the Federal Mediation and Conciliation Service (herein referred to as the "Service," except that for sixty days after the date of the enactment of this Act such term shall refer to the Conciliation Service of the Department of Labor). The Service shall be under the direction of a Federal Mediation and Conciliation Director (hereinafter referred to as the "Director"), who shall be appointed by the President by and with the advice and consent of the Senate. The Director shall receive compensation at the rate of $12,000* per annum. The Director shall not engage in any other business, vocation, or employment.

FUNCTIONS OF THE SERVICE

SEC. 203. (a) It shall be the duty of the Service, in order to prevent or minimize interruptions of the free flow of commerce growing out of labor disputes to assist parties to labor disputes in industries affecting commerce to settle such disputes through conciliation and mediation.

(d) Final adjustment by a method agreed upon by the parties is hereby declared to be the desirable method for settlement of grievance disputes arising over the application or interpretation of an existing collective-bargaining agreement. The Service is directed to make its conciliation and mediation services available in the settlement of such grievance disputes only as a last resort and in exceptional cases.

NATIONAL EMERGENCIES

SEC. 206. Whenever in the opinion of the President of the United States, a threatened or actual strike or lock-out affecting an entire industry or a substantial part thereof engaged in trade, commerce, transportation, transmission, or communication among the several States or with foreign nations, or engaged in the production

*Pursuant to Public Law 90-206, 90th Cong., 81 Stat. 644, approved Dec. 16, 1967, and in accordance with Sec. 225(f)(ii) thereof, effective in 1969, the salary of the Director shall be $40,000 per year.

cf goods for commerce, will, if permitted to occur or to continue, imperil the national health or safety, he may appoint a board of inquiry to inquire into the issues involved in the dispute and to make a written report to him within such time as he shall prescribe. Such report shall include a statement of the facts with respect to the dispute, including each party's statement of its position but shall not contain any recommendations. The President shall file a copy of such report with the Service and shall make its contents available to the public.

SEC. 208. (a) Upon receiving a report from a board of inquiry the President may direct the Attorney General to petition any district court of the United States having jurisdiction of the parties to enjoin such strike or lock-out or the continuing thereof, and if the court finds that such threatened or actual strike or lock-out—

(i) affects an entire industry or a substantial part thereof engaged in trade, commerce, transportation, transmission, or communication among the several States or with foreign nations, or engaged in the production of goods for commerce; and

(ii) if permitted to occur or to continue, will imperil the national health or safety, it shall have jurisdiction to enjoin any such strike or lock-out, or the continuing thereof, and to make such other orders as may be appropriate.

SEC. 209. (a) Whenever a district court has issued an order under section 208 enjoining acts or practices which imperil or threaten to imperil the national health or safety, it shall be the duty of the parties to the labor dispute giving rise to such order to make every effort to adjust and settle their differences, with the assistance of the Service created by this Act. Neither party shall be under any duty to accept, in whole or in part, any proposal of settlement made by the Service.

(b) Upon the issuance of such order, the President shall reconvene the board of inquiry which has previously reported with respect to the dispute. At the end of a sixty-day period (unless the dispute has been settled by that time), the board of inquiry shall report to the President the current position of the parties and the efforts which has been made for settlement, and shall include a statement by each party of its position and a statement of the employer's last offer of settlement. The President shall make such report available to the public. The National Labor Relations Board, within the succeeding fifteen days, shall take a secret ballot of the employees of each employer involved in the dispute on the question of whether they wish to accept the final offer of settlement made by their employer as stated by him and shall certify the results thereof to the Attorney General within five days thereafter.

SEC. 210. Upon the certification of the results of such ballot or upon a settlement being reached, whichever happens sooner, the Attorney General shall move the court to discharge the injunction, which motion shall then be granted and the injunction discharged. When such motion is granted, the President shall submit to the Congress a full and comprehensive report of the proceedings, including the findings of the board of inquiry and the ballot taken by the National Labor Relations Board, together with such recommendations as he may see fit to make for consideration and appropriate action.

**CONCILIATION OF LABOR DISPUTES IN THE HEALTH CARE INDUSTRY

SEC. 213. (a) If, in the opinion of the Director of the Federal Mediation and Conciliation Service a threatened or actual strike or lockout affecting a health care institution will, if permitted to occur or to continue, substantially interrupt the delivery of health care in the locality concerned, the Director may further assist in the resolution of the impasse by establishing within 30 days after the notice to the Federal Mediation and Conciliation Service under clause (A) of the last sentence of section 8(d) (which is required by clause (3) of such section 8(d)), or within 10 days after the notice under clause (B), an impartial Board of Inquiry to investigate the issues involved in the dispute and to make a written report thereon to the parties within fifteen (15) days after the establishment of such a Board. The written report shall contain the findings of fact together with the Board's recommendations for settling the dispute, with the objective of achieving a prompt, peaceful and just settlement of the dispute. Each such Board shall be composed of such number of individuals as the Director may deem desirable. No member appointed under this section shall have any interest or Involvement in the health care institutions or the employee organizations involved in the dispute.

(c) After the establishment of a board under subsection (a) of this section and for 15 days after any such board has issued its report, no change in the status quo in effect prior to the expiration of the contract in the case of negotiations for a contract renewal, or in effect prior to the time of the impasse in the case of an initial bargaining negotiation, except by agreement, shall be made by the parties to the controversy.

TITLE III

SUITS BY AND AGAINST LABOR ORGANIZATIONS

SEC. 301. (a) Suits for violation of contracts between an employer and a labor organization representing employees in an industry affecting commerce as defined in this Act, or between any such labor organizations, may be brought in any district court of the United States having jurisdiction of the parties, without respect to the amount in controversy or without regard to the citizenship of the parties.

(b) Any labor organization which represents employees in an industry affecting commerce as defined in this Act and any employer whose activities affect commerce as defined in this Act shall be bound by the acts of its agents. Any such labor organization may sue or be sued as an entity and in behalf of the employees whom it represents in the courts of the United States. Any money judgment against a labor organization in a district court of the United States shall be enforceable only against the organization as an entity and against its assets, and shall not be enforceable against any individual member or his assets.

(c) For the purposes of actions and proceedings by or against labor organizations in the district courts of the United States, district courts shall be deemed to have jurisdiction of a labor organization (1) in the district in which such organization maintains its principal offices, or (2) in any district in which its duly authorized officers or agents are engaged in representing or acting for employee members.

(d) The service of summons, subpena, or other legal process of any court of the United States upon an officer or agent of a labor organization, in his capacity as such, shall constitute service upon the labor organization.

(e) For the purposes of this section, in determining whether any person is acting as an "agent" of another person so as to make such other person responsible for his acts, the question of whether the specific acts performed were actually authorized or subsequently ratified shall not be controlling.

**Pursuant to Public Law 93-360, 93d Cong., S. 3203, 88 Stat. 396-397. Title II of the Labor Management Relations Act, 1947, is amended by adding Sec. 213.

RESTRICTIONS ON PAYMENTS TO EMPLOYEE REPRESENTATIVES

Sec. 302. (a) It shall be unlawful for any employer or association of employers or any person who acts as a labor relations expert, adviser, or consultant to an employer or who acts in the interest of an employer to pay, lend, or deliver, or agree to pay, lend, or deliver, any money or other thing of value—

(1) to any representative of any of his employees who are employed in an industry affecting commerce; or

(2) to any labor organization, or any officer or employee thereof, which represents, seeks to represent, or would admit to membership, any of the employees of such employer who are employed in an industry affecting commerce; or

(3) to any employee or group or committee of employees of such employer employed in an industry affecting commerce in excess of their normal compensation for the purpose of causing such employee or group or committee directly or indirectly to influence any other employees in the exercise of the right to organize and bargain collectively through representatives of their own choosing; or

(4) to any officer or employee of a labor organization engaged in an industry affecting commerce with intent to influence him in respect to any of his actions, decisions, or duties as a representative of employees or as such officer or employee of such labor organization.

(b)(1) It shall be unlawful for any person to request, demand, receive, or accept, or agree to receive or accept, any payment, loan, or delivery of any money or other thing of value prohibited by subsection (a).

(2) It shall be unlawful for any labor organization, or for any person acting as an officer, agent, representative, or employee of such labor organization, to demand or accept from the operator of any motor vehicle (as defined in part II of the Interstate Commerce Act) employed in the transportation of property in commerce, or the employer of any such operator, any money or other thing of value payable to such organization or to an officer, agent, representative or employee thereof as a fee or charge for the unloading, or the connection with the unloading, of the cargo of such vehicle: Provided, That nothing in this paragraph shall be construed to make unlawful any payment by an employer to any of his employees as compensation for their services as employees.

(c) The provisions of this section shall not be applicable (1) in respect to any money or other thing of value payable by an employer to any of his employees whose established duties include acting openly for such employer in matters of labor relations or personnel administration or to any representative of his employees, or to any officer or employee of a labor organization, who is also an employee or former employee of such employer, as compensation for, or by reason of, his service as an employee of such employer; (2) with respect to the payment or delivery of any money or other thing of value in satisfaction of a judgment of any court or a decision or award of an arbitrator or impartial chairman or in compromise, adjustment, settlement, or release of any claim, complaint, grievance, or dispute in the absence of fraud or duress; (3) with respect to the sale or purchase of an article or commodity at the prevailing market price in the regular course of business; (4) with respect to money deducted from the wages of employees in payment of membership dues in a labor organization: Provided, That the employer has received from each employee, on whose account such deductions are made, a written assignment which shall not be irrevocable for a period of more than one year, or beyond the termination date of the applicable collective agreement, whichever occurs sooner; (5) with respect to

money or other thing of value paid to a trust fund established by such representative, for the sole and exclusive benefit of the employees of such employer, and their families and dependents (or of such employees, families, and dependents jointly with the employees of other employers making similar payments, and their families and dependents): Provided, That (A) such payments are held in trust for the purpose of paying, either from principal or income or both, for the benefit of employees, their families and dependents, for medical or hospital care, pensions on retirement or death of employees, compensation for injuries or illness resulting from occupational activity or insurance to provide any of the foregoing, or unemployment benefits or life insurance, disability and sickness insurance, or accident insurance; (B) the detailed basis on which such payments are to be made is specified in a written agreement with the employer, and employees and employers are equally represented in the administration of such fund, together with such neutral persons as the representatives of the employers and the representatives of employees may agree upon and in the event the employers and employee groups deadlock on the administration of such fund and there are no neutral persons empowered to break such deadlock, such agreement provides that the two groups shall agree on an impartial umpire to decide such dispute, or in event of their failure to agree within a reasonable length of time, an impartial umpire to decide such dispute shall, on petition of either group, be appointed by the district court of the United States for the district where the trust fund has its principal office, and shall also contain provisions for an annual audit of the trust fund, a statement of the results of which shall be available for inspection by interested persons at the principal office of the trust fund and at such other places as may be designated in such written agreement; and (C) such payments as are intended to be used for the purpose of providing pensions or annuities for employees are made to a separate trust which provides that the funds held therein cannot be used for any purpose other than paying such pensions or annuities; (6) with respect to money or other thing of value paid by any employer to a trust fund established by such representative for the purpose of pooled vacation, holiday, severance or similar benefits, or defraying costs of apprenticeship or other training program: Provided, That the requirements of clause (B) of the proviso to clause (5) of this subsection shall apply to such trust funds; or (7) with respect to money or other thing of value paid by any employer to a pooled or individual trust fund established by such representative for the purpose of (A) scholarships for the benefit of employees, their families, and dependents for study at educational institutions, or (B) child care centers for preschool and school age dependents of employees: Provided, That no labor organization or employer shall be required to bargain on the establishment of any such trust fund, and refusal to do so shall not constitute an unfair labor practice: Provided further, That the requirements of clause (B) of the proviso to clause (5) of this subsection shall apply to such trust funds*; or (8) with respect to money or any other thing of value paid by any employer to a trust fund established by such representative for the purpose of defraying the costs of legal services for employees, their families, and dependents for counsel or plan of their choice: Provided, That the requirements of clause (B) of the proviso to clause (5) of this subsection shall apply to such trust funds: Provided further, That no such legal services shall be furnished: (A) to initiate any proceeding directed (i) against any such employer or its officers or agents except in workman's compensation cases, or (ii) against such labor organization, or its parent or subordinate bodies, or their officers or agents, or (iii)

*Sec. 302(c)(7) has been added by Public Law 91-86, 91st Cong. S. 2068, 83 Stat. 133, approved Oct. 14, 1969; Sec. 302(c)(8) was added by Public Law 93-95, 93d Cong. S. 1423, 87 Stat. 314-315, approved Aug. 15, 1973.

against any other employer or labor organization, or their officers or agents, in any matter arising under the National Labor Relations Act, as amended, or this Act; and (B) in any proceeding where a labor organization would be prohibited from defraying the costs of legal services by the provisions of the Labor-Management Reporting and Disclosure Act of 1959.

(d) Any person who willfully violates any of the provisions of this section shall, upon conviction thereof, be guilty of a misdemeanor and be subject to a fine of not more than $10,000 or to imprisonment for not more than one year, or both.

(e) The district courts of the United States and the United States courts of the Territories and possessions shall have jurisdiction, for cause shown, and subject to the provisions of section 17 (relating to notice to opposite party) of the Act entitled "An Act to supplement existing laws against unlawful restraints and monopolies, and for other purposes," approved October 15, 1914, as amended (U.S.C., title 28, sec. 381), to restrain violations of this section, without regard to the provisions of sections 6 and 20 of such Act of October 15, 1914, as amended (U.S.C., title 15, sec. 17, and title 29, sec. 52), and the provisions of the Act entitled "An Act to amend the Judicial Code and to define and limit the jurisdiction of courts sitting in equity, and for other purposes," approved March 23, 1932 (U.S.C., title 29, secs. 101–115).

(f) This section shall not apply to any contract in force on the date of enactment of this Act, until the expiration of such contract, or until July 1, 1948, whichever first occurs.

(g) Compliance with the restrictions contained in subsection (c)(5)(B) upon contributions to trust funds, otherwise lawful, shall not be applicable to contributions to such trust funds established by collective agreement prior to January 1, 1946, nor shall subsection (c)(5)(A) be construed as prohibiting contributions to such trust funds if prior to January 1, 1947, such funds contained provisions for pooled vacation benefits.

BOYCOTTS AND OTHER UNLAWFUL COMBINATIONS

SEC. 303. (a) It shall be unlawful, for the purpose of this section only, in an industry or activity affecting commerce, for any labor organization to engage in any activity or conduct defined as an unfair labor practice in section 8(b)(4) of the National Labor Relations Act, as amended.

(b) Whoever shall be injured in his business or property by reason of any violation of subsection (a) may sue therefore in any district court of the United States subject to the limitations and provisions of section 301 hereof without respect to the amount in controversy, or in any other court having jurisdiction of the parties, and shall recover the damages by him sustained and the cost of the suit.

RESTRICTION ON POLITICAL CONTRIBUTIONS

SEC. 304. Section 313 of the Federal Corrupt Practices Act, 1925 (U.S.C., 1940 edition, title 2, sec. 251; Supp. V, title 50, App., sec. 1509), as amended, is amended to read as follows:

SEC. 313. It is unlawful for any national bank, or any corporation organized by authority of any law of Congress to make a contribution or expenditure in connection with any election to any political office, or in connection with any primary election or political convention or caucus held to select candidates for any political office, or for any corporation whatever, or any labor organization to make a contribution or expenditure in connection with any election at which Presidential and Vice Presidential electors or a Senator or Representative in, or a Delegate or Resident Commissioner to Congress are to be voted for, or in connection with any primary election or political convention or caucus held to select candidates for any of the foregoing offices, or for any candidate, political committee, or other person to accept or receive any contribution prohibited by this section. Every corporation or labor organization which makes any contribution or expenditure in violation of this section shall be fined not more than $5,000; and every officer or director of any corporation, or officer of any labor organization, who consents to any contribution or expenditure by the corporation or labor organization, as the case may be, in violation of this section shall be fined not more than $1,000 or imprisoned for not more than one year, or both. For the purposes of this section "labor organization" means any organization of any kind, or any agency or employee representation committee or plan, in which employees participate and which exists for the purpose, in whole or in part, of dealing with employers concerning grievances, labor disputes, wages, rates of pay, hours of employment, or conditions of work.

TITLE V

DEFINITIONS

SEC. 501. When used in this Act—

(1) The term "industry affecting commerce" means any industry or activity in commerce or in which a labor dispute would burden or obstruct commerce or tend to burden or obstruct commerce or the free flow of commerce.

(2) The term "strike" includes any strike or other concerted stoppage of work by employees (including a stoppage by reason of the expiration of a collective-bargaining agreement) and any concerted slow-down or other concerted interruption of operations by employees.

(3) The terms "commerce," "labor disputes," "employer," "employee," "labor organization," "representative," "person," and "supervisor" shall have the same meaning as when used in the National Labor Relations Act as amended by this Act.

SAVING PROVISION

SEC. 502. Nothing in this Act shall be construed to require an individual employee to render labor or service without his consent, nor shall anything in this Act be construed to make the quitting of his labor by an individual employee an illegal act; nor shall any court issue any process to compel the performance by an individual employee of such labor or service, without his consent; nor shall the quitting of labor by an employee or employees in good faith because of abnormally dangerous conditions for work at the place of employment of such employee or employees be deemed a strike under this Act.

Labor-Management Reporting and Disclosure Act of 1959, As Amended

[Revised text¹ showing in bold face new or amended language provided by Public Law 89-216, as enacted September 29, 1965. 79 Stat. 888]

Definitions

(29 U.S.C. 402)

Sec. 3. For the purposes of titles I, II, III, IV, V (except section 505), and VI of this Act—

(a) "Commerce" means trade, traffic, commerce, transportation, transmission, or communication among the several States or between any State and any place outside thereof.

(b) "State" includes any State of the United States, the District of Columbia, Puerto Rico, the Virgin Islands, American Samoa, Guam, Wake Island, the Canal Zone, and Outer Continental Shelf lands defined in the Outer Continental Shelf Lands Act (43 U.S.C. 1331–1343).

(c) "Industry affecting commerce" means any activity, business, or industry in commerce or in which a labor dispute would hinder or obstruct commerce or the free flow of commerce and includes any activity or industry "affecting commerce" within the meaning of the Labor Management Relations Act, 1947, as amended, or the Railway Labor Act, as amended.

(d) "Person" includes one or more individuals, labor organizations, partnerships, associations, corporations, legal representatives, mutual companies, joint-stock companies, trusts, unincorporated organizations, trustees in bankruptcy, or receivers.

(e) "Employer" means any employer or any group or association of employers engaged in an industry affecting commerce (1) which is, with respect to employees engaged in an industry affecting commerce, an employer within the meaning of any law of the United States relating to the employment of any employees or (2) which may deal with any labor organization concerning grievances, labor disputes, wages, rates of pay, hours of employment, or conditions of work, and includes any person acting directly or indirectly as an employer or as an agent of an employer in relation to an employee but does not include the United States or any corporation wholly owned by the Government of the United States or any State or political subdivision thereof.

(f) "Employee" means any individual employed by an employer, and includes any individual whose work has ceased as a consequence of, or in connection with, any current labor dispute or because of any unfair labor practice or because of exclusion or expulsion from a labor organization in any manner or for any reason inconsistent with the requirements of this Act.

(g) "Labor dispute" includes any controversy concerning terms, tenure, or conditions of employment, or concerning the association or representation of persons in negotiating, fixing, maintaining, changing, or seeking to arrange terms or conditions of employment, regardless of whether the disputants stand in the proximate relation of employer and employee.

(h) "Trusteeship" means any receivership, trusteeship, or other method of supervision or control whereby a labor organization suspends the autonomy otherwise available to a subordinate body under its constitution or bylaws.

(i) "Labor organization" means a labor organization engaged in an industry affecting commerce and includes any organization of any kind, any agency, or employee representation committee, group, association, or plan so engaged in which employees participate and which exists for the purpose, in whole or in part, of dealing with employers concerning grievances, labor disputes, wages, rates of pay, hours, or other terms or conditions of employment, and any conference, general committee, joint or system board, or joint council so engaged which is subordinate to a national or international labor organization, other than a State or local central body.

(j) A labor organization shall be deemed to be engaged in an industry affecting commerce if it—

(1) is the certified representative of employees under the provisions of the National Labor Relations Act, as amended, or the Railway Labor Act, as amended; or

(2) although not certified, is a national or international labor organization or a local labor organization recognized or acting as the representative of employees of an employer or employers engaged in an industry affecting commerce; or

(3) has chartered a local labor organization or subsidiary body which is representing or actively seeking to represent employees of employers within the meaning of paragraph (1) or (2); or

(4) has been chartered by a labor organization representing or actively seeking to represent employees within the meaning of paragraph (1) or (2) as the local or subordinate body through which such employees may enjoy membership or become affiliated with such labor organization; or

(5) is a conference, general committee, joint or system board, or joint council, subordinate to a national or international labor organization, which includes a labor organization engaged in an industry affecting commerce within the meaning of any of the preceding paragraphs of this subsection, other than a State or local central body.

(k) "Secret ballot" means the expression by ballot, voting machine, or otherwise, but in no event by proxy, of a choice with respect to any election or vote taken upon any matter, which is cast in such a manner that the person expressing such choice cannot be identified with the choice expressed.

(l) "Trust in which a labor organization is interested" means a trust or other fund or organization (1) which was created or established by a labor organization, or one or more of the trustees or one or more members of the governing body of which is selected or appointed by a labor organization, and (2) a primary purpose of which is to provide benefits for the members of such labor organization or their beneficiaries.

(m) "Labor relations consultant" means any person who, for compensation, advises or represents an employer, employer organization, or labor organization concerning employee organizing, concerted activities, or collective bargaining activities.

(n) "Officer" means any constitutional officer, any person authorized to perform the functions of president, vice president, secretary, treasurer, or other executive functions of a labor organization, and any member of its executive board or similar governing body.

73 Stat. 520.

73 Stat. 521.

67 Stat. 462.

61 Stat. 136.
29 U.S.C. 167.
44 Stat. 577.
45 U.S.C. 151.

(o) "Member" or "member in good standing", when used in reference to a labor organization, includes any person who has fulfilled the requirements for membership in such organization, and who neither has voluntarily withdrawn from membership nor has been expelled or suspended from membership after appropriate proceedings consistent with lawful provisions of the constitution and bylaws of such organization.

(p) "Secretary" means the Secretary of Labor.

(q) "Officer, agent, shop steward, or other representative", when used with respect to a labor organization, includes elected officials and key administrative personnel, whether elected or appointed (such as business agents, heads of departments or major units, and organizers who exercise substantial independent authority), but does not include salaried nonsupervisory professional staff, stenographic, and service personnel.

(r) "District court of the United States" means a United States district court and a United States court of any place subject to the jurisdiction of the United States.

TITLE I—BILL OF RIGHTS OF MEMBERS OF LABOR ORGANIZATIONS

Bill of Rights
(29 U.S.C. 411)

Sec. 101. (a)(1) Equal Rights.—Every member of a labor organization shall have equal rights and privileges within such organization to nominate candidates, to vote in elections or referendums of the labor organization, to attend membership meetings and to participate in the deliberations and voting upon the business of such meetings, subject to reasonable rules and regulations in such organization's constitution and bylaws.

(2) Freedom of Speech and Assembly.—Every member of any labor organization shall have the right to meet and assemble freely with other members; and to express any views, arguments, or opinions; and to express at meetings of the labor organization his views, upon candidates in an election of the labor organization or upon any business properly before the meeting, subject to the organization's established and reasonable rules pertaining to the conduct of meetings: Provided, That nothing herein shall be construed to impair the right of a labor organization to adopt and enforce reasonable rules as to the responsibility of every member toward the organization as an institution and to his refraining from conduct that would interfere with its performance of its legal or contractual obligations.

(3) Dues, Initiation Fees, and Assessments.—Except in the case of a federation of national or international labor organizations, the rates of dues and initiation fees payable by members of any labor organization in effect on the date of enactment of this Act shall not be increased, and no general or special assessment shall be levied upon such members, except—

(A) in the case of a local organization, (i) by majority vote by secret ballot of the members in good standing voting at a general or special membership meeting, after reasonable notice of the intention to vote upon such question, or (ii) by majority vote of the members in good standing voting in a membership referendum conducted by secret ballot; or

(B) in the case of a labor organization, other than a local labor organization or a federation of national or international labor organizations, (i) by majority vote of the delegates voting at a regular convention, or at a special

convention of such labor organization held upon not less than thirty days' written notice to the principal office of each local or constituent labor organization entitled to such notice, or (ii) by majority vote of the members in good standing of such labor organization voting in a membership referendum conducted by secret ballot, or (iii) by majority vote of the members of the executive board or similar governing body of such labor organization, pursuant to express authority contained in the constitution and bylaws of such labor organization: Provided, That such action on the part of the executive board or similar governing body shall be effective only until the next regular convention of such labor organization.

(4) Protection of the Right to Sue.—No labor organization shall limit the right of any member thereof to institute an action in any court, or in a proceeding before any administrative agency, irrespective of whether or not the labor organization or its officers are named as defendants or respondents in such action or proceeding, or the right of any member of a labor organization to appear as a witness in any judicial, administrative, or legislative proceeding, or to petition any legislature or to communicate with any legislator: Provided, That any such member may be required to exhaust reasonable hearing procedures (but not to exceed a four-month lapse of time) within such organization, before instituting legal or administrative proceedings against such organizations or any officer thereof: And provided further, That no interested employer or employer association shall directly or indirectly finance, encourage, or participate in, except as a party, any such action, proceeding, appearance, or petition.

(5) Safeguards Against Improper Disciplinary Action.—No member of any labor organization may be fined, suspended, expelled, or otherwise disciplined except for nonpayment of dues by such organization or by any officer thereof unless such member has been (A) served with written specific charges; (B) given a reasonable time to prepare his defense; (C) afforded a full and fair hearing.

(b) Any provision of the constitution and bylaws of any labor organization which is inconsistent with the provisions of this section shall be of no force or effect.

Civil Enforcement
(29 U.S.C. 412)

Sec. 102. Any person whose rights secured by the provisions of this title have been infringed by any violation of this title may bring a civil action in a district court of the United States for such relief (including injunctions) as may be appropriate. Any such action against a labor organization shall be brought in the district court of the United States for the district where the alleged violation occurred, or where the principal office of such labor organization is located.

Retention of Existing Rights
(29 U.S.C. 413)

Sec. 103. Nothing contained in this title shall limit the rights and remedies of any member of a labor organization under any State or Federal law or before any court or other tribunal, or under the constitution and bylaws of any labor organization.

Right to Copies of Collective Bargaining Agreements
(29 U.S.C. 414)

Sec. 104. It shall be the duty of the secretary or corresponding principal officer of each labor organization, in the case of a local labor organization, to forward a copy of each collective bargaining agreement made by such labor

73 Stat. 522

73 Stat. 523

organization with any employer to any employee who requests such a copy and whose rights as such employee are directly affected by such agreement, and in the case of a labor organization other than a local labor organization, to forward a copy of any such agreement; and such officer shall maintain at the principal office of the labor organization of which he is an officer copies of any such agreement made or received by such labor organization, which copies shall be available for inspection by any member or by any employee whose rights are affected by such agreement. The provisions of section 210 shall be applicable in the enforcement of this section.

Information as to Act
(29 U.S.C. 415)

Sec. 105. Every labor organization shall inform its members concerning the provisions of this Act.

TITLE II—REPORTING BY LABOR ORGANIZATIONS, OFFICERS AND EMPLOYEES OF LABOR ORGANIZATIONS, AND EMPLOYERS

Report of Labor Organizations
(29 U.S.C. 431)

Sec. 201. (a) Every labor organization shall adopt a constitution and bylaws and shall file a copy thereof with the Secretary, together with a report, signed by its president and secretary or corresponding principal officers, containing the following information—

(1) the name of the labor organization, its mailing address, and any other address at which it maintains its principal office or at which it keeps the records referred to in this title;

(2) the name and title of each of its officers;

(3) the initiation fee or fees required from a new or transferred member and fees for work permits required by the reporting labor organization;

(4) the regular dues or fees of other periodic payments required to remain a member of the reporting labor organization; and

(5) detailed statements, or references to specific provisions of documents filed under this subsection which contain such statements, showing the provisions made and procedures followed with respect to each of the following: (A) qualifications for or restrictions on membership, (B) levying of assessments, (C) participation in insurance or other benefit plans, (D) authorization for disbursement of funds of the labor organization, (E) audit of financial transactions of the labor organization, (F) the calling of regular and special meetings, (G) the selection of officers and stewards and of any representatives to other bodies composed of labor organizations' representatives, with a specific statement of the manner in which each officer was elected, appointed, or otherwise selected, (H) discipline or removal of officers or agents for breaches of their trust, (I) imposition of fines, suspensions, and expulsions of members, including the grounds for such action and any provision made for notice, hearing, judgment on the evidence, and appeal procedures, (J) authorization for bargaining demands, (K) ratification of contract terms, (L) authorization for strikes, and (M) issuance of work permits. Any change in the information required by this subsection shall be reported to the Secretary at the time the reporting labor organization files with the Secretary the annual financial report required by subsection (b).

(b) Every labor organization shall file annually with the Secretary a financial report signed by its president and treasurer or corresponding principal officers containing the following information in such detail as may be necessary accurately to disclose its financial condition and operations for its preceding fiscal year—

(1) assets and liabilities at the beginning and end of the fiscal year;

(2) receipts of any kind and the sources thereof;

(3) salary, allowances, and other direct or indirect disbursements (including reimbursed expenses) to each officer and also to each employee who, during such fiscal year, received more than $10,000 in the aggregate from such labor organization and any other labor organization affiliated with it or with which it is affiliated, or which is affiliated with the same national or international labor organization;

(4) direct and indirect loans made to any officer, employee, or member, which aggregated more than $250 during the fiscal year, together with a statement of the purpose, security, if any, and arrangements for repayment;

(5) direct and indirect loans to any business enterprise, together with a statement of the purpose, security, if any, and arrangements for repayment; and

(6) other disbursements made by it including the purposes thereof;

all in such categories as the Secretary may prescribe.

(c) Every labor organization required to submit a report under this title shall make available the information required to be contained in such report to all of its members, and every such labor organization and its officers shall be under a duty enforceable at the suit of any member of such organization in any State court of competent jurisdiction or in the district court of the United States for the district in which such labor organization maintains its principal office, to permit such member for just cause to examine any books, records, and accounts necessary to verify such report. The court in such action may, in its discretion, in addition to any judgment awarded to the plaintiff or plaintiffs, allow a reasonable attorney's fee to be paid by the defendant, and costs of the action.

(d) Subsections (f), (g), and (h) of section 9 of the National Labor Relations Act, as amended, are hereby repealed.

(e) Clause (i) of section 8(a)(3) of the National Labor Relations Act, as amended, is amended by striking out the following: "and has at the time the agreement was made or within the preceding twelve months received from the Board a notice of compliance with sections 9 (f), (g), (h)".

Report of Officers and Employees of Labor Organizations [deleted]
(29 U.S.C. 432)

Reports Made Public Information
(29 U.S.C. 435)

Sec. 205. (a)[2] The contents of the reports and documents filed with the Secretary pursuant to sections 201, 202, 203, and 211 shall be public information, and the Secretary may publish any information and data which he obtains pursuant to the provisions of this title. The Secretary may use the information and data for statistical and research purposes, and compile and publish such studies, analyses, reports, and surveys based thereon as he may deem appropriate.

[2] Prior to amendment by section 2(a) of Public Law 89-216, the first sentence of section 205(a) read as follows: "Sec. 205. (a) The contents of the reports and documents filed with the Secretary pursuant to sections 201, 202, and 203 shall be public information, and the Secretary may publish any information and data which he obtains pursuant to the provisions of this title."

Retention of Records
(29 U.S.C. 436)

SEC. 206. Every person required to file any report under this title shall maintain records on the matters required to be reported which will provide in sufficient detail the necessary basic information and data from which the documents filed with the Secretary may be verified, explained or clarified, and checked for accuracy and completeness, and shall include vouchers, worksheets, receipts, and applicable resolutions, and shall keep such records available for examination for a period of not less than five years after the filing of the documents based on the information which they contain.

Criminal Provisions
(29 U.S.C. 439)

SEC. 209. (a) Any person who willfully violates this title shall be fined not more than $10,000 or imprisoned for not more than one year, or both.

(b) Any person who makes a false statement or representation of a material fact, knowing it to be false, or who knowingly fails to disclose a material fact, in any document, report, or other information required under the provisions of this title, shall be fined not more than $10,000 or imprisoned for not more than one year, or both.

(c) Any person who willfully makes a false entry in or willfully conceals, withholds, or destroys any books, records, reports, or statements required to be kept by any provision of this title shall be fined not more than $10,000 or imprisoned for not more than one year, or both.

(d) Each individual required to sign reports under sections 201 and 203 shall be personally responsible for the filing of such reports and for any statement contained therein which he knows to be false.

Civil Enforcement
(29 U.S.C. 440)

SEC. 210. Whenever it shall appear that any person has violated or is about to violate any of the provisions of this title, the Secretary may bring a civil action for such relief (including injunctions) as may be appropriate. Any such action may be brought in the district court of the United States where the violation occurred or, at the option of the parties, in the United States District Court for the District of Columbia.

TITLE III—TRUSTEESHIPS

Purposes for Which a Trusteeship May Be Established
(29 U.S.C. 462)

SEC. 302. Trusteeships shall be established and administered by a labor organization over a subordinate body only in accordance with the constitution and bylaws of the organization which has assumed trusteeship over the subordinate body and for the purpose of correcting corruption or financial malpractice, assuring the performance of collective bargaining agreements or other duties of a bargaining representative, restoring democratic procedures, or otherwise carrying out the legitimate objects of such labor organization.

Unlawful Acts Relating to Labor Organization Under Trusteeship
(29 U.S.C. 463)

SEC. 303. (a) During any period when a subordinate body of a labor organization is in trusteeship, it shall be unlawful (1) to count the vote of delegates from such body in any convention or election of officers of the labor organization unless the delegates have been chosen by secret ballot in an election in which all the members in good standing of such subordinate body were eligible to participate, or (2) to transfer to such organization any current receipts or other funds of the subordinate body except the normal per capita tax and assessments payable by subordinate bodies not in trusteeship: *Provided,* That nothing herein contained shall prevent the distribution of the assets of a labor organization in accordance with its constitution and bylaws upon the bona fide dissolution thereof.

(b) Any person who willfully violates this section shall be fined not more than $10,000 or imprisoned for not more than one year, or both.

Enforcement
(29 U.S.C. 464)

SEC. 304. (a) Upon the written complaint of any member or subordinate body of a labor organization alleging that such organization has violated the provisions of this title (except section 301) the Secretary shall investigate the complaint and if the Secretary finds probable cause to believe that such violation has occurred and has not been remedied he shall, without disclosing the identity of the complainant, bring a civil action in any district court of the United States having jurisdiction of the labor organization for such relief (including injunctions) as may be appropriate. Any member or subordinate body of a labor organization affected by any violation of this title (except section 301) may bring a civil action in any district court of the United States having jurisdiction of the labor organization for such relief (including injunctions) as may be appropriate.

(b) For the purpose of actions under this section, district courts of the United States shall be deemed to have jurisdiction of a labor organization (1) in the district in which the principal office of such labor organization is located, or (2) in any district in which its duly authorized officers or agents are engaged in conducting the affairs of the trusteeship.

(c) In any proceeding pursuant to this section a trusteeship established by a labor organization in conformity with the procedural requirements of its constitution and bylaws and authorized or ratified after a fair hearing either before the executive board or before such other body as may be provided in accordance with its constitution or bylaws shall be presumed valid for a period of eighteen months from the date of its establishment and shall not be subject to attack during such period except upon clear and convincing proof that the trusteeship was not established or maintained in good faith for a purpose allowable under section 302. After the expiration of eighteen months the trusteeship shall be presumed invalid in any such proceeding and its discontinuance shall be decreed unless the labor organization shall show by clear and convincing proof that the continuation of the trusteeship is necessary for a purpose allowable under section 302. In the latter event the court may dismiss the complaint or retain jurisdiction of the cause on such conditions and for such period as it deems appropriate.

Complaint by Secretary
(29 U.S.C. 466)

SEC. 306. The rights and remedies provided by this title shall be in addition to any and all other rights and remedies at law or in equity: *Provided,* That upon

73 Stat. 530.

73 Stat. 532.

73 Stat. 531.

73 Stat. 533.

452

the filing of a complaint by the Secretary the jurisdiction of the district court over such trusteeship shall be exclusive and the final judgment shall be res judicata.

TITLE IV—ELECTIONS

Terms of Office; Election Procedures
(29 U.S.C. 481)

Sec. 401. (a) Every national or international labor organization, except a federation of national or international labor organizations, shall elect its officers not less often than once every five years either by secret ballot among the members in good standing or at a convention of delegates chosen by secret ballot.

(b) Every local labor organization shall elect its officers not less often than once every three years by secret ballot among the members in good standing.

(c) Every national or international labor organization, except a federation of national or international labor organizations, and every local labor organization, and its officers, shall be under a duty, enforceable at the suit of any bona fide candidate for office in such labor organization in the district court of the United States in which such labor organization maintains its principal office, to comply with all reasonable requests of any candidate to distribute by mail or otherwise at the candidate's expense campaign literature in aid of such person's candidacy to all members in good standing of such labor organization and to refrain from discrimination in favor of or against any candidate with respect to the use of lists of members, and whenever such labor organizations or its officers authorize the distribution by mail or otherwise to members of campaign literature on behalf of any candidate or of the labor organization itself with reference to such election, similar distribution at the request of any other bona fide candidate shall be made by such labor organization and its officers, with equal treatment as to the expense of such distribution. Every bona fide candidate shall have the right, once within 30 days prior to an election of a labor organization in which he is a candidate, to inspect a list containing the names and last known addresses of all members of the labor organization who are subject to a collective bargaining agreement requiring membership therein as a condition of employment, which list shall be maintained and kept at the principal office of such labor organization by a designated official thereof. Adequate safeguards to insure a fair election shall be provided, including the right of any candidate to have an observer at the polls and at the counting of the ballots.

(d) Officers of intermediate bodies, such as general committees, system boards, joint boards, or joint councils, shall be elected not less often than once every four years by secret ballot among the members in good standing or by labor organization officers representative of such members who have been elected by secret ballot.

(e) In any election required by this section which is to be held by secret ballot a reasonable opportunity shall be given for the nomination of candidates and every member in good standing shall be eligible to be a candidate and to hold office (subject to section 504 and to reasonable qualifications uniformly imposed) and shall have the right to vote for or otherwise support the candidate or candidates of his choice, without being subject to penalty, discipline, or improper interference or reprisal of any kind by such organization or any member thereof. Not less than fifteen days prior to the election notice thereof shall be mailed to each member at his last known home address. Each member in good standing shall be entitled to one vote. No member whose dues have been withheld by his employer for payment to such organization pursuant to his voluntary authorization provided for in a collective bargaining agreement shall be declared in-

eligible to vote or be a candidate for office in such organization by reason of alleged delay or default in the payment of dues. The votes cast by members of each local labor organization shall be counted, and the results published, separately. The election officials designated in the constitution and bylaws or the secretary, if no other official is designated, shall preserve for one year the ballots and all other records pertaining to the election. The election shall be conducted in accordance with the constitution and bylaws of such organization insofar as they are not inconsistent with the provisions of this title.

(f) When officers are chosen by a convention of delegates elected by secret ballot, the convention shall be conducted in accordance with the constitution and bylaws of the labor organization insofar as they are not inconsistent with the provisions of this title. The officials designated in the constitution and bylaws or the secretary, if no other is designated, shall preserve for one year the credentials of the delegates and all minutes and other records of the convention pertaining to the election of officers.

(g) No moneys received by any labor organization by way of dues, assessment, or similar levy, and no moneys of an employer shall be contributed or applied to promote the candidacy of any person in an election subject to the provisions of this title. Such moneys of a labor organization may be utilized for notices, factual statements of issues not involving candidates, and other expenses necessary for the holding of an election.

(h) If the Secretary, upon application of any member of a local labor organization, finds after hearing in accordance with the Administrative Procedure Act that the constitution and bylaws of such labor organization do not provide an adequate procedure for the removal of an elected officer guilty of serious misconduct, such officer may be removed, for cause shown and after notice and hearing, by the members in good standing voting in a secret ballot conducted by the officers of such labor organization in accordance with its constitution and bylaws insofar as they are not inconsistent with the provisions of this title.

(i) The Secretary shall promulgate rules and regulations prescribing minimum standards and procedures for determining the adequacy of the removal procedures to which reference is made in subsection (h).

Enforcement
(29 U.S.C. 482)

Sec. 402. (a) A member of a labor organization—

(1) who has exhausted the remedies available under the constitution and bylaws of such organization and of any parent body, or

(2) who has invoked such available remedies without obtaining a final decision within three calendar months after their invocation,

may file a complaint with the Secretary within one calendar month thereafter alleging the violation of any provision of section 401 (including violation of the constitution and bylaws of the labor organization pertaining to the election and removal of officers). The challenged election shall be presumed valid pending a final decision thereon (as hereinafter provided) and in the interim the affairs of the organization shall be conducted by the officers elected or in such other manner as its constitution and bylaws may provide.

(b) The Secretary shall investigate such complaint and, if he finds probable cause to believe that a violation of this title has occurred and has not been remedied, he shall, within sixty days after the filing of such complaint, bring a civil action against the labor organization as an entity in the district court of the

73 Stat. 534.

73 Stat. 533.

the United States in which such labor organization maintains its principal office to set aside the invalid election, if any, and to direct the conduct of an election or hearing and vote upon the removal of officers under the supervision of the Secretary and in accordance with the provisions of this title and such rules and regulations as the Secretary may prescribe. The court shall have power to take such action as it deems proper to preserve the assets of the labor organization.

(c) If, upon a preponderance of the evidence after a trial upon the merits, the court finds—

(1) that an election has not been held within the time prescribed by section 401, or

(2) that the violation of section 401 may have affected the outcome of an election,

the court shall declare the election, if any, to be void and direct the conduct of a new election under supervision of the Secretary and, so far as lawful and practicable, in conformity with the constitution and bylaws of the labor organization. The Secretary shall promptly certify to the court the names of the persons elected, and the court shall thereupon enter a decree declaring such persons to be the officers of the labor organization. If the proceeding is for the removal of officers pursuant to subsection (h) of section 401, the Secretary shall certify the results of the vote and the court shall enter a decree declaring whether such persons have been removed as officers of the labor organization.

(d) An order directing an election, dismissing a complaint, or designating elected officers of a labor organization shall be appealable in the same manner as the final judgment in a civil action, but an order directing an election shall not be stayed pending appeal.

Application of Other Laws
(29 U.S.C. 483)

Sec. 403. No labor organization shall be required by law to conduct elections of officers with greater frequency or in a different form or manner than is required by its own constitution or bylaws, except as otherwise provided by this title. Existing rights and remedies to enforce the constitution and bylaws of a labor organization with respect to elections prior to the conduct thereof shall not be affected by the provisions of this title. The remedy provided by this title for challenging an election already conducted shall be exclusive.

TITLE V—SAFEGUARDS FOR LABOR ORGANIZATIONS
Fiduciary Responsibility of Officers of Labor Organizations
(29 U.S.C. 501)

Sec. 501. (a) The officers, agents, shop stewards, and other representatives of a labor organization occupy positions of trust in relation to such organization and its members as a group. It is, therefore, the duty of each such person, taking into account the special problems and functions of a labor organization, to hold its money and property solely for the benefit of the organization and its members and to manage, invest, and expend the same in accordance with its constitution and bylaws and any resolutions of the governing bodies adopted thereunder, to refrain from dealing with such organization as an adverse party or in behalf of an adverse party in any matter connected with his duties and from holding or

73 Stat. 536.

acquiring any pecuniary or personal interest which conflicts with the interests of such organization, and to account to the organization for any profit received by him in whatever capacity in connection with transactions conducted by him or under his direction on behalf of the organization. A general exculpatory provision in the constitution and bylaws of such a labor organization or a general exculpatory resolution of a governing body purporting to relieve any such person of liability for breach of the duties declared by this section shall be void as against public policy.

(b) When any officer, agent, shop steward, or representative of any labor organization is alleged to have violated the duties declared in subsection (a) and the labor organization or its governing board or officers refuse or fail to sue or recover damages or secure an accounting or other appropriate relief within a reasonable time after being requested to do so by any member of the labor organization, such member may sue such officer, agent, shop steward, or representative in any district court of the United States or in any State court of competent jurisdiction to recover damages or secure an accounting or other appropriate relief for the benefit of the labor organization. No such proceeding shall be brought except upon leave of the court obtained upon verified application and for good cause shown which application may be made ex parte. The trial judge may allot a reasonable part of the recovery in any action under this subsection to pay the fees of counsel prosecuting the suit at the instance of the member of the labor organization and to compensate such member for any expenses necessarily paid or incurred by him in connection with the litigation.

(c) Any person who embezzles, steals, or unlawfully and willfully abstracts or converts to his own use, or the use of another, any of the moneys, funds, securities, property, or other assets of a labor organization of which he is an officer, or by which he is employed, directly or indirectly, shall be fined not more than $10,000 or imprisoned for not more than five years, or both.

Making of Loans; Payment of Fines
(29 U.S.C. 503)

Sec. 503. (a) No labor organization shall make directly or indirectly any loan or loans to any officer or employee of such organization which results in a total indebtedness on the part of such officer or employee to the labor organization in excess of $2,000.

(b) No labor organization or employer shall directly or indirectly pay the fine of any officer or employee convicted of any willful violation of this Act.

(c) Any person who willfully violates this section shall be fined not more than $5,000 or imprisoned for not more than one year, or both.

Prohibition Against Certain Persons Holding Office
(29 U.S.C. 504)

Sec. 504. (a) No person who is or has been a member of the Communist Party [8] or who has been convicted of, or served any part of a prison term resulting from his conviction of, robbery, bribery, extortion, embezzlement, grand larceny, burglary, arson, violation of narcotics laws, murder, rape, assault with intent to

[8] The U.S. Supreme Court, on June 7, 1965, held unconstitutional as a bill of attainder the section 504 provision which imposes criminal sanctions on Communist Party members for holding union office (U.S. v. Brown, 381 U.S. 437, 85 S. Ct. 1707).

kill, assault which inflicts grievous bodily injury, or a violation of title II or III of this Act,[9] any felony involving abuse or misuse of such person's position or employment in a labor organization or employee benefit plan to seek or obtain an illegal gain at the expense of the members of the labor organization or the beneficiaries of the employee benefit plan, or conspiracy to commit any such crimes or attempt to commit any such crimes, or a crime in which any of the foregoing crimes is an element, shall serve or be permitted to serve—

73 Stat. 537

(1) as a consultant or adviser to any labor organization,

(2) as an officer, director, trustee, member of any executive board or similar governing body, business agent, manager, organizer, employee, or representative in any capacity of any labor organization,

(3) as a labor relations consultant or adviser to a person engaged in an industry or activity affecting commerce, or as an officer, director, agent, or employee of any group or association of employers dealing with any labor organization, or in a position having specific collective bargaining authority or direct responsibility in the area of labor-management relations in any corporation or association engaged in an industry or activity affecting commerce, or

(4) in a position which entitles its occupant to a share of the proceeds of, or as an officer or executive or administrative employee of, any entity whose activities are in whole or substantial part devoted to providing goods or services to any labor organization, or

(5) in any capacity, other than in his capacity as a member of such labor organization. that involves decisionmaking authority concerning, or decisionmaking authority over, or custody of, or control of the moneys, funds, assets, or property of any labor organization,

during or for the period of thirteen years after such conviction or after the end of such imprisonment, whichever is later, unless the sentencing court on the motion of the person convicted sets a lesser period of at least three years after such conviction or after the end of such imprisonment, whichever is later, or unless prior to the end of such period, in the case of a person so convicted or imprisoned, (A) his citizenship rights, having been revoked as a result of such conviction, have been fully restored, or (B) if the offense is a Federal offense, the sentencing judge or, if the offense is a State or local offense, the United States district court for the district in which the offense was committed, pursuant to sentencing guidelines and policy statements under section 994(a) of title 28, United States Code, determines that such person's service in any capacity referred to in clauses (1) through (5) would not be contrary to the purposes of this Act. Prior to making any such determination the court shall hold a hearing and shall give notice of such proceeding by certified mail to the Secretary of Labor and to State, county, and Federal prosecuting officials in the jurisdiction or jurisdictions in which such person was convicted. The court's determination in any such proceeding shall be final. No person shall knowingly hire, retain, employ, or otherwise place any other person to serve in any capacity in violation of this subsection.

(b) Any person who willfully violates this section shall be fined not more than $10,000 or imprisoned for not more than five years, or both.

[9] The following text shows changes made by Public Law 98-473, Oct. 12, 1984, 98 Stat. 2031, 2133, 2134, and by Public Law 100-182, Dec. 7, 1987, 101 Stat. 1266, 1268. Public Law 99-217, Dec. 26, 1985, 99 Stat. 1728, changed the effective date for the amendment made by Public Law 98-473, 98 Stat. 2031, from Nov. 1, 1986, to Nov. 1, 1987; Public Law 100-182, 101 Stat. 1266, made that amendment applicable only to crimes committed after Nov. 1, 1987.

(c) For the purpose of this section—

(1) A person shall be deemed to have been "convicted" and under the disability of "conviction" from the date of the judgment of the trial court, regardless of whether that judgment remains under appeal.

(2) A period of parole shall not be considered as part of a period of imprisonment.

(d) Whenever any person—

(1) by operation of this section, has been barred from office or other position in a labor organization as a result of a conviction, and

(2) has filed an appeal of that conviction,

any salary which would be otherwise due such person by virtue of such office or position, shall be placed in escrow by the individual employer or organization responsible for payment of such salary. Payment of such salary into escrow shall continue for the duration of the appeal or for the period of time during which such salary would be otherwise due, whichever period is shorter. Upon the final reversal of such person's conviction on appeal, the amounts in escrow shall be paid to such person. Upon the final sustaining of such person's conviction on appeal, the amounts in escrow shall be returned to the individual employer or organization responsible for payments of those amounts. Upon final reversal of such person's conviction, such person shall no longer be barred by this statute from assuming any position from which such person was previously barred.

73 Stat. 537

Extortionate Picketing
(29 U.S.C. 522)

SEC. 602. (a) It shall be unlawful to carry on picketing on or about the premises of any employer for the purpose of, or as part of any conspiracy or in furtherance of any plan or purpose for, the personal profit or enrichment of any individual (except a bona fide increase in wages or other employee benefits) by taking or obtaining any money or other thing of value from such employer against his will or with his consent.

(b) Any person who willfully violates this section shall be fined not more than $10,000 or imprisoned not more than twenty years, or both.

73 Stat. 540. 29 U.S.C. 522.

Retention of Rights Under Other Federal and State Laws
(29 U.S.C. 523)

SEC. 603. (a) Except as explicitly provided to the contrary, nothing in this Act shall reduce or limit the responsibilities of any labor organization or any officer, agent, shop steward, or other representative of a labor organization, or of any trust in which a labor organization is interested, under any other Federal law or under the laws of any State, and, except as explicitly provided to the contrary, nothing in this Act shall take away any right or bar any remedy to which members of a labor organization are entitled under such other Federal law or law of any State.

(b) Nothing contained in titles I, II, III, IV, V, or VI of this Act shall be construed to supersede or impair or otherwise affect the provisions of the Railway Labor Act, as amended, or any of the obligations, rights, benefits, privileges, or immunities of any carrier, employee, organization, representative, or person subject thereto; nor shall anything contained in said titles (except section 505) of this Act be construed to confer any rights, privileges, immunities, or defenses upon employers, or to impair or otherwise affect the rights of any person under the National Labor Relations Act, as amended.

44 Stat. 577; 45 U.S.C. 151.

61 Stat. 136; 29 U.S.C. 167

Effect on State Laws
(29 U.S.C. 524)

Sec. 604. Nothing in this Act shall be construed to impair or diminish the authority of any State to enact and enforce general criminal laws with respect to robbery, bribery, extortion, embezzlement, grand larceny, burglary, arson, violation of narcotics laws, murder, rape, assault with intent to kill, or assault which inflicts grievous bodily injury, or conspiracy to commit any of such crimes.

Criminal Contempt
(29 U.S.C. 528)

Sec. 608. No person shall be punished for any criminal contempt allegedly committed outside the immediate presence of the court in connection with any civil action prosecuted by the Secretary or any other person in any court of the United States under the provisions of this Act unless the facts constituting such criminal contempt are established by the verdict of the jury in a proceeding in the district court of the United States, which jury shall be chosen and empaneled in the manner prescribed by the law governing trial juries in criminal prosecutions in the district courts of the United States.

Prohibition on Certain Discipline by Labor Organization
(29 U.S.C. 529)

Sec. 609. It shall be unlawful for any labor organization, or any officer, agent, shop steward, or other representative of a labor organization, or any employee thereof to fine, suspend, expel, or otherwise discipline any of its members for exercising any right to which he is entitled under the provisions of this Act. The provisions of section 102 shall be applicable in the enforcement of this section.

Deprivation of Rights Under Act by Violence
(29 U.S.C. 530)

Sec. 610. It shall be unlawful for any person through the use of force or violence, or threat of the use of force or violence, to restrain, coerce, or intimidate, or attempt to restrain, coerce, or intimidate any member of a labor organization for the purpose of interfering with or preventing the exercise of any right to which he is entitled under the provisions of this Act. Any person who willfully violates this section shall be fined not more than $1,000 or imprisoned for not more than one year, or both.

TITLE VII OF THE CIVIL RIGHTS ACT OF 1964, AS AMENDED

An Act

To enforce the constitutional right to vote, to confer jurisdiction upon the district courts of the United States to provide injunctive relief against discrimination in public accommodations, to authorize the Attorney General to institute suits to protect constitutional rights in public facilities and public education, to extend the Commission on Civil Rights, to prevent discrimination in federally assisted programs, to establish a Commission on Equal Employment Opportunity, and for other purposes.

Be it enacted by the Senate and House of Representatives of the United States of America in Congress assembled, That this Act may be cited as the "Civil Rights Act of 1964".

* * * * *

TITLE VII—EQUAL EMPLOYMENT OPPORTUNITY [1]

DEFINITIONS

SEC. 701. For the purposes of this title—

(a) The term "person" includes one or more individuals, *governments, governmental agencies, political subdivisions,* labor unions, partnerships, associations, corporations, legal representatives, mutual companies, joint-stock companies, trusts, unincorporated organizations, trustees, trustees in bankruptcy, or receivers.

(b) The term "employer" means a person engaged in an industry affecting commerce who has *fifteen* or more employees for each working day in each of twenty or more calendar weeks in the current or preceding calendar year, and any agent of such a person, but such term does not include (1) the United States, a corporation wholly owned by the Government of the United States, an Indian tribe, or *any department or agency of the District of Columbia subject by statute to procedures of the competitive service (as defined in section 2102 of title 5 of the United States Code), or* (2) a bona fide private membership club (other than a labor organization) which is exempt from taxation under section 501(c) of the Internal Revenue Code of 1954, *except that during the first year after the date of enactment of the Equal Employment Opportunity Act of 1972,* persons having fewer than *twenty-five* employees (and their agents) shall not be considered *employers.*

(c) The term "employment agency" means any person regularly undertaking with or without compensation to procure employees for an employer or to procure for employees opportunities to work for an employer and includes an agent of such a person.

(d) The term "labor organization" means a labor organization engaged in an industry affecting commerce, and any agent of such an organization, and includes any organization of any kind, any agency, or employee representation committee, group, association, or plan so engaged in which employees participate and which exists for the purpose, in whole or in part, of dealing with employers concerning grievances, labor disputes, wages, rates of pay, hours, or other terms or conditions of employment, and any conference, general committee, joint or system board, or joint council so engaged which is subordinate to a national or international labor organization.

(e) A labor organization shall be deemed to be engaged in an industry affecting commerce if (1) it maintains or operates a hiring hall or hiring office which procures employees for an employer or procures for employees opportunities to work for an employer, or (2) the number of its members (or, where it is a labor organization composed of other labor organizations or their representatives, if the aggregate number of the members of such other labor organization) is (A) *twenty-five* or more during the first year after the *date of enactment of the Equal Employment Opportunity Act of 1972, or* (B) *fifteen* or more thereafter, and such labor organization—

(1) is the certified representative of employees under the provisions of the National Labor Relations Act, as amended, or the Railway Labor Act, as amended;

(2) although not certified, is a national or international labor organization or a local labor organization recognized or acting as the representative of employees of an employer or employers engaged in an industry affecting commerce; or

(3) has chartered a local labor organization or subsidiary body which is representing or actively seeking to represent employees within the meaning of paragraph (1) or (2); or

(4) has been chartered by a labor organization representing or actively seeking to represent employees within the meaning of paragraph (1) or (2) as the local or subordinate body through which such employees may enjoy membership or become affiliated with such labor organization; or

(5) is a conference, general committee, joint or system board, or joint council subordinate to a national or international labor organization, which includes a labor organization engaged in an industry affecting commerce within the

---

[1] Includes 1972 amendments, made by P.L. 92-261 printed in Italic.

meaning of any of the preceding paragraphs of this subsection.

(f) The term "employee" means an individual employed by an employer, *except that the term 'employee' shall not include any person elected to public office in any State or political subdivision of any State by the qualified voters thereof, or any person chosen by such officer to be on such officer's personal staff, or an appointee on the policymaking level or an immediate adviser with respect to the exercise of the constitutional or legal powers of the office. The exemption set forth in the preceding sentence shall not include employees subject to the civil service laws of a State government, governmental agency or political subdivision.*

(g) The term "commerce" means trade, traffic, commerce, transportation, transmission, or communication among the several States; or between a State and any place outside thereof; or within the District of Columbia, or a possession of the United States; or between points in the same State but through a point outside thereof.

(h) The term "industry affecting commerce" means any activity, business, or industry in commerce or in which a labor dispute would hinder or obstruct commerce or the free flow of commerce and includes any activity or industry "affecting commerce" within the meaning of the Labor-Management Reporting and Disclosure Act of 1959, *and further includes any governmental industry, business, or activity.*

(i) The term "State" includes a State of the United States, the District of Columbia, Puerto Rico, the Virgin Islands, American Samoa, Guam, Wake Island, the Canal Zone, and Outer Continental Shelf lands defined in the Outer Continental Shelf Lands Act.

(j) The term "religion" includes all aspects of religious observance and practice, as well as belief, unless an employer demonstrates that he is unable to reasonably accommodate to an employee's or prospective employee's, religious observance or practice without undue hardship on the conduct of the employer's business.

"(k) The terms, 'because of sex' or 'on the basis of sex' include, but are not limited to, because of or on the basis of pregnancy, childbirth or related medical conditions; and women affected by pregnancy, childbirth, or related medical conditions shall be treated the same for all employment-related purposes, including receipt of benefits under fringe benefit programs, as other persons not so affected but similar in their ability or inability to work, and nothing in section 703(h) of this title shall be interpreted to permit otherwise. This subsection shall not require an employer to pay for health insurance benefits for abortion, except where the life of the mother would be endangered if the fetus were carried to term, or except where medical complications have arisen from an abortion: Provided, That nothing herein shall preclude an employer from providing abortion benefits or otherwise affect bargaining agreements in regard to abortion".

EXEMPTION

Sec. 702. This title shall not apply to an employer with respect to the employment of aliens outside any State, or to a religious corporation, association, *educational institution,* or society with respect to the employment of individuals of a particular religion to perform work connected with the carrying on by such corporation, association, *educational institution,* or society of its *activities.*

DISCRIMINATION BECAUSE OF RACE, COLOR, RELIGION, SEX, OR NATIONAL ORIGIN

Sec. 703. (a) It shall be an unlawful employment practice for an employer—

(1) to fail or refuse to hire or to discharge any individual, or otherwise to discriminate against any individual with respect to his compensation, terms, conditions, or privileges of employment, because of such individual's race, color, religion, sex, or national origin; or

(2) to limit, segregate, or classify his employees *or applicants for employment* in any way which would deprive or tend to deprive any individual of employment opportunities or otherwise adversely affect his status as an employee, because of such individual's race, color, religion, sex, or national origin.

(b) It shall be an unlawful employment practice for an employment agency to fail or refuse to refer for employment, or otherwise to discriminate against, any individual because of his race, color, religion, sex, or national origin, or to classify or refer for employment any individual on the basis of his race, color, religion, sex, or national origin.

(c) It shall be an unlawful employment practice for a labor organization—

(1) to exclude or to expel from its membership, or otherwise to discriminate against, any individual because of his race, color, religion, sex, or national origin;

(2) to limit, segregate, or classify its membership, *or applicants for membership* or to classify or fail or refuse to refer for employment any individual, in any way which would deprive or tend to deprive any individual of employment opportunities, or would limit such employment opportunities or otherwise adversely affect his status as an employee or as an applicant for employment, because of such individual's race, color, religion, sex, or national origin; or

(3) to cause or attempt to cause an employer to discriminate against an individual in violation of this section.

(d) It shall be an unlawful employment practice for any employer, labor organization, or joint labor-management committee controlling apprenticeship or other training or retraining, including on-the-job training programs to discriminate against any individual because of his race, color, religion, sex, or national origin in admission to, or employment in, any program established to provide apprenticeship or other training.

(e) Notwithstanding any other provision of this title, (1) it shall not be an unlawful employment practice for an employer to hire and employ employees, for an employment agency to classify, or refer for employment any individual, for a labor organization to classify its membership or to classify or refer for employment any individual, or for an employer, labor organization, or joint labor-management committee controlling apprenticeship or other training or retraining programs to admit or employ any individual in any such program, on the basis of his religion, sex, or national origin in those certain instances where religion, sex, or national origin is a bona fide occupational qualification reasonably necessary to the normal operation of that particular business or enterprise, and (2) it shall not be an unlawful employment practice for a school, college, university, or other education institution or institution of learning to hire and employ employees of a particular religion if such school, college, university, or other educational institution or institution of learning is, in whole or in substantial part, owned, supported, controlled, or managed by a particular religion or by a particular religious corporation, association, or society, or if the curriculum of such school, college, university, or other educational institution or institution of learning is directed toward the propagation of a particular religion.

(f) As used in this title, the phrase "unlawful employment practice" shall not be deemed to include any action or measure taken by an employer, labor organization, joint labor-management committee, or employment agency with respect to an individual who is a member of the Communist Party of the United States or of any other organization required to register as a Communist-action or Communist-front organization by final order of the Subversive Activities Control Board pursuant to the Subversive Activities Control Act of 1950.

(g) Notwithstanding any other provision of this title, it shall not be an unlawful employment practice for an employer to fail or refuse to hire and employ any individual for any position, for an employer to discharge any individual from any position, or for an employment agency to fail or refuse to refer any individual for employment in any position, or for a labor organization to fail or refuse to refer any individual for employment in any position, if—

(1) the occupancy of such position, or access to the premises in or upon which any part of the duties of such position is performed or is to be performed, is subject to any requirement imposed in the interest of the national security of the United States under any security program in effect pursuant to or administered under any statute of the United States or any Executive order of the President; and

(2) such individual has not fulfilled or has ceased to fulfill that requirement.

(h) Notwithstanding any other provision of this title, it shall not be an unlawful employment practice for an employer to apply different standards of compensation, or different terms, conditions, or privileges of employment pursuant to a bona fide seniority or merit system, or a system which measures earnings by quantity or quality of production or to employees who work in different locations, provided that such differences are not the result of an intention to discriminate because of race, color, religion, sex, or national origin, or shall it be an unlawful employment practice for an employer to give and to act upon the results of any professionally developed ability test provided that such test, its administration or action upon the results is not designed, intended or used to discriminate because of race, color, religion, sex, or national origin. It shall not be an unlawful employment practice under this title for any employer to differentiate upon the basis of sex in determining the amount of the wages or compensation paid or to be paid to employees of such employer if such differentiation is authorized by the provisions of section 6(d) of the Fair Labor Standards Act of 1938, as amended (29 U.S.C. 206(d)).

(i) Nothing contained in this title shall apply to any business or enterprise on or near an Indian reservation with respect to any publicly announced employment practice of such business or enterprise under which a preferential treatment is given to any individual because he is an Indian living on or near a reservation.

(j) Nothing contained in this title shall be interpreted to require any employer, employment agency, labor organization, or joint labor-management committee subject to this title to grant preferential treatment to any individual or to any group because of the race, color, religion, sex, or national origin of such individual or group on account of an imbalance which may exist with respect to the total number or percentage of persons of any race, color, religion, sex, or national origin employed by any employer, referred or classified for employment by any employment agency or labor organization, admitted to membership or classified by any labor organization, or admitted to, or employed in, any apprenticeship or other training program, in comparison with the total number or percentage of persons of such race, color, religion, sex, or national origin in any community, State, section, or other area, or in the available work force in any community, State, section, or other area.

OTHER UNLAWFUL EMPLOYMENT PRACTICES

SEC. 704. (a) It shall be an unlawful employment practice for an employer to discriminate against any of his employees or applicants for employment, for an employment agency, *or joint labor-management committee controlling apprenticeship or other training or retraining, including on-the-job training programs,* to discriminate against any individual, or for a labor organization to discriminate against any member thereof or applicant for membership, because he has opposed any practice made an unlawful employment practice by this title, or because he has made a charge, testified, assisted, or participated in any manner in an investigation, proceeding, or hearing under this title.

(b) It shall be an unlawful employment practice for an employer, labor organization, employment *agency, or joint labor-management committee controlling apprenticeship or other training or retraining, including on-the-job training programs,* to print or publish or cause to be printed or published any notice or advertisement relating to employment by such an employer or membership in or any classification or referral for employment by such a labor organization, or relating to any classification or referral for employment by such an *employment agency, or relating to admission to, or employment in, any program established to provide apprenticeship or other training by such a joint labor-management committee* indicating any preference, limitation, specification, or discrimination, based on race, color, religion, sex, or national origin, except that such a notice or advertisement may indicate a preference, limitation, specification, or discrimination based on religion, sex, or national origin when religion, sex, or national origin is a bona fide occupational qualification for employment.

EQUAL EMPLOYMENT OPPORTUNITY COMMISSION

SEC. 705. (a) There is hereby created a Commission to be known as the Equal Employment Opportunity Commission, which shall be composed of five members, not more than three of whom shall be members of the same political party. *Members of the Commission shall be appointed by the President by and with the advice and consent of the Senate for a term of five years. Any individual chosen to fill a vacancy shall be appointed only for the unexpired term of the member whom he shall succeed, and all members of the Commission shall continue to serve until their successors are appointed and qualified, except that no such member of the Commission shall continue to serve (1) for more than sixty days when the Congress is in session unless a nomination to fill such vacancy shall have been submitted to the Senate, or (2) after the adjournment sine die of the session of the Senate in which such nomination was submitted.* The President shall designate one member to serve as Chairman of the Commission, and one member to serve as Vice Chairman. The Chairman shall be responsible on behalf of the Commission for the administrative operations of the Commission, and *except as provided in subsection (b),* shall appoint, in accordance with the *provisions of title 5, United States Code, governing appointments in the competitive service, such officers, agents, attorneys, hearing examiners, and employees as he deems necessary to assist it in the performance of its functions and to fix their compensation in accordance with the provisions of chapter 51 and subchapter III of chapter 53 of title 5, United States Code, relating to classification and General Schedule pay rates: Provided, That assignment, removal, and compensation of hearing examiners shall be in accordance with sections 3105, 3344, 5362, and 7521 of title 5, United States Code.*

(b)(1) There shall be a General Counsel of the Commission appointed by the President, by and with the advice and consent of the Senate, for a term of four years. The General Counsel shall have responsibility for the conduct of litigation as provided in sections 706 and 707 of this title. The General Counsel shall have such other duties as the Commission may prescribe or as may be provided by law and shall concur with the Chairman of the Commission on the appointment and supervision of regional attorneys. The General Counsel of the Commission on the effective date of this Act shall continue in such position and perform the functions specified in this subsection until a successor is appointed and qualified.

(2) Attorneys appointed under this section may, at the direction of the Commission, appear for and represent the Commission in any case in court, provided that the Attorney General shall conduct all litigation to which the Commission is a party in the Supreme Court pursuant to this title.

(c) A vacancy in the Commission shall not impair the right of the remaining members to exercise all the powers of the Commission and three members thereof shall constitute a quorum.

(d) The Commission shall have an official seal which shall be judicially noticed.

(e) The Commission shall at the close of each fiscal year report to the Congress and to the President concerning the action it has taken; the names, salaries, and duties of all individuals in its employ and the moneys it has disbursed; and shall make such further reports on the cause of and means of eliminating discrimination and such recommendations for further legislation as may appear desirable.

(f) The principal office of the Commission shall be in or near the District of Columbia, but it may meet or exercise any or all its powers at any other place. The Commission may establish such regional or State offices as it deems necessary to accomplish the purpose of this title.

(g) The Commission shall have power—

(1) to cooperate with and, with their consent, utilize regional State, local, and other agencies, both public and private, and individuals;

(2) to pay to witnesses whose depositions are taken or who are summoned before the Commission or any of its agents the same witness and mileage fees as are paid to witnesses in the courts of the United States;

(3) to furnish to persons subject to this title such technical assistance as they may request to further their compliance with this title or an order issued thereunder;

(4) upon the request of (i) any employer, whose employees or some of them, or (ii) any labor organization, whose members or some of them, refuse or threaten to refuse to cooperate in effectuating the provisions of this title, to assist in such effectuation by conciliation or such other remedial action as is provided by this title;

(5) to make such technical studies as are appropriate to effectuate the purposes and policies

of this title and to make the results of such studies available to the public;

(6) to *intervene* in a civil action brought *under section 706* by an aggrieved party *against a respondent other than a government, governmental agency, or political subdivision.*

(*h*) The Commission shall, in any of its educational or promotional activities, cooperate with other departments and agencies in the performance of such educational and promotional activites.

(*i*) All officers, agents, attorneys, and employees of the Commission shall be subject to the provisions of section 9 of the Act of August 2, 1939, as amended (the Hatch Act), notwithstanding any exemption contained in such section.

PREVENTION OF UNLAWFUL EMPLOYMENT PRACTICES

SEC. 706. (*a*) *The Commission is empowered, as hereinafter provided, to prevent any person from engaging in any unlawful employment practice as set forth in section 703 or 704 of this title.*

(*b*) Whenever *a charge is filed by or on behalf of a* person claiming to be aggrieved, or by a member of the Commission, *alleging* that an employer, employment agency, labor *organization, or joint labor-management committee controlling apprenticeship or other training or retraining, including on-the-job training programs,* has engaged in an unlawful employment practice, the Commission shall *serve a notice of the charge (including the date, place and circumstances of the alleged unlawful employment practice) on* such employer, employment agency, labor *organization, or joint labor-management committee* (hereinafter referred to as the "respondent") *within ten days, and shall make an investigation thereof. Charges shall be in writing under oath or affirmation and shall contain such information and be in such form as the Commission requires. Charges* shall not be made public by the Commission. If the Commission *determines* after such investigation that there is *not* reasonable cause to believe that the charge is true, *it shall dismiss the charge and promptly notify the person claiming to be aggrieved and the respondent of its action. In determining whether reasonable cause exists, the Commission shall accord substantial weight to final findings and orders made by State or local authorities in proceedings commenced under State or local law pursuant to the requirements of subsections (c) and (d). If the Commission determines after such investigation that there is reasonable cause to believe that the charge is true,* the Commission shall endeavor to eliminate any such alleged unlawful employment practice by informal methods of conference, conciliation, and persuasion. Nothing said or done during and as a part of such *informal* endeavors may be made public by the *Commission, its officers or employees, or used as evidence in a subsequent proceeding* without the written consent of the *persons concerned.* Any *person who makes* public information in violation of this subsection shall be fined not more than $1,000 or imprisoned *for* not more than one *year, or both. The*

Commission shall make its determination on reasonable cause as promptly as possible and, so far as practicable, not later than one hundred and twenty days from the filing of the charge or, where applicable under subsection (c) or (d) from the date upon which the Commission is authorized to take action with respect to the charge.

(*c*) In the case of an alleged unlawful employment practice occurring in a State, or political subdivision of a State, which has a State or local law prohibiting the unlawful employment practice alleged and establishing or authorizing a State or local authority to grant or seek relief from such practice or to institute criminal proceedings with respect thereto upon receiving notice thereof, no charge may be filed under subsection (a) by the person aggrieved before the expiration of sixty days after proceedings have been commenced under the State or local law, unless such proceedings have been earlier terminated, provided that such sixty-day period shall be extended to one hundred and twenty days during the first year after the effective date of such State or local law. If any requirement for the commencement of such proceedings is imposed by a State or local authority other than a requirement of the filing of a written and signed statement of the facts upon which the proceeding is based, the proceeding shall be deemed to have been commenced for the purposes of this subsection at the time such statement is sent by registered mail to the appropriate State or local authority.

(*d*) In the case of any charge filed by a member of the Commission alleging an unlawful employment practice occurring in a State or political subdivision of a State which has a State or local law prohibiting the practice alleged and establishing or authorizing a State or local authority to grant or seek relief from such practice or to institute criminal proceedings with respect thereto upon receiving notice thereof, the Commission shall, before taking any action with respect to such charge, notify the appropriate State or local officials and, upon request, afford them a reasonable time, but not less than sixty days (provided that such sixty-day period shall be extended to one hundred and twenty days during the first year after the effective *date* of such State or local law), unless a shorter period is requested, to act under such State or local law to remedy the practice alleged.

(*e*) A charge under *this section* shall be filed within *one hundred and eighty* days after the alleged unlawful employment practice *occurred and notice of the charge (including the date, place and circumstances of the alleged unlawful employment practice) shall be served upon the person against whom such charge is made within ten days thereafter,* except that in *a* case of an unlawful employment practice with respect to which the person aggrieved has *initially instituted proceedings with a State or local agency with authority to grant or seek relief from such practice or to institute criminal proceedings with respect thereto upon receiving notice thereof,* such charge shall be

461

filed by *or on behalf of* the person aggrieved within *three hundred* days after the alleged unlawful employment practice occurred, or within thirty days after receiving notice that the State or local agency has terminated the proceedings under the State or local law, whichever is earlier, and a copy of such charge shall be filed by the Commission with the State or local agency.

(f)(1) If within thirty days after a charge is filed with the Commission or within thirty days after expiration of any period of reference under subsection (c) or (d), the Commission has been unable to secure from the respondent a conciliation agreement acceptable to the Commission, the Commission may bring a civil action against any respondent not a government, governmental agency, or political subdivision named in the charge. In the case of a respondent which is a government, governmental agency, or political subdivision, if the Commission has been unable to secure from the respondent a conciliation agreement acceptable to the Commission, the Commission shall take no further action and shall refer the case to the Attorney General who may bring a civil action against such respondent in the appropriate United States district court. The person or persons aggrieved shall have the right to intervene in a civil action brought by the Commission or the Attorney General in a case involving a government, governmental agency, or political subdivision. If a charge filed with the Commission pursuant to subsection (b) is dismissed by the Commission, or if within one hundred and eighty days from the filing of such charge or the expiration of any period of reference under subsection (c) or (d), whichever is later, the Commission has not filed a civil action under this section or the Attorney General has notified a civil action in a case involving a government, governmental agency, or political subdivision, or the Commission has not entered into a conciliation agreement to which the person aggrieved is a party, the Commission, or the Attorney General in a case involving a government, governmental agency, or political subdivision, shall so notify the person aggrieved and within ninety days after the giving of such notice a civil action may be brought against the respondent named in the charge (A) by the person claiming to be aggrieved, or (B) if such charge was filed by a member of the Commission, by any person whom the charge alleges was aggrieved by the alleged unlawful employment practice. Upon application by the complainant and in such circumstances as the court may deem just, the court may appoint an attorney for such complainant and may authorize the commencement of the action without the payment of fees, costs, or security. Upon timely application, the court may, in its discretion, permit the *Commission,* or the Attorney General in a case involving a government, governmental agency, or political subdivision, to intervene in such civil action *upon certification* that the case is of general public importance. Upon request, the court may, in its discretion, stay further proceedings for not more than sixty days pending the termination of State or local proceedings described in subsections *(c) or (d) of this section or further* efforts of the Commission to obtain voluntary compliance.

(2) Whenever a charge is filed with the Commission and the Commission concludes on the basis of a preliminary investigation that prompt judicial action is necessary to carry out the purposes of this Act, the Commission, or the Attorney General in a case involving a government, governmental agency, or political subdivision, may bring an action for appropriate temporary or preliminary relief pending final disposition of such charge. Any temporary restraining order or other order granting preliminary or temporary relief shall be issued in accordance with rule 65 of the Federal Rules of Civil Procedure. It shall be the duty of a court having jurisdiction over proceedings under this section to assign cases for hearing at the earliest practicable date and to cause such cases to be in every way expedited.

(3) Each United States district court and each United States court of a place subject to the jurisdiction of the United States shall have jurisdiction of actions brought under this title. Such an action may be brought in any judicial district in the State in which the unlawful employment practice is alleged to have been committed, in the judicial district in which the employment records relevant to such practice are maintained and administered, or in the judicial district in which the aggrieved person would have worked but for the alleged unlawful employment practice, but if the respondent is not found within any such district, such an action may be brought within the judicial district in which the respondent has his principal office. For purposes of sections 1404 and 1406 of title 28 of the United States Code, the judicial district in which the respondent has his principal office shall in all cases be considered a district in which the action might have been brought.

(4) It shall be the duty of the chief judge of the district (or in his absence, the acting chief judge) in which the case is pending immediately to designate a judge in such district to hear and determine the case. In the event that no judge in the district is available to hear and determine the case, the chief judge of the district, or the acting chief judge, as the case may be, shall certify this fact to the chief judge of the circuit (or in his absence, the acting chief judge) who shall then designate a district or circuit judge of the circuit to hear and determine the case.

(5) It shall be the duty of the judge designated pursuant to this subsection to assign the case for hearing at the earliest practicable date and to cause the case to be in every way expedited. If such judge has not scheduled the case for trial within one hundred and twenty days after issue has been joined, that judge may appoint a master pursuant to rule 53 of the Federal Rules of Civil Procedure.

(g) If the court finds that the respondent has intentionally engaged in or is intentionally engaging in an unlawful employment practice charged in the complaint, the court may enjoin the respondent from engaging in such unlawful employment practice, and

order such affirmative action as may be appropriate, which may include, but is not limited to, reinstatement or hiring of employees, with or without back pay (payable by the employer, employment agency, or labor organization, as the case may be, responsible for the unlawful employment practice), or any other equitable relief as the court deems appropriate. Back pay liability shall not accrue from a date more than two years prior to the filing of a charge with the Commission. Interim earnings or amounts earnable with reasonable diligence by the person or persons discriminated against shall operate to reduce the back pay otherwise allowable. No order of the court shall require the admission or reinstatement of an individual as a member of a union, or the hiring, reinstatement, or promotion of an individual as an employee, or the payment to him of any back pay, if such individual was refused admission, suspended, or expelled, or was refused employment or advancement or was suspended or discharged for any reason other than discrimination on account of race, color, religion, sex, or national origin or in violation of section 704(a).

(h) The provisions of the Act entitled "An Act to amend the Judicial Code and to define and limit the jurisdiction of courts sitting in equity, and for other purposes," approved March 23, 1932 (29 U.S.C. 101–115), shall not apply with respect to civil actions brought under this section.

(i) In any case in which an employer, employment agency, or labor organization fails to comply with an order of a court issued in a civil action brought under this section, the Commission may commence proceedings to compel compliance with such order.

(j) Any civil action brought under this section and any proceedings brought under subsection (i) shall be subject to appeal as provided in sections 1291 and 1292, title 28, United States Code.

(k) In any action or proceeding under this title the court, in its discretion, may allow the prevailing party, other than the Commission or the United States, a reasonable attorney's fee as part of the costs, and the Commission and the United States shall be liable for costs the same as a private person.

SEC. 707. (a) Whenever the Attorney General has reasonable cause to believe that any person or group of persons is engaged in a pattern or practice of resistance to the full enjoyment of any of the rights secured by this title, and that the pattern or practice is of such a nature and is intended to deny the full exercise of the rights herein described, the Attorney General may bring a civil action in the appropriate district court of the United States by filing with it a complaint (1) signed by him (or in his absence the Acting Attorney General), (2) setting forth facts pertaining to such pattern or practice, and (3) requesting such relief, including an application for a permanent or temporary injunction, restraining order or other order against the person or persons responsible for such pattern or practice, as he deems necessary to insure the full enjoyment of the rights herein described.

(b) The district courts of the United States shall have and shall exercise jurisdiction of proceedings instituted pursuant to this section, and in any such proceeding the Attorney General may file with the clerk of such court a request that a court of three judges be convened to hear and determine the case. Such request by the Attorney General shall be accompanied by a certificate that, in his opinion, the case is of general public importance. A copy of the certificate and request for a three-judge court shall be immediately furnished by such clerk to the chief judge of the circuit (or in his absence, the presiding circuit judge of the circuit) in which the case is pending. Upon receipt of such request it shall be the duty of the chief judge of the circuit or the presiding circuit judge, as the case may be, to designate immediately three judges in such circuit, of whom at least one shall be a circuit judge and another of whom shall be a district judge of the court in which the proceeding was instituted, to hear and determine such case, and it shall be the duty of the judges so designated to assign the case for hearing at the earliest practicable date, to participate in the hearing and determination thereof, and to cause the case to be in every way expedited. An appeal from the final judgment of such court will lie to the Supreme Court.

In the event the Attorney General fails to file such a request in any such proceeding, it shall be the duty of the chief judge of the district (or in his absence, the acting chief judge) in which the case is pending immediately to designate a judge in such district to hear and determine the case. In the event that no judge in the district is available to hear and determine the case, the chief judge of the district, or the acting chief judge, as the case may be, shall certify this fact to the chief judge of the circuit (or in his absence, the acting chief judge) who shall then designate a district or circuit judge of the circuit to hear and determine the case.

It shall be the duty of the judge designated pursuant to this section to assign the case for hearing at the earliest practicable date and to cause the case to be in every way expedited.

(c) Effective two years after the date of enactment of the Equal Employment Opportunity Act of 1972, the functions of the Attorney General under this section shall be transferred to the Commission, together with such personnel, property, records, and unexpended balances of appropriations, allocations, and other funds employed, used, held, available, or to be made available in connection with such functions unless the President submits, and neither House of Congress vetoes, a reorganization plan pursuant to chapter 9, of title 5, United States Code, inconsistent with the provisions of this subsection. The Commission shall carry out such functions in accordance with subsections (d) and (e) of this section.

(d) Upon the transfer of functions provided for in subsection (c) of this section, in all suits commenced pursuant to this section prior to the date of such transfer, proceedings shall continue without abatement, *all court orders and decrees shall remain in effect, and the Commission shall be substituted as a party for the United States of America, the Attorney General, or the Acting Attorney General, as appropriate.*

(e) Subsequent to the date of enactment of the Equal Employment Opportunity Act of 1972, the Commission shall have authority to investigate and act on a charge of a pattern or practice of discrimination, whether filed by or on behalf of a person claiming to be aggrieved or by a member of the Commission. All such actions shall be conducted in accordance with the procedures set forth in section 706 of this Act.

EFFECT ON STATE LAWS

SEC. 708. Nothing in this title shall be deemed to exempt or relieve any person from any liability, duty, penalty, or punishment provided by any present or future law of any State or political subdivision of a State, other than any such law which purports to require or permit the doing of any act which would be an unlawful employment practice under this title.

VETERANS' PREFERENCE

SEC. 712. Nothing contained in this title shall be construed to repeal or modify any Federal, State, territorial, or local law creating special rights or preference for veterans.

RULES AND REGULATIONS

SEC. 713. (a) The Commission shall have authority from time to time to issue, amend, or rescind suitable procedural regulations to carry out the provisions of this title. Regulations issued under the section shall be in conformity with the standards and limitations of the Administrative Procedure Act.

(b) In any action or proceeding based on any alleged unlawful employment practice, no person shall be subject to any liability or punishment for or on account of (1) the commission by such person of an unlawful employment practice if he pleads and proves that the act or omission complained of was in good faith, in conformity with, and in reliance on any written interpretation or opinion of the Commission, or (2) the failure of such person to publish and file any information required by any provision of this title if he pleads and proves that he failed to publish and file such information in good faith, in conformity with the instructions of the Commission issued under this title regarding the filing of such information. Such a defense, if established, shall be a bar to the action or proceeding, notwithstanding that (A) after such act or omission, such interpretation or opinion is modified or rescinded or is determined by judicial authority to be invalid or of no legal effect, or (B) after publishing or filing the description and annual reports, such publication or filing is determined by judicial authority not to be in conformity with the requirements of this title.

NONDISCRIMINATION IN FEDERAL GOVERNMENT EMPLOYMENT

SEC. 717. *(a) All personnel actions affecting employees or applicants for employment (except with regard to aliens employed outside the limits of the United States) in military departments as defined in section 102 of title 5, United States Code, in executive agencies (other than the General Accounting Office) as defined in section 105 of title 5, United States Code (including employees and applicants for employment who are paid from nonappropriated funds), in the United States Postal Service and the Postal Rate Commission, in those units of the Government of the District of Columbia having positions in the competitive service, and in those units of the legislative and judicial branches of the Federal Government having positions in the competitive service, and in the Library of Congress shall be made free from any discrimination based on race, color, religion, sex, or national origin.*

(b) Except as otherwise provided in this subsection, the Civil Service Commission shall have authority to enforce the provisions of subsection (a) through appropriate remedies, including reinstatement or hiring of employees with or without back pay, as will effectuate the policies of this section, and shall issue such rules, regulations, orders, and instructions as it deems necessary and appropriate to carry out its responsibilities under this section. The Civil Service Commission shall—

(1) be responsible for the annual review and approval of a national and regional equal employment opportunity plan which each department and agency and each appropriate unit referred to in subsection (a) of this section shall submit in order to maintain an affirmative program of equal employment opportunity for all such employees and applicants for employment;

(2) be responsible for the review and evaluation of the operation of all agency equal employment opportunity programs, periodically obtaining and publishing (on at least a semiannual basis) progress reports from each such department, agency, or unit; and

(3) consult with and solicit the recommendations of interested individuals, groups, and organizations relating to equal employment opportunity.

The head of each such department, agency, or unit shall comply with such rules, regulations, orders, and instructions which shall include a provision that an employee or applicant for employment shall be notified of any final action taken on any complaint of discrimination filed by him thereunder. The plan submitted by each department, agency, and unit shall include, but not be limited to—

(1) provision for the establishment of training and education programs designed to provide a maximum opportunity for employees to advance so as to perform at their highest potential; and

(2) a description of the qualifications in terms

of training and experience relating to equal employment opportunity for the principal and operating officials of each such department, agency, or unit responsible for carrying out the equal employment opportunity program and of the allocation of personnel and resources proposed by such department, agency, or unit to carry out its equal employment opportunity program.

With respect to employment in the Library of Congress, authorities granted in this subsection to the Civil Service Commission shall be exercised by the Librarian of Congress.

(c) Within thirty days of receipt of notice of final action taken by a department, agency, or unit referred to in subsection 717(a), or by the Civil Service Commission upon an appeal from a decision or order of such department, agency, or unit on a complaint of discrimination based on race, color, religion, sex, or national origin, brought pursuant to subsection (a) of this section, Executive Order 11478 or any succeeding Executive orders, or after one hundred and eighty days from the filing of the initial charge with the department, agency, or unit or with the Civil Service Commission on appeal from a decision or order of such department, agency, or unit until such time as final action may be taken by a department, agency, or unit, an employee or applicant for employment, if aggrieved by the final disposition of his complaint, or by the failure to take final action on his complaint, may file a civil action as provided in section 706, in which civil action the head of the department, agency, or unit, as appropriate, shall be the defendant.

(d) The provisions of section 706(f) through (k), as applicable, shall govern civil actions brought hereunder.

(e) Nothing contained in this Act shall relieve any Government agency or official of its or his primary responsibility to assure nondiscrimination in employment as required by the Constitution and statutes or of its or his responsibilities under Executive Order 11478 relating to equal employment opportunity in the Federal Government.

INDEX

Bargaining *cont.*
   duty to provide bargaining
      information, 162–65
   employer's duty, 153–62
   impasse, 147–48, 154, 155, 160,
      202
   inception and duration of the
      obligation, 139–44
   negotiation process, 144–51
   notice requirements, 144–46
   order, 89–94, 102
   ratification procedures, 150, 152–
      53
   relationship, anti-trust laws, 263–
      65
   remedies for refusal, 170–71
   subjects, 151–53
      mandatory, 151–52, 153, 162,
         168
   tentative agreements, 149–50
   units. *See* Appropriate bargaining
      unit
   waiver of bargaining rights, 156–
      57
Bargaining duty of successor
      employer, 165–68
   alter ego employer, 163, 168
   double breasted operation, 163,
      168–69
   duty to arbitrate, 285–86
   remaining in same industry, 166–
      67
   retaining prior workforce, 165–66
   successorship clauses, 167–68, 250,
      285–86
   successor's rights, 167
Bargaining orders, 89–94, 102
Bargaining tactics, 146–50, 153, 156,
      161
Bargaining units. *See* Appropriate
      bargaining unit; Collective
      bargaining units
BASF Wyandotte Corporation decision,
      106–7
Basic capital decisions, bargaining
      obligation, 158
Beck decision, 304, 305, 306, 309
Belknap v. *Hale* decision, 194, 414
Benefits
   changes during election campaign,
      85
   employer promises of, 84–85
Bildisco decision, 160
"Bill of Rights of Members of Labor
      Organizations," 4, 327–29,
      335, 342
Binding arbitration, 289
Blocking charge, NLRB procedures,
      92
Board regulation of campaign
      statements, 80–85
   abuse of Board processes, 81–82
   employer free speech, 82–85
   Hollywood Ceramics Doctrine, 81
   misrepresentations, 80–81
Boeing Co. decision, 340
Bogus work, featherbedding, 259
Bona fide occupational qualifications
      (BFOQ), 364, 375–76, 379–
      80, 382

Bond, bargaining subject, 152
Bottom line concept, employment
      discrimination, 372–74
Boulwareism, 149, 151
Bowen decision, 357
Boycotts, 199, 236, 260–61. *See also*
      Secondary boycotts
   consumer, 222–25, 229
Boys Market decision, 198, 199, 204
Breach of contract
   successorship clauses, 167–68
   suit to enforce contract, 271–74,
      284–85
   as unfair labor practice, 153–62,
      288
Bruckner Nursing Home decision, 108
Buffalo Forge decision, 199–201, 204
Burns Detective decision, 165–68, 250,
      285–86
Business justification for
      employment practice, evidence
      of, 369–70
Business operations
   cessation during picketing, 219–20
   duty to bargain over changes in,
      157–60
Business Services by Manpower
      decision, 195

Campaign tactics, representation
      elections. *See* Board regulation
      of campaign statements;
      Elections (NLRB)
Captive audience doctrine, 78
Carbon Fuel decision, 197, 198
Carey v. *Westinghouse* decision, 285
Catholic Bishop of Chicago decision, 12
CBS decision, 257
C cases. *See* Unfair labor practice
C & C Plywood decision, 156, 161,
      288
Central Hardware decision, 77
Certification
   AC petition to amend, 33
   joint, 45
   procedures for, 25
Certification bar, 57
Certification revocation, 395
Certified public accountant, dues
      protest and use of, 308
Certified union, 30, 139–40
Check-off, 171, 310–11, 314
   authorizations, 140–41
   contractual provisions, 317–19
City Disposal decision, 110–11, 112,
      201
Civil Rights Act of 1964, 1, 34, 302,
      348, 362–408
   affirmative action, 396–98
   arbitration and, 394–95
   disparate treatment and disparate
      impact discrimination, 366–74
   processing requirements and suit
      procedures, 383–87
   religious and age discrimination,
      379–83
   remedies, 362–65, 387–92
   reverse discrimination, 395–96
   sex discrimination, 374–79

Civil Rights Acts of 1866 and 1871
      (Reconstruction Acts), 365–
      66, 392–94, 400
Civil Rights Restoration Act, 365–66
Civil rights violations (employment).
      See also specific headings
      pertaining to age, race, and
      religious discrimination
   arbitration remedies, 394–95, 401
   EEOC remedies, 383–94
   judicial remedies, 387–92
   NLRB remedies, 395
Class actions, 387–88
Clayton Act, 260, 261, 262, 263, 266
Clayton decision, 356
Clear Pine Mouldings decision, 190
Closed shops, 302
Coalition bargaining, 147
Coercive activity
   requirement for under LMRA
      Sections 8(a)(1) and 8(a)(3),
      119–28
   work assignment disputes,
      requirement for NLRB
      jurisdiction, 254, 255–56
Collateral estoppel, doctrine of, 235
Collective bargaining, 1–3, 33, 34,
      41, 47, 84, 102, 104, 113. *See
      also* Bargaining
   conflicting policies of antitrust
      laws and, 260
   duty to bargain, 153–62
Collective bargaining agreements. *See
      also* Arbitration; No-strike
      clause
   enforcement of, 271–92
   federal v. state court jurisdiction,
      271–74, 413–15
   NLRB jurisdiction to enforce,
      153–62, 170–71, 288–92
   supervisor conduct in
      administering, 337
Collective bargaining functions test,
      union security clauses, 304–10
Collective bargaining units, 39–70,
      153
   election procedures and timing,
      56–61
   exclusion of employees, 48–55
   factors in determining, 39–48
   voter eligibility, 61–64
Collyer Doctrine, 161, 289, 290–91,
      292, 293
Commerce standard, 12–13
Common law, status of union at,
      299–300, 333–34
Commonly owned companies, 225–
      26
Common situs picketing, 214–15
Communications to third parties as
      protected activity, 117
Communications Workers v. *Beck*
      decision, 304
Community of interest, 39–40, 41,
      42, 45, 47, 49, 53, 64, 66, 67,
      169
Comparable worth theory, 379
Competing employee groups,
      jurisdictional disputes, 256–57